American Congregations

American Congregations

VOLUME 1

Portraits of Twelve Religious Communities

EDITED BY

James P. Wind and James W. Lewis

The University of Chicago Press
Chicago and London

JAMES P. WIND is a program director in the Religion Division of the Lilly Endowment in Indianapolis, Indiana. JAMES W. LEWIS is Executive Director of the Louisville Institute for the Study of Protestantism and American Culture.

Published with the generous assistance of The Lilly Endowment, Inc.

The University of Chicago Press, Chicago 60637
The University of Chicago Press, Ltd., London
© 1994 by The University of Chicago
All rights reserved. Published 1994
Printed in the United States of America
03 02 01 00 99 98 97 96 95 94   1 2 3 4 5

ISBN: 0-226-90186-6 (cloth)

Library of Congress Cataloging-in-Publication Data

American congregations / edited by James P. Wind and James W. Lewis.
    p. cm.
   Includes bibliographical references and indexes.
   Contents: v. 1. Portraits of twelve religious communities—v.
 2. New perspectives in the study of congregations.
    1. United States—Religion. 2. Religious institutions—United
States. 3. Church work. I. Wind, James P., 1948–   . II. Lewis,
James Welborn.
BL2525.A525 1994
291.6'5'0973—dc20   94-4136

CONTENTS

ILLUSTRATIONS

PREFACE

THANKS TO A GRANT FROM the Lilly Endowment, Inc., the University of Chicago Divinity School initiated the Congregational History Project in 1987. Based in the Divinity School's Institute for the Advanced Study of Religion, the project was codirected by James P. Wind and James W. Lewis. Convinced that American congregations are both extremely important and strangely ignored by historians, the Congregational History Project sought to focus fresh scholarly attention on American congregations by means of three major programs—a publication project, a dissertation competition, and a seminar on congregational history.

The publication project produced the two-volume *American Congregations*. The first volume, *Portraits of Twelve Religious Communities*, includes historical essays on twelve significant and diverse North American congregations. Building on these historical studies, the essays in the second volume, *New Perspectives in the Study of Congregations*, reflect on the various contexts of American congregations, the congregational tasks of faith formation and theological reflection, and the role of congregational leadership—all with the history of at least twelve particular congregations firmly in mind.

As an investment in the future of congregational studies, the Dissertation Fellowship program sought to identify and support promising new scholars studying the congregational dimension of American religious life. During the three years of the program, seventeen scholars, working in a variety of academic disciplines, were named Dissertation Fellows.[1]

The Congregational History Project seminar included each year's Dissertation Fellows as well as a variety of scholars with an interest in the congregation.[2] During its five meetings, the seminar explored the relationship between congregational history and congregational studies and reviewed the draft chapters of both volume 1, *Portraits of Twelve Religious Communities*, and volume 2, *New Perspectives in the Study of Congregations*. In addition, each Dissertation Fellow presented his or her dissertation project to the seminar.

The three-part Congregational History Project was unified by common attention to several core tasks. First, the project sought to transcend scholarly provincialism by assembling a group of scholars who work from various methodological perspectives. While seeking to identify the genius, or distinctive character, of the congregation as a religious institution, the project also attempted to broaden the descriptive horizon by studying a group of congregations that reflect significant religious and cultural diversity. As its name implies, the Congregational History Project sought to advance the historical understanding of the congregation, but it also encouraged participation by traditional theological disciplines which have contributed infrequently to the conversation about congregations. In addition, the project attempted to clarify the strategic position of the congregation on the borderline between the public and private spheres of American life. Finally, to a limited extent the project attempted to assess the significance of congregational studies for American religious history, theological education, and religious studies.

The codirectors of the Congregational History Project wish to acknowledge our deep indebtedness to a long list of people who have assisted at various stages. Perhaps our largest debt of gratitude is to Robert W. Lynn, of the Lilly Endowment, Inc., who first directed our attention to the important topic of congregational studies and worked with us in securing generous funding for the inquiry. Equally supportive has been Craig Dykstra, Robert Lynn's successor at the Endowment and our valued colleague.

We also enjoyed the consistent institutional support of colleagues at the Divinity School of the University of Chicago, including a former dean, Franklin I. Gamwell, and the current dean, W. Clark Gilpin. The deans' administrative assistants, Sandra Peppers and the late Delores Smith, were always helpful in many ways. Jennie Browne, a Ph.D. student at the Divinity School, was a valued and energetic research assistant, indexer, and good friend. In addition, we owe special thanks to Chicago's distinguished historian, Martin E. Marty, for advice and counsel from the very beginning of the project.

We are grateful to the members of the seminar of the Congregational History Project for their sage advice throughout the project. For their hard work and patience with our never-ending editorial suggestions, we express our thanks to the authors of both volume 1 and volume 2. As the two volumes neared publication, we relied on the extraordinary editorial skills of Helen Creticos Theodoropoulos and, especially, Barbara Hofmaier. We would also like to thank Alan G. Thomas, our editor at the University of Chicago Press, for his wisdom and good judgment.

Finally, to our spouses, Kathleen Wind and Marcia Lewis, we owe much more than gratitude for their patience and support in this and many other ventures.

NOTES

1. Timothy R. Allan, Kevin P. Demmitt, Dana Fenton, Karla Goldman, Shirah Weinberg Hecht, Timothy I. Kelly, Carol A. Kitchen, Fred Kniss, Doris O'Dell, Kristin Park, Mark A. Peterson, Joseph T. Reiff, Beth Barton Schweiger, Susan Myers Shirk, Clinton Stockwell, William Sutton, and Wayne L. Thompson.

2. In addition to the Dissertation Fellows, regular seminar participants included: Dorothy C. Bass, Eileen Brewer, Don S. Browning, Phil Devenish, Jay Dolan, Carl Dudley, Robert Franklin, Franklin I. Gamwell, Langdon Gilkey, E. Brooks Holifield, L. DeAne Lagerquist, Martin E. Marty, R. Stephen Warner, James W. Lewis, Jack Wertheimer, and James P. Wind.

Introduction

JAMES P. WIND AND JAMES W. LEWIS

IN AN ESSAY ENTITLED "The Work of Local Culture" novelist and essayist Wendell Berry celebrates the memory of our distinctive rural communities and mourns their destruction by modern commercial, industrial society. For Berry, "there is no more important work" than the making of local culture, a process he likens to an old wooden bucket in which the decaying and dying fragments of life are gathered and converted into the good black dirt out of which new life can spring. Berry does not discuss religious congregations in his essay. But the congregational histories to follow are nothing less than case studies of this very work of creating local cultures out of the accumulation of pasts that Americans bring into their places of worship.

Like Berry's buckets, congregations are important, if for the most part unglamorous. Although the importance of congregations is not primarily a matter of numbers, the numbers are impressive. According to the National Council of Churches, in 1990 there were at least 350,337 congregations in the United States, down only slightly from 350,481 in 1989.[1] Moreover, the diversity of these groups is astounding as are the many reasons for their importance. Clearly they are important to those who find within them a source of religious meaning. But they are also important to scholars of American religion, including American religious historians. As historian E. Brooks Holifield has noted, the local congregation preceded that most American of religious institutions, the denomination.[2] Indeed, congregations preceded most other permanent institutions in America. This is not to say that America is distinctively religious. But it is to say that American religion has been, and by and large remains, distinctively congregational.

Some clarification of our terms is in order. First by "congregation" we mean a body of "people who regularly gather to worship at a particular place." "Congregation," as we use it then, is an inclusive term

1

limited neither to those Protestant churches known as Congregational, nor to the other Protestant groups with a congregational church polity.[3] In this book, for example, we use "congregation" to refer to Roman Catholic parishes, a Jewish synagogue, a Muslim mosque, a Swaminarayan Hindu temple, a Mormon ward, a Greek Orthodox cathedral, as well as to a variety of Protestant gatherings, new and old, large and small. Despite its Protestant overtones, the term has the benefit of emphasizing the persistently communal nature of religion in America. And unlike such terms as "meeting," the term "congregation" emphasizes the distinctively religious purpose of the gathering.

The basic elements of this definition are four. A congregation requires a body of people. Despite the important role of individual religious leaders, an important theme in many of the chapters to follow, there can be no congregation without the group. Even the Swaminarayan priest, who often ministers to the images in his temple alone, does so on behalf of the group. By "congregation," then, we denote an organizational pattern that places considerable power in the hands of the local body of lay members, even where (as in Greek Orthodoxy and Roman Catholicism) official polity invests authority in the hands of the clergy and a remote hierarchy.

Second, the congregation is not an occasional or ad hoc meeting but requires intentional, regular assembly. This gathering may be daily mass at St. Peter's Catholic Church or a once-a-month preaching service at Mt. Hebron Baptist Church. But an occasional revival meeting or a Bible study group, for example, does not constitute a congregation.

Third, the people who gather regularly do so for worship, a term representing the distinctively religious dimension of human life. Congregations are not, of course, the sole location of the sacred. Private devotions and individual meditation have long been a part of the American religious landscape. Our history is also replete with mass religious happenings—the Cane Ridge revivals, Billy Graham's crusades, or Pope John Paul II's great public masses, for example. But alongside these manifestations of individual and mass spirituality, Americans have continued to flock in large numbers to church, to synagogue, to temple, both for those activities that can be done only in a group—corporate worship, high holy day services, and so forth—but also for support of their private devotional practices. In addition, congregations typically include a full menu of other organizations, such as women's societies, youth groups, self-help groups, and athletic teams. But, ideally at least, these diverse activities are integrally related to the religious identity of the congregation.

Finally, the group of people that convenes regularly for worship does so at a particular place. To put it another way, congregations have represented sacred space for much of American religion. Altar, pulpit, anxious bench, the synagogue ark containing the Torah scrolls, and, more recently, the Hindu images of Krishna and Radha—these, among others, have symbolized the sacred for Americans. Particular places have been important, even for a pilgrim people. Over time, these places become repositories of religious experience, gathering and condensing tradition, practice, and memory. Congregations, then, are groups of people who gather regularly to worship at a particular place.

The twelve congregational histories in this book provide readers with an unprecedented introduction to this local level of American religion. Unlike the denominational histories, biographies of exceptional leaders, or social movement narratives that make up so much of the literature about modern religious history, these chapters focus on the basic unit of religion in America, the local congregation. Astonishingly, although the congregational story of American religion is now entering its fifth century, this is the first collection of critical historical portraits of a broad variety of American congregations. We do not claim that interpreters of American life have completely ignored the settings in which most Americans actually encounter the sacred, locate their lives in contexts of transcendent traditions and referents, or organize their experience, concerns, and commitments. But in fact congregations generally have remained in the background of other stories and have served as stages for somebody else's speeches. Here, for the first time, they move into the foreground, turning our attention to the institutions where American religion was and is believed and practiced.

This sampler of American religion introduces us to a variety of distinctive local religious cultures which have developed in the American environment. Some, like Center Church in New Haven, Connecticut, or Mt. Hebron Baptist Church near Leeds, Alabama, trace their stories back into colonial and frontier periods of American history. Others, like the Swaminarayan Hindu Temple in suburban Chicago and Calvary Chapel in Costa Mesa, California, are the most recent manifestations of the congregational phenomenon, the latest attempts to create local religious worlds for Americans.

No single book-length collection of congregational histories—even one as thick as this one—could ever represent adequately the variety of congregational cultures that have enriched the American landscape—and continue to do so. Yet, this collection does remind us of both the diversity of local religion and the pervasiveness of congregational patterns. As readers move from chapter to chapter they move from the world of German Jews in Cincinnati, to Black Methodists in Baltimore, to Lebanese Muslims in Northern Canada, to Irish Catholics in San Francisco, to Latter-day Saints in Salt Lake City. In each case, we see how an individual congregation fashioned a particular world of belief and behavior out of a bewilderingly complex set of materials. Great religious traditions, denominational identities, ethnic and racial heritages, familial, economic, regional, and local pasts mix with American modernity to render each place of worship different from every other, even when they seek, as the Mormon wards do, to look alike. Our authors kept searching for ways to describe the genius of each congregation studied. One of the advantages of gathering these individual portraits into a gallery is that such comparison allows the distinctive identity, or particular genius, of each congregation to emerge.

These chapters draw upon many of the great interpretive themes used to make sense of American religious life, but with a key difference, localization. Usually in the foreground of religious history, these themes look different here as they blend into a congregational background and interrelate with other dynamics of North American life. To begin with one of the most timely topics, the two chapters that frame the collection raise the question of the fate of mainline American religion. Center Church in New Haven reminds us of Puritan beginnings and of the burdens of handing on a way of life from one generation to the next. Nowhere, perhaps, is this poignant task better illustrated than in America's congregations. In varying ways all of our twelve congregations struggle with the challenge of communicating the faith to their young, one of their most important and yet frustrating tasks.

Across the continent, on the other hand, Calvary Chapel reminds us of revivalism, one of the primary engines of American religion. At Calvary Chapel grand interpretive themes again take on local color as the converts the mainline seems unable to produce have come so rapidly to the Reverend Chuck Smith's church that it choreographs parking and broadcasts the service throughout its expansive campus (including the parking lots!) so that all may find a place there.

These two congregations tell us that part of the American story is the breakdown of established ways of life and the decline of once vital institutions. But they also illustrate, in very specific ways, the other side—the energy, institutional creativity, and resourcefulness of American religion. As Center Church searches for something to revive it and as Calvary Chapel booms, one wonders if the old line is dying, if a new mainline is coming to life, or if American religion, as Robert Wuthnow has suggested, is being fundamentally restructured.[4]

If questions about the existence or nonexistence of a mainline in American religion, the transmission of faith to the next generation, and revivalism have their congregational dimensions, so do questions about ethnicity, race, and cultural accommodation. The histories of St. Peter's Church, St. Boniface Parish, and Annunciation Cathedral show us how congregations have served as especially important "way stations" or places of cultural negotiation for American newcomers. Central to these stories are: clergy who function like political bosses on behalf of their congregation's members, helping them find jobs and utilize the political systems of their neighborhoods; parish schools which simultaneously teach old-world customs and values as they prepare children for life in a new world; complex organizational networks which employ sodalities, women's organizations, youth groups, and ethnic clubs to provide total institutions at the same time that they teach people voluntary and organizational skills for life in the wider society. Beneath the surface of the women's society dinners and the Sunday School curriculum debates are enormously complex collisions of cultures, and congregations prove to be especially important places for watching the processes of accommodation and resistance, transformation and dissolution, that are a recurring feature in the history of this nation of immigrants.

But these congregational histories tell us still more. First, the chapters about the Muslim *mosque* and the Swaminarayan Temple remind us that the process of cultural negotiation continues and help us see the pivotal role that congregations still play. It would, of course, be misleading to suggest that congregations are the only places that mediated or still mediate between cultures in America; clearly public schools, local businesses, and media do so. But these essays remind us that congregations provide access to deep, perhaps fundamental dimensions of that negotiation which may be less visible if we look only elsewhere.

Equally fascinating are congregational struggles with discipline. In each case, old strategies for preserving ways of life are fought over, accommodated, and retrieved from the past. There are excommunications in these histories, and censorship and punishment too. But there are also countless efforts to teach religious ways of life through acts of compassion, programs of education, and patterns of organization. These stories all point to breakdowns of discipline and abandonments of specific disciplinary standards and practices. But they also give evidence of the continuing struggle to create new disciplines and new identities which are adequate for life in the American environment. They also raise the question of whether the discipline currently being fostered within our congregations is more that of the American way of life than the way of the cross, the observance of Torah, or obedience to Allah.

An especially important discovery that comes from the study of these local cultures modifies our conventional wisdom about the division of modern life into public and private spheres. For most of this century congregations have been viewed as private places which, along with the family, are removed from the world of government and the world of business, and critics have regularly faulted congregations for their private preoccupations and public irrelevance.[5] Yet these histories tell another story. In each case we find a congregation fashioning a distinctive relationship with its particular public. In some cases, as in Rockdale Temple or Sugar House Ward, the congregation reaches directly into civic life, contributing officeholders, responding to major public needs. In other cases the congregation selects one public, an ethnic one in the case of St. Peter's Parish, the Cathedral of the Annunciation, or the Muslims of Lac Le Biche, and cares for its needs over against those of other publics, whether those publics are around the corner or back home in the old country. But in each case the congregation serves as a place of public formation and mediation. A specific group of people and their needs is addressed; their needs are in turn advocated or protected vis-à-vis other groups. Frequently, congregations play pivotal and complex mediating roles between individual worlds and the public sphere, as indicated by the economic creativity of Bethel A.M.E. Church and the reform politics of Rockdale Temple.

Not to be missed in this connection are the colorful ways in which congregations deepen our pluralism. The festival life of St. Peter's Church, both in its earlier Irish and now in its Hispanic days, shows us how congregations keep alive ways of life and teach their people styles of plural belonging. The way that the members of Annunciation Cathedral refought the Greek Venizelist-Royalist controversy during and after World War I, even to the point of striking blows at the altar, indicates the serious cultural negotiations these congregations do. Under the

6

seemingly petty conflicts that turn so many people away from these places of worship are fundamental questions about human identity and purpose, about meaning, about right and wrong, about the ultimate character of human life and the universe.

Breaking those stereotypical understandings of the relationship between public and private spheres and coming to a fuller appreciation of the religious dimensions of pluralism cast new light as well on conventional wisdom about the secularization of American society. Clearly the persistence of religious congregations undermines the thesis in its simplest form. But a closer look at actual congregational histories illustrates a more complex relationship between the sacred and the secular. In a way these two dimensions of human life meet in religious congregations, where the secular informs the sacred sphere as much as the sacred inspires the secular. And in an interesting twist on the thesis that persons become progressively more secular in the American context, we learn in this volume that Swaminarayan Hindus tend to become more religious in the New World than they were in the old.

Although in this volume we did not set out to produce case studies of American religious leadership, great battles over lay versus clerical leadership, religious authority, and discipline appear regularly in these histories. Catholics clash over trusteeship, often starting their parishes under trustee leadership, then centralizing authority in the hands of the clergy. But after Vatican II they find themselves in the midst of a leadership crisis as seminary enrollments decline and parish councils and new understandings of priesthood emerge. The story of the rabbinate in Rockdale Temple teaches us volumes about the fate of American clergy. There, in a tradition that did not include the model of clergyman, we find a type of rabbi emerging that professionalizes ethos-bearing. The clergyperson becomes the hired representative religious figure, carrying the weight of a tradition that members still want borne but cannot embody fully in their own lives. We watch Mormons struggle to avoid accommodating to the paid clergy model, and we see fresh outcroppings of the American clerical paradigm in the Muslim and Swaminarayan congregations. At the same time that these congregations professionalize they also borrow other leadership models and techniques from the culture—boards of trustees, Robert's Rules of Order, and congregational minutes. These histories show us how the clergy and the congregations they serve are caught up in a great national debate about religious leadership and how that leadership has evolved in certain professional and democratic directions while always adapting to local realities.

In addition to professional religious leaders, these essays make room for a fascinating variety of notable men and women. Inventor-philanthropist Cyrus McCormick strides across the history of Chicago's Fourth Presbyterian Church, as does one of its alleged heretics, David Swing, and the indefatigable social worker Vera Eberhart. Bethel A.M.E. Church of Maryland features such noted African-American leaders as Daniel Payne, Richard Allen, and Frederick Douglass. Cincinnati's famous reform mayor, Murray Seasongood, enjoyed a power base in Rockdale Temple, but he did not cast nearly as large a shadow over Reform Judaism as did its dominant rabbi, Max Lillienthal. Dorothy Day appears in the story of St. Peter's Church, as does Cesar Chavez. But here these movers and shakers appear not in splendid isolation but as part of the local stories that spill over into the larger ones that make up our American culture.

This locating of individuals within congregational stories makes several contributions to our understanding of American religion. First, it allows us to see that, while Americans are restless pilgrims, often moving, like Orestes Brownson, William James, or Dorothy Day, through a variety of religious traditions and institutions, they also have sacred places, loci of the sacred where people can return and be shaped by a great tradition, week after week, year after year. Second, they remind us that, as Robert Bellah and company recently have in *The Good Society*, we habitually deceive ourselves into thinking that we live in an individualistic world, when in fact our lives are decidedly shaped by patterns of connection and interdependence called institutions. All too often our stories of American religion obscure the connections, the institutional contexts, which make possible the individual flourishes and creativity that catch our attention.

Among the many lessons of congregational history, evident throughout the chapters which follow, is the distinctively congregational pattern of religion in North America. This claim is not to deny the vital importance of other, more individualized religious manifestations, be they the secular piety of American Transcendentalists or the privatized religion of contemporary Americans. This important, nontraditional side of the American religious story richly deserves the greater scholarly attention it is currently receiving. But it is still the case that the story of religious experience is rarely just an individual story. Consequently the American religious story is as much a story of religious groups as of religious individuals.

But there is more to our claim about the congregational pattern of

American religion than the observation that religion is frequently a group affair. As sociologist Stephen Warner points out in his chapter in *New Perspectives in the Study of Congregations* (volume 2 of *American Congregations*), religious groups in America tend to assume a congregational pattern.[6] From Center Church to Calvary Chapel, the American religious experience has been predominantly a congregational one in which leaders and members share authority in a varied and complicated fashion. To overlook the congregational character of American religion is thus to overlook much of the source of American religious vitality. This is one lesson we have learned from the congregational stories that follow.

We have also discovered that congregations represent an essential religious link between past and present. Congregations have been part of American history from the first page. In fact, the phenomenon of religious gathering reaches back to the kivas and longhouses of those Native Americans who inhabited this land before the European newcomers arrived. To be sure, the colonial newcomers often established congregations in the new world in order to establish independence from the religious constraints of the old, and as a result the theme of religious freedom has been a constant in American historiography. Tragically, that new pursuit of freedom to congregate often came at the expense of Native American sacred places and ways.

In the nineteenth century other American congregations were established in order to forge strong ties to the old world and to establish symbolic boundaries around a particular religious group (often, but not always, an ethnic group as well). Many congregations expressed their new world freedom and cultivated the old world ways simultaneously.

For centuries writers have told the stories of these congregations. William Bradford's celebrated *History of Plimoth Plantation* (written from 1620 to 1648), for example, may be seen as a congregational history, telling the story of Scrooby congregation's migration first to Holland and then to New England. Usually these congregational histories have been celebratory, uncritical accounts written by members of the congregations for various congregational occasions. After decades in which professional historians have looked elsewhere, some recent scholars have discovered, as indicated by the chapters in this volume, that congregations are unusually rich sources of historical information.

There are, of course, many ways to study a congregation's history. Some of the following essays bear an initial similarity to the old-fashioned "clergy-centered" parish history of the anniversary booklet as they organize their narratives around priests, pastors, and rabbis. Others look suspiciously like ethnographic and sociological inquiries. The statistically inclined will be delighted to find that there is a new use for church records here and that those dusty books really do have stories to tell. The methodological pluralism of these essays should help create new debates about the most adequate ways to uncover the historical treasures within these local cultures. But they also should be viewed as early attempts in a new field of historical inquiry—congregational history.

On the one hand, as both of us have pointed out previously, this turn to the lived religious experience of congregating Americans is part of a broader historiographical attention to social history.[7] The great social movements that make up so much of the American story are strands in the fabric of congregational history. Urbanization, suburbanization, the labor movement, the rise of the so-called knowledge class, the great struggle for equality of women and blacks, and the powerful countermovements that sought to block them—these are part of the local histories of American congregations. In this respect, congregational histories are analogous to histories of cities, labor unions, and cultural institutions that illuminate broader historical phenomena by concentrating on local institutions and attending to the rank and file as well as leadership elites. Congregational histories, for example, have told us much, and can tell us still more, about the religious experience of American women.[8]

But congregational history is not just social history; it is also religious history. As Brooks Holifield has observed, a desire to understand what is "distinctively religious within diverse cultural settings" also lies behind the rise of congregational history.[9] In order, that is, to understand the *religious* experience of men, women, and children in America, scholars have turned to that complex set of local institutions in which most Americans have chosen to express their religious convictions. This is not to say that religion in America is merely local and institutional. But any account of it that omits the local and institutional—the congregational—is woefully inadequate.

One reason congregations have been overlooked is that existing interpretive frameworks have focused attention elsewhere. As Martin E. Marty observed in *A Nation of Behavers*, the writing of American religious history has been guided by four maps, or interpretive frameworks. The first of them, drawn primarily between 1492 and 1776, organized accounts of religious experience around theological and territorial boundaries, focusing, for example, on the experience of Quakers in Pennsylvania, Anglicans in Virginia, or Congregationalists in New England. After the American Revolution, denominational categories supplanted the theological-territorial ones. This second set of maps prevailed until the 1960s and produced a long tradition of denominational histories of Lutherans, Quakers, Unitarians, Catholics, Mormons, and so forth. Beginning in the 1960s historians employed political maps to chart the interactions of the religious groups with the polis, the human city; and issues of church and state, civil religion, and democracy supplanted those of creed or institution. In the 1970s, responding to the rise of social history, Marty proposed a fourth map which grouped Americans, on the basis of religious behavior, into mainline, evangelical/fundamentalist, pentecostal/charismatic, civil religious, and new religious groups.[10]

In the congregational histories that follow, readers will note elements of all four maps. Thus these congregational histories represent an attempt to draw the fourth kind of behavioral map in such a way that the other three approaches to history writing are incorporated rather than abandoned. Consequently, traditional theological and denominational stories move in and out of these accounts of local religious worlds. The battles over scriptural interpretation, the second coming of Jesus, polygamy, Zionism, and priestly authority that are so central to the various denominational histories of America are all fought here, but with local variations and solutions. Fourth Presbyterian Church is distinctively Presbyterian, even in the 1990s, when its Magnificent Mile location in the midst of Chicago's most cosmopolitan neighborhood might tempt us to doubt the significance of denominational heritages. Pre- and post-Vatican II forms of Catholicism are palpable and still determinative in the Catholic parishes studied here, and the Divine Liturgy of Eastern Orthodoxy continues to shape the life of Maryland's Greek Americans in ways that St. John Chrysostom might recognize. But again, the histories presented are not merely mini-versions of great theological debates or denominational histories. They are local creations, where specific groups of people fashion distinctive local cultures that bear but also subtly shape the larger traditions of which they are a part.

For far too long American religious historiography has focused on the white Protestant mainstream, ignoring much of the rich tapestry that is American religion. Recently scholars have pointed out the deficiencies of this privileging of a Protestant center and have urged that the story of American religion be reinterpreted. In this volume we have sought to move beyond preoccupation with the white Protestant establishment in order to attend to the varied congregational experiences of other religious groups in America. Clearly we have not exhausted the story of the rich panoply of American congregations. For example, neither Asian or Hispanic Protestants appear in these pages, despite their increasing presence and importance in American society. But we have moved beyond the Protestant mainstream to include African-American Protestants, evangelical Protestants, and a broad variety of ethnic religious experience including Roman Catholic, Greek Orthodox, Jewish, Hindu, and Muslim. In so doing, we see how the religious story in the American context often becomes a congregational story. We have also been reminded of the rich diversity of the American religious experience and of the manifold ways in which American congregations have contributed to the lives of individuals and groups. We have, in a word, discovered just how interesting and important the local American religious story really is.

NOTES

1. Constant H. Jacquet, Jr., and Alice M. Jones, eds., *Yearbook of American and Canadian Churches 1991* (Nashville: Abingdon Press, 1991), p. 265. Although we frequently use the term "America," we are referring to North America generally and the United States in particular. Aside from the story of one Muslim group in Canada, this volume focuses on the history of congregations in the United States. A more systematic comparison of congregational history in the United States and Canada is yet to be written.

2. E. Brooks Holifield, "The Historian and the Congregation," in *Beyond Clericalism: The Congregation as a Focus for Theological Education,* ed. Joseph C. Hough, Jr., and Barbara G. Wheeler (Atlanta: Scholars Press, 1988), p. 90.

3. James P. Wind, *Places of Worship: Exploring Their History* (Nashville: American Association for State and Local History, 1990), pp. xvi–xvii.

4. Robert Wuthnow, *The Restructuring of American Religion: Society and Faith Since World War II* (Princeton: Princeton University Press, 1988).

5. For a brief overview of literature advancing that argument, see Wind, *Places of Worship,* pp. 107–10.

6. R. Stephen Warner, "The Place of the Congregation in the Contemporary American Religious Configuration," in James P. Wind and James W. Lewis, eds., *New Perspectives in the Study of Congregations,* vol. 2 of *American Congregations* (Chicago: University of Chicago Press, 1994).

7. Wind, *Places of Worship,* pp. 110–14; James W. Lewis, *The Protestant Experience in Gary, Indiana, 1906–1975: At Home in the City* (Knoxville: University of Tennessee Press, 1992), pp. 7–13.

8. A particularly fine example is Joan R. Gunderson, *"Before the World Confessed": All Saints Parish, Northfield, and the Community, 1858–1985* (Northfield, Minn.: Northfield Historical Society, 1987).

9. E. Brooks Holifield, "Recent Studies of the American Synagogue," *Religious Studies Review* (July 1991): 201.

10. Martin E. Marty, *A Nation of Behavers* (Chicago: University of Chicago Press, 1976).

ONE

A New England Congregation
Center Church, New Haven, 1638–1989

HARRY S. STOUT AND CATHERINE BREKUS

IT IS SUNDAY, October 27, 1989, a beautiful New England day in late fall. Multihued, aged trees stand like colorful sentinels from a distant past, surrounding Center Church on the old green and lending it a quiet dignity. The church's steeple, white-columned portico, and window frames have been freshly painted as part of the church's recent 350th anniversary celebration. Inside, 140 polished white pews sit in orderly ranks before the elevated pulpit, and an encircling balcony above gives a combined seating capacity of 1,000. On the walls surrounding the pews are plaques commemorating the great pastors who guided the congregation over the centuries. The names—Davenport, Pierpont, Noyes, Whittelsey, Stuart, Taylor, and their distinguished successors—all remain in view, bearing witness to a noble and storied past. Behind the pulpit stands a magnificent stained-glass window recreating the first worship service in 1638. In the basement crypt lie the remains of James Pierpont, Joseph Noyes, Chauncy Whittelsey, and other notables, including Jared Ingersoll, the ill-fated colonial stamp-tax collector, and Margaret Arnold, widow of Benedict Arnold.

At 9:45 people begin to enter the sanctuary, reenacting a ritual of gathering for public worship that is now in its 18,252d consecutive week. The most recent pastor, Peter Ives, resigned over the summer to take another pulpit in Massachusetts. In his place is the Reverend Edward Couch, an acting minister. Around us, worshipers gather in small clusters that can't begin to fill the cavernous sanctuary. Clearly the congregation has shrunk to a shadow of its former self. In all, there are forty-two women and twenty-six men, a total of sixty-eight people. Most are past retirement age; none appears to be under eighteen. There are three black women, and the rest of the congregation is white. The special music is professional and inspirational. But the congregation's singing of such traditionally triumphant hymns as "Immortal, Invisible, God Only Wise," or "Stand Up, Stand Up for Jesus" is perfunctory and lacking in vital energy.

This particular Sunday is "Stewardship Sunday," and the people listen to a twelve-minute sermon entitled "What's Going On Here?" The minister speaks eloquently about Center Church's noble past to inspire members' giving in the present. Following the service, all enjoy one another's company over coffee. In some ways the coffee hour, set in the back of the church, is more spirited than the service, which seems unreal in the huge surroundings.

What *is* going on here? To all outward appearances, Center Church is approaching the end of its history even as it has just finished celebrating its 350th anniversary. Like many other once majestic, inner-city Protestant churches, Center Church has been cast ignominiously from "mainline" to "sideline." Although a congregation still worships at Center Church, it is possible that the building will soon become a museum. Significantly, one of the most active current projects at the church is a drive to raise funds to protect the crypt in the basement. The church's large endowment—well over a million dollars—could see to its preservation. The cost, of course, would be the surrender of a living voice in the ongoing history of the New Haven community. The church would be entombing itself, preserving the legacy of those buried in the crypt rather than preparing for future generations.

Many recent observers have tried to explain the reasons for the decline of Protestant mainline churches in modern America. In his 1988 address to the Presbyterian General Assembly, Thomas W. Gillespie, president of Princeton Theological Seminary, argued that the demise of the mainline is the result of "our inability over the past quarter of a century to transmit our faith to our own children."[1] By giving the children a bland, tolerationist theology where anything goes as long as it's ethically sensitive, Gillespie maintained, mainline churches have unwittingly undermined the distinctiveness of their own tradition, cutting themselves off from their past and their future.

This case study confirms Gillespie's insight, although it also suggests that his view is both incomplete and shortsighted. For Center Church and other inner-city churches, suburbanization, race, and increasing mobility, not just a bland theology, have frustrated attempts to create a vital, intergenerational membership. And although Gillespie sees this problem as one of fairly recent vintage, Center Church members

TABLE 1

Pastors of Center Church, New Haven, 1639–1989

PASTORS	NO. OF NEW MEMBERS ADMITTED
John Davenport (1639–1668)	266*
Nicholas Street (1668–1684)	11*
James Pierpont (1685–1714)	434
Joseph Noyes (1716–1758)	508
Chauncy Whittelsey (1758–1787)	265
Joseph Dana (1789–1805)	90
Moses Stuart (1806–1810)	202
Nathaniel Taylor (1812–1822)	372
Leonard Bacon (1825–1866)	1,249
George Leon Walker (1868–1873)	186
Frederick Noble (1875–1879)	150
Newman Smyth (1882–1908)	421
Oscar Maurer (1909–1943)	1,756
David Beach (1943–1960)	701
Frederick Smith (1961–1969)	160
Bruce Whittemore (1971–1983)	411
Peter Ives (1983–1989)	40

*In this and all subsequent tables and figures, membership records for Davenport's and Street's ministries are incomplete.

since the Revolutionary era have been struggling to find ways to transmit their piety to future generations.

This study is an intellectual and social history of Center Church, New Haven, from its origins in 1638 to the present. We know much about "Puritan" theology and the great preachers who occupied Center Church's pulpit (see table 1), but hardly anything about the people in the pews. Nor do we know what happened to Puritan congregations over time. Without ignoring ministers or institutional changes, we hope to go beyond them to examine the social and communal experiences that shaped the congregation over its 350-year history. Although numerous histories and rich biographies of major ministers at Center Church have been written, the *congregation* has been virtually ignored.[2] Certainly ministers helped to shape the experiences and mission of the congregation. But clergymen responded to their congregations as much as they shaped them, creating a link between abstract thought and concrete policies that can be seen only from the "bottom up."

One of the first American congregations still in existence, Center Church is in many respects an ideal test case. Because its history parallels European-American history from the first seventeenth-century settlements to the present, it offers a baseline along which any other congregation might be measured. Insofar as Center Church ministers and members played leading roles in the events and movements that shaped their age, moreover, it has had more than a merely local significance. Whether supplying soldiers for the Revolution, contributing female members to charitable and interdenominational agencies in the nineteenth century, or providing leaders to the twentieth-century World Council of Churches, Center Church has been at the forefront of civil and religious leadership throughout American history. Our longitudinal study allows us to locate recent trends and patterns at Center Church in the largest possible perspective. In particular, we can see how the cyclical pattern of "rise and decline" in church membership and vitality is an old story whose roots go back to the colonial era. Present declines in church membership are neither novel nor irreversible. Rather they have recurred throughout Center Church's history and can be correlated with outside changes in culture and community.

Like many other New England congregations, Center Church's early members were meticulous record-keepers. From their complete membership lists, it is possible to determine the age, gender, familial connection, migration patterns, and place of birth for every new member. With the aid of a computer, we coded information on each member, some 7,379 in all, and applied statistical tests to discover patterns of continuity and change over a 350-year period.[3] Besides raw membership data, a great number of sermons, pamphlets, yearbooks, histories, and biographies survive that enable us to correlate broad social patterns of congregational change with changes in ethnic composition, institutional identity, theological orientation, and social programs in the New Haven community.[4] In short, Center Church provides an ideal setting for an examination of social and intellectual change in one congregation over the whole course of American history.

When we began organizing this study we resisted overly facile divisions based on arbitrary "centuries" or external "events" like the Great Awakening, the American Revolution, the Industrial Revolution, or the world wars; we wanted the data to sort themselves according to their own internal ordering patterns. Yet we discovered as we analyzed the data that there have been two periods of dramatic change in the church— one at the end of the eighteenth century, at the time of the American Revolution, and the other at the end of the nineteenth century, at a time of massive immigration and increasing geographical mobility. Our essay therefore has three parts corresponding roughly to the colonial era, the nineteenth century, and the twentieth century. In a sense, each part can stand by itself and can bear comparison with other congregations and events in those years. Yet a continuity binds all three together: namely, the congregation's persistent belief in its own religious and historical importance. Ultimately, then, in this study, we are examining the church's continuing life cycle, passing from youth to maturity to old age.

A Puritan Church

In the spring of 1638, a small band of English Puritans led by the Reverend John Davenport founded a "new haven" in eastern Connecticut. Like many other Puritans who had fled from religious persecution in England, Davenport and his followers hoped to create a purer church in America. When on April 25, 1638, they met for their first worship service, they reenacted a drama that lay at the center of every New England community. In constituting their communities as "Bible Commonwealths," these Puritan founders ceased to be marginalized Old World "fanaticks" and became instead *the* culture-shaping force in the New World. As the newly empowered religious establishment, the Puritan founders believed their New World experience represented a new chapter in human history and the basis for a self-contained and self-perpetuating "American" identity.[5] For the next century and a half the men and women who founded and ministered to these congregations held uncontested sway over the souls and consciences of their communities.

Like all seventeenth-century Connecticut and Massachusetts churches, Center Church originated as a "congregational" church. All religious authority resided in the local congregation and was institutionalized through the simple but profoundly important mechanism of a common pledge, or "covenant," between the inhabitants and the men they had chosen to be their rulers in church and state. In answer to the question, "What makes a church a church?" John Davenport explained that a church exists whenever "local believers join willingly together in a Christian communion and orderly covenant." No higher synod or episcopacy would impose its will on the local church. At the same time, however, each particular church existed as part of a larger common mission, leading Davenport to add that

> although particular churches be distinct and severall independent bodies, every one as a city compact within itself, without subordination under or dependence upon any other but Jesus Christ, yet are all churches to walk by one and the same rule, and by all means convenient to have the counsell and help one of another when need requireth, as members of one body.[6]

Very soon after arriving in New Haven, on a day spent in fasting and prayer, the inhabitants pledged to one another in a "plantation covenant" that they would live according to Scripture "in matters that concern the gathering and ordering of a Church" as well as in "all public offices, which concern civil order, [such] as choice of magistrates and officers, making and repealing of laws, dividing allotments of inheritances, and all things of like nature."[7] Founding a church was the inhabitants' most pressing concern, but they proceeded slowly and with caution. For fourteen months, as they surveyed the land and began building houses, they attended "private meetings wherein they that dwelt nearest together gave their accounts one to another of Gods Gracious work upon them and prayed together and conferred to their mutual edification."[8] Finally, in June 1639, they chose the seven among them whom they believed were godly enough to be the "pillars," or founders, of the church. In a solemn ceremony on August 22, 1639, these pillars formally gathered a church, calling it the "First Church of New Haven," and ordained "ruling" and "teaching" elders. (During the early nineteenth century, First Church became known as Center Church—the name it still bears today—because of its location on the New Haven Green between the Trinity Episcopal and United Congregational churches.)

Seldom in the history of New World settlement was so much invested in so little as a promise to submit to God's Word in orderly congregations. Instead of dedicating themselves to liberty and pluralism, these men and women vowed to subordinate their self-interest and personal gain to a common orthodoxy defined by the pastor and congregation. This orthodoxy would be imposed on all members of the community, whether they were church members or not. Family, state, and economy would all coexist for no higher end than to further the interests of the local congregation. In fact, until New Haven's union with Connecticut in 1665, only full church members were allowed to vote. There was, in other words, no separation of church and state; religious faith represented at once private piety and public policy. In New Haven, as elsewhere in New England, there was no police force, clerical episcopacy, standing army, or aristocracy to preserve order and cohesion— nothing but the members' covenant.

The central purpose of Center Church congregation, like that of other Puritan congregations, was spiritual and evangelistic. Through their covenanted society, Puritans perceived themselves as embarking on a great "errand" to redeem the world. The focus of this redemption was spiritual and, ultimately, eschatological.[9] Social conformity, material well-being, political order, and liberty were all understood instrumentally as subordinate to the task of implementing a "Congregational Way" that the world would want to emulate. Paradoxically, Puritan congregations combined an intensely insular and self-contained local order with a spiritual vision that was global and even cosmic in scope. If their evangelistic mission was ever forgotten, as Davenport warned in a later election sermon, then they would "have a sad reckoning."[10]

Throughout the formative decades of the seventeenth century, New Haven's autonomy was complete. Not only did the church exist unto itself, but the town and surrounding neighbors existed as an independent colony, distinct from the Connecticut colonies centered in Hartford and the Connecticut River Valley, and the Massachusetts Bay colony centered in Boston. The Reverend Davenport, together with his friend and chief magistrate, Theophilus Eaton, enjoyed immense (though not unchecked) power in defining both church orthodoxy and civil law. New Haven's laws, modeled directly on the Hebrew Bible, were the strictest in New England.[11] Center Church stood out as the most Puritan church in Puritan New England and established religious and cultural assumptions that prevailed into the twentieth century. Grammar schools, catechisms, and thrice-weekly sermons instilled an instinctual, self-contained identity as a Bible commonwealth that would only grow stronger with age. There were no rival political institutions or com-

1.1 South view of Center Church's first meetinghouse (replaced 1670). Reprinted from Edward Lambert, *History of the Colony of New Haven* (New Haven: Hitchcock & Stafford, 1838); courtesy of New Haven Colony Historical Society.

peting churches to refract the founders' vision. Nor were there any rival speakers challenging the monolithic voice of the pastor as God's "viceregent."[12]

From its inception, Center Church was both the spiritual and the geographical center of the town. It represented the public square in which and through which corporate identity could be discovered. Constructed in 1640 on the town green, the first building was a plain, fifty-foot-square log structure. Inside, simplicity was the rule, and furnishings were limited to a slightly elevated pulpit for the pastor and long benches for the worshipers. All worshipers were "seated" in permanent locations according to their rank, age, and office, with men and women on opposite sides of the church and children at the back or along the aisles.[13]

Every Sunday morning at nine o'clock, the townspeople were summoned together by the beating of a drum. Failure to attend services could be punished by fine and, ultimately, banishment. During the week there were prayer meetings at the church on Tuesday evenings, public lectures on Wednesday, and many private prayer meetings in people's homes. But Sunday, especially, was set aside as a day of worship. From sundown on Saturday to sundown on Sunday, all inhabitants did no work, and the pious dedicated themselves only to worshiping God.

During the morning service, the pastor offered an opening prayer, the teacher read and interpreted a chapter of Scripture, and the ruling elder led the congregation in the singing of a psalm. Unaccompanied by any musical instruments, the elder first sang a verse alone, then paused as the congregation sang it after him. After the psalm, the congregation stood as the pastor delivered his sermon, which could often last for more than an hour. Following precooked meals at the homes of those closest to the meetinghouse, the congregation reconvened in the afternoon at two o'clock. Again, attendance was required of all the inhabitants. The pastor prayed, the elder led the singing of a psalm, and then the teacher preached. Afterward, any baptisms would be performed, and as the afternoon grew late, contributions were collected. Rather than passing around baskets, the people approached the deacon's seat at the front with their voluntary offerings: charitable giving was thus less an individual or private affair than a public ceremony in which all philanthropy was channeled through the church.

In content, Center Church sermons invariably followed a schema of "sin-salvation-service" in which the pastor pointed to the people's sins, testified to God's grace as the only way of salvation, and then enjoined them to a lifetime of grateful, obedient service to the dictates of God's Word. Throughout, the spiritual and eternal overwhelmed more immediate "temporall" concerns of state, society, and commonwealth. True, saving faith, Davenport explained, was "to know Jesus to be the Messiah." This "knowledge," he continued, in words echoed throughout New England pulpits, involved not only the rational "understanding" but also the "will and affections." Such knowledge was rooted in the experience of conversion—a transforming realization that forever changed the life of the saint. The conversion experience did not happen overnight, indeed it often stretched out over years, but it was discernible. In the certainty that reflected his own experience and that of his parishioners, Davenport asserted: "For all that know Christ in a right manner, can tell, that there was a time when they did not thus know Christ as now they do."[14]

In addition to hearing sermons, the Center Church congregation paid close attention to its devotional and sacramental life.[15] Once a month, the morning service closed with the celebration of the Lord's Supper. In addition, infant baptism was offered to all church members, thus imbuing covenant theology with a strong genealogical confirmation. These mutually reinforcing social practices and ritual activities subordinated all to the spiritual vision and mission of a "people of the Word."

An essential component of congregational uniformity was spiritual oversight and discipline. On Sunday afternoon, as required, any cases of discipline were aired before a meeting of the full members of the congregation. The most serious offenses could be met with excommunication— a penalty with both religious and social consequences. At these times also, full church members would hear the testimonies of prospective new members and vote on whether to admit them. Through the ritual activities of punishment and acceptance, powerful cultural norms of conformity and voluntary subordination were perpetuated across the generations.[16]

Although everyone was legally required to attend the church and was subject to its discipline, only those who could testify to an experience of saving grace were admitted to membership. By this means, the congregation hoped to combine power—in its capacity to compel everyone in the community to sit under the Word—with purity—in its exclusion of those who had not experienced conversion. These "visible saints" were the foundation of the church.[17] Only full members could partake of the Lord's Supper, and they alone could vote in town elections.

Before presenting their testimonies to the church congregation, prospective members faced a committee composed of an elder and a group of church members. If there were no objections to a person's membership, he or she would then be required to make a profession of faith before the members of the congregation, who would vote their acceptance by raising their right hands.[18]

For those who were not accustomed to speaking in public, this experience could be intimidating. Indeed, in a contemporary church in Dedham, Massachusetts, one woman, known only to the records

as "Brother Hindsell's wife," approached the front of the congregation, but "being fearful," fainted at the sound of her own voice.[19] In
the early years of the First Church, while Davenport was minister, it is
probable that only men, not women, were required to speak aloud before the congregation. In more than one sermon Davenport referred to
the rule of Timothy (1 Timothy 2:12) which forbade women to speak in
church, and in congregations like the First Church of Boston, women
made their professions privately, sitting quietly as the pastor read their
words to the congregation.[20] Gender distinctions carried over into other
areas as well; Puritan women could neither vote nor hold church office,
and like the women of Corinth, they were "commanded to be under
obedience."

Clergymen argued over the qualifications for church membership
throughout the seventeenth century. The first founders of the Congregational churches had assumed (somewhat arrogantly) that God had not
only regenerated them but in the future would regenerate their progeny.
That expectation led to a crisis, as many second-generation children
failed to become "visible saints." For example, during Davenport's ministry at Center Church, 56 percent of the members never had a child join
the church (see fig. 1).[21] Ministers were in a quandary when many of
these second-generation Puritans brought their children to be baptized.
Could a child be baptized if one of his or her parents had never become
a full church member? John Davenport adamantly believed that the answer was no, but at a synod held in Boston in 1662, other New England
divines disagreed with him. They argued that those among the second
generation who had been baptized were "half-way" members who, as
long as they agreed to "own the covenant" and lead upright lives, could
baptize their children. Until his death, Davenport denounced the Half-
Way Covenant as impure, but at Center Church, as in many other New
England churches, the congregation overruled their pastor and quietly
accepted the covenant during the 1680s.[22]

Having described the cultural and doctrinal axes of Center Church,
we turn now to the membership records. Before Robert Pope's pioneering study of New England congregational records published in 1969,
no scholars had ever studied actual church membership figures.[23] Instead they relied solely on literary evidence produced for the most part
by the clergy. Yet sermon-based studies tell us little about empirical realities at the congregational level. In particular, they say little about
patterns of decline or vitality. Who were the men and women who
joined Center Church, and when in their lives did they join? Was church

FIGURE 1

Family Connections of New Members
1639–1989

A 1639–1787

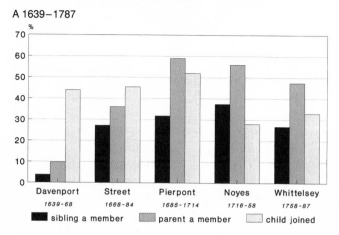

B 1789–1908

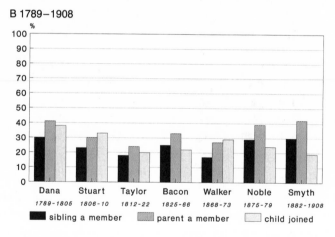

C 1909–1989

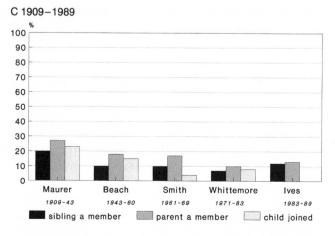

TABLE 2

New Members Admitted in Each Decade,
1639–1989

DECADE	NO. ADMITTED	DECADE	NO. ADMITTED
1639–1650	189	1820–1830	346
1650–1660	33	1830–1840	399
1660–1670	43	1840–1850	337
1670–1680	2	1850–1860	270
1680–1690	142	1860–1870	234
1690–1700	147	1870–1880	303
1700–1710	88	1880–1890	176
1710–1720	133	1890–1900	164
1720–1730	124	1900–1910	113
1730–1740	218	1910–1920	832
1740–1750	77	1920–1930	506
1750–1760	44	1930–1940	307
1760–1770	86	1940–1950	283
1770–1780	98	1950–1960	503
1780–1790	69	1960–1970	185
1790–1800	60	1970–1980	393
1800–1810	228	1980–1989	65
1810–1820	182	TOTAL: 7,379	

membership primarily an affair for the old, for adults, or for children, and what, in turn, does this tell us about the interconnections of church and society? In like manner, we need to explore discipline. Were Center Church members excommunicated? When, if ever, did excommunication disappear? And what does this tell us about internal cohesion and larger social involvements? Finally, family and mobility patterns need to be explored. Who were the central families at Center Church? Did many move away after joining? Until now, these questions have gone unanswered.

First, how many men and women joined Center Church? As table 2 shows, more people were admitted in the 1680s than in the 1660s. From surviving church records (which in these early years are incomplete) it appears that only 43 people joined the church between 1660 and 1670, but between 1680 and 1690, 142 were admitted. Clearly, "decline" was not irreversible. Center Church survived the crisis of the Half-Way Covenant and emerged as a thriving institution that continued to grow more powerful throughout the seventeenth and eighteenth centuries.

Equally as significant are the ages of new members at joining. In theological terms, age at membership reflects assumptions about spiritual maturity. Yet its correlation (or lack thereof) with social coming-of-age yields important insights into the interrelationships of church membership and communal leadership. It is our assumption that the more church membership conveys social authority and economic privilege, the more membership will be limited to the socially empowered adults of the community. Conversely, as church and community become disassociated, and as corporate identity is separated from the church, the more the membership will include individuals who are not yet fully empowered by their society.

From a rich fund of New England town studies completed in the 1970s, it is clear that children did not marry until their mid or late twenties and did not inherit property until their thirties because of the long life-expectancy of the founding generation. This meant that they remained "children" or "adolescents" dependent on their parents until rather late in their lives.[24]

How old were these children when they joined the church? By grouping together those who joined during each pastorate and ranking them by age, it is clear that church membership in the colonial era was almost always a matter for responsible adults. The vast majority of members admitted during Davenport's ministry were over the age of twenty-five; 71 percent were between fifteen and forty-six. The fact that one child under sixteen was admitted reveals there that were no theological proscriptions against childhood membership. Rather the impetus was social. Given the power of the laity in Congregational churches, and the power of the church in the community, new members were expected, indeed *required* to be mature and socially responsible. Boston's famous pastor John Cotton explained that "Noe man fashioneth his house to his hangings, but his hangings to his house."[25] If the church was to direct and model social and political institutions, then its members must be the same adults who would exercise authority in the community.

The pattern of mature membership continued unchanged throughout the seventeenth and eighteenth centuries until the American Revolution.[26] During James Pierpont's ministry, between the years of 1685 and 1714, the children of the founders came of age and began joining the church as young adults. As the children inherited property, voted, and began having families of their own, their descendants also joined the church. Of the 333 members admitted during Pierpont's ministry, the majority (67 percent) joined between the ages of twenty and thirty-five. Only one child joined under the age of fifteen. Conversely, the very elderly also failed to become members. Ministers routinely reminded their listeners that the elderly were too steeped in their ways to join. At Northampton, Massachusetts, the famed preacher-theologian Jonathan Edwards (related by marriage to James Pierpont) warned that old people "won't be so likely to be Christians . . . as those that are Converted in their youth."[27] Membership patterns at Center Church bear these warnings out. Throughout Pierpont's ministry, only two members over the age of sixty joined the congregation.

During Joseph Noyes's ministry (1716–58), membership patterns remained the same.[28] And by the third and fourth generations, membership had become somewhat routinized. Most people joined the church in their twenties. The one exception to this pattern occurred during the great mid-eighteenth-century revivals known as the "Great Awakening," which drew many youths into New England churches. In 1736, Jonathan Edwards wrote in his *Narrative* that "there was a considerable revival of religion last summer at New Haven. . . . this flourishing of religion still continues."[29] The revival he described is confirmed in the membership records. In 1734, Noyes admitted 17 new members, but in 1735 he admitted 45, in 1736 he admitted 56, and in 1737, 36. Many of these new members were young. Indeed, between 1720 and 1730, Noyes admitted only 49 new members who were twenty-five or under, but between 1730 and 1740, he admitted 82—an increase of 79 percent.

Clearly *revival*, in the gradual language of stages, had become the primary recruiting mechanism of Center Church, and it remained so well into the nineteenth century. Yet the radicalism of many of the eighteenth-century revivals divided the congregation into two competing factions: conservative "Old Lights" versus anti-ministerial "New Lights."[30] After the popular itinerant James Davenport accused the Reverend Noyes of being an "unconverted" minister, a "hypocrite, a wolf in sheep's clothing, and a devil incarnate," the congregation was unable to maintain even a semblance of unity.[31] In 1742, a group of Center Church members, encouraged in part by Noyes's brother-in-law, James Pierpont, seceded to form the White Haven Church on the grounds that "the preaching and conduct of the Rev. Mr. Noyes had been in great measure unprofitable to them."[32] Several years later, in 1753, in response to student complaints, President Clap of Yale decided to hold worship services in College Hall rather than send his students to hear a pastor they clearly disliked. This marked the beginnings of Yale College Church and ended the virtual monopoly that Center Church pastors enjoyed with the college's students.[33]

Obviously, the Great Awakening was one of the most turbulent periods in Center Church's history. However, because of the formation of alternative churches to absorb dissidents, the standards and practices of membership at Center Church were affected only briefly. When Chauncy Whittelsey began his twenty-nine-year ministry at Center Church in 1758, the revivals had peaked and the age patterns had again stabilized. If anything, the age at membership during Whittelsey's tenure *rose* slightly as new members over the age of thirty increased from 26 percent to 36 percent. Again, the very oldest and youngest did not join.

In turning from social practice to theology, we see that for the most part the preaching reflected social reality; it was young adults who were joining Center Church. From Davenport through Whittelsey, Center Church ministers spoke of salvation in gradualistic terms correlated with the life cycle. All pointed out that the Holy Spirit *could* effect saving grace in youth, but that his "general pattern" was to work gradually, "convicting" sinners in a series of stages that began in youth but did not cross the threshold of grace until early adulthood. Under the methodical gospel preaching of their ministers, Center Church members internalized the language of gradualism and learned to label every stage of their spiritual experience, from "humiliation" to "saving faith" to "true obedience." Such labeling gave them a vocabulary for self-examination and a basis for personal hope in the knowledge that childhood guilt and rebellion were necessary prerequisites to the healing work of the Holy Spirit. In addition, the language of stages provided an objective standard by which ministers and congregations could judge the maturity of aspiring members in reference to the general social norms of the community. Theology and adult membership were mutually reinforcing. The steady stream of adult admissions confirmed ministers in the infallible "truth" of their gradualist theology, thus completing a seamless web of theological teaching and congregational behavior. As long as a core of young adults continued to enter the church in significant numbers, the church could remain the frame on which the hangings of society, politics, and economics rested.

Given the power the laity enjoyed in the Congregational system, and their social status as land-owning adults, one wonders how important the settled ministers were in the recruitment of new members. It is clear from looking at the annual rate of new members joining that, despite substantial lay powers, the ministers were essential to the recruitment process. Center Church accepted new members only when a settled minister was in place. In the vacancies between Pierpont's and Noyes's ministries (1714–16), and between Whittelsey's and Dana's ministries (1787–89), only six new members joined, and those were transfers from other churches rather than new converts.[34] In theory, the congregation and "ruling" (lay) elders could admit new members. But in practice they did not. Although many early studies may have erred in exaggerating the importance of "elite" ministers to the virtual exclusion of the laity, the ministers clearly *were* perceived as central and essential to the primary evangelistic mission of the congregation. Quite simply, without ministers preaching conversion and revival there would be no revival. When later ministers abandoned the language of revival, the recruitment of new members suffered.

Congregations took their covenant pledges of church membership seriously, and their pastors also viewed their covenant with the church as a permanent bond. There was no sense of the ministry as a separate "profession," nor did ministers think of "moving on." In 1667, after New Haven's forced union with Connecticut, John Davenport was so disillusioned by the fate of his colony that he accepted a call to the First Church in Boston, but the public reaction was so strong (in both New Haven and in Boston) that no subsequent colonial minister at Center Church left his congregation. All either retired or died in office. This stability strengthened the bonds linking pastor and congregation into a church "family"—the metaphor most frequently favored to describe the structure of the congregation.

Equally as significant as age at membership and ministerial leadership at Center Church are questions related to the marital status of new members and familial interconnections. Of particular interest here is the extent to which the same core of interconnected families dominated church membership from generation to generation. In his pathbreaking study of the Puritan family, completed fifty years ago, Edmund S. Morgan observed a pattern of "tribalism" in Puritan towns where church

FIGURE 2

Marital Status of New Members
1639–1787

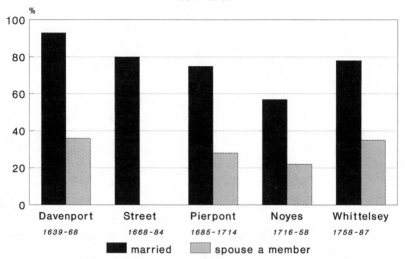

families increasingly concentrated their energies and attention toward their own perpetuation at the center of churches and communities throughout New England. Although ostensibly concerned with Indian missions and the salvation of the "heathen," the Puritans' major evangelistic thrust was inward.[35]

To what extent do Morgan's insights into Puritan tribalism characterize the membership of Center Church? It is clear that the majority of members during Davenport's ministry arrived and joined as married adults (see fig. 2). Of the 224 members who joined in that period, only 3 percent were single. There were actually more widowed members (4 percent) during Davenport's ministry than single members.

Given the fact that most of New Haven's first inhabitants arrived in families, the predominance of married members is not surprising. As the second generation came of age during the pastorate of Nicholas Street, Center Church's second minister, the number of single members rose to 20 percent—a figure that increased to 42 percent during Noyes's ministry. Yet throughout the colonial era, the majority of members, ranging from 56 to 96 percent, were married at the time they joined—a striking confirmation of Morgan's thesis. Of the married members joining Center Church in the colonial era, many were married to one another and even came forward together to apply for church membership.

Of all the married people joining the church between 1700 and 1720, 47 percent either followed a spouse into the church or joined in the same year.

When we extend our analysis of the kinship webs from married couples to new members who had brothers or sisters in the church, the tribalistic patterns become even clearer. Between one-fourth and one-third of new members had siblings in the church (see fig. 1 for family connections of new members). This figure peaked during Noyes's third- and fourth-generation ministry, when 37 percent could point to brothers or sisters among the fellowship, a figure that was not matched during any minister's tenure in office.

Colonial members of Center Church not only shared their pews with spouses and siblings but, in many cases, with their parents as well. From the second generation on, the majority of new members had a parent who belonged to the church. Throughout the ministries of Pierpont and Noyes, roughly 60 percent of all new members joined the church after or in the same year as a parent did. This reflects both the strong tribalism of Center Church members and the demographic patterns of long life-expectancy that allowed parents to survive long into the lives of their children, and even of their grandchildren.[36] Only with Whittelsey's ministry, in the midst of the upheavals of the American Revolution, did the number of new members with parents in the church dip below 50 percent.

Just as many new members at Center Church joined with their siblings and parents, so also did they produce children who followed them into the church. Throughout the ministries of Street and Pierpont, between 40 and 50 percent of new members had at least one child join the Center Church congregation. With Noyes's ministry, this figure dropped off: 67 percent had no children join, a pattern that reflects, at least in part, the creation of a new, competing congregation at White Haven formed out of the controversy over the "Great Awakening." Of those members whose children joined, most had one or two children follow them into membership, though cases where three or more joined were not rare. Indeed, some, like Samuel and Sarah Alling, lived to see six of their children become church members.[37]

Did the particular families who joined Center Church vary from generation to generation, or did the same core of families enter with each new generation? To answer this question, we sought out the surnames that recurred most regularly, and we labeled as *pillar families* those whose surnames appeared at least fifteen times in the records. A striking pattern emerged; we discovered that the great majority of new members throughout the colonial era were attached to a core of pillar families whose names continued to appear on church rolls through the seventeenth and eighteenth centuries and beyond (see fig. 3). Families like the Atwaters, the Pierponts, and the Mixes replenished the church membership lists over many generations. Many of these families also dominated lay leadership positions in every generation.

The presence of pillar families among new members peaked during the ministry of Joseph Noyes. Of the 508 members who joined under Noyes, 411, or 81 percent, were pillars. But this was not an aberration. Throughout the colonial era, the percentage of pillar families among new members held constant at around 75 percent—an extraordinary confirmation of tribalism, not only *within* but *between* a core of close-knit families.

Tribalism, it is clear, was a multigenerational phenomenon that persisted throughout the colonial era. Indeed, Center Church's identity as a cohesive, interconnected "tribe" grew more rather than less pronounced with each passing generation. Despite frequently voiced fears of "declension" and loss of spiritual resolve, the children and grandchildren absorbed and perpetuated the mission of their parents, and the congregation became more rather than less "Puritan" with each passing generation.

Closely allied to tribal patterns at Center Church were patterns of high residential stability. Local town studies of geographic mobility have shown that New England communities were extraordinarily stable and resistant to the forces of atomism that plagued other colonies to the south. Covenant pledges were taken with the same seriousness as marriage vows and proved to be powerfully effective in thwarting the urge to "go West." Few inhabitants left the towns in which they were born until at least the fourth generation, when land began to run out.[38]

Within Center Church, mobility rates were similarly low. The vast majority of new members in the colonial era were born, grew up, and died in New Haven. Through Whittelsey's ministry, nearly 90 percent of new members were native New Havenites (fig. 4). In theory, church members could leave their church and community if they gave proper cause and received a letter of "dismission" from their home congregation. Yet 83 percent of new members admitted between 1600 and 1700

FIGURE 3
"Pillar Members" Admitted by Each Pastor
1639–1989

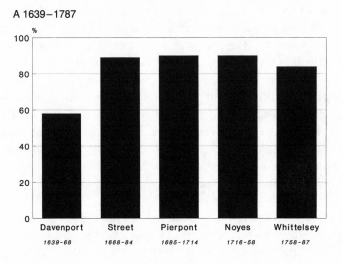

A 1639–1787

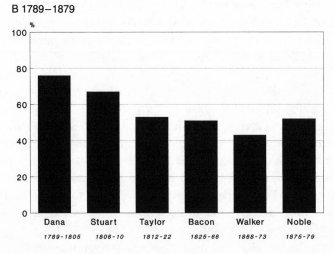

B 1789–1879

and 72 percent of new members admitted between 1700 and 1800 re-mained members throughout their lifetimes—in sharp contrast to the pattern of the nineteenth and twentieth centuries. Pillars, in particular, rarely left the church, which suggests a level of internal stability unri-valed in seventeenth- and eighteenth-century colonial societies.

Nor surprisingly, just as few members left New Haven's close-knit

FIGURE 3

(continued)

C 1882–1989

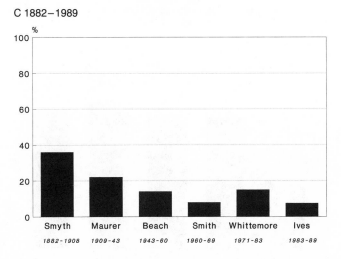

membership, few were added as transfers from other Congregational churches outside New Haven. Transfer memberships never amounted to more than 2 percent of new members in any colonial minister's pastorate. Indeed, Center Church's growth was almost entirely self-generated and self-perpetuated. There was no significant missionary impulse in New Haven, nor was there any attempt to evangelize neighboring towns or communities. Church, community, family, and faith coexisted; none of these single parts could construct an identity or existence independent of the whole.

Statistical measures for the effectiveness of Puritan culture in molding a corporate identity are difficult to come by. Without diaries, survey data, or personal statements it is difficult to know how seriously Center Church congregation members took their ministers' "errand" as their own. One exciting measure, however, first suggested by the historian Daniel Scott Smith in his demographic study of Hingham, Massachusetts, is the use of biblical names in the naming of children.[39] Recognizing that child-naming is a profoundly significant ritual, Smith reasoned that any impulse to construct a Bible commonwealth or a "New Israel" would be reflected in the frequent use of biblical names for children. And indeed, the seventeenth-century "Geneva Bible" used by most first-generation Puritans included a glossary of biblical names together with their meanings for the purpose of child-naming. In looking at

FIGURE 4

New Members Admitted by Each Pastor
Who Were New Haven Natives
1639–1989

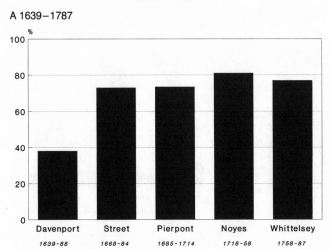

A 1639–1787

	Davenport	Street	Pierpont	Noyes	Whittelsey
	1639-68	1668-84	1685-1714	1716-58	1758-87

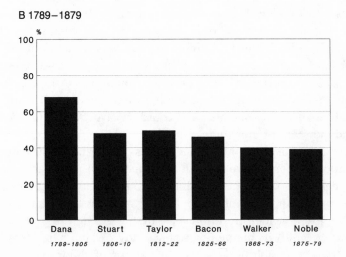

B 1789–1879

	Dana	Stuart	Taylor	Bacon	Walker	Noble
	1789-1805	1806-10	1812-22	1825-66	1868-73	1875-79

child-naming patterns in Center Church (fig. 5), we see a remarkable confirmation of Puritan biblicism. Many of the founders converted to Puritanism as adults and so retained their English family names. But beginning with their children—the second generation—biblical names predominated among the members. For example, Caleb and Mehetabel

FIGURE 4

(continued)

C 1882–1989

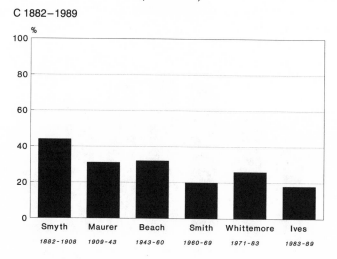

Hotchkiss (themselves named after biblical figures) had three children who joined the church: Caleb, Rachel, and Nehemiah. Caleb, Jr., in turn, became the proud father of a son he christened Jonah.[40] It is unlikely that the high percentages of members who had biblical names were merely a reflection of the popularity of names like John or Sarah. Although the membership lists contain many examples of traditional names like Matthew, Mark, and Elizabeth, they are also liberally sprinkled with more eccentric and self-consciously biblical names like Azariah, Enos, Ephraim, Abiah, Zaccheus, Eleazar, and Eliakim.[41]

Throughout the pastorates of Pierpont, Noyes, and Whittelsey, we see a pattern of enduring biblicism: over 80 percent of new members had biblical names. Indeed, the practice became even more common among the third and fourth generations than it had been among the first and second. In this sense, the high point of the Bible commonwealth did not come in the first two generations, as most ministers (and historians) assumed, but in the third and fourth generations. By Joseph Noyes's pastorate, fully 86 percent of all new members had biblical names. Again, it appears from the statistical evidence that a religious decline was more perceived than real—at least in the colonial era. Throughout, the ministers guided new members who had absorbed their biblical identity, and mission, at the most formative level.

To guarantee the perpetuation of that mission, it was essential that

FIGURE 5

New Members with Biblical Names
1639–1960

A 1639–1810

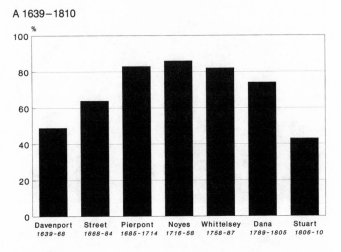

B 1812–1960

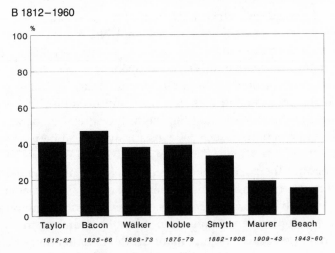

members—as a congregation of pure, visible saints—be disciplined by both the pastor and his congregation. With so much riding on the "Congregational Way," pastors and laity alike served as watchdogs, overseeing the pastor's theology and their fellow members' practice. Cases of heresy, gross impropriety, or rebellion were grounds for excommunication. This decision, like those on ordination and membership, was arrived at by the whole congregation.

The most famous case illustrating the assumptions and procedures for excommunication was that of Anne Eaton. Anne Eaton was the wife of Theophilus Eaton, the governor of the colony and a close personal friend of John Davenport's. But this did not exempt her from discipline. In 1644, she aroused Davenport's ire by publicly questioning his views on baptism, believing it should be restricted to regenerate adults. Davenport responded by preaching against her beliefs from the pulpit, but she was heard muttering "it is not so" as he spoke. Ostentatiously, she left her seat at the front of the church whenever he baptized an infant. He then visited her at home, accompanied by both the teacher of the church, William Hooke, and the magistrate, but according to him she behaved with "such contemptuous carriage" that they soon left.[42]

Eaton clearly posed a threat to Davenport's authority. Alarmed by her large number of followers, both male and female, he couldn't help but compare her to Anne Hutchinson, the "divine rebel" whose excommunication he had attended in Boston in 1638. Like Hutchinson, Eaton was an outspoken, contentious woman whose opinions posed a serious threat to the religious stability of the community. Davenport may have hesitated to punish Eaton because of his affection for her husband, but ultimately he prized the purity and power of his church over personal feelings. After visiting her at home once again to urge her to change her views, Davenport instigated disciplinary proceedings against her. On July 14, 1644, she was called to testify in front of the congregation.

Although Davenport's dispute with Eaton was theological, the transcript of the trial reveals that he strategically dodged many of the religious issues she had raised. He chose to censure her "scandalous walking in her family" rather than the substance of her beliefs. As a woman, Eaton was particularly vulnerable to such a line of attack. Davenport portrayed her as an aggressive, quarrelsome woman who refused to submit to the authority of both her minister and her husband. According to testimony given by various servants and witnesses, Eaton was guilty of seventeen "offenses" against her family. To name just a few, she had hit and pinched several servants; she had accused her stepdaughter of being pregnant out of wedlock; and she had slapped her mother-in-law "twice on the face with the back of her hand." She had also told her husband "with much heat of Spirit" that she would prefer to live without him.[43]

Out of respect for her husband, in the summer of 1644 the church voted only to admonish Eaton rather than excommunicate her. However, after nine months, when she still "continued obstinate," they voted to excommunicate her, the most severe punishment they could offer. In Davenport's words, excommunication

> is Spiritual, and for ever, upon impenitent persons. It is greater than Earthly kings and Magistrates can do; they can bind a Male-factor hand and foot . . . but this Censure binds the Soul and Conscience, delivers them to Satan, and excludes obstinate impenitent sinners from the Kingdom of God.[44]

Members of the congregation, apart from relatives, were required to treat an excommunicate as an outcast, without "civil familiarity," "so as may make him ashamed."

Cases like Eaton's were relatively rare but regular enough to confirm that the church's powers were real. During Davenport's ministry, three members besides Eaton were excommunicated. All three were men, and their offenses ranged from theft to bestiality to falsehood and defamation. Following Davenport's ministry, only two other excommunications were recorded in the colonial era, both during Whittelsey's ministry. A man was excommunicated for fornication, and a woman was excommunicated for intemperance. Interestingly, with the exception of Eaton, all of these excommunicated members were the first of their family to join the church. As such, they lacked the strong family connections that might have kept them within the discipline of the congregation or, alternatively, protected them from prosecution.

The number of Center Church excommunications rose in the nineteenth century. The absence of excommunications between Davenport and Whittelsey suggests less a dilution of standards and purity than an educated membership who policed themselves and prevented others from going too far. In addition, many religious offenses in colonial New Haven were civil offenses as well, punishable by the civil magistracy. For example, several of Eaton's followers were not full church members and so could not be excommunicated, but they did face stiff fines imposed by the civil court.[45]

Turning from discipline to gender, we see some fascinating patterns that appeared early on and shaped Center Church throughout its history. First, and most dramatically, far more women than men became church members. From Center Church data, it is clear that the "feminization" of Congregationalism began far earlier than the eighteenth century, where most historians have dated it.[46] In every twenty-year period from 1660 to the American Revolution, women constituted an ever-growing majority of new converts. As figure 6 illustrates, between 1660

FIGURE 6

Membership by Gender
1639–1989

A 1639–1760

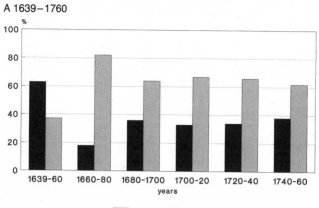

B 1760–1880

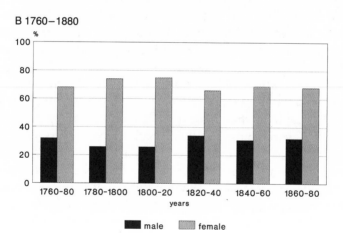

C 1880–1989

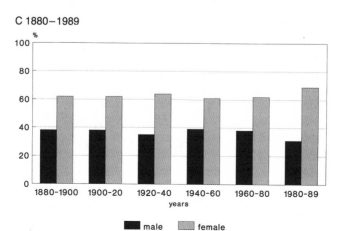

and 1680, women made up 82 percent of new members, and from 1680 to 1700, 64 percent. In the eighteenth century, about 720 women joined Center Church—a figure exceeding the total membership of men from *both* the seventeenth and the eighteenth centuries. Statistics from other Congregational churches suggest that this phenomenon was not confined to Center Church. In New Haven's White Haven Church in 1796, only 36 of its 158 members were male. Between 1796 and 1805, 78 new members were admitted, but only 25 of them were men.[47] And in Boston's Congregational churches between the years of 1730 and 1769, women comprised 59 percent of all new members.[48]

Why did more women than men join the church? Perhaps women's distinct experiences made them more thoughtful about their spiritual condition. Both bearing and rearing children were hazardous enterprises in the colonial era. Pregnancy was a particularly fearful time for women as they confronted their own and their children's mortality. Death often appeared suddenly and without warning. Out of the 465 people in Center Church who died between the years of 1763 and 1786, many were children—114 were under the age of two, and another 52 were between the ages of two and five.[49]

Women may also have been more attracted to the church because it offered them a public identity, a visible role in the creation of a "city on a hill." Although in the colonial period public and private spheres tended to be overlapping and fluid, "good wives" were not normally expected to speak in public or exercise a leadership role.[50] Instead, within the hierarchy of the Puritan state and family they were supposed to be humble and submissive. When Abigail Noyes, the eldest daughter of the Reverend James Pierpont, died in 1768, Chauncy Whittelsey used the occasion of her funeral sermon to urge the women in his audience to "aspire after the ornaments of Godliness, Charity, and a meek and quiet spirit, from the example of holy *women* of old."[51] The church defined and limited women's piety, but it also offered them their only opportunity for public self-expression.

The early predominance of female members became self-perpetuating. By the end of the seventeenth century, ministers and laypeople alike simply expected women to be godly. As Cotton Mather remarked in 1691, "there are far more godly women in the world than there are godly men."[52] Faced with growing numbers of women in their congregations, ministers tailored their sermons to suit their audience. Although many historians have argued that the first Puritans saw women as weak or even evil (because of the taint of Eve's sin), others have recognized that perceptions of women changed as they swelled the pews.[53] As early as the 1690s, ministers were using the typology of the female as a model for the regenerate. By the revivals of the 1740s, ministers such as Jonathan Edwards frequently employed the metaphor of a mystical marriage to explain the convert's relationship to Christ. They described new converts as "brides" of Christ, who were expected to exemplify the virtues that colonial culture equated with "femininity"— submission, devotion, and purity.[54] As historian Leigh Erik Schmidt has argued, men as well as women could be "brides of Christ," but this relationship required men to "transform their sexual identity and subvert their status."[55] In contrast, women found it easier to imagine themselves in this relationship because of their social experiences as "good wives."

By the nineteenth century, women's enthusiastic participation in church life had made them the religious centers of their families. However, our data suggest that throughout the colonial period, until the years surrounding the American Revolution, men, not women, were expected to be the primary religious carriers in the family. One suggestive piece of evidence for this interpretation is that men were often more likely to have a biblical name than women (a pattern that would reverse after the Revolution as the church became even more thoroughly "feminized"). Between 1660 and 1680, 62 percent of the men but only 43 percent of the women who were admitted had biblical names. Between 1720 and 1740, 91 percent of men but only 80 percent of women who were admitted had biblical names. On the level of naming, colonial parents appeared to be singling out their sons more frequently than their daughters for a biblically inspired destiny.

Pillar families in particular seem to have pressured their sons to convert. The majority of *both* female and male converts were pillars, and in sheer numbers there were more female than male pillars. Yet a greater *percentage* of men than women came from pillar families; when a man entered the church, he was more likely to be surrounded by parents and siblings than a woman. Between 1760 and 1780, for example, 55 percent of men had a parent in the church and 34 percent had a sibling in the church, in contrast to 44 percent of the women who had a parent and 23 percent a sibling in the church (see fig. 7).

Despite women's increasing influence in the pews, male pillars had been raised in the expectation that they would become bulwarks of the church. In the Puritan's world, the father was second only to the minister in religious authority. As the head of the family, the man was

FIGURE 7

Family Connections by Gender
1760–1780

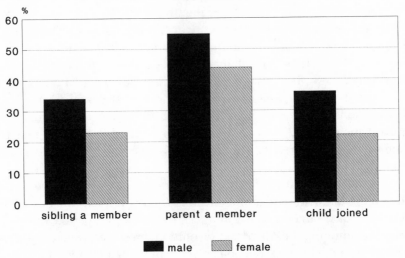

entrusted with the care of his wife's and children's souls. As John Cotton explained, "when we undertake to be obedient" to God, we undertake not only "in our owne names, and for our owne parts, but in the behalfe of every soul that belongs to us . . . our wives, and children, and servants, and kindred, and acquaintance, and all that are under our reach."[56] Apparently men took this responsibility seriously. Throughout the colonial period, a greater percentage of male than female converts had children who eventually joined the church. In this sense, the "feminization" model does not apply to the colonial era. Rather, fathers and sons were essential carriers of the faith.[57]

For most Puritans, conversion occurred in adulthood, after marriage and parenthood. For men in particular, as we have seen, marriage meant not only new economic but new spiritual duties. They tended to convert when they were well into adulthood. For example, between 1680 and 1700, 54 percent of new male members were between the ages of thirty-one and forty-six. The vast majority (95 percent) were married, and many were parents. Although the scarcity of records means that our sample for this variable is small, the data are provocative nevertheless. Of the 80 men admitted between 1680 and 1700, 70 percent were parents.

When we compare these statistics to those on women members,

clear differences become apparent. Gender norms seem to have affected the timing of conversion. Most significant here is the large number of women (more than double the number of men) who joined when they were young and single.[58] These figures suggest that conversion occurred at different times in the male and female life cycles. Men were expected to join the church when they attained maturity, which they defined as becoming the head of a household. Women, on the other hand, may have been expected to reach maturity at an earlier age. For them, church membership was not linked to taking on political responsibilities or inheriting land. Disconnected from the larger male framework of communal leadership, women may have been seen as "mature" as soon as they reached a marriageable age and accepted their subordinate place within the Puritan hierarchy.

The increasing numbers of women joining the church at younger ages had important consequences. Most notably, religion began to be "feminized." Recognizing that there are no intrinsic "feminine" or "masculine" qualities, we can nevertheless reconstruct the values eighteenth-century people attributed to women and see if they gained in emphasis as female membership gained in numbers. Barbara Welter has argued that "feminization" began after the American Revolution, but our data suggest that its roots can be found even earlier. As men drifted away from the church, ministers "softened" their sermons to fit the needs of their new female audience. Ministers had inherited conceptions of women as "softer" and more emotional, and they emphasized those values to meet the perceived needs of the majority in their audience. We have already seen how, by using the metaphor of the convert as the bride of Christ, ministers demanded that converts imagine themselves in female terms. Other developments only added to the identification of women with religion. In sermons and hymns, ministers increasingly portrayed Christ as loving, submissive, and humble, and over time they abandoned the idea of infant damnation (a concept that may have been particularly difficult for mothers to accept).[59] Certainly individual men could continue to identify with Christ, but culturally, the constellation of values revolving around love, nurture, and submission was perceived as "feminine."

While it is risky to draw connections between particular social configurations and particular theological orientations, it does appear that the feminization of New England congregations coincided with the great evangelical revivals of George Whitefield and the "Great Awakening." The causes of the revivals and its consequences were many and varied.

But surely one contributing factor was feminization. The emphasis on "affections" and experience in the sermons of revivalists like Whitefield coincided with increasing numbers of women members who had been denied access to higher religious training, and whose interests therefore tended to be, generally speaking, less theological than experiential.[60] This increasingly experiential sense of religion appeared in the mid-eighteenth century and suffused *both* Arminian and Calvinist congregations. All turned to "heartfelt" sensation that had its origins in the "New Birth." Clearly many factors related to consumerism and the rise of a market economy led to this new heart-centered conception of faith and, in this sense, feminization did not "cause" the theological shift. Nevertheless increasing numbers of female members, closed off from higher education and denied roles in theological formulations like catechisms, covenants, or creeds, surely provided a receptive soil for the new ideas.

The feminization of the church contributed to a profound theological transformation. When viewed from the congregational level, the most striking transformation in Puritanism was not the transition "from piety to intellect" described by Perry Miller in his analysis of male Harvard and Yale graduates, but its opposite, a transition from intellect, where doctrinal knowledge informed membership, to piety, where the *experience* of grace mattered more than formal creeds and catechisms.

Despite signal changes in feminization and a theology of sentiment, the most striking finding to emerge from our study of church membership in the colonial period is its extraordinary stability. Certainly great events like King Philip's War (the bloody war with native tribes during 1675–76), the adoption of the Half-Way Covenant, and the 1690 Act of Toleration affected the lives of the congregants, yet none of these events substantially altered the patterns of stability and continuity that persisted generation after generation. Even the "Great Awakening," which divided the church into two competing factions and resulted in the formation of both the Yale College Chapel and the White Haven Church, did not affect the internal demographic, cultural, and theological continuity of the church. From first to last, the congregants saw themselves as "Puritans" sent on a great errand into the wilderness.

That identity—both tribal and biblical—grew steadily stronger with each passing generation. Every new year confirmed the congregants' identity as a "People of the Word" bound in a "peculiar" covenant with God. Every year, that is, until 1776. When, in 1776, New Haven citizens found themselves catapulted into what one participant termed "the greatest event taking place in the present Age," the members of

1.2 South view of Center Church's second meetinghouse (1670–1757). Reprinted from Henry T. Blake, *Chronicles of the New Haven Green* (New Haven: The Tuttle, Morehouse & Taylor Press, 1898); courtesy of New Haven Colony Historical Society.

Center Church congregation found that their lives—and their congregation—would never again be the same. As the colonial era passed, they left behind their Puritan roots to enter a new, mature phase as a Yankee congregation.

A Yankee Congregation

For a century and a half, Center Church congregation had existed as an insular, self-contained "Puritan church." The members were *Puritan* in the sense that they were Congregational in polity, tribal in demographic structure, and evangelical in their commitment to the New Birth and a Bible commonwealth. They were a *church* in the sociological sense of being state-supported and autonomous, a public institution whose norms molded the civic community.

In the years following independence, however, all this changed. As we examined our data for the Revolutionary era, every graph and table pointed to a sudden, remarkable transformation that was more radical and far-reaching than any that had appeared in the earlier life of the Center Church congregation and that would not be equaled again until the twentieth century. The War for Independence, it soon became clear, meant far more than political rebellion against a colonial tyrant. It meant the start of an internal revolution that transformed every institution, including the congregation, according to the new republican orthodoxy of individualism, voluntarism, and the separation of church and state.[61] After 1840, the church recovered from the shocks it had experienced in the Revolution, but only partially. In stark contrast to the colonial era, the most salient fact of life within the Center Church congregation throughout the nineteenth century was change, not stability.

The closing decades of the eighteenth century were turbulent ones in American society. The Revolutionary era encompassed not only a political transformation but the fruition of cultural and economic changes that had begun decades earlier. In New England, an economy based on self-sufficient farming was giving way to a market economy. Many of the first Puritan settlers, including those in New Haven, had planned to be merchants rather than farmers, and throughout the seventeenth century they traded meat, fish, and lumber with colonists in the West Indies. In the eighteenth century, trading expanded even further, and many families no longer depended on household manufacturing to supply all their clothing and food. Instead, farmers used the income they made from selling their surplus crops to purchase what they needed.

The Revolution only accelerated these changes. The exigencies of war meant that manufacturing increased, especially in the iron and weapons industries. And as the market with England closed, Americans expanded their trade to lucrative outlets with other countries including France, Spain, and the Netherlands.

These economic changes had far-reaching effects on New England's culture and values. The Puritans believed in working hard in order to glorify God, yet they also believed in a fixed social hierarchy and deference to superiors. Ironically, as their work ethic made them successful, their wealth and their social mobility posed a challenge to their hierarchical, tightly ordered way of life. As Richard Bushman has argued in *From Puritan to Yankee: Character and the Social Order in Connecticut*, the expansion of trade led to acquisitiveness and social fragmentation.[62] In addition, economic change uprooted traditional institutions of church and state, leaving the "public square" deserted.[63] Instead of looking to established institutions, individuals confronted a society in which there were no authoritative guardians proclaiming a public orthodoxy. The creation of the new American individual, it soon became clear, was as much a cause for anxiety as for celebration.

The Revolution not only accelerated economic changes, but it also represented the triumph of an entirely new set of cultural values. More and more, the logic of the marketplace became a shaping metaphor for American society, a metaphor that placed unprecedented emphases on individualism and on private, voluntary associations as the repository of personal values and meaning. Life in the new republic would be different from life in the Puritan colonies. Instead of advocating hierarchy and deference like their Puritan foreparents, "Yankees" rebelled against authority and celebrated social mobility. Instead of subordinating all interests to the church and its civic Bible commonwealth, they prized individualism and shifted the locus of religious faith from public policy to private conscience. And in place of an inscrutable, all-powerful deity they increasingly celebrated their free will, which assured self-made individuals that in spiritual terms they could become self-made saints.

Religious changes only added to the turmoil. Throughout New England, Protestant dissenters—Methodists, Baptists, or simply "Christians"—were forming new churches to compete with the Congregational establishment. These churches took the republican celebration of individualism and popular sovereignty to its logical culmination in movements that severed connections to all "Old World" creeds and college-educated "priests."[64]

The problems of the Congregational churches were compounded by internal rivalries and divisions. As we have seen in New Haven, the "Great Awakening" had divided many congregations in two. Competition between "New Lights" and "Old Lights" created healthy controversy and vitality but also fragmented many Congregational churches. By 1782, there were five rival churches in New Haven: four Congregational and one Episcopal. And this was only the start. After 1818 in Connecticut, Congregational churches were officially disestablished and could no longer rely on state support. In the new republic, churchgoing would be voluntary rather than required. Neither Center Church, nor the Congregational churches collectively, exercised sole religious authority in the town as they had earlier. Indeed, they were forced to compete with other churches for members. By the end of the eighteenth century, John Davenport's First Church officially became known as Center Church, denoting its central location on the green. Center Church no longer stood alone in the middle of New Haven. On one side, the White Haven Church, which had been formed during the Great Awakening, reminded the congregants of past schisms. On the other, Trinity Church represented the Anglican establishment that the original Puritans had so desperately fled.

Because of the proliferation of churches, Center Church was no longer the largest congregation in town, although it remained the wealthiest. According to Yale president Ezra Stiles, in 1782 Center Church had 900 members, while Fair Haven had 950 and White Haven had 800. In 1796, when Fair Haven and White Haven merged, calling themselves the United Church, their combined numbers must have been quite considerable. In wealth, however, the advantage went to Center. In 1811 the United Society had a respectable $4,682 in its fund for the support of its ministry, while Center Church had $11,685.10.[65]

Despite its continuing wealth, the future of Congregationalism was uncertain in the years immediately following the Revolution. Religious toleration inspired tremendous growth among such new sects as the Universalists and the Shakers, but membership in the old, established Congregationalist churches began to decline. In New Haven, according to the Reverend Oscar Maurer, the Yale College Chapel was reduced to only about four or five members before being revitalized under the presidency of Timothy Dwight.[66] In fact, by 1808 Connecticut's General Assembly had become so concerned about the spread of new religious ideas that they passed a law making deism a felony.[67]

In all this political and religious turmoil, Center Church continued to grow, although somewhat slowly. Between 1770 and 1800, 227 new members joined.[68] Although these numbers were smaller than in previous decades, they attested to the continuing appeal of the church and the strength of its leadership. Chauncy Whittelsey, the pastor when the war first broke out, was not known for his inspired preaching—the missionary David Brainerd once remarked that he had "no more grace than a chair"—but he did manage to hold together a congregation of divided loyalties. According to Ezra Stiles, there were between twenty and thirty Loyalist families in the congregation. The most notorious Loyalist was the local stamp collector, Jared Ingersoll, who suffered grievously at the hands of the patriotic "Sons of Liberty." Yet because of Whittelsey's diplomacy, even Ingersoll stayed and was eventually buried in the crypt beneath the new meetinghouse.

Whittelsey himself was a leading patriot in the revolutionary cause. Like many other New England clergymen, he played an important role as a catalyst of the Revolution.[69] When, on October 18, 1774, New Haven patriots voted to send relief to Boston's beleaguered inhabitants, Whittelsey was at the head of the line. In the spring of 1775, a regiment of New Haven troops that included members of Center Church set out for Boston under the command of Colonel Benedict Arnold, and Whittelsey offered prayers for their safe delivery.

For his unstinting efforts on behalf of the patriot cause, Whittelsey was invited to deliver Connecticut's 1778 annual election sermon. In that sermon, delivered in the midst of war, Whittelsey reminded his hearers of the old Puritan truism that, next to a belief in the existence of God, a belief in his providence was most important. While uncertain about the immediate outcome of particular battles, Whittelsey had no doubt that America's long-term destiny was providentially glorious. Despite disturbing news of military setbacks, he consoled his listeners with the certainty of a great future:

> At this day the prospect evidently is, that a new Empire, under the providence of God, is now rising up, in the western world; a prospect, which from the beginning of the controversy [with England], has from time to time, grown brighter and brighter.[70]

If pushed to describe the shape of that "new Empire," he undoubtedly would have painted it as New England's Bible commonwealth writ large. And like most of the clergy, he assumed that ministers like himself would continue to guide and direct the morals of the people so that they would retain God's favor as an "elect nation." Neither he nor any of his peers had any sense that this revolution would be far more transforming than anything they imagined—so powerful, in fact, that it would deprive them (and their congregations) of the privileged place they had once enjoyed in New England society.

Following Whittelsey's death in 1787, the vacancy in the pulpit was filled by James Dana, who in January 1789 was elected and ordained pastor by the congregation. In his former pastorate at Wallingford, Connecticut, Dana had fallen under censure for his supposed Unitarian views. Although exonerated of the charge and declared to be solidly "moderate" in his Calvinist theology by Yale president Ezra Stiles, Dana continued to encounter fierce resistance from his more Calvinist clerical peers in New Haven. Samuel Austin, pastor of the Fair Haven Church, and Jonathan Edwards, Jr., pastor of the White Haven Church, both "New Divinity" heirs of Jonathan Edwards, Sr., refused to "hold fellowship" with him. This rupture with New Haven's other Congregational churches provided a graphic illustration of life in the new republic. Henceforth there would be no single "establishment," and each congregation would compete for members as a voluntary organization.

Like Whittelsey, his predecessor, Dana was not known for fervent revival preaching or path-breaking theology. But he did manage to avoid large-scale defections or losses of new members and actually admitted ninety new members during his sixteen-year ministry. As before, most of these new members came from pillar families in New Haven who had long-standing local connections to the church.

Despite increases, the small rate of growth in the Dana era was a warning sign. The Puritans had prized the cohesiveness of their communities, but many of New Haven's rising generation were participating in a massive westward population movement. In addition, when the threat of war passed, many new immigrants began entering New Haven and other northern cities in search of new opportunities. All these changes insured that the old self-perpetuating, tribalistic ethos would also change. New Haven was changing and so, inevitably, were its churches. Families would separate, pillars would move away, children would declare their independence from their parents and join new religious movements, new immigrants would move to New Haven with new faiths. Eventually, even theology would have to catch up to the vast demographic transition that marked the formal end of the Puritan tribe and the Bible commonwealth.

But exactly how would the church respond to this demographic crisis? One response, long favored in Congregational churches, was revival. And, in fact, the next two pastors, Moses Stuart (1806–10) and Nathaniel Taylor (1812–22), were powerful preachers who actively sought revival. They called themselves "Calvinist," yet at the same time they recast the old Puritan theology in ways that gave increasing scope to free will and self-determination. Taylor gained national recognition as the architect of a "New Haven Theology" that modified the old doctrines of total depravity and unconditional election. When he later moved to the faculty of Yale Divinity School, his students carried his teachings and example throughout the new republic.

Born as Americans rather than colonists, Stuart and Taylor instinctively brought a new republican ethos into the pulpit with them. They celebrated the new creed of self-reliance and they redefined conversion, disconnecting it from family responsibilities and stressing its individual qualities. This orientation, we will see, was as much a response to changed circumstances as it was the product of abstract theological reasoning. As New Haven's population grew and pillar families dispersed or transferred to competing churches, potential converts had to be sought in the wider community.[71]

Moses Stuart first took the pulpit of Center Church during the winter of 1804–5, when Dana was ill. Although young, he was an accomplished theologian and biblical scholar who bridged the gap between moderate Calvinism and the Edwardsean "New Divinity" far more effectively than Dana. Like many learned clergymen, he imbibed deeply from the wells of both Scottish commonsense realism and a softened Calvinism. Gone was the idealism of Jonathan Edwards with its unwavering adherence to unconditional election, and in its place was a simple appeal to the senses to validate the empirical claims of Christianity and to experience Christ *now*.[72] During the first winter at Center Church, Stuart aroused so much excitement that the congregation did not want him to leave. When Dana returned from his illness, they urged him to accept Stuart as a colleague in the pulpit. Dana refused, little realizing the price he would pay. In 1805, the church's ruling body, the First Society, voted "its consent that Dr. Dana retire from his pastoral labors," even though he had expressed no intention of retiring. In effect, even though Dana had devoted sixteen years of his life to the congregation, they dismissed him against his will.

Stuart's evangelical, heartfelt preaching complemented his scholarly knowledge of Scripture; for him, revival was rooted in the latest biblical scholarship.[73] Compared to the 90 new members Dana had admitted during his sixteen-year pastorate, Stuart brought in 202 new members over only four years through a program of successive revivals. Many of these new members were not from pillar families but were the first in their families to join the church. In just a few years, the mission and membership of the church had changed radically.

In 1810, after a brief but successful ministry at Center Church, Stuart announced that he would leave to accept a position as professor of sacred literatures at the newly founded Andover Seminary. He left a legacy of revival preaching and innovative theology to his successor, Nathaniel Taylor, an equally powerful preacher and brilliant theologian who later won national recognition for his modified Calvinism. Like Stuart, Taylor proved to be a charismatic, dynamic preacher whose ten-year ministry brought nearly four hundred new members into the church. His preaching was conversionist in theme, modeled closely on the revivalist theology of his mentor, Yale's president Timothy Dwight. President Dwight had counseled all his students to preach in commonsense, practical terms that any farmer could understand. Taylor took these lessons to heart and led several notable revivals in 1815, 1816, 1820, and 1821. The 1820 revival was so successful that Taylor's successor, Leonard Bacon, recalled how on one day, over seventy people, "old and young and of every condition in life filled these aisles, as they came from their seats to take the vows of God upon them."[74] But like Stuart, Taylor would not remain. In 1822, over the objections of his congregation, Taylor resigned at Center Church to become Dwight Professor of Didactic Theology at the newly established Yale Divinity School.

The forced removal of Dana and the resignations of two preachers as beloved and successful as Stuart and Taylor suggest that a profound transition was taking place among the clergy in the early republic. Through these examples we see confirmation of a changing conception of the Congregational ministry, moving from office to profession.[75] Ever since the bitterness caused by Davenport's resignation, Center Church pastors had remained with their congregations until death or retirement. But in the new republic, ministers came and went according to their personal and professional self-interest, and congregations "shopped" for the pastors who best suited their needs. In the process, the churches themselves became less prestigious. In the colonial era, ministers preferred major pulpits to college appointments: Increase Mather had gone so far as to turn down the presidency of Harvard College to retain his Boston pulpit. But by the nineteenth century, this was no longer the case. The academy began to surpass the pulpit in prestige and influence, depriving local congregations of leading intellectuals. Individualism and the separation of church and state, it is clear, struck at the very heart of the Congregational Way.

In 1814, Center Church spent $35,000 to construct, over the old graveyard, an impressive new meetinghouse that was the most majestic and imposing church on the green.[76] Physically, this new meetinghouse symbolized the changes taking place in the church's cultural identity. Instead of being plain and unadorned, the exterior of the church was ornate and neoclassic in style, as reminiscent of Rome as of the colonial past. Inside, the elaborate altar and pulpit signaled a new era, at once

1.3   In the middle is Center Church's third meetinghouse (constructed 1757). Photograph of William Giles Munson, "View of the New Haven Green in 1800" (oil on canvas, c. 1830, gift of the Botwinik Foundation, Inc. in memory of Harris & Hyman Botwinik); courtesy of New Haven Colony Historical Society.

triumphant and American, even as the old was preserved in the tombs below.

By 1815, the congregation had changed as much as the physical structure of their meetinghouse. The first index of fundamental changes in Center Church congregation is age at membership: increasing numbers of new members were under the age of sixteen. Five percent of new members in Stuart's ministry were children who were born as Americans, who knew of their colonial past only indirectly as "history." Another 15 percent of new members were adolescents between the ages of sixteen and nineteen. Together, this meant that one in every five new members of Center Church was a young person under the age of twenty. Between 1820 and 1840, the percentage of converts under twenty-five rose to 53 percent, the highest percentage of young members admitted in any twenty-year period since the brief upheaval of the Great Awakening.

In the colonial era, when the Puritan church and the New Haven community had been almost identical, and when church membership had been equated with coming-of-age, children were rarely admitted. Once Center Church had lost that position, however, and church membership was no longer linked with communal responsibility, children began to be accepted. Although one had to be an adult, particularly a male adult, to guide the new democratic society, church membership and political power were no longer coextensive. The altered construction of the community, state, and nation, together with an increasingly experiential theology, meant that children were now fit candidates for spiritual regeneration and church membership.

Moses Stuart was the first minister at Center Church to institutionalize childhood membership as both a complement and an alternative to a revival-driven ministry centered on the adult community. He began by proposing semiannual periods of instruction in which the children should be catechized. This practice continued to grow, so that by the mid-nineteenth century, children were expected to attend "Sabbath school" weekly. Educating children in religion became one of the most important functions of the church. Many of the church manuals that survive from the latter half of the nineteenth century contain detailed information about how many students attended Sabbath school, what they learned, and how many experienced conversion.[77] In the nineteenth century, unlike the seventeenth and eighteenth centuries, ministers and laypeople expected their children to experience saving grace.

At the same time that increasing numbers of children joined churches like Center Church, church leaders altered their theological orientation. As we have tried to show in this study, theological change does not take place in a social vacuum. In the same way that the "Great Awakening" was in some sense a response to feminization, a changing theology of conversion may well have been shaped by the growing number of child members. Theologically, ministers tended to shift their emphases in conversion preaching from nature to nurture. In the colonial era, conversion was understood in the context of total depravity and unconditional election. In this framework, God initiated salvation by "breaking the will" of sinners and transforming their (adult) nature from unregenerate to regenerate.[78] Without ever giving up their conversionist rhetoric, ministers at Center Church stressed a more natural process of domestic conversion in which a child might grow up never knowing he or she was *not* a Christian.

When, in 1847, Horace Bushnell (a prominent student of Nathaniel Taylor's) published his classic treatise *Christian Nurture*, he was giving theological voice to what had already become a sociological reality in

FIGURE 8

Marital Status of New Members
1789–1908

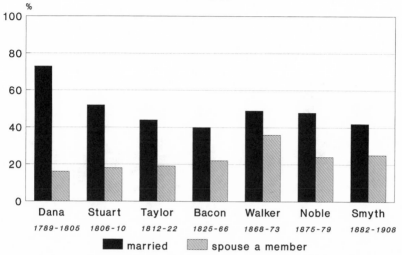

congregations like Center Church. Too often, Bushnell complained, American congregations relied on revivals to build churches, while at the same time neglecting their own youth. Instead of relying exclusively on convulsive conversion experiences, which grew ever wilder among the new denominations, he wanted "the child . . . to grow up a Christian, and never know himself as being otherwise." This new emphasis on nurture comported well with established practices of congregations like Center Church.[79]

The younger ages at membership marked a decisive break with the Puritan past. Equally dramatic was the corresponding increase in single members. In the colonial era, three-quarters of new members had been married at the time they joined, and often their spouses were also members of the church. However, beginning with Stuart's ministry and continuing until the middle of the nineteenth century, single members dominated the membership lists. During Stuart's tenure only 52 percent of new converts were married, and only 18 percent of these had a spouse in the church. This trend continued during Taylor's pastorate, when only 44 percent were married, and only 19 percent of these had a spouse in the church (fig. 8). In the same way that Center Church was now differentiated from the community as one more voluntary association, it was also losing its identity as a church "family."[80]

FIGURE 9

New Members Who Were First in Their Families
to Join the Church
1639–1989

A 1639–1760

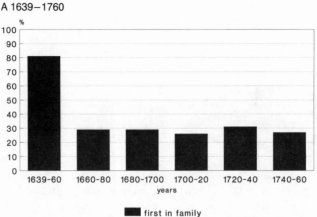

first in family

B 1760–1880

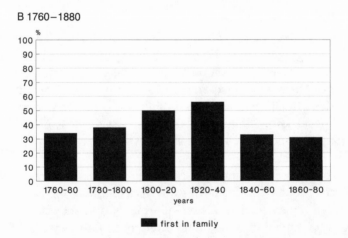

first in family

The contagion of individualism that swept the new republic did not
bypass religion. Church membership at Center Church was becoming a
more individualized experience, increasingly detached from tribal connections. Pastors like Horace Bushnell and Nathaniel Taylor realized
that their pleas for family religion were tilting against the windmills of
the American republic. Too late, they recognized that they had become
the victims of their own revolutionary rhetoric.[81]

Children could be catechized, but this did not insure the participa-

FIGURE 9

(*continued*)

C 1880–1989

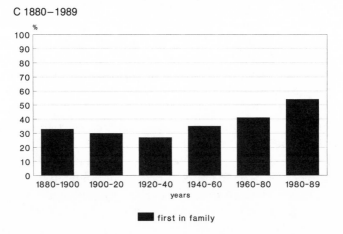

first in family

tion of the whole family in the ongoing life and operations of the con-gregation. One useful index to this transformation is the increasing number of converts who were first in their family to join the church. With the exception of the first generation, converts who were "first" never made up more than 30 percent of new members in any twenty-year period until 1760–1780 (fig. 9). However, that percentage began to rise at the turn of the century, peaking between 1820 and 1840 when 56 percent of the members admitted had no spouse, sibling, parent, or child in the church. Even more significant, many were failing to incor-porate their children (fig. 1). Fewer than 25 percent of new members had parents in the church, and fewer than 25 percent of those same members introduced their children to church membership. During Taylor's min-istry, 80 percent of the 372 new members failed to have even one child join the church. From this we can see how the well-documented failure of contemporary mainline congregations to incorporate their children into the church is, in fact, the product of trends set in motion a century earlier.

In the wake of the Revolution, seemingly overnight, the church had lost its tribal identity. A graph of the percentage of pillars entering the church reveals just how abruptly the institution was transformed (see fig. 3). Throughout the colonial period, the majority of new members had strong family connections within the church. Parents had passed on their church membership to their children, who in turn perpetuated the Congregational Way. Yet in the aftermath of the Revolution, the per-centage of pillar members drastically declined, falling from 70 percent of the new members admitted between 1780 and 1800 to less than half (46 percent) between 1820 and 1840. For the first time in Center Church's two-century history, the majority of new members were not from pillar families.

Several factors may help to explain the loss of tribalism. Certainly some of the children and grandchildren of the pillar members simply lost interest in the church and chose to devote their energies to more secular pursuits. Opportunities for ordinary people, particularly men, proliferated in the early republic and drew dynamic energies away from the church. In the colonial era, Center Church could draw on the finest talent to provide leadership and identity. Increasingly in the nineteenth century, however, the church found itself competing with other institu-tions and losing valuable leaders.

A further drain on Center Church resources was undoubtedly trans-fer to other churches in New Haven. From 1820 to 1865, New Haven's population jumped from eight thousand to fifty thousand. In corre-sponding manner, the number of Congregational churches grew from two to ten, in addition to three mission stations supported by all the Congregational churches. One of these—Davenport Church—had been founded by twenty-five Center Church members as a mission outreach. Others openly competed with Center Church for Congregational mem-bers. Although the majority of New Haven's inhabitants were still Con-gregational, the appearance of other competing denominations was equally impressive. By 1865, Center Church competed with seven Epis-copal churches, six Methodist churches, four Baptist churches, a Uni-versalist church, and a Lutheran church. To this still-Protestant majority were added three Roman Catholic churches and a Reform synagogue of German Jews.

Even more significant than intratown transfers in accounting for the loss of tribalism was geographic mobility. The postrevolutionary genera-tions were restless generations whose children and grandchildren moved west in ever-growing numbers. The migration of Connecticut inhabitants to the north and west continued unabated through the nine-teenth century. The toll on Center Church was heavy. As one would expect, throughout the history of the church, members who had been born in New Haven were more likely than other converts to have rela-tives in the church. Yet beginning with Stuart's ministry, new members born in New Haven numbered less than three-quarters of those admitted to membership. By Taylor's ministry the number of new members born in New Haven had dropped to about 50 percent.[82]

In looking more generally at dismissal patterns, we see that the number of new members who eventually left Center Church increased with every generation. Before Stuart's ministry, ministers could count on a persistence rate of 70 percent or better, but with Stuart that rate dropped to 58 percent. In Center Church's experience, the Age of Jackson was the era of peak mobility and movement out of the church. At the very time when the population growth should have meant massive increases in membership, the outmigration of new members made the gains considerably lighter.

With no covenant pledges binding them permanently to their church, nearly half of Center Church's new members in the early nineteenth century left the congregation. Most were *not* simply transferring to other New Haven churches. New Haven church transfers never accounted for more than 18 percent of Center Church dismissals and were generally less. In addition, many of those who transferred were relocating to one of the many smaller missionary churches Center Church had helped to create in New Haven's poorer neighborhoods, such as the Davenport Church or the Lebanon Mission. A minority of members, however, do seem to have "shopped" for a church, and often Center Church lost more members to its competition than it gained. For example, during Taylor's ministry, 59 members were dismissed to local churches, but only 17 members were admitted from them.

Yet if Center Church lost members to dismissals, they also gained members admitted from other churches outside New Haven, and in many cases, even outside Connecticut. Members in good standing from other Congregational churches could be admitted to Center Church as long as they had a letter from their minister. By Taylor's pastorate, 24 percent of new members were admitted by certificate. By 1878, there were so many transfers that the church covenant had to be revised. Transferring members were now required to "recognize your obligation to *this church* in particular."[83]

As Puritan tribalism disappeared at Center Church, so also did the Puritan church with its vision of a Bible commonwealth. Ministers continued to preach, and members continued to experience conversion, but the deeply inculcated vision of a New Israel disappeared. Nowhere is this more dramatically registered than in the abrupt decline in new members who had biblical names. Before Stuart's ministry, new members with biblical names amounted to about 83 percent of all admissions (fig. 5). During Stuart's ministry that figure dropped dramatically to 43 percent. At first glance, the correlation between an abrupt decline in biblical names and political independence is bewildering. How could an external event like the Revolution affect the intensely personal and religious decision to name one's child? Yet clearly, it *did*. The Bible commonwealth, understood as a coercive and exclusive social order, had disappeared, and with it, the determination to identify one's children with biblical heroes.

The rapid influx of new members and the disappearance of old families meant that discipline became particularly important as a means of preserving internal harmony and cohesion. Center Church could preserve its distinctiveness (and loyalties) only if it was willing to supervise and enforce a standard of belief and behavior from within. There were no longer any external codes or agencies the congregation could rely upon to preserve its identity. If the church's discipline disappeared, so would its distinctiveness. In Stuart's and Taylor's ministries discipline was actively enforced through the pastor and a standing committee elected by the congregation, who met monthly to preside over all complaints and transgressions. As large numbers of new members joined the church during revivals, they required oversight and supervision so that their young faith could be shaped into a life of "sanctified obedience."

Sixteen members admitted between 1800 and 1820 and nine members admitted between 1820 and 1840 were excommunicated. Their offenses ranged from "belief in universal salvation" to "connivance and support of immoral practices at home" to "stealing and contumacy." Intemperance was one of the most frequent causes for disciplinary action: eight men and one woman were expelled from the church for it. As was true in the colonial period, the majority of members excommunicated between these years lacked family connections in the church. Nineteen of them were the first in their family to join the church. And, as in earlier years, men tended to be excommunicated much more frequently than women. Even though women were the clear majority in the church, only six of the twenty-five members excommunicated in these years were female.

Despite the large number of members who were excommunicated between 1800 and 1840, the church no longer had the coercive powers that it had enjoyed in Puritan times. When Anne Eaton was excommunicated, there were powerful and inevitable consequences. Discipline was much less effective in the nineteenth century. A case in point is the famous Nancy Garfield trial in 1816. Garfield, accused of becoming pregnant before marriage, simply refused to appear before the church's discipline committee. Unrepentant, she claimed that she had had a secret wedding. Nathaniel Taylor and his committee found themselves helpless to do anything except take her name off the membership list, not for adultery but "for the sin of falsehood and for contemptuously refusing to receive any communication from this Church." In a biting letter to Taylor, Garfield accused him of being less powerful than his clerical predecessors. A happier result might have ensued, she taunted, if only "the rulers of your Church, had constituted you its Pastor, in *fact* as well as in *name.*" [84]

To be an effective instrument for social cohesion and enforcement of group standards, excommunication had to be tied to communal norms and statutes. In the new republic, however, where all churches were voluntary organizations with no preferred legal standing, an excommunicated member could simply transfer to another church or denomination with no penalty or loss of status in the community. This, in fact, was exactly what Garfield did in 1817, when she transferred next door to Trinity Church, prompting an angry Nathaniel Taylor to ask Rector Henry Crosswell:

> By what rule of the Gospel, by what principle of Christianity does your Church open the arms of protection to the offending member of another—invite and welcome to its embrace the accused and the convicted and thus to the utmost of their power counteract the efficacy of that discipline which Christ has established for their SALVATION? [85]

In fact, Crosswell had every "right" in the new republic to admit whomever he wished, and Garfield lived out her days a contented member of Trinity Church.

Although attenuated by the new liberties of the republic, discipline still occupied an important role in the life of the congregation. Garfield's rebellion was dramatic, but it was countered by many other, less sensational cases where members accepted their discipline, repented, and eventually returned to the church. When later generations of Center Church members abandoned discipline, they lost the internal sanctions that elevated congregational loyalty and made membership valuable.

During these decades of turbulence, men's and women's church experiences diverged as dramatically as they had in the colonial period. Most strikingly, women continued to dominate church membership lists. Of the 410 new members admitted between 1800 and 1820, 75 percent were women (fig. 6). In the nineteenth century as a whole, women outnumbered men two to one.[86] Visually, the disparity in the pews would have been obvious to any casual observer. By 1870, only 162 of the 577 members of the church were men.[87]

How can we explain this decline in male members? Clearly the Revolution marked an important turning point for men's church involvement.[88] Unlike women, who were still expected to subordinate their personal interests to their families' welfare, men embraced a new individualism that gave them faith in their power to mold their own destiny. A recent study of nineteenth-century conversion narratives suggests that men, unlike women, found it difficult to believe that they were helpless before God. For example, in 1807 the *Connecticut Evangelical Magazine* published the account of a man who initially strove for salvation by "breaking off from all my evil conduct. I endeavoured to build up a righteousness of my own." Many men now believed they could bring about their own salvation by behaving ethically.[89] In such a climate, church membership may have seemed less important to them than it had to earlier generations of men. They were not as psychologically "needy" as their Calvinist precursors.

Men may have also been less attracted to Center Church because they had so many alternative outlets for public expression. The church was no longer the center of the community. Male organizations like political clubs and Masonic lodges proliferated in the years after the Revolution.[90] In contrast, women's public role was restricted to church activities.

Finally, theology was becoming even more compatible with perceived "feminine" virtues. Indeed, at Center Church, the church covenant and the profession of faith were rewritten in 1832 to reflect a new, more maternal view of God. Instead of giving warnings about a strict Father who elected some to eternal life "out of his mere good pleasure," the new profession assured members that "God has had compassion on sinful men." Rather than warning sinners that justification and sanctification "are not bestowed as the reward of any merit," the new profession affirmed that "God offers forgiveness to all men; and that every sinner, who turns to God, by repentance, with faith in his Son, is freely pardoned and will be saved." The requirements for membership had also become more "feminized." The earlier covenant had been short and had demanded dedication and humility. The 1832 version was longer

FIGURE 10

Family Connections by Gender
1800–1820

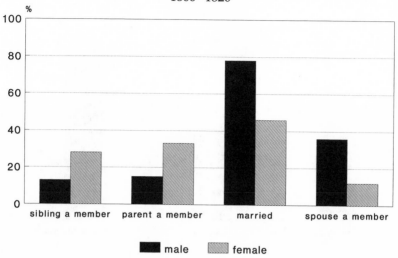

and demanded more self-denial and submission. The convert was urged (twice) to "give up" himself or herself and also to "serve" God, to be "at his disposal," and to behave with "submission." This language of resignation and obedience fit the realities of women's lives, but men may have found it less appealing. Instead of being raised to be submissive, men had been taught to be self-reliant and independent.[91]

In response to many of these cultural changes, the patterns of male and female membership established during the colonial period were altered. First, beginning with the twenty years between 1780 and 1800, women rather than men were more likely to have a sibling or parent in the church. The disparity was greatest between the years of 1800 and 1820, when out of 410 new members admitted, 33 percent of the women had a parent in the church and 28 percent had a sibling, while only 15 percent of the men had a parent in the church and 13 percent had a sibling (fig. 10).

These differences can be partially explained by greater mobility of men (fig. 11). In a culture that celebrated the opportunities for self-advancement, many men left their hometowns in search of success. Between 1800 and 1820, 58 percent of new female members but only 37 percent of new male members had been born in New Haven. In

FIGURE 11

Gender Differences in Mobility
of New Members
1800–1820

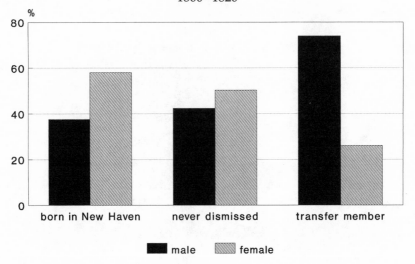

addition, among those members men were also more likely to be dismissed to another congregation. Fifty percent of the women admitted never left the church, compared to 42 percent of the men.

But men's greater mobility can only partially explain why they had fewer family members in the church than women. More important, cultural norms and values encouraged women to join the church but discouraged men. As women continued to fill the pews and theology became more "feminized," families now expected women, rather than men, to be the primary religious carriers in the family. As has so often happened in American history, experience outpaced ideology or, in this case, theology. What began as sociological fact had now become the moral norm. And nowhere was this more evident than in the striking reversal in the gender patterns of biblical naming. During the colonial period, parents had chosen to endow their sons with biblical names more often than their daughters. However, after the Revolution (when biblical name usage declined in the aggregate), parents who continued to choose biblical names were more likely to name their *daughters* after biblical characters than their sons. Of all the church members born between 1820 and 1840, 48 percent of the women but only 39 percent of the men had biblical names.[92]

Women at Center Church had become more important than ever before in transmitting piety to their families, especially to their husbands. Although the majority of *both* men and women joined the church before they were thirty, men were still more likely than women to be married and to have a spouse in the church. Indeed, the majority of men who joined the church did so either after or in the same year as their wives. For example, Eli Whitney did not become a member until 1858, twelve years after his wife Sarah joined. Between 1800 and 1820, 78 percent of the men admitted were married, and 36 percent of them had a spouse in the church; in contrast, only 46 percent of the women admitted were married, and only 12 percent of them had a spouse in the church. Because the majority of men admitted were not older than the women, their greater tendency to be married and to have a spouse in the church was not a reflection of age. Clearly, Center Church women played a major role in influencing their husbands' decisions to join the church, and within the congregation they discovered a realm of power and influence that belied their status as the "weaker sex."[93]

As men's energies were devoted to more secular pursuits, women became the mainstay of the church's benevolent activities. These activities, in turn, represented the most active component of church life outside of worship. The voluntary ethos that infused the new nation was often organized and expressed through local congregations.[94] Center Church women formed groups like the Independence Club, created in 1891 to help working girls learn traditionally feminine activities such as singing and sewing.[95] Perhaps their most successful venture was the creation of the Ladies Home Missionary Society in 1851, an organization dedicated to helping missionaries and their families by sending them clothing and other supplies. The Ladies Home Missionary Society made it clear that they took their work seriously—in their words, they were not a "tea drinking society." Each year they sewed and collected several thousands dollars' worth of goods. When they celebrated their twenty-fifth anniversary in 1876, they calculated that they had donated a total of $62,766.72 since their founding. Their work was so impressive that in 1868 one male member referred to them as "the life of the church."[96]

Women dedicated not only their time to voluntary organizations but their money. As in the colonial era, philanthropy continued to be understood in corporate terms: the church was the primary repository of funds and provider of outlets for charity. Yet within this continuity, women played an increasingly dominant role, maintaining Center Church's reputation as one of the most affluent churches in town.

Throughout the nineteenth century, Center Church made large donations to various benevolent organizations. By 1883, their charities included the YMCA, the City Missionary Society, the United Workers, the New Haven Orphan Society, the Home for the Friendless, the New Haven Aid Society, the General Hospital Society, the Connecticut Training School for Nurses, and the Board of Organized Charities. Individual members of the congregation were so wealthy that on February 12, 1888, when the Reverend Newman Smyth explained that the church needed $25,000, they managed to raise the money among themselves in only half an hour. Women made many of the church's largest donations. When the congregation began to raise money for the Home for Aged and Destitute Women, for example, a member named Miss Susan Trowbridge contributed land worth $3,800, and Miss Maria Tuttle left a legacy of $7,500. In 1894, a Mrs. Fitch left a legacy of $109,000 to be distributed through the church.[97]

Patterns of change that had begun during the ministries of Stuart and Taylor continued throughout the nineteenth century, and pastors were helpless to counteract them. For one, geographic mobility continued to pose a problem for Center Church. By the time of George Leon Walker's ministry, nearly three-quarters of the new members were added through transfer rather than first admission—a startling figure that suggests the increasing inability of Center Church to "church" new members through the mechanism of revival. Local revivals depended for their pool on new generations coming of age in the community and then staying put. The age of Stuart, Dwight, and Taylor was the last age of revival in the old evangelical sense of widespread, dramatic conversions. With increased mobility, membership came more through transfer than revival.

The church also seemed unable to recapture the widespread interest or support of men. Although many male members were just as dedicated and pious as the female members, women continued to be more active and numerous within the congregation. They played a disproportionate role in supplying energy, money, and leadership. In written reports and commemorations, men recognized women's leadership, though not to the extent they might have. In 1876, a resolution entitling the "sisters of the church" to vote in calling a new pastor was tabled, and later action indefinitely postponed. Women's right to vote was not formally recognized until 1910, when Center Church merged with Davenport Church. Women may not have pressed for voting rights for reasons of their own. Ironically, when men proposed to allow them membership in the ruling First Society, the women refused "on the ground that since they [the women] were doing most of the church work, the men ought to attend to the society's business."[98]

Despite the many instances of decline after the Revolution, especially in male involvement, the second half of the nineteenth century was also a time of growth and vitality for the church. Many of the most dramatic changes that had occurred after the Revolution were partially reversed during the years after 1840. By the middle of the nineteenth century, more people than ever were becoming members. In 1860, the church offered three services on Sundays—one in the morning, one in the afternoon, and one at night—as well as a lecture every Tuesday evening, a monthly "concert of prayer for the conversion of the world," and a monthly "preparatory" lecture preached on the Friday evening before the celebration of the Lord's Supper. Center Church also offered its members access to a library of religious books that numbered almost 1,500 by 1875.[99]

After the disruptions of the Revolution, membership patterns had stabilized. For example, as the revivals waned, the youth of the converts during the post-Revolutionary years gave way to a more mature membership. For the first time in the history of the church, a significant percentage of middle-aged members were admitted. Between 1860 and 1880, 33 percent of the members admitted were over forty-six, while between 1880 and 1900, the number rose to 46 percent. Greater mobility meant that more people were being accepted by certificate from distant churches, and many of these transfers tended to be older. Thus even as the strategy of childhood membership and nurture failed, the life and community presence of the congregation were sustained through other means.

Of all the partial recoveries made in the latter half of the nineteenth century, perhaps the most important was the incorporation of new families into the church. Although Center Church would never again be home to an entrenched, multigenerational membership, this modified tribalism did stem the earlier losses in significant ways. Not only were many new members older, but they were much more likely to have relatives in the church than those who had joined in the aftermath of the Revolution. Many of the pillar families were gone, but during the pastorates of Leonard Bacon and George Leon Walker, Center Church once again became a family-based institution. To give just a few examples, the percentage of new members admitted who had a parent in the church rose from 24 percent between 1820 and 1840 to 39 percent between 1840

FIGURE 12

Family Connections of New Members
1760–1880

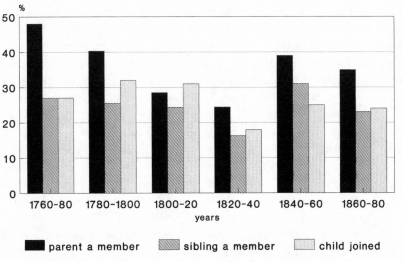

parent a member   sibling a member   child joined

and 1860 (fig. 12). In the same years, the percentage of new members admitted who had a sibling in the church rose from 16 percent to 31 percent. Despite continuing mobility, new members managed to pass on their piety to their children more often than their predecessors had. Between 1820 and 1840, only 18 percent of the members admitted had a child who eventually joined the church, but for members admitted between 1840 and 1860, that number increased to 25 percent.

By the mid-nineteenth century, Center Church had recovered from many of the dislocations caused by the Revolution. Unlike the Revolutionary era, during which great numbers of Americans ceased joining the churches, the Civil War did not lead to a decline in church membership. At Center Church, ministers joined their congregation in opposition to slavery, and there were no internal divisions or disaffections. Just as the church had managed to hold together its membership during the Revolution, it adopted a centrist position during the Civil War. Both Nathaniel Taylor and Leonard Bacon wrote and spoke actively on the antislavery issue, identifying themselves as ardent foes of both slavery *and* abolitionism. Like many in their congregation, they endorsed the colonization of freed slaves in Africa rather than immediate emancipation. As war grew near, they denounced the South. Following the Kansas-Nebraska Act in 1854, Taylor and Bacon expressed their outrage in public meetings and in 1856 supported the newly formed Republican party. For many Center Church families, the war meant personal loss and anguish.[100] Yet its effects on Center Church's membership were minimal.

Center Church weathered the crises of the Revolution and the Civil War. Yet by the end of the nineteenth century, its identity and sense of history had fundamentally changed. Gone was the rhetoric of a Bible commonwealth binding past, present, and future into one seamless web. Center Church could no longer point to an immediate, self-contained "errand," nor could it see itself as "Puritan" in having an exclusive state establishment. Church members became detached from their history even as they celebrated it. As Americans in a new republic where church and state were separate and where different religions had to coexist, Center Church members began looking back on their past and realizing that they now had a history that was distinct from their own present.

Disconnected from their past, ministers reminded members of their Puritan legacy even as they redefined it in terms compatible with a new republican ideology. In 1838, the Reverend Leonard Bacon delivered a commemorative sermon series to celebrate Center Church's bicentennial. In it he carefully rehearsed the Puritan past. The story was poignant but carefully rendered to comport with a new Yankee identity. Civic intolerance, Hebrew law, state support, and strict discipline were ignored or defended as part of the "spirit of the age"—an age whose time had clearly passed. Bacon's emphasis was on piety (now sentimentalized and softened to accommodate a nurturing theology), learning (epitomized by Yale College, now as much a training ground for lawyers and lovers of knowledge as ministers), and liberty. In Bacon's retelling of Center Church history, the original members were so Yankee as to be only dimly recognized as Puritans. In the terminology of historian Nathan Hatch, Bacon and his congregants had become "civil millennialists" who had engrafted Old World Calvinism onto their new republican identity and commitment to the dawning "American Way of Life."[101]

In closing his thirteen "discourses," Bacon neatly fused Puritan past with republican present. In his words, the Puritans

subdued the wilderness, and planted a land now sown; that we might dwell in a land adorned with culture, and enriched with the products of industry and art. . . . They came to the world's end, away from schools and libraries, and all the fountains of light in

71

the old world; that we and our children might inhabit a land, glorious with the universal diffusion of knowledge. They were exiles for truth and purity, they like their Savior were tempted in the wilderness; that the light might make us free, and that the richest blessing of their covenant God might come on their posterity.[102]

Center Church continued to celebrate its past somewhat longingly in commemorative publications and speeches, but it would never again be the same Puritan church that John Davenport had founded two centuries before. Yet if not Puritan, they were still part of a recognized Protestant majority with a self-defined responsibility for moral oversight and custody of the American destiny. Instead of looking inward to pillar families and their offspring, the Yankee church reached outward to the community and to charitable organizations. Through these agencies, Center Church participants could still perceive themselves as creating a model society, an ideal Christian world. In 1870, one member affirmed that "this church is indeed a city set on a hill; its light cannot be hid. Its example is looked to, its influence is felt throughout New Haven and in other communities."[103] Like their Puritan ancestors, they were on an errand, but now it was America's errand, and they were the self-appointed guardians of the new order. There was still room for optimism and the triumphalism to which their building testified. But, like mainline churches throughout urban America, their moment was quickly passing.

Religious Outsiders

In 1889, as the nineteenth century drew to its close under Newman Smyth's ministry, Center Church celebrated its 250th anniversary. Over the centuries, the congregation had sat under twelve ministers spanning eight generations. In that same period, over three thousand men, women, and children of all social ranks had experienced conversion, joined Center Church, and lived out their lives participating in the church's many agencies and activities. Together the clergy and the congregation had successfully guided Center Church along its changing course, providing strong local leadership in New Haven and national direction to the great denominational agencies and missions that constituted the Protestant establishment. Certainly, on its 250th anniversary, Center Church had reason to celebrate. Even as the congregation extolled its illustrious past, however, new changes threatened its existence and steadily distanced it from its once central position in New Haven society. Center Church had survived the dislocations of the American Revolution, but in the twentieth century its members faced even more difficult challenges.

Center Church had been dramatically transformed in the nineteenth century. Ideologically, the congregation had been forced to adjust to a new republican ethos that shifted its orientation from established church to voluntary organization. And socially, members had learned to cope with the exodus of colonial pillar families. Still, despite these changes, deep connections tied Center Church members to their colonial past and to the center of New Haven life. Religious, genealogical, and racial similarities bound the members together. In New Haven, white Protestants continued to represent the great majority of inhabitants, and Center Church, the oldest white Protestant congregation in the city, managed to make the transition from Puritan to Yankee. As a center of revival, moreover, Center Church represented the spiritual heart of the community. Despite its increasing activities on behalf of charity and community uplift, the church's main identification and efforts remained evangelistic, both at home and abroad.

In the twentieth century, however, Center Church lost its identity as a spiritual institution at the center of New Haven life. This time, the catalyst was not ideological, as it had been after the Revolution, but social, ethnic, and demographic. Beginning in the 1890s, Roman Catholic Polish and Italian laborers entered New Haven in growing numbers that soon supplanted the white Protestant majority. By 1930, only about a quarter of the population (28 percent) were whites born of native parents. The new immigrants were overwhelmingly Catholic. By 1933, 57 percent of the heads of New Haven families were Catholic, and only 29 percent were Protestant.[104] Congregational churches were no longer the majority in New Haven. In 1890 there had been a total of 64 churches in New Haven, including 18 Congregational and 8 Catholic. By 1935, in a city of 106 churches, Congregational churches had shrunk to 12, and Catholic churches had increased to 19. Three of the buildings that had once been used for Congregational worship had now become Catholic churches.[105]

As the century wore on, the new Roman Catholic majority in New Haven was joined by a growing population of black laborers, part of the great exodus of freedmen to northern cities. Although blacks constituted only 3 percent of the population in 1930, by 1970 they had increased to 26 percent.[106] During the seventeenth, eighteenth, and nineteenth centuries at Center Church, some black members had been admitted, but they had never made up more than one percent of the new members.[107] The first black member, listed only as "Jinny," joined in 1714, followed three years later by "Mingo" and "Sanders." By 1826, Center Church had admitted 34 black members. Unfortunately, very little is known about these pioneers; the membership lists do not provide any information about their dates of birth or marital status, or even whether they had family members in the church. Pero Sume joined the church in 1743, followed a year later by Dinah Sume, but the church records do not indicate whether they were siblings or spouses, or whether they were even related. In fact, we know that they were black only because their names on the membership rolls were followed by the adjective "colored."

We can only speculate about these black members' experiences in the church. But it is telling that after a white member of Center Church named Simeon Jocelyn helped to create the city's first black church in 1824, Temple Street Congregational, most black Protestants chose not to join the fellowship at Center Church. Between 1826 and 1839, Center Church accepted only one black member; it had admitted 18 between 1809 and 1826. By 1825, Temple Street's membership had already swelled to 100. Other black churches soon followed, such as the First African Methodist Episcopal Bethel Church and the Zion African Methodist Episcopal Church, and they too flourished.[108]

Coinciding with this massive immigration of Roman Catholics and blacks was an equally significant (and not coincidental) outmigration of old Protestant families to such neighboring suburbs as Branford, Orange, Hamden, and Guilford. Although the population of New Haven had been growing dramatically through the nineteenth and early twentieth century—the population doubled from 81,298 in 1890 to 162,655 in 1920—by 1930 this surge had subsided. Falling birthrates were partly to blame, but equally important were the increasing numbers of middle-class whites moving to the suburbs. Between 1920 and 1930, New Haven's population remained stationary, while the population of the surrounding suburban towns grew from 42,834 to 71,001. New Haven's population actually began to decrease after 1960, falling from 152,048 to 137,707 by 1970. In 1980, there were 212,413 people living in New Haven's suburbs compared with 125,787 living in the city itself.[109]

Surprisingly, despite the pressures of suburbanization, large numbers of Center Church members were never dismissed to other churches (fig. 11). The nineteenth century was the highwater mark of mobility and migration out of New Haven to other churches. By the twentieth century, new members either stayed or, as sociologist Robert Wuthnow's recent study suggests, simply left the church altogether.[110] Many members were not leaving for other churches but rather had become disengaged from church membership entirely.

The new social realities of a changing New Haven pushed Center Church congregation ever more to the fringes of New Haven society. Its entrenched identity as a Puritan Congregationalist or "mainstream Protestant" church made it difficult for the congregation to accommodate the new needs of the community. Once the center of piety and corporate morality, Center Church reluctantly found itself on the sidelines of New Haven life and politics.

Alongside social changes in the New Haven community was a profound intellectual revolution in Protestant theology in which Center Church's ministers played a leading role. At the same time that Center Church was becoming marginalized in the New Haven community, such ministers as Newman Smyth and Oscar Maurer identified it as being on the cutting edge of a new theology. Shaped by ideas emerging out of leading theological institutions like Andover Seminary and Yale Divinity School, this new theology gave the church national prominence but ironically distanced it from New Haven's new immigrants, who were more attuned to a traditional, "conservative" conversionist theology. As in other Protestant churches, the gap separating pulpit and pew grew steadily wider.[111]

In his monumental *Religious History of the American People*, Sydney E. Ahlstrom identified the late nineteenth and early twentieth centuries as the period of the greatest theological shift since the Reformation.[112] The chief catalysts in this transformation were science, particularly the theory of evolution identified with Darwin, and positivistic naturalism, which moved away from supernatural definitions of faith to a "natural theology." Relativism had become the new Protestant keyword. Rather than reading the Bible literally, new critics read it as poetry or metaphor, stripping biblical texts of their "myths" in order to recover their enduring ethical and moral principles.

With the new hermeneutics, all the old creeds, formulations, and eternal verities were questioned and criticized. As theology embraced history and science, Protestants were profoundly divided into "liberals" and "fundamentalists." The long period of cooperation in mainline churches degenerated into a series of theological debates and "heresy" trials that persisted well into the twentieth century, leaving the once-dominant Protestant Establishment in a shambles.[113]

At Center Church this revolution in thought had particularly far-ranging consequences, because many of its ministers played a leading role in the new liberalism, both from the pulpit and in the press. One of the most important national leaders in the defense of Protestant liberalism was Center Church's Newman Smyth. Although not the most powerful preacher in Center Church's history, he was the most prolific scholar and contributed his pen to the liberal cause with all the fervor of a twentieth-century pilgrim. Along with United Church's pastor, Theodore Munger, Smyth shaped a "New Theology" every bit as innovative and influential as Nathaniel Taylor's earlier "New Haven Theology."

Like many Protestant liberals, Smyth never had a conversion experience.[114] Instead he immersed himself in modern science as a student at Yale and led the way in designing a "natural theology" that looked less to ancient texts in the search for truth than to "nature's progressive self-revelation."[115] In his 1912 Taylor Lectures (named for Nathaniel Taylor) delivered at Yale Divinity School, he built on a lifetime of study in science and religion (his *Through Science to Faith* was widely read and reprinted), to present what he titled a *Constructive Natural Theology*. Central to this theology was a profound faith in the new science's ability to transform and outfit Christian faith for the twentieth century.

Absent from Smyth's natural theology were calls to revival or conversion, once the hallmarks of Center Church's religious impulse. In one especially controversial statement, Smyth questioned the orthodox teaching (on which foreign missions depended) that "heathens" who had never heard the gospel were eternally lost. Instead, he suggested the possibility of a "future probation" when they would be given a second chance.[116] Through modern science and philosophy, together with the ethical legacy of the gospel, humankind had the tools to fashion a new, more progressive modern faith.

Such modern views fit well with the relatively well-educated, liberal-minded congregation Smyth addressed. Yet it marked a radical divide from both his predecessors in the Center Church pulpit and from the ordinary parishioners in the New Haven community. His theology was vital, but it spoke to a shrinking minority of New Haven's population.

Between the New Haven Theology of Taylor and the New Theology of Smyth came a steady erosion of ministerial status and influence. Congregations no longer understood the subtleties of the New Theology, and ministers looked to one another for support. Ironically, by reverencing science so adamantly the ministers lost some of the reverence they had once enjoyed. The result was an inability to command revivals in the magisterial manner of the "pulpit giants" who had preceded them.[117]

Many of Smyth's ideas were taken over and elaborated by his successor in the pulpit, Oscar Maurer. By the time of Maurer's ministry the church had become a national voice for theological liberalism, and Sunday sermons often defined and commented on liberal themes. It remained to be seen if these sermons could repeople and revitalize the congregation as Nathaniel Taylor's had done so successfully a century earlier. Like other liberal ministers throughout twentieth-century America, Maurer sought to educate his congregation in the new learning and to bridge the gap between modern scholarship and popular belief. This is clearly what his congregation wanted as well, or at least the congregation's leaders. After all, they selected their own ministers, and by choosing Maurer they signaled their desire to retain a position of national visibility and leadership.

Maurer's educational aims can be seen in virtually all of his preaching. In his sermon "The Spirit of Truth," he underscored the new orthodoxy of historical relativism with the doctrine that truth had not been entirely revealed in Scripture but was progressive and ongoing. There is, he proclaimed, a "progressive revelation of God" in nature and history. Those who "take it [that] the scriptures are all written, the revelations all finished, [and] the creeds all formulated" are "contemptuous of the present." So too were those who harkened back to the old highly personalistic religion of revival and supernatural conversion. In another sermon, "Faith Plus," Maurer expressed his disdain for preaching geared to "what a past generation called conversion." He complained that many of those who "claimed to have been converted" never changed their lives or the condition of their society. In his words, "The upshot of their philosophy seemed to be that it was worth wallowing in the gutter-dirt in order to be lifted out and made clean, and they rather suspected people who had not had a similar experience."[118]

Alongside liberalism's theological innovation came a new emphasis on ethics and morality. Henceforth churches would be judged less by their beliefs than by their actions—what they did to improve a rapidly changing, urbanized America. This "social gospel," whose classical theological exposition was Walter Rauschenbusch's *Christianity and the Social Crisis* (1907), began in cities, where a new population of foreign immigrants and blacks made Protestant ministers aware of their growing irrelevance. From Leonard Bacon's antislavery agitation to Newman Smyth's advocacy of labor rights, Center Church had long been a voice for social reform.[119] Under Maurer's ministry that reforming impulse continued, but in its modern guise it became severed from its identification with revival and was elevated as an end in itself. In a sermon entitled "Signs of Hope in American Life," Maurer praised the new "American" preaching that was "prevailingly ethical." He asserted, "the social teachings of Jesus and their application to the betterment of human relations is the burden of the pulpit message."[120] When not tied to conversion and revival, this orientation became national in scope and abstracted from particular spiritual concerns. After highlighting the "social burden of the gospel," Maurer went on to address issues like higher education, industry, race, international relations, and peace. Certainly, these were central and pressing national concerns, but none were immediately relevant to the personal spiritual needs of the hearers.

A social gospel that was separated from revival inevitably changed the tone and content of the congregation's worship. Indeed, the church came to be defined more as a social agency than as a spiritual or supernatural presence. At Center Church, the ministers devoted themselves to uplifting the citizens of New Haven, many of whom were no longer Center Church members. In 1913, Center Church initiated a "Forum" for discussion of civic issues, a program that later became known as the Center Church Institute. Discussions centered on such issues as "Shall We Extend the Franchise to Women?" "Prohibition," "What Shall We Do About War?" and "Can We Christianize the Social Order: How?"[121] The institute represented a shift in the church's identity away from local revival and foreign missions to social reform. Such an "instituted" church, George Leon Walker explained,

> aims not merely to unite its members in worship, Christian nurture, and benevolence by the ordinary channels of endeavor, but to touch the surrounding community at many points, providing reading-rooms, gymnasiums, and bowling-alleys, clubs for boys and girls, healthful amusement and instruction for the tempted and the homeless, all designed to make the gospel more effective in the upbuilding of an upright, self-respecting, Christian manhood and womanhood.[122]

If the New Theology provided clear social imperatives and programs, and a refreshing reconciliation of science and religion for educated seekers, it was unclear whether it would appeal to inner-city audiences. With revival and conversion no longer at the center of congregational life and mobilization, what shape would the congregation assume?

From virtually every statistical index used in this study, it is apparent that the congregation underwent decisive changes in the early twentieth century. Many of these changes took place during the ministry of Oscar Maurer. In the same way that Moses Stuart's pastorate served as a bellwether of change from the eighteenth to the nineteenth century, Maurer's much longer pastorate from 1909 to 1943 represented the beginning and maturation of a new era. In this period spanning two world wars and vast population movements to northern cities and suburbs, Center Church underwent yet another transformation, from Yankee congregation to an inner-city "institutional church."

On the level of church membership, the transformation proved to be a failure. Programs and platforms proliferated, but the congregation shrank. Membership growth did not keep pace with either New Haven population figures or earlier rates of growth in Center Church history. A significant number of new members joined Center Church in this period—1,770—but that number failed to maintain the pace of growth set in the eighteenth and nineteenth centuries. For example, between 1830 and 1840, at a time when New Haven's population numbered approximately 10,000, Center Church admitted 399 members. Seventy years later, between 1900 and 1910, the population was eight times as large, but only 113 new members were admitted. The number admitted hadn't been so low in any decade since the end of the eighteenth century (see table 2). In absolute terms, Center Church's membership had fallen from 563 in 1880 to 396 in 1909.[123]

Other Congregational churches were also suffering. One of these, Davenport Church, had originally been founded by a group of Center Church members. In the flush of nineteenth-century missionary work, Center Church had created many smaller churches throughout New Haven. Although Davenport had been fairly successful, the changing composition of New Haven forced it to close its doors in 1910, sending its members back to Center Church. At a time when the church's membership figures were falling, this merger with Davenport proved timely: 438 new members were admitted in 1910, and Center Church's membership surged from 396 in 1909 to 819 in 1911.[124]

Throughout the twentieth century, Center Church sustained its membership largely through mergers with neighboring congregations and transfers from other churches. If revivals had represented, in

George Leon Walker's phrase, "the characteristic feature of Congregational religious life" for two centuries, that was no longer the case. Few new members in this century were converted under the preaching of Center Church's ministers. During the colonial period, only about 10 percent of the members admitted had transferred from other churches. In the nineteenth century, the number admitted by certificate increased to 30 percent, and in the twentieth it soared to 70 percent.

The decrease in conversions at Center Church demonstrates empirically that, at the congregational level, the church no longer identified itself as an active spiritual presence organized around evangelistic activities designed to "win" young adults or covenanted children to Christ. Clearly, there was a connection between social and theological changes. As conversions decreased, the former rhetoric of conversionist preaching also declined, meaning that the two trends mutually reinforced each other. The effect was that Center Church became a congregation of transfer members, a church whose members turned to the socially inspired words of Smyth and Maurer to make sense of their increasing spiritual and personal isolation from the New Haven community.

Center Church's growing inability to draw from a pool of New Haven natives is reflected in figure 4. In the colonial era virtually all new members had been born in New Haven. In the nineteenth century, that number dropped to one-half, and by the twentieth century it had dipped below one-third. The turning point came during Oscar Maurer's pastorate, when only 31 percent of the new converts admitted were born in New Haven. Most new members came from Connecticut or other states in the Northeast, but there were also transfers from the Midwest, the West, the South, and even foreign countries. Between 1900 and 1920, 10 people were admitted from the South, 44 from the West and Midwest, and 12 from other nations.

Because of the large number of transfer members, the majority of men and women admitted in this century have been married adults (transferring members tend to be older than other members). Between 1900 and 1920, 75 percent of the new members between the ages of twenty-six and thirty, and 86 percent of those over sixty had transferred from other churches. These men and women had come of age and converted in their hometown churches but had moved to New Haven in their adulthood in search of better jobs or educational opportunities. At least 51 percent of the members admitted in this century have been married, and many of them (37 percent, the highest percentage in any cen-

FIGURE 13
Marital Status of New Members
Admitted in Each Century
1639–1989

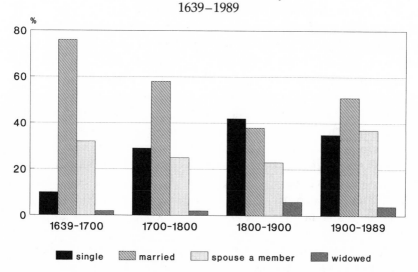

tury) entered the church either in the same year as their spouse or after their spouse (fig. 13).

Although the majority of the members admitted in this century have been married adults who transferred from other churches, a significant percentage of children also joined. Children numbered prominently among those who hadn't transferred from other churches. During the nineteenth century, the number of members admitted who were between the ages of sixteen and nineteen had increased. In the twentieth century, however, members were accepted at an even earlier age. This both reflected and reinforced a major shift in theological orientation. By 1900, membership at Center Church was rooted less in a communal coming-of-age or a conversion experience than in childhood education and nurture in the principles of a Christian life and faith. Much of this education centered on an effective Sunday school, which during David Beach's ministry was combined with the program of United Church next door. Twenty-eight percent of the new members accepted in the twentieth century were under sixteen years of age, compared with only 5 percent in the nineteenth century and less than 1 percent in the seventeenth and eighteenth centuries. If, in the nineteenth century, church membership at Center Church had increasingly come to be seen as "women's business," in the twentieth century it had become "children's business." The church hosted local divisions of children's clubs, like the Camp Fire Girls and the Boy Scouts, and even sponsored yearly children's days when children were the focus of the service.[125] In 1925, for example, the congregation gathered on a Sunday morning to celebrate the Sunday school's "graduation." This day was also set aside for the baptism of infants and a ceremony for seven-year-olds. The pastor gave every child who had turned seven his or her own Bible.[126]

Clearly, the meaning of church membership had changed. A significant percentage of the converts who had never belonged to a Congregational church—in other words, nontransfers—were young. Between 1940 and 1960, 44 percent of first-time new members were under twenty. In earlier centuries, significant numbers of new members had converted between the ages of twenty and twenty-five as they reached adulthood. In the twentieth century, however, membership was no longer linked to marriage and family. Instead, it had become an adolescent rite of passage.

Maurer's pastorate was identified with a time of major changes in the congregation. The character of Center Church as a family of interconnected families virtually disappeared during Maurer's ministry. Under Leonard Bacon, George Walker, and Frederick Noble, the church had partially regained the familial character that it had lost in the years immediately following the Revolution. However, that recovery proved to be temporary. Few new Center Church members had parents or siblings in the church. During Maurer's ministry, only 20 percent of the members admitted had a sibling in the church, and only 27 percent had a parent (fig. 1). For most new members, one's in-church "family" consisted solely of spouses; there was no longer any clear sense of continuity from generation to generation.

As intergenerational familial networks disappeared, so did pillar families (see fig. 3). Although the percentage of new members admitted from pillar families declined in the nineteenth century, they had still represented about 40 percent of new members. With Maurer's ministry, that percentage declined to 22 percent. The families that had helped to perpetuate Center Church's membership generation after generation were moving to the suburbs or other states or were simply losing interest in church membership altogether. Most recently, during Peter Ives's ministry, only 7 percent of the 40 new members belonged to pillar families.

Women still made up the clear majority of new converts, but they did not continue to increase in the numbers that they had in previous centuries. Between 1940 and 1960, 39 percent of the new members admitted were men, the highest percentage in any twenty-year period excepting the first generation of Puritans (fig. 6). The number of new female members had more than doubled from the seventeenth through the nineteenth centuries, but from the nineteenth through the twentieth centuries, the number of women admitted grew only modestly, from 1,794 to 1,991. Clearly, the relative increase in the percentage of male members signaled less an increase in male piety and congregational involvement than a decrease in female involvement.

Women no longer sustained the church as they had in the nineteenth century. The number of societies dwindled. So too did the benevolent giving, contributed and administered mostly by women's societies. With Center Church no longer at the center of the community, charitable giving declined, and members set apart church "tithes" from "charitable giving," which they determined individually on a case-by-case basis.

How can we understand this apparent decrease in women's involvement and commitment to Center Church? Clearly the loss of pillar families who had long-standing commitments to the congregation was significant. But equally important were larger changes taking place in American culture. The "women's movement" had entered a new and more assertive phase. Just as men had left the church after the Revolution to make their mark in other institutions, women's economic and political gains, especially their increasing employment, provided them with new opportunities and diverted their energies away from church activities. Although Center Church tried to lure them back again, offering a Business Women's Group that met conveniently in the evening (unlike the Ladies Home Missionary Society and the Women's Federation, which usually met during the day), many women had lost interest in the church.[127]

As men's and women's "spheres" were no longer as rigidly separated in the twentieth century, their patterns of church membership also converged. The differences that had marked men's and women's experiences of church membership became less sharp after 1900. For two centuries men had been more likely to come from pillar families than women. By the twentieth century that difference had virtually disappeared. Between 1920 and 1940, 19 percent of men and 20 percent of women were pillars.

In looking at biblical name usage, a similar pattern appears. Between

FIGURE 14

Family Connections by Gender
1920–1940

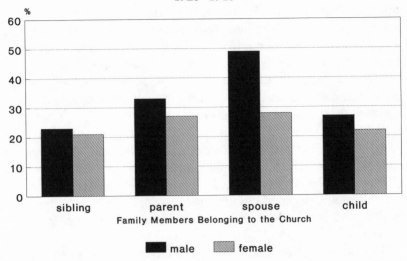

Family Members Belonging to the Church

■ male   ▨ female

1920 and 1940, the disparity in men's and women's tendency to have a biblical name was so slight as to be insignificant—a significant departure from the nineteenth century. Fifteen percent of the men and 17 percent of the women had a biblical name. Most striking here is the decrease in biblical name usage for *all* new members (fig. 5). This shift was symptomatic of a profound cultural transformation. Quite simply, the new modern themes of preaching had reversed cultural priorities. Colonial church members had tried to submerge their present into the biblical past. In contrast, twentieth-century church members sought to submerge and reinterpret the biblical past into their modern present. With such a reversal, biblical names could not possibly have the significance for the twentieth century that they had enjoyed earlier among either men or women.

Throughout the nineteenth century, women had been more likely to have a parent or sibling in the church than men, but in the twentieth century that distinction disappeared as well (fig. 14).[128] Measures of men's and women's mobility also point to new similarities. In the nineteenth century, women members were slightly more likely to be born in New Haven, while a greater percentage of men had been transferred from or dismissed to other churches. In the twentieth century, however, these differences no longer existed.[129]

Even age differences faded. For example, between 1920 and 1940, 19 percent of the men and 17 percent of the women joined before they were sixteen.[130] Although a slightly greater percentage of women than men joined who were over sixty (11 percentage of women and only 7 percent of men), this disparity can be explained by women's longer life-expectancies in the twentieth century.

Men's and women's converging ages at membership reflected their increasing equality of experience in the twentieth century. This convergence can also be explained by the severing of church membership from conversion experiences and a "testimony of grace." Membership became a function of "graduating" from Sunday school membership classes rather than experiencing "conversion," a dramatic turning away from sin. In the eighteenth and nineteenth centuries, cultural expectations about the timing of men's and women's membership, as well as the different responsibilities of the sexes, had meant that conversion often occurred at different points in their life cycles. In the twentieth century, however, adolescent boys and girls have both been expected to join the church after completing a preparatory program of religious and moral instruction.

In all of these similarities, one significant difference remained. A greater percentage of men than women still had a spouse in the church. Between 1920 and 1940, for example, 49 percent of men but only 28 percent of women had a spouse in the church (fig. 14). In other words, men still tended to follow their wives into the church more often than vice versa. Apparently, even in the twentieth century women continued to play a more dominant role in convincing their husbands to join the church. In this sense, the theme of feminization lives on.

Between 1900 and 1940, Center Church approached an unprecedented demographic crisis, one that culminated in the latter half of the twentieth century. While it is true, as sociologist R. Stephen Warner has recently argued, that demographic change does not "define destiny" for particular congregations, it surely delimits opportunities, particularly over the long haul.[131] Recent studies of "decline" in the mainline churches have, for the most part, begun with World War II.[132] Yet from this study, it is clear that the patterns were set well in advance. As early as 1914, declining attendance led New Haven churches to sponsor an "Everybody-at-Church Sunday." Members were urged to bring their friends and relatives to Sunday services with them, in the hope of "breaking . . . a non-church-going habit on the part of many."[133] Later, in 1942, the *Center Church Chronicle* pleaded, "the support that your

1.4 Photograph, c. 1945, of Center Church's fourth meetinghouse (completed 1814), photographer unknown; courtesy of New Haven Colony Historical Society.

church most needs is your personal attendance upon each service. Why not get the church-going habit? It will help your community, your church, yourself most of all."[134] Post–World War II developments were less a "new trend" or "sudden reversal" than the culmination of changes set in motion a half-century earlier.[135]

Since World War II, the familial base of the church has eroded even further. Between 1960 and 1980, 41 percent of the new converts admitted were the "first" in their family to join the church. Between 1980 and 1988, that number increased to 54 percent (fig. 9). Although many members (especially men) have continued to join the church in the same year that their spouse joined or after their spouse, smaller percentages have had parents or siblings in the church than ever before. Between Maurer's and Beach's ministries, which ended in 1943 and 1960 respectively, the number of new members with siblings in the church dropped from 20 percent to 10 percent, and has remained at about 10 percent through subsequent ministries (fig. 1). Of the new members accepted during Maurer's ministry, 27 percent had a parent in the church, but during Beach's ministry that number dropped even further to 18 percent. Most recently, in Peter Ives's ministry, only about 10 percent of the new members admitted had a parent in the church.

In like manner, new members with children joining have virtually disappeared. Of all the members accepted during Bruce Whittemore's pastorate (1971–83), 92 percent never had a child join the church. Nor were there any revivals. The lack of conversion preaching, together with the "youth movement" of the 1960s, diverted children—particularly children of mainline churches—into other outlets for social reform and activism.[136] The dependence on transfer members continued. During Frederick Smith's ministry (1961–69), 62 percent of new members were admitted by certificate rather than profession of faith. Ninety-one percent of the members admitted during Bruce Whittemore's pastorate (1971–83) were transfers from other churches.

Currently, Center Church is on the verge of extinction as a self-perpetuating, spiritual organism. Historically, the great strength of Congregationalism was its covenant theology. But essential to that theology was the concept of a genealogical succession of God's promises from "generation to generation." And that succession, in turn, depended on mobilization strategies like revival or child nurture. Without that succession there could be no real meaning attached to covenant in the traditional sense of the term. Nor, for that matter, could there be the same meaning to church identity.

As we have seen, Center Church was in trouble as early as the 1930s and 1940s.[137] But the extent of the crisis was partially hidden by unions with other area congregations in trouble themselves. The church had been rejuvenated by the merger with Davenport Church in 1910, and it gained another 215 new members in 1951 after Humphrey Street Church closed down.[138] Another boost came in 1970 when Edgewood Church shut its doors, sending Center Church 325 more members. Because many of the members coming from Edgewood were young, Center Church may have hoped to regain its familial character. But even these two large influxes of members could not inject new life into the congregation. By 1989 Center Church had only 320 recorded members, of which only about 115 were active.[139]

The remaining Center Church members continued with their idea of an institutional church. Appeals to covenant, conversion, and evangelical mission virtually disappeared. Efforts on behalf of the disadvantaged—the homeless, the poor, and the unemployed—became Center Church's primary function and a rallying point for its identity. Yet the congregation had not created any stable identity as a community *church*. Instead of being a *part* of the community in which they existed, they had almost become a detached service agency.

In all this community activity, the once central activity of gospel preaching and adult conversion moved steadily to the sideline. The preaching ministry of the church declined. Afternoon services languished and were replaced for a time with vesper services directed to community issues. Between the two world wars even the vesper services stopped. So too did traditional emphases on the Sabbath as a day when the congregation would come together as a body. Sociologist Benton Johnson, writing about Presbyterians, sees in the disappearance of vesper services and Sabbath observance a "paradigm for a larger process of change":

> This process involves the erosion of commitment to the churches' "old agenda" of social and spiritual concerns. Observance of the Sabbath, including faithful church attendance, was part of that old agenda, and so was learning the Bible, refraining from worldly amusements, dressing modestly, abstaining from intoxicating beverages, and much more. Some of these items involved prohibitions, others involved commandments; many were "hard" in the sense of requiring a high level of commitment. What has been happening is a process of *de*-commitment to the old agenda items, of *de*-energization within the ranks of the church. . . .[140]

In like manner, discipline has virtually disappeared. In fact, Center Church recorded no excommunications after George Leon Walker's ministry. In 1895, one church member defended the lack of discipline by arguing that the present membership "with their clearer light and larger knowledge and greater opportunities are more securely implanted in the essentials of a churchly and Christian life than their progenitors were."[141] By the time of Oscar Maurer's pastorate in the early 1900s, discipline was barely a memory, leading him to conclude, "it is probable that excommunication would not be regarded, nowadays, as a serious social stigma nor as an effective method of maintaining the standards of church membership." Maurer did not realize that discipline continued to be enforced within many more "conservative" or "evangelical" movements—movements that would thrive in the 1970s and 1980s.[142] Like Sabbath observance, discipline was hard, but with that hardness came a tempering that stiffened resolve and bound members in a community of sacrifice as well as of service.

It is easy to trace Center Church's present crisis to nonconversionist theology. But that is too simple. Such a theology was itself a response to decreasing conversions in urban congregations and the perceived irrelevance of old verities to a modern world. In part, both theological innovation and congregational decline were products of the inexorable course of demographic change. Ironically, while twentieth-century pastors were adept at identifying the force of historical relativism in the abstract, they could not foresee how the effects of demography and mobility, once set in motion, would eventually undermine the very churches they hoped to save with their new orthodoxy. Theological innovation, no matter how modern, could not counter the sheer force of numbers.

Whatever questions are raised about Center Church's new tactics and strategies, its present crisis has been brought on by demographic changes. With a shrinking "pool" of converts in the white adult population of New Haven, the evangelical impulse invariably weakened. What use were sermons oriented primarily to the salvation of the soul when the numbers of souls in the pews were constantly shrinking? In this sense, theology *had* to shift to respond to changing social realities in New Haven (and in northern cities generally where "mainstream" churches had once dominated) just as surely as theology had shifted in the nineteenth century to meet the changing ideological realities of the new republic.

To respond to the crisis in the church after the Revolution, Moses Stuart and Nathaniel Taylor had thrown open the church doors to the wider New Haven community. But in the twentieth century, that community is international and multiracial. So far, the strong commitment of Center Church members to their historical identity as a white mainline church has kept them from taking the radical step of offering their congregation as a spiritual home to New Haven's inner-city residents.

As the religious mission of Center Church shifted, so too did its understanding of its history. As early as 1922 Center Church had begun opening its doors to touring visitors seven days a week, and in 1928 an endowment was established for maintaining the building and its crypts. In Maurer's words, the church was becoming a "religious monument . . . which in a peculiar sense belongs to the people of New Haven." As the church lost a coherent identity as a spiritual force in the present, it looked increasingly to the past for meaning.

Center Church has always celebrated its past in terms relevant to its present. In the era of Leonard Bacon, this meant a celebrated past minus the "harder" doctrines of total depravity and unconditional election. Nevertheless, in his creedal foundations and conversionist rhetoric, Bacon retained more than he discarded. By the twentieth century, however, the chasm separating Center Church from its history was of such social and theological breadth that the past became a museum or a monument. The church no longer represented the community or maintained a theological continuity built on revival and conversion.

In 1938, Oscar Maurer delivered, and later published, a series of addresses celebrating Center Church's 300th anniversary. Many of his themes simply acknowledged and repeated Bacon's earlier discourses in describing the courage and willpower of the Puritan founders. And like Bacon, he reduced the Puritan civic legacy to republican themes of virtue, love of liberty, and learning. Maurer concluded that three major convictions "characterize the Puritan mind": veneration for the "sovereignty of God" (minus the vicarious atonement of Christ), a belief in the "Moral Dignity of Man" (asserted without reference to original sin), and a love of "Liberty Under Law." Nowhere in his discourses did Maurer emphasize the intensive lay spirituality (as opposed to morality) that characterized church members, nor did he celebrate patterns of revival through communal and childhood conversion. Center Church's agenda was now so different as to be hardly recognizable. Its orientation had shifted from the individual soul at war with itself to the pressing social problems of world war and urban violence. The obstacles Maurer's Puritans faced were not so much hard hearts and sinful natures as tangible, outward enemies in a violent world. Maurer never mentioned Puritan biblicism, hell-fire preaching, or strict discipline. Instead, he remembered a civic Puritanism, a Puritanism more compatible with twentieth-century liberal Protestantism.

Contained in Maurer's celebration was a tacit confession that Center Church's original position and mission were no longer viable. Turning to the present and the future, he passed over church growth, personal spirituality, and communal revival—hallmarks of an earlier age—and considered larger, global issues instead. For Maurer, the "wilderness" once faced by the Puritans had changed in modern society. It was no longer the wilderness of an unsettled Indian territory or of an industrializing New Haven. Instead, Center Church now confronted the dangers of an international wilderness, a world that seemed to have lost its moral center—and a world that was abstracted from the local world of worship and spirituality. Rather than calling on modern-day Congregationalists to scrutinize their own souls, he asked them to direct the "Puritan" principles of worship, moral dignity, and liberty toward the world. In his words,

> If we are faithful to them [Puritan values], they will enable us to cope with the social jungle in which we are wandering. We shall do well to apply them to the problems which are perplexing us: the problem of self-control; the problem of national self-government in terms of the present day; the problem of a just and humane industry; the problem of civilized race-relations; the problem of international peace. These are the modern wildernesses to be overcome. In the name of all that was brave and holy in the past, for the sake of a better life and a freer spirit in the years that lie ahead, let us sign a new compact between God and one another, and move out together toward these spiritual frontiers.[143]

Although Center Church desperately tried to remain alive as an effective voice in the New Haven community, membership continued to decrease. No longer either Puritan church or Yankee congregation, the members of Center Church seemed to have become religious outsiders, strangers in their own land.

Epilogue

As this essay is being completed, Center Church has hired two copastors, Campbell Lovett and Shepard Parsons, who were installed on October 27, 1991. Both the pastors and the congregation have reaffirmed their determination to continue as New Haven's oldest continuing congregation. Worship attendance through 1992 averaged 110, and 30 new members have been received. Of these, 95 percent reside in New Haven, and 85 percent of these new members are under forty-five years of age.[144] Both the pastors and the congregation are determined that Center Church will not "become a museum," and they are exploring new links with the community and neighboring churches.[145]

Whether Center Church survives, and in what form, is a question that goes beyond the scope of this essay. But the present-day Center Church congregation encompasses more than the living. Like a vast extended family, the congregation is the product of the habits, customs, and values established by many generations. Center Church's future is inextricably tied to its past. In the words of the poet T. S. Eliot,

Time present and time past
Are both perhaps present in time future,
And time future contained in time past.

NOTES

The authors would like to acknowledge the help of the Reverend Peter Ives and the board of Center Church for allowing us access to church records. The Reverend David Beach, pastor of Center Church for almost twenty years, graciously granted us an interview a few months before his death. We would also like to thank Robert Boyd for teaching us to use Systat and Carol Brekus for helping us with Harvard Graphics. Nancy Cott, James Lewis, James Wind, Jan Shipps, Brooks Holifield, Scott Cormode, Gretchen Townsend, Susan Stout, and Erik Sontheimer all provided helpful comments and criticisms. Most important, we owe a special debt of gratitude to Deborah Stout, who devoted long hours to data entry.

1. Thomas W. Gillespie, "Meeting the Intellectual Challenge with Faith," Address to the 1988 General Assembly, Presbyterian Church U.S.A. For a similar argument, see Roger Finke and Rodney Stark, *The Churching of America, 1776–1990* (New Brunswick: Rutgers University Press, 1992), pp. 231–33.

2. In Sidney Mead's magisterial biography of Nathaniel Taylor, for example, the only Center Church people who appeared in his chapter on Taylor's ministry at Center Church were three who were excommunicated. Sidney Mead, *Nathaniel William Taylor, 1786–1858, a Connecticut Liberal* (Chicago: University of Chicago Press, 1942).

3. The membership records for John Davenport's and Nicholas Street's ministries (1639–84) are incomplete. A printed list of First Church members was published by Franklin Bowditch Dexter in 1914. See his *Historical Catalogue of the Members of the First Church of Christ in New Haven, Connecticut* (New Haven: n.p., 1914). For members admitted since 1914, we used the church's manuscript membership lists at the parish house. The church's records list approximately 7,500 members. Our number is slightly smaller because we did not enter information on members who were admitted twice (some seem to have moved away from New Haven only to return at a later time).

4. The Center Church parish house contains not only membership records but First Church manuals (1820, 1832, 1862–1930), weekly calendars, issues of

the *Center Church Chronicle* (1930–present), catalogues of the church Sabbath school, United and Center Church school agendas (1934–43), papers of the 250th, 275th, and 300th anniversaries of First Church, Ladies Home Missionary Society papers and annual reports, Women's Federation papers and reports, endowment reports, and finance records.

5. On Puritan self-perceptions and subsequent historical realities, see Sacvan Bercovitch, *The Puritan Origins of the American Self* (New Haven: Yale University Press, 1975).

6. John Davenport, *The Profession of Faith of that Reverend and Worthy Divine . . .* (London, 1642), p. 8.

7. Quoted in Leonard Bacon, *Thirteen Historical Discourses . . .* (New Haven: Durrie and Peck, 1839), p. 18.

8. *New Haven Colonial Records 1638–1649*, pp. 15–17. Most other New England congregations followed this same process. See the account of Dedham congregation's formation in Kenneth Lockridge, *A New England Town: The First Hundred Years* (New York: W. W. Norton, 1970).

9. Perry Miller, "Errand into the Wilderness," in *Errand into the Wilderness* (Cambridge: Harvard University Press, 1956), and Sacvan Bercovitch, *The American Jeremiad* (Madison: University of Wisconsin Press, 1978).

10. John Davenport, *A Sermon Preached at the Election . . .* (Cambridge, 1670), p. 13.

11. See Gail Sussman Marcus, " 'Due Execution of the Generall Rules of Righteousnesse': Criminal Procedure in New Haven Town and Colony, 1638–1658," in *Saints and Revolutionaries: Essays on Early American History*, ed. David D. Hall, John M. Murrin, and Thad W. Tate (New York: Norton, 1984), pp. 99–137. See also Isabel MacBeath Calder, *The New Haven Colony* (New Haven: Yale University Press, 1934).

12. The monolithic shaping power of Puritan preaching is traced in Harry S. Stout, *The New England Soul: Preaching and Religious Culture in Colonial New England* (New York: Oxford University Press, 1986).

13. For an example of church seating arrangements, see the proceedings of the General Court, held March 10, 1646, reprinted in Bacon, *Thirteen Discourses*, pp. 310–12.

14. John Davenport, *The Knowledge of Christ Indispensably Required of all Men* (London, 1653), p. 8.

15. See Charles Hambrick-Stowe, *The Practice of Piety: Puritan Devotional Disciplines in Seventeenth-Century New England* (Chapel Hill: University of North Carolina Press, 1982), and E. Brooks Holifield, *The Covenant Sealed: The Development of Puritan Sacramental Theology* (New Haven: Yale University Press, 1974).

16. On discipline, see Emil Oberholzer, *Delinquent Saints: Disciplinary Action in the Early Congregational Churches of Massachusetts* (New York: Columbia University Press, 1956).

17. Edmund Morgan, *Visible Saints: The History of a Puritan Idea* (Ithaca: Cornell University Press, 1963).

18. For an account of the procedure to become a member, see George Selement and Bruce Wooley, eds., *Thomas Shepard's Confessions* (Boston: Massachusetts Historical Society, 1981) in the *Collections of the Colonial Society of Massachusetts* 58, pp. 18–21.

19. Ibid., p. 19.

20. Ibid., p. 20. See also John Davenport, *The Power of Congregational Churches . . .* (London, 1672), p. 97.

21. Because of space limitations, we have not been able to include tables or graphs for every statistic that we cite. However, for those who would like to look more closely at the data or use it for comparative studies, copies of tables are available at the Sterling Memorial Library, Yale University, New Haven, Connecticut.

22. See Robert G. Pope, *The Half-Way Covenant: Church Membership in Puritan New England* (Princeton: Princeton University Press, 1969), and Gerald Francis Moran, "The Puritan Saint: Religious Experience, Church Membership, and Piety in Connecticut, 1636–1776" (Ph.D. diss., Rutgers University, 1974). There is no written record of the acceptance of the Half-Way Covenant, but an unusually large number of baptisms were recorded as soon as James Pierpont became minister in 1685. See Bacon, *Thirteen Discourses*, p. 177.

23. Pope, *The Half-Way Covenant*. Other statistical studies of church membership include Darrett Rutman, *Winthrop's Boston: Portrait of a Puritan Town, 1630–1649* (Chapel Hill: University of North Carolina Press, 1965), and Moran, "The Puritan Saint." Many historians have argued that the Half-Way Covenant represented the decline of the Puritan church. In his two-volume opus *The New England Mind*, Perry Miller used the Half-Way Covenant as a symbol for the Puritans' loss of piety. Miller's work influenced a generation of scholars, who found evidence of "declension" in everything from town politics to witchcraft trials. For two examples, see Kenneth Lockridge, *A New England Town*, and Paul Boyer and Stephen Nissenbaum, *Salem Possessed: The Social Origins of Witchcraft* (Cambridge: Harvard University Press, 1974). However, recent works have challenged his view on a number of fronts. For a sampling of these see Hambrick-Stowe, *Practice of Piety*; Bercovitch, *American Jeremiad*; Stout, *New England Soul*; and Christine Heyrmann, *Commerce and Culture: The Maritime Communities of Colonial Massachusetts, 1690–1750* (New York: W. W. Norton, 1984). In "Declension, Gender, and the 'New Religious History,'" in *Belief and Behavior: Essays in the New Religious History*, ed. Philip Vandermeer and Robert Swierenga (New Brunswick: Rutgers University Press, 1991), we have argued that the concept of declension is flawed because it does not account for the persistence of piety among women congregants. Many historians have equated declension with the feminization of church membership.

24. Philip J. Greven, *Four Generations: Population, Land, and Family in Colonial Andover, Massachusetts* (Ithaca: Cornell University Press, 1970), and *The Protestant Temperament: Patterns of Child Rearing, Religious Experience, and the Self in Early America* (New York: Knopf, 1977).

25. John Cotton, "Letter from Mr. Cotton to Lord Say and Sele," reprinted in

The Puritans: A Sourcebook of Their Writings, ed. Perry Miller and Thomas H. Johnson, rev. ed., in 2 vols. (New York: Harper and Row, 1965), 1:209.

26. This was not true for every New England congregation. In Andover, Massachusetts, for example, age at membership dropped steadily throughout the eighteenth century. See Philip J. Greven, "Youth, Maturity, and Religious Conversion: A Note on the Ages of Converts in Andover, Massachusetts, 1711–1749," *Essex Institute Historical Collections* 108 (1972): 119–34.

27. Jonathan Edwards, "Sermon on 2 Chronicles 34:2–3," November 1734. We are indebted to Eileen Duggan for pointing this sermon out to us.

28. Under Noyes, 438 members joined the congregation as young adults. Thirty-nine percent were between twenty and twenty-five years of age at the time they joined. Only two children joined under the age of fifteen, and only two members were over sixty.

29. Quoted in Bacon, *Thirteen Discourses,* p. 206.

30. The most notorious revivalist was James Davenport, the grandson of John Davenport, whose enthusiasm prompted discord and separation. See Harry S. Stout and Peter Onuf, "James Davenport and the Great Awakening in New London," *Journal of American History* 70 (December 1983): 556–78.

31. Quoted in Bacon, *Thirteen Discourses,* p. 214.

32. Ibid., p. 217.

33. Ralph Henry Gabriel, *Religion and Learning at Yale: The Church of Christ in the College and University, 1757–1957* (New Haven: Yale University Press, 1958), pp. 1–3.

34. Members of other Congregational churches could transfer their membership to the First Church with a letter from their minister.

35. Edmund S. Morgan, *The Puritan Family: Religion and Domestic Relations in Seventeenth-Century New England* (New York: Harper and Row, 1944).

36. Indeed, grandparents were almost a New England "invention" in that so many could be found within New England communities. See Greven, *Four Generations,* pp. 103–74.

37. Samuel Alling joined the church in 1686, and his wife followed him in 1692. Their children—Samuel, Roger, Sarah, Daniel, Caleb, and Esther—all became members. See Dexter, *Historical Catalogue.* During James Pierpont's ministry (1685–1714), 18 percent of new members had three or more children join.

38. See Greven, *Four Generations,* pp. 175–260.

39. Daniel Scott Smith, "Child-naming Practices, Kinship Ties, and Change in Family Attitudes in Hingham, Massachusetts, 1641 to 1880," *Journal of Social History* 19 (1985): 541–66. See also David Hackett Fischer, *Albion's Seed: Four British Folkways in America* (New York: Oxford University Press, 1989), pp. 93–97.

40. Mehetabel and Caleb Hotchkiss joined the church together in 1711. Caleb, Jr., became a member in 1734, Rachel in 1735, and Nehemiah in 1760. Jonah joined in 1773. See Dexter, *Historical Catalogue.*

41. For a sampling, see Dexter, *Historical Catalogue.*

42. "Mrs. Eaton's Trial," *New Haven Colony Historical Society Papers* 5:143, 136. The original trial transcript is contained in the Records of the First Church of New Haven, vol. 1, pp. 17–23, at Center Church Parish House. For a discussion of the Eaton trial, see Lillian Handlin, "Dissent in a Small Community," *New England Quarterly* 59, no. 2 (1985): 193–220.

43. "Mrs. Eaton's Trial," pp. 138, 143.

44. John Davenport, *The Power of Congregational Churches* . . . , p. 132.

45. See Charles Hoadly, ed., *Records of the Colony and Plantation of New Haven from 1638 to 1649* (Hartford, 1657), pp. 242–46, 253–54, 256–57, 173, 279. Like Eaton, Ezekiel Cheever, the schoolmaster, was disciplined by the church, but he was not excommunicated. See "The Trial of Ezekiel Cheever before the Church at New Haven, Connecticut," in *Connecticut Historical Society Collections* 1:22–51.

46. See Barbara Welter, "The Feminization of American Religion," in *Clio's Consciousness Raised*, ed. Marty Hartman and Lois Banner (New York: Harper Torchbooks, 1973); Ann Douglas, *The Feminization of American Culture* (New York: Knopf, 1977); and Richard Shiels, "The Feminization of American Congregationalism, 1730–1835," *American Quarterly* 33 (1981): 46–62.

47. Samuel W. S. Dutton, *The History of the North Church in New Haven* (New Haven: A. H. Maltby, 1842).

48. Shiels, "Feminization of American Congregationalism," p. 48.

49. Timothy Dwight, *A Statistical Account of the Towns and Parishes in the State of Connecticut* (New Haven: Walter and Steele, 1811), vol. 1, no. 1.

50. The best general discussion of women's lives in colonial America is Laurel Thacher Ulrich, *Good Wives: Image and Reality in the Lives of Women in Northern New England, 1650–1750* (New York: Knopf, 1982).

51. Chauncy Whittelsey, *A Sermon Occasioned by the Death of Mrs. Abigail Noyes* (New Haven: Thomas and Samuel Green, 1768), p. 25.

52. Quoted in Shiels, "Feminization of American Congregationalism," p. 46.

53. See Lonna M. Malmsheimer, "Daughters of Zion: New England Roots of American Feminism," *New England Quarterly* (September 1977): 484–504, and "New England Funeral Sermons and Changing Attitudes toward Women, 1672–1792" (Ph.D. diss., University of Minnesota, 1973).

54. Ruth H. Bloch, "Women, Love, and Virtue in the Thought of Edwards and Franklin," in Barbara B. Oberg and Harry S. Stout, eds., *Benjamin Franklin, Jonathan Edwards, and the Representation of American Culture* (New York: Oxford University Press, 1993), pp. 134–51. Morgan, *Puritan Family*, 161–68; Margaret W. Masson, "The Typology of the Female as a Model for the Regenerate: Puritan Preaching, 1690–1730," *Signs* 2, no. 2 (1976): 304–15; and Amanda Porterfield, *Feminine Spirituality in America: From Sarah Edwards to Martha Graham* (New York: Oxford University Press, 1971). This marital language continued into the nineteenth century.

55. Leigh Erik Schmidt, *Holy Fairs: Scottish Communions and American Revivals in the Early Modern Period* (Princeton: Princeton University Press, 1989), pp. 164–65. Schmidt was summarizing the work of Caroline Bynum Walker. See her "'. . . And Woman His Humanity': Female Imagery in the Religious Writings of

the Later Middle Ages," in *Gender and Religion: On the Complexity of Symbols,* ed. Caroline Walker Bynum, Stevan Harrell, and Paula Richman (Boston: Beacon Press, 1986).

56. Quoted in Morgan, *Puritan Family,* p. 7.

57. For example, between 1660 and 1680, 75 percent of the men and 60 percent of the women admitted had one or more children who became church members, and later, between 1740 and 1760, 35 percent of the men and 29 percent of the women admitted had at least one child who joined the church.

58. For example, between 1680 and 1700, 56 percent of women converts but only 26 percent of men converts were between the ages of sixteen and thirty. In addition, 28 percent of new female members but only 5 percent of new male members were young and single. And finally, between the same years, 51 percent of the women, as opposed to 70 percent of the men, were parents.

59. Welter, "Feminization of American Religion." See also Douglas, *Feminization of American Culture.* Douglas has been challenged by many critics. For a sampling, see David S. Reynolds, "The Feminization Controversy: Sexual Stereotypes and the Paradoxes of Piety in Nineteenth Century America," *New England Quarterly* 53 (1980): 96–106, and Darrel M. Robertson, "The Feminization of American Religion: An Examination of Recent Interpretations of Women and Religion in Victorian America," *Christian Scholar's Review* 8, no. 3 (1978): 238–46. For a more general overview of the literature on women and religion in America, see Elizabeth B. Clark's "Women and Religion in America, 1780–1870," in *Church and State in America: A Bibliographic Guide,* ed. John F. Wilson (New York: Greenwood Press, 1986), 1:365, 413, and the bibliography in *Journal of Women's History* 3, no. 3 (1992): 141–77.

60. On revivals and sensation see Harry S. Stout, *The Divine Dramatist: George Whitefield and the Rise of Modern Evangelicalism* (Grand Rapids: Eerdmans, 1991). On women's relative interest in theological disputes see Stephen R. Grossbart, "Seeking the Divine Favor: Conversion and Church Admission in Eastern Connecticut, 1711–1832," *William and Mary Quarterly* 46, no. 4 (October 1989): 696–740.

61. Two superb analyses of the interconnections of republican ideology and religion in the new republic are Jon Butler, *Awash in a Sea of Faith: Christianizing the American People* (Cambridge: Harvard University Press, 1990), and Nathan O. Hatch, *The Democratization of American Christianity* (New Haven: Yale University Press, 1989).

62. Richard Bushman, *From Puritan to Yankee: Character and the Social Order in Connecticut, 1690–1765* (Cambridge: Harvard University Press, 1967). On the nineteenth-century market revolution, see Charles Sellers, *The Market Revolution: Jacksonian America, 1815–1846* (New York: Oxford University Press, 1991).

63. This privatization of religion is traced in Richard John Neuhaus, *The Naked Public Square: Religion and Democracy in America* (Grand Rapids: Eerdmans, 1984).

64. See Hatch, *Democratization,* and Gordon S. Wood, "Evangelical America and Early Mormonism," *New York History* 61 (1980): 359–86.

65. Dwight, *Statistical Account*, p. 45.

66. Oscar Edward Maurer, *A Puritan Church and Its Relation to Community, State, and Nation* (New Haven: Yale University Press, 1938), p. 91. White Haven Church, which had been formed during the Great Awakening after a Center Church schism, admitted only 96 new members in the twenty-five years between 1769 and 1795. See Dutton, *History of the North Church*.

67. Maurer, *Puritan Church*, p. 91.

68. These numbers were comparatively small. For example, between 1700 and 1730, at a time when New Haven's population was smaller, 345 new members had joined.

69. On the role of the clergy, see Alice M. Baldwin, *The New England Clergy and the American Revolution* (New York: Frederick Unger, 1958).

70. Chauncy Whittelsey, *The Importance of Religion* (New Haven, 1778), p. 17.

71. In "The Rise of the Evangelical Conception of the Ministry in America, 1607–1850," in *The Ministry in Historical Perspective*, ed. H. Richard Niebuhr and Daniel Williams (New York: Harper and Brothers, 1956), Sidney Mead traces the evolving conception of evangelism from being family-based to being communal.

72. On the importance of commonsense realism for religion in this period, see Theodore Dwight Bozeman, *Protestants in the Age of Science: The Baconian Ideal and Ante-Bellum American Religious Thought* (Chapel Hill: University of North Carolina Press, 1977).

73. On Stuart's innovative role in critical biblical scholarship, see Mark A. Noll, *Between Faith and Criticism: Evangelicals, Scholarship, and the Bible in America* (New York: Harper and Row, 1986), p. 14.

74. Quoted in Mead, *Nathaniel William Taylor*, p. 68.

75. Donald M. Scott, *From Office to Profession: The New England Ministry, 1750–1850* (Philadelphia: University of Pennsylvania Press, 1978).

76. Maurer, *Puritan Church*, p. 95.

77. For an example, see *Manual of the First Church of New Haven for 1865*, Appendix D, p. 38. On Sunday schools, see Anne Boylan, *Sunday School: The Formation of an American Institution* (New Haven: Yale University Press, 1989).

78. See Greven, *Protestant Temperament*.

79. Horace Bushnell, *Christian Nurture* (New Haven: Yale University Press, 1916), p. 49.

80. The only exception to this pattern in the nineteenth century appears during the pulpit vacancy between 1866 and 1868. Of the 45 members admitted in this period, slightly over half had a spouse in the church. In large measure, however, this figure reflects returning Civil War soldiers and Yale students.

81. Even as he urged a church built on the foundations of family nurture, Horace Bushnell conceded how difficult this would be: "All our modern notions and speculations have taken a bent toward individualism. . . . In matters of religion we have burst the bonds of church authority, and erected the individual mind into a tribunal of judgment within itself. . . . While thus engaged, we have

well nigh lost, as was to be expected, the idea of organic powers and relations." See Bushnell, *Christian Nurture*, p. 75.

82. This pattern of geographic mobility in the churches was not unique to New Haven. See also Paul E. Johnson, *A Shopkeeper's Millennium: Society and Revivals in Rochester, New York, 1815–1837* (New York: Hill and Wang, 1978), Appendix B, pp. 158–61.

83. *Manual of the First Church of Christ in New Haven for 1878.* The emphasis is ours.

84. Mead, *Nathaniel William Taylor*, p. 73.

85. Ibid., 74.

86. Between 1800 and 1900, 845 men and 1,794 women were admitted to the church.

87. *Manual of the First Church of Christ in New Haven for 1870.*

88. For a more extended discussion, see Stout and Brekus, "Declension, Gender, and the 'New Religious History.'"

89. Susan Juster, "'In a Different Voice': Male and Female Narratives of Religious Conversion in Post-Revolutionary America," *American Quarterly* 41 (March 1989): 47.

90. See Paul Goodman, *Towards a Christian America: Antimasonry and the Great Transition in New England, 1826–1836* (New York: Oxford University Press, 1988), pp. 80–102. For an excellent discussion of men's political culture in the years after the Revolution, see Paula Baker, "The Domestication of Politics: Women and American Political Society, 1780–1920," *American Historical Review* 89 (June 1984): 620–47.

91. *Manual of the First Church of Christ in New Haven for 1820* and *Manual of the First Church of Christ in New Haven for 1832.*

92. The only exception to this pattern occurred among pillar families who, in the spirit of Puritan tradition, continued to name their sons after biblical heroes. More of their sons than daughters eventually joined the church. Men constituted a higher percentage of pillar members throughout the nineteenth century.

93. See Mary P. Ryan, "A Women's Awakening: Evangelical Religion and the Families of Utica, New York, 1800–1840," *American Quarterly* 30 (Winter 1978): 602–23. Ryan suggests in her study of church membership records from four Utica, New York, churches that women often helped to convert their male relatives.

94. Timothy Smith, *Revivalism and Social Reform* (New York: Abingdon, 1957).

95. Other groups that they founded included the Home for Aged and Destitute Women, established in 1868, and the Women's Foreign Missionary Society, begun in 1870.

96. *Manual of the First Church of Christ in New Haven for 1876; Manual of the First Church of Christ in New Haven for 1868*, p. 59.

97. *Manual of the First Church of Christ in New Haven for 1869; Manual of the First Church of Christ in New Haven for 1894.*

98. Maurer, *Puritan Church*, p. 159. The First Society was also known as the Ecclesiastical Society.

99. *Manual of the First Church of Christ in New Haven for 1875*.

100. There are no statistics available for the number of Center Church men who were killed or wounded in combat.

101. Nathan O. Hatch, *The Sacred Cause of Liberty* (New Haven: Yale University Press, 1977).

102. Bacon, *Thirteen Discourses*.

103. "Report of the Pastor's Aid Society," in *Manual of the First Church of Christ in New Haven for 1870*.

104. Thelma A. Dreis, compiler, *A Handbook of Social Statistics of New Haven, Connecticut* (New Haven: Yale University Press, 1936), p. 127. According to Dreis, 12 percent were Jewish, 6 percent belonged to "other sects," and 15 percent had no preference.

105. *The One Hundredth Anniversary Yearbook of the Church of the Redeemer Congregation, New Haven, Connecticut, 1838–1938* (New Haven: Whaples-Bullis, 1938).

106. The first figure is from Dreis, *Handbook*. The second is cited in Daniel Y. Stewart, *Black New Haven, 1920–1977* (New Haven: Advocate Press, 1977), p. 43.

107. Statistics on black members admitted in the twentieth century are not available. In the twentieth century, church records no longer specified whether a member was black or not.

108. See Robert Austin Warner, *New Haven Negroes: A Social History* (New Haven: Yale University Press, 1940; rpt. New York: Arno Press, 1969), pp. 80–84. At least six of Center Church's black members transferred to join one of the new African churches in 1829.

109. See "The Rise of Metropolitan New Haven, 1860 to 1980," in *New Haven: An Illustrated History*, ed. Floyd Shumway and Richard Hegel (Woodland Hills, Calif.: Windsor Publications, 1981).

110. Robert Wuthnow, *The Restructuring of American Religion: Society and Faith Since World War II* (Princeton: Princeton University Press, 1988).

111. See Jeffrey K. Hadden, *The Gathering Storm in the Churches* (Garden City: Doubleday, 1969).

112. Sydney E. Ahlstrom, *A Religious History of the American People* (New Haven: Yale University Press, 1972), pp. 763–84.

113. William R. Hutchison, *The Modernist Impulse in American Protestantism* (Cambridge: Harvard University Press, 1976), and George M. Marsden, *Fundamentalism and American Culture: The Shaping of Twentieth-Century Evangelicalism, 1870–1925* (New York: Oxford University Press, 1980).

114. Hutchison, *Modernist Impulse*, p. 78.

115. Cynthia Eagle Russett, *Darwin in America: The Intellectual Response, 1865–1912* (San Francisco: Freeman Press, 1976), pp. 37–38.

116. Hutchison, *Modernist Impulse*, pp. 84, 167. Hutchison points out that

many of Smyth's thoughts on future probation were derived from Isaac A. Dorner of Berlin.

117. Edwin S. Gaustad, "The Pulpit and the Pews," in *Between the Times: The Travail of the Protestant Establishment in America, 1900–1960,* ed. William A. Hutchison (Cambridge: Harvard University Press, 1989), pp. 21–47.

118. Oscar Maurer, "Faith Plus," in *Center Church Sermons* (New Haven: privately printed), p. 7.

119. Hutchison, *Modernist Impulse,* p. 238.

120. Maurer, "Signs of Hope in American Life," in *Center Church Sermons,* p. 13.

121. Calendars of Center Church activities for April 5, 1914, March 7, 1915, April 4, 1915, and December 6, 1925.

122. George Leon Walker, *A History of the Congregational Churches in the United States* (New York, 1894), p. 423.

123. For membership figures, see *Manual of the First Church of Christ in New Haven for 1880,* and *Manual of the First Church of Christ in New Haven for 1909.*

124. *Manual of the First Church of Christ in New Haven for 1909,* and *Manual of the First Church of Christ in New Haven for 1911.*

125. The church calendar for the week of May 20, 1928, contains announcements for meetings of both the Boy Scouts and the Camp Fire Girls.

126. For two examples of "Children's Day," see the calendar of Center Church activities for June 14, 1914, and June 14, 1925.

127. For a typical announcement of a Business Women's Group meeting, see the *Center Church Chronicle,* March 12, 1944. On women's employment opportunities in the twentieth century, see Alice Kessler-Harris, *Out to Work: A History of Wage Earning Women in America* (Oxford: Oxford University Press, 1982). On the feminist movement and weakening religious commitment, see Wuthnow, *Restructuring of American Religion,* pp. 225–35.

128. Between 1900 and 1920, 31 percent of the men and 28 percent of the women admitted had a parent in the church. In that same period, 21 percent of the men and 22 percent of the women admitted had a sister or brother who was a member.

129. For example, between 1900 and 1920, 32 percent of men and 31 percent of women members were born in New Haven, 76 percent of men and 79 percent of women were transfer members, and 75 percent of both men and women were never formally dismissed from the church. Men were no longer more mobile than women.

130. During the same years, 9 percent of the men and 7 percent of the women joined between the ages of sixteen and nineteen.

131. R. Stephen Warner, "Mirror for American Protestantism: Mendocino Presbyterian Church in the Sixties and Seventies," in *The Mainstream Protestant 'Decline': The Presbyterian Pattern,* ed. Milton Coalter et al. (Louisville: Westminster/John Knox Press, 1990), pp. 220–21.

132. On recent trends, see Ahlstrom, *Religious History,* pp. 1079–96; Wade

Clark Roof and William McKinney, *American Mainline Religion: Its Changing Shape and Future* (New Brunswick: Rutgers University Press, 1987); Wuthnow, *Restructuring of American Religion;* and Dean R. Hoge and David A. Roozen, eds., *Understanding Church Growth and Decline: 1950–1978* (New York: Pilgrim Press, 1979).

133. Calendar of Center Church activities, January 11, 1914. In 1930, Center Church sponsored "Loyalty Sunday": "as an expression of our loyalty to Jesus Christ and to the principles which are the reasons for the church's existence, Let Us Go To Church, bringing our family and friends with us." See the *Center Church Chronicle,* October 26, 1930.

134. *Center Church Chronicle,* October 18, 1942.

135. One older study did, in fact, date the decline in mainline churches earlier, in ways that correspond to our findings. See Arthur M. Schlesinger, Sr., "A Critical Period in American Religion, 1875–1900," *Massachusetts Historical Society Proceedings* 64 (1930–32), reprinted in John M. Mulder and John F. Wilson, eds., *Religion in American History: Interpretive Essays* (Englewood Cliffs: Prentice-Hall, 1978), pp. 302–17.

136. Sydney Ahlstrom, "The Traumatic Years: American Religion and Culture in the 1960s and 1970s," *Theology Today* 26 (1980): 504–22.

137. During this period, the number of new members admitted fell from 506 between 1920 and 1930, to 307 between 1930 and 1940, to 283 between 1940 and 1950 (table 3). In a 1960 essay, Robert T. Handy identified this period as one of general "depression" in the Protestant establishment. See "The American Religious Depression, 1925–1935," *Church History* 29 (1960): 3–16.

138. See "The Joint Report Concerning a Possible Merger of the Humphrey Street Church and Center Church in New Haven, Connecticut, January, 1951." A copy of this report is in the Center Church vault at the Parish House.

139. Diana Scott, "Church Uneasily Awaits Future," *New Haven Independent,* September 7, 1985, p. 1.

140. Benton Johnson, "On Dropping the Subject: Presbyterians and Sabbath Observance in the Twentieth Century," in *The Presbyterian Predicament: Six Perspectives,* ed. Milton J Coalter et al. (Louisville: Westminster/John Knox Press, 1990), p. 105.

141. "From 1865 to 1895, Being a Chapter in the History of this Church by the Clerk, Read at Its Annual Meeting, Jan. 13, 1895," in *Manual of the First Church in New Haven for 1895,* p. 58.

142. Dean M. Kelley, *Why Conservative Churches Are Growing* (New York: Harper and Row, 1972).

143. Maurer, *Center Church Sermons.*

144. New attendance and membership figures were communicated by the Reverend Campbell Lovett.

145. "New Team Aims to Enliven Oldest Church," *New Haven Register,* June 15, 1991, p. 1.

T W O

"A Special Feeling of Closeness"
Mt. Hebron Baptist Church, Leeds, Alabama

WAYNE FLYNT

M Y INITIAL VISITS TO Mt. Hebron Baptist Church demonstrated many of the persistent themes of evangelical rural religion in America: crises within rural society reflected in the church; extreme individualism and traditionalism; fundamentalist theology; lack of class barriers; democratic polity; ambivalence about the believer's relationship to the world; and a strong sense of community. My first visit came on a cold winter's morning in February 1989. A young layman filled the pulpit in place of the pastor, who was ill. The young man had recently responded to God's "call" to preach and was taking Bible courses to prepare for his new career. He made the day's announcements, then stepped back into the choir where he added his voice to a choir of six. When the anthem ended, he moved into the pulpit, opened his Bible, and instructed his congregation to turn in the New Scofield reference Bible to the page from which he read (a passage from Revelation 3).

His exegesis concerned the hypocrisy of the ancient church at Sardis. His application focused on religion ·in America. He denounced large churches which, like Sardis, had neglected their true mission to win souls for the lesser task of meeting the needs of the community. Selecting an agricultural analogy, he compared the modern church to a hull which when opened contained no bean. But his jeremiad was not confined to the empty churches of urban America. Even Mt. Hebron showed signs of spiritual decay. Like all the other powerless churches, it was shackled to tradition and had forsaken the ministry of soul-winning. The enfeeblement of the church reflected the moral collapse of the nation. Americans had forsaken Christian values. The old verities and benchmarks no longer anchored American society.

His homily completed, he began the invitation, issuing a general call for professions of faith and transfers of membership. No one came.

More earnestly now, he admonished the deacons to come forward as a pledge of their prayers for the renewal of Mt. Hebron. Then he asked all members who would join in this commitment to come and stand with him. Gradually the congregation of sixty or so thinned to three adolescents sitting to my left, each apparently determined to resist the invitation, but each also wavering. Finally one of them, a girl, rose slowly and headed for the side aisle, followed in a moment by her two male companions. Now the entire congregation made a semicircle at the front of the church, all of them facing my wife and me who were now the only persons still seated. Noting our obvious discomfort, the young minister quickly dismissed the service with prayer and hurried to speak to us. He greeted us warmly, apologized for any embarrassment he might have caused, but added that the spiritual fires of Mt. Hebron had burned low and only the infusion of new fuel could set the spirit aflame again.

Easter night my wife and I returned to hear Pastor James Blair preach. Obviously more comfortable in the pulpit than the young layman had been, he proclaimed a gospel of renewal and hope. Repeatedly citing the absolute authority of the Bible and using no notes, he paced from one side of the pulpit to the other. He delivered his extemporaneous message in conversational style, not in the random shouts that might have punctuated pulpit oratory in an earlier age. An occasional dramatic gesture was his only concession to bygone days.

Such descriptions have long been the stuff of humorous undergraduate lectures and disdainful academic scholarship. Yet the nexus between those services and Mt. Hebron's historical experience contains far more profound meaning.

Believers at Mt. Hebron expressed their faith through a set of sacred symbols shared by all: the Cross, believer's baptism, the Lord's Supper, extending the right hand of fellowship, laying-on-of-hands for those set apart for special ministry, and the use of special designations such as "brother" and "sister." The sacred symbols and rituals of the church produced consecrated behavior—worship, discipline, revivals, singings, homecomings—which shaped the life of generations of believers. They wrestled with questions of suffering and community disaster, not considering how to avoid suffering but how to make physical pain, personal loss, or worldly defeat meaningful and how to comfort those who experienced it. The motivations and expectations growing from powerful religious symbols gave meaning to life and helped determine right conduct in one's relations to neighbors. Encounter and commitment mattered more than detachment and analysis in the religious cosmos of

Mt. Hebron. At the core of religion was the "drive to make sense out of experience, to give it form and order," a drive which was as real and pressing as biological needs.[1]

Religion operated in two ways. On one level it provided meaning that allowed a person to make sense out of the realities of existence. But it served a social function as well by relating persons to a sacred community made up of people who perceived reality in similar ways and shared common symbols and aspirations. After all, there were many "realities" within Alabama's rural society: moonshining, violence, indigence, alienation, incest, wife and child abuse, and financial corruption, to name only a few. So the distinctive evangelical Christianity practiced at Mt. Hebron integrated people into a very specific "reality" within many competing realities, a concrete and sacred "world" within many larger worlds. The shared symbols touched people at different points with varying strength. Sometimes a person sought to pull away, but the web exerted even greater effort to keep the wayward pilgrim within the sacred community.

Evangelical Protestantism enabled a rising lower and middle class on the southern frontier to achieve identity and solidarity. The new birth on which this new community rested resulted from a conscious act of choice. The order and discipline which this community required replaced the former disorder and social anarchy of a chaotic frontier. Special symbols of social intimacy such as laying-on-of-hands, greetings with a kiss, and extending the right hand of fellowship became powerful bonds for this spiritual community. And the community was expansive enough to offer a place for the poor, for women, and for African Americans living within a secular society which offered no such opportunities.

Bivocationalism bound the religious community into an especially democratic arrangement. All that was needed for a Baptist minister to preach was a sense of divine calling; education, even literacy, was not a prerequisite. Because churches often consisted of poor folks and because members often believed a minister should work at secular tasks to earn a living, salaries, when paid at all, remained low. This assured that no professional class of ministers remote from a people would arise.[2] Such a religion might seem excessively individualistic; indeed, its primary thrust was toward the individual, a thrust which suited it nicely to southern culture. But southern evangelical religion often transcended this personal ethos for a more collective approach to the world, as in Bible, tract, and education efforts, home and foreign mission societies, and programs for the poor, blind, and Indians.[3]

Mt. Hebron Baptist Church was a product of the first phase of settlement of the Alabama frontier. Located in the Upper Cahaba River Valley in the southern foothills of the Appalachian Mountains, the region was settled at the end of the First Creek War (1812–14). Tennessee soldiers who had fought across eastern Alabama in Andrew Jackson's army received land through lease-sale agreements. Many of the pioneer families came from Tennessee, obtained their lands in this way, and began farms and Mt. Hebron Church at almost the same time. Many families that were to play a major role in the life of the church settled in the decade after 1815.

Hezekiah Balch Moor and his wife Virginia (Gincy) left Tennessee with their two children in late 1816 or early 1817. They came by ox cart and settled near the St. Clair-Jefferson county line in the northern part of the valley. Moor had served as a physician under the command of General Andrew Jackson and claimed a grant of land. The third of his fifteen children, Joseph, born in 1817, was ordained to preach at Mt. Hebron and became moderator of the Canaan Baptist Association. The church also ordained Hezekiah Moor, Jr., who pastored Bethel Baptist, a mission of Hebron located in St. Clair County.[4]

John McLaughlin and his wife, Margaret, claimed bounty land in 1821. He had soldiered through the valley under the command of General John Coffee, one of Jackson's lieutenants. He fought again in the Second Creek War (1834–36) as a member of McAdory's 4th Mounted Alabama Infantry. McLaughlin led a family resettlement from Tennessee that resulted in his brother purchasing land in the northern end of the valley adjacent to his. Like the Moors, the McLaughlins produced large families. William C. McLaughlin, the second son, who was born in 1821, bought land next to his father and served as the eighth pastor of Mt. Hebron, affectionately known to inhabitants of the valley as "Pastor Billy."[5]

The Mitchell Pool family came to the region from South Carolina in 1819 with six daughters and three sons. The Pools settled in the southern end of the valley near where Mt. Hebron was organized. Among the twelve charter members of the church were three Pools: John, Huldah, and William.[6]

An Indian trail split the Cahaba Valley, running southwest from the future village of Ashville in St. Clair County to Montevallo in Shelby County. In the 1820s the trail became a stagecoach route, called the Ashville-Montevallo Road, with inns and post offices at frequent intervals. Flanked by the Cahaba River on the north and mountain ridges to the south, it was not ideal farming country. Unlike the rich bottomland of the Tennessee Valley in northern Alabama or the magnificent ebony soil of the central Alabama Black Belt, this earth yielded a good living only to the hardiest and most determined. Early settlers staked out claims to an entire section of 640 acres or more, and some acquired the slaves necessary to farm such extensive domains; but more typical were small yeoman farmers who scratched out a living on twenty to forty acres worked by hordes of their "younguns." Rural traditions and values took firm root. Seventh-generation descendants of these early settlers still live in the valley, some on the same land originally cleared by their ancestors.[7] Descendants of some founders of Mt. Hebron still claim a place in the pews each Sunday.

Mt. Hebron Church owed its existence to the Reverend Hosea Holcombe, a legendary figure who in 1818 pastored the first Baptist congregations in the region. A Virginian of limited formal education, Holcombe had entered the ministry in 1805 and moved to South Carolina where he preached for thirteen years before joining the westward movement into Alabama. While in South Carolina he came under the influence of Luther Rice and Richard Fuller, Baptist leaders who pioneered foreign missions and led in the establishment of the State Convention of South Carolina. Holcombe retained their evangelical fervor, founding five churches in the region that would one day become Birmingham.[8]

When Holcombe arrived in the state in 1818, Alabama was part of the "Old Southwest," still a raw frontier quite unlike the more sophisticated and stable Atlantic seaboard from which he had come. He later estimated that in 1820 the new state contained no more than fifty Baptist churches, all small and struggling.[9] Problems abounded. Creek Indians still posed a psychological threat if not a physical one. The Creek War of 1812–14 had opened eastern Alabama to settlement, but Creeks remained on some of their lands until their removal in the late 1830s. The Upper Cahaba Valley was just to the north of the Creek Nation in a no-man's-land between Creeks, Cherokees, and Chickasaws, hunted by each but occupied by none. The first settlers moved into the valley only months after the decisive Battle of Horseshoe Bend in 1814, and Mt. Hebron began services only five years after that bloody engagement. Violence, drunkenness, and disorder accompanied the general anxiety about safety from Indian attack. Internal migration, the severing of family and community ties occasioned by moving, the arduous labor entailed in clearing new land and building houses and farm buildings, all added to the perils of marginal land and difficult transportation. The

Cahaba River was not navigable, and transportation for five-hundred-pound cotton bales was difficult if not impossible. The valley produced corn, wheat, potatoes, and many other food crops but relatively little cotton. The marginality of the economy compounded problems inherent in pioneer life: extreme individualism, competitiveness, and a spirit of noncooperation. Added to all these problems, illness, disease, and frightfully high rates of infant mortality created a theological climate of fear and impending doom. Many early settlers had families by multiple wives because of the high female mortality rates in childbirth. Gincy Moor—wife of Hezekiah, mother of fifteen children, two of them sons ordained at Mt. Hebron—died in 1862; Hezekiah later married a widow and began a second family. John C. Pool, descendant of one of Mt. Hebron's charter members, died along with four of his children in a February 1884 tornado. Inscriptions on tombstones in the cemetery behind Mt. Hebron Church speak eloquently of the impermanence of life on the Alabama frontier.

Evangelical religion offered a coherent view of every person's place within this capricious world. To women facing the perils of childbirth, to men confronting drought or flood, the simple message of good news dispensed by rural congregations was welcome. Religion contained obvious social benefits for such congregations. It brought isolated people together, provided young people opportunities for courtship, and offered a community center for activities. But first and foremost the gospel of the fall, redemption, and ultimate vindication and glory of humanity provided balm for the soul. Tiny quarter-time churches allowed an opportunity for socializing only once a month or at infrequent camp meetings or protracted revivals. But comfort for the soul, the certainty that God was in charge and would work his will from among all the discordant and evil events of life, provided constant solace.

Nor was such religion escapist. Despite much Zion talk about ultimate causes and destinations—Canaan land, the New Jerusalem, Heaven—the Baptists of the Upper Cahaba Valley lived very much in the real world amidst real problems. But most of these problems were beyond their control: natural disasters such as droughts, floods, tornadoes, deaths in childbirth, and diseases; and man-made disasters such as wars, depressions, and political oppression. They exerted all the efforts of hard work and citizenship that were within their power, voting for those who favored their causes and influencing policy. Alabama was as close to a pure white democracy as America knew at the time, providing universal manhood suffrage, a legislature controlled by poor and yeoman farmers, and a tax system which taxed according to one's wealth. For problems that resisted such efforts, they had to trust in the providence of God. There is no evidence that evangelical religion kept the people of Mt. Hebron in a syrupy world of religious platitudes. Quite to the contrary, some members owned slaves, fashioned a defense of their peculiar institution from Scripture, and condemned many of the sins believed to be rife among their social betters, the large planters and aristocracy. Antebellum tirades against gambling, drinking, the theater, and dancing were as much rooted in class grievances as in theology.

The symbols and rituals of evangelical religion, its rousing hymns and thunderous sermons, provided a providential message for a frontier folk. Sin and depravity threatened on every hand. One needed only to look about to observe the consequences of such wickedness. The wage of sin was death. But praise be to God who from his abundant grace offered a gospel of redemption and renewal, of entry into a holy community of restoration and ultimate glory! The much-maligned camp meeting revivals offered hope not only to individual souls but to the community of the saved. Salvation created not only a new person but a new community, a people of God. It was this need—for self-discipline and restraint, for order and meaning, to control violence within families and among neighbors, this necessity for one to live responsibly in relations with friends and community—which nourished the crop that Hosea Holcombe harvested. The Great Revival that began at Cane Ridge, Kentucky, in 1800 had set the forces in motion. And as that revival swept across the South, conditions in the Cahaba Valley were ideally suited for religious awakening.[10]

Hosea Holcombe brought his message to a responsive community. During the last week of August 1819, some seventy-five days before Alabama became a state, seven men and five women established Mt. Hebron Baptist Church. Holcombe preached one service a month, and William White donated land in what was then Shelby County but would ultimately be included in Jefferson County. As early as 1827 the congregation had a building. In 1836 the expanding congregation relocated and rebuilt. A tornado destroyed this building in 1884. The new building was much like the former one, a white frame structure with tower to the left of the front entrance, and two doors, one opening into the women's side of the church, the other into the men's domain. This building could no longer contain the crowds by 1922, and the congregation constructed a larger edifice, which burned after being struck by lightning in 1954. The present building—a low, simple brick structure—lacks the simple elegance of the earlier frame buildings or the ecclesiastical grandeur of the typical Greek revival church. The location of all the buildings since 1838 is a too-small plot beside the strategic Montevallo-Ashville Road. It nestles in a valley five miles south of Leeds, a New South industrial town that began about 1881 in the shadow of Birmingham, which is located in Jones Valley across several mountain ridges to the west. There in the southern part of the Upper Cahaba Valley the little church beamed forth its light.

The founders provided an "Abstract of Principles" which provides ample insight into their mission. They formed Mt. Hebron Church because all who were "favored with the dispensation of God" should "embrace his covenant, acknowledge his government, profess his name and unite in the faith and fellowship of the gospel." A strong sense of religious community prevailed among them as they covenanted "to endeavor to keep the unity of the spirit in bonds of peace," to meet together at "all convenient seasons," "to sympathize with each other and to pray with and for each other," and to contribute part of their substance to conduct worship and help needy members. Because of the "diversity of sentiment among professing Christians," they believed it necessary to adopt a set of principles, namely: belief in one true God which was three persons in the Godhead; faith in the Old and New Testaments as the "word of God" and the only rule of faith and precept; God's "free electing love" expressed through Jesus Christ which beckoned "God's chosen" to be "called, regenerated, and sanctified"; man's original sin and incompetence to save himself; justification by the righteousness of Christ through faith; the certainty of a final judgment; the practice of baptism and the Lord's Supper ordinances for all "regularly Baptized" true believers; the ministration of a "regularly Baptized," "called," and ordained minister; resurrection of the dead; eternal punishment for the wicked and joy for the righteous; the sanctity of the Lord's day; the obligation to support the gospel; and the duty "to pay . . . conscientious regard to civil government and to give our support as an ordinance of God." [11]

"Rules of Decorum" reflected the democracy of the southern frontier. At church conferences held monthly, motions made and seconded would be put to a vote. A simple majority would prevail but must act with "due respect to the minority, and if possible convince them, but if they cannot, the minority shall submit to the majority." To assure order, the rules provided that a member who chose to speak should rise to his feet and address the moderator. Upon being recognized, the member could speak on the subject under debate "without casting reflections" on any member who had spoken previously. No member could speak more than three times on a single subject without permission of the church, nor miss more than one conference without sending an excuse. If a member missed twice without excuse, the congregation appointed a delegate to cite the miscreant to attend the next meeting. No member could bring charges against another without first "taking gospel steps" to resolve the conflict, and any member accusing another without sufficient evidence had to satisfy the accused.[12]

Taken together, the "Abstract of Principles" and "Rules of Decorum" provided a doctrinal basis for Baptist polity. The modest Calvinism of the abstract still allowed for aggressive proselytizing. The formation of the church created a special religious community, set apart from the world, which covenanted to associate together, help one another in physical need, live in peace, and accept a common body of doctrine rooted in Scripture and in historic Reformation Christian practice. Aside from the distinctive Baptist requirement to be "regularly Baptized" (i.e., immersed), the abstract was neither narrow nor sectarian. The decorum assured that democracy and order would prevail in their proceedings just as they hoped it would permeate secular society. If the sacred community prevailed, it would require Herculean efforts by God's chosen community, efforts of attendance, involvement, and commitment not required or even possible elsewhere in their lives.

Discipline

Historian Donald Mathews contends that the terms "order" and "discipline" were central to the southern evangelical's conception of the Christian life. After carefully studying antebellum evangelicals in Mississippi, historian Randy J. Sparks agreed that "the disciplinary process was at the very heart of the evangelical experience."[13] Evangelical churches made heavy demands on their members as part of a separate and holy fellowship. The purpose of such discipline was not to punish the wanderer but to recall the person to faith and to full fellowship within the community. Since Baptists believed that once a sinner was saved the person could not "fall from grace," the purpose of church discipline had more to do with the boundaries of a sacred community than with assurance of salvation. Bound together in the wonder of Christ's redeeming love, Baptists believed that the sins of a brother or sister inflicted pain on the entire family. In the life of Mt. Hebron, congregational disciplining of a member compared closely to parental restraint of a child. The intent was not to exclude the child from the family but to clarify the boundaries of accepted conduct, to forewarn that, if an offspring valued participation in the family, then that child must observe certain standards of conduct. Such restrictions were not designed to hinder the rebellious so much as to keep the family coherent, stable, and mutually committed. The scriptural basis of such discipline was Matthew 18:15–17.

Words became important symbols in Mt. Hebron's disciplining. The congregation began the process by "citing" a brother or sister, a process that involved appointing a committee of two or three men to investigate and bring the wayward one before the next church conference. Usually the accused appeared promptly and either "acknowledged" the sin and asked forgiveness or "gave satisfaction" to the congregation. Only when the accused refused to appear, would not deny the charge, or, if acknowledging it, would not repent, did the congregation act. In fact the conference seemed anxious not to take action, repeatedly delaying decisions and appointing new committees to reason with the accused. Only when all efforts at reconciliation failed did the congregation "exclude" or "excommunicate" the brother or sister from "fellowship." Clearly, this threatened loss of place in a valued community was a powerful stimulus to reform. Most accused either energetically and promptly denied the charge or repentantly confessed their sins and asked forgiveness. No sin seemed too grievous to forgive; confessions of immorality, alcoholism, gambling, dancing, slander, swearing, fighting, swindling, all received immediate forgiveness and restoration.

Mt. Hebron's members realized the poor clay from which humanity was crafted and offered the most generous conditions of restoration. They cited their brothers for "drinking too much" or "drinking to excess," not for drinking. They encouraged inquiries about ethical conduct that might be unclear. And periodically the church simply wiped the ethical slate clean in what might be called a "Baptist dispensation": past sins forgiven but from this day on members must abide by strict ethical standards!

Sins against family weighed more heavily than personal impiety such as drinking, dancing, or swearing. The wording of one 1830 disciplinary action was particularly harsh: Brother Lungley was "excommunicated for inconstance in marrying another man's wife. . . ." But the congregation anxiously awaited repentance. In September 1857 the church cited Brother Marion McDanal for "immoral conduct." When he acknowledged that he had "done wrong and gave satisfaction" of his repentance, "he was acquitted."[14]

During the first decades, the church primarily disciplined personal habits on a disordered frontier. But as the frontier receded, the congregation cited members more frequently for sins against the collective community. The first such reference appeared in March 1841, when the congregation excluded Brother John Kelley "for violating the law of our state. . . ." Ten years later, in October 1851, amid the prosperity of the cotton boom in the Gulf South, the church brought charges against Brother D. A. Ellington for taking illegal tolls at his mill. In January 1853 the congregation excluded Brother John Watson for passing worthless paper banknotes for genuine money. In March 1866, the church cited Brother Isaac Looney for signing over his property to his wife in order to avoid paying his debts. Although personal ethical grievances still predominated, the church increasingly sought to stabilize the life of a society beyond the sacred community. Paradoxically, after the defeat of the Confederacy in 1865, the church seemed to renew its devotion to controlling the private lives of its members and chastening society. During the 1870s and 1880s the church handled an unprecedented number of cases as if to make up for the sins that must have caused the awful judgment of God between 1861 and 1865.[15]

By the last three decades of the nineteenth century the church faced an unprecedented crisis, which it also sought to contain with church discipline. Until these decades Mt. Hebron had absorbed Methodists and Presbyterians into its fellowship but seldom lost its own. When such an event had occurred, the culprit was usually a woman who left for another denomination either because of marriage or discontent with Mt. Hebron. In either circumstance the church had acted firmly and harshly, excluding them from membership. But these isolated instances paled in comparison to the "comeoutism" of the 1870s.

What triggered the crisis is hard to tell, but it clearly involved a deep sense of dissatisfaction with mainstream evangelical southern churches. The exodus of members from Baptist and Methodist congregations swelled the Church of God, the Holiness Church, and other Pentecostal and Holiness sects. Departing members resented the church's growing assimilation of secular culture and yearned for a purer ecclesiastical order. Spreading poverty and rising rates of tenancy increased class divisions within churches. Political divisions between conservative Bourbon (Redeemer) Democrats and independent-minded and more radical Greenbackers, Grangers, Alliancemen, and Populists split congregations. Fueled by a multitude of causes, tension mounted in this rural Zion.[16] As with all other matters of discord and disharmony, members relied on church discipline to contain the damage to their sacred community, which they increasingly perceived in sectarian form.

Periodically Mt. Hebron had expelled members for heresy, but the church's rigid adherence to its original statement of principles and the denominational loyalty of its pastors minimized the influence of schism. Mt. Hebron's one concession to Baptist heterodoxy came in 1868 during a period when it had trouble retaining a regular pastor. The church voted to adopt foot-washing as an ordinance.

More serious trouble arose in September 1871, when the congregation excluded seven people for joining another church. Mt. Hebron expelled others in October, and in November church minutes mentioned the new congregation by name, Sherman's Church, so named for a man who lived in the vicinity of Mt. Hebron. Three more members left Mt. Hebron for Sherman's Church in January (all were excluded) and others apparently followed (approximately thirteen in all), contributing no doubt to the congregation's steady decline in membership from 109 in 1861 to 35 in 1902 (though the largest percentage of this loss resulted from the withdrawal of black members). Luckily Sherman's Church was short-lived and only a momentary threat. In addition to excluding heretical members, the congregation took steps to shore up denominational loyalty. In October 1877 members voted to add "Baptist" to the official title of the church, and in July 1878 the congregation elected delegates to the Baptist State Convention. Although the church had been active in regional associations—the Cahaba Association in 1819, the Mt. Zion Association in 1823, the Canaan Association in 1833, and the Cahaba Valley Association in 1867—this is the first reference to participation in the state convention.[17]

The ecclesiastical rigor of church discipline appeared more severe than it really was. Not only did members immediately forgive a penitent sinner, they also softened the language of discipline. Even when a committee cited a member, it did so in ways that symbolized the unity of the sacred community. Minutes referred to miscreants as "Brother" and "Sister" even when they had committed sins of adultery and heresy. If the sinner proved recalcitrant, the congregation excluded the slacker;

but the break in fellowship was often temporary. One principal function of the annual summer revival was to call the excluded to repentance and renewal. Seldom did a revival season pass without joyous reunions as sinners reentered the sacred circle. Church clerks filled the minutes with symbolically significant words. Those guilty of acts of "nonfellowship" were "excluded from fellowship," then later "made a statement to the community" and were "restored to fellowship." Of 376 members who belonged to the church between 1819 and 1865, the church excluded fifty-five. Of these fifty-five, the church restored at least ten to fellowship. No doubt the extreme pride and individualism so renowned among southerners caused many disciplined members to join other denominations or leave the church entirely. But this cultural pattern only accentuates the significance of those who repented of their sins with contrite and humble hearts.

One function of discipline was to define the boundaries of sacred community. This function encouraged members to challenge vague or ambivalent teachings by asking for clarification. Better to avoid a breach in fellowship by asking interpretations of doctrine than to risk exclusion.

During the frontier stage of Mt. Hebron's existence, when community mattered the most and individualism posed a threat to church order, the minutes contain many inquiries resolved in conference. In January 1837 a church conference resolved that none of its members should make or sell "ardent spirits unless for medical purposes." Any member who became drunk more than twice would be excluded. In May 1839 Brother Hezekiah Moor, Jr., inquired as to whether it was wrong for a member of Mt. Hebron to take his or her seat "among the world, and not among the members of the Church" during communion. The answer helped strengthen the sacred community; the congregation voted that such practice was wrong. During communion members should sit among their own. More mundane inquiries poured in: Was it wrong to "pitch dollars on the Sabbath day in sport"? Yes! Was it "consistent with Christianity for a man to marry his wife's niece"? The congregation believed such practice "to be consistent." In December 1852 members resolved against "dancing, playing cards for sport or otherwise, nor engage in vain plays nor allow the same in his or her house."[18]

The "Hebronites," as they were called within the community, also tempered church discipline with periodic wholesale revisions, reversals, and suspensions. These occurred mainly when social, economic, and political unrest threatened to engulf the church.

The first such crisis began in 1861. Although hostile armies did not traverse the Cahaba Valley, Mt. Hebron did not escape unscathed. A partial list of church members who served in Confederate armies contains seven names among the congregation of 104. Lists of church members in 1865 indicate that one-third of the members were slaves, so nearly 10 percent of the total white membership (and 27 percent of the estimated white males) fought in the conflict. This put an extraordinary strain on the church. In October 1861 Bradley White wrote from his bivouac in Auburn, acknowledging his sins and asking restoration. The church not only restored him, it also appointed White and three of his comrades-in-arms from Mt. Hebron to "watch over each other" and inform the church of any "misdemeanor" committed while in service. Letters of acknowledgment soon arrived from two other soldiers seeking absolution at long range. It was granted, though not without some resistance in one case. Thus did the sacred community extend itself even to distant battlefields, to men in danger of their lives. But it is unlikely that the soldiers or members back home paid much attention to misdemeanors during the next half-decade. In the preoccupation with surviving, discipline declined.

With war ended and the disaster of Reconstruction descending, Mt. Hebron had to rethink its theology. Convinced that a just God must have acted according to his will, how could a southerner make sense out of historical tragedy? Had a decline in Christian conduct precipitated the ruinous outcome of the war? In February 1866 the church resolved to "strike out all complaints against those that have taken any act in plays and dancing, drinking and so on and commence with our resolution and inforce them strictly." What followed was the most rigorous application of church discipline in Mt. Hebron's history. Members scrambled to qualify previous sins under terms of the "wipe out law," and the congregation granted generous terms. A rash of exclusions followed, the severity of which threatened the fragile stability of the church. Realism once more outweighed moral judgment. In February 1867 the church agreed "to suspend rules against parties and drinking for the present and inforce them strictly hereafter." For a while the church relied on arbitration of disputes rather than on punitive discipline.

When this crisis passed, cases of discipline mounted rapidly during the remainder of the century. Exclusions, the withdrawal of black members, and the heresy of Sherman's Church reduced the congregation to only 35 members in 1902, the smallest figure since the early days of the

2.1   Mt. Hebron Baptist Church, 1895. Photograph courtesy of Lou Arnold and the congregation of Mt. Hebron Baptist Church. Courtesy of Special Collection, Samford University Library, Birmingham, Alabama.

church. Mt. Hebron abandoned church discipline altogether in 1904. The only recorded cases of exclusion between the Populist revolt which divided the church in 1892–93 and the end of church discipline in 1904 were cases involving members who joined another denomination. The steady membership decline ended what the Populist revolt had begun: the luxury of exclusion in a church barely able to attract enough members to survive.

Although the church took no formal action to suspend discipline in 1904, no further cases appeared in the minutes until the congregation adopted a new order of decorum amid another historic crisis in December 1934. In that month the congregation issued a blanket dispensation similar to the ones it had granted in 1866 and 1867. Members voted "to let the past conduct be the past and forget and never allow it to come up in the church"; but "from this date on we do agree to comply with all the church rules and decorum of this Hebron Baptist Church." This discipline primarily affected polity and procedures, not personal conduct. Deacons had to attend church conferences. If the church appointed a committee to hear grievances between members, the decision reached by the committee would be final. If the committee could not agree, it would turn the matter over to the entire church for action. Active members must attend church at least once a month unless providentially hindered. All grievances or charges of misconduct would be referred to a church committee created for that purpose.

The renewal of church discipline was short-lived. At church conferences the moderator would ask for "acknowledgments," and occasionally a member would confess a sin and ask prayers and forgiveness. The last such recorded confession occurred in September 1945. Discipline had become a matter of individual conscience, and confession a method of maintaining harmony within the church family, not a way by which the sacred community imposed its standards through collective action.

The decline of discipline after 1900 demands an explanation. At its most basic level, discipline functioned as a method of establishing and preserving values and defining the boundaries of acceptable conduct within the religious community. But the twentieth century brought a more complex definition of values. Matters such as dancing were no longer moral issues that were as central or as compelling as they had once been. The congregation had more difficulty imposing its values upon an increasingly pluralistic and tolerant society. At the same time, the religious community successfully imposed many of its notions upon the secular society. Progressive reforms such as prohibition made the state a partial arbiter of private conduct and lessened the need for church discipline. If discipline was designed to keep the world out of the church, it was less necessary in a time when world and church seemed to be converging. Right conduct was subsumed under broader notions of good citizenship and community conformity. Protestant standards of personal conduct permeated society, and true Americanism became synonymous for a while with what had once been the ethos of Mt. Hebron.

African Americans

The relationship of church discipline to religious community is nowhere more apparent than in the way it affected African-American slaves and women. It was in the historic tangent where southern evangelical Christianity touched race and gender that Mt. Hebron left its most lasting impact upon secular society.

Baptist attitudes toward slavery underwent a slow metamorphosis between the Revolutionary War and the Civil War. The zeal for freedom following 1776 confirmed the abolitionist sentiments of many Baptists.

But the expansion of cotton cultivation and slavery muted such sentiment and gradually turned southern evangelicals into ardent defenders of slavery. They rationalized that a literal reading of Scripture supported slavery, and that the presence of so many slaves constituted an unparalleled opportunity for evangelism. Actually they made only halfhearted efforts at evangelizing slaves until the creation of the Southern Baptist Convention (SBC) in 1845. After that date they frequently favored teaching blacks to read the Bible, among other reforms. Following the creation of a regional church, secular southerners could no longer oppose reforms by arguing that they stemmed entirely from meddling Yankee abolitionists-evangelicals.

Several keys unlock the complex relationship between black and white Baptists. Although African Americans did not experience religious equality, they did obtain rights not granted by secular governments. Under Alabama law after 1832, slaves could not be taught to read and write, could not testify in court, or meet separately in groups. Informal social contacts between the races were governed by a complex hierarchical caste system which denied all forms of social equality. Yet within evangelical churches slaves entered a religious community by an act of free will (commitment to Christ or transferal of membership). They were baptized in the same creeks with whites, offered the same "right hand of Christian fellowship," were brought before the church for discipline in the same way, were exonerated, forgiven, excluded, and restored in the same process, allowed to give testimony, sometimes preached to both black and white congregations, and worshiped in the same services with whites (though often in a separate area of the building).[19] White evangelicals often taught them to read Scripture (a violation of the law) and recognized the sanctity of their marriages and the inviolability of their families.

The extent of shared rituals varied from congregation to congregation. Black churches existed in cities, but rural congregations usually combined races both for purposes of economy of effort and ease of social control. That way whites could monitor how ministers interpreted Christianity to blacks. Some rural churches used the terms "Brother" and "Sister" uniformly without regard to race; others used such familiar terms only for white members. Some minutes recorded only the first names of slaves but the full names of whites. Membership lists sometimes separated the names of whites and slaves; others mixed them; some omitted the names of slaves altogether. In matters of discipline slaves sometimes testified against slaves, sometimes acknowledged their own sins, sometimes were the objects of charges by whites, and infrequently watched passively as whites cited other whites for mistreatment of slaves. In extremely rare cases slaves testified against whites.[20]

Even if whites intended the gospel as a form of social control, slaves often appropriated the symbols and rituals in different ways. Masters expected obedience as the result of the Christian message; but slaves obtained a sense of joy, meaning, and spiritual liberation. Different perceptions of spiritual symbols and white notions of black inferiority assured that the sense of religious community experienced by blacks and whites would be different.[21] Within each racially mixed church three sacred communities existed: whites with whites, blacks with blacks, and whites with blacks.

Mt. Hebron tended toward the liberal end of this continuum of Christian relationships. Of 376 names recorded in church minutes between 1819 and 1865, 51 were names of slaves and 2 those of free blacks. The church book recorded only the first names of slaves and always listed them as "a servant of . . ." (e.g., "Pattey, a servant of R.S. Shepherd"). Their names are listed chronologically among whites in the order in which they joined Mt. Hebron, not separately by race. In many cases slaves joined the church although their masters did not belong. That seems to be the case with planter R. S. Shepherd, who was not listed among church members although eleven of his slaves were. Other slaves joined at the same time as their masters. Peter and Mark, servants of John McDanal, were listed as numbers 134 and 135, and McDanal as member number 136. Mary and Pattey, servants of B. White, came as members 193 and 194; Nancy E. White, presumably B. White's wife, came as member 192. Many slaves joined long before their masters and may even have influenced the whites to join. John, a servant of Isaac Cameron, entered Mt. Hebron as member number 72; his mistress, Sara Cameron, became member 100. Rose, servant of William Watson, joined the church (number 78) long before her master (number 266).

The church did not remain all white for long after its founding. In October 1825 Peter, "a colored person, servant of John McDanal," joined. Most slaves came by profession of faith, though some came by letter of transfer. Usually the congregation routinely dismissed slaves when they desired to transfer elsewhere (perhaps because they were sold to another plantation). A curious exception to that pattern occurred in March 1829, when the church granted letters of dismissal to "black brethren" belonging to a Dr. Shackleford. But at a June meeting white member Jesse Sparks reported that three of the "black brethren belonging to Dr. Shackleford, wish their letters to remain in this church." This intriguing conflict between Shackleford, his slaves, and the church is not further explained, although in December the blacks did request their letters that the church had first granted, then retained. Whatever the complex factors operating in this case, obviously the congregation respected the right of the three slaves to determine for themselves whether or not to request their letters. However Shackleford obtained their transfer, whether through persuasion or coercion, the church would not grant the letters so long as the three slaves resisted. Only when they themselves sought their letters did the church honor the requests.

When a slave is mentioned in church proceedings, the prefix "black brother" or "black sister" is usually appended, although no slave was accorded a last name. That was not the case with the free men of color. Ned Potter joined Mt. Hebron on June 14, 1832, and is always called by his full name when mentioned in the minutes. Like many of his white brethren, he fell victim to church discipline. In July 1833 two white men cited Porter. In August the congregation excluded him from fellowship for drunkenness and swearing. In February 1855 the church received by letter Isaac Johnson, "a colored man." Although the minutes do not specify whether he was slave or free man, the use of his full name suggests that he was a free man of color.

Slaves also answered frequently to charges. Church minutes record the names of seven male slaves subjected to discipline and two females. In January 1836 members excluded Bob and Abram for quarreling on the Sabbath. In August 1852 the church excluded Elijah for lying. Allegations of unruly and disorderly conduct typified charges against black males: the church cited two for quarreling, two for fighting, one for lying, one for nonattendance, and one for Sabbath violation.

The two females cited seemed to have committed offenses that struck more fundamentally at the racial order. In March 1846 a two-man committee cited "Sister Julia," a slave of C. Thompson. They charged that she disobeyed her master and ran away. For this offense the church excluded her. In September 1858 the church cited Mary, a slave belonging to a man named Herring, for "unchristian conduct." The church appointed her master, apparently a church member, "to inform her of the charge and report to next conference her reply." This practice differed from the normal practice of allowing members personally to answer charges made against them. Because her master investigated the charge and presented her reply, it is no surprise that the membership excluded her.

Having a white reply for a slave was uncharacteristic of earlier discipline cases. In February 1848 two men appeared before the church to acknowledge that they had engaged in fighting in self-defense. Brother Lowery was white, Brother George was a slave. Both spoke in their own defense, and each asked to be retained. The church forgave them and retained fellowship with both men. George was not so lucky the second time around. When he acknowledged the same sin seventeen months later, the church excluded him from fellowship.[22]

The strangest episode in the interracial history of Mt. Hebron occurred in 1854, and demonstrates the way in which close religious fellowship blurred the secular boundaries of race. In January 1855 the congregation considered a report that "some brethren" had attended "a Negro ball, and engaged with the blacks in dancing." The church appointed an unusually large committee of five white men to investigate. The committee reported in January 1855 that several church members had attended a gathering on the Shepherd plantation during the Christmas holidays. At least eleven of Shepherd's slaves belonged to the church, so such an assembly might not seem strange except for the circumstances. Whites other than masters seldom visited slaves in their own cabins. Furthermore, the committee reported that "one or two [white] members engaged with them in [fiddling and dancing] . . . (to wit) Samuel P. Dyers, Leonard B. McDonald, Manson Glass, Bradley White, Smith White, and Samuel W. White."

The entire congregation took up the charges in February. Three of the accused gave "satisfaction" and were retained. But the other three failed to exonerate themselves and were excluded from fellowship.

Barely four months after the resolution of the interracial Christmas dance, the church cited Sister Audea Harris. The sensational report alleged that Harris had been seen visiting the Negro quarters on the Shepherd plantation. Harris explained through the committee to the July church conference that she had been processing Mrs. Shepherd's will. As part of those duties she had "called at a negro cabin but says she has not made a habit of visiting" Negro houses and "disapproves such conduct." The church accepted her explanation and took no action.[23]

The two episodes reveal much about race relations. The unusual length and detail of the account in church minutes and the unprecedented size of the investigating committee indicates the extent of concern. Having brought the two races together in sacred community, white members now scrambled to define the limits of their fellowship. Whites and blacks could share hymns, communion, baptism, the right hand of fellowship, discipline, and sermons; but they could not share the slave quarters or fiddle and dance together. The specter of six white males dancing with black women at a Christmas party was bad enough. But a female church member frequenting a slave cabin alone raised sexual questions of even greater magnitude. Mt. Hebron Church, having first blurred racial distinctions in the process of defining religious community, now tried desperately to reorder and redefine those distinctions within a larger secular society that absolutely would not tolerate acts of racial iconoclasm.

This close attention to church discipline reflects Mt. Hebron's concern for the spiritual welfare of its slave members. But the interest appears in other aspects of church life as well. In January 1828 members agreed to build an addition to the meeting house for "the accommodation of Black persons." Apparently between 1825 when the first slave had joined and this addition some three years later, slaves had worshiped with whites. The new addition allowed the spatial separation within the building which whites deemed necessary. This symbol of hierarchy and separation indicates both the limits of community and the determination of white members to minister to the spiritual needs of slaves even at considerable inconvenience and the allocation of precious financial resources.

Four years later, in March 1832, "Brother Anthony," slave of Willis H. Jones, was "liberated by the church to preach the Gospel so long as he keeps in good order." "Liberate" did not mean to free physically, which was beyond the power of the church in any case. But use of the term, which the church minutes do not employ when describing ordination of whites, is significant, as is the unusual qualification (so long as he "keeps in good order"). One may assume Anthony kept in "good order" and continued his ministry of preaching to his flock in Mt. Hebron and environs because the minutes make no further mention of him.

Of course the Civil War and emancipation altered all of these arrangements, but not so suddenly as one might expect. Denominational leaders in Alabama differed sharply over the future course of black-white relations when the war ended. The Rev. I. T. Tichenor, a distinguished minister, businessman, and college administrator, chided Alabama Baptists in 1865 for having tolerated antebellum laws which denied blacks the ability to learn to read Scripture. White Baptists should welcome freedmen into church fellowship, teach them to read the Bible, and share communion with them.

Not all Alabama Baptists agreed with this proposal. Some churches established committees to speed the withdrawal of black members, and one association in the Tennessee Valley refused to accept a black church into its fellowship, urging black Baptists to create an association of their own. Many white Baptists expressed triple concerns: fear that blacks would want to remain with them; fear lest meddling northern Baptists try to proselytize among them, thereby working both religious and political mischief; and fear lest blacks create churches under the leadership of ignorant and overtly political black pastors. In a variety of ways whites made it clear that any continued relationship would be on their terms, not on terms of religious or social equality. Interracial churches would not select black pastors, deacons, Sunday school teachers or other officers. Nor did most white churches make much effort to dissuade black members when they began to leave.[24] Blacks chose to create churches which they controlled, which met their religious needs, and which allowed them to realize the full possibilities of religious community. But the fact that the patterns of their churches so closely matched the ones from which they came confirms the strong element of biracial community even in the churches that slavery wrought. Given the paternalism or outright hostility of many whites, it is no surprise that virtually all blacks withdrew from interracial Baptist churches during Reconstruction, and most did so within months of emancipation.

Once again Mt. Hebron proved an exception to the rule. Perhaps the relatively small number of blacks living in the Upper Cahaba Valley and the stable and long-term religious association inhibited quick resolution of the issue. Whatever the cause, separation occurred slowly. In October 1865, six months after the Civil War ended, the church received "black sister Emley by letter." The familiar designation of "Sister" remained, but so did the condescendingly familiar given name without surname. The church continued to exercise discipline over both races. In March 1866 the congregation considered charges of immoral conduct against Salley, a "black sister," and excluded her. In January 1872 the church excluded a black member, now listed by full name as Alse Mc-Danal, because he had joined the exodus to the heretical Sherman's Church, which apparently was interracial. The final reference to black members in church records occurred in November 1873 when sisters Mary and Matilda Looney transferred their letters. After that date the church consisted of white members only, reflecting the broader patterns of segregation spreading rapidly across southern society.

Ironically, however, the Looney sisters were not the last black persons to attend Mt. Hebron. Despite hardening racial lines and the steady progress of Jim Crow laws, local tradition and Christian good-will once again defied stereotypes in the twentieth century. Present member Margie Poole Martin remembers a black woman who attended the church. An elderly couple, the Jim Doroughs, hired the black woman to live with them and help them with chores. She accompanied them to church "just as regular as can be." The church building contained a large pot-bellied stove, and a bench nearby belonged to her.[25] So in the twentieth century as in the nineteenth, community existed within community. The congregation exempted a single black woman from racial exclusion but made sure she had her own bench, to emphasize that racial boundaries still mattered in congregational life.

Women

Evangelical churches divided by race also designated roles according to gender. Baptists in early Virginia and South Carolina represented a backcountry frontier people opposed to a Tidewater gentry dominated by men. The history of discipline within these early churches reveals how forcefully evangelicals attacked so-called masculine virtues—competitiveness, violence, gambling, drinking, swearing, horseracing, and Sabbath desecration (especially hunting on the Sabbath). Added to this inferential evidence is the fact that most congregations were disproportionately female (one estimate claims a ratio in all southern churches of 65 percent female to 35 percent male). Although male evangelicals were as "manly" as their secular counterparts, they belonged to churches which glorified "feminine" virtues such as nonviolence, emotional expressiveness, kindness to neighbor and stranger, humility, and pursuit of collective rather than individual goals.[26] One of the strengths of religious community was its capacity to encourage and nourish human growth and potential, "motherly" characteristics within the complex division of roles according to gender.

"Family religion" became common in the South. Society at first expected the male head of family to establish religious standards for his family. But when males shirked this responsibility, pressure shifted toward women as pivotal in the public and private life of evangelicalism. In the process of directing and arbitrating the family's religious life, many women consciously or unconsciously experienced a fascinating metamorphosis paralleling the religious experience of slaves. Evangelical religion became a force for restraining abusive husbands and rowdy sons, a method of establishing "psychological distance" between themselves and worldly husbands, which allowed them, for the best of theological reasons, to place loyalty to God above obedience to husband in at least the most sacred spheres of life. Christianity allowed women to secure both a separate sexual identity and a group gender identity. In time they could speak and vote their minds in church conferences.

The church also provided antebellum women their chief means of public identity. The great awakening that swept the South after the Cane Ridge revival of 1800 even allowed women to become "exhorters." Such women appeared in a formal role to urge sinners to respond to the tugging of the Holy Spirit.[27] And the separate doors and seating within frontier churches must not be considered exclusively a matter of sexual separation. Segregating women and girls from men encouraged emotional bonding with other women. Mt. Hebron experienced many of these patterns. Although males slightly outnumbered females in the first few months of the church's existence—seventeen men and eleven women among the first twenty-eight members—the pattern quickly became more typical. New members added during 1828 included eleven white and three black females, six white and two black males, or a total of fourteen women to only eight men. A ten-day camp meeting in October 1849 brought in twenty-eight white and three black women, nineteen white and two black men, for a total of thirty-one females to only twenty-one males. By December, 1865, Mt. Hebron contained twenty-six male members and forty-seven females, a ratio of 65 percent female to 35 percent male, virtually identical to one historian's estimate for the southern church.[28] Interestingly, the church in 1865 divided the membership list by gender, whereas previously it had listed names in the order in which persons had joined the church.

Religious symbols confused gender identification. As with black slaves, women shared freely and equally in most of the common rituals. Like blacks, they initiated a relationship to Christ and his church by an act of free will. The congregation extended baptism, the right hand of fellowship, communion, and discipline without regard to gender. But other practices stemmed from women's separation into a sphere reserved for them. Like blacks, they sat in a separate section of the church, and this segregation lasted at least until the 1920s, within the memory of women who still belong to Mt. Hebron.[29] Like blacks, women were excluded from leadership roles within the church. No woman's name appears as an officer or as member of any committee until February 1830, when a Sister Nance served on a committee to cite another woman for a discipline violation. But appointing a woman to a discipline committee was not common practice. In infrequent cases where the church appointed women to such committees, the accused was also a woman. Women never investigated charges against men, but men frequently conducted investigations involving women. Although the evidence is not conclusive, it appears that women did attend church conferences from the early years of the church, but it is not clear when they began to vote on ecclesiastical matters. Certainly they were considered full members of the church from the moment of their profession of faith and baptism.

Throughout the history of Mt. Hebron, disciplinary matters most clearly revealed the complex gender relations within the sacred community. From the first recorded case of discipline in 1826 until the last in 1904, church minutes describe at least 242 cases brought before the church. Of these complaints 181 accused men (172 citations of white men, 7 of slaves, and 2 of free blacks) and 61 charged women (58 white, 2 slaves, 1 free black). So in a church 65 percent female, women stood accused of only 25 percent of the ethical and religious violations. The 35 percent minority of men committed 75 percent of the breaches of acceptable conduct.[30]

Analysis of the types of offenses committed reveals gender differences even more sharply. Although women held no offices, they strongly influenced the ethical standards of the church. The "sin" most frequently cited in discipline cases was alcohol abuse. It is now clear that excessive consumption of alcohol often accompanies other activities destructive to family and community values: fighting, gambling, wife and child abuse, adultery, and other "disorderly" conduct. Of the fifty-four cases of "excessive drinking," "too much drinking," "intoxication," "whiskey-making," and so on, all involved males and all but one a white male. So far as the formal discipline of Mt. Hebron was concerned, drunkenness was an exclusively male sin and the one most frequently cited. Of the eighteen cases of swearing cited in church minutes, every one involved white males. Gambling, cardplaying, disorderly conduct, and Sabbath violation appear as exclusively male sins, as do a series of unethical business practices (unlawful use of public funds, swindling, and overcharging). Charges of quarreling, fighting, and anger affected twenty-three men but only one woman. The church also excluded one man for wife abuse.

Conversely, some categories of "sin" belonged to women. Charges of heresy resulted in the exclusion of three women but were never brought against a man.

A few moral breaches seemed to affect both sexes. The church cited thirty-two men and twenty women for dancing, six women and five men for falsehood/slander, eight men and four women for nonattendance, fifteen men and thirteen women for joining another denomination, and four men and two women (one of them a free black woman) for immorality/adultery.

Quite clearly discipline meted out by Mt. Hebron served to protect women and families from the worst aspects of frontier life and to socialize and "civilize" males in a way defined by females. This fact tends to mitigate the absence of women on committees appointed to cite wayward members. They might not often serve on such committees, but they heard the charges and they either cast votes or influenced decisions on whether or not to exclude miscreants.

Another curiosity of disciplinary proceedings was the frequency with which women rejected the jurisdiction of the church over their private conduct. Such cases usually involved dancing, as did an instance in 1857. After being cited for this violation in February, Sister Martha Jane Byram acknowledged the conduct in a March conference but refused to "make satisfaction"; the church excluded her from fellowship. In April 1869 Sister Jiney McDanal also refused to give satisfaction on dancing charges and met the same fate. Many other members charged with dancing asked forgiveness at that same conference, and the church retained them in fellowship. In 1852 Elizabeth Hall obtained a letter dismissing her from Mt. Hebron. But in May of that year the conference excluded her and asked that she return the letter. Sister Hall refused a man's request for her letter and the church voted to report her to the association. She finally capitulated to this threat in July.

Women frequently left Mt. Hebron for other denominations, but often this decision involved marriage or the dictates of husbands or families. Some incidents of exclusion of women for joining Presbyterian or Methodist churches carry the mitigating reference in church minutes that the sister *had married* and joined another denomination. Church minutes for September 1832 refer to "Sister Annie" who "to satisfy her family, joined the C. Presbyterians." No such clarifying reference ever appears in regard to a male.

Another crisis of conscience and family loyalty could occur when the congregation cited a spouse or family member. On numerous occasions independent-minded members of Mt. Hebron refused to recant and were excluded. Often family members remained loyal to them and requested a "letter of dismission" as protest against church action. Unless a member remained in good standing, that person could not transfer membership to another Baptist church. So an excluded person would often "give satisfaction" in order to return to good standing, then immediately request a church letter of dismissal allowing transfer to another Baptist church. Frequently the unoffending spouse would also request a letter. Many such cases appear in church minutes, and in all but two cases they involved a wife loyally supporting her aggrieved husband.[31] Twice the church charged women with offenses, and their husbands loyally stood by them. In August 1839 the church found Sister Mary Whitfield guilty of slandering Elizabeth Kelley and excluded her. At the same meeting, her husband George Washington Whitfield requested that his name be withdrawn from church rolls. In March 1851 Sisters Harris and McDanal and Brother McDonald investigated an "evil report" circulating about Sister Elizabeth McDanal. Two of the members accepted the report as true (it seems likely that the Sister McDanal on the inquiring committee was a relative and perhaps dissented), and the church excluded Elizabeth McDanal. In May a relative, John McDanal, requested his letter, and in January 1852 Elizabeth's husband William requested dismissal. In May 1853 William, Elizabeth, and Francis McDanal, another relative of the prominent family, moved their letters back to Mt. Hebron. In April 1880 the church cited Mollie Courson for dancing, and she immediately acknowledged her sin. But in August Ann Courson, probably Mollie's mother, requested a letter of dismissal. Clearly family ties often meant more to spouses and family members than good relations with a sacred community.

What is equally fascinating is the infrequency with which a wife left the church when the church cited her husband. In fact the recorded cases of family solidarity in such crises makes even more significant the numerous exceptions to this pattern. Usually after the church cited a man the minutes contain no reference to a wife seeking a letter of dismissal. Although the case is not altogether certain, it appears that most women chose loyalty to Christ and his church over loyalty to spouse, perhaps because many devout women believed the discipline meted out to their husbands was entirely appropriate. Such a case occurred in July 1848, when Mt. Hebron members excluded William Watson for hunting on the Sabbath. Sister Watson remained an active member of the church, and in November 1848 served on a committee to cite a sister who had joined the Presbyterian Church.

Because the central function of the church was preaching and the primary task of deacons and trustees was fund-raising and administration of church business, women obviously did not fit into the hierarchical structure of Mt. Hebron. During much of the nineteenth century services consisted of nothing more than preaching once a month on Saturday followed by a church conference. Annual camp meetings and protracted revivals afforded women few roles other than preparing meals or boarding a visiting preacher.

Development of a more complex educational structure after 1900 extended greater opportunities to women. The Woman's Missionary Union (WMU) provided a place for women to develop leadership and parliamentary skills and socialize with other women. It also became Mt. Hebron's primary advocate of missions, especially of community ministry to the poor and sick.

Mt. Hebron's most important denominational affiliation was the annual associational meeting. The early records of the church mention no delegates elected to the Alabama Baptist or Southern Baptist conventions, but the church seldom failed to send a delegation to the nearby associational meetings. The church always elected male messengers until 1919. During the years between 1900 and 1917 Alabama and Southern Baptists furiously debated the propriety of allowing women to serve as messengers (delegates) to the statewide denominational meeting. Many biblical literalists insisted that this reform contradicted Scripture. Mt. Hebron's minutes contain no reference to the issue. But seven years after the state convention allowed women to serve as messengers (1912) the church apparently elected its first female delegate to the association when it selected Mr. and Mrs. G. C. Chaney.[32] It may not be altogether coincidental that this rural Baptist congregation elected its first woman messenger in 1919, the same year Congress approved the nineteenth amendment extending to women the right to vote. In 1921 the church again selected the Chaneys as well as Mr. and Mrs. A. L. Dorough and Mrs. Ellen Moore, giving women a three-to-two majority. Since many of the male members had begun working in coal mines and steel mills by the 1920s, they could not attend the day-long associational meetings. Although male messengers often attended in the evening, women regularly outnumbered men during the daytime sessions which made policy and transacted business, none of which of course was binding on the fiercely independent local Baptist congregations.

Hard times during the 1930s further eroded male dominance. With men desperately seeking employment or demoralized by the Great Depression, women assumed a larger role in church life. They had long furnished all Sunday school teachers except for the two men's classes. A historic event occurred on February 23, 1930, when the pastor, a Howard College student, asked a prominent WMU leader, Mrs. McDanal, to conduct a prayer meeting. The Reverend W. Albert Smith was no liberal or theological iconoclast, but the church was experiencing difficulty finding a man willing to serve as deacon or in other leadership roles, so Mrs. McDanal's service seems to have been more an act of ministry in time of need than an example of theological liberalism.

Other breakthroughs occurred four years later. Previously, business matters had been largely beyond the influence of female members, though they had proven quite adept at raising money for missions through the WMU. But on December 16, 1934, the church appointed Mrs. Joe Dorough as secretary of donations. That same month the church revised its decorum to reestablish a committee to hear grievances or complaints of misconduct toward members. It appointed Mrs. Annabel Moore as one of three committee members.

Post–World War II social upheaval accelerated the pace of change within the church. Mt. Hebron's Sunday school organization in May 1946 listed female teachers for twelve of fourteen Bible classes. When the church selected messengers to the associational meeting in September 1947, it elected four women, and it again elected an all-female contingent a year later. Women regularly led in prayer at church meetings, and in February 1958 a female missionary to migrant workers spoke from the pulpit at a regular Sunday morning worship service. During Youth Sunday in March 1957, a boy "brought the morning message and Earline McLaughlin spoke on missionaries at the evening service." Although the minutes do not clarify the difference between a male "bringing a message" and a female "speaking" at a service, apparently the church regarded both as regular services. At the end of Miss McLaughlin's "speech," she gave an invitation, and Margaret Ann Skelton accepted Christ as her savior, undoubtedly the supreme test of a "sermon" from a Southern Baptist pulpit.

Numerous subtle tensions over gender surfaced in the 1960s. Women began to resist the traditional annual all-day singing because they had to cook to feed the singers, most of whom were not members of the church. When the church left the matter of refreshments for the annual revival to the discretion of the WMU, the ladies decided that everyone should bring a supper on the Saturday evening of the revival, in place of a few women preparing refreshments for each night of the services. Their work re-tiling the nursery floor, making curtains, raising money for new choir robes and church kitchen equipment left little time for preparing refreshments. Obviously Mt. Hebron's women had decided their Christian ministry did not consist mainly of preparing meals for men.

In the summer of 1964 the church employed a female choir director to replace a man who had resigned. Her modest pay of twenty dollars a week barely covered her travel expense, but Mrs. Davis served faithfully and well. She tried to resign in 1969, but the entire church gave a banquet in her honor and persuaded her to stay on until 1974. In September 1975 the deacons proposed to raise money to build an educational building and entrusted the task of being the fund-raising chairman to Mrs. Ester Oglesby, who was nursery director and teacher of the woman's Sunday school. The deacons instructed her to select her own committee members. When Mt. Hebron's pastor resigned in 1981, the church elected a pulpit committee consisting of three deacons and their wives, who would elect their own chairman.

The good folk of Mt. Hebron through the generations insisted on rigid adherence to biblical admonitions regarding the subordination of women and the hierarchical nature of the family. Yet the church did respond in numerous ways to societal shifts in the understanding of the appropriate role of women in society. Women established their own networks whereby they raised money for missions and held offices from president down within the WMU. Many established the priority of Christ in their lives even when husbands did not share the same vision. They influenced the church's concept of proper ethical conduct and molded Mt. Hebron's use of discipline toward social objectives that helped protect them from violence, drunkenness, and discord. They might not hold the offices of pastor or deacon, but they made their voices heard nonetheless.

Pastors

The men who provided leadership to Mt. Hebron were as unpredictable a group as the women who filled the pews. Few generalizations fit all of them, though some do provide helpful categories. Between 1819 and 1980 the church employed thirty-six pastors. "Employed" is almost too strong a word to describe their relationship to the congregation. Most were bivocational men who earned a primary salary in a secular vocation. Others studied at nearby Howard College, the leading Baptist institution in the state. The fortuitous proximity of the college allowed the church to use faculty and ministerial students as revival speakers, interim pastors or guest preachers when pastors were ill or out of town, and regular pastors. In fact Mt. Hebron had a long association with the eastern end of Jones Valley, later the East Lake suburb of Birmingham. Hosea Holcombe, pastor of Ruhama Baptist in East Lake, founded Mt. Hebron. In 1887 Howard College moved from Marion to East Lake, across the street from Ruhama Church, continuing the close relationship.

During most of its history Mt. Hebron, like most rural churches in the South, was quarter-time. Throughout the nineteenth century members met once a month, usually on Saturday. During the 1920s the church experimented with services twice a month, but reverted to older traditions by the early years of the Depression. Not until the late 1930s did the church begin weekly services on a regular basis.

Because the membership consisted mainly of farmers and working-class people, the church struggled financially. This fact limited what it could pay pastors and embroiled it in financial crises. Low pay kept its pastors poor, as both church records and oral history attest.

Not until the 1960s did the church select a pastor for an indefinite period of time. Before that, members elected their pastor annually. The process followed the most elemental democratic practice, with members lining up behind their favorites. Many times the church conducted a kind of preach-off, bringing in several visiting preachers for trial sermons, then voting to elect the one which the congregation liked best. Such elections were often temporarily divisive. In September 1945 members nominated three candidates for pastor. Then they voted on whether to conduct a secret ballot or a public, standing vote, and decided on the latter. The beloved former pastor (1935–44), Fred E. Maxey, received twenty-three votes, a preacher named Fullmer got twelve, and the Reverend Earnest Faulkner was elected with twenty-nine. At the same conference, members elected Mrs. Fred Maxey, Jr., daughter-in-law of the former pastor, church clerk. Whether because of the rejection of his father or for some other reason, Fred Maxey, Jr., and his family left the church and affiliated with Bold Springs Presbyterian Church, though they rejoined Mt. Hebron in 1953. In 1948 the church unanimously decided to delay calling a preacher for three months in order to hear a variety of them, but split sixteen-to-eleven over whether to pay visiting preachers. After one of the deepest splits in Mt. Hebron's history in 1954, members voted on two nominees by having all who favored the Reverend Jim Brunner move to one side of the auditorium (thirty-two moved to his side) and those preferring the Reverend Gene Crocker (a former pastor) to stand on the other side (thirty-four moved to his side, giving him the pastorate). In September 1947 a member proposed calling a pastor for an indefinite period of time in conformity with general Baptist practice, but members tabled the motion by a three-to-one vote. In 1959 the church voted on whether to keep the present pastor, the Reverend Albert I. Bowman, or to elect a new one. The vote of thirty-five-to-thirteen favored a change.

Low pay contributed to the general instability. In the nineteenth century many rural Baptists believed the church should not pay the pastor a regular salary. He was one of the people, though divinely called, and should earn his living by the sweat of his brow like his parishioners. What was good for Paul and Silas was good enough for Mt. Hebron.

The long tradition of bivocationalism had some salutary effects. It guaranteed a pastor close to the people, one who spoke their language, shared their beliefs, and knew their problems. No gulf of formal education or theological learning stood between pastor and people. Although many church historians have depicted this practice as a liability to spiritual maturity, it was most certainly a stimulus to growth. Rural Baptist churches became the churches of the common people. Affluent planters and businessmen, the well-educated and the culturally refined, might find a more hospitable worship environment, but the plain people flocked to Baptist churches.

From their meager earnings the plain folk gave what they could, which was never very much. During the early years members subscribed money in various special solicitations for the pastor's salary, associational offerings, mission gifts, building funds, and other causes. By the 1930s the church followed the Southern Baptist pattern of adopting a single, unified budget which included all items. The church also urged members to adopt the biblical principle of the tithe. This change over time in church finances is clearly reflected in historic patterns. In August 1837 Mt. Hebron's members decided it was "not expedient to employ a minister to ride and preach for us next year." For the remainder of the year the church did without a regular parson while soliciting funds for a salary in the future. In October 1906, with membership near a historic low, members raised eighteen dollars for a pastor. In November 1921 the church anguished over how much to pay the preacher. Not until 1935 did the church begin to consider a parsonage. During the middle 1930s the church paid the pastor only twenty dollars a month, when it could raise that much. But some members still walked to church themselves, and many others still traveled by wagon. By 1948 postwar prosperity and the emphasis on tithing and a unified budget allowed the church to raise the salary to twenty-five dollars a week, though the Reverend Eugene Crocker recommended cutting his salary in 1950 because low contributions made it impossible to fully pay him anyway. In a move which reflected the church's precarious finances, members voted in 1951 to raise Crocker's salary to fifty dollars a week if the church could pay that much, or to forty-five dollars if it could not. The church raised the salary to fifty-five dollars a week in 1954, to three hundred a month in 1960, four hundred in 1966, five hundred in 1974, and 160 dollars a week in 1980. The beloved Reverend Willie B. Harris, who served a record seventeen years as pastor between 1962 and 1978, earned his primary living at a local company and had to terminate his pastorate when the company moved to Atlanta in 1978.

Irregularity of pastoral leadership may explain Mt. Hebron's occasional flirtation with heterodoxy. During the years when the church adopted foot-washing (1868) and lost many of its members to the heretical Sherman's Church (1871), the congregation apparently had no regular pastor. Although minutes from the Reconstruction period are fragmentary, they list no names of pastors from 1855 until 1874, and contain another gap from 1874 until 1878. Nor is a pastor listed for the critical years from 1897 until 1902, years of economic decline and political turmoil when church membership dropped. Conversely, when the church began to rely heavily on the state denominational college for its pastors, it became much more orthodox, adopting Southern Baptist literature and organizational structure.

Despite its problems, lack of pay did not keep Mt. Hebron from attracting a steady supply of able pastors. The first, Hosea Holcombe, was the premier denominational leader of his time in Alabama. During his years as pastor of Ruhama, Mt. Hebron, and numerous missions, he helped establish the Alabama Baptist Convention in 1823, became its first domestic missionary, served for six years as its president (1833–38), helped establish a manual labor institute, wrote the first history of Alabama Baptists (1840), and fiercely resisted the antimissionary Primitive Baptists, who took over many congregations and led them out of the missionary fold.[33] Although Mt. Hebron apparently lost members to the antimissionary movement, it remained loyal to Holcombe's vision through good times and bad.

Subsequent pastors were like Holcombe in that their evangelical zeal outweighed their theological education. They came mostly from the area. The eighth pastor (1874, 1892–94), the Reverend C. McLauglin, grew up in the church, son of one of the valley's earliest settlers. The Reverend Joseph Moor and his brother Hezekiah, Jr., also descended from early families and grew up in the church. Mt. Hebron ordained Joseph in May 1847 and Hezekiah in November 1856. Hezekiah became pastor of Mt. Hebron's mission church, Bethel Baptist.

The Moor brothers were only two of nine men ordained by Mt. Hebron, which also licensed (indicating permission to preach) eight of its sons to the ministry. Although the congregation respected the right of any man, however simple, to hear and respond to God's call to preach, it did exercise careful scrutiny. The name of Anthony, the slave "liberated by the church to preach the Gospel," does not appear in the church history. Nor do the names of two white members licensed to preach.[34] The church licensed John Lowery in 1854 but later asked him to surrender his license because he had not used it. In August 1874 the church licensed J. W. Owens to preach, but in September reconsidered its action and recalled his license, though it did grant him the "liberty to exercise in public at home."

Jacob Lawler served Mt. Hebron as its third pastor in 1829–30. Lawler moved from his native North Carolina to Tennessee and from there to Alabama in 1814. Elected a Shelby County judge in 1825, he soon began preaching also. Although he continued to pastor churches until his death in 1838, he did not seek to escape the temporal into some ethereal world. He served as a state legislator, receiver of public monies, United States congressman, and as trustee of the University of Alabama.[35]

Infrequent services and limited pastoral duties made such dual careers possible. The Reverend Henry Cox, who pastored Mt. Hebron in 1833 and again from 1838 until 1844, agreed to preach "as often as convenient." When reelected pastor in 1843 by the apparently satisfied congregation, Cox consented "to attend occasionally."[36] His duties consisted of one preaching service and one church conference per month plus occasional funerals and marriages, all performed for a congregation of only fifty or so members.

Between 1829 and 1981 minutes contain the names of thirty-four pastors together with their terms of office. Their tenures averaged only 3.4 years, and even that figure is distorted by two long terms of ten and seventeen years. Deleting those two periods of service, the remaining thirty-two pastors averaged only 2.7 years. So continuity of leadership was not characteristic of the church.

The Reverend W. Albert Smith (1929–32) was born in 1905 in Clay

County, Alabama, one of the state's poorest white counties. His father—a ne'er-do-well who farmed, traded horses, and cut meat—did not set a good example for the boy. Jealous and occasionally violent, he abused his wife and ultimately caused her to leave him, though they never formally divorced. The gentle Albert survived both the poverty and the domestic violence of his childhood. He worked in a textile mill to help buy necessities, although such efforts delayed his high school graduation until he was twenty-one. A mill church afforded the peace and serenity lacking in his family. His decision to enter the ministry led him to the Baptist college in Birmingham in 1919. Despite help from the mill's owner, a job became imperative. Mt. Hebron called him as pastor in 1929, and he continued to lead the church until he graduated in 1932 and headed for Southwestern Baptist Theological Seminary in Fort Worth, Texas. The pay of twenty dollars per month at Mt. Hebron did not include eggs and vegetables, which members lavished on their pastor, nor gargantuan country meals eaten in their homes. Smith was remembered as a good pastor and a kind person; his age, particularly, appealed to the youth. He enjoyed being with them and shared their fishing trips and baseball games.[37] After struggling through seminary during the depths of the Depression, he and his wife returned to Alabama where he became pastor of a series of small-town churches and a respected denominational leader.

Although vigorously Bible-oriented and unquestioning of biblical authority, Smith seldom if ever mentioned "literalism" or "inerrancy." The necessity to minister to vast human needs left him no time for biblical polemic. Perhaps he was fundamentalist in the elemental sense of that term. But at Southwestern he came into contact with critical approaches to biblical scholarship and seemed to have no trouble reconciling science, history, and biblical authority. He took for granted biblical miracles, the virgin birth of Christ, the authority of the Bible, the atonement, and the bodily resurrection, and assumed other Baptists did also. But he lacked a fundamentalist temper. He was tolerant and open-minded, and avoided controversies both at Mt. Hebron and at his later charges. He was far ahead of his times on racial issues. While pastoring in the Tennessee Valley, he drove to Courtland once a week to teach theology to black Baptist preachers, often accompanied by his two youngest children, one of whom vowed to grow up to become "a black Baptist preacher." He kept his openness and tolerance on racial issues pretty much to himself during the tumultuous years of the 1950s and early 1960s, but like Mt. Hebron he represented a Christian ethic that personalized race relations in such a way as to remove some hard edges from racism.

The Reverend Fred E. Maxey represents a different tradition in the pastoral history of the church. Maxey became pastor following a good deal of conflict over a new order of decorum in December 1934. He conducted a three-week revival in the church during March 1935, with five professions of faith to show for his efforts. Apparently church members were impressed because, when their current pastor resigned in April 1935, they immediately employed Maxey to take his place. Thus began a ten-year tenure that became one of the best loved in the church's history.

Unlike Albert Smith, Maxey came from another state and religious tradition. A native of Virginia, he practiced law and became a labor negotiator before moving to Taylor's Valley in southwestern Virginia in 1922. A religious skeptic when he arrived, he was converted in 1924 at the Walnut Grove Church of the Brethren. That church licensed him to preach, and Maxey became an evangelist, preaching in tabernacles, brush arbors, tents, store buildings, and barns in twenty-six states. He also held pastorates in Texas and Indiana before coming to Alabama. His skills as a speaker and his aggressive evangelistic style served him well. Maxey arrived in Leeds in January 1935, to preach a city-wide revival. He rented an old theater building and preached the first night to an audience of forty, who apparently came thinking they would see a movie. Maxey had neither fuel for a fire nor money to buy any, so a Baptist preacher-miner provided some coal for the theater's stove. The revival continued into February and attracted the attention of some Mt. Hebron members, who invited Maxey to preach a revival at Mt. Hebron, perhaps unaware that he belonged to a different denomination.

At the time, in February 1935, Maxey published a newsletter for supporters entitled "Christo-Centric." He headed his publication with the theological description: "Fundamental," "Undenominational," "Pre-Millennial." His February letter described the eight "Dispensations." His dispensational premillennialism identified him firmly with the fundamentalist tradition of the nineteenth century. However, the prospect of a new base of operations in Alabama, and perhaps some changes in his own doctrinal beliefs, led him to become a Baptist and the new pastor of Mt. Hebron in April 1935. The next newsletter listed Leeds, Alabama, as its home and omitted from its masthead the three words "Fundamental," "Undenominational," and "Pre-Millennial."[38] Whether this change reflected the economic desperation of the Depression, an opportunistic change of course, or the culmination of a long theological odyssey, is uncertain.[39] Although Mt. Hebron would not have disputed fundamental theology, it was not a fundamentalist church in the sense of strident, intolerant dogma or interdenominational commitment to restrictive theology or to a political program. Had members thought much about theological questions, they would have affirmed the fundamentals propounded by Maxey's publication. But they were too busy surviving to waste time on such idle speculation.

The Maxeys had five children, too many to feed on a salary of twenty dollars a month, so members gave them food. So poor were they that when Maxey departed for one revival he left his wife and children only large bags of red beans and rice which became their diet three meals a day until he returned.

Though he lacked formal theological training, Maxey possessed a keen legal mind and considerable skills as a communicator. His background as a labor negotiator in the Appalachian coal fields served him well at Mt. Hebron, where a number of his members were miners.

The church proved amazingly tolerant of his constant absences as he preached at revivals, perhaps because when he preached at Mt. Hebron he did so with such good effect. A three-week revival he preached in September 1935 brought eight additions. So popular was he that church minutes during his decade-long tenure ceased mentioning an annual call, and in December the church committed itself to building his family a parsonage, the church's first.

Although a traditional evangelist in theology, Maxey was innovative in the structure of his meetings. He held preaching services at night and Bible studies in the morning. After his revivals ended, he conducted sessions to train new converts and involve them in church life. He also divided men and women into separate groups and talked to them about marriage relationships and sex. Although he always had his wife attend the sessions with women, some men objected to the meetings and would not allow their wives to attend. Those who came heard Maxey's frank advice that sex was an important aspect of marriage and should not be considered dirty or a chore. God intended sex to be a joyous and wonderful part of life.

Maxey also proved unorthodox in his political and racial ideologies. His skills in labor arbitration brought a tempting offer. During the Franklin D. Roosevelt administration a Department of Labor official visited Maxey in Leeds and offered him the princely sum of fifteen thousand dollars a year to work for the Labor Department as a negotiator.

His inability to provide for his family tempted him to take the post, but in the end he remained at Mt. Hebron. He did use his ties to the Democratic administration, however. People on welfare or without food contacted him frequently, and he intervened with the state welfare bureaucracy to obtain work for them. His assistance even extended to blacks who visited the parsonage seeking help. Maxey tried to aid them with relief administrators, an activity which apparently did not sit well with some local folk. On one occasion Maxey received a telephone threat from the Ku Klux Klan warning him to stop interceding for Negroes. In East Tennessee he preached a sermon entitled "The Cross of Christ or the Cross of the Klan," and the hooded order sent a delegation to visit his service and warn him to stop meddling in race relations. But Maxey's best-kept secret was his flirtation with the Communist party. The party had established its southern base of operations in Birmingham, and Maxey began to write for one of its newspapers, the *Southern News Almanac*. His "Pulpit in Print" column charged the church with failing to live up to its biblical mandate to care for the poor and proclaimed Jesus to be a radical. He tried to fuse Christianity and Marxism, and spoke at rallies opposing the poll tax and advocating the right of blacks to vote. Although it is unlikely that his congregation knew the extent of his radicalism, it is worth remembering that many of them were tenant farmers and coal miners who had much to gain from a more just economic order. Certainly his radical egalitarian racial ethic was wildly at variance with the world of his parishioners, which makes his continued popularity with older members of the congregation even more remarkable.[40]

Apparently his skills as evangelist and negotiator mitigated any opposition within Mt. Hebron about his frankness over issues of sexuality, his personal contacts with blacks, or his frequent absences. His close ties with Democratic officials, his assistance in getting poor members relief jobs, his evangelistic preaching, and his thorough Bible studies endeared him to members. Annabel Moore reminisced about her favorite minister: "He taught me so much about the Bible and how to live close to God and meant very much to me." The entire community respected the Maxey family, and Leeds residents later elected his grandson mayor.

Connections

Mt. Hebron's warm relationship with Maxey reflects its long tradition of connectedness to churches of other denominations. Nor was this unusual for rural congregations, which often behaved quite differently from denominations that sought to draw distinctions between their doctrines and practices and those of sister groups. Mt. Hebron's members did not confine community to a narrow sphere. The congregation evidenced a keen interest in the religious life of the valley and the church universal of which it recognized itself to be only a small part.

Members of Mt. Hebron assumed a role of leadership in the various Baptist associations to which the church belonged. The church first elected delegates to the Cahawba Association in August 1825. Pastors and members served terms as moderator (chief officer) and on many of its committees.

During special occasions at nearby Methodist and Presbyterian churches, Mt. Hebron often suspended its own services so members could attend the others. Because all the churches in the valley conducted services only once a month, devout Christians often attended a different church each week, developing Christian friendships across denominational lines. The Great Revival of 1800–1820 had created a southern evangelical church remarkably similar in its basic conception of the acts of God, the nature and destiny of humanity, the reality of sin, and the imperative of repentance and salvation.[41] Children who grew up in one church moved easily to another, depending on friendships, marriage, and personal preferences. Concepts such as Fundamentalism and neo-Orthodox theology, ecumenism or parochial denominationalism played little role in the religious life of the valley. Methodists and Presbyterians, who were kin and neighbors of Mt. Hebron members, might dispute small matters of polity and practice but united on larger issues of meaning and purpose. Of eight members interviewed in 1989, everyone mentioned family connections to nearby Methodist and Presbyterian churches. Annabel Moore grew up in a Methodist family before joining Mt. Hebron. Maggie Dee Wilkinson's family belonged to Bold Springs Presbyterian Church before joining Mt. Hebron in 1952, but had often attended the Baptist church for singings, homecomings, decoration days at the cemetery, and for revivals. J. T. Poole's father was also Presbyterian, though the family attended Mt. Hebron so regularly that many members assumed he was Baptist.[42]

As late as 1946 members of other denominations held offices in the Sunday school. Although all church officers belonged to Mt. Hebron, newly joined members often held these posts. The church elected Fred Maxey, Jr., Sunday school superintendent in July 1953 after his family returned from Bold Spring Presbyterian Church in January. Members elected a man baptized in March 1953 as Baptist Training Union director in July.

The ease with which members moved back and forth across denominational lines reflected the simplicity of joining Mt. Hebron. All one had to do was profess faith in Christ or express desire to become a member. If the person had been previously baptized by immersion, even within a non-Baptist church, the congregation admitted the brother or sister without further action. For instance, on September 13, 1964, members accepted a new member by statement of previous baptism from Chelsea Church of God. But when Fred Maxey, Jr., joined from a Church of the Brethren background, the congregation decided they had better baptize him again to make sure it was done properly. That night they took him down to the creek on Edwards' farm, turned their car lights on, and immersed him in the waters. Members thereafter called him a "moonlight Baptist."

Lack of emphasis on doctrine explains this ease of movement as well as the periodic heterodoxy of Mt. Hebron. People unaccustomed to Southern Baptist literature, organization, and procedures adopted whatever material and mode of operation made sense to them. In 1945 each Sunday school class voted on its literature. Some used Southern Baptist material; others used the independent fundamentalist Scofield Bible literature. In May 1946 the congregation voted to use only Southern Baptist Sunday school literature; but in September 1948 the church decided to try International Sunday school materials for two months. During the 1930s and 1940s the church adopted the standard Baptist church organizations: Training Union, Women's Missionary Union, brotherhood and youth programs. In 1956 members adopted a "standard" Sunday school graded according to age. By this period earlier flirtations with foot-washing were an aberration of the past. In fact when a member requested use of the church building in order to christen her baby, the church clerk wrote that "this is against the rules of a Baptist church," and members unanimously denied the request.

Although the church developed close ties to the local association and to a lesser extent with the state convention, its connection to the Southern Baptist Convention was remote. The Women's Missionary Union followed the lead of the national women's group more closely than it followed any other segment of the church. But the national WMU had no formal ties to the SBC and was a fully independent auxiliary. Not until 1979, the first year of fundamentalist victory within the denomination, did Mt. Hebron's minutes record a messenger to the Southern Baptist Convention's annual meeting. Although the pastor and his wife often traveled to the convention after 1979, few lay people could afford such a trip. Hence the battle for control of the denomination remained remote to Mt. Hebron. When asked how church members viewed the convention-wide controversy over the inspiration, authority, and inerrancy of Scripture, Annabel Moore responded: "We discussed that some, but when they have conventions they almost get in a fight. It has been in the news and we're so sorry about that, but in Hebron Church, it's just lovely now and we'd never think about having any trouble or anything. Everybody loves each other and why we just enjoy our life as we meet there on Sundays and prayer meetings."[43]

Mt. Hebron's connections to its community confounds the traditional notion that fundamentalist churches ignore secular social institutions. Just as Fred Maxey reached out to unemployed members and the community's blacks during the 1930s, the church had existed within both sacred and secular communities. Distinctions between the two became blurred. Because the farming area south of Leeds had no school, Mt. Hebron established one before the Civil War. Classes met in the church until the community joined together about 1915 to build a schoolhouse adjacent to the church. In 1859 John G. Moor, descendant of a prominent pioneer family which also furnished many members to Mt. Hebron, taught the school. Prominent families—among them the McDaniels, Baileys, DeShazos, Moors, Doroughs, and Fosters—sent their children to the school. It continued to prosper after the turn of the century until the rural consolidation and school-bus programs finally caused its discontinuance in 1942.[44] During the Depression, Auburn University home-demonstration agents used the school building as a community center to teach poor families how to make mattresses and learn crafts to supplement incomes. After the school closed in 1942, the Mt. Hebron Extension Homemaker's Club turned the building into a clubhouse and community center for educational and social programs—canning, sewing, cooking, and hygiene. Many female church members joined large crowds of women attending the monthly meetings.[45] In 1951 the church voted to cooperate with the Home Demonstration Club and Mt. Hebron Cemetery Association in repairing the well at the clubhouse, which all three would then use.

Recalling club meetings, Annabel Moore spoke of "wonderful memories" of a time before women worked for salaries, when they had time on their hands and enjoyed spending it together.[46] So the ties of community that developed within Mt. Hebron expanded outward to a larger secular community.

Mission

If asked to name the central function of Mt. Hebron, most members will not answer: to discipline members, forge community, or build schools. Members defined the primary function of their congregation as winning people to faith in Christ and enrolling them in his church. But people won to faith in Christ are not simply related in a new way to their creator. They are related in a new way to other believers.

The church directed much of its energy and resources toward conversion. In the early years, revivals, camp meetings, or protracted meetings formed the central agenda of the church. One such protracted meeting in July 1838, conducted with four other churches, added sixty-one members. As early as October 1827, members decided to "hold meeting" in the neighborhood of a Captain Nance. This revival at Hopewell Meeting House attracted enough new members to justify services there every third Saturday. In December members voted to name this new "arm of the church" "Bethel." But disagreements soon troubled the fellowship. Members stopped attending Bethel, the mission declined, and the mother church chided its offspring for accepting a member who came from a Separate Baptist Church without requiring re-baptism. Finally in December 1832 Mt. Hebron dismissed sixteen of its members to reconstitute Bethel. In 1845 Mt. Hebron appointed six brethren to meet on fourth Sundays at a cabin on Bear Creek for services. Four years later the church established a campground for meetings and also began services in a settlement where many members had joined Mt. Hebron during an October revival. A protracted meeting of ten days in September 1858 added fifteen new members by profession of faith, six by letter, and seven by restoration to fellowship. By 1858 the church had established a mission on "Shole" (Shoal) Creek which flourished during the next few years. As a result of such evangelistic outreach, Mt. Hebron's membership grew from 107 in 1856 to 133 in 1858. The loss of black members and the Sherman Church schism reduced membership from 100 members in 1869 to 72 in 1871. Although Mt. Hebron experimented with different meeting-times and weekends for services, membership declined throughout most of the remainder of the century. The church could not obtain pastors, drifted away from Baptist doctrine, and seemed to lose its evangelistic zeal. Perhaps Reconstruction, rural poverty, the spread of sharecropping, and political dissension simply left its members too little money and energy.

Whatever the reason for decline, conditions improved after 1902. Revivals became more frequent and successful. The community seemed to stabilize. A 1910 revival added eight members by profession of faith; seven more came in August 1913, and twelve more joined in a September 1921 meeting. The 1920s brought such prosperity that the church temporarily began services twice a month. Fred Maxey strengthened this resurgence during his pastorate in the 1930s. A revival he preached in July 1938 added thirteen members by profession of faith, and his September 1939 meeting brought in eighteen more. He began morning and evening services weekly.

Another expression of the church's missionary interest came in the form of contributions. From its earliest association with the Cahawba Association, Mt. Hebron donated money to what Baptists then called "domestic missions." In 1830 the church could contribute only three dollars, but it faithfully gave what it could. By 1832 Mt. Hebron had doubled its original gift. In 1846 several members pledged one dollar each to the cause of domestic missions. By 1950 the church determined to send the entire evening offering for statewide missions, and the following year the church added a twenty-dollar donation toward purchase of a mission bus for Howard College. Mt. Hebron also tithed its income (10 percent) to the Cooperative Program of the Southern Baptist Convention, which in 1925 replaced individual fund drives with a single unified budget. As the church became increasingly aware of local needs, it shifted emphasis in 1956, allocating 1 percent of its funds for associational missions, 2 percent for state missions, and 7 percent for the Cooperative Program, a formula it modified again in 1963 and 1964. Increasing financial needs among local people required an allocation of 2 percent each for local and associational missions and 6 percent for the Cooperative Program. For a church that perpetually experienced financial woes, such an allocation of funds demonstrated its historic commitment to missions. And figures did not include special WMU offerings for foreign and home missions at Christmas and Easter.

The Persistence of Community

The geographical area in which Mt. Hebron Church functioned changed dramatically between 1819 and the 1980s. The valley had begun as a rural frontier; by the 1870s, Leeds had become an industrial suburb of

Birmingham. Whereas Mt. Hebron's members had originally been farmers, more of its male members began to mine coal or work in iron and steel mills. By the 1970s the community experienced additional dislocation resulting from the steady decline of smoke-stack industry and the growth of economic sectors of the economy which did not well suit the folk south of Leeds. Urban sprawl south of Birmingham moved slowly up the Cahaba Valley toward the church, threatening to overwhelm it with apartments, condominiums, and fashionable housing projects. With Leeds moving south and Birmingham moving north, the rural-minded Mt. Hebron community seemed an anachronism. Their narrow strip of rural Alabama had contracted to less than ten miles by 1990. Sunday school enrollment steadily declined from more than a hundred in 1967 to barely 50 in the early 1980s. Perhaps the sense of community was more important when life was risky and people were powerless. As life stabilized and conditions improved, the sense of community was not restricted to the religious life of Mt. Hebron.

Each change within the larger community left its impact on Mt. Hebron. Each infusion of new members created tensions between old-timers basically satisfied with the church and its work, and younger, more aggressive newcomers bent on change.

Almost all of the current members who are in their seventies and eighties grew up in farm families. Of seven current members interviewed, each one grew up on a farm. The father of one was a farmer-miller, another a farmer-carpenter, a third a farmer-coal miner, but all seven traced their values and origins to rural life. None had very much education. Only one continued beyond high school, obtaining secretarial training at a business college. Most of them did not finish high school. Of five interviewees who listed occupations, one became a farmer, one mined coal and worked for a steel manufacturing company, and three women married men who became coal miners, industrial workers, or farmers. The economic fluctuations of the Birmingham coal and steel district affected them dramatically. Tied to a farm economy in the nineteenth century, Mt. Hebron was suspended between agricultural and industrial worlds in the twentieth.

Because so many of the members of Mt. Hebron represented families with deep ties to the valley, membership represented more than a joyous occasion of conversion. Joining Mt. Hebron became a way of identifying with one's roots, of continuing tradition, and affirming family. Although most accepted Christ during revivals, a gradual process usually led to conversion, not a dramatic emotional experience.[47]

Once bound together in sacred fellowship, members, who were neighbors and often also relatives, helped with each other's needs. In the early days such concern did not find its way into church minutes. But by the 1930s the decline of farming and the perilous cycles of industry had created new problems. An economy built around subsistence farming had given way to an industrial wage system. Layoffs, depressions, recessions, plant closings, catastrophic diseases, high medical bills, all these and more, brought new problems to the valley. A membership so small and close that the church cut its own Christmas tree and drew names for presents could not ignore human misery.

Historically the church had expressed part of its concern through local missions. This heritage had provided the church a vision larger than itself. The women of the WMU best exemplified this tradition. Though small in number they regularly adopted an orphan from the Baptist Children's Home to support, gave clothes to needy families and Birmingham's Jimmy Hale Mission, prepared meals for widowed black women at holiday seasons, visited and cared for elderly members, contributed to the sick who could not afford medical care, and performed a multitude of other charitable services. After World War II this impulse toward sharing became global. In June 1946 the church voted twenty-five dollars for world relief and rehabilitation.

In 1952 young pastor Gordon T. Walker expanded this world vision. Deeply concerned about the spiritual welfare of postwar Europe, Walker joined a Youth for Christ team bound for France and Germany. The church granted him a three months' leave of absence. In long, detailed letters from Berlin, Walker described the wretched conditions in refugee camps. He told of helping a displaced couple in their twenties who had no coats and only the clothes they wore. When he returned, he preached about the poverty, the emptiness of state-supported churches, and the judgment of God on humanity. These sermons obviously touched an emotional current within the congregation. Layman Fred Maxey, Jr., proposed that all contributions over one hundred dollars collected the first Sunday of each month be given to a clothing station sponsored by evangelicals in France. The church also gathered 161 boxes of clothes for refugees.

Despite these global efforts, members reserved their greatest concern for friends and neighbors. In January 1947 the church appointed a committee for the needy. In November 1948 members voted to buy radio batteries for a poor family. In 1954 members gave eighty dollars to buy a wheelchair for a member.

By the 1960s the growing number of community financial problems convinced members of Mt. Hebron that individual acts of charity must give way to a more systematic policy. So the church voted to redistribute missions spending, and created a local missions budget of 2 percent of all contributions available for those in need. During the next three decades, Mt. Hebron appropriated thousands of dollars to help its own members and people who lived in the community: in 1965, fifteen dollars to the Hyde family; in 1966, fifty dollars to the Albert Chambers family; 1967, thirty-five dollars to Mrs. Flora Yarbrough; 1970, fifty dollars to a local family whose house burned and fifty-five to the Phillips children; 1971, seventy-five dollars to Jerry Thompson, whose house had burned, and fifty dollars to church member Archie Dison, who had been sick and unable to work. In 1972 the church gave Dison additional money and in 1973 provided funds to a seriously ill member. In 1974, Mt. Hebron loaned money to Eddie Gosnell, a church member, to pay his tuition at Howard College, allowing him to repay the loan by mowing the church lawn and from earnings on a summer job. By the fall of 1977 the church provided Bertha Mae Chambers between thirty and forty dollars per month and assisted the Larry Standifer family as well. In 1979 members helped the Steve Atkinson family, which had lost a son. Because demands on the local missions funds had been so great, the church had to limit appropriations to fifty dollars a month, less than the Atkinsons needed. A member solved this dilemma by contributing two hundred fifteen dollars, to be added to the fifty dollars from local mission funds. By the fall of 1979 at least one person received the maximum fifty dollars from the local funds every month, and many months the church helped several families.

Mt. Hebron demonstrated its concern for the community in other ways as well. In 1967 the church began a community youth program open to all white families. Available to any "young people of the community" over the age of eight, the program used the old schoolhouse as a recreation building. The church appropriated seventy-five dollars for film rental, and a local man coordinated the program. Every other week the church showed films and sponsored recreation.

Although members responded to a changing society as best they could, tensions between old ways and new were inevitable. Members with roots that sometimes extended back seven generations valued the plot of land on which four successive church buildings had stood. Debates over the shape and location of church buildings seem trivial to casual observers. But to Mt. Hebron's people and to many other Christians such matters were of great consequence. Two entrance doors and separate seating for men, women and children, and slaves had reflected a profound white male notion about the hierarchical arrangements of Christianity. A plain, unadorned church building with a pulpit in the front center emphasized the role of preacher, proclamation, and conversion. And location tied people to their roots, to ancestors now departed. On this ground members had attended their first Christian services and their first school. Here their ancestors lay beneath the sod of a cemetery gently sloping up the hill behind the church. Nearby they had disappeared beneath the baptismal waters of the Little Cahaba River and risen to new life in Christ. But members who joined during the 1930s, 1940s, and 1950s had fewer ties to the community and more concern with parking places and youth programs, sufficient building space for a spacious sanctuary, and an education building for an expanding Sunday school. The differences finally came to a head in 1954.

The crisis was precipitated by a fire that destroyed Mt. Hebron Church. Until then all had seemed well within the congregation. The missionary journey of the Reverend Gordon Walker had energized the church and added to its membership. Rising income during these prosperous years allowed the church to increase the pastor's salary. Energetic new members held most church offices and brought a level of enthusiasm to Mt. Hebron unseen in years. In fact members had begun to remodel the church when lightning struck the building on August 9, 1954. Within forty-five minutes the building, which had been constructed of heart pine in 1922, had burned to the ground.

In a spirit of unity and dedication the congregation vowed to rebuild and set about the task of raising money. All went well until the planning committee recommended that the church authorize it to negotiate the purchase of six acres a short distance away. The new site would provide room for a larger building and adequate parking. The church would sit back farther off the road, allow the parsonage to be located elsewhere, and permit expansion of the cemetery. Opponents of this move cited added expense and sentimental attachment to the place of their ancestors.

At a business meeting on August 29, 1954, Fred Maxey, Jr., proposed to buy the new site, and the Reverend Walker seconded his motion; fifty-four members supported the motion and only six opposed it. But when the church voted whether to build on the old site or the new, forty-five voted for the old site and only thirty-six for the new. On October 17 Walker announced at a Sunday morning service that he believed

God wanted the church to revote on the site of the new church. He believed God desired the congregation to move. Walker asked those who favored the new site, or at least were willing to support it, to move to the left side of the church. Those who believed God meant the re-building to occur on the current site should stand to the right. Those who were neutral or unsure of God's will should abstain from voting. The vote went overwhelmingly for the new site, forty-four to eighteen. But that night the deacons called another church conference. They an-nounced that they had conferred with another pastor, who had advised them that in a case where two votes occurred with varying results, a third vote should be held. Furthermore, only baptized members of Mt. Hebron or those who had come by letter could vote. The minutes record no additional ballot, but Walker resigned in December, announcing his plan to enter seminary. The vote to name his replacement, a thirty-four/ thirty-two split, confirmed the deep division within the church. On De-cember 12, forty-eight members, including Fred Maxey, Jr., the Rever-end Walker, and most key Sunday school officials and church officers transferred to Leeds First Baptist Church; four additional members left the following Sunday.[48] The fifty-two members who departed shortly afterwards formed a new congregation, Valley View Baptist Church. The thirty members who remained at Mt. Hebron began to plan how to re-build on the location so dear to them. Thanks to the sacrifices of those who remained and the generosity of one of their more affluent mem-bers, Mt. Hebron moved into its new building in 1955.

Those who remained behind perceived the issue as a dispute over the location of the church. The leader of those who left understood the controversy in more complex terms. Maxey believed that the Reverend Gordon Walker, young and brimming with evangelical zeal, had led the church toward strong commitment to evangelism and church growth; but Walker "was young, was inexperienced, and I think said things in-stead of approaching people where they were." Maxey also explained the crisis as more fundamental than merely a dispute over location of the church. Members disagreed over growth. The Maxey-Walker faction wanted the church to move in a different direction, to reach new people, and build educational space; older members remained satisfied with the church as it was, more committed to its traditional course.[49]

Although some members exchanged harsh words and many left, this split was only the worst of many in the life of Mt. Hebron. Anti-mission Baptists had left for the Primitive Baptists early in the nineteenth century. During subsequent decades, members left because church discipline offended them. In 1871 a substantial number had left for Sherman's Church. And without exception those on both sides of the 1954 controversy who were interviewed in 1989 maintained that individual relationships with the community remained good. Fred Maxey, Jr., believed that the split had left no lasting effect; he loved his neighbors and they loved him. Annabel Moore was one of only four members who withdrew, then later returned to Mt. Hebron. She remembered the strong feelings on both sides, but also believed time had healed the wounds. Now the members of Valley View "love us and we love them." The chairman of Mt. Hebron's deacons at the time of the dispute, who remained at the old site, visited older members seeking advice during the controversy, then talked with those who threatened to leave. But he could not reconcile the two groups. Margie Poole Martin believed that those who left did not depart as enemies of the ones who stayed. As years passed, they returned to visit Mt. Hebron on Memorial Day and other occasions.[50]

The Calvinist cosmology that had allowed their forefathers to make religious sense out of flood and drought, war and pestilence, served them as well. Margie Poole Martin described the split as a way of forming a new and prosperous church. T. C. West explained that every event, even the lightning that destroyed the church building and the split, "works for the best for them who love God (Romans 8:28)." Annabel Moore recalls that when the split occurred and those who left formed Valley View Baptist Church nearer Leeds, "there wasn't a building anywhere around Valley View, so it must have been God's leading because all of a sudden houses sprang up all around it." Fred Maxey, Jr., expressed a similar theology: "I don't think the Lord is the author of confusion, but I think he allows [it] to happen and now we are reaching people that Mt. Hebron would have never reached and no one else in Leeds has reached."

Although Mt. Hebron slowly recovered and even grew momentarily (Sunday school attendance returned to above a hundred in the 1960s), the space limitations and traditionalism of its members continued to hinder the church. By the 1980s Valley View flourished and Mt. Hebron languished, its Sunday school attendance reduced to fifty or so faithful souls. In 1982 the Reverend James Blair became pastor and injected new energy into the congregation. Like so many of his predecessors, Blair is a bivocational minister and sells building materials as well as preaching.

2.2   Mt. Hebron Baptist Church, 1992. Photograph by Peter H. Branum.

Under his ministry the church has grown slowly to a Sunday school attendance of 60, with 90 in worship services and a resident membership
of 188 (1989).

But not all churches are expected to grow, expand, and begin new
programs. In some locales caught between old ways and new, between
farms and cities, between tradition and modernity, between the elderly
and the young, perhaps it is enough just to survive and to provide a
place of meaning and caring. In 1989 Mt. Hebron's sense of sacred community seemed as strong for those who remained as ever before.

In some ways the members have changed. None we interviewed
favored reinstituting church discipline. Margie and J. T. Poole could not
remember Mt. Hebron excluding a member and did not think it a good
idea. T. C. West remembered an uncle who lived up a hollow from the
valley who once gave a dance and was turned out of the church. West's
father played the banjo and one of the deacons played the fiddle for the
dance. The church cited all three, but his father and the deacon asked
forgiveness for a deed neither believed to be wrong: "It hurt the church.
Some of them never did come back. My uncle who had the dance, he
moved his membership down to the Presbyterian Church." Though a
fine Bible scholar and deacon, West saw no good purpose to such a

practice. Annabel Moore also remembered exclusions. The church turned out two members during her lifetime: "I never had such feeling in my life. It was like God had shut the door on them. I don't believe in it. I would not vote for it and I didn't. . . . It was the coldest feeling I ever had. It broke my heart because one of them was my friend, a lady, and the other was making whiskey and selling it." Maggie Wilkinson agreed, opposing exclusion on biblical grounds, believing as Baptists do that "once saved always saved; you might stray, but you'll come back. When you stray, people need to pray for you, not push you out."[51]

Tastes in theology also changed with the passing years. T. C. West contrasted preaching "intended to frighten you—that you were going to hell for what you did and what you didn't do"—to modern sermons that emphasize love. He remembered such shouting in Mt. Hebron that boys who could not stand the pressure would jump out of the windows during services. Explaining his own theology he reasoned: "Fear is misleading to people who don't understand. With the fear of God, it's not that you're scared of him, that's not it. You love him enough to want to do what he says, that's the fear of God."[52]

In other ways members have changed little. For them Mt. Hebron still represents an anchor of stability in a turbulent world. They rely on its fellowship for their social activities, treasure its sense of community, and draw strength from it during times of personal trouble. Although elderly members are concerned that conditions have changed, that they see less of each other than they once did, and that they have less time to help one another, they still believe Mt. Hebron contains a special closeness and fellowship.

Conversion remains at the core of religious experience at Mt. Hebron. Annabel Moore grew up the youngest child in a family that did not attend church. Her mother died when she was a small girl, and her father, left with eight children to rear, did the best he could. She eloped at age sixteen, and became a Christian after the birth of her first child. Maggie Wilkinson accepted Christ at the age of twelve or thirteen during a 1934 revival. T. C. West responded to a series of tragedies which subjected him to emotional stress.[53]

But conversion has never been an end in itself. Extending the right hand of fellowship follows conversion and baptism. This historic and symbolically important gesture involves more than a physical ritual. It opens a sacred inner community to a child, stranger, or newcomer. Of course the new convert now determines the boundaries of sacred community rather than the church doing so with discipline as in the old days. But if one seeks it, this inner community works as well as it ever did. The testimony of four members makes this clear.

Remembering the Great Depression of the 1930s, Annabel Moore recalls typical Sunday mornings: she would draw water from her well, gather vegetables from her garden, cook lunch over a wood stove, then gather her children for their walk down the road to church (the Moores had no car). She described her life during those years not in the bleak hues of depression but in the warm tones of community: "Wonderful life! We'd come back home and . . . a lot of times the preacher would eat with us." Asked if she still spent more time in church activities than in other social involvements, she responded that the church "*is* our social life." Maggie Wilkinson agreed that she and her husband had few social outlets beyond the church. T. C. West also agreed, saying he attended church functions four or five times a week, "every time the door is open."[54]

Every person interviewed talked about "a special feeling of closeness" at Mt. Hebron. One member claimed that because members grew up together, "I don't think it's [closeness] nowhere else but here." Margie Poole Martin added: "We're more like brothers and sisters than we are neighbors." J. T. Poole, asked to name the best attribute of Mt. Hebron, did not hesitate: "Make a stranger feel at home."[55]

Once again recalling the 1930s, Annabel Moore explained: "Times were very difficult but I tell you we visited each other, we quilted for the church, and we had the best time . . . ; we were close to each other and saw each other all the time." Both Annabel Moore and Maggie Wilkinson experienced tragedy—the loss of their spouses and illness. And each time they suffered, the church responded. This love moved them deeply. Moore explained: "I just have the deepest feeling. I'm the happiest, I feel it's heaven when I get down there and sing and worship with the others. It's just part of my life and I don't reckon the door ever opened that I wasn't there." Maggie Wilkinson added: "Everyone loves one another. Most people who live there have lived there all their lives. . . . Everyone knows what you need, you don't have to call them, they'll come to help you." T. C. West reminisced about church neighbors who had helped build his house and later surrounded him with love when his wife died: "It has been a wonderful place to live, this valley. I tell you right now there's plenty of love over here."[56]

Young women work now, and their social lives no longer revolve exclusively around the church. The pluralism of a hectic secular world has eroded exclusive loyalties to Mt. Hebron. But enough of the old ways survive that a young bivocational lay preacher could still base his sermon, the first I ever heard there, on a sacred community set apart from the world. Conversion was central to his vision. Ancient traditions both bound members of Mt. Hebron together as family and hindered their divine mission. So urgent was the task that all members must choose sides, come forward, and stand beside their preacher in a symbolic gesture of separation from the world and commitment to each other. That February 1989 Sunday morning their faith drew more heavily from their past than any of them realized.

NOTES

1. Clifford Geertz, *The Interpretation of Cultures: Selected Essays* (New York: Basic Books, 1973), pp. 90–125, 140.

2. Donald Mathews, *Religion in the Old South* (Chicago: University of Chicago Press, 1977), pp. 84–87.

3. Anne C. Loveland, *Southern Evangelicals and the Social Order, 1800–1860* (Baton Rouge: Louisiana State University Press, 1980), pp. 161–62.

4. History Committee, Leeds Bicentennial Commission, Leeds, Alabama, *Leeds . . . Her Story* (Anniston: Higginbotham, 1979), p. 45.

5. Ibid., p. 56.

6. Ibid., p. 60.

7. Ibid., pp. 7–8. Cahaba is spelled two ways in Alabama place-names: Cahaba and Cahawba.

8. A. Hamilton Reid, *Baptists in Alabama: Their Organization and Witness* (Montgomery: Paragon Press, 1967), pp. 47–49; Davis C. Woolley, "Hosea Holcombe: Pioneer Alabama Baptist Historian," *Alabama Review* 14 (January 1961): 6–8.

9. Hosea Holcombe, *A History of the Rise and Progress of the Baptists in Alabama* (Philadelphia: King and Baird, 1840), p. 44.

10. Dickson D. Bruce, Jr., *And They All Sang Hallelujah: Plain-Folk Campmeeting Religion, 1800–1845* (Knoxville: University of Tennessee Press, 1973), pp. 4–93; John Boles, *The Great Revival, 1787–1805: The Origins of the Southern Evangelical Mind* (Lexington: University Press of Kentucky, 1972), pp. 119–30, 169–81, 191, 195; William G. McLoughlin, *Revivals, Awakenings, and Reform* (Chicago: University of Chicago Press, 1978), pp. 131–35.

11. Mt. Hebron Church Book and Minutes, 1819–1983, Alabama Baptist Historical Collection, Samford University Library, Birmingham, Alabama. Archivist Elizabeth Wells suggested this church because its minutes are nearly complete since its creation in 1819. Such care with church records was not unusual among rural churches. Clerks obviously assumed their duties with an enormous sense of responsibility. As this essay makes clear, their task gained enhanced

importance from the central role of kinship within the congregation. They preserved not just the records of a church but the history of kin across generations.

12. Ibid.

13. Mathews, *Religion in the Old South*, p. 42; Randy J. Sparks, "'A Wholesome, Godly Discipline': Race and Gender in Mississippi Evangelical Disciplinary Actions, 1806–1870," manuscript in possession of author. I am grateful to Professor Sparks for sharing his findings with me. Professor Larry James also presented a paper at the 1981 Southern Historical Convention entitled "Church Discipline in Antebellum Mississippi and Louisiana Baptist Churches" regarding the same topic.

14. Mt. Hebron Church Book and Minutes.

15. Dan Cloyd, "Prelude to Reform: Political, Economic, and Social Thought of Alabama Baptists, 1877–1890," *Alabama Review* 31 (January 1978): 48–64.

16. For insights on religious divisions within the southern church, 1870–1900, see: David Edwin Harrell, Jr., "Religious Pluralism: Catholics, Jews, and Sectarians," in *Religion in the South*, ed. Charles Reagan Wilson (Jackson: University Press of Mississippi, 1985), 59–82; Wayne Flynt, "One in the Spirit, Many in the Flesh: Southern Evangelicals," in *Varieties of Southern Evangelicalism*, ed. David E. Harrell, Jr. (Macon: Mercer University Press, 1981), pp. 23–44; Mickey Crews, "From the Back Alleys to Uptown: A History of the Church of God (Cleveland, Tennessee)," Ph.D. diss., Auburn University, 1988, pp. 24–52.

17. Herschel Edwin Campbell, "A Struggle for Life" (the story of Mt. Hebron Baptist Church), pp. 9–10, unpublished church history, copy in Alabama Baptist Historical Collection, Samford University Library.

18. Mt. Hebron Church Book and Minutes.

19. John Boles, Introduction, *Masters and Slaves in the House of the Lord*, ed. John Boles (Lexington: University Press of Kentucky, 1988), pp. 13–18. This important book challenges many traditional notions about the subservient role of slaves in antebellum southern churches and argues that the relationships were quite complex. In many churches blacks had rights not available to them in secular society.

20. Larry M. James, "Biracial Fellowship in Antebellum Baptist Churches," in ibid., pp. 38–50; Randy Sparks, "Religion in Amite County," in ibid., pp. 62–72.

21. Ibid., pp. 37 and 78.

22. All descriptions of discipline come from Mt. Hebron Church Book and Minutes.

23. Ibid.

24. See Robert E. Praytor, "From Concern to Neglect: Alabama Baptists' Religious Relationship to the Negro, 1823–1870" (M.A. thesis, Samford University, 1971), pp. 30–73.

25. Oral history with J. T. Poole and Margie Poole Martin, Leeds, Alabama, May 1, 1989, by Peter Branum. My thanks to Mr. Branum for his superb work as my research assistant.

26. Sparks, "A Wholesome, Godly Discipline," quoting Mathews, *Religion in the Old South*, pp. 47–48; Rhys Isaac, *The Transformation of Virginia, 1740–1790* (Chapel Hill: University of North Carolina Press, 1982); and Bertram Wyatt-Brown, *Southern Honor: Ethics and Behavior in the Old South* (New York: Oxford University Press, 1982).

27. Mathews, *Religion in the Old South*, pp. 101–24.

28. Mt. Hebron Church Book and Minutes.

29. Oral history with Margie Poole Martin.

30. This discrepancy is consistent with the pattern discovered by Randy Sparks in his investigation of 1,169 cases of church discipline in Mississippi between 1806 and 1870. White men were most frequently cited, and only about one-tenth of the charges involved white women, with dancing accounting for almost half (in Mt. Hebron, 20 of 58 disciplinary cases against white women involved the charge of dancing). See Sparks, "A Wholesome, Godly Discipline."

31. Examples abound. In December 1840 the church excluded Davidson McGuire for abuse of alcohol, and Sara McGuire requested a letter of dismissal in September 1841. In May 1882 the church excluded Jonathan D. Shugart for intoxication, and Alice Shugart requested her letter in July. They subsequently joined another denomination. In April 1891 the church lodged charges of drunkenness and profanity against J. H. Hudson, and in June excluded him from membership. His wife sought a letter of dismissal in April, but the church withheld her letter because charges were pending against her husband. In July he finally acknowledged his sins, was restored to fellowship, and both promptly requested and were granted letters of dismissal.

32. Church minutes during the second decade of the century are incomplete, so the church may have elected a female messenger somewhat earlier than this.

33. Reid, *Baptists in Alabama*, pp. 48–49.

34. Campbell, "A Struggle for Life," appendices 3 and 4.

35. Ibid., p. 7.

36. Mt. Hebron Church Book and Minutes, March 1843.

37. Interview with Dorothy Smith Flynt and Everett Smith, July 18 and 30, 1989; oral history with J. T. Poole and Margie Poole Martin.

38. "Christo-Centric," February 1935 and undated issue, copies in author's possession.

39. Oral history with Fred E. Maxey, Jr., May 18, 1989, Leeds, Alabama, by Peter Branum. Maxey claims that his father became a Baptist after arriving in Alabama, but that his study of theology and his evangelistic efforts led him to Baptist doctrine.

40. Ibid.; Robin D. G. Kelley, *Hammer and Hoe: Alabama Communists During the Great Depression* (Chapel Hill: University of North Carolina Press, 1990), pp. 196–97, 214.

41. Boles, *The Great Revival*, pp. 183–203; Samuel S. Hill, Jr., *Southern Churches in Crisis* (Boston: Beacon Press, 1967), pp. 20–39.

42. Oral histories with J. T. Poole, Margie Poole Martin, Fred E. Maxey, Jr.;

T. C. West, April 30, 1989, Leeds, Alabama, by Peter Branum; Annabel Moore and Maggie Dee Wilkinson, April 18, 1989, Leeds, Alabama, by Peter Branum; Eloise Dison and Carla Dison Lawly, April 30, 1989, Leeds, Alabama, by Peter Branum.

43. Oral history with Annabel Moore and Maggie Dee Wilkinson.

44. History Committee, *Leeds . . . Her Story*, p. 168.

45. Oral history with Annabel Moore and Maggie Dee Wilkinson.

46. Ibid.

47. Oral histories with T. C. West, J. T. Poole, and Margie Poole Martin.

48. Mt. Hebron Church Book and Minutes.

49. Oral history with Fred Maxey, Jr.

50. Oral histories with J. T. Poole, Margie Poole Martin, Fred E. Maxey, Jr., T. C. West, Annabel Moore, and Maggie Dee Wilkinson.

51. Oral histories with J. T. Poole, Margie Poole Martin, T. C. West, Annabel Moore, Maggie Dee Wilkinson, Eloise Dison, and Carla Dison Lawly.

52. Oral history with T. C. West.

53. Oral histories with Annabel Moore, Maggie Dee Wilkinson, and T. C. West.

54. Ibid., and oral history with Eloise Dison and Carla Dison Lawly.

55. Oral history with J. T. Poole and Margie Poole Martin.

56. Ibid., and oral histories with Eloise Dison, Carla Dison Lawly, Annabel Moore, Maggie Dee Wilkinson, and T. C. West.

THREE

From Synagogue-Community to Citadel of Reform: The History of K. K. Bene Israel (Rockdale Temple) in Cincinnati, Ohio

JONATHAN D. SARNA AND KARLA GOLDMAN

It was in the month of October, 1816, that a young man arrived in New York from the shores of Great Britain, to seek a home and a residence in the New World. This individual's name was Joseph Jonas, from Plymouth, in England. He had read considerably concerning America, and was strongly impressed with the descriptions given of the Ohio river, and had therefore determined to settle himself on its banks, at Cincinnati. This he was encouraged in by a relative he met with in New York. On arriving at Philadelphia, he was persuaded to settle in that city, and took up his residence for a short time with the amiable family of the late Mr. Samuel Joseph (peace be unto him.) He here became acquainted with the venerable Mr. Levi Philips, who took a great interest in him, using many persuasive arguments not to proceed to Ohio. One of them was frequently brought to his recollection: "In the wilds of America, and entirely amongst gentiles, you will forget your religion and your God."[1]

JOSEPH JONAS, the author of this memoir, and the man generally considered to be the "founding father" of the Cincinnati Jewish community, "solemnly promised . . . never to forget his religion nor forsake his God." For two years, following his arrival in the city in 1817, he worshiped alone. Then, when more settlers arrived, holiday services were conducted. In 1821, local Jews purchased a small plot of land to serve as a cemetery.[2] Finally, in 1824, "a majority of the Israelites in Cincinnati" assembled at the home of Jonas's brother-in-law, Morris Moses, and formed a congregation, "Kahl aKodish Bene Israel," "for the purpose of glorifying our God, and observing the fundamental principles of our faith, as developed in the laws of Moses."

Seventy years later, Dr. David Philipson, rabbi of what had now become known as K.K. Bene Israel (Holy Congregation of the Children of Israel), and later as Rockdale Temple, commemorated the anniversary of his congregation's founding by compiling its only published history, a volume entitled "The Oldest Jewish Congregation in the West." He explained that the story of Bene Israel's development needed to be told. It was, he wrote, the first Jewish congregation west of the Alleghenies, and "it presents, in the course of its existence, the gradual development of religious thought that may be taken as characteristic of the reform movement in Judaism in this country."[3]

Philipson overstated his case. No one synagogue can claim to be "characteristic"; each in its own way is unique. Nevertheless, as "the oldest Jewish congregation in the west," the premier Reform congregation of Cincinnati, and as a leading member of the Union of American Hebrew Congregations, the organization of Reform temples in North America, Bene Israel did serve as a model for congregations around the country. If its longevity, eminence, and traditions rendered it somewhat distinctive, its origins, stages of development, and ongoing challenges have indeed been typical of many American synagogues, even those outside of the sphere of Reform.

The Synagogue-Community

Cincinnati's new congregation perceived itself as a frontier outpost of Judaism. "The fiat had gone forth," Jonas reported in his memoir, published in 1844, "that a new resting place for the scattered sons of Israel should be commenced, and that a sanctuary should be erected in the Great West, dedicated to the Lord of Hosts, to resound with praises to the ever-living God." Earlier, in an 1825 appeal for funds, addressed to "the Elders of the Jewish Congregation at Charleston," the same theme was expressed. Leaders of the new congregation portrayed themselves as veritable pioneers, "scattered through the wilds of America," doing all in their power to "promote Judaism" in a frontier "where a few years before nothing was heard but the howling of wild Beasts, and the more hideous cry of savage man." The appeal proceeded to paint a glowing picture of how, slowly but surely, the spiritual wilderness was being conquered: a room had been "fitted up for a synagogue," two Torah scrolls procured, a burial ground purchased, there was even a ritual slaughterer (*shochet*) for kosher meat. If only enough money could be raised for a synagogue, the leaders pleaded, they were certain that "hundreds" of Jews within a 500-mile radius, particularly the Jews of New Orleans "who now know and see nothing of their religion," would travel to Cincinnati, at least for the holidays.[4]

Although no synagogue was built until 1836, Cincinnati was already home, by 1830, to approximately one hundred Jews, the bulk of them, like Jonas, from Britain. The time had come to organize the congregation on a more formal and legal basis. On January 8, 1830, the state awarded the congregation a charter under the name "Kal A Kodesh Beneh Israel (Holy Congregation of Children of Israel)." Within a short time, it would become known as "K.K. Bene Israel," its official name to this day.[5]

In calling Bene Israel a "holy congregation," its leaders had in mind the kind of synagogue that they had known in England (whether they followed the Sephardic Spanish rite, or, as Jonas did, the Ashkenazic German one), and that existed in most American Jewish communities into the first quarter of the nineteenth century. This was the model of the all-embracing "synagogue-community" that both controlled all aspects of Jewish life and commanded allegiance from every Jew dwelling or sojourning within its ambit:

> In this phase of Jewish history [Martin Cohen writes], the synagogue reinforced the basic values which . . . perpetuated the optimism, morality, creativity and compassion which traditionally have shaped Jewish life. Socially it was the place where Jews met, commented on events, communicated their needs, planned their charities, adjudicated their disputes, and held their life cycle events. In the synagogue bridegrooms were given recognition, mourners comforted, strangers fed and housed, and the *herem*, or ban of excommunication, pronounced against recalcitrant members.[6]

In New York, Philadelphia, and Charleston, the synagogue-community had, by 1830, begun to break down under pressure from religious dissenters as well as new immigrants who, in the spirit of American religious freedom and voluntarism, spurned communal discipline and formed competing synagogues of their own.[7] But in Cincinnati, where the Jewish community was still relatively small and homogeneous, Bene Israel could still attempt to recreate a traditional Jewish communal structure.

Of course, the congregation could not, as in some European countries, compel all Jews to belong to the synagogue—its state charter specifically restricted membership to those "who may apply and be accepted." But it could attempt to enforce traditional conceptions of community upon those who did choose to join. Thus, in the event that two members fell into dispute, the congregants were expected to accept the congregation's jurisdiction over the conflict.[8] Fines could also be levied on those who misbehaved or refused to assume congregational office. In return for placing themselves under communal discipline, members enjoyed the satisfaction of knowing that their religious and community needs would be taken care of. Congregational leaders assumed responsibility for overseeing the cemetery, for ensuring the supply of kosher meat and of Passover matzah, for educating the young, tending the sick, burying the dead, providing loans to members, relieving the poor, and most of all for organizing religious services whenever appropriate.

The greatest danger to this "holy community" was precisely what Joseph Jonas had been warned about back East: "In the wilds of America, and entirely among Gentiles, you will forget your religion and your God." Most who came under the umbrella of the Cincinnati congregation were familiar with traditional European Jewish communities, but they had also experienced, in Cincinnati or en route to the Ohio city, life outside the bounds of a traditional community. This experience together with the limited religious resources of those "scattered through the wilderness" resulted in a certain flexibility when it came to observing the strictly mandated practices of domestic and synagogue life. Thus, Joseph Jonas noted two early innovations influenced by Portuguese Jewish custom and the fact that the congregation was composed entirely of "young people": "we . . . introduced considerable choral singing into our worship, in which we were joined by the sweet voices of the fair daughters of Zion," and "our Friday evening service was as well attended for many years as the Sabbath morning." With the arrival of more traditional Jews from Germany, "old customs . . . conquered" and thereafter women seldom sang out with the men. But, according to Jonas, at least a few hymns sung by the entire congregation continued to prevail.

Although the early adherents of Bene Israel struggled to introduce the communal institutions and services that would enable them to worship and live as traditional Jews in a traditional community, their orthodoxy was limited by the realities of their environment. The congregation itself was invested with no particular religious authority. As these new Americans cast about for an authentic basis for their religious structures and decisions, resolutions generally reflected whatever the group could agree upon. They had to rely upon their own knowledge and experience in making judgments on issues ranging from the propriety of their ritual slaughterer to the conduct of their religious services. Nevertheless, by 1840, many of the institutions necessary to leading an observant Jewish life were in place.

Bene Israel's leaders recognized that one of the greatest dangers of settling in the wilderness was that "many Jews are lost in this country from not being in the neighborhood of a congregation[;] they often marry with Christians, and their posterity lose the true worship of God for ever."[9] Seeking an antidote, they wrote stiff provisions into Bene Israel's constitution denying membership to anyone "united in marriage contrary to the laws and regulations of the Jewish Religion," and warning existing members that anyone "marrying out of the pale of the Jewish Religion" would have his membership summarily canceled. Then, apparently to prevent intermarrieds from surreptitiously arranging to be buried in the Bene Israel cemetery, the constitution, in its sternest single provision, directed the cemetery superintendent (the "Gabah Beth Hiam") "not [to] suffer any corpse to be Burried in the congregational Burial Ground without a written order from a majority of the vestry, under a penalty of five hundred dollars and a forfeiture of his membership."[10]

Yet even as the congregation sought to protect Jewish religious identity, members took great pride in their participation in the broader non-Jewish community.[11] Jonas himself boasted that "the Israelites have been much esteemed and highly respected by their fellow citizens, and a general interchange of civilities and friendships has taken place between them." In 1834, the congregation as a whole took obvious pleasure in the fact that "fifty-two gentlemen of the Christian faith, our fellow citizens" donated twenty-five dollars each toward the building of a synagogue. When the synagogue was dedicated, just before Rosh Hashanah (the Jewish new year) in 1836, the crowd of Christians was so great that many had to be turned away; there was only sufficient room for "the clergy and the families of those gentlemen who so liberally had given donations towards the building." From the beginning, then, Bene Israel's leaders faced a tension common to Jews throughout the modern world: they sought to strengthen Jewish religious identity and prevent intermarriage even as they worked to promote closer neighborly relations with the Christian "fellow citizens" among whom they dwelt.

The dedication of the new synagogue building—the first synagogue west of the Allegheny Mountains—marked Bene Israel's coming of age. Jews and Christians joined together to celebrate the occasion, and the ceremony received a great deal of attention.[12] Here was an important indication that Cincinnati had moved beyond frontier status and was becoming a major American metropolis. This sense of emergence, of tradition transplanted, was even symbolized in the synagogue's architecture. Constructed according to ancestral custom, with a woman's gallery, a reader's platform (*taybah*) near the west end of the sanctuary opposite the large frontal ark, and with "two marble painted slabs containing the Decalogue in gold letters," the building evoked memories of Judaism in more established communities, a feeling that was heightened by the structure's "handsome dome" and its five brass chandeliers that had previously hung in the oldest synagogue in America, Shearith Israel's Mill Street synagogue in New York. The only modest innovation introduced into the building was the arrangement of seats. Earlier American synagogues had followed the Sephardic (Spanish and Portuguese) practice of seating worshipers along the walls; Bene Israel followed the Ashkenazic (German) practice, soon to become widespread, of seating worshipers across the floor.[13] This was akin to local Christian seating patterns and reflected a growing shift toward Ashkenazic modes of worship, as Sephardic Jews became a diminishing minority of the nation's Jewish population, and their long hegemony over Jewish religious practices in North America came to an end.

With its new edifice in place, Bene Israel hastened to expand its activities. It purchased adjacent land for a new cemetery, established a Hebrew school to provide religious education for young people, and hired its first paid functionaries to serve as *chazan* (reader), *shochet* (ritual slaughterer), and *shamas* (sexton). As another measure of its improving status, the congregation, in 1838, contributed funds to aid Charleston's Beth Elohim congregation, whose synagogue had been destroyed in a fire. In this traditional way, Bene Israel signaled that it had emerged from its period of dependency, when it required aid from other Jews to develop and grow; it now felt secure enough to act like an established congregation, able to extend a helping hand to other Jews in need.[14]

Bene Israel's rapid development took place against a backdrop of unprecedented urban growth. "From the mid-1820s to the mid-1850s," a student of this period writes, "Cincinnati was perhaps the nation's premier boomtown. Its population nearly doubled each decade, its economy grew and diversified, and physically and culturally it was rapidly transformed from a rough frontier town into one of the nation's leading and most urbane cities."[15] Jesup W. Scott, writing in Charles Cist's *Cincinnati* in 1841, predicted "that within one hundred years from this time, Cincinnati will be the greatest city in America, and by the year of our Lord two thousand, the greatest city in the world." Jews, recognized as being among the founders of the city, shared in this buoyant mood. Many Jews took full part in Cincinnati's commercial expansion and rose, literally, from rags to riches. As Cincinnati developed into a major destination for German immigrants coming to America, it also became the destination for many German Jews who came as part of an accelerating wave of German immigration to America in the 1840s. The city's Jewish population multiplied tenfold (from 100 to 1,000) between 1830 and 1840, and reached 2,500 just ten years later.[16]

While all of Cincinnati's Jews may not have been members of Bene Israel, the synagogue's leaders could certainly claim that their congregation represented the Jews of Cincinnati and quite naturally equated their synagogue community with the growing Jewish community of Cincinnati. In 1841, the congregation was forced to build new seats for both men and women in the Broadway Street synagogue which they had dedicated only five years previously.[17] According to Joseph Jonas, "a number of the seats were sold for a sum much more considerable than the expense of the alterations." Apparently, the purchase of synagogue seats had become, for some, a form of conspicuous consumption, a socially sanctioned means of demonstrating that one had financially arrived while supporting the synagogue at the same time.

But rapid growth also brought with it a host of problems for the congregation. First, there were inevitable tensions between "old-timers" and "newcomers." Members who had come to Cincinnati in the 1810s and 1820s, primarily English and Dutch Jews, had built Bene Israel and felt a sense of ownership about it; they expected those who came later to show them deference. Second, many of the newcomers were German Jews. They differed both in culture and in language from the old-timers, and the two interacted only with difficulty. Finally, there were significant liturgical differences between the two groups. While they shared basic prayers in common, their forms, formulas, customs, observances, and traditional melodies were quite distinct.[18]

The result—well-nigh inevitable given America's religious pattern—was the creation of a new synagogue: K.K. B'nai Yeshurun, organized informally in 1840 and on a more formal basis, with a constitution, a year later. Most of the new synagogue's founders were German immigrants, who, if they had been members of Bene Israel at all, had not been active there. What they sought now was a new congregation that followed their ancestral customs and ran on their terms. Separate congregations of German Jews already existed in Philadelphia (1802) and New York (1825), and in both cities the ideal of the unified synagogue-community had soon given way to what might be termed a "community of synagogues." In these cities, communal and organizational ties, rather than a common synagogue, now bound Jews together. In Cincinnati, even before Bene Yeshurun was founded, Bene Israel's monopoly on Jewish life had been partially broken by independent mutual aid and philanthropic organizations created in the 1830s.[19] Many other Jews in the community remained unaffiliated; they opted out of the "holy community" altogether.[20]

The challenge posed by B'nai Yeshurun, however, was much more direct and provocative. Knowing this, the founders of the new congregation began its constitution, dated September 19, 1841, with an elaborate justification:

> WHEREAS, The wise and republican laws of this country are based upon universal toleration, giving to every citizen and sojourner the right to worship according to the dictates of his conscience, and
> WHEREAS, Also the mode of worship in the established synagogue of our beloved brethren, K.K.B.Israel, in this city, is not in accordance with the rites and customs of the said German Jews,
> *Therefore,* We, the undersigned, bind ourselves under the name of the congregation, K.K.B.Yeshurun, to use our best exertions to support a synagogue by that name, and to worship therein according to the rites, customs and usages of the German Jews. . . .[21]

Actually, although nobody is known to have mentioned the fact at the time, the constitution was not original. It had been cribbed, almost word for word, from the 1826 constitution of the synagogue's namesake, Congregation B'nai Jeshurun of New York.[22] The success of New York's experiment with multiple synagogues (six of them by 1840) may have persuaded the Cincinnatians that a second synagogue in their own city would do no harm. History proved them correct, for the new congregation effectively put an end to the outdated practice of equating one congregation with the entire organized Jewish community, and set the stage for the formation of additional synagogues. Within a decade two more had been founded: K.K.Ahabeth Achim (1847) and K.K.Shaar Hashomayim (1850).[23]

Redefining the Community

The resulting move from synagogue-community to a community of synagogues (or, at least, a multisynagogue community) carried profound implications for Bene Israel. The congregation was forced to adjust its self-image and reorient itself to a new religious environment where congregations competed with one another for members and status. Of course, Bene Israel still maintained the prestige that came with being the city's first synagogue. But as Cincinnati synagogues began to organize themselves on a subethnic, "country of origins" basis, primacy turned out to be of little advantage. Owing to the somewhat British cast of Bene Israel's service, Jews from Franconia and Bavaria often preferred to worship at the more Germanic B'nai Yeshurun, where over 90 percent of all members (1840–75) were of German origin. Germans also predominated at Ahabeth Achim located in the solidly German neighborhood of Over-the-Rhine. Polish Jews, meanwhile, worshiped first at Shaar Hashomayim, which dissolved in 1852, and later at Adath Israel.[24] Through all of this, the membership of Bene Israel remained relatively heterogeneous. English and Dutch Jews, while no longer a majority, remained an influential minority, and the growing number of Germans in the congregation continued to respect their authority, even though this meant that many potential members were lost to the competition.[25]

The growing number of religious options for Cincinnati's Jews emphasized anew the voluntary nature of synagogue membership in America. Disgruntled worshipers came to understand that Bene Israel needed them more than they needed it. This was, of course, a necessary corollary of religious freedom. To paraphrase Sidney Mead, what synagogues gave up with religious freedom was coercive power. Resting on the principle of free, uncoerced consent, they became voluntary associations, equal before, but independent of, the civil power and each other.[26] Bene Israel had to learn to adjust to this new situation, and it did so slowly.

Bene Israel's bylaws, for example, continued to assume that the congregation should exercise a certain authority over members' lives, just as synagogues had done traditionally. The belief that Jews should govern themselves was likewise reflected in the requirement that all civil cases between members first be submitted to the board of the congregation and only then be left to the arbitration of civil authorities. Any member who charged a fellow member in civil court without first bringing the case before the vestry was liable to a fine of fifty dollars.[27]

Yet, where cases were brought before the vestry in the 1840s and 1850s, often one party, and sometimes both, questioned the congregation's authority over noncongregational matters—a sign that the traditional understanding of the synagogue's role was already severely strained. In 1844, for example, four years after B'nai Yeshurun's founding, a Bene Israel member was threatened with a fine "for having sued Mr. N. Malzer in court, without having his complaint first brought before the congregation." The defendant, Mr. Solomon Samuel, insisted that the synagogue had no standing in the case, for he explained "that it was his wife who had sued Mr. Malzer, and that his Wife was not bound to our By Laws."[28] Such an excuse would scarcely have been appropriate in a traditional Jewish community where men were responsible for the actions of their wives, and all alike were governed by the authority of the powerful synagogue-community. In voluntaristic Cincinnati, however, it offered synagogue officials a graceful way out. They referred the matter to the congregation, and in all likelihood no fine was ever collected. Disputes over communal authority persisted at Bene Israel, but by the Civil War the whole system of communal control was a dead letter: coercion had given way to persuasion.

Persuasion, in turn, implied competition. To attract new members and even, in some cases, to hold on to existing ones, Bene Israel had to demonstrate that it was at least as good, if not better, than its B'nai Yeshurun rival. B'nai Yeshurun, of course, faced the same challenge in reverse. (Competition from the smaller synagogues, by contrast, was negligible, owing to their location and the character of their membership.) As a result, the two synagogues alternately emulated and attacked one another. Both sought to attract new dues-paying members, principally German Jews, so earlier disputes, based on country of origin, were muted. Instead, rivalry between the two synagogues largely expressed itself in disputes over matters of piety; each accused the other of being religiously illegitimate. Lay leaders of the two congregations used the national Jewish press to accuse one another of insufficient piety, and of condoning ritual laxity, especially in the sensitive area of *shechitah*, kosher slaughtering.[29] Vituperative charges and countercharges by each congregation against the other's *shochet* filled minute books and kept tempers on edge.

Even as each questioned the other's legitimacy, however, they carefully noted, and sometimes shamelessly copied, the other's successful innovations. In 1842, both came out with similarly worded bylaws.[30] In 1846, B'nai Yeshurun laid the cornerstone for an impressive new building, and a month later Bene Israel decided that it had better look to move as well. That same year, when B'nai Yeshurun hired Rabbi James K. Gutheim as "lecturer and reader," Bene Israel separately contracted with him to address their congregation on occasion as well. When Gutheim subsequently introduced various aesthetic reforms at B'nai Yeshurun, Bene Israel hurried to approve similar ones.[31]

Aesthetics, indeed, came to play an increasingly important role at Bene Israel, in part because it felt threatened by B'nai Yeshurun's moves in this area, and in part because religious services had hitherto been marked by a raucousness that was now seen as quite out of keeping with developing ideas about what was appropriate to a religious setting. Congregants at midcentury wanted their synagogues to be beautiful, their worship orderly and meaningful, and the behavior of their fellow congregants thoroughly decorous. This development, of course, was not confined to Cincinnati. In nineteenth-century Europe, both Sephardic and German Jews sought to promote synagogue decorum, hoping, thereby, not only to make worship more meaningful but also to improve the image of Jews in the eyes of their neighbors. In America, rules "to promote solemnity and order" were already introduced into the 1805 bylaws of Congregation Shearith Israel in New York. These became far more widespread with the immigration of German Jews, some synagogues issuing full-scale "rules of order." It soon became clear, Leon Jick observes, "that the chaotic, self-governing congregation was to be a training school in propriety."[32]

At Bene Israel, the new proprieties included a precise system for distributing in rotation such synagogue honors as the privilege of being called up before the Torah (rather than at auction, as had sometimes been done before); rules requiring men to wear their prayer shawls during divine services; resolutions designed to keep "poor boys" in "good order," so that they might recite their prayers in "proper order" and not wander into the women's section; and a decision to "put in force" an old decree that "no girl or boy under 5 years old shall be allowed to be in the Shool [synagogue], or any girl in the Shool below." The aim in each case was to minimize potential distractions, like crying babies or violations of sexual spheres, so as to create a "proper" atmosphere for prayer, and "a due respect and reverence for the precepts of our holy religion."[33] Later resolutions asked individuals to recite their prayers "in a low tone of voice, so as not to interfere with the Hazan [reader] or Chorus," and mandated that "no person shall interrupt or correct either the Hazan during the service or reading the Torah."[34]

The tendency of all of these changes was to transform male congregants from active participants in the religious service into passive observers. The growing concern with aesthetics undermined the feeling that the synagogue was an everyday place where one might feel comfortable acting in common, even disreputable ways.[35] New expectations for synagogue behavior defined the sanctuary as a special place marked by a solemn and "proper" atmosphere. The sanctuary needed to be more elegant, more dignified than the common spheres of life. A special code was introduced instructing the reader to wear a special black robe at particular times and to behave in an especially dignified way.[36]

Although in its concern with aesthetics, and in other ways, Bene Israel seemed simply to be aping the modernizing initiatives of B'nai Yeshurun, the emergence of the new congregation also prompted the older synagogue to express anew its fidelity to tradition, as if in contrast to B'nai Yeshurun. Thus, in 1846, the secretary accounted for the recent addition of twenty new members as exhibiting "on the part of our Brethren here a regard for perpetuating in its primitive holiness the tenets and principles of our holy Religion." The secretary, however, hastened to explain that the congregation itself had no intention of backing away from modernity. Instead, the accession of new members would enable it "to conduct its affairs with that liberality which must command the respect and esteem of all men."[37] Two years later, when Bene Israel followed B'nai Yeshurun's lead and resolved to form a choir, the congregation's leaders walked the same thin line. Rather than trumpet the innovation, they made it "clearly understood that no alteration or diminishment shall take place in our present form of Divine Service or Prayers" as a result.[38] Given the diversity of Bene Israel's members and the desire to attract as many new members as possible, this pragmatism is understandable. The congregation sought to be modern and traditional, like B'nai Yeshurun and different from it—all at the same time.

Bene Israel also responded to the B'nai Yeshurun challenge by expanding the role of the synagogue in several traditional areas. In 1847, for example, the trustees learned that the *mikveh* (ritual bath) necessary for the ritual observance of laws of marital purity, which had hitherto been operated by a private establishment in Cincinnati, was closing down. They therefore took it upon themselves to open a new *mikveh* so that they might "supply this requisite convenience, and tend to keep up with strictness the time honored laws of Judaism." They backed up this commitment with an expenditure of more than $1,000, furnishing a bath to serve the wives of members and nonmembers alike.[39] Similarly, in early 1848, the matzas committee was instructed to oversee the installation of a special oven at the back of the synagogue "for the purpose of baking Matzas for the ensuing Passover."[40] Again, the matzas were sold not just to members but to the community at large. Bene Israel thus attempted to solidify its position by reasserting its traditional communal role. While it could not by such actions recreate the old synagogue-community, it did indicate its continuing sense of responsibility for the community; it would not withdraw into itself.

Yet, for all this, the congregation's priorities did change. As aesthetics and the need to compete with B'nai Yeshurun became paramount, the congregation paid less attention to older concerns, like religious tradition and Jewish learning. While questions dealing with Jewish law and practice continued to arise, their resolution was left to a shrinking number of educated members who were able to read the prayers and guide the congregation along traditional lines. But the knowledge and authority of these few was itself open to question. For example, the Committee on Religious Rules, in 1846, considered the question of whether Joseph Jonas should be "disqualified from reading [i.e., leading] prayers during the year succeeding the demise of his Father." The revealing answer, preserved in the minutes, reads as follows: "That according to the [blank] which is our standing Laws to be guided by, it is strictly forbidden. . . ." Actually, the answer is not correct; the supposedly "strict" prohibition is disputed by several major authorities, and all agree that where another prayer leader is unavailable, the mourner may assume the task.[41] What is even more telling than this error, however, is the "blank" left in the record. The secretary was apparently unfamiliar with the text (presumably the sixteenth-century code of Jewish law known as the *Shulchan Aruch*) that served as the congregation's "standing Laws" and had to check, or find somebody else to fill in the proper words in Hebrew. This was a change from the early days when the congregation's secretary—usually a communal leader on the way up—possessed a traditional Jewish education and inserted Hebrew into the minutes in a familiar and comfortable hand. Now, when Hebrew appeared in the records at all it was written in ornate calligraphy, a sign that ability to write it could not be taken for granted. Indeed, Hebrew literacy had declined to the point where the language could be written out only by experts—and they, significantly, paid special attention to aesthetics.

In many ways, then, Bene Israel by midcentury had become entirely different from the frontier congregation of 1824. Where the founders had sought to transplant tradition and to create a "holy community" in Cincinnati, the synagogue now faced competition and the need to come to terms with American religious norms, by which they felt they were being judged, and according to which, increasingly, they came to judge themselves. Coercion had given way to persuasion, learning to aesthetics, and dignity and decorum had become the watchwords of the day. As a result, the synagogue was becoming ever more rarefied; it took on a special aura that set it apart from the normal tenor of life. Like the Hebrew words in the minute books, it at once became less familiar and more ornate. And sometimes it became a blank that members forgot to fill in at all.

Reform Comes to Cincinnati

The history of Bene Israel, indeed of Cincinnati Judaism as a whole, changed in 1854 with the appointment of Isaac Mayer Wise as rabbi of B'nai Yeshurun.[42] Born in Steingrub, Bohemia, in 1819 and trained in Germany, Wise immigrated to the United States in 1846 and quickly established himself as a "Reformer." In his first major pulpit, at Congregation Beth El in Albany, he stirred controversy with a series of ritual modifications aimed at improving decorum; he also organized a mixed choir. These innovations helped precipitate his firing, led to a memorable melee on the holiday of Rosh Hashanah when the congregation's president lashed out at him and knocked off his hat, and soon resulted in the founding of a new congregation, Anshe Emeth, which he served as rabbi until being called to Cincinnati. How much B'nai Yeshurun's leaders knew of all this when they appointed him (and agreed to his unprecedented demand for a life contract) is not clear, but they surely realized that they were getting one of the most able young men then serving in the American rabbinate: a leader who combined within himself traditional and modern learning, boundless energy and ambition, facility in both German and English, and remarkable personal charisma.[43]

In accepting the B'nai Yeshurun position, Wise made clear that he shared the vision of those who hired him. He promised to elevate his new synagogue into a "model congregation for the whole West and South," and pledged to "maintain and defend the honor of our sacred faith opposite all religious sects." He was, he pointed out, "a friend of bold plans and bold schemes."[44] In Cincinnati, where bold planners and grand schemers already envisioned their city becoming the greatest city in America if not the world, Wise felt right at home.

Meanwhile, over at Bene Israel, the future looked bleak. Wise's "synagogue was progressing while ours was fast sinking," one member wrote. He revealed that Bene Israel was hampered by "a burdensome debt . . . and bad government." Part of the blame apparently lay with an earlier decision to spend $40,000 on a larger synagogue, erected on the same site (plus adjoining lots) of the former one, at Sixth and Broadway. The new synagogue was completed in 1852, but by then many Jews had moved out of this declining downtown area; a $10,000 debt remained.[45] The more serious threat, however, was Wise himself. In the past, Bene Israel had proudly eschewed appointing a rabbi and relied upon the knowledge and leadership of its own members. They, in turn, had looked upon B'nai Yeshurun's need for a minister (it had seven different "rabbis" in ten years) as evidence of the younger congregation's weakness: "It is true we have only a reader. Yet our Synagogue is daily opened for prayers, and well attended."[46] Now the tables had turned, and B'nai Yeshurun with its new rabbi was steadily attracting former Bene Israel members away, while B'nai Yeshurun adamantly refused to share him even on a co-equal basis. Suddenly, Bene Israel's stalwart and outspoken traditionalists found themselves on the defensive, particularly as Wise with his dynamic plans for reform waved aside the ritual issues that they had always found so important. As membership eroded, Bene Israel was left with but one sensible option: it had to find a rabbi who could compete. Fortunately for the congregation, Rabbi Max Lilienthal accepted the challenge.

Born and educated in Munich, where he received both his doctorate and his ordination, Lilienthal (1814?–1882) was by training and inclination a *modern* rabbi. While still in his twenties, he had played a significant role in Russia's controversial effort to modernize Jewish education, working under S. S. Uvarov, the country's minister of national enlightenment. He resigned under somewhat mysterious circumstances soon after his marriage and immigrated to New York, where he arrived in 1845.[47] There, he served for a time as "chief rabbi" of the city's "United German-Jewish community," and subsequently founded a private Jewish boarding school, which he and his wife led with great success until Bene Israel called him away.[48] On June 5, 1855, thirteen months after Wise's own arrival in the city, Lilienthal assumed his new position.

Lilienthal and Wise had been friends back in New York, and had served together on a short-lived rabbinical court. Whether or not Wise actually recommended Lilienthal for the Cincinnati job, he knew that Lilienthal had grown increasingly sympathetic toward moderate religious reforms.[49] Lilienthal himself confirmed this in his preliminary meeting with the Bene Israel trustees when he told them that, as rabbi, he would seek to abolish the sale of synagogue honors, alter the manner of saying the *misheberach* petitionary prayers, and urge that "some certain prayers now said in many shools [synagogues] . . . be abolished."[50] Once settled, he set in motion a steady process of reforms. The system for distributing synagogue honors was changed, suggestions for "some alterations" in prayers were proposed, and serious efforts were made to institute a choir that would include women. In July, Lilienthal conspicuously absented himself from the traditional Tisha B'Av services which commemorate, with fasting and lamentation, the destruction of the first and second temples in Jerusalem. Such an observance, Lilienthal maintained, mourned what should be celebrated: the dispersion of Jews over the face of the earth, enabling them to carry their message to humanity.[51]

From the start, Lilienthal promised "to go hand in hand, in all matters concerning reform, with his beloved friend Dr. Wise." Together, the two men saw themselves as the harbingers of *American* Judaism, a legitimate heir to the Judaism practiced by different waves of Jewish immigrants. They believed, in other words, that the modernized Judaism that they consciously sought to establish in Cincinnati would in time be recognized as the rite, or *minhag*, of *all* American Jews, displacing the various rites that then divided them. This was a logical Jewish counterpart to the "Cincinnati dream." The city that represented the future of America as a whole, the "gateway to the west," would, they hoped, shape American Jewry's destiny as well.[52]

Not all Bene Israel members bought into this dream. A vocal traditionalist minority that had for some time been fighting efforts to change time-tested practices in the congregation withdrew after losing a close August 1855 congregational vote on reforms, and founded a new and traditional synagogue, aptly named Shearith Israel, the remnant of Israel. Rid of his opponents, Lilienthal continued on his course, recruiting new members and redefining the synagogue along more progressive lines.[53]

In the decades that followed, moving in fits and starts and usually following B'nai Yeshurun's lead, the congregation enacted a whole series of aesthetic and liturgical reforms, including shorter and more decorous services, vernacular prayers, organ music, mixed seating, limitations on the use of traditional prayer shawls, and, finally, "monitors" to preserve order and "to prevent the egress of all persons during divine services unless in cases of urgent necessity." Congregational leaders quite self-consciously sought both to abolish practices that seemed in "straight contradiction with the present requirements of decorum and morality" and to regulate the disorder caused by the many voices and movements of autonomous worshipers. Other proposals aimed to shorten, translate, or alter those portions of the prayer service which were deemed too long, incomprehensible, or jarring to modern ears.[54] Through these changes, members hoped to create a service that was more understandable, more pleasing, and less in conflict with the beliefs and assumptions that guided the lives of enlightened Americans. At the same time, and as a further indication of its changing sense of its own role, the congregation stopped overseeing kosher food and the *mikveh*. These, it argued, were communal responsibilities that all local congregations should share in.[55]

Yet even as the congregation was abandoning the last vestiges of the old synagogue-community, it refused to abandon its role as representative of the Jewish community, symbolizing Cincinnati Judaism to the outside world. As such, it sought to project as positive an image of the Jew as possible. This explains the bulk of the changes introduced at Bene Israel during the Lilienthal years. It also explains much about Lilienthal's own rabbinate. Reinterpreting the traditional rabbinic role, Lilienthal became the first rabbi in Cincinnati's history, and one of the first anywhere, to take an active role in civic affairs. During the course of his more than two decades of leadership, he served on the city's Board of Education, became a regent of McMicken University, actively participated in local philanthropic, social, and cultural organizations, and reputedly became the first American rabbi to preach in a Christian pulpit.[56] He was, according to Isaac M. Wise, the "mediator" between Jews and Gentiles in the city. While he also worked closely with Wise on behalf of religious reforms, church-state separation, the Union of American Hebrew Congregations (founded 1873) and Hebrew Union College (founded 1875), it was usually Wise who focused on the Jewish community's needs and Lilienthal who involved himself with the general community. In this way, as in many others, the two rabbis complemented one another. Their relationship, which did much to advance the

Cincinnati Jewish community's reputation, was captured, in a few phrases, by a contemporary journalist:

> What Wise suggested, Lilienthal supported, and what Lilienthal pacified, Wise promoted. What Wise wounded, Lilienthal healed, and what Lilienthal whitewashed, Wise exposed. Where Wise wanted to lead, Lilienthal gracefully followed, and where Lilienthal wisely warned, Wise laudably obeyed.[57]

The esteem in which Lilienthal was held by Cincinnatians was never better demonstrated than in 1868, when he accepted a call to become the rabbi of Temple Emanu-El in New York. His wife had recently died, and he was frustrated, for his congregation had still not delivered on its resolution of five years before, "to build a temple with all the necessary improvements . . . in a more suitable part of the city."[58] The competition, meanwhile, had built an imposing new edifice, B'nai Yeshurun's so-called Plum Street Temple, dedicated in 1866. Use of the word "temple" there was not accident; the new edifice, equipped with an organ, choir loft, and pews for the mixed seating of men and women, symbolized Reform Judaism's break with the past, its renunciation of any hope for redemption, and the rebuilding of the temple in Jerusalem.[59] Lilienthal believed that Bene Israel needed a "temple" too. He pointed to the "spirit of the age" as well as to the need "to impress the minds of the rising generation" in seeking to persuade cost-conscious congregants, who knew that Bene Israel still owed money on its 1852 building, to support his proposal.[60] But, as David Philipson later recalled, "after the foundation for the new building had been dug the work dragged along. Subscriptions were slow in coming in, and the hands of the building committee were bound by a resolution of the congregation, prohibiting the building committee from making contracts or proceeding with the work on the temple until the classification on pews had reached seventy-five thousand dollars."[61] Lilienthal eventually lost hope, and when the Emanu-El offer arose, he accepted it.

His Cincinnati congregants, clearly shocked, tried to persuade him to change his mind. They spoke of the loss "which will be felt by the community in general," and promised to renew their efforts to raise necessary funds. At the same time, sixteen of Cincinnati's most prominent non-Jewish leaders, headed by Judge Bellamy Storer, addressed an extraordinary letter to Bene Israel's trustees asking them to persuade their rabbi to withdraw his resignation; they considered him too valuable a citizen for the community to lose. At a meeting convened at Judge Storer's home, Lilienthal gave in and consented to stay. Presumably as part of the agreement, the cornerstone for Bene Israel's magnificent new Mound Street Temple was laid just ten weeks later. Shortly before the high holidays of 1869 the congregation moved in.[62]

The new temple reinforced the image that Bene Israel sought to project to the wider world. Outside, the building conveyed a positive picture of Jews and Judaism. It made a distinct contribution to the city's skyline, and was an edifice that Jews felt proud to show off to their Christian neighbors. Inside, the worship appeared no less pleasing. It was both aesthetically beautiful and thoroughly decorous. Rabbi Lilienthal, now one of the most respected men in the city, only enhanced the congregation's sense of self-esteem. His message spelled out in words what Bene Israel's new building tried to express in bricks and mortar: the idea that "the public at large will judge our religion according to the decency we display on every public occasion," and the corollary, that "we cannot do enough to improve the order and decorum of all public rituals in our religion."[63] Julius Freiberg, the congregation's president, raised these pronouncements to the level of a religious duty. "Our members," he reported with pride in 1873, "seem to have but one aim before them, that of elevating our beloved Congregation and Judaism in general in the eyes of all men."[64]

How to achieve this lofty aim was not always certain. At the very first congregational meeting held in the new temple, for example, the congregation was asked to consider "the nonobservance by some members of the Congregation of the rule and custom of sitting in the Temple during Divine Service with the head covered."[65] The "nonobservance," of course, was a reform motivated by the Western Protestant idea that heads should be uncovered as a sign of respect. This was further from Jewish tradition than most Bene Israel Jews were prepared to move in 1869, but after several years of discussion and an 1873 resolution by B'nai Yeshurun permitting their members to dispense with head-coverings, a split congregation voted, in 1875, to offer congregants the right to pray bareheaded; traditional headgear would henceforward be required only of the rabbi and the reader.[66]

The compromise is revealing, for it shows that, more and more, Judaism at Bene Israel was becoming a vicarious experience. Worshipers watched and listened but rarely participated themselves. At best, they were passive: sung to, spoken to, told when to stand and when to sit. This yawning gap between pulpit and pew was underscored by new rules, promulgated in 1871, that required paid officers of the congregation—and only them—to observe the Sabbath. Efforts to enforce congregation-wide Sabbath observance had long since been abandoned.[67] The requirement (later abandoned) that the rabbi and reader maintain their skullcaps, even as congregants discarded them, likewise emphasized the role of the congregation's spiritual leaders as "symbolic exemplars" and guardians of the faith. So long as *they* upheld a modicum of tradition, members felt free to do as they pleased.

By the late 1870s, then, the course of Reform seemed to be running smoothly. With a respected rabbi, a magnificent (non-Jewish) professional choir, a growing membership, and ever more affluent congregants, President Freiberg happily reported that Bene Israel's "social position" had attained an "enviable eminence."[68] Congregants sat decorously and followed along as the rabbi, reader, and choir created a service that was inspiring, impressive, and edifying.

Yet beneath the surface it was apparent that all was not well at the temple. Attendance was down, and not just on weekdays (already in 1865, some people seem to have been paid to attend so that the requisite *minyan* [quorum] for the twice-daily weekday services could be maintained)[69] but also on the Sabbath. As early as 1873, Freiberg bemoaned the fact that sometimes more gentiles were present in the synagogue than Jews.[70] Later, he complained that most of the Jews who did come to synagogue, at least on Saturday morning, were women and children. This phenomenon, a counterpart to the "feminization" that characterized Protestantism of this era, only seemed to emphasize the fact that the temple had become marginal to the lives of its members. "The real old Jewish feeling and devotion which characterized us in former times," Freiberg lamented, "has declined."[71] The question, as Bene Israel entered the closing decades of the nineteenth century, was whether the Judaism that replaced that of "former times" would suffice.

The Wrong Rabbi

On April 5, 1882, Max Lilienthal died after a short illness. He had served Bene Israel faithfully for twenty-seven years, and now he was widely mourned. "The funeral obsequies," according to David Philipson, "were among the most impressive ever held" in Cincinnati.[72] Finding someone to replace Lilienthal would be difficult, finding someone of equal stature, impossible. America had only just begun to train its own rabbis at this time, and the first Hebrew Union College ordination would not occur until the following year. To be sure, many congregations imported German rabbis to fill their pulpits. That, however, was not an option for Bene Israel, for too many of its members were not native German speakers. Instead, the congregation turned to an English-born rabbi named Raphael Benjamin (1846–1906), who was then serving in Melbourne, Australia. They hoped that his relative youth (he was thirty-six), his background in education, and his fine homiletical style would win young people back to the temple.[73]

Unfortunately, Raphael proved the wrong man for the job. His conception of the rabbinate turned out to be narrowly congregational, rather than broadly communal as Lilienthal's had been, and he never established a firm base of support. The new rabbi did devote a great deal of time to pastoral calls, the religious school, and his weekly sermons. He refused, however, to be drawn into the many outside activities that carried with them the status that Bene Israel's congregants wanted their rabbi to have. He also refused to succeed his predecessor as professor of history at Hebrew Union College, a position of some status, even when assured that the post would bring him honor and likewise do honor "to the congregation he represents." For a congregation that saw itself as a harbinger of what American Judaism should be, and that also had to compete with Isaac M. Wise's Plum Street Temple, this was intolerable. Exasperated lay leaders tried to explain to Benjamin that Bene Israel, "the pioneer of Judaism in the west," had "to stand at the head and take the lead in every good object calculated to advance and elevate our faith among ourselves, as likewise in the eyes of all Nations."[74] But Benjamin, who never understood the role of "symbolic exemplar" that the congregation demanded of him, felt that he carried all that he could handle ministering to the needs of Bene Israel's more than 300 members. When new demands were placed upon him, he complained of lack of time. As a result, in 1888, when his contract was up for renewal, the board voted 13–1 that "a change will be best for the welfare of the congregation."[75] While Benjamin moved on to a new position in New York, the congregation searched for someone who more closely approximated its ideal of what a Bene Israel rabbi should be.

The Right Rabbi

To replace Benjamin, Bene Israel's leaders turned to a twenty-six-year-old American-born rabbi, raised in Columbus, Ohio, trained at Hebrew Union College, and ordained at its first ordination in 1883. His name was David Philipson, and he would be associated with the congregation for the next sixty-one years.[76] Philipson had been a great favorite of Max Lilienthal's and believed that the older rabbi, had he not died so suddenly, would have selected him as his successor.[77] When Bene Israel did make its approach, he was already in Baltimore, serving as rabbi of Har Sinai Congregation. Although he was happy in Baltimore, and had turned down several offers from other congregations, he accepted the Cincinnati call. "Cincinnati exerted a spell that I could not withstand," he later explained. He believed that the center of Reform activity, the home of his eminent teacher, Isaac M. Wise, and of Hebrew Union College "would afford him greater scope."[78]

Philipson soon took up where Lilienthal had left off. Modeling his career upon that of his beloved predecessor, he became active in the general community, especially in cultural, philanthropic, and civic affairs. He also taught at Hebrew Union College, offering classes in Semitic languages and homiletics. Most important of all, he, like Lilienthal, advocated and practiced a Judaism that was cultured, respectable, solemn, impressive, and not too demanding of its adherents. Once again congregants could now bask in their rabbi's reflected glory. "Thank God," the president reported in 1888, "the troubles are over and the future is bright."[79]

Philipson moved quickly to establish his authority. He took command of the religious school and, over the objections of the board of trustees, invited a Unitarian minister to address the annual Thanksgiving Day service.[80] He then turned his attention to the more vexing problem of pews that sat empty week in and week out, while their owners spent the Jewish Sabbath at work. Philipson's classmate, Joseph Krauskopf, faced with a similar problem a few months earlier at Congregation Keneseth Israel in Philadelphia, had solved it by inaugurating a series of "Sunday Lectures" that attracted Jews and Gentiles alike. Philipson now proposed a similar idea to the trustees of Bene Israel.

The issue aroused great passions. Rabbi Isaac Mayer Wise at B'nai Yeshurun had long opposed Sunday services in any form, even when disguised as only a lecture, for being a "violation of Jewish custom." To him, and to many others, the traditional Sabbath was a lasting symbol of Jewish identity, a critical boundary line between Jews and Christians that Reform should not dare to breach. Wise advocated instead an embellished Friday evening service for those who needed to work on the Sabbath day. Yet Philipson, believing that Friday evening services had not succeeded at B'nai Yeshurun, viewed Sunday lectures as a necessary and pragmatic reform—a counterpart, not a replacement, for traditional Sabbath day services. In his diary, he blasted Wise for "throwing the firebrand of discord into the ranks of my congregation." He was angry at Wise, once his teacher and hero, for trying to thwart him.[81]

But thwarted he was. In 1888, the board of trustees narrowly endorsed Philipson's request to introduce Sunday lectures, but the congregation rejected the move, inviting Philipson instead to choose the "most propitious" time on any day during the week "except Sunday" for his lectures. When, the next year, Philipson tried to assert his authority by beginning a Sunday lecture series without prior congregation approval, the result was a large and chaotic public debate at which "great tumult ensued." A pledge that no "religious services of any kind" would ever be "connected with such lectures" failed to calm the waters. Philipson and the board had no choice but to back down, and the Sunday talks were discontinued. In 1891, when Philipson again asked for permission to speak on Sundays, he was thwarted once more. Reluctantly, he acceded to a board request to deliver the lectures on Friday nights instead.[82]

Many members of Bene Israel continued to feel uncomfortable about Jews gathering for religious activities on Sunday; they saw this as a threat to Judaism's integrity. Much as they sympathized with their rabbi's goal of creating Jewish functions for those who regularly missed services on Saturday, they did not share his vision of how this should be done. Philipson, however, did not give up; he merely bided his time. In 1909, when he once again moved to introduce Sunday lectures, the time was right and they were approved. Ten years later, when he expanded these into Sunday morning services, they were approved too. By then, Philipson's authority within the congregation had expanded to the point that dissenters, if any remained, kept quiet. Yet in the end, Sunday services failed to become a major part of Philipson's program for American Judaism, and failed to become firmly entrenched in his own temple. Sunday services also faced considerable resistance within the Reform movement as a whole. As a result, in 1930, following a congregational referendum on the subject, they were discontinued. Ironically, they were replaced by an embellished late Friday night worship service beginning at 7:45 P.M. (which, depending on the time of the year, was either earlier or later than traditional Sabbath eve services, which are held at sundown).[83]

The Sunday-service controversy pointed up a major change that had taken place at Bene Israel. The congregation's foremost objectives of achieving financial security, a large membership, and of "elevating our beloved Congregation and Judaism in general in the eyes of all men" had essentially been attained. Now the overriding concern was how to keep Jews connected with their religion and its institutions. Philipson believed that the synagogue was the key to Jewish survival. He was willing to push the limits of Judaism in order to make the synagogue into a comfortable space for Cincinnati's acculturated Jews. To his mind, Sunday services were justifiable if they brought Jews into the synagogue. While some of his congregants, for symbolic reasons, opposed special Sunday devotions, they fully agreed with their rabbi's larger aim. As a result, during Philipson's tenure, Bene Israel took on a wide range of new functions, all of them designed to bring Jews, especially Jewish men, back into the synagogue on a more frequent basis.

Complaints about poor synagogue attendance dogged Philipson from the beginning. Even with modernized services, the congregation's presidents had continually to plead for members' attendance. Julius Freiberg, Bene Israel's president for twenty years, was particularly concerned about the problem, and referred to it in his last annual address to the congregation in 1890:

> The attendance of members during the year, with the exception of the great holidays and Shevuoth, has been steadily on the decrease. Of course, we often have a goodly congregation of women and children, and I must confess that I am always delighted to see them, but at the same time, I would have been delighted much more if I had the pleasure of seeing our members in the Temple, if only occasionally.[84]

Recruitment of new and potentially more active members was one possible solution. New members had the additional advantage of helping to offset a growing deficit. But recruitment, as well as regular attendance by current members, was stymied in the 1890s by the accelerating movement of affluent Jews out of Cincinnati's downtown region, into the hilly suburbs around the city. As early as 1894, David Philipson had called attention to this problem, stating that the time had come "for the erection of a house of worship in the new residential section, miles away from the present structure." His president, Philipson later recalled, considered him *"meshugge"* (crazy) for making such a suggestion.[85] But ten years later, buoyed by hopes that a new location would bring Jews back to the synagogue, the congregation broke ground for a new temple on Rockdale and Harvey Avenues in Avondale, the suburb that had become home to many of Cincinnati's German Jews.

A Temple on a Hill and a Synagogue-Center

Completed in 1906 and dedicated amidst considerable fanfare, the new 1,500-seat "Temple on the Hill" was a modern, dignified structure featuring an impressive portico adorned with classical columns and a lofty pediment bearing the universalistic message "My House Shall be a House of Prayer for All Peoples." In its very architecture, as Lance Sussman has observed of synagogue architecture of this era, it expressed the idea "that Judaism was an ancient and integral part of Western Civilization" and "that the Jewish heritage was based on lofty, noble ideals that contributed to the strength and stability of society."[86] Here was an architectural answer to the congregation's twentieth-century problem, a statement in stone explaining why Jews should come back to the synagogue. Formal in every way, it was built on a grand scale that was meant to impress outsiders and to reflect positively on the stature of the congregation within.

The move to Avondale marked a new era in the history of Bene Israel. Two years before, while the move was being planned, the congregation had mourned the death at age ninety-eight of Elinor Moses, wife of Phineas Moses, one of the Bene Israel's 1824 founders. The congregation's leaders recognized the symbolic impact of her demise, for it "removed the one personal link that joined the first days of our Congregation with the present time." The president reassured congregants that Mrs. Moses had been "familiar with the removal which we are about to make to the hill-top." He implied that she was the connection, the legitimating tie, between the old pioneers and the new temple. For all intents and purposes the "single tie" to the "earliest pioneer days" had now been irrevocably severed.[87]

As in its previous incarnations, the new congregation quickly became known by the name of the street upon which it was built. The inauguration of "Rockdale Temple," like the consecration of the Mound Street Temple before it, also led congregants to expect some transformation of their Judaism and its place in their lives. Accordingly, the new temple promulgated a new, modern constitution. It abandoned the old

3.1 Rockdale Temple as it appeared at its dedication in 1906. Photograph courtesy of both the Collection of the Public Library of Cincinnati and Hamilton County and the American Jewish Archives, Cincinnati Campus, Hebrew Union College-Jewish Institute of Religion.

fines, several outmoded offices, and, most revealingly, the explicit rules of decorum that were now observed as a matter of course.

As expected, the early years at Rockdale and Harvey Avenues in the hilltops of Avondale were triumphant ones. Although women continued to dominate the Sabbath morning congregation, attendance was deemed to be almost satisfactory. And according to the congregation's presidents, high holy day services were everything that the new majestic environment suggested they should be: solemn, imposing, and marked by a "profound religious spirit."[88] Yet by far the most important change that took place at Rockdale—paralleling a development that transformed many Orthodox, Conservative, and Reform congregations in the early twentieth century—was a process of redefinition. The synagogue was transmuted from a house of worship into a synagogue-center, a focal point for Jewish activities of every sort. This marked the triumph of earlier efforts to promote the synagogue as the central institution of Jewish life. But the result, somewhat unintended, was that home religion declined.

The synagogue responded to this decline by transplanting tradition-

ally domestic rituals into the sanctuary. Home rituals, like candle lighting, now became synagogue rituals. The synagogue also became the
favorite place to celebrate the Sabbath, holidays, and life-cycle events,
many of which had formerly been celebrated, at least in part, at home.
In time, the synagogue, located in the heart of the Cincinnati Jewish
community, also accommodated a wide variety of clubs and organizations, some of which it had itself initiated. In short, Rockdale, like many
another modern synagogue, now aimed to go beyond "mere" worship
to promote a broader sense of Jewish social cohesiveness as a bulwark
against assimilation. Like the "institutional church," a parallel development in American Protestantism, it blurred many of the distinctions between the religious and the secular, on the theory that deed was more
important than creed. Mordecai Kaplan, who best articulated the
synagogue-center ideology, explained the idea this way:

> The Jewish milieu provided by the home, basic as it is to Jewish
> life, cannot suffice. There is need for some additional *locus* where
> the cultural and social aspects of Jewish civilization might find a
> far wider scope for expression and enjoyment than is possible in
> the home. That *locus* should be the synagogue, not the congrega-
> tional synagogue which exists in American-Jewish life today, but
> the synagogue reconstructed to meet the new needs which have
> arisen in Jewish life. . . . It should be a neighborhood center to
> which all Jews to whom it is accessible should resort for all reli-
> gious, cultural, social and recreational purposes.[89]

As early as 1906, Rockdale's trustees permitted the local branch of
the National Council of Jewish Women to use the temple's schoolrooms.
A year later, the temple provided space for a Hebrew Union College
lecture series, B'nai B'rith meetings, and the Ladies' Sewing Society. By
1909, temple president J. Walter Freiberg characterized the congregational home as a "center of Jewish communal life." The next president,
Alfred M. Cohen, reiterated the point: "the policy of the Trustees," he
announced in 1913, "has been to make the school building a Jewish center, and it is such in the widest sense."[90] These activities expanded in
the next decade with the establishment of a sisterhood, youth group,
men's club, and boy and girl scout troops. There was also a formal Rockdale Temple Center for young people, which in conjunction with a similar group at Wise Temple (the new name adopted by B'nai Yeshurun
upon Isaac M. Wise's death) sponsored parties, lectures, and outings.
Inevitably, some complained that the congregation had forgotten its

raison d'être, "the worship of God, according to the precepts of Israel."[91] But the new view—that the congregation should work to bring Jews into the synagogue and make them feel a part of it—generally triumphed. And judged by this standard, rather than by attendance at weekly services, Rockdale thrived, for its building bustled with life all week long.

The active role of women was the most salient aspect of the general growth in temple activities which marked the synagogue-center. Despite Reform's attempt to emancipate women from the limited role assigned to them by traditional Judaism, and despite the preponderance of women in the weekly congregation, there had been no distinctive or organized role for women connected with the congregation since the disappearance of the benevolent societies that had been part of the original synagogue-community. Given how thoroughly religion was equated with the "gentler sex" during this era, and given how important female participation had become in many Christian church communities, it seems strange that women at Bene Israel were restricted to the roles of attendee and "member's wife" until the end of the nineteenth century. The problem was that with the sphere of the synagogue reduced to the sanctuary, the only nonreligious activity associated with the congregation was governance, which remained, without apparent objection, firmly in the hands of male officers and trustees. It was only toward the end of the century that the educational and professional advancement of women in other spheres began to make female exclusion from synagogue governance seem outmoded.

The expansion of temple activities that marked the rise of the synagogue-center created opportunities to find places for women within the congregation that went beyond their seats in the sanctuary. In 1900, women were accorded the right to join Bene Israel as full members even if they were not, as had previously been necessary, widows of former male members. "The experience of late years has demonstrated the necessity for reliance upon the women of Israel to fill our pews each Sabbath," the president reminded the congregation. He argued that membership would provide at least "a slight recognition of the obligation" owed by the congregation to these faithful attendees. Yet very few women availed themselves of their new privilege. Most continued to affiliate through their fathers or husbands.[92]

Once women had been certified as potential members in their own right, the congregation's leadership continued to enlarge the possibilities for women to contribute their energies to the temple in a manner thought to be in keeping with their character and interests. "There are many things in connection with the school," the school committee explained in 1903, "that ladies are particularly apt in doing." They asked for the creation of a ladies' auxiliary to the school committee which would undertake such tasks as "the beautifying of the school-rooms, the arranging of entertainments [holiday parties for the children] . . . and the like."[93] With the move to Rockdale, a Ladies Auxiliary (later Women's House) Committee was set up under the chairmanship of Mrs. J. Walter (Stella Heinsheimer) Freiberg to take responsibility for the "care and supervision" of the temple's interior.[94] While these auxiliaries brought institutional recognition to the few women who were appointed to serve on them, Bene Israel's (male) leadership was not prepared to place women on the congregation's governing committees. Even as the Women's House Committee was being formed, the board of trustees responded to a request from the Cincinnati section of the National Council of Jewish Women by stating that "they did not deem it advisable at this time" to place "a lady member of the Temple" on the Choir Committee.[95] (Therese Strauss, who had been trained as an opera singer, became the first woman appointed to a nonauxiliary congregational committee when she was made a member of the choir committee in 1919.)

In 1913, the National Federation of Temple Sisterhoods (NFTS), an organization intended to connect the efforts of temple women's organizations throughout the country was founded at a meeting of the Union of American Hebrew Congregations in Cincinnati. Aware of the imminent emergence of NFTS, David Philipson sponsored the formation of a sisterhood at Rockdale Temple—another indication that change at the temple proceeded from the top down. Rockdale's sisterhood quickly grew into one of the most active contributors to temple activities. Within the developing synagogue-center there was much "within the sphere of women's labor" that could be accomplished, and the sisterhood soon assumed responsibility for temple, school, communal, and Reform movement-wide activities, including fund-raising. Rockdale's president, Alfred M. Cohen, took note of the new status women had won when he began the 1913 congregational meeting with the salutation "Brethren and sisters." Never before had women been officially welcomed.[96]

Within twelve months, the sisterhood had proved its worth, and drew high praise for serving, in Cohen's words, "delicately and unobtrusively the cause we love so well."[97] By 1925 the sisterhood boasted 745 members (total synagogue membership, including all male heads of households and widows, was 792), and was involved in the full range of activities that the synagogue had taken under its wing—entertainments, holiday observances, the religious school, social and philanthropic work within the community, and more. Sisterhood leaders even participated in leading the services for a special Women's Sabbath which began in 1923 and became an annual event.[98] Rockdale also exercised national leadership in the sisterhood movement, again led by Mrs. J. Walter Freiberg, who served several terms as NFTS president.

After the passage of the Nineteenth Amendment (women's suffrage) in 1920, women came to play a greater role in the governance of Rockdale Temple. They were invited to congregational meetings, allowed to serve on major committees, and in 1924 two were elected to the temple's board of trustees. Sisterhood paved the way for this development. It nurtured a cadre of women leaders and marked out distinctive roles for women to play within the expanded world of the synagogue-center.

Men, however, continued to dominate congregational affairs. As lay leaders, they embodied the central values that the congregation as a whole espoused. The most prominent lay leader of Bene Israel during the second half of the nineteenth century was Julius Freiberg, one of Cincinnati's leading citizens. A close ally of Max Lilienthal, he had overseen the transition from "shool" to temple, as well as the consolidation of Reform practice within the worship service. As president of the Union of American Hebrew Congregations, he also advocated the Lilienthal-Wise version of American Judaism on the national level. Freiberg was by trade a distiller, and he understood that his leadership in the Jewish community was an intrinsic part of his general status within the Cincinnati community. He achieved enviable success in both realms, so much so that the Cincinnati Chamber of Commerce and Merchants' Exchange, in eulogizing him, declared that "no merchant, manufacturer or citizen of our beloved Cincinnati has contributed more to its good name, its development, growth and prosperity than did he."[99]

Julius' son, J. Walter Freiberg, followed in his father's footsteps. He too sought to exemplify success in two realms, playing a major role both in Cincinnati civic life and in Jewish religious life. Like his father, he also presided over Bene Israel as well as the Union of American Hebrew Congregations (his wife, Stella, meanwhile, presided over Bene Israel's sisterhood and the National Federation of Temple Sisterhoods). He too was described at his death as an "ideal citizen." As a Jewish lay leader, he exemplified the creed that his congregation preached to all who would listen: "only in religion is the Jew distinctive from his fellow American."[100]

Lay leadership notwithstanding, it was the rabbi, David Philipson, who stood at the center of the temple's activities.[101] He led the worship, he explained what Judaism meant, he showed how Jewish ideals could be put into practice, he defended Judaism to the Gentile community, and he represented Jews in the community at large. With the death of Isaac Mayer Wise in 1900, Philipson assumed Wise's mantle and was recognized as Cincinnati's premier rabbi. For many Rockdale Temple members, he actually personified Judaism. They experienced it vicariously through him.

Philipson had participated in the famed Pittsburgh Rabbinical Conference in 1885 that drew up the "Pittsburgh Platform," a statement of Reform Jewish principles. These formed the basis for his conception of Judaism, a variation of what would later be known as Classical Reform Judaism. Every Rockdale congregant knew Philipson's basic credo: "We are Jews in Religion, Americans in Nationality." He elaborated on his beliefs in a 1909 address to the Union of American Hebrew Congregations where he set forth what he later called "the creed of the American Jew" and the essence of his lifelong message:

> We repudiate the fiction of a Jewish race but we recognize the ob-
> ligation of our Jewish birth; we have been born into a great heri-
> tage: a heritage of the spirit. We are members of a religious
> community, a religious people, a *goy kadosh;* we are held together
> as Jews, not by political, national, or racial ties, but by religious
> bonds. We are an historic community, molded by historic forces. If
> solidarity there be among us, it is a religious solidarity, not a na-
> tional or a racial. Nationally, I feel attached to my American brother
> of whatever faith or non-faith. Religiously I am bound to my Jewish
> brother. . . .[102]

Philipson's sermons reiterated these themes and defended them against critics. He particularly lambasted political Zionism: "To my mind," he wrote in his autobiography, "political Zionism and true Americanism have always seemed mutually exclusive. No man can be a member of two nationalities, a Jewish and an American. . . . There is no middle way." He considered Zionism "fraught with danger to the welfare of Jews in this country."[103]

Whereas the Zionist vision was focused abroad and looked to create a Jewish homeland in Palestine, Philipson's vision was firmly rooted in American soil. He, like many Cincinnati Jews, cherished a civic ideal, a mission to work for "the public weal." Education, culture, philanthropy, social work, and especially good government stood among the leading causes that he embraced, often in a spirit of civic pride and *noblesse oblige*. Looking back over his career, he boasted that he had given himself "fully and without stint to every upward movement for the welfare of my city and its citizens."[104]

Philipson played a particularly important part in the movement to clean up city government in Cincinnati. As early as 1889, just one year after he assumed his position at Bene Israel, he defended his right to speak out against political corruption:

> when . . . purity of purpose and honesty in action have made way for the crookedness of the politician and the wire-pulling of the ringleader, when devotion to the best interests of the people is sacrificed to private ambition and aggrandizement, then it is high time for the pulpit to say its word and to use its influence in the attempt to stay the corruption, for laxity in these things cannot fail to react on the general life of the people.[105]

A few years later, he attacked the political machine of "Boss" George B. Cox from the pulpit, and called on his congregants to vote it out of office. In 1905, along with other local clerics, he worked for good government (and against Cox) through the Honest Elections Committee. In 1909, he publicly supported John W. Peck, the Democratic reform candidate for mayor, against the machine (he explained that he was "speaking as a citizen of Cincinnati and not as a rabbi of the congregation"). Ultimately, his student, congregant, and friend, Murray Seasongood, backed by many Rockdale Temple members and Philipson himself, spearheaded an anticorruption campaign that resulted in the passage of a new city charter in 1924, and Seasongood's own election as the city's first reform mayor two years later. To be sure, some of Philipson's congregants opposed his political involvements and backed other candidates. What is significant, however, and this Seasongood himself recognized, is that Philipson regarded "citizenship and the fearless discharge of civic duty as a religious obligation." Judaism so defined burst the bounds of the synagogue, and even of the synagogue-center, and entered into the public arena. Politics became one more way of expressing one's Jewish faith.[106]

Patriotism offered still another way. Devotion to America played a central role in Philipson's Judaism, and he made certain that it was prominently reflected in both the worship and the activities of his temple. An American flag stood on his pulpit dais, he regularly preached on patriotic themes, and he invited patriotic organizations to use Rockdale's facilities for their meetings. During and after World War I, when patriotic hysteria was at its height, Philipson became an apostle of Americanism, "called upon continually to speak in the interest of democracy for which the United States and the European allies were fighting." In a lecture distributed nationwide in two hundred thousand copies, he declared America "truly chosen" by God to make the world safe for democracy:

> I have the firm conviction that, just as in the prophet's vision, Israel of old was chosen and called for service, so in this latest age of the world's history, this nation has been called for service, this nation has been chosen. I hear the voice of the Lord speaking to America through the prophet even as He spake to ancient Israel: "I the Lord have called thee in righteousness and have taken hold of thy hand and kept thee and set thee for a covenant of the peoples, for a light of the nations. . . ."[107]

The experience of World War I did much to solidify Philipson's creed within his congregation. Following their rabbi's lead, Rockdale congregants participated wholeheartedly in the war effort both within the temple and without: sending their sons off to fight, working for the Red Cross, contributing funds, adopting (along with the other Reform congregations of the city) a regiment, raising an American flag and singing patriotic songs. Philipson encouraged Bene Israel's congregants to believe that their patriotic efforts were, in effect, an expression of their Judaism.

After the war this same commitment to patriotic piety justified the temple's efforts to strengthen its synagogue-center activities. Congregants wanted to prove that "the ultimate goal of our faith [is] . . . the making of better men and better citizens."[108] Unable to sustain a real community based around worship, Rockdale, like other synagogues and temples, attempted to provide services and activities—including sewing, music, dance, and drama—that would bring the temple as a community back into the lives of area Jews. These activities, more than Sabbath services or education, provided members with a sense of belonging and mission. In turn, they made the temple itself seem vibrant and vital.

On January 18, 1924, K.K.Bene Israel/Rockdale Temple celebrated its centennial. There was much to be joyful about. The congregation boasted over 700 members ("of the highest class") and was growing at a rate of more than forty new members a year. It had long before surpassed its competition, which had declined somewhat since Isaac M. Wise's death in 1900, and it now claimed to be "the largest and most influential" congregation "in the entire middle west." Its members included many of the leading Jews and citizens of the city, among them Murray Seasongood and Alfred M. Cohen. David Philipson, the city's premier rabbi, was a towering figure within the Cincinnati community, a leader within the Reform movement in Judaism (whose history he had written), and, in the eyes of many, the "Dean of American rabbis." Rockdale and its rabbi had, indeed, become Cincinnati institutions; they were well established, filled a recognizable niche, and symbolized religious continuity.[109]

Being connected with these "institutions" was for local Jews itself a mark of status. This was symbolized on Yom Kippur eve when "full-dress ushers (in tails and white ties) met the worshipers at the doors." Journalist Alfred Segal, who recalled this scene years later, pointed out that "one of the profane could feel himself to be a gate crasher at an exclusive party."[110] For the elite, however, Rockdale with its magnificent sanctuary represented the perfect synthesis of religion, community responsibility, and cosmopolitan elegance. This was its distinguishing genius, underscored in 1928 when the congregation grandly celebrated Philipson's fortieth anniversary as its rabbi. To mark the occasion, community leaders, Jewish and non-Jewish alike, outdid one another in singing the rabbi's praises and enumerating his many achievements.[111]

Yet even as Philipson was being feted, dark clouds were gathering on Rockdale's horizon. The overwhelming wave of immigration from Eastern Europe that began in the 1880s and ended with the immigration restriction legislation of 1924 had forever changed the face of American Jewry. Millions of these new American Jews took little interest in the denationalized religious expression that Philipson and Bene Israel had championed. Although German Jews remained institutionally, if not numerically, dominant in Cincinnati, even there the tide was shifting. The growing influence of Zionism and the changing nature of American Jewry and American Judaism served to increasingly isolate a congregation that had celebrated itself in 1924 as "THE AMERICAN CONGREGATION."

In the 1920s, both Wise Temple and the Reading Road Temple, mired in hard times, brought a new generation of Reform rabbis into their pulpits. Their mandate was to chart new directions and programs, to reinvigorate Reform Judaism, and to win young people back into the synagogue. They enjoyed some striking successes. In a direct challenge to David Philipson, both of the new rabbis, James G. Heller and Samuel Wohl, also spoke out strongly on behalf of Zionism. "I stand in proud isolation in my universalistic advocacy of Judaism," Philipson admitted wistfully to his diary in 1927. Not only did the city's other Reform rabbis and Hebrew Union College professors disagree with his anti-Zionist interpretation of Judaism, but he found himself "frequently laughed to scorn."[112]

Although Rockdale flourished through much of the 1920s, these were difficult years for Reform Judaism throughout the United States. The nationwide "religious depression," the growth of secularism and Jewish secularism, the emergence of East European Jewry, the rise of Conservative Judaism, of European and American anti-Semitism—all of these posed significant challenges to the buoyant optimism that had characterized Reform Judaism in the previous era. The nation's economic collapse in 1929 made conditions still more difficult; throughout the country synagogue membership and income declined and the American dream was called into question.[113]

Rockdale was scarcely able to meet these challenges. The easy assumption of prosperity and affluence which the congregation had so conscientiously attempted to express in the temple building and in divine services was quickly undermined by the prevailing economic conditions. Rockdale was hardly immune to the times; at least two members committed suicide. Moreover, both membership and financial receipts declined sharply, forcing the congregation to make do on less and less.[114] The disillusionment of the Depression years, and the looming threat of totalitarianism in Europe could not but deflate the optimistic faith in the future and in the promise of American life that had long marked Bene Israel and its rabbis. In addition, Philipson himself was weakening.

As conditions worsened in the next decade, even some of Philipson's most ardent admirers wondered if he was just hanging on. By now into his seventies, the rabbi had lost much of his effectiveness: his sermons became repetitive, sometimes tearful, and frequently out of touch with the times. Rockdale's message, as a result, became increasingly negative—*against* Jewish nationalism, *against* the proposed World Jewish Congress, *against* the Jewish Center movement, *against* allegedly radical trends within the Central Conference of American Rabbis.

Emblematic of Rockdale's decline was the victory that Rabbi Eliezer Silver, the dynamic new leader of Cincinnati Orthodox Jewry (mostly East European immigrants) scored against it in 1932. Silver had acquired a lot at Hickory and Burnet Avenues, near Rockdale, for construction of a new community *mikveh*, the same kind of ritual bath that Bene Israel itself had constructed eighty-five years earlier. Neighbors, including many Jews, opposed the new building and challenged it on zoning grounds. In a letter to the *Cincinnati Enquirer*, Philipson explained that the *mikveh* was "entirely foreign to our modern interpretation of Jewish faith and practice." "The large body of Jews who have given Cincinnati so prominent a position among the Jewish communities of the United States," he claimed, fully agreed with him. Ex-mayor and Bene Israel stalwart Murray Seasongood led the battle to keep the *mikveh* out. But the Orthodox community, claiming to represent 65 percent of the city's Jews, fought back. It questioned Philipson's leadership of the Jewish community, pointed out divisions within the Reform camp, and reminded Philipson that the earliest Jews in the city were Orthodox. More importantly, Rabbi Silver secured the services of Robert A. Taft, himself a skillful politician, to defend the *mikveh* in court. Unwilling to fight the case on these terms, Seasongood dropped it, and the *mikveh* was eventually built.[115] The episode demonstrated how much had changed in Cincinnati Jewish life and heightened Rockdale's sense of embattlement.

In 1938, David Philipson finally retired. He was seventy-six years old, and had served at Rockdale for a full half-century. Pursuit of that milestone, which he believed would constitute a record for rabbinical service, helped to keep him going.[116] Now as Nazism menaced world Jewry, calling into question many of the assumptions upon which Philipson had staked his career, a change was long overdue. Would Rockdale take the opportunity to move back into the mainstream of Reform Judaism? Would it follow other Reform temples and embrace Zionism? Would it even be able to maintain its status with Philipson gone? These were only some of the questions faced by the congregation as it looked forward to its fourth rabbi in 115 years.

A Tradition of Anti-Traditionalism

Victor Reichert, the man selected as Philipson's successor, was no stranger to Rockdale Temple. He had come to the congregation in 1926, fresh out of Hebrew Union College, when he was appointed to serve as Philipson's assistant. Two years later, he was made associate rabbi. Thereafter, he bided his time and stood in Philipson's shadow, always according the senior rabbi the utmost respect, and garnering praise for his geniality, his accommodating nature, his diligence, and his scholarly sermons. Meanwhile, his own work in the congregation focused on pastoral duties, as well as such themes as social justice, interfaith relations, and especially Jewish education and scholarship where he strove to set a personal example. These remained his priorities when he succeeded Philipson as Rockdale's senior rabbi.

Reichert had been a safe choice for the congregation. He was a known quantity, and there was every reason to expect that he would move in familiar directions. Moreover, with Philipson continuing on as emeritus, a position he held until his death in 1949, a certain deference remained important. Reichert, ever the gentleman, could be depended upon to maintain proprieties. Nobody expected the amiable rabbi to achieve Philipson's stature in the community or in the Reform movement. Nor was he considered likely to return the temple to its former pinnacle of glory among the Reform congregations of the Midwest. But at a time when those who were successfully gaining national reputations in the Reform movement were either proponents of Zionism or of a Judaism that sought to break down the formalism and limitations of Judaism as practiced at places like Rockdale, the congregation was content to be removed from the fray. If not a David Philipson, Reichert was certainly an exemplary pastor: well liked, well respected, eager to lend a sympathetic ear. That, the congregation decided, was just what it needed at this juncture in its history.

Like Philipson and Lilienthal before him, Reichert reached out to the general community. He also seconded Philipson's opposition to Zionism, albeit without the vehemence that characterized his predecessor (or for that matter, his own older brother, Rabbi Irving Reichert, a founder of the American Council for Judaism).[117] Reichert preferred, as much as possible, to maintain a lower-keyed, gentler rabbinate. He was a "spiritual, scholarly, sincere and affable" rabbi,[118] rather than a fiery prophet.

Although nonworship congregational activities would continue to expand at Rockdale, especially in the 1950s, the temple, under Reichert, no longer saw itself as the bustling synagogue-center for the entire Jewish community that it had been in prior decades. With the mass movement of Jews up to Avondale, an independent Jewish Community Center Association had been formed, and in 1935 it opened up a facility of its own on Reading Road. The new Jewish Community Center absorbed many of the secular and youth activities that Rockdale (and later the Wise-Rockdale Center) had once housed and maintained.[119] Its success also signaled an important shift in the Jewish community's balance of power, one that would, over time, considerably weaken the synagogue to the benefit of communal agencies that embraced all Jews: Orthodox, Conservative, Reform, and unaffiliated alike.

At Rockdale, this development encouraged a new and far narrower vision of what the congregation should be. No longer did the temple seek to ride the wave of the future. No longer did it see itself as a community center. No longer did it even seek to play a leadership role within the Reform movement as a whole, especially once the Union of American Hebrew Congregations moved from Cincinnati to New York in 1948. Instead, it sought to preserve and perpetuate Reform Judaism according to its own traditions, as preached by Max Lilienthal and David Philipson.

This is not to say that the congregation barred newcomers; to the contrary, they were welcomed. During the 1930s, when many German Jews emigrated to Cincinnati, fleeing from Nazi Germany, Rockdale assisted them. Members whose own families had come from Germany in the nineteenth century believed that Bene Israel would provide the proper religious setting for these new German immigrants as well. Of course, the immigrants themselves, even if they were Reform Jews, found American Reform Judaism as practiced at Rockdale alien and bizarre. Those used to praying with their heads covered, for example, were shocked to discover that they needed to remove their head-coverings or leave.[120] Most joined other more traditional congregations, or founded their own. But some, because of family connections or because they liked it, did join Rockdale and still express lifelong appreciation for the welcoming hospitality and beneficial assistance that it showed to them.

Increasingly, Rockdale also attracted members from East European Jewish backgrounds. This population brought temple membership above 1,000 families in 1948.[121] (The family-centeredness of the synagogue was underscored in this period by grouping members into "family units," a procedure that was also administratively easier now that both men and women were accepted as full members.) But the new members did not bring about change. Given the numerous other congregational options available in Cincinnati, it was presumed that the Jews who came to Rockdale wanted the elegant and undemanding religious environment that was its hallmark. Newcomers were expected to conform to Rockdale's traditions, not vice versa.

The vehemence with which Rockdale stalwarts defended their ancestral traditions, even when their own record of attendance at weekly services was poor, suggests that "tradition" at the temple had come to symbolize a matter of transcendent importance, something that members considered to be desperately worth preserving and gravely in danger of slipping away. Rockdale tradition represented more than just the memory of the ancestors who had immigrated to Cincinnati in the nineteenth century, rising from rags to riches to give the community its shape, although that was not unimportant. At an even deeper level, "tradition" represented the lofty *vision* of those ancestors, their sense that they were creating "a sort of paradise for the Hebrews," a "promised land," located in what they expected to become America's greatest city. Reform Judaism as it had developed at Rockdale, with its stress on aesthetics, its minimalist ritual, and its emphasis on interfaith relations and civic duty, was part and parcel of that lofty vision. Now the vision stood in danger of collapsing. Cincinnati, in Reichert's day, was neither the urban center that the first immigrants envisaged, nor the model community that their children strove to create; in fact, newcomers saw it as just one more midwestern metropolis. Rockdale's stalwarts, who had grown up believing in the "Cincinnati dream," could not quite face up to this collapse. The fact that their magnificent temple was showing its age and was becoming more and more isolated within an increasingly black urban environment, that Zionism (the antithesis of everything they stood for) was on the rise, that the Reform movement was no longer centered in Cincinnati, and that the majority of the city's Jews were of East European origin and knew nothing of the city's heritage—all this was more than they could absorb. "Tradition" thus became a form of escape. It enacted a symbolic return to days gone by when the congregation was at its height and hopeful dreams abounded.[122]

Reichert was careful to preserve a great deal of Rockdale tradition, and during his first eleven years on the job he regularly called upon the "living symbol" of that tradition, Rabbi-emeritus David Philipson, to deliver prayers and sermons.[123] Temple activities, while less tradition-bound, also moved in well-established patterns. During World War II, members contributed heavily to the war effort. The Sisterhood women knitted, crocheted, and baked cookies, served as hostesses for the USO, conducted first-aid classes, organized blood banks, sold war bonds, and assisted in the communal effort to resettle Jewish refugees from Nazi Germany. Men joined them in several of these activities, and were, in addition, involved in war production, civilian defense, and, of course, the armed forces. After the war, adult education became more of a temple priority. Classes, lectures, study groups, and discussion groups promised to give members "a new outlook on the world we live in." None of them were particularly well attended. Rabbi Reichert, meanwhile, continued his varied pastoral activities, the most characteristic feature of his rabbinate, and also participated in "larger communal activities, Jewish and general." Like his predecessors, he invited congregants to bask in his reflected glory by keeping them well informed of his many speaking engagements, awards, and recognitions.[124]

For all of the emphasis on tradition, however, Rockdale did introduce some innovations during the Reichert years. In part, the new postwar emphasis on Jewish (as opposed to "Rockdale") tradition and the acceleration of temple activities reflected a nationwide return to religion that enlivened both churches and synagogues in the 1950s. The innovations may also have reflected the impact that revelations about the Nazi destruction of European Jewry made upon the congregation, although this is more difficult to gauge. In January 1946, the congregation's president, Alex Frieder, recalled the "cataclysmic, world tottering" year just past, but failed to mention the atrocities and the death camps. He did, however, call upon the congregation to prepare for "the days ahead, so foreboding and ominous," with "a return to God." The following year, echoing Christian calls for a return to the church, he again exhorted congregants to "return to our faith and our synagogues," but this time his call was clearly placed within a Jewish context. He sought to ensure that "the six million Jewish martyrs [will] not have died in vain."[125]

Whether on account of the Holocaust or not, the postwar years did bring about a growing acceptance of symbolic ceremonialism, particularly among those concerned with religious education. Under Lilienthal and Philipson, Bene Israel had succeeded in intellectualizing Judaism and in discarding forms of Jewish expression that Classical Reform Judaism characterized as primitive or odd. Reichert relaxed some of this rigidity. As soon as Philipson retired, he reintroduced the bar mitzvah ceremony for those boys who wanted it. In 1947, Rockdale erected an outdoor *sukkah*, or temporary hut for the fall holiday of *Sukkot* (Tabernacles), recalling Israel's forty years of wandering in the desert. Where, under Philipson, the congregation had hung fruits from the ceiling and celebrated an indoor harvest festival, now the outdoor *sukkah*, once rejected as "primitive," was praised as a "beautiful traditional festival symbol."[126]

When Stanley Brav came to Rockdale as associate rabbi in 1948, he sought to encourage more of a return to traditionalism. Over the objection of some congregants, he began to chant the blessing over the wine (*kiddush*) at Friday night services. One of his daughters also became Bene Israel's first bat mitzvah. But these were all relatively minor ceremonial changes that could be justified on the basis of Philipson's own realization that Reform needed to recover "the warmth of religious emotion" which had been too quickly discarded.[127] They did not do serious violence to temple tradition as old-timers understood it. When Brav went further and sought to enforce the temple's stated but neglected requirement that Hebrew language instruction and weekday classes be compulsory for religious-school students, that was different. More than 500 members, an astonishingly large turnout, showed up at a special congregational meeting at which the new requirements were challenged and debated.[128] Following an impassioned speech by Murray Seasongood, who argued that Rockdale had produced thousands of fine Jews and fine Americans who knew no Hebrew whatsoever, the stipulation was abolished.[129] The message was clear. A majority of members, for all the latitude they extended to their rabbis, still expected them to adhere to the limits of "Rockdale tradition." Small-scale changes designed to attract new members or to satisfy younger ones were tolerated. But a serious breach with congregational tradition, as Brav's requirements were perceived to have been, would generate swift and divisive opposition, and would, in the end, fail decisively.

A year later, in 1954, Brav himself left Rockdale, having been informed that he would never succeed Reichert as senior rabbi. He privately blamed the rebuff on members of a "ruling clique," determined to have their own way in the congregation and to carry on as their fathers had done, without change. In fact, as the large turnout against the teaching of Hebrew suggests, opposition was much more widespread; the Lilienthal-Philipson tradition still carried great weight with members. Brav and forty-two like-minded congregants, having failed to reform Rockdale from within, now formed a more ritually-traditional Reform temple, Temple Sholom, located in the northern suburbs of Cincinnati where many Jews were then moving.[130]

In the wake of Brav's departure, both Rockdale's president and the director of its religious school wondered aloud about the congregation's future. "Are we, as members," they asked, "living in the glory of the past?" They warned congregants that "every institution which has a heritage is endangered by inertia, by timidity, by complacency, by a reluctance to keep abreast of progress."[131] The warning, however, fell largely on deaf ears. There seemed at that time little to worry about, for membership and activities increased during the 1950s, fueled by the baby boom, a nationwide religious revival, and the energies of many of Rockdale's women. Social groups within the congregation—the Sisterhood, the Men's Club, and the youth groups—showed particularly large gains. Their meetings drew impressive crowds, frequently larger than those at weekly services. Sparse attendance at Sabbath prayers did arouse some concern, and members were reminded, as part of an interfaith campaign to promote religion in American life, that "the family that prays together stays together."[132] But for the most part, the vitality of Rockdale's organizational life warded off fears that the congregation as a whole was suffering from lethargy.

Moreover, subtle changes were taking place. Increasingly, for example, Rockdale included among its stated goals such items as the need "to perpetuate Judaism as a way of life," "to cultivate a love and understanding of the Jewish heritage," and "to stimulate fellowship with Jews everywhere." Where once it had been enough for the temple to be the locus of religion, now members were expected to "feel" Jewish themselves and to bring the practice of Judaism into their homes. One postwar religious-school class reflected this new mood in its very title: the "Joy and Importance of Feeling that I am a Jew."[133]

The young state of Israel helped to shape this new attitude toward Judaism. With the establishment of the state in 1948, and its immediate recognition by the United States government, anti-Zionism faded at Bene Israel. The first stirrings of Israel-consciousness began to filter into selected areas of temple life: the youth groups reported how much they enjoyed Israeli dancing; the sisterhood advertised the "lovely Israeli items on display" in their gift shop.[134] Still, there remained a real concern, especially among temple stalwarts, that this change, like the others, should not result in Rockdale's becoming "too Jewish," as Rabbi Brav was perceived to have been. While leaders understood that the "glory of the past"—the Rockdale tradition—might have to be modified, they insisted that it not be totally compromised.

In 1962 Rabbi Victor Reichert retired. He was sixty-five, had spent thirty-six years with the temple, and now saw his own name added to the list of those who had decisively shaped Rockdale's path, along with Joseph Jonas, Max Lilienthal, and David Philipson. After 139 years, the congregation could still tell its history in the lives of four great men.

Rockdale had turned inward during the Reichert years, and had lost much of its national prestige. Yet it remained conscious of its distinguished heritage and committed to keeping its noble past alive. Year in and year out, it faithfully preserved its own brand of elegant, nondemanding worship services that stirred memory and evoked past glory. This was Rockdale's tradition, for better or for worse, and a powerful group of temple laymen guarded it closely. The loyalty inspired by tradition was perhaps Rockdale's greatest asset. It would sustain the congregation during the turbulent period that lay ahead.

Confronting a Changing World

The sixties were difficult years for Rockdale Temple. For a congregation that depended on tradition and rested on its laurels, the challenges of physical and spiritual change posed formidable threats to its identity and very existence. Having had but four senior rabbis in its entire history, the congregation now saw three more in the eight years from 1962 to 1970. By decade's end, the temple's home on Rockdale Avenue, designed to symbolize monumentality, grandeur, and permanence, stood abandoned: its interior in ruins, its stained-glass windows destroyed, its grand exterior boarded up, its grounds "decrepit and untidy."[135] Brought into disturbing conflict with a changing world, the congregation responded by retreating geographically and religiously. It stiffened its resistance against all innovations, especially those that seemed to threaten Rockdale's own venerable traditions.

Following Victor Reichert's retirement, Murray Blackman, who had served as his associate and co-rabbi since 1956, was promoted to senior rabbi. Admired as an eloquent orator, Blackman was well liked by many in the congregation, but a minority dissented. At a congregational meeting to elect Blackman, "a number of members expressed critical disapproval of Rabbi Blackman's discharge of his pastoral duties and adverse criticism of his leadership as a congregational Rabbi." Forty-two of the hundred or so members present indicated in their votes that Blackman did not have their full support.[136]

Stung by this criticism, Blackman struggled in the years that followed to win his critics over. He regularly reported to the board of trustees on his involvement in community affairs, on his radio appearances, and particularly on the number of pastoral calls that he had made and the time he devoted to pastoral counseling. He tried not to make waves and felt constrained from advocating any large-scale changes that might provoke controversy. Yet dissatisfaction continued. In the area of pastoral care, for example, the role of the rabbi had expanded considerably under Reichert. Prodded and assisted by his wife, Louise, he had been scrupulous about calling on new members, visiting those in hospital, and comforting the bereaved. This was in line with a general twentieth-century trend toward a larger pastoral role for clergy and reflected a belief, evident at Rockdale and in synagogues throughout the country, that earlier rabbis had focused too heavily on the mind and neglected the soul. Blackman carried forward Reichert's initiatives in this area, but with less success. Even his wife came in for criticism, some alleging that she was less interested in congregants' personal needs than her predecessor had been.[137]

Blackman again ran into trouble on the one occasion when he did challenge temple tradition, seeking to abolish the annual congregational Passover seder on the grounds that the holiday was meant to be observed at home with the family. Resistance developed, and the sisterhood proposed, as a compromise, that the congregational seder be moved to the second night of the holiday, giving families the chance to celebrate together on the first night. This seemed to the congregation like a happy means of reconciling temple tradition and family togetherness, and was accepted. Blackman, who feared that the celebration of two seders might be misinterpreted as a return to "Orthodox practice," was overruled, another indication that in the absence of strong rabbinic leadership in congregational affairs authority had begun to shift back to the laity.[138]

Blackman enjoyed no more success in his campaign to promote greater attendance at worship services. Although he appealed to the board of trustees to "set the pace for the rest of the Congregation" by attending services themselves, the message fell on deaf ears.[139] In this case, as in so many others, his priorities turned out to be different from those of the congregation.

The central problem that Rockdale faced during Blackman's tenure was a demographic one. As Jews moved out to the northern suburbs, the congregation's continued existence at the corner of Rockdale and Harvey Streets became less and less tenable. Even in the 1940s it had become evident that the center of Cincinnati's Jewish population was beginning to shift. This was one of the factors that encouraged Stanley Brav to found Temple Sholom in the new area of Jewish settlement. In 1955, Rockdale itself spent $95,000 to purchase a site on Dawn Road in Roselawn to hold for "future needs." Plans were announced to open a satellite Sunday and mid-week afternoon Hebrew school on the site, to supplement Rockdale's overcrowded educational facility where every available space "including rest rooms" was being utilized for class-rooms. But a fundraising campaign fell far short of expectations and the property was never developed. Ultimately, the idea was abandoned "due to substantial resistance to consider any move from [the] present location." [140]

By the time Murray Blackman became associate rabbi at Rockdale, in 1956, the area for several blocks around the temple was already largely inhabited by black families. Thousands of poorer blacks crowded into the area in the next decade when the predominantly black West End neighborhood of the city (previously the home of Cincinnati's Jews) was torn down to accommodate highway and redevelopment projects. With social and recreational facilities lacking and the racial climate in the area becoming ever more tense, the movement of white Jewish families to the north accelerated. The temple became isolated.

Blackman, now senior rabbi, understood that, unless it moved, "the congregation would diminish in size and in vigor." [141] More and more members were calling for a new building program, complaining that Rockdale had become too inconvenient to get to. Some resigned to join one of the two small Reform congregations established in the northern suburbs already. [142] By the mid 1960s, the Dawn Road site had been abandoned as unsatisfactory, in part because Jews were already moving further north. After an extensive search for a more appropriate site for the temple, the congregation settled upon a property in the village of Amberley, which a member offered to them at a price below market value. Across the street from Brav's congregation and right next door to the site where Isaac M. Wise Temple planned to move, it was "the only feasible site available." Brushing aside concerns that "all three of the major Reform Congregations would be located adjacent to one another," the temple's leaders decided to push ahead. [143] They believed, rightly as it turned out, that historical loyalties, as well as the very real social and ideological differences separating the different Reform temples from one another would allow all three to maintain their distinctive identities and bases of support even as they sat side by side in Amberley. [144]

A massive fund-raising campaign for the projected $2,480,000 needed to construct the new Bene Israel was announced in 1966.[145] Meanwhile, the temple at Rockdale and Harvey, which had hardly been given a "lick and a promise" since the congregation first thought about moving back in the 1950s, was looking increasingly shabby and membership had plunged into the 700s.[146] This posed a financial crisis, so even while the new building-fund campaign went forward, the congregation's board tried, without much success, to encourage congregants to increase their regular dues voluntarily in order that the operating expenses of the old temple might still be covered.[147]

Ground was broken at the Amberley site in January 1967. Everyone hoped that building would proceed rapidly to effect as smooth a transition as possible. But a series of tumultuous shocks lay ahead. First, in April 1967, Murray Blackman, to everyone's surprise and shortly after his contract had been renewed by the congregation, announced that he was resigning from Rockdale in order to fulfil "long range personal and professional objectives" as the rabbi of St. Thomas in the Virgin Islands.[148] Actually, there had been signs before that Blackman was unhappy at Rockdale, and some members were certainly unhappy with him. But for a congregation that had enjoyed almost eight decades of stable rabbinic leadership, and had not seen a senior rabbi leave for another pulpit since Raphael Benjamin departed for New York in 1888, the idea that someone could find a more satisfying position than at Rockdale was almost inconceivable—a sure sign that something was wrong. It was arranged that Victor Reichert would serve as interim rabbi until the congregation could hire a new spiritual leader.

Even before Blackman left town, a second and still more serious crisis arose. Congregants departing a June service in honor of the temple's confirmation class found themselves caught up in the midst of a full-blown urban riot. Fortunately, although a few cars were hit by stones and bricks, no one was seriously hurt. Beyond a few broken windows, there was no significant damage to the temple either, although the confirmation service itself—a service wherein teenage boys and girls publicly declare their adherence to Judaism—had to be shifted to the Jewish Community Center in Roselawn.[149] But the violence, and the tense racial situation that the riot reflected, raised questions about whether it was safe to continue holding any services and activities in Avondale. Meanwhile, the projected completion of the new facility in Amberley was still more than a year away.

The board of trustees wrestled with two factors in deciding what to do, "one being practicality and the other the moral issue." It knew that many members would not be happy having to come to Avondale for services, much less to bring children there for religious school, but it felt uncomfortable, particularly given the liberal and ethical tenets of Reform Judaism, about fleeing the beloved temple from fear of the surrounding black population. Besides, without a building where would the congregation go? Some members felt, in addition, that it would be difficult to explain to children why the congregation was running away rather than staying and trying to help. In the end, then, and not without serious misgivings, the board decided to continue holding services and religious school in Avondale, "with adequate protection" provided.[150]

One prominent member of the 1967 Rockdale board still recalls the somber mood of the congregation at that time. If ground had not already been broken in Amberley, he believes, the congregation would probably have collapsed altogether, for it could certainly not attract new congregants to Avondale and was having trouble holding on to its existing ones.[151] Weekly worship services in the vast sanctuary attracted no more than forty or fifty individuals. There was no sense of spiritual dynamism, no institutional activity, just a barely concealed feeling of fear at what might happen next as the ghetto seethed on the brink of another explosion.

Into this maelstrom marched Rabbi David Hachen, Blackman's replacement as senior rabbi.[152] The board, in selecting him, made a conscious decision to steer Rockdale in a new direction. "We knew we had to move from the kind of classical Reform we'd had in order to survive," one member of the selection committee recalls.[153] Hachen, who represented the more traditional wing of the Reform movement but who also had ties both to Cincinnati and to Rockdale (his wife was a Cincinnatian and his brother served on the Rockdale board) seemed like the ideal person to chart a middle ground between Rockdale tradition and contemporary Reform.

Hachen's first year was a trying one. Following the assassination of Dr. Martin Luther King, Jr., on April 4, 1968, rioting broke out in Cincinnati, and fear gripped the community. Thereafter, use of the building by members was severely curtailed, and temporary arrangements were made to use other facilities for most temple functions until the new sanctuary in Amberley could be readied.[154] At the same time, in a move aimed at conciliation, the congregation's leaders invited "highly responsible" black community groups serving the area's youth to utilize what was left of the temple's facilities free of charge. High-minded members felt that in this way the congregation "could make a real contribution to the community" as well as establish "the possibility of a permanent future use of the building," perhaps at city expense.[155] More cynical members considered the program a cheap way of protecting the congregation against further vandalism and violence. Soon, community groups took over much of the facility, painting the temple's social hall red and black. Security was provided by young, armed black men patrolling the temple grounds. Regular Jewish worship continued to be held in the building each Sabbath and on holidays, but under extremely trying conditions. On one occasion, a bullet was shot through one of the windows during a religious service.[156]

While Rockdale's building, its symbol of tradition and majesty for so many years, was being physically assaulted from without, other symbols of Rockdale traditionalism came under attack from within. Hachen, mindful of his mandate to lead Rockdale into a new era, energetically set about teaching new courses, meeting with members at informal gatherings in private homes, and reintroducing rituals and ceremonies, like *Havdalah*, the brief service separating Sabbath from the work week, that Reform Jews elsewhere had come to find meaningful. He also brought more Hebrew into the worship service and toned down its air of formality. This mixture of personal warmth and greater religious traditionalism seemed to him to be both what the congregation needed at this juncture in its history and what its leaders had asked him to provide.[157] But he, and many members of the board as well, underestimated the pull of Rockdale's own sense of tradition: the austere Judaism expounded by Max Lilienthal, David Philipson, and Victor Reichert. Like the temple building itself, this was part of the congregation's heritage and ethos. It was what made members feel at home at Rockdale, part of their very identity as Jews.

Within four months of Hachen's arrival at Rockdale, he already faced criticism about "certain aspects of rituals and traditions" that made some members feel uncomfortable. Those with "complaints or differences of opinion" were encouraged to meet him face-to-face so he could explain his position.[158] Classical Reform turned out to have more defenders than Hachen had realized. Even more than by his ritual innovations, however, members felt distressed at the rabbi's adamant refusal to perform mixed marriages (without conversion). True, David Philipson had not performed them either, but Victor Reichert did, within limits, and quite a number of members and their children were themselves intermarried. Was the rabbi implying that they were not good Jews? Would he deny members' children who sought to intermarry the right to be wed by a rabbi? Intermarriage, of course, was a volatile and emotional issue not only at Rockdale but within the Reform movement as a whole, for it cut to the heart of the whole question of Jewish identification, raising such issues as who is a Jew, what are the responsibilities of a Jew, and what distinguishes Jews from other Americans. Rockdale Jews were not used to confronting these kinds of difficult questions, and many reacted angrily to Hachen's view that Judaism sometimes imposed inconvenient burdens; that was not the kind of Judaism that they had traditionally been taught. While Hachen defended his position in a lengthy document distributed to all members and at a public discussion of the question sponsored by the temple's brotherhood (its men's club), the issue continued to simmer. Some members, particularly those with children whose marriages (intermarriages) Hachen had refused to perform, resigned.[159]

The mood of the congregation at this time was captured in a poll of the members on the question of what the new temple in Amberley should be called. Precedent suggested that it be named the Ridge Road Temple after its new location. The congregation might also have gone back to using the name Bene Israel, its official name. But a clear majority of the members elected instead to retain the name "Rockdale Temple," with all that it implied.[160] They thus sought symbolically to maintain the traditions established over the sixty-seven years at that location. In a tumultuous period, they yearned for continuity, a new temple that would remind them of the old, of what they had been and what they stood for. They were not looking for changes, and certainly not for "inconvenient burdens."[161]

David Hachen, of course, had a different agenda, and within a year it was clear that he and the congregation were on a collision course. Given the fragile condition of the congregation, the need to raise substantial funds, and the desire to win back old members once the move to Amberley was accomplished, there was a general desire to avoid the kind of controversy that Hachen engendered. Since reconciliation seemed impossible, the board had little choice but to request the rabbi's resignation. On March 21, 1969, it was announced to the congregation.[162]

Hachen's resignation marked the end of efforts to radically transform Rockdale. Having tasted change and found it bitter, the congregation returned to its own traditions, resolving to carry Rockdale's time-tested ethos out with it to suburbia. With that, the sense of proceeding "from crisis to crisis," seemed to abate.[163] In May, the congregation moved into its new facility in Amberley. By the fall, it had a new rabbi, Harold Hahn. He effected change much more slowly, and did, on a case by case basis, perform intermarriages. At the same time, his personality and warmth drew members back to the temple and promoted reconciliation.

Problems remained back on Rockdale Avenue where black militant groups demanded that the congregation deed the old temple to them, if not outright then for a symbolic payment of $400 paid at the rate of $1 per year for 400 years. To back up their demands, they refused to let anyone from the temple enter the building in order to collect the congregation's historic and religious property.[164] When the congregation stopped paying the building's utility fees, the place fell into a shambles. On September 14, 1970, it was fire-bombed and mostly destroyed amidst continuing unrest in the neighborhood.[165] Today, the temple no longer exists: it was razed by the city and the site was converted into a playing field.

Conclusion

Having begun in 1824 as an all-embracing synagogue-community, Bene Israel had, over the years, withstood a whole series of changes and challenges. Competition from other synagogues, membership secessions, aesthetic and ritual reforms, ideological innovations, great rabbis, new synagogue buildings, changing attitudes toward women, contraction into a worship-focused congregation, expansion into a synagogue-center, identification with Classical Reform Judaism, confrontations with developments in Cincinnati urban life, encounters with new developments within American Jewish life—all these and more shaped the congregation. They created its unique ethos and tradition.

At the same time, like synagogues across the length and breadth of the United States, Bene Israel also experienced through the years a wide variety of competing pressures and demands. Jewish tradition, American society, various old world customs, the rabbis it hired, the officers it elected, the members it sought to attract and hold, the Reform movement to which it adhered, and in time its own heritage and traditions all pulled it in different, sometimes contradictory, directions. Repeatedly, Bene Israel struggled to reconcile all of these conflicting forces and to find its own path. The history of the congregation, as well as its future, lie in the effort to keep to that path: to move ahead, twisting and turning as conditions do, without losing its way.

APPENDIX

K. K. Bene Israel Membership

YEAR	NUMBER OF MEMBERS	COMPOSITION	MILESTONE
1846	108		
1848	126		
1850	138		
1855			Max Lilienthal arrives.
1869	216		Mound Street temple opens.
1871	166		
1872	167	Includes 9 widows	
1873	187	178 men, 9 widows	
1874	197	170 men	
1875	200		
1876	205		
1877	206	190 men, 15 widows	
1878	214	199 men, 15 widows	
1879	236	Includes 18 widows	
1880	228	Includes 20 in arrears	
1882	279	Includes 255 in good standing	Raphael Benjamin arrives.
1883	301		
1884	307		
1886	287	All in good standing (AIGS)	
1888	299	AIGS, includes 30 widows	David Philipson arrives.
1889	302	AIGS, includes 34 widows	
1892	331		
1893	341		
1894	316	Plus 29 in arrears	
1895	317	Plus 26 in arrears	
1896	351		
1897	359	Includes 22 in arrears	
1898	354	Includes 22 in arrears	
1899	363	Includes 28 in arrears	
1900	367	Includes 23 in arrears	Women can become associate members.

CHAPTER THREE

K. K. Bene Israel Membership (*continued*)

YEAR	NUMBER OF MEMBERS	COMPOSITION	MILESTONE
1901	396		
1902	395	Includes 371 in good standing	
1903	418	Includes 9 in arrears	
1904	440	420 in good standing	
1905	430	407 in good standing	
1906	475		Rockdale temple opens.
1907	467	455 in good standing	
1912	480		
1917	499		
1918	531		
1919	520		
1920	575		
1921	643		
1922	716	697 members and 19 estates	
1923	678		
1924	767		
1925	792		
1926	823		
1927	930		
1928	950		
1929	940		
1930	942		
1931	889		
1932	819		
1933	782		
1934	750		
1935	721		
1936	716		
1937	704		
1938	731		Victor Reichert becomes senior rabbi.
1939	778	Representing 2,000 people.	

K. K. Bene Israel Membership (*continued*)

YEAR	NUMBER OF MEMBERS	COMPOSITION	MILESTONE
1941	800		
1945	899		Begin to count by families?
1947	961		
1948	1,014		
1950	1,089		
1953	1,083		
1954	1,059	"Families"	
1955	1,062		
1956	1,064		
1957	1,075		
1958	1,057	"Families"	
1959	1,054		
1960	1,054		
1961	1,045		
1962	1,063		Murray Blackman becomes senior rabbi.
1967			David Hachen becomes senior rabbi.
1970	850	"Real membership"	Temple in Amberley opens. Harold Hahn becomes senior rabbi.

NOTES

1. Joseph Jonas, "The Jews in Ohio" (1843), reprinted in Morris U. Schappes, ed., *A Documentary History of the Jews in the United States, 1654–1875* (New York: Schocken, 1971), pp. 223–35. This famous memoir, the best primary source on early Cincinnati Jews, was originally printed in the *Occident* 1 (1844), and is also reprinted in Jacob R. Marcus, *Memoirs of American Jews, 1775–1865* (Philadelphia: Jewish Publication Society, 1955), vol. 1, pp. 203–15. Unattributed quotations below are taken from this work.

2. The cemetery was needed to bury Benjamin Lape, a Jew by birth, who had lived in Cincinnati as a Christian but on his deathbed asked to be buried "according to the rites of the Jewish faith." See David Philipson, *The Oldest Jewish*

Congregation in the West [*Bene Israel, Cincinnati*] *Souvenir of Seventieth Anniversary, 1824–1894* (Cincinnati, 1894), pp. 26–27. Jews frequently established cemeteries prior to synagogues, for worship could always be conducted in a private home.

3. Philipson, *Oldest Jewish Congregation*, p. 3.

4. Letter "To the Elders of the Jewish congregation at Charleston," from J. Joseph, Joseph Jonas, D. J. Johnson, Phineas Moses, July 3, 1825, American Jewish Archives, Cincinnati Ohio (hereafter: AJA), also reprinted in David Philipson, "The Cincinnati Community in 1825," *Publications of the American Jewish Historical Society* 10 (1902), pp. 97–99; reprinted in Schappes, *Documentary History*, pp. 177–179.

5. The original charter is reprinted in *Charter By-Laws and Regulations of Kal A Kodesh Beneh Israel . . .* (Cincinnati, 1859), pp. 3–4. For a variant spelling of the congregation's name, see Joseph Jonas's 1836 consecration address to the congregation, excerpted in Jonathan D. Sarna and Nancy H. Klein, *The Jews of Cincinnati* (Cincinnati: Center for the American Jewish Experience, 1989), p. 28.

6. Martin A. Cohen, "Synagogue: History and Tradition," in *The Encyclopedia of Religion*, ed. Mircea Eliade (New York: Macmillan and Free Press, 1987), vol. 14, p. 212.

7. Jonathan D. Sarna, "The Evolution of the American Synagogue," in *The Americanization of the Jews*, ed. Robert M. Seltzer and Norman J. Cohen, forthcoming, and Leon A. Jick, *The Americanization of the Synagogue, 1820–1870* (Hanover, N.H.: Brandeis University Press, 1976), p. 21.

8. "By Laws of Kal A Kodesh Beneh Israel," K. K. Bene Israel Trustee Minutes, 1842, Cincinnati, Ohio (Congregation Bene Israel Records, AJA; all manuscript sources come from the Congregation Bene Israel Collection at the AJA, unless otherwise noted).

9. Philipson, "Cincinnati Community," p. 28.

10. "Congregation Bene Israel, Cincinnati, Ohio Charter an[d] By-Laws, 1842–1843," Article 5, Section 4, in KKBI Trustee Minutes, 1842.

11. See Jonathan D. Sarna, "'A Sort of Paradise for the Hebrews': The Lofty Vision of Cincinnati Jews," in Sarna and Klein, *Jews of Cincinnati*, pp. 1–21.

12. [Samuel Osgood], "First Synagogue in the West," *The Western Messenger* 2 (October 1836): 204.

13. Rachel Wischnitzer, *Synagogue Architecture in the United States* (Philadelphia: Jewish Publication Society, 1955), p. 37; for a full description and sketch of the building, see Sarna and Klein, *Jews of Cincinnati*, p. 31.

14. As it turned out, the $119.50 that Bene Israel members sent to Beth Elohim was more than it received from any other American Jewish community outside of South Carolina; see Charles Reznikoff and Uriah Z. Engelman, *The Jews of Charleston* (Philadelphia: Jewish Publication Society, 1950), pp. 137, 294. Doubtless, some at Bene Israel recalled that in 1825 the Charleston congregation had aided them (see above, n. 4).

15. Stephen G. Mostov, "A 'Jerusalem' on the Ohio: The Social and Economic History of Cincinnati's Jewish Community, 1840–1875" (Ph.D. diss., Brandeis University, 1981), pp. 54, 61.

16. Ibid., pp. 105–41; Maxwell Whiteman, "Notions, Dry Goods, and Clothing: An Introduction to the Study of the Cincinnati Peddler," *Jewish Quarterly Review* 53 (April 1963): 306–21; Sarna and Klein, *Jews of Cincinnati*, pp. 4–7, 36–40.

17. K. K. Bene Israel (hereafter: KKBI) Vestry Minutes, February 24, 1841.

18. Joseph Jonas alludes to these differences in his memoir (in Schappes, *Documentary History*, p. 227). See also I. M. Wise's comments on "minhag" reprinted in James G. Heller, *As Yesterday When It Is Past: A History of the Isaac M. Wise Temple—K.K.B'nai Yeshurun—of Cincinnati in Commemoration of the Centenary of Its Founding* (Cincinnati: Isaac M. Wise Temple, 1942), pp. 19–20.

19. Mostov, "A 'Jerusalem' on the Ohio," pp. 147–48.

20. Synagogue membership figures were far smaller than Jewish population estimates might lead one to expect. Even in 1851, when Cincinnati housed four synagogues, an estimated 22 percent of the city's Jews were unaffiliated. See Mostov, "A 'Jerusalem' on the Ohio," p. 150.

21. Reprinted in Heller, *As Yesterday*, pp. 26–27.

22. See the text in Israel Goldstein, *A Century of Judaism in New York* (New York: B'nai Jeshurun, 1930), pp. 55–56. A different section of the B'nai Jeshurun constitution was appropriated by Congregation Covenant of Peace in Easton (1842); see Joshua Trachtenberg, *Consider the Years: The Story of the Jewish Community of Easton, 1752–1942* (Easton: Temple Brith Sholom, 1944), p. 237.

23. Mostov, "A 'Jerusalem' on the Ohio," pp. 151, 155.

24. Ibid., pp. 151–58.

25. The increasing numerical importance of German members at Bene Israel was reflected in the 1859 bylaws, which were printed in both English and German, Bylaws file.

26. Sidney E. Mead, *The Lively Experiment: The Shaping of Christianity in America* (New York: Harper & Row, 1976), p. 113.

27. By Laws of Kal A Kodesh Beneh Israel, 1842–43, Bylaws file.

28. KKBI Vestry Minutes, May 12, 1844.

29. See, for example, *Occident* 10 (1852): 219–21, 311; 11 (1853): 63–71, 162–75, 569–72; and the tendentious account in I. Harold Sharfman, *The First Rabbi: Origins of Conflict between Orthodox and Reform* (Malibu: Joseph Simon/Pangloss Press, 1988), pp. 296–300.

30. It is difficult to determine which set of bylaws served as a model for the other, or whether Bene Israel had any bylaws before 1842. It is also possible that both congregations borrowed their bylaws from somewhere else. (See bylaw files in KKBI and K. K. B'nai Yeshurun collections.)

31. Heller, *As Yesterday*, pp. 32–41; KKBI Trustee Minutes, November 15, 1846; May 15, 1846; February 12, 1848; May 9, 1848.

32. Jick, *The Americanization of the Synagogue, 1820–1870*, pp. 115–16; Jakob J. Petuchowski, *Prayerbook Reform in Europe* (New York: World Union for Progressive Judaism, 1968), pp. 105–27. This understanding of the role of aesthetics in Jewish worship has been influenced by Riv-Ellen Prell, *Prayer and*

CHAPTER THREE

Community: The Havurah in American Judaism (Detroit: Wayne State University Press, 1989).

33. KKBI Vestry Records, May 8, 1843; KKBI Minutes, esp. Nov. 11, 1846; August 1, 1847; May 9, 1848.

34. KKBI Trustees, February 12, 1848.

35. KKBI Vestry records, June 6, 1843. "Mr. Simon Cohen, Jacob Hilf and Jacob Ayer made quite a noise outside of the Shool . . . during divine service also W J Myer cursed all the Vestry."

36. KKBI Trustees, September 26, 1847.

37. Ibid., November 1, 1846.

38. Ibid., February 12, 1848.

39. Ibid., April 7, 1847, January 30, 1848.

40. Ibid., January 30, 1848. The Bene Israel matzas committee usually worked together with a similar committee from B'nai Yeshurun in overseeing matzah production.

41. Ibid., July 25, 1846. See the *Shulchan Aruch* (Code of Jewish Law), Yoreh Deah, 376.14 and especially the commentary of Y. M. Epstein, *Aruch HaShulchan,* who reviews the various opinions.

42. The two paragraphs that follow are taken, with slight revisions, from Sarna, "'A Sort of Paradise for the Hebrews,'" in Sarna and Klein, *Jews of Cincinnati,* p. 14.

43. Isaac M. Wise, *Reminiscences* (1901; 2d ed., New York: Central Synagogue of New York, 1945); James G. Heller, *Isaac M. Wise: His Life, Work and Thought* (New York: Union of American Hebrew Congregations, 1965), pp. 124–83; Naphtali J. Rubinger, "Dismissal in Albany," *American Jewish Archives* 24 (November 1972): 161–62; Jick, *The Americanization of the Synagogue, 1820–1870,* pp. 115, 121–29, 154–55.

44. Quoted in Mostov, "A 'Jerusalem' on the Ohio," p. 170.

45. Samuel Bruel, "Affairs in Cincinnati," *Occident* 13 (December 1855): 458–64.

46. Dr. Mayer and N. Malzer, "Congregation B'nai Jeshurun, Cincinnati," *Occident* 11 (June 1853): 162–75.

47. On this chapter in Lilienthal's life, see Michael Stanislawski, *Tsar Nicholas and the Jews* (Philadelphia: Jewish Publication Society, 1983), pp. 69–96.

48. David Philipson, *Max Lilienthal: His Life and Writings* (New York, 1915); Hyman B. Grinstein, *The Rise of the Jewish Community of New York, 1654–1860* (Philadelphia: Jewish Publication Society, 1945); Morton J. Merowitz, "Max Lilienthal (1814–1882)—Jewish Educator in Nineteenth-Century America," *Yivo Annual* 15 (1974): 46–65.

49. While several sources claim that Lilienthal was hired upon Wise's recommendation, David Philipson, in his biography of Lilienthal, says that the recommendation came from "prominent Jewish families" whose sons attended Lilienthal's New York boarding school (*Max Lilienthal,* p. 59).

50. KKBI Board of Trustees Minutes, June 5, 1855; see I. M. Wise's reminiscence of Lilienthal in *The Hebrew Review* 2 (1881–82): 184–90.

51. KKBI Trustees, August 1, 1855; *Occident* 13 (December 1855): 460.

52. *Occident* 13 (December 1855): 459; Sarna, "A Sort of Paradise for the Hebrews," in Sarna and Klein, *Jews of Cincinnati*, p. 14.

53. *Occident* 13 (December 1855): 462–64; KKBI Trustees, September 9, 1855; September 16, 1855.

54. KKBI Congregational Minutes, October 28, 1865; November 10, 1867.

55. KKBI Trustees, November 5, 1854 ("scheta" [ritual slaughter] committee is omitted in appointment of new congregational committees), May 17, 1857; October 25, 1857.

56. See L. Hearn, "Cincinnati Saints," quoted in Sarna and Klein, *Jews of Cincinnati*, p. 50.

57. *St. Louis Jewish Tribune* (1883), reprinted in Sarna and Klein, *Jews of Cincinnati*, p. 86.

58. KKBI Trustees, April 8, 1863.

59. See Heller, *Isaac M. Wise*, pp. 377–79.

60. KKBI Trustees, April 8, 1863.

61. Philipson, *Oldest Jewish Congregation*, pp. 53–54.

62. KKBI Trustees, March 24, 1868; Congregational Minutes, April 2, 1868; Sarna and Klein, *Jews of Cincinnati*, p. 56.

63. KKBI Trustees, October 14, 1877.

64. KKBI Congregational Minutes, October 19, 1873.

65. Ibid., September 4, 1869.

66. For head-covering discussion, see ibid., September 4, 1869; October 11, 1874; February 28, 1875; September 5, 1875; September 26, 1875; October 31, 1875.

67. Ibid., October 19, 1873.

68. Ibid., November 5, 1876.

69. KKBI Trustees, April 9, 1865; May 21, 1865. The tradition of paying old or idle men to make a *minyan* was brought over from Europe; see *Encyclopedia Judaica* (Jerusalem, 1972), vol. 12, col. 67, s.v. "minyan."

70. KKBI Congregational Minutes, October 19, 1873.

71. Ibid., October 29, 1884.

72. Philipson, *Oldest Jewish Congregation*, p. 65.

73. For a sketch of Benjamin's career, see *Universal Jewish Encyclopedia* (1948), vol. 2, p. 185.

74. KKBI Congregational Minutes, October 28, 1883.

75. Letter from Raphael Benjamin to Board of Trustees, December 27, 1883, in KKBI Congregational Minutes; KKBI Trustees, June 11, 1888.

76. On Philipson, see Douglas Kohn, "The Dean of American Rabbis: A Critical Study of the Life, Career and Significance of David Philipson, as Re-

flected in His Writings" (Rabbinic Thesis, Hebrew Union College-Jewish Institute of Religion, 1987); and David Philipson's autobiography, *My Life As An American Jew* (Cincinnati: 1941). Philipson was the congregation's first rabbi to be ordained in America. Lilienthal had been ordained in Germany and Benjamin in England.

77. Philipson, *My Life*, pp. 8, 57.

78. Ibid., p. 57; KKBI Congregational Minutes, June 17, 1888.

79. KKBI Congregational Minutes, October 14, 1888.

80. Philipson, *My Life*, pp. 61–63.

81. See Kerry M. Olitzky, "The Sunday-Sabbath Movement in American Reform Judaism: Strategy or Evolution," *American Jewish Archives* 34 (April 1982): 79; Philipson's diary (with valuable annotations) as reproduced in Stanley F. Chyet, "Isaac Mayer Wise: Portraits by David Philipson," in Bertram W. Korn, *A Bicentennial Festschrift for Jacob Rader Marcus* (Waltham, 1976), esp. pp. 85–88.

82. KKBI Congregational Minutes, November 25, 1888; December 15, 1889.

83. Ibid., October 29, 1911; October 31, 1915; October 27, 1922; 1930 *Yearbook*. In 1913, Bene Yeshurun also introduced "short talks . . . and also some musical numbers" on Sunday morning; see Heller, *As Yesterday*, p. 177. For the larger Sunday debate in Reform Judaism, see Michael A. Meyer, *Response to Modernity: A History of the Reform Movement in Judaism* (New York: Oxford University Press, 1988), pp. 290–92; Sidney L. Regner, "The Rise and Decline of the Sunday Service," *Journal of Reform Judaism* (Fall 1980): 30–38; and Kerry M. Olitzky's articles in *American Jewish Archives* 34 (1982): 75–82; *Journal of Reform Judaism* (Summer 1984), pp. 66–71; and *American Jewish History* 74 (1985): 356–68.

84. KKBI Congregational Minutes, November 6, 1890.

85. Philipson, *My Life*, p. 95.

86. Lance Sussman, "The Suburbanization of American Judaism as Reflected in Synagogue Building and Architecture, 1945–1975," *American Jewish History* 75 (September 1985): 32.

87. KKBI Congregational Minutes, "President's Report," October 16, 1904.

88. Ibid., October 31, 1909; October 27, 1912; October 25, 1908.

89. Mordecai M. Kaplan, *Judaism as a Civilization* (New York: Schocken, 1967; orig. ed., 1934), p. 425; Marshall Sklare, *Conservative Judaism* (New York: Schocken, 1972; orig. ed., 1955), pp. 129–45; Deborah Dash Moore, *At Home in America: Second Generation New York Jews* (New York: Columbia University Press, 1981), pp. 123–47. Sklare (p. 305) points out that Kaplan and his followers were not themselves leaders of the synagogue-center movement "but in reality their role was confined chiefly to reflecting some of the contemporary developments." For discussions of Orthodox synagogue-centers, see Aaron I. Reichel, *The Maverick Rabbi* (Norfolk: Donning, 1984), pp. 87–327, and Leo Jung, *The Path of a Pioneer* (New York: Soncino, 1980), pp. 63–92. For a general discussion of the American synagogue-center, see David Kaufman, "'Shul with a Pool': The Synagogue-Center in American Jewish Life, 1875–1925" (Ph.D. diss., Brandeis University, 1993).

90. KKBI Congregational Minutes, "President's Report," October 28, 1906; KKBI Trustees Minutes, October 27, 1907; October 31, 1909; October 26, 1913.

91. KKBI 1930 Yearbook, "President's Report."

92. KKBI Congregational Minutes, October 28, 1900; Trustees Minutes, October 16, 1904.

93. KKBI Congregational Minutes, October 25, 1903.

94. KKBI Letterbook, letter of KKBI secretary to Mrs. J. Walter Freiberg, November 2, 1906.

95. Ibid., letter from secretary of KKBI to Mrs. Stella S. Rosenberg, secretary, Cincinnati Section, Council of Jewish Women, November 2, 1906.

96. KKBI Congregational Minutes, October 26, 1913.

97. Ibid., October 25, 1914.

98. KKBI 1925 Yearbook, "Annual Report of the President," "Report of the Rockdale Avenue Temple Sisterhood"; KKBI Trustees Minutes, April 5, 1923.

99. "Memorials in Honor of Julius Freiberg," 1906, AJA.

100. KKBI Congregational Minutes, October 20, 1921; KKBI Trustees Minutes, May 5, 1921.

101. Until 1914, Philipson was joined on the pulpit by a cantor. Morris Goldstein—cantor, composer, and artist—had preceded Philipson at Bene Israel; he served the congregation until his death in 1906. When his successor, Joseph Mandelberg, resigned in 1914, Philipson himself began to read the prayers, joined only by the choir (KKBI Congregational Minutes, October 25, 1914). From this time on, all spiritual activities at the temple were consolidated within the rabbi's sphere.

102. Philipson, My Life, 203.

103. Ibid., pp. 72, 277; see Kohn, "The Dean of American Rabbis," pp. 159–202.

104. Philipson, My Life, pp. 72, 169–70; see Sarna, "'A Sort of Paradise for the Hebrews,'" in Sarna and Klein, Jews of Cincinnati, p. 9.

105. American Israelite, November 17, 1889, reprinted in Philipson, My Life, pp. 72–73.

106. Philipson, My Life, pp. 67–68; Zane Miller, Boss Cox's Cincinnati (Chicago, 1968), pp. 134, 269; Sarna, "'A Sort of Paradise for the Hebrews,'" in Sarna and Klein, Jews of Cincinnati, p. 12.

107. Philipson, My Life, pp. 270–75.

108. KKBI Congregational Minutes, October 31, 1920; October 20, 1921.

109. The proceedings of the "Centennial Pageant" are reprinted in the 1924 edition of Philipson, The Oldest Jewish Congregation.

110. Alfred Segal, quoted in Philipson, My Life, p. 497.

111. For the 1928 festivities, see Addresses and Testimonials on the Occasion of Rev. Dr. David Philipson's Fortieth Anniversary with Congregation Bene Israel, Cincinnati, Ohio, November 3, 1928 (Cincinnati, 1928).

112. Quoted in Philipson, My Life, pp. 361–62.

113. Meyer, *Response to Modernity*, pp. 296–98; 303–7. For the larger setting, see Sydney E. Ahlstrom, *A Religious History of the American People* (New Haven: Yale University Press, 1972), pp. 895–931; Robert T. Handy, "The American Religious Depression, 1925–1935," *Church History* 29 (1960): 3–16.

114. Interview with Victor and Louise Reichert, November 1988.

115. "Voices from the People," *Cincinnati Enquirer*, May 6, 1932, and May ?, 1932 (clippings at American Jewish Archives). See also Aaron Rakeffet-Rothkoff, *The Silver Era: Rabbi Eliezer Silver and His Generation* (New York: Feldheim, 1981), pp. 82–87.

116. See Kohn, "Dean of American Rabbis," p. 137: "He had considered retiring earlier, but he decided to keep going to round out a half century in one congregation: 'This will stand as the record in this country. For that reason and that reason alone I am continuing.'"

117. See Fred Rosenbaum, *Architects of Reform* (Berkeley: Magnes Museum, 1980), pp. 125–46.

118. KKBI 1939 *Yearbook*, p. 10.

119. Sarna and Klein, *Jews of Cincinnati*, p. 141.

120. Gunther Plaut, one of five German seminary students who were brought out of Germany to study at Hebrew Union College, recalls his first Sabbath service in America at Rockdale Temple, for which they dressed as they would have in Germany. After the service he and his friends were greeted by Philipson, who wrathfully informed them: "If you ever appear here again with those things [hats] on your heads I will have you physically removed." Gunther Plaut, *Unfinished Business, an Autobiography* (Toronto, 1981), p. 55.

121. 1948 *Yearbook*, "President's Report."

122. See Sarna, "'A Sort of Paradise for the Hebrews,'" passim.

123. After World War II, Reichert did privately advocate some changes in Rockdale tradition, including the introduction of daily religious services conducted by lay members and "greater warmth and participation in our Sabbath service through singing and new ceremonials." There is no evidence that these proposals were ever formally presented to the temple board. See Victor E. Reichert to Ira Abrahamson (December 12, 1945 and n.d. [1945/46]), Rockdale Temple Papers (uncatalogued, loose archival material found at Rockdale Temple, Cincinnati, Ohio; hereafter: RTP).

124. KKBI 1942, 1947, 1949, *Yearbook*.

125. KKBI 1945 *Yearbook*, pp. 5–6; 1946 *Yearbook*, pp. 5–6.

126. KKBI 1947 *Yearbook*, pp. 5, 7.

127. Philipson, *My Life*, pp. 325–27.

128. Some of the requirements actually dated back to 1940, but they were apparently not strenuously enforced; see KKBI 1940 *Yearbook*, p. 26.

129. KKBI 1953 *Yearbook*, p. 9; interview with Stanley Brav, June 1989; interview with Victor and Louise Reichert, June 1989.

130. Stanley R. Brav, *Dawn of Reckoning: Self Portrait of a Liberal Rabbi* (Cin-

cinnati, 1971), pp. 195–197; interview with Brav, June 1989; and KKBI 1954 *Yearbook*.

131. *1954 Yearbook*, pp. 9–10.

132. KKBI 1949 *Yearbook*, "President's Report."

133. KKBI By-Laws, 1951; KKBI 1946 *Yearbook*, p. 9.

134. KKBI 1953 *Yearbook*, p. 34; 1956 *Yearbook*, p. 31; 1957 *Yearbook*, p. 28.

135. KKBI Trustees Minutes, October 9, 1969. Trustee minutes after February 11, 1960, are found in Rockdale Temple, Cincinnati, Ohio.

136. Congregational Meeting, March 13, 1962, RTP.

137. KKBI Board of Trustees, November 15, 1962; January 9, 1964, in which Blackman reports that he visited 300 hospitalized congregants over the last year; interviews with Victor and Louise Reichert, June 1989, and Elizabeth Trager, June 1989.

138. For Passover seder discussion, see KKBI Trustees Minutes, February 14, 1963; April 11, 1963; May 9, 1963; and June 13, 1963.

139. KKBI Board of Trustees, September 10, 1964; interview with Victor and Louise Reichert, June 1989.

140. 1955 *Yearbook*, p. 6; 1956 *Yearbook*, p. 7; 1957 *Yearbook*, p. 11; December 11, 1966, letter to the congregation, RTP.

141. KKBI Trustees, "Minutes of Board of Governors," November 10, 1963.

142. See, for example, "President's Report to the Congregation," April 20, 1964, RTP; KKBI Trustees, October 11, 1962; February 14, 1963.

143. Board of Governors meeting, November 10, 1963; congregational meeting minutes, June 30, 1965, RTP.

144. The high school religious education for all of Cincinnati's Reform temples is combined within Cincinnati's Reform Jewish High School.

145. KKBI Trustees, December 11, 1966.

146. Ibid., November 13, 1963.

147. Congregational meeting, December 18, 1966, RTP.

148. Letter, Murray Blackman to Henry Hersch, April 13, 1967, RTP.

149. Sarna and Klein, *Jews of Cincinnati*, p. 173.

150. KKBI Trustees, August 29, 1967.

151. Interview with Philip Cohen, June 1989.

152. KKBI Trustees, August 29, 1967.

153. Philip Cohen interview.

154. See KKBI Trustees, April 1968, and following.

155. KKBI Trustees, April 11, 1968; April 24, 1968.

156. Interviews with Philip Cohen, David Hachen, Marcia Lowenstein, June 1989.

157. Letter from Hachen to congregation, January 15, 1968, RTP; interview with David Hachen, June 1989.

CHAPTER THREE

158. KKBI Trustees, April 11, 1968.

159. Letter from Henry Hersch to congregation, November 5, 1968, RTP; letter from David Hachen to congregation, November 5, 1968, RTP; KKBI Trustees, October 10, 1968; February 13, 1969; interview with Roslyn and Albert Freiberg, September 1988.

160. Letter from Philip S. Cohen to Board of Rockdale Temple, January 16, 1969, RTP.

161. When a member requested that the rabbi officiate at the b'ris of his grandson on the third day after birth, the man could not understand why Hachen would maintain that the circumcision, to be in accordance with Jewish law, had to be on the eighth day. Hachen interview.

162. Letter from Val Friedman to congregation, March 21, 1969. One hundred and thirteen families (and perhaps 400 signatures) responded with a petition questioning why he had resigned and the apparently undemocratic way in which the whole matter was handled by the board of trustees. KKBI Trustees, April 10, 1969.

163. "President's Message—1968," RTP.

164. Letter, Henry Hersch to Rev. W. E. Crumes, July 1, 1969, RTP; KKBI Trustees, January 8, 1970.

165. "Once-proud Rockdale Temple now prey of vandals," *Cincinnati Post*, December 26, 1972, Near Print file, AJA.

FOUR

A Social History of the Bethel African Methodist Episcopal Church in Baltimore: The House of God and the Struggle for Freedom

Lawrence H. Mamiya

CATCHING SIGHT OF THE twin Gothic spires, a Sunday visitor to the Bethel A.M.E. Church in Baltimore in 1991 might first remark that the church from a distance resembles many other church edifices. But then a large black and white sign comes into view, posted in front of the church steps on Druid Hill Avenue, which loudly proclaims "Free Southern Africa" to all passersby; another sign by the church office reads "Let's End U.S. Support for South Africa." The increasing feeling that this church is perhaps "different" from most churches, black or white, is confirmed by the large, vibrant, and colorful mural on the front wall of the sanctuary. Painted in 1977, the mural depicts the artist's vision of the pilgrimage of African Americans in the United States from slavery and oppression to hope and liberation. Black people in scenes from everyday life appear in a bright rainbow of acrylic colors—green, blue, lavender, red, orange, and gold. The mural ascends from the blue and lavender of slavery and oppression to the top, where a child is being held up to a gold cross and a pulsating sun in the background, symbols of freedom and a hopeful future. Unlike most sanctuary murals in black churches which depict Jesus (usually white-skinned) as the good shepherd, Bethel's mural does not depict Jesus as a person at all; the cross is the symbol for Jesus.[1] Finally, the enthusiastic and at times ecstatic worship service, packed with 1,700 people for each of two morning services, differs from the decorum of the traditional A.M.E. service. As a five-piece instrumental ensemble provides background music, the pastor and the members hold their outstretched arms with palms upward and call upon the power of the Holy Spirit to descend upon them, chanting, "Send the Spirit. Send the Spirit." Bethel's worship service now has a Pentecostal feel: the emphasis upon the power of the Holy Spirit and the liveliness of contemporary gospel music have produced a much more emotionally laden atmosphere than that generally found in A.M.E. churches.

How did one of the oldest, most prestigious, and most solidly middle-class black churches in the A.M.E. denomination become part of the neo-Pentecostal movement? The term *neo-Pentecostal* in this chapter refers to a charismatic movement among middle-class black churches (like those in the A.M.E. Church) that has grown considerably over the past two decades. In contrast to the traditional black Pentecostal churches like the Church of God in Christ, black neo-Pentecostal churches tend to have a more educated clergy and laity; to place a greater emphasis upon progressive politics and community outreach; and to emphasize glossolalia, or speaking in tongues, as a private prayer-language more than as a large corporate event in worship services. What factors led to this development? How does an ecstatic and enthusiastic worship style relate to Bethel's historic past? And what are the implications of neo-Pentecostalism not only for Bethel but also for the A.M.E. Church and for other black churches?

The history of the Bethel congregation can be summarized as a journey toward and a struggle for freedom. *Freedom* has achieved the status of an ultimate value in the sacred cosmos of the African American community, but its meanings have changed in different historical circumstances: for 250 years freedom meant freedom from bondage; during Reconstruction it meant the right to vote; and in the twentieth century it carried the connotations of political, economic, and social equality. During each stage of this struggle for freedom, the pastors and the members of Bethel made contributions. In addition, Bethel sought to be a central holistic institution in the black community, constantly involving itself in political, economic, and social issues as well as in the tasks of spiritual nurture. In the process the church had to deal with the tensions between accommodation and resistance toward American mainstream values and practices and with the recovery of Afrocentrism, which places a premium upon identification with Africa and an African heritage. The first half of this chapter focuses on the events and personalities of Bethel's rich past during the nineteenth and twentieth centuries until the civil rights period. The remainder presents an analysis of Bethel's history since 1975, when its membership grew from 600 members to over 7,000 in less than a decade.

The Black Methodist Movement in Baltimore

Maryland was founded as an English province in 1634, and the dominant religious influence until the War of Independence was the Anglican Church. Slavery began in the colony during the first few years of its existence, probably between 1638 and 1639, when it was first mentioned in two acts of the provincial assembly. In 1755 slaves constituted 24.3 percent of the whole population, free Negroes 5.2 percent, and whites 70.5 percent. However, within a century Maryland and its chief port city of Baltimore had the largest free black population in the United States prior to the Civil War. This rapidly growing free black population plus the stimulus of the revivals of the first Great Awakening were the preconditions for the development of black churches like Bethel in Baltimore.

In 1760 the Reverend Robert Strawbridge, a local preacher from Ireland, brought Wesleyan Methodism to Maryland, and free blacks and slaves were greatly attracted to a common people's religion that seemed to cut across not only class lines but also the insurmountable barrier of race. Methodists preached the same gospel to all classes, and they established mixed congregations where the two races worshiped "in harmony." Reflecting on stories and memories of older members of the Strawberry Alley meetinghouse from the 1780s, Bishop James Handy of the A.M.E. Church wrote that the white and colored members "sat on the same seats, and when they died, were buried in the same church yard or burial ground." But much of the harmony described by Handy began to disappear by 1785, when many white Methodists began the practice of treating their African members differently.

In the late eighteenth century some black Methodists became dissatisfied with their treatment in white churches and began holding their own prayer meetings in individual homes. At the same time, a group of leaders at the predominantly black Sharp Street Methodist Episcopal Church became dissatisfied and eventually split off. Both groups came together in 1801 to hire their first teacher and preacher, Daniel Coker. The earliest evidence for the existence of the independent black Methodist "prayer bands" in the city of Baltimore comes from the journal of Richard Allen, the founder of African Methodism. In a journal entry dated 1785 Allen wrote, "My lot was cast in Baltimore, in a small meeting-house called Methodist Alley. . . . I had some happy meetings in Baltimore." Allen's reference to the small meetinghouse called Methodist Alley probably refers to the Strawberry Alley meetinghouse, one of the two early Methodist churches from which Bethel traces its origin (the other being Lovely Lane, the first meetinghouse in Baltimore). He was probably preaching to some of the black people who would later found Bethel Church.

Sometime during 1785 or 1786 white Methodists in the Lovely Lane and Strawberry Alley meetinghouses began to restrict black members to the gallery and also banned blacks from taking communion with whites at the altar. In addition, the Christmas Conference of 1784 had enabled the ordination of white preachers only; black preachers were left unordained until 1800, sixteen years later. A certain "restlessness" appeared among the black members of the Methodist Episcopal Church. In 1787, about three weeks before Richard Allen and Absalom Jones founded the Free African Society in Philadelphia, a Colored Methodist Society in the form of an independent prayer group was established in Baltimore. Bishop Handy wrote:

> The men would meet and discuss the situation and in 1787 an independent prayer meeting, led by Jacob Fortie, was held in a house near the Belair market. This prayer meeting culminated in the formation of a Colored Methodist Society, which was organized in the boot-black cellar of Caleb Hyland. This society continued to grow as they held prayer meetings from house to house, and about the year 1797, they received a great addition in the person of Mr. Stephen Hill, who, by his ability and piety, gave strength to the little band.[2]

It is important to note that these early independent prayer bands were in actuality "house churches," the most rudimentary form of the Christian congregation that corresponds to New Testament teaching— "where two or three are gathered in my name, there I am in their midst" (Matt. 18:20).

The independent group of Bethelites also used the African Academy, founded in 1797 as the first school in Baltimore for educating blacks, as their place of worship. They claimed the main teacher at the academy, Daniel Coker, as their pastor from 1801 until 1817. On May 9, 1815, this separatist group of black Methodists assembled and selected the name "The African Methodist Bethel Society." With Daniel Coker as its leader, the group included the Gilliard family, Charles Hackett, Don Carlos Hall, and Stephen Hill. When it was established as a formal church, Bethel had about 633 members who were led by Daniel Coker as preacher, along with seven trustees. They purchased property on

Fish Street (now Saratoga Street) from John Carman, a white abolitionist, for their church building.

The Founding of the A.M.E. Church

While he was still an escaped slave in Baltimore in 1808, Daniel Coker's eloquent preaching, teaching, and leadership skills so impressed the key members of the Colored Methodist Society, who were part of the core group that formed Bethel Church, that they hid him for a while and sought to purchase his freedom with the aid of some white abolitionists. Eventually he was asked to become the first pastor of Bethel. "He is said," wrote Daniel Payne, a later pastor, "to have been a man of uncommon talent, and he possessed more information on all subjects than usually fell to the lot of colored men of his day."[3] Coker's intellectual and spiritual leadership was indispensable in the founding of both Bethel Church in Baltimore and the African Methodist Episcopal Church, one of the first black denominations and the first national organization among African Americans.

Coker conducted what we now call a tent-making ministry: he worked full time at another job and also pastored the church. His main livelihood was his work as a teacher in a day school (the former African Academy) that became attached to the Methodist Episcopal church on Sharp Street, but his real love was the ministry. He had about 17 students in the school when he began and more than 150 students when he left the school in 1815 to found Bethel Church. Besides his role as pastor, Coker served as the manager and teacher of the newly formed Bethel Church Charitable School.

After the formal organization of Bethel Church in Baltimore in 1815 and the achievement of freedom of Bethel Church in Philadelphia (later called Mother Bethel) from white ecclesiastical control in the early months of 1816, black Methodists from five churches along the eastern seaboard gathered in Philadelphia to make an Ecclesiastical Compact and to hold the first General Convention. Bethel-Baltimore's delegation of six members was the largest, and of the three leaders who displayed distinguished leadership at the convention, two were from Baltimore—Daniel Coker and Stephen Hill—and the third was Richard Allen of Philadelphia. At the convention, Daniel Coker was elected as the first bishop of the A.M.E. Church, but he resigned the next day in favor of Richard Allen, who was duly elected and consecrated as the founding bishop.[4] The convention passed the following resolution, offered by

Stephen Hill of Bethel, which organized the African Methodist Episcopal Church as a denomination:

Resolved, that the people of Philadelphia, Baltimore, and all other places, who shall unite with them, shall become one body under the name and style of the African Methodist Episcopal Church of the United States of America and that the book of Discipline of the Methodist Episcopal Church be adopted as our Discipline until further orders, except that portion relating to Presiding Elders.[5]

The choice of the term *African* as part of the name of the denomination had the unintended consequence of inaugurating what we now call an "Afrocentric" tradition among the independent black Methodists, which helped them to identify with Africa and to value their African heritage. Although the term *African* was commonly used during this period to identify black people, other possible choices were *Negro* and *colored*. With the passage of time, *African* proved to be a wise choice: it not only meant separation from white ecclesiastical control, but it also stood for independence and the preservation of an African American cultural heritage.

Though the name differed, the doctrine and the connectional polity of the Methodist Episcopal Church were adopted wholesale and published in the A.M.E. *Book of Discipline* without any significant changes. The original disagreement of the members of the A.M.E. denomination was not with matters of belief or structure but with the failure of white Methodists to treat them equally with respect and Christian love. As in the Methodist Episcopal Church, baptism of full-fledged members was accomplished by a symbolic sprinkling of water on the head of a convert rather than by the complete immersion required by the Baptist sects. In accord with the patriarchy of the time, only male members could vote.

In regard to polity, under the connectional system adopted, each church was not an entity unto itself but was connected at different levels to offices of the national body. The categories of ministerial leadership included the following: the licensed *local preacher*, an assistant to the pastor; the *ordained deacon*, who performed all ministerial functions except administering the sacraments; the *elder*, usually the pastor of a local church; the *presiding elder*, who supervised a district or circuit of local churches; and the *bishop*, who oversaw an episcopal district of two or more annual conferences.[6] An *annual conference* was composed of at least two districts supervised by presiding elders. Bishops were elected at

General Conferences of the whole denomination, held every four years. The annual conference of Baltimore was usually held at Bethel Church throughout the nineteenth and early twentieth centuries.

The major positions for lay leadership at a church like Bethel included the Board of Stewards (responsible for finances) and the Board of Trustees (responsible for property). Positions for women like stewardess and deaconess, however, were created only later in the nineteenth century as a result of pressures from women. Deaconesses ministered to the sick and the poor, and they remained unordained (though male deacons were ordained). Stewardesses assisted the pastor in the rites of Holy Communion and baptism, but they had no responsibility for church finances. Women were not ordained as elders in the A.M.E. Church until 1948. Laity could also be active as class leaders, Sunday school teachers, ushers, members of choirs and the missionary society, or leaders of the young people's department and a few other lay organizations like the women's auxiliary.

The Methodist system mandated that the baptized adult membership of a local church like Bethel be divided into "classes" led by lay "class leaders." Bethel's classes in the nineteenth century met weekly on different evenings, except Wednesdays when prayer meetings were held. Class sizes varied, with some classes having as many as 200 members. The larger classes and their charismatic leaders always posed the threat of schism.

The tasks of the class and the class leader were to strengthen members' faith and to exercise moral discipline over their behavior. Minutes from the monthly meetings of Bethel's Official Board (composed of class leaders, trustees, and stewards, along with the pastor) often reported that "members were growing in the faith," and sometimes they recorded the common moral infractions of members like "drinking," "quarreling and fighting," and infrequently "adultery." Punishments included warnings, periods of suspension from membership, and at the worst, expulsion from the church. Black churches like Bethel thus provided a system of social control within urban and rural black communities. In addition to serving a disciplinary function, the Official Board received financial reports of monies received and paid out.

The clergy and lay positions at Bethel and in the A.M.E. Church as a whole provided an alternative status system for people who were marginalized by the larger society.[7] In black churches like Bethel the "invisible people" in the United States—domestics and maids, porters and janitors—were given respect and dignity. In their positions as head of the ushers, trustee, steward, or Sunday school teacher, they gained recognition and status in a caring community.

Forging A Congregational Identity

Education was a major concern in Baltimore's black community of 20,000 freed persons and 5,000 slaves in the early nineteenth century, and it became a major task of black churches to provide for rudimentary education in Sunday schools or day schools or both. Clergy were often considered the best-educated persons in a black community, and both Bethel's Sunday school and day school (the Bethel Church Charitable School) were led by its pastor, Daniel Coker. The Sunday school had begun in 1815, but by the early 1830s attendance had dwindled so that efforts had to be made in 1836 to start another one. According to a report ("The Condition of the Coloured Population of the City of Baltimore") written by two white clergymen, the Reverends Robert J. Breckenridge and Andrew B. Cross, for the *Baltimore Literary and Religious Magazine* in 1838, "The Bethel coloured church in Saratoga, formerly called Fish street, has a Sabbath school attached to the congregation." Organized by a "few coloured young men, of good moral religious dispositions," the Sabbath school had nine teachers and an enrollment of eighty. Although the flood of 1838 had destroyed the library of "one thousand Sabbath school books" that Coker had started, funds were raised to start another library.[8] Sunday schools like Bethel's often involved the memorization of Bible stories and the teaching of rudimentary reading skills. Because these schools usually provided the only education available for blacks, the Colored Sabbath School Union of Baltimore was formed to give direction to the schools and teachers. Its preamble stated that they were "to aid and assist in the mental, moral, and religious instruction of our people in every way and manner which we think will contribute to our best interests both for time and eternity."[9]

In 1818 Daniel Coker, Bethel's first pastor, was charged with a grave moral offense, probably adultery. The A.M.E. system of discipline applied to clergy and laity alike, so following a church trial, Coker was expelled from the A.M.E. Church. He resigned his pastorate, and the fledgling black congregation and denomination survived their first major crisis. The Reverend Henry Harden, an early lay founder of the Colored Methodist Society, was appointed to replace him. Although Coker was reinstated a year later, he was by then deeply involved in the activities of the Maryland branch of the American Colonization Society and finally decided to emigrate to the society's colony in Liberia. On February 6, 1820, Coker left New York for West Africa as the first black foreign missionary. The emigration debate became heated and divisive among black people, especially in Baltimore. The members of Bethel, however, were influenced by the participation of their former pastor and tended to support the colonization scheme, particularly the idea of sending black missionaries to Africa to evangelize. Throughout its history, the Bethel congregation supported the African missions of the denomination, particularly in Liberia and later in South Africa. Returning missionaries also spoke at Bethel and helped to reinforce the congregation's identification with Africa.

Accommodation and Controversy:
The Pastorate of Daniel Alexander Payne

From 1816 to 1853, Bethel's congregation more than doubled in size—from 633 to about 1,504 members—becoming the largest and the leading black church in Baltimore (see table 1).[10] Bethel's growth was fueled by four factors: first, the decline in the number of slaves in Baltimore (from 4,357 in 1820 to 2,218 in 1860) and the rapid increase in the number of free blacks in the city (from 10,326 in 1820 to 25,680 in 1860, making it the largest free black population in the United States); second, the participation of highly talented laypeople like George Hackett and Isaac Myers, described below; third, the leadership of outstanding pastors like the Reverend Daniel Payne; and fourth, a massive revival that occurred in Baltimore in 1842 (as a late wave of the Second Great Awakening), converting many of the unchurched.[11]

Daniel Payne was born of free parents in Charleston, South Carolina, on February 4, 1811. In 1835 Payne fled from South Carolina after the authorities forced him to close his own school because of fears of slave revolts like Denmark Vesey's in 1822 and Nat Turner's in 1831. After attending Lutheran Seminary in Gettysburg, Pennsylvania, Payne was ordained a Lutheran minister in 1837. He pastored a Lutheran church in Troy, New York, for two years and also started a school in Philadelphia before joining the A.M.E. Church in 1840. Ironically, it was the negative attitude of the clergy and members of the A.M.E. Church toward education that had led him to join the Lutheran church earlier. In his autobiography, he wrote about his experience with the A.M.E. Church in Charleston:

It was a common thing for the preachers of that church to introduce their sermons by declaring that they had "not rubbed their heads against college walls," at which the people would cry, "Amen!"; they had "never studied Latin or Greek," at which the people would exclaim, "Glory to God!"; they had "never studied Hebrew," at which all would "shout."[12]

Payne's career in the A.M.E. Church was directed toward changing these black folk attitudes by focusing on both clergy and lay education alike. Although Payne can be viewed as an accommodationist, he and other church leaders in the mid-nineteenth century faced the enormous task of providing uplift for the masses of the still enslaved and the newly freed black people, most of whom were illiterate and still hampered by the segregation of schools and the prohibition against teaching slaves. Consequently, a black folk culture often substituted for education and knowledge, especially in the churches, which were for a long period of time the only independent large-scale institutions. Payne raised a major issue that would continue to be debated among future generations: how much of black folk culture should be preserved as part of the ethnic heritage of African Americans, and how much could be discarded?

Payne was the pastor of Bethel Church from 1845 to 1849. As a result of the large increase in membership from the Second Great Awakening, it was obvious that the church had outgrown its building, for which the final debt payment had been made in 1838. When Payne arrived, however, two large classes of 150 persons each were meeting at the church, led by a local preacher, the Reverend Nathaniel A. Peck. Like his predecessor, H. C. Turner, Payne tried to divide the large classes into smaller ones, but he encountered objections and quite a bit of hostility. When Payne attempted to lead the Bethel membership in building a new house of worship, he again met significant opposition from Peck's faction. Payne nevertheless won the vote for the new building and proceeded, while Peck and his followers withdrew from the church. The membership raised a fund of $5,000 (a third of the cost of the building) in 1846, and a cornerstone was laid in 1847. Within a year an imposing Romanesque structure, costing $16,000, was erected and consecrated.

Although some pastors might have rested after the successful completion of a new building, Payne moved on to other important changes. He strengthened Bethel's Sunday school and educational programs, and he taught in Bethel's day school. He was also responsible for purchasing an organ in 1847, thus making Bethel the first black church in Baltimore and the first A.M.E. church in the nation to have instrumental music. For Payne, however, the organ was more than a symbol of instrumental music in worship; he wanted to change the whole style of worship to a more "dignified form" as outlined in the A.M.E. *Book of Discipline.*

In almost all black churches of whatever denomination in the nineteenth century, worship blended European, American, and African forms. Enslaved Africans did not come to North America as blank slates; rather they had been socialized in African ethnic cultures permeated by traditional religion. The degree to which the African cultural heritage has survived over the generations has become a matter of intense scholarly debate, but the emerging consensus is that a unique African American subculture was formed out of the interaction of influences from Europe, North America, and Africa.[13] In religion, the African deities and spirits in the black sacred cosmos of the slaves in the U.S. were largely replaced by Christian beliefs in the Trinity. While the substance of beliefs was the same as in mainstream Christianity, the valences of some beliefs tended to differ. For example, black people in the nineteenth century favored the Old Testament view of God as a vengeful paladin who brings divine retribution for such sins as the enslavement of the Israelites in the Exodus stories. Jesus, as one of the oppressed who understands, was referred to more often in black worship than in white worship, and the doctrine of the Holy Spirit found resonance in the spirit dimension of African religions. Forms of worship also differed: the antiphonal singing, the rhythmic swaying of a black congregation and its choir, the "call and response" between preacher and congregation with shouts of "Well?" or "Amen." Enslaved and freed Africans also composed their songs, reflecting their experiences and hopes. On the whole, black worship services tended to be more emotional and enthusiastic than those of their white counterparts, many times bordering on the ecstatic.

The greatest difference between black and white forms of worship in the nineteenth century was in the attitude toward dancing as a part of worship. In traditional African music, singing always involved dancing; there was no separation. In the evangelical Christianity that spread among the slaves, however, dancing was viewed as sinful. In black religious culture it was rationalized that dancing involved crossing one's feet, and if one did not cross the feet but slowly shuffled from side to side, then one was not dancing but "shouting." As music historian Eileen Southern points out, "Only songs of a religious nature were sung, and the feet must never be crossed (as would happen in the dance). Among strict devotees, the feet must not even be lifted from the ground."[14] Ritual forms like the "ring-shout" developed in black churches, with worshipers rhythmically shuffling around the room in a circle; this shout was sometimes performed in the worship service but more usually afterward, and it could last for three or four hours. While ring-shouts were more common in rural black churches on Southern plantations, there is some evidence that they also occurred at urban churches like Bethel.

Worshipers clapped their hands, stomped their feet, performed ring-shouts, and sometimes "fell out," overcome by the power of the Holy Spirit, often shaking and trembling, with their voices breaking into cries and shouts. They also sang songs composed of repetitive rhythms and simple, catchy rhymes. Some of these songs have been preserved as "Negro spirituals," but the vast majority have disappeared. Derisively called "cornfield ditties," these songs had lyrics like the following:

> Ashes to ashes, dust to dust.
> If God won't have us, the devil must.

> I was way over there where the coffin fell;
> I heard that sinner as he screamed in hell.[15]

Bethel's order of worship for Sunday morning services followed the traditional evangelical format inherited from the Methodist Episcopal Church: the invocation; the congregational singing of several songs from hymnals; the reading of Scripture lessons; prayers; the preaching of the sermon by the pastor; the collection of offerings; announcements; the altar call; and the benediction. Songs sung by a trained choir were introduced into A.M.E. churches like Bethel after 1841, and it took some time before choirs were accepted as a part of the service.[16] Although the format was the same, however, often the content, the cultural style of worship, and the length of the service differed. Preachers like Coker and Harden had learned the peculiar black style of preaching by a period of apprenticeship to older black preachers and through the constant practice of a repetitive and rhythmic delivery that included humming, whooping, and even singing. The sung sermon (or large parts of the sermon) was a major stylistic contribution of the black oral tradition. Clergy like Daniel Payne, who rejected much of black folk culture, had a more difficult time mastering the nuances of the black preaching style, and they were subjected to more criticism from their congregation. The high point of the service was to worship and glorify God by achieving the experience of mass catharsis: a purifying explosion of emotions that eclipses the harshness of reality for a season and leaves both the preacher and the congregant drained in a moment of spiritual ecstasy. Thus the preaching received far greater weight in black churches like Bethel than other aspects of ministry like counseling or teaching.

This emphasis upon emotive preaching also led to a greater stress upon the *charismatic* style of leadership among black preachers in contrast to the *bureaucratic* style of careful record-keeping and efficient church administration. Clergy who could preach in the style described above and who had demonstrated personal charisma were more highly valued than those who were merely good administrators. Although, following A.M.E. polity, Bethel's clergy were assigned to the congregation by the bishop of the Second Episcopal District, the congregation tried to influence the bishop's choice of candidate and also decisions about length of tenure. Throughout Bethel's history a number of church schisms occurred because congregational members followed a popular and charismatic preacher when the time limit of the appointment (in the nineteenth century, usually five years) was reached. Because the systems of slavery and racial segregation resulted in a paucity of secular leadership positions for black people, especially among males, the pastors of a leading black church like Bethel had far greater authority and power than their white counterparts. They were treated with extreme deference, and their exercise of power at times bordered on the authoritarian. The position of bishop of the A.M.E. Church was even more powerful because it was the highest leadership post to which a black man could aspire before the Civil War and the creation of black colleges.

The singing at Mother Bethel Church in Philadelphia, described by Russian traveler Paul Svinin in 1811, is probably similar to the worship practices carried on at Bethel Church in Baltimore. The minister was reading the psalms, wrote Svinin, and

> At the end of every psalm the entire congregation, men and women alike, sang verses in a loud, shrill monotone. This lasted about half an hour. When the preacher ceased reading, all turned toward the door, fell on their knees, bowed their heads to the ground and set up an agonizing, heart-rending moaning. Afterwards, the minister resumed the reading of the psalter and when he had finished sat down on a chair; then all rose and began chanting psalms in chorus, the men and women alternating, a procedure which lasted some twenty minutes.[17]

As Southern points out, the key features of the singing in this service included the choral response given by the congregation to the reading of each psalm and the singing of psalms in alternation by men and women. Both aspects are related to the African tradition of antiphonal singing. "The loudness of the singing and the 'heart-rending moaning' are also typically found in the African tradition—the singers singing with all their might and becoming totally involved in the experience."[18] The practice of singing psalms was taught to black slaves by John Eliot and Cotton Mather during the colonial period, and it was continued by freed blacks in the nineteenth century. An emotional quality characterized not only the preaching but also the singing and the prayers at Bethel's services.

As noted by Svinin, the reading of the psalms alone, accompanied by the congregation's antiphonal choral response, took about an hour, reflecting a consciousness of time in the African heritage different from that of the Anglo-Protestant tradition, where time is to be used efficiently and economically. Time in African American culture was less hurried and less concerned with functional efficiency; one took as much time as was needed to complete a task. Events could begin fifteen minutes to an hour later than an announced starting time: they began when people got there and not at any precise point. This cultural view of time was also carried into black worship. "Sacred time" was not measured by a clock but was carried by the emotional quality of the events that were occurring. The preacher and the congregation took as much time as was needed to reach those emotional high points in their worship of God. Thus "going to church" in the black community usually meant an all-day event. Sunday morning worship services at Bethel were three to five hours long and were followed by an evening service.

The length of the worship services gave rise to two phenomena: an informal atmosphere and the church dinner. An informal atmosphere, where congregants could move about the sanctuary as they needed without being considered disruptive, allowed parents to bring babies and young children into the worship service. The tradition of the Sunday church dinner met the demands of feeding hungry congregants who spent all day in church. A church kitchen and a place to eat (a fellowship hall) thus were crucial elements in the architecture of black church edifices, and each of the buildings that the Bethel congregation occupied during its three moves met these requirements. Bethel's kitchen and cooks acquired an enviable reputation in Baltimore's black community. After the church dinner and before the evening service, the various lay organizations, auxiliaries, and boards met to conduct their business.

Bethel Church at mid-century had the reputation of being an "enthusiastic church." In a letter to the editor of the *Baltimore Clipper* in 1840, one critic complained about the too enthusiastic and too boisterous worship services emanating from the church. To him, the services sounded more like a "corn-husk," with "hundreds of negroes assembled together for purpose of 'worship' making night hideous with their howls, dancing to the *merry* song of some double-lunged fellow, who glories the more his *congregation* yells." In conclusion the writer asked, "Should an entire neighborhood be disturbed daily by these rioters—because some well meaning persons choose to say they are free to worship?"[19]

Although there is no extant description of nineteenth-century worship services in Bethel's historical documents, this letter to the editor from a white neighbor near the church gives some indication. We learn that the services were enthusiastic and loud with the singing of cornfield ditties, that there was some dancing, and that they were held almost daily, usually at night. Bethel, then, seems to have been the center for social and recreational activity in the community. It is not known how Sunday morning worship differed from these nightly events, but from Payne's reactions, it is obvious that Sunday worship at Bethel shared some of these features.

In their article on the conditions of the black population in Baltimore in 1838, the white clergymen Breckenridge and Cross offer a similar assessment of public worship at black churches like Bethel:

> With respect to religion and the public worship of God while much ignorance, infidelity, neglect, carelessness and indifference prevail among a great multitude, others are *less attentive to order and decorum in public worship* both on the Sabbath and at weekly prayer meetings. *A degree of fanaticism, and wildfire, and religious enthusiasm,* perhaps, in some cases, prevail among others of the coloured people in some places in the city, when they meet together. The excitements at the meetings in Sharp Street, *Bethel* and Asbury are some times considerable; and much noise prevails occasionally among the people assembled together at night meetings. (Emphasis added)[20]

Some educated A.M.E. clergy like Payne would have agreed with the white complainant and the clerical observers; moreover, Payne also considered these worship forms to be "ridiculous and heathenish." He saw "ring-shouts" and "cornfield ditties" as manifestations of ignorance, not as aspects of African culture that should be preserved. Payne's major goal was an educational uplift of the clergy, laity, and the general A.M.E. Church so that they could become a part of the American mainstream.[21]

Although the issues surrounding these differences in worship style surface again for the Bethel congregation and the A.M.E. Church in the late twentieth century, when black people collectively are attempting to recover their roots and ethnic heritage, Payne's attempt to foster a more dignified mainstream worship service at Bethel was successful. Indeed, his influence on worship traditions at Bethel and upon the A.M.E. denomination was so strong that one must speak of pre- and post-Payne eras.[22] Before Payne, Bethel's congregational worship was enthusiastic, filled with rituals, songs, and dances from black folk culture; after him, worship followed the emphasis upon the "order and decorum" of the Methodist Episcopal *Book of Discipline*, which the A.M.E. Church adopted. The organ that Payne introduced at Bethel in 1847 also tended to cut down on the more spontaneous hand clapping and foot stomping that accompanied a cappella singing.

Between 1818 and 1820 Bethel's Don Carlos Hall had helped to produce the first official *A.M.E. Hymnal*, which replaced an earlier hymn book edited by Richard Allen. Because of widespread illiteracy among the black population and a paucity of hymnals, however, the hymn-lining tradition, in which a leader called out the lines of a song, continued into the twentieth century. Bethel and the whole A.M.E. Church gradually succumbed to a more assimilationist ethos that began to disdain the enthusiastic and spontaneous worship rituals of black folk culture. From the late nineteenth century into the twentieth, the black folk religious culture was carried by the Holiness-Pentecostal movement, first in rural churches and later in urban storefront churches.

Daniel Payne's four years at Bethel were filled with controversy, and the largest, the "Rebellion of 1849," occurred in the last year of his pastorate. Payne's own records contain the only account of the controversy, which was evidently the culmination of grievances against the changes Payne had introduced. The triggering incident was an attempt by members of the Ebenezer A.M.E. Church, Bethel's mission church among poorer blacks in Baltimore, to buy their land and church building from Bethel. Although the trustees of Ebenezer were willing to purchase the church property for about $1,000, Payne sought Bethel's approval to sell it to them for $10. The majority voted for approval—with only male members voting, according to the church polity of this period—but five trustees were dissatisfied with this outcome. Money was not the issue for them; they did not want to give up the power of controlling Ebenezer. The vote was taken twice at their prompting, and they lost each time. Finally, a resolution of the Baltimore Quarterly Conference of October 22, 1848, declared the actions of the five trustees to be "antimethodistic and rebellious," giving the first evidence of a brewing controversy.

The trustees were unsuccessful in this affair, but from then on they and their cohorts made Payne's final year miserable. They were raucous at church meetings and even used clubs in attempting to enforce the resolutions they passed at the quarterly conference. Even though the chancery court of the city warned these five trustees in February 1849, they continued their obstructions.

Finally, they were brought to a church trial before Bethel's quarterly conference for discipline. They came with their wives and supporters, two of whom were armed with "a cudgel and a slugshot." After the testimony of witnesses, when it seemed that conviction was certain, the rebels shouted, "It is enough!" and attacked the conference officers. Payne was uninjured, but the conference secretary, the Reverend Darius Stowe, was bloodied by a blow. The city police were called to restore order and arrest the culprits. When the trouble continued after they posted bail, the conference finally sat in judgment and expelled the five members for "rebellion against the spiritual and temporal government of the church," a decision that was reaffirmed by the Baltimore Annual Conference.[23] Although Payne maintained that only these five were expelled and that forty-five of their supporters withdrew from the church, Bethel's membership records reveal that 20 members were expelled for participating in the 1849 rebellion. The rebellion was a culmination of resentments building among some members of the Bethel congregation against Payne's authoritarian ways, especially his forcing changes in worship style. The sale of Ebenezer only provided the excuse for a further challenge to Payne's authority by some disenchanted members. His reputation had so spread among black Methodists in Baltimore that when he was appointed to become the pastor of the Ebenezer A.M.E. Church, whose independence Payne had supported, the members of that congregation refused him. Ebenezer's chief steward explained their reasons to Payne bluntly: "The people say they have no objection to your moral character. They believe you are a Christian gentleman; but they say you have too fine a carpet on your parlor floor, and *you won't let them sing the cornfield ditties,* and if any one of them should invite you to dine or take tea with him, you are too proud to do it." (Emphasis added.)[24]

Payne's rejection by the Ebenezer congregation was fortuitous for the entire A.M.E. Church because it freed him to undertake the arduous task of traveling throughout the United States and Canada to do interviews, collect historical documents, and write the first history of the denomination. Much of what we know about Richard Allen, Daniel Coker, the first annual conferences, and the whole first generation of A.M.E. bishops and churches comes from Payne's historical digging. For example, in the attic of Richard Allen's family he found a box of papers containing Allen's journal, his letters, and the minutes of the annual conferences, recorded by his son. Though irascible and demanding, Daniel Payne was a deep visionary and a thinker, and he ranked at the top of all black clergy in the nineteenth century. Although he was the pastor of Bethel for only four years, he introduced more changes in the life of that congregation than any other of Bethel's pastors until 1975. When he became the bishop of the Second District in the 1860s, Payne continued to influence the worship life of Bethel by ordering that Scriptures be read responsively by the congregation.

From 1816 to 1860, the membership of Bethel's congregation grew steadily, reaching a peak of 1,500 members between 1850 and 1860 (see table 1). Bethel also increased in influence. Given its size and its importance in the founding of the denomination, the pastorate there was viewed as a stepping-stone toward the bishopric. Because the church could finance its pastor's extensive travels to other episcopal districts to solicit support, as well as provide a network of campaigners at the General Conference, Bethel's candidates for the office had a built-in advantage. Fifteen of Bethel's pastors went on to be consecrated as bishops in the A.M.E. Church, so Daniel Payne was part of a long line of influential Bethelites (see table 2).

The Congregation in the Streets

While most congregational studies have tended to focus on the private life of the congregation at worship, describing its sacred rituals, such a perspective is inadequate for understanding the ministry of churches like Bethel, which also included dynamic social outreach programs. A holistic ministry was carried out at Bethel, and attention to spiritual nurture was accompanied by outreach programs involving politics, economics, and social welfare. Bethel was blessed with highly talented laypeople, freed men and women who were not only active leaders in their church but active participants in the larger community, engaging the most difficult issues of their time. Far from being isolated actors, these people were part of a social network that found its center at Bethel. Yet a focus on the activities of key church members like George Hackett and Isaac Myers is also legitimate. Their efforts constitute an important contribution to Bethel's mission in the streets of Baltimore in the nineteenth century.

George Hackett, the Abolitionist Movement, and Black Economic Development

The origins of Bethel Church, as mentioned above, were tied to the abolitionist movement in the city. The first building to house the church, on Fish Street, was owned by John Carman, a white abolitionist associate of the Quaker Elisha Tyson. At Tyson's urging, Carman sold the property to the more radical black Methodist faction within the Colored Methodist Society. Because of the clandestine nature of the operation, it is extremely difficult to find definite evidence of the involvement of many black churches in the Underground Railroad to help fugitive slaves, but there is some evidence that Bethel participated. Before the purchase of his freedom, Daniel Coker was a fugitive slave who was hidden by the first members of Bethel in the Colored Methodist Society, which included Charles Hackett. In 1806 Hackett's wife bore George Alexander Hackett, who became Bethel Church's strongest link to the Underground Railroad and to initiatives toward black economic development in the nineteenth century.[25]

Because his father was one of Bethel's founding trustees, George Hackett was raised in the church, attended the church school that Coker founded, and in 1828 married Mary Jane Gilliard, the daughter of Jacob Gilliard, Jr. After ten years as a seaman, Hackett became an independent businessman, running first a livery stable and later a coal yard. As a layperson, he held major leadership positions at Bethel and was influential in the national church. His years at Bethel also overlapped the pastorates of the Reverends Daniel Payne and James A. Shorter, who became the sixth and the ninth bishops of the A.M.E. Church, respectively. From the 1840s to the 1860s, George Hackett rose to prominence as the leading black political figure in Baltimore.

The major political battle of Hackett's career occurred in 1859, when

Colonel C. W. Jacobs, a member of Maryland's House of Delegates from the Eastern Shore, introduced a bill that would either re-enslave or expel the free black populace of the state. Following John Brown's raid on Harper's Ferry in October 1859, slaveowners like Jacobs felt threatened by the large free black population. Hackett took the lead in organizing black opposition to the Jacobs bill for the next two years. Petitions were circulated, and blacks held weekly meetings to formulate their position. The majority of these meetings were held at Bethel.

On February 9, 1860, all the black opponents to the Jacobs bill gathered at Bethel at 3 A.M. and observed a whole day of prayer and fasting against the evil decree. At this service preaching was followed by prayer and singing, and outstanding black clergy, including the Reverends Henry McNeil Turner, Harrison Webb, William Waters, Hiram Revels, Noah Davis, and Moses Clayton, were invited to preach. Indignation services, as they were called, originated with the Bethel congregation in the mid-nineteenth century to mobilize the black community and publicly express its views on serious black offenses. For example, another indignation service at Bethel in 1882 protested the expulsion of Bishop Payne from a first-class railroad car.

Only after a long struggle was the Jacobs bill defeated. Hackett also organized the Protection Association, a group formed to protect free blacks against enslavement. Along with Bethel's pastor, the Reverend John Mifflin Brown, he wrote numerous letters to the *Weekly Anglo-African*, criticizing Jacobs' proposals. Pastor Brown came to Bethel from New Orleans, where he had been arrested five times for refusing to prohibit slaves from attending his church meetings. During his pastorate at Bethel, Brown was elected president of the Moral Mental Improvement Society, which met at the church on the first Sunday of each month; it was considered one of the city's leading literary and debating societies. Most of the members of the debating societies were male, but occasionally women presented essays. Bethel's outreach programs into the community were concerned with both the political issue of abolitionism and the educational and moral development of individuals.

Risking life and limb, George Hackett was a man of action who received more than ten death threats during his lifetime. During the Civil War years, before Maryland's slaves were freed, Hackett conducted his own underground railroad on the Eastern Shore plantations. His activities increased after the Emancipation Proclamation of 1863 when many of Maryland's slaveholders refused to abide by the decree. Reminiscent of the famed "conductor" Harriet Tubman, Hackett would frequently "hire a wagon, go on a plantation, fill it with slaves, and with a six-barrelled revolver in each hand, defy the master to prevent it."[26] He also helped to recruit black soldiers for Baltimore's 30th and 31st Colored Regiments during the Civil War.

Racial discrimination in employment has been a perennial problem for black workers throughout American history. In 1865 the white caulkers in Baltimore wanted to exclude black caulkers from the shipyards, so they went on strike and succeeded in driving blacks from their jobs. George Hackett, along with several other laymen from Bethel Church (Isaac Myers, William F. Taylor, John W. Locks, and Causeman Gaines), took a lead in solving this problem. They organized their own shipyard, the Chesapeake and Marine Railway and Drydock Company, which became the first example of black people forming a joint stock company for their own benefit.[27] Begun as early as 1866, within a year the company had 100 black workers earning an average daily wage of $3. It also employed white and black mechanics. The company lasted until 1884, one year after a national recession caused enormous financial difficulties.

This example of black economic development differed somewhat from other economic initiatives that black churches were involved in during the late nineteenth century. Black-owned banks and black insurance companies were created after 1880 by black churches, fraternal orders, and beneficial societies, usually under ministerial leadership. But this first black-owned shipyard was managed and operated by laypeople from one church. Although these men were of comparatively modest means, they willingly risked their hard-earned resources to try to deal with the problem of racial discrimination in employment.[28] Their example, a real testimony to Christian faith in action, gives an insight into the social ministry of many congregations, both black and white: namely, it is very rare for an *entire* congregation to become involved in a social ministry, beyond contributing funds or attending meetings. Most of the daily work of congregational social ministries is carried out by a few members who are highly motivated and display individual initiative.

Hackett was also involved in founding two key black institutions in Baltimore. With others from Bethel and the larger black community, he helped to establish the Douglass Institute in 1865. This cultural center was named after the Baltimorean who was the first acknowledged national leader among black people, the abolitionist Frederick Douglass. The Douglass Institute and the Bethel and Sharp Street churches were the central meeting places for Baltimore's black community. Hackett served as a member of the executive committee of the institute, and he also helped to establish the Gregory Aged Women's Home in 1867. Mary Ann Prout, a member and Sunday school teacher at Bethel Church, became president of the association in charge of the home, while George Hackett served as its superintendent.[29]

Isaac Myers, Sunday Schools, Black Businesses, and Public Education

Just as Bethelite George Hackett dominated Baltimore's black politics from the 1840s to the 1860s, another member from Bethel, Isaac Myers, took over in the 1870s and 1880s. Myers was an active lay leader and for many years the supervisor of Bethel's Sunday school, once acclaimed by the national head of A.M.E. Sunday schools to be the "best Sunday School in the world" and the "largest black Sunday School in the state."[30] In 1869 Myers, along with Bethelites H. J. Brown and A. Ward Handy, helped to found the African Methodist Sunday School Union. Handy was elected president.

Sunday schools or church schools were very important in black history because they often were the first places where many black people learned the rudimentary skills of reading and sometimes writing. For the vast majority who grew up in the Bible Belt of the rural South, reading God's Word for themselves was the highest priority. In his classic study, *The Education of the Negro Prior to 1861*, Carter G. Woodson pointed out that "although cloaked with the purpose of bringing the blacks to God by giving them religious instruction, the institution permitted its workers to teach them reading and writing when they were not allowed to study such in other institutions."[31] While the Sunday school at Bethel still relied on teachers reading Bible stories and students memorizing them, a major change after the Civil War was the use of John Comley's *Speller* for teaching the basic skills. Students could now learn to spell and begin reading words without relying on rote memory. Sunday schools in black churches usually had adult classes as well as children's. In the 1880s John Murphy, Sr., a member of Bethel, sold copies of the *Sunday School Helper* to Bethel and other churches to help students with their lessons. In 1838 the Sunday school at Bethel Church had reported approximately 80 persons in attendance.[32] Under Myers's leadership, Bethel's Sunday school increased to more than 250 students.

In Baltimore, Bethel Church became the site of numerous conventions focused on Sunday schools. In 1878, for example, a National

Convention of Sunday Schools was convened at Bethel with 200 representatives from different states. The following year a local interdenominational Convention of Colored Sunday Schools of Baltimore City and County was also held at Bethel, and in 1881 the African Methodist Sunday Schools held its convention there. Myers was an active leader in each of these conventions. His skill at organizing people was also used by Bethel's pastor, the Reverend James Handy, in furthering the cause of the National Camp Meeting, an evangelical branch of Methodism. Myers also organized fund-raising meetings for the Monumental Literary Association, which sponsored speakers and activities and was located across the street from Bethel. In 1879, for example, the association invited the Reverend Richard Cain, an A.M.E. minister and former congressman, to speak at Bethel on "The Future of the Colored Race."[33]

Myers's organizing efforts also extended to the concerns of the small black businessman and the black laborer. The owner of a successful coal yard, Myers understood from the inside the difficulties that black workers had encountered in getting jobs since the large-scale immigration of Europeans had begun in the 1840s and increased in the late 1870s. As part of his Christian concern, Myers initiated a national labor movement among black workers. He brought mechanics and tradesmen together in Baltimore and throughout the state to form a permanent organization that would look after the interests of black skilled workers. He constantly supported their efforts, and in 1881 he wrote a letter to the *People's Advocate*, complaining that black workers were being pushed out of the trades by the large influx of foreigners. Myers was also the organizer and president of the first Colored Industrial Fair of Maryland held in October 1888. When black entrepreneurs experienced great difficulty in securing loans from white banks, Myers, with the aid of Bethel members, organized the Colored Building and Loan Association of Baltimore. With other lay leaders from Bethel, Myers became concerned about the problem of poorly paid, aging black clergy in the A.M.E. denomination at large, and he led his fellow congregants to found the Aged Ministers Home of the A.M.E. Church of Baltimore. Myers's efforts in organizing labor and other self-help groups made him a leading Republican politician on the national level.

The burning political issue of this period in Baltimore, however, was public education, especially the appointment of black teachers to staff local public schools, and Myers got involved on this front also. This issue had been raised earlier in the Black Border States Convention meetings in the 1860s under George Hackett. Prior to the Civil War, black children were taught by black teachers in black schools like Bethel's day school. After 1865, however, the city's school board took over the management of black schools from the Baltimore Association for the Moral and Educational Improvement of the Colored People. Most of the black teachers were soon dismissed from their positions, and within a decade there were no black teachers in the public schools of Baltimore. It is ironic that when African Americans sought to become part of the mainstream public schools, black teachers who taught in the independent schools (which were largely housed in black churches like Bethel) lost their jobs. Isaac Myers was prominent in helping to organize the campaign for hiring black teachers in public schools, and numerous meetings were held for more than a decade. He was assisted by the Reverend James H. A. Johnson, a member of Bethel and a graduate of Princeton Theological Seminary, who published public letters throughout 1879 in the *Morning Herald*, arguing the case for black teachers.

From December 5 to December 8, 1879, a series of indignation meetings, combining worship and protest, were held at Bethel Church on the school issue. The Reverend James Johnson, presiding elder from the Hagerstown District, moderated the meetings, and speakers included William E. Matthews and Frederick Douglass. Douglass noted in his speech that his old "gray head" was still on the side of "freedom and equality; justice and fair play." Moreover, he said, "We are only following the line marked out for us by Bethel Church more than fifty years ago—the principle of the assertion and dignity of manhood, and Bethel Church can be in no better service than it exercises this evening."[34]

Another indignation meeting was held at Bethel on January 6, 1881, when the school board refused to honor its pledge to hire black teachers by the first of the year. The meetings and sustained vigorous protest of the black community continued for seven years before Roberta Sheridan was hired as the first black teacher at the Waverly Colored Public School in the fall of 1888.

The Bethel congregation, which numbered from 1,200 to 1,500 during the 1870s and 1880s, provided both the leadership and support for these school protests. The pastors of Bethel and talented lay leaders such as Myers spearheaded the movement, while many church members helped to mobilize the community.

Bethel's unique development of the indignation meeting underscored the holistic dimension of its ministry, which embraced the political, economic, and social aspects of life along with the spiritual. In fact, Bethel's indignation meetings can be seen as forerunners of the "mass meeting" developed in the civil rights movement of the twentieth century, which also used song, preaching, and prayer combined with political protest.

As powerful as the Bethel congregation was in its social ministries, however, it continued to serve as spiritual nurturer, comforter in times of sorrow and death, house of mercy for the suffering, provider of role models for young people, and counselor for the distraught; consecrations of new babies, baptisms, weddings, revivals, and funerals were performed. Bethel was still the place where those who suffered the daily indignities of racism could cry openly or shout for joy among those who understood. It was the place where God's spirit could renew the souls of black folk in worship to face another day, another week.

Bethel and Mutual Aid Groups in the Nineteenth Century

Besides its active involvement in politics and in the spiritual life of its members, Bethel played an important role in the social organizations of Baltimore's black community: the fraternal orders, lodges, and beneficial societies. During the 1780s Prince Hall, a Methodist minister from the West Indies, received permission to establish the Prince Hall Masonic Lodge for people of color. The orders and lodges followed society's rules for racial segregation, but they quickly became status symbols for the black elite. Groups like the Masons, the Oddfellows, and the Elks and their female counterparts like the Daughters of the Eastern Star were "parallel institutions" that provided the same opportunities for social advancement among blacks that they did for whites. Throughout the nineteenth century and into the first half of the twentieth century, the orders and lodges of African Americans provided for mutual aid for educational and cultural enrichment. The beneficial societies, many of which were founded in churches, provided for the sick, bereaved, orphaned, and widowed. They offered a combined form of health and burial insurance, and one of their primary functions in fact was to provide for decent funerals. Many black people, including occupational groups, became members. Both the beneficial societies and the orders and lodges were quasi-religious institutions. They also played an important economic role in black communities: along with churches they provided the needed capital to develop independent black banks and black insurance companies.

In Baltimore, several of these groups were spawned at Bethel Church and met there, and many Bethel members were leaders. George

Hackett, for example, was a founding member of two groups that were initiated at Bethel, Rising Star of Daniel A. Payne Lodge of the Good Samaritans and the Good Intent Building Association. Bethelite Mary Ann Prout organized an affiliate of the national organization of the Order of St. Luke in 1856 that met at the church. Perhaps the most active member, however, was the Reverend James A. Handy, who pastored Bethel from 1875 to 1877 and who had grown up in the church from the age of five. In 1848 Handy, along with others like Daniel Payne, George Hackett, and Helmsley Nicholas, founded the Good Samaritan order. The first Samaritan Temple was attached to Bethel Church. Handy was also deeply involved with the Masons. In 1876 he was elected the grandmaster of the lodge and Causeman Gaines, another Bethelite, was deputy grandmaster. Other men from Bethel like Isaac Myers, George Watkins, George Myers, Jacob Seaton, and Hiram Watty were also active in the Masons. In addition, Handy was a founding member of the Baltimore chapter of the Nazarites, a beneficial society that was established in 1854.

One of the most important mutual aid groups was the Ladies Sewing Circle of Bethel Church. During the late 1850s, the Reverend John Mifflin Brown, Bethel's pastor, had high praise for the activities of this group. The circle aided the poor of the city by giving them food, clothing, and fuel. It had helped about 200 people during the winter by buying 100 cords of wood and in another effort had donated 500 loaves of bread to be distributed to the poor. In the early spring of 1860, Eliza A. Tilghman, George Hackett's daughter, presented a check for $600 on behalf of the Ladies Sewing Circle to the trustees of Bethel Church. The trustees in turn gave a "grand dinner" for the circle with the head table seating about 309 honorees.

Besides mutual aid activities, the lodges, beneficial societies, and the Ladies Sewing Circle also sponsored picnics. The Oddfellows had a picnic on August first of each year, as did the Ladies Sewing Circle and the Barbers' Association. The black community of Baltimore established a tradition that continues to this day. The first week of August has been a time for citywide picnics, and Bethel's congregation has participated in that tradition with its family-church picnics in August throughout its history.

All these groups—the mutual aid societies, beneficial societies, fraternal orders and lodges, and even the Ladies Sewing Circle of Bethel—were examples of the black self-help tradition that stemmed in large part from black churches like Bethel. Prior to the establishment of any social welfare system and under the great pressures exerted by both an oppressive system of racial discrimination and the added burdens of newly freed slaves, black people influenced by this self-help tradition responded in heroic ways.

Challenges at the Turn of the Twentieth Century

The family of John Henry Murphy, Sr., had deep roots in Baltimore and Bethel Church. Both Murphy and his father Benjamin were slaves who had been freed by the passage of Maryland's 1864 Emancipation Act. It isn't clear exactly when they joined Bethel Church, but it was probably before the Civil War.[35] Ben Murphy (1813–82) was a self-taught but talented musician who served as the choir director at Bethel for more than a decade. His son John Murphy, Sr., served as a sergeant in the Civil War and, like Hackett, Myers, and Reverend Handy, his contemporaries, he was also active in the orders and lodges. Although the Murphys became part of the black elite in the twentieth century, they did not start out with inherited wealth. The small black elite of Baltimore usually consisted of one or two generations of freed persons, at least high-school educated, who were able to become independent entrepreneurs or professionals. The elite also included schoolteachers (because education was highly valued in the black community) and the pastors of large churches like Bethel.

John Murphy, Sr., was not only a former slave and Civil War veteran but also a whitewasher and janitor. However, his association with some of the black elite at Bethel and his participation in the intellectual and political events held at the church eventually led him to purchase the *Baltimore Afro-American* newspaper for $200 in 1890 from William Alexander, an entrepreneur who helped to stimulate the growth of black Baptists in Baltimore and to establish the Insurance Society, a black insurance company. It was rumored that Murphy had borrowed the money from his wife, Martha, who became one of the cofounders of the YWCA in the black community in 1896.[36]

As with so many other institutions, the emergence of the black press, especially newspapers, occurred in the "cultural womb" of black churches.[37] John Murphy served for many years as the chairman of the board of trustees of Bethel Church and also as the superintendent of its Sunday school. He had learned about the newspaper business in the course of producing the *Sunday School Helper,* a paper which he sold at Bethel and other churches as a primer for Sunday school lessons for children and adults. At Bethel he could gather news about the events of the black community in Baltimore. But Murphy did not limit his newspaper coverage to Baltimore. A nearly defunct paper when he bought it, the *Baltimore Afro-American* became a well-respected weekly, and with its circulation of 14,000, it had the largest black readership in the Middle Atlantic states.[38]

Another leader during this period was the Reverend Levi Coppin, pastor of Bethel Church from 1881 to 1883 (during the height of the educational struggles in Baltimore) and the twenty-third bishop of the A.M.E. Church. Coppin was appointed to the Second Episcopal District for two terms, from 1908 to 1916.[39] In many ways he was a key actor in the church's acquisition of a new building and its move to the present site on Lanvale Street and Druid Hill Avenue. As early as 1881 during his tenure at Bethel, he saw that

> Bethel could not remain indefinitely in Saratoga St., among the iron foundries and hold a leading place among the Churches. When Bethel was organized in the latter part of the eighteenth century, colored people sought a secluded spot for their Churches. In a back alley; behind the woods; where they could sing and pray late and loud without disturbing the "white folks." Bethel, down on the "marsh" was in a good place at first, but in 1881, times had changed, and were still changing rapidly.

Coppin claimed that he was offered $45,000 for the Saratoga Street site. Though he had an opportunity to buy the Presbyterian church, parsonage, and schoolhouse on Baltimore and Lord Streets, the project did not meet the approval of some older members, who threatened to riot. With recollections of Daniel Payne's difficulties, Coppin took the threat seriously and withdrew. Nevertheless, what the pastor could not accomplish in 1881, the Baltimore City Council did in 1909. The council passed an ordinance to widen Saratoga Street, but the church building was in the way. Faced with the condemnation of its building, the congregation voted to purchase the building of St. Peter Episcopal Church. The members put down $20,000 cash on a $90,000 building and took out a fifteen-year mortgage. As bishop of the district, Coppin approved the negotiations. He wanted to see "dear old Bethel" restored "to her pristine glory, the leading Church among our people in the Monumental City." The congregation had been located at Saratoga Street for 113 years, and Bethel's pastor, the Reverend Daniel G. Hill, wrote upon leaving: "How the mind is refreshed and strengthened as it reviews the important part [Bethel] has played in the substantial development of the Christian life today which truly affords so much comfort and sustaining power to the fathers, mothers, and children of this generation."[40] In 1910 Hill competently oversaw the move into the new church building at 1300 Druid Hill Avenue.

The minutes of the Official Board meetings occasionally pointed to tensions that sometimes existed between the power and authority of the pastor and that of the board of trustees. On December 18, 1916, the minutes recorded that a Sister Edith Murray had given a verbal report of the work she was doing at the solicitation of the pastor (Reverend J. W. Saunders). "A motion to adopt the report was discussed and Mrs. Murray was commended for the work she did, but some of those taking part in the discussion contended that the work should be reported to the Financial Board. The motion to adopt was lost, but the pastor ruled that it did not matter whether or not we passed it. It was going to be because he wanted it, and it was only a courtesy on his part in bringing the matter before the Board."[41] The power and authority that the pastor of a large black church like Bethel could wield was considerable, and sometimes that authority moved in an authoritarian direction, overruling trustees and lay leaders.

Although Bethel at the outbreak of World War I was a thriving church with "hundreds of new members," many of whom were part of the urban migration from rural areas in the South, Bishop Coppin reported that the church struggled with the weight of the enormous $70,000 debt it had incurred.[42] The church membership had dipped below 1,000 at the turn of the century but was now back to its peak of 1,500 members. Several pastors who had followed Hill could not significantly reduce the debt, and the interest payments put a stranglehold on the programs and plans of Bethel. Bishop Coppin along with other A.M.E. bishops saw the need to eliminate the debt as soon as possible. Fortunately, they had a secret weapon to combat church indebtedness in the talented and able Reverend William Sampson Brooks.

The Fiscal Conservatism and Radical Activism
of the Reverend William Sampson Brooks

Educated, charismatic, and organized, William Sampson Brooks gained a national reputation among African Methodist Episcopalians as a great fund-raiser and shepherd of church growth. Before coming to Bethel, he had eliminated the $14,000 indebtedness of the St. Paul A.M.E. Church in St. Louis, Missouri, in one year. Brooks had broken all fund-raising records among A.M.E. churches in 1912.

Although he had already been appointed to St. Paul Church in Wichita, Kansas, Brooks was eventually transferred to Bethel in Baltimore in 1917 to tackle the largest church debt that the denomination had ever seen. John Murphy, Sr., publisher of the *Baltimore Afro-American*, chairman of Bethel's board of trustees, and superintendent of the Sunday school, traveled to Kansas City to convince Brooks to become Bethel's pastor. When Brooks arrived, Bethel's debt stood at about $55,000. With his accustomed gusto and discipline, he organized all of the church members at Bethel into fund-raising units. He also preached frequently about the need to be financially responsible. With Murphy's help, Brooks organized programs that attracted interdenominational audiences from all black churches to Bethel. Working together, they raised $12,000 during Brooks's first year and $12,000 in his second.[43] On June 16, 1919, Brooks organized a rally that broke all the records: in one night he raised $33,000, enough to eliminate Bethel's debt completely. Word spread quickly in the city and throughout the denomination of Brooks's $33,000 rally! As Bishop Coppin recalled, "it would seem indeed" that Brooks and Bethel "had won a victory unlike any financial accomplishment in the long and eventful history of the Church."[44]

At the beginning of Brooks's pastorate, someone had written in the *Christian Recorder:* "if Brooks can clear Bethel of debt he should be made bishop at the next General Conference."[45] Apparently, there was a broad consensus on this, both within the A.M.E. Church and without. When the General Conference met in St. Louis in 1920, it appeared that the whole city of Baltimore, blacks and whites, Baptists and others, were rooting for Brooks and calling for his election. Brooks was consecrated the forty-fourth A.M.E. bishop in 1920.

It would be a mistake, however, to view Brooks's pastorate at Bethel as being occupied wholly with financial matters, fund-raising, and burning the mortgage. Though his accomplishments in matters of finance were unsurpassed, Brooks was also acutely aware of the pressing political issues facing his people. In the area of finance and fund-raising, he was a conservative, but in political matters he was a radical, expounding a position of black nationalism. Brooks's radicalism is best shown in an event he helped to cosponsor at Bethel with the Baltimore division of the Universal Negro Improvement Association, led by William D. Rankin. The featured speakers were Marcus Garvey, the founder and head of the UNIA, and Ida B. Wells-Barnett, the antilynching crusader who was elected as the UNIA's delegate to a peace conference in Versailles. The meeting was scheduled for Wednesday, December 18, 1918, at 8 P.M. Throughout its history, Bethel Church had provided a forum for a variety of controversial political activists including Frederick Douglass, Frances Ellen Watkins Harper, the Reverend Henry Highland Garnett, and the Reverend Henry McNeil Turner. But the political radicalism represented by Wells-Barnett and Garvey on the same program went far beyond the norm even for Bethel. The program was monitored by several agents from the Office of the Director of Military Intelligence, the precursor of the Federal Bureau of Investigation.[46] This event not only reflected upon the church's role as a public forum for Baltimore's black community but also demonstrated its emphasis upon the African heritage and its links with initiatives toward black independence.

The Reverend William Sampson Brooks did more than play host for Wells-Barnett's and Garvey's visits. Apparently, he became one of the few black clergy nationwide openly to support Garvey's militant black nationalism. Black clergy were deeply divided concerning Garvey's movement, and some prominent New York clergy like the Reverend Adam Clayton Powell, Sr., of the Abyssinian Baptist Church, a few doors down from the UNIA's Liberty Hall, spoke out strongly against Garvey, as did some leading black intellectuals like W. E. B. DuBois.[47] Brooks, who had just ended his appointment at Bethel in May 1920, was not deterred by such criticism.[48] On the evening of July 25, 1920, he gave a stirring speech on the spirit of Garveyism to a record crowd at Liberty Hall in Harlem. After elaborating that the spirit of Garveyism meant the spirit of self-reliance, self-denial, self-sacrifice, and the spirit of freedom for Africa, Brooks concluded:

I can see before me the spirit of Garveyism, stimulating, inspiring, unifying and sweeping 400,000,000 black people of the world until they march out on the plains of Africa, under the banner of the Red, the Black and the Green; ready, if need be, to die, that the cause nearest and dearest to their hearts may live—live—that Africa may at last be free, and that Ethiopia may again stretch forth her hand to God, and become a great people.[49]

Brooks's speech and participation in Garvey's UNIA movement illustrate the large degree of independence given to black clergy by their churches and their denominations. Very few other black professionals could have made the same speech without suffering political or economic consequences, in 1920 or even in the present. It is a credit to the A.M.E. Church and the Bethel congregation that Brooks's support of the Garvey movement did not affect his election as bishop, which occurred several months after the speech.

The speeches of Ida Wells-Barnett and Marcus Garvey at Bethel Church and Brooks's support of the UNIA were in continuity with several dominant themes running through Bethel's own history: black independence as illustrated in the separation from the Methodist Episcopal Church; support of emigration generally, whether to Africa or to states outside of the South; and Ethiopianism, which has to do with the redemption of Africa and African redemption of the world. Ethiopianism is a part of Bethel's Afrocentric heritage, relating as it does to the quest for identity and the preservation of African ethnic contributions in the midst of the assimilative pressures of the larger society. More than any other pastor at Bethel until recently, Brooks represented the tradition of independence, resistance, and Afrocentrism. He also showed that one person can combine administrative skills, fiscal expertise, and a charismatic personality.

Church Schism and the Creation of New Churches

While Brooks's ministry represented some of the positive, identity-affirming traditions at Bethel, the Reverend Frederick Douglas's tenure brought schism and division. Named after the famous abolitionist of the nineteenth century, Douglas was appointed to Bethel after Brooks, and he built upon his predecessors' accomplishments. (His name has often contributed to historical misidentifications, including the spelling of his surname, which had a single s but sometimes appears with a double s like his famous namesake's.)[50] Douglas was a great preacher, and the church's historical notes indicate that the Easter services he conducted were among the "greatest ever." He was a church builder in more ways than one. While his preaching ability attracted great numbers of people, he was also a skillful carpenter and built the church's restroom for women with the aid of the sexton, Mr. Chambers. But Douglas's ministerial career at Bethel was not entirely smooth: in June and July 1921 he faced a church trial on a charge of adultery. Although the examining committee finally exonerated him, the complainant threatened to take her case to civil court before it was finally settled.[51]

Douglas was a very popular preacher who won the loyalty of many members. Unfortunately, according to the rules laid down by the A.M.E. Church at the time, pastors could be appointed to a local church for a maximum of five years only. The A.M.E. denomination was attempting to preserve the eighteenth-century rule of itinerancy for pastors, keeping them in the traditional Methodist circuit, and both pastors and bishops were subject to the itinerant rule. Douglas, however, wanted to continue his work with the congregation, so he finally broke with the A.M.E. Church and founded his own independent church. At the end of his tenure in 1925, he formed the Douglas Memorial Community Church, taking about four hundred Bethel members with him. Bethel's membership in that year was estimated at 1,400 to 1,500 members.

The schism led by Douglas was not the first in Bethel's history; others had occurred in the nineteenth century, particularly during Daniel Payne's pastorate. Schisms, however, were only one path to the creation of new churches. Large churches like Bethel sometimes appointed "missionaries" whose task was to create a mission church, usually in a poor neighborhood. The Ebenezer A.M.E. Church was the first of such mission churches to sprout from Bethel in 1826. The "mother church" would also provide additional members and sometimes financial support for her mission churches. The creation of new churches and the commissioning of older members to support them is one way a large church like Bethel can create room for new members. It is estimated that throughout its history, Bethel has contributed to the creation of at least twenty new churches in Baltimore and the surrounding area (see table 3).

Following the exodus led by Douglas, the Reverend C. Harold Stepteau pastored Bethel from 1925 to 1930. Although Reverend Stepteau was an outstanding preacher and orator in his own right, he had very little success in getting those who had left Bethel to return. In 1930 Bethel's membership stood at 1,000, with 420 pupils in the Sunday school, led by 23 teachers. Twenty conversions were recorded in that year, and the value of the church property was estimated to be $1 million. [52] Financial records show that Stepteau was also paid a salary of $60 a week in April 1930, the same amount that Douglas received in 1925. Although Stepteau helped to stabilize Bethel's congregation after the schism, even greater problems—economic ones—began to be felt at the end of his pastorate.

The Depression Years

Because black people had very little invested in Wall Street, the stock market crash of 1929 did not affect Bethel's members immediately. The effects of the Great Depression, however, grew steadily as more and more people were thrown out of jobs and the lines of the homeless and hungry increased. By 1939 about 65 percent of whites and 92 percent of blacks nationwide were considered poor.[53]

Bethel's Official Board minutes of January 6, 1931, and July 10, 1931, give insights into the economic difficulties beginning to grip the black community both at Bethel and in Baltimore at large. The minutes from January 6 indicate that "the need for some ready money to meet necessary bills in January was brought to the attention of the Board. It was agreed to request the congregation to bring an extra collection of $0.50 on the fourth Sunday to assist the trustees to meet these emergency bills." Apparently, the financial situation of the church worsened during the interim so that at the July 10 meeting the pastor (the Reverend A. Chester Clark) requested salary reductions of 10 percent for all paid officers and other help, beginning with his own. He recommended that the amount be placed in an emergency fund to meet the obligations facing them.

In spite of extremely tight finances, however, Bethel church members continued their outreach to the larger black community. On November 15, 1930, Clark and the trustees agreed to let the social welfare department of the city of Baltimore use its half-acre church basement for feeding and sheltering unemployed and poor people, as well as for providing industrial, educational, and social programs for them.[54] Besides setting up this soup kitchen in cooperation with the social welfare department, Bethel also experimented with spreading the gospel by broadcasting its worship services on radio in 1932. In its use of the new technology, the church was following in the footsteps of the black pioneer of religious broadcasting, Elder Lightfoot Solomon Michaux of the Church of God in Washington, D.C., who became one of the first radio evangelists in 1929.[55]

Even in economically desperate times, it was still important for the people at Bethel to "take care" of their pastor in a fitting and suitable manner. Because real estate prices were plummeting during this period, Bethel's trustees took out a mortgage on a larger parsonage for their pastor at 2027 McCulloh Street. Clark was willing to sacrifice 10 percent of his salary, but the church members would repay him with more comfortable living quarters. This illustrates a long-established tradition in black religion: the "vicarious satisfaction" that church members derive from the status and prestige of their pastor or leader. No matter how poor their own material circumstances, they take pride in ensuring that their pastor enjoys the material benefits—a Cadillac or a beautiful home—that they cannot have.[56]

The City-Wide Young People's Forum became a significant black organization during the Depression years, sponsoring programs that aimed to develop the intellectual and moral talents of poor young people. Led by a community activist, Juanita Jackson, the forum held most of its meetings in Bethel's sanctuary, and it became an important vehicle for the church's teenagers and young adults.[57] Along with the Baltimore chapter of the National Urban League, forum members picketed and boycotted the city's chain stores, which refused to hire Negro clerks. They also protested segregation at the Enoch Pratt Public Library and held mass meetings to demonstrate against the Williams lynching in Salisbury, Maryland, in 1932 and the Armwood lynching in Princess Anne, Maryland, in 1933.[58]

These examples from the forum not only underscore Bethel's public role but remind us that many of the activities associated with direct action, picketing, boycotts, and demonstrations also occurred before the civil rights movement. The interwar period, especially the 1930s, has been sometimes labeled the time of the "deradicalization of black churches," of quietism and withdrawal from the public arena of politics.[59] But for Bethel's congregation, especially for its young people, this thesis is contradicted. Even though the effects of the Depression had reduced the church's income by two-thirds, members of Bethel found creative ways to support its social ministry, from providing a soup kitchen to participating in political protests. Reminiscent of Bethel's large "indignation meetings" in the 1870s and 1880s, which had resulted in the hiring of Baltimore's first black public-school teacher, similar meetings took place during 1937 as the black community pushed the city to hire black police officers. With its 1,600-seat sanctuary and its long-established tradition of involvement in political and community affairs, Bethel was a natural center for this new phase of the struggle for black equality. With the church packed to capacity, city and police officials finally acceded to public pressure. A black woman and member of Bethel, Violet Hill Whyte (the daughter of Daniel Hill, a former pastor of Bethel) became the first black police officer in Baltimore. Her husband, George S. Whyte, served as Bethel's Sunday school superintendent, and their daughter, Esther Bailey, continued to serve the church as an active layperson into the 1990s.

While Bethel maintained a public outreach ministry to the community, it also attempted to serve its own members through individual acts of charity. The following entries from the Official Board minutes of July 3 and September 25, 1931, provide examples:

> Sister Minnie Jones states that Sister Margaret White was in a very bad condition and she had been informed that the money given her from this church has been taken from her and something should be done to get her in the home. Sister Madden made a motion that our pastor be empowered to appoint a committee to get her in the city hospital. Brother Dodd reported the amount of $3.44 was taken up at the church conference on Monday and out of it $2.00 was given to Sister Glascoe as charity and the balance of $1.44 was put in the treasury of the Poor Fund.

As the economic depression deepened, frequent entries in the minutes concerned the need of the trustees to borrow money from their mortgage fund in order to pay their bills. Bethel's financial records show a steep decline in income. For example, the total for plate offerings for the month of October 1932 (five Sundays) was $38.71. Prior to the Depression, from 1925 to 1929, plate offerings had been averaging between $100 and $150 per week.[60]

Just as the nation did not recover from the effects of the Depression until World War II, Bethel Church did not recover from its financial doldrums until that period, when new rural migrants from the Deep South began to join the church. Its financial records for the 1940s showed that the church first matched and then surpassed its pre-Depression income levels from tithing and plate collections. The church's membership averaged about 1,200 during this period. The Reverend James Reese, who served Bethel from 1940 to 1948, also proved to be an astute manager of church finances. He paid off the balance that the trustees had borrowed from the mortgage fund, bought the grounds of the parsonage, retired all floating debts from the Depression years, and improved the property of the church and parsonage. Reese's careful stewardship gave Bethel a firm foundation in both finances and membership before it entered the turmoil and challenges of the civil rights era.

On May 30, 1953, the members of Bethel Church held a special memorial service to honor the work of two outstanding people in the congregation's past: Bishop Sampson Brooks, who had rescued the church from its huge debt, and John H. Murphy, Sr., who had founded the *Baltimore Afro-American* and served as chairman of Bethel's trustees and as superintendent of its Sunday school. Bishop Brooks's plaque was presented by Eva Proctor, president of the Sampson Brooks Sunshine Circle at Bethel, and the W. Sampson Brooks Lodge of the Elks was also present in full force. These two lay organizations, one a women's group and the other a fraternal order, witness to a common practice at Bethel and at other black churches: by naming themselves after someone they revered, lay groups attempted to keep alive the memories of heroic individuals. In doing so they preserved both the history of their congregation and black religious history, which were often ignored by mainstream church historians. John Murphy's plaque was presented by his son, Carl, president of the *Baltimore Afro-American*, on behalf of African American newspapers in the United States. Bryant's sermon that Sunday morning was entitled "The Deeds of Great Men Live After Them." The bronze plaques, hung in the front foyer of Bethel's sanctuary, help the congregation to preserve its own memory and to identify the important role of its leaders in African American history.

Two typical events sponsored by lay groups in this period were a hairstyle and hat fashion show and a drive to collect trading stamps. Although a fashion show might seem frivolous to some, it had important meaning in the black community. Because the physical features of African Americans were often denigrated in the larger society and because racial discrimination excluded black participation in fashion, it was not unusual for lay groups, especially women's groups, to sponsor fashion shows in the black community's only independent institution, the church. In the context of the extreme depersonalization that occurs among an oppressed people, there was a subtle theological underpinning for fashion shows sponsored by black churches: "to love God and to love your neighbor as *yourself.*" Long before the black consciousness movement of the 1960s, these social affairs underscored the insight that black was indeed beautiful. The fashion shows can also be seen as part of a pattern of accommodation and resistance to the dominant culture. While the styles of fashion were influenced by the larger society and can be viewed as accommodationist, the fact that the event was held at all, using black women as models, showed a degree of resistance to the depersonalizing forces of an unequal and segregated society. The fashion shows were also part of the development of "parallel institutions" in the black community mentioned above. The hairstyle and hat show held at Bethel on February 25, 1916, drew an audience of 200 women with

50 models participating. Almost all of the black hairdressers in Baltimore participated in the event, which gives some indication of the church's social influence. The show was sponsored by the Women's Day committee, led by Mayme Tilghman and assisted by Edith Bryant, the pastor's wife. In June 1962, Tilghman, who was president of Bethel's Laymen League, also led the campaign to collect 2,300 Merchants Green Trading Stamps, to be used for the purchase of a new school bus for the Sunday school. More than 1,000 adult members of the church and 100 Sunday school children participated in the stamp drive. There was even a "licking committee" to paste loose stamps into books.[63]

Under the leadership of Bishop Frank Madison Reid, Sr., the Second Episcopal District sponsored the first stewardship seminar ever held in the A.M.E. Church to teach clergy and laity about responsible stewardship and the handling of church finances. The two-day seminar held on April 30 and May 1, 1962, at Bethel Church brought in consultants from the salary department of the A.M.E. Church as well as from the National Council of Churches and the Maryland Council of Churches. This seminar was important for Bethel because afterward, for the first time in its history, the church adopted a budget. In the past the congregation had always kept records of its assets and debits, but it had followed no overall rational budget plan that allocated expenses in view of income. Expenditures were usually tied to the whims of the pastor or the generosity of the head steward. The mishandling of finances through the lack of budgets and record keeping has remained a constant source of problems and schisms in black churches.

The Civil Rights Years

The fifteen years of the Reverend Harrison J. Bryant's pastorate at Bethel illustrate how flexible the A.M.E. itinerant system had become. His career in Bethel's pulpit was the longest in the church's history, and the dates (1949 to 1964) also span the crucial beginning years of the civil rights movement in the United States. A courageous man of quiet dignity who was nearing his ninetieth birthday, Bishop Emeritus Harrison Bryant recounted in an interview how he was called to the ministry in a conversion experience at the St. Stephen A.M.E. Church in South Carolina at the age of ten.[61] Forced by his family's poverty to drop out of school, he later struggled to complete his high school, college, and seminary education. In 1945 he was appointed to St. John A.M.E. in Baltimore. Bryant's success at rebuilding St. John A.M.E. after a fire had demolished the building and in retiring its mortgage in four years led to his promotion to Bethel's pulpit.[62]

The impact of the fledgling civil rights movement did not reach Baltimore until 1958, although the Mongomery Improvement Association, led by the Reverend Dr. Martin Luther King, Jr., finally won its victory in desegregating that city's public transportation in 1956. Both the minutes of the A.M.E. Preachers' Meeting for Baltimore and its vicinity and Bethel's Official Board minutes reflected the growing concerns about the need to desegregate public schools.[64] At the Bethel meeting, the Reverend Harrison Bryant reported on the landslide voting against school integration in Little Rock, Arkansas. This was to be expected, he said, because only a few thousand approved of integration in that city. He also observed that fighting about integrating schools in Virginia was still going on and that only fourteen Maryland counties had integrated schools.

During Maryland's desegregation struggle in the 1960s, Bryant, his family, and some Bethel members worked with the National Association for the Advancement of Colored People (NAACP), the Congress for Racial Equality (CORE), and the Interdenominational Ministerial Alliance to desegregate the stores, restaurants, movie theaters, beaches, and parks in Baltimore. In 1963 Bryant was arrested and jailed during a demonstration to open Gwynn Oak Park to all people. He was also one of the honorary chairmen who mobilized the largest civil rights "March for Baltimore" on March 30, 1964, when some 4,000 demonstrators, led by Dick Gregory, pushed for an end to segregation in all spheres, especially in housing.[65]

The march was supported by many white clergy, including Jewish rabbis. The majority of Bethel's members supported Pastor Bryant's civil rights activities. Bethel's long history of sociopolitical involvement by its pastors and lay leaders did not lead to the kind of divisions and fractious debates that activist clergy in the movement faced in many white churches and some black ones. According to the Quarterly Conference minutes of June 10, 1963, Bethel had 1,489 members on its rolls with 2 new members and 8 baptisms (7 infants and 1 adult).

The year 1964 was a memorable one for Harrison Bryant because his year-long campaign for episcopal office was successful. Bryant was so popular as a preacher that if he had not been elected to the bishopric that year, the Bethel congregation was ready to request his reappointment. In 1965 the newly elected bishop was assigned to the episcopal district of South Africa, and the Reverend Frank Madison Reid, Jr., was appointed to Bethel. Bryant's departure from Bethel led to a gradual but noticeable decline in the congregation's membership from 1,500 to about 1,100 members in succeeding years. The loss of a popular and charismatic preacher seemed to account for the decline.

As an activist who had marched with Martin Luther King, Jr., in Selma, Alabama, Frank Reid continued the tradition of active participation in the civil rights arena that Bryant had established at Bethel. The local newspapers cited three events that demonstrated the congregation's continued involvement. The first event was a farewell reception at Bethel on November 2, 1965, for Bishop Bryant and his wife. It was through Bishop Bryant's involvement in the problems of South Africa that the Bethel congregation developed a special sensitivity toward apartheid in that country, a decade before the rise of the anti-apartheid movement in the United States.

The second event, held at Bethel and sponsored by the Baltimore branch of the NAACP (of which Pastor Reid was vice president), celebrated the Honorable Thurgood Marshall's appointment as the solicitor general of the U.S. by President Lyndon Johnson in 1965. A native Baltimorean, Marshall was especially remembered by the national civil rights community for his prosecution of the case that led to the Supreme Court's decision in *Brown vs. the Board of Education* in 1954, which provided the legal legitimation for the civil rights movement.

The third event occurred during the week of May 17, 1966, when the members of Bethel celebrated the 150th anniversary of the founding of the A.M.E. Church as one of the first black denominations. The celebration began on Tuesday evening with "A Salute to History," which featured several outstanding women in the civil rights movement: Rosa Parks, the seamstress who had sparked the Montgomery bus boycott; Gloria Richardson, who had led the protest movement in Cambridge, Maryland; and Vivian Malone, the first black graduate of the University of Georgia. The congregation's celebration of these women's achievements was one of the first public recognitions of their important role in the civil rights struggle. It also showed that the Bethel congregation was more open to recognizing the role of women than most other black churches.[66]

After the passage of the Voting Rights Act in 1965 and the rise of the black power militants in 1966, the civil rights movement was gradually eclipsed by the increasing involvement of the United States in the Vietnam War. This shift was acknowledged by the members of Bethel Church and by the Baltimore Annual Conference in the resolutions adopted in 1967 at its 151st session. Frank Reid, Bethel's pastor, headed the committee that drafted the resolutions. In the main resolution the A.M.E. Church condemned the killing and maiming of human life "by all parties fighting in Vietnam." It supported a general cease-fire and asked President Johnson and Congress to "find new ways toward peace." The resolution supported the right of the antiwar demonstrators to protest if they did so in an orderly and responsible manner. Other resolutions reflected the church's response to social issues. One called for local churches to sponsor government nonprofit housing developments. Another emphasized the need for increased financial support for programs in Johnson's War on Poverty like Head Start, the Youth Corps, and Medicare. Under Reid's leadership, a Head Start program was instituted at Bethel Church with 200 children in the first class. He also led the drive to retire Bethel's $40,000 mortgage.

The Reverend Frank Madison Reid, Jr., followed in the footsteps of his father, Bishop Frank Reid, Sr., when he was elected as the ninety-fourth bishop of the A.M.E. Church in 1972, the fourteenth pastor of Bethel to be elevated to episcopal office. This pattern has occurred twice in Bethel's history, with two Bishop Reids and two Bishop Bryants; Frank Reid III, Bethel's present pastor, may well be elevated in due time. This phenomenon of sons following their fathers into the ministry is not unusual among black churches.

From 1968 to 1975 the Reverend Walter Hildebrand served as Bethel's pastor. He was considered to be a steadfast, scholarly pastor, known for his skill in conducting Bible classes. He also had a strong, beautiful voice for singing and preaching. The period of Hildebrand's pastorate was also a time of great turmoil within black communities. After the assassination of Martin Luther King, Jr., on April 4, 1968, several hundred urban riots took place across the nation, and Baltimore itself experienced some street violence. At the same time, the black consciousness movement was spreading in the U.S., with its emphasis upon black power, black pride, and the slogan "black is beautiful." The national black community's commitment to working for civil rights and integration was giving way to a growing sense of separation.

Bethel's membership had stood at 1,100 during Reid's pastorate, but by the end of Hildebrand's tenure in 1975 it had fallen below 600. Several factors may have led to the decline: the turmoil and conflict of the time; the confusion of struggling with a new group identity; and Pastor Hildebrand's more scholarly demeanor in the pulpit. (The lack of a charismatic preacher has often been cited as the major factor in the decline of black church membership.) Despite the decline, however, Hildebrand did continue Bethel's tradition of activism and outreach. For example, in 1970 Bethel was one of the three churches chosen by the Community Action Agency of Baltimore to become one of the summer Head Start centers. The programs provided educational, social, medical, dental, and psychological services for children. Fifty-four children participated in Bethel's Head Start center. Another event during Hildebrand's pastorate was the recovery of Bethel Church's historical papers, including financial records, and Official Board minutes from boxes in the church belfry, where they had been covered with pigeon droppings. Hildebrand, the church sexton, and two scholars, Dr. Bettye Collier-Thomas and Dr. Bettye Gardener, aided in the rescue mission.[67]

According to interviews with several long-time lay members, Bethel's worship services under Hildebrand's leadership met the A.M.E. standard of "order and decorum." Music during worship services consisted of traditional anthems and hymns from the *A.M.E. Hymnal*. The lively gospel music and songs that became popular in Baptist and Pentecostal churches in the 1960s were not played at Bethel because they detracted from the orderliness of worship. Very few members, if any, shouted, fell out, or cried during the services. Such emotional responses belonged in the sanctified storefront churches. The Bethel congregation, like the A.M.E. church as a whole, seemed to have become fully assimilated into the dominant culture. Although the official membership list recorded some 600 members, only about half regularly participated in church activities.[68] This active core of largely black middle-class members, however, was vital to the future growth of the church from 1975 to 1989, a period when Bethel was transformed from a "large" 600-member church into a megachurch of 6,000 to 7,000 members.

The Rise of the Neo-Pentecostal Movement:
The Ministry of the Reverends John and Cecilia Williams-Bryant

A visit to Bethel Church on a Sunday morning in 1991 reveals the changes that have been part of its most recent history. Seated behind the pastor near the elevated pulpit area are a female associate pastor, a bishop emeritus, several church trustees and stewards, and a lay leader in charge of security. A "mother of the church," usually one of the older and more respected female members, also sits on the dais. On the congregation's left side, a "signer" translates the worship service for the deaf members in the church and the television audience; on the right, a drummer's beat blends softly with the keyboard, guitar, bass, and saxophone. The sixty members of the men's chorus, outfitted in dark suits and ties, are seated on elevated rows behind the pulpit. Other key lay leaders usually sit in the first two rows so that they can assist the pastor during the altar call, when as many as thirty people come forward every Sunday, seeking either to join the church or to convert and renew their faith. A few lay leaders station themselves in the back of the church by the vestibule at the front entrance, keeping a watchful eye on the order of the service. Women ushers have white dresses and white gloves, sometimes with a colored banner or insignia indicating the ushers' group they are part of. Men ushers have dark suits and sometimes wear white gloves. Each of Bethel's two morning worship services—at 8:00 and 11:00—attracts 1,200 to 1,700 worshipers, and cars are double-parked for several blocks around the church. About 400 people attend the church's Sunday evening service at 6:00, which accommodates the members who work on Sunday mornings (for example, the maids, cooks, and janitors at the big downtown hotels).

At a recent eleven o'clock service, during a very lively anthem by the instrumental group, the church members were clapping rhythmically, and several people got up near the front rows and started to do the "holy dance." A man dressed in an African dashiki and carrying a parasol went into jerky spasms, possessed by the Holy Spirit. Members of the congregation cried out, "Hallelujah!" and "Come Holy Spirit!" But there was no speaking in tongues en masse as is customary in a Pentecostal service. During the sermon the pastor, the Reverend Frank Reid III, became emotionally caught up and descended from the pulpit. With a wireless microphone pinned to his lapel, he began running up and down the aisles of the church, trying to illustrate that "you can't hide from God." Delighted by the pastor's spontaneity and antics, the congregation stood up, applauding and cheering him on. About forty new members joined Bethel on that Sunday during the altar call. Each new member was met by a lay leader and taken to a back room where they could discuss membership or conversion. Daniel Payne would certainly be astounded by what is going on in worship services at the contemporary Bethel.

At the center of a still developing neo-Pentecostal movement in the entire A.M.E. denomination are the Reverends John and Cecilia Williams-Bryant. The son of Bishop Harrison Bryant, Bethel's longest-serving pastor, John Bryant was appointed to Bethel in 1975. He had served as the pastor of the St. Paul A.M.E. Church in Cambridge,

Massachusetts, from 1970 to 1975. Within those five years St. Paul's had grown from 200 members to 1,200 members, so Bryant had come to Bethel with the reputation of church builder. He had also come with the reputation of doing some "far out" things: St. Paul's had become known in A.M.E. circles as a "rocking church." According to Bryant, his wife, the Reverend Cecilia Williams, contributed to their joint ministry by working with the women of the church.[69] Because women make up at least two-thirds or more of black congregations, that task alone was quite formidable. Williams was eased into her role as associate minister gradually so that the congregation would be comfortable seeing her as a leader—first in prayer meetings, Bible studies, and Sunday evening services and then in the regular Sunday morning worship services. Her role as the first female associate minister at Bethel stirred some controversy, but much of it was muted as the congregation began to see the successful ministry of their first clergy couple.

As pastor, Bryant worked with all members, but the couple shared one salary. When he arrived at Bethel, there were 600 members on the rolls, but an average of only 200 to 250 people attended Sunday worship. On his first Sunday he counted 310 people, with 10 new members joining; in all the previous year Bethel had gained only 12 new members. This auspicious beginning in church growth is significant because the church has had new members join every Sunday since 1975 through 1988, when Bryant was elected bishop, and this pattern has continued into 1993.

John Bryant described himself as being a "mediocre" and "troublesome" kid growing up in a highly talented family. Named after the first church his father pastored in Baltimore, St. John A.M.E., he barely graduated from high school and Morgan State University in Baltimore because he "partied too much." In the midst of applying to Methodist-related seminaries at Drew and Boston universities, he decided instead to heed the advice of a famous black preacher, the Reverend Dr. Samuel Proctor, to "go first to Africa" because "you haven't seen or done anything yet." His Peace Corps experiences in Liberia were important to his identity and spiritual formation. In the Peace Corps he could be himself and escaped being labeled as the son of Bethel's pastor or the younger brother of three highly talented older siblings. In Liberia he encountered the "spirit dimension" of Africans, who understood the holistic connection between the material and the spiritual. His observations and his own experiences with this spirit dimension in healing ceremonies and in unexplainable occurrences deepened his conviction about its significance for his ministry and for the A.M.E. Church.

Later, reflecting upon his training at the School of Theology at Boston University, Bryant concluded that to separate mind from feeling (as was encouraged in academia) was "to weaken and not to strengthen." Christians could emote and celebrate, he felt, and still be deeply grounded theologically. Finally, Bryant applied these insights to his reflections on the history of the A.M.E. Church and Bethel:

> I also maintain that the A.M.E. Church made its greatest strides when it was not ashamed of its feelings. But in trying to be accepted by the white world and trying to be sophisticated, they threw all of that out. One of the great fathers of the A.M.E. Church, Daniel Payne, who was a great blessing to the Church with his emphasis on education, also saw it the exact same way. That if we are going to be an educated and sophisticated people, we've got to stop participating in what he called "cornfield ditties," "the sand dances," and all the rest. He told them don't act like "heathens." "You have to learn how to sit—erect and proper in the House of the Lord." . . . Payne dominated more than anybody else in the past in the mood and style of the mainline force of the Church. So I always maintained that the style that I have adopted is not "new." But it is a "renaissance," a return to the old [a recovery of the emotional side of African Americans and African Methodism in worship].[70]

Besides his Peace Corps experience in Africa and his struggles with the deficiencies of seminary education in Boston, a third factor that pushed Bryant in the direction of emphasizing the Holy Spirit was traditional Pentecostalism. While pastoring his first church, Bethel A.M.E. of Fall River, Massachusetts, he learned more about the doctrines of the Holy Spirit and the techniques used by black Pentecostals from Bishop Young of the Church of God in Christ (COGIC) in Boston. Among black denominations, it was COGIC that upheld the banner of the Holy Spirit, while the others had let it slip. COGIC members believed that accepting Jesus as one's personal savior was not enough; a person needed "the baptism of the Holy Spirit," which is evidenced by such "gifts of the Spirit" as "speaking in tongues." Bryant felt that his own denomination had emphasized "the Father" and "the Son" of the Trinity and had largely neglected the Holy Spirit.

St. Paul A.M.E. in Cambridge had added a thousand new members in a few years, and Bethel in Baltimore grew from 600 to 7,000 members in a decade. What accounted for this remarkable growth in church membership? According to Bryant the winning formula was an "emphasis on the Holy Spirit" and "active involvement in the community"— a recognition that "the Spirit is always given to do." This approach, Bryant felt, overcame the difficulties that Christian churches succumbed to when they stressed only one side of the dialectic. For example, traditional Pentecostal churches that emphasize the Holy Spirit usually have very little or no involvement with the world. Likewise liberal churches can become deeply involved in the community with an array of social action projects but remain relatively empty on Sunday mornings, with no emphasis on worship, praise, and the Holy Spirit. The combination, for Bryant, was biblical because "Jesus fed folk. He delivered folk. And he led them in prayer." Bryant continued,

> One must ask the question, "Holy Spirit for what?" What are we going to do? If all we are doing is jumping up and down in the air, speaking in other tongues, saying "yea, the Spirit is with us," that's fine. But I preach all the time that that is taking the gravy and leaving the Spirit. The meat of the Holy Spirit is for our empowerment. It's for our liberation and development. It's for our strength as a people. And it has been that.

At St. Paul and Bethel, Bryant began to develop an "outreach ministry"—an economic development ministry, a ministry to prisons, a ministry to whole persons; "I try to think of as many needs as people have and try to address those."

Another factor that has influenced growth at Bethel has been an emphasis on "black awareness." Black cultural elements have been consciously introduced: the mural in the sanctuary, the five-piece instrumental ensemble (drums, electric guitar, organ, piano, and bass) in the worship service. The focus of the brightly colored mural has been on black people as black Christians, not merely as Christians who happen to be black. Bryant's experience with murals went back to St. Paul's in Cambridge, where he had asked an artist to paint scenes from the everyday life of black people. The negative reactions from some of the older members were intense: "One woman said, 'Get that big old black woman with big black legs down!' And the woman looked just like her. They would say, 'Why don't you have a dove, or Jesus with some sheep?' I would say to them, 'I don't see any doves in Cambridge, no sheep around. But up there is us and the Lord with us.'" The diehards in the St. Paul congregation finally began to accept the mural when some white schools in the area started to send their art classes to the church to study it. After his first year at Bethel, Bryant decided to have a mural painted when the church had to be renovated. He invited Yvonne Evert, a graduate student in art at Howard University, to attend services for a few weeks in order to "get a feel for the congregation," and then decide what to paint. Bethel's mural did not arouse the extremely negative reactions as had the mural at St. Paul's, but it continued to draw the interest of people, even those who may not have liked it. The mural said to people, "This is a different place. Difference is here." It also said, "Unashamedly, I'm black!! No accident. And I've got a history of God in my blackness. And I've got a reason to celebrate God in my blackness, for my blackness. And you need to know how to live as black folk."

The strongest negative criticisms to these cultural innovations at Bethel came when Bryant introduced the musical ensemble, especially the drums, in the same year that the mural was painted. For the older members the use of drums in worship was "too secular." For Bryant not only did the drums symbolize an important connection to African culture, they were reminders that slave masters had banned the use of drums throughout most of the South because they were instruments of communication as well as music. Their use in church was a recovery of the past. The musical ensemble played traditional Methodist hymns and black spirituals, but they also began to introduce the livelier, upbeat, more celebratory modern gospel music. That music has helped to attract black young people to church, as another study has shown.[71] Obviously, both the emphasis upon black identity and the use of gospel music with drums during worship reiterate the themes of Afrocentrism and resistance to total cultural assimilation that have been an important part of the congregation's history.

Several things helped to quell the negative reactions of older church members. The first, according to Bryant, was that "I was their son"—a son of Bethel who had grown up in the church. With the first changes, the older members had said inquisitively, "What is this boy talking about now? What's he going to do? There was a love there. That was to my benefit." The second factor was the enormous church growth. From Bryant's first Sunday service, Bethel Church began to grow (see table 4). "The growth was the real key to my success. There were people at Bethel who never liked what I was doing, especially when I brought the drums and instruments in," said Bryant. "But the critics were gradually silenced because they were outnumbered by the crowds that were attracted by the innovations." As Bethel Church grew in numbers and in prominence, both in the public press and in the denomination, the old church leaders still wanted to be leaders because they now had followers to lead. But these new members were also "potential place takers." For years the old leaders had complained, "Well, we are the faithful few, the faithful remnant, and without us where would this church be?" Now, however, younger people were turning up and asking, "Boy, I would love to be a trustee. What do you have to do to be a trustee?" The church's growth gave Bryant freedom from his traditionalist critics. Finally, as part of his strategy of coming to terms with the older members of Bethel, Bryant poured himself into the whole spiritual ministry— worship, preaching, Bible study, prayer meetings, and "love feasts" (gatherings to celebrate an engaged couple's wedding plans). "That won the old people," he said, and "I think my age excited the young people. I was thirty-one years old, the youngest pastor in Bethel's history."

After solidifying Bethel's internal worship life, Bryant began an outreach ministry by buying a dilapidated old rowhouse near the church for $1,700, fixing it up, and using it as a distribution point for giving out free clothes and food. "I think the older people finally liked what they saw on the whole: the church was beginning to grow, and more and more people started coming." The church leaders began consciously to count as the numbers soared to 700, 800, 1,000, 1,200, and beyond. In the first few years, the congregation rose to sing "O for a Thousand Tongues to Sing," to celebrate every 100 new members that were added. Bryant's goal was to make Bethel Church known as "the Holy Ghost Headquarters."

Besides the Outreach Center set up in 1976, Bethel's ministry to the community also involved reinvigorating the programs of Freedom House and establishing a women's center in 1977. Founded in 1970, Freedom House had the primary aim of preserving the inner city as a wholesome place for all to live by cooperation between the police department and the neighborhood residents. In 1977 John Peters, a member of Bethel and the president of Freedom House, also added a full-employment program, "Jobs Now," to the earlier police-community campaign against crime. Every Tuesday at Bethel Church, Peters assembled representatives from utility companies, banks, industry, and federal, state, and municipal agencies to talk directly to the unemployed. Pastor Bryant was the finance chairman of Freedom House.[72]

Under the leadership of the Reverend Cecilia Williams-Bryant, the pastor's wife, and Bethel laywomen Carol A. Talley and Millicent G. White, the church established the women's center on October 1, 1977. Staffed by volunteer professionals, the center focused on providing both group and individual counseling to women, as well as establishing educational programs. Women could learn how to read, and they could also take up to four college credit courses at the center. The credit for the college courses was from Morgan State University; financial aid was available to those who couldn't afford to pay. Staff members from Morgan State University's Women's Center and the University of Maryland Cooperative Extension Program assisted the church women in setting up the new center, but Bethel Church funded the entire program. The center also established a weekly "Women-Together Luncheon," which brought participants in the counseling program together with outstanding women from the local community who became role models for women at the center. Since 1976, as part of their annual Women's Day observance, Bethel Church has instituted the African rite of passage called "Kwandulukwa Ntu," or "Going Back Into History." The ritual, which includes classes and counseling by older women, helps young women make the transition from adolescence to adulthood. Black churches that arose from the evangelical tradition, as Bethel did, do not pay any attention to the rite of confirmation; thus a rite of passage to adulthood is lacking. By creating its own rite of passage based on African tradition, the congregation was again asserting its resistance to mainstream American culture and returning to its African heritage. "We feel that a lot has happened in the past ten years to diminish what was once called the strong black woman," said the Reverend Cecilia Williams-Bryant in connection with the women's center and other church programs for women. "Black women's closeness to the church began to decline with the whole political consciousness thing. A lot of the problems that we are in today are because people no longer decide for themselves what their lives will be—they just go along and accept what comes. We're here to tell them that they can have some impact on their own lives. That's the message that our Women's Center will try to convey."[73]

In 1976 Pastor John Bryant began a Labor Day sunrise service that has become a Bethel tradition, combining both worship and social ministry. The worship service was dedicated to the unemployed, and members were asked to bring with them either information about a job, a new pair of shoes, or some canned goods as their offering. The 6:00 A.M. service attracted 1,500 persons. The front altar was filled with brand-new shoes for poor people, especially children who needed shoes for school. Information on over 100 jobs was brought in, and unemployed persons were matched with those jobs.[74] The idea was to have the church community share the fruits of their labor with the poor and unemployed and to begin the process of freeing people from the bondage of unemployment.

During Bryant's ministry, numerous other programs were started, including a food co-op, an energy co-op, and a federal credit union for church members, a community library, a prison visitation program, aerobics classes, martial arts training, a singles' club, and a rural development committee to help churches outside Baltimore develop community programs, especially in poor black communities on Maryland's Eastern Shore. Bethel also reached back to its origins in 1815, when the church also housed the Bethel Church Charitable School; in 1983 the Alphonso MacLaren Christian Academy was established, providing a Christian and academic education for children from kindergarten through the second grade. A church drama ministry was started, and the worship committee experimented with modern dance performances in regular worship services by the Marie Brooks Children's Dance Research Theater, which encouraged Bethel to develop its own dance group.

In 1984 the church started an annual tradition called "homecoming day" when all who have been associated with Bethel's past and present get together for food and fellowship after the eleven o'clock service in mid-September. More than 2,500 people attended the first homecoming. "Often the 8 o'clock crowd doesn't know the 11 o'clock crowd," said Bryant. "Homecoming is a chance for us to get to know who the family is." Present and former members of Bethel drive long distances to be present at homecoming. Although the congregation has always had programs of social outreach in the past, these programs have become much more extensive in Bethel's present ministry. They reflect the impact of the congregation's larger membership and financial base, and also Bryant's view that a church like Bethel should attempt to "dominate its community," returning to the central role it held in the nineteenth century when it was the premier institution in Baltimore's black community.

After an unsuccessful attempt in 1984, John Bryant was elected bishop of the A.M.E. denomination in 1988, Bethel's fifteenth pastor to serve in that office. The question of a replacement for Bryant at Bethel became a major concern in the denomination and in the Second District because Bethel had become the largest A.M.E. church in the nation.[75]

The appointment of the Reverend Frank Madison Reid III to succeed Bryant was apt for several reasons. First, Reid was a Bryant protégé, having attended St. Paul's in Cambridge while he was at Harvard Divinity School. Second, he too was a "son of Bethel," having grown up in the church while his father was the pastor, and Reid, like Bryant, was the son of an A.M.E. bishop. Third and foremost, Reid was a successful pastor, having built the 500-member Ward A.M.E. Church in Los Angeles into a congregation of 5,000. Using the formula of his mentor, Reid had built Ward into a church that was known for its enthusiastic, spirit-filled worship and its activist community outreach, and now he was returning to Bethel.

A 1989 Congregational Survey

On July 9, 1989, with the consent and cooperation of Reverend Reid and Bethel's trustees and ushers, I and several assistants were able to conduct a congregational survey at Bethel. We passed out surveys to those attending the two morning worship services; from the estimated 2,800 persons attending services that morning, 898 usable surveys were returned.[76] The purposes of the survey were to obtain a profile of the members, to allow them to express their views about the ministry of Bethel Church, and to assess the impact of the neo-Pentecostal movement on their lives. The profile indicated that 85 percent of the respondents were members of Bethel Church, and 14 percent were not. In response to the question, "In what year did you join the church?" answers ranged from 1914 to 1989. About 9 percent of the respondents had joined Bethel Church before 1975, and more than 75 percent had joined Bethel after 1975. More than three-fourths of the member-respondents, then, had joined Bethel during the ministries of either Bryant or Reid. The influence of the neo-Pentecostal movement in contributing to the growth of Bethel's membership has been enormous. The survey also indicated that close to two-thirds of this growth resulted from membership transfers from other churches and that about one-third of the new members had no prior church membership.

A Demographic Profile of the Congregation

The profile showed that 29 percent of the respondents were male, and about 70 percent were female, which correlates closely with the national average for black church membership, one-third male and two-thirds

4.1 Exterior view of Bethel African Methodist Episcopal Church, 1992. Courtesy of Bethel A.M.E. Church.

female.[77] The median level of education among the respondents was in the category of "some college" (about two-thirds of the sample—66.7 percent—checked the categories of "some college," "college graduate," or "graduate school," giving an indication that the majority of Bethel's members are in the middle class). The median income of the respondents was in the $20,000–$29,000 range, with 26 percent earning more than that level and 25 percent earning less. The data indicated that about 76 percent of Bethel's respondents were above age thirty.

Of those responding, 58 percent claimed that they attended church once a week, while 32 percent attended two or three times a month.

Only 7 percent attended once a month or less, and fewer than 1 percent had never attended church before. The survey also asked whether they participated in Bethel Church activities other than Sunday worship. About half of the respondents indicated that they participated in church activities other than worship, and 46 percent said they did not. The data on church attendance and participation indicate that Bethel Church has been able to attract a very loyal and quite active membership. Comparisons with Gallup surveys indicate that Bethel's attendance and active participation rates are much higher than the national average for black churches: for weekly attendance, 58 percent for Bethel versus 44 percent nationally; for loyalty and participation in church activities other than worship services, 50 percent for Bethel versus 37 percent nationally.[78] Bethel members participate in a host of groups and ministries: Sunday school; one of eight choirs; the weeknight classes that are part of the Methodist class system; Women's Day activities; the credit union; ushers; youth ministries; Bible study; economic development committee; Lenten committee; married couples ministry; women's ministry; men's Bible class; senior citizens' groups; missionary committee; children's chapel; scholarship committee; substance abuse ministry; altar guild; stewards and trustees; black history workshops; deaf and sign-language ministry; radio and television ministry; hospitality; evangelism ministry; boot camp (a Bible training camp for new converts and those who wish to deepen their spiritual life); prison ministry; Bethel Bible Institute; and New Life Ministry (orientation and training for new members). Except for some of the traditional A.M.E. groups (the Methodist class system, Sunday school, choir, Bible study, altar guild, ushers, stewards, and trustees) that were present at Bethel before 1975, the majority of the lay groups came into existence with the congregation's neo-Pentecostal phase. These smaller groups are important in providing spiritual nurture and person-to-person contact in the megachurch that Bethel has become.

Religious Experiences and Gifts of the Spirit

In order to assess the influence of the neo-Pentecostal movement in the lives of church members, the survey asked questions about religious experiences and experiences of the gifts of the Holy Spirit. In response to the question, "Have you ever had a religious experience that was a particularly powerful religious insight or awakening?" 51 percent said yes, and 23 percent said no. In the qualitative section, some respondents elaborated on their religious experiences by citing incidents when they were miraculously healed from a life-threatening illness or when a serious automobile accident had been averted. Others spoke of their experiences of being in a "calm and soothing presence."

As follow-up questions, the survey asked, "Have you yourself experienced the gifts of the Holy Spirit?" and "If yes, describe the gifts." Although 30 percent said no, more than half of the respondents (59 percent) answered affirmatively: 14 percent said they had experienced "speaking in tongues"; 16 percent, "prophecy"; 2 percent, "interpretation of tongues"; 26 percent, "healing," and 21 percent, "other." Although more chose the category of healing as their gift from the Holy Spirit than any other category, more than half of these meant that they had experienced healing in their lives rather than that they had the ability to heal others. This interpretation is evident from the responses in the qualitative section of the survey.

The Bethel congregation differs from traditional Pentecostal churches in that only 14 percent of the respondents claimed that they had received the gift of glossolalia, or speaking in tongues. In traditional Pentecostalism, the focus is on receiving the gift of tongues, and it is not unusual for mass sessions of glossolalia to occur in worship services. At Bethel, large sessions of tongue-speaking have not occurred during worship services. Rather, glossolalia is viewed by the pastor and church leaders mainly as a prayer language to be used in solitude or in small prayer groups. Mass sessions of glossolalia have thus not been encouraged by the leaders of worship, but this practice should not be considered a reassertion of the old tradition of "order and decorum," because other aspects of the worship service do not reflect that concern. As John Bryant commented in his interview, he had difficulty understanding how speaking in tongues could occur in large Pentecostal churches upon the command of one person and then stop when that person stopped.

Views on Political Involvement and on Women as Pastors

Replicating questions from earlier Gallup surveys and national studies, the survey polled the Bethel respondents about their views on church involvement in politics, civil rights militancy, and women as pastors of churches. In response to the question, "Should Bethel A.M.E. Church keep out of political matters, or should the church express its views on day-to-day social and political questions?" the vast majority, 80 percent, supported the position that Bethel should express its views; only 4 percent felt that the church should keep out of politics. Gallup surveys in March 1957 and February 1968 indicated that 68.4 percent of 231 nonwhites and 46.4 percent of 2,000 whites favored a prophetic role for the church in social issues. Bethel's congregation has shown a higher level of support for social involvement than did Gallup's national sample, a finding that is consonant with the church's past history of social activism in the nineteenth century and during the Depression of the 1930s.[79]

On the question of civil rights militancy ("How would you feel about the clergy of Bethel Church taking part in protest marches on civil rights issues? Would you approve or disapprove of this?"), 81 percent of the members responding approved of civil rights militancy by their clergy, while only 2.2 percent said they disapproved (the remainder gave no response). The level of support for civil rights militancy among Bethel's members is similar to the comparative data provided by the Gallup survey in 1965 at the peak of the civil rights movement, in which 88 percent of 235 nonwhite respondents supported militancy and only 30.5 percent of 2,205 white respondents did.[80] In a 1986 in-house study of the Leadership Training Institute of the Second Episcopal District of the A.M.E. Church, of which Bethel is a part, 71 percent of 127 A.M.E. lay leaders approved of civil rights militancy by their clergy.[81]

The strength of the members' approval or disapproval of a woman as the pastor of a church was also assessed. More than a third of the respondents (35 percent) said they "strongly approved" of a woman pastor, and 44 percent felt they "approved." About 6 percent said they "strongly disapproved," while 4 percent said they "disapproved." The level of support for women pastors among Bethel's congregational members—78.5 percent—is similar to that expressed by A.M.E. lay leaders of the Second District, among whom 77 percent approved and only 7 percent disapproved.[82] The high level of support for women clergy by Bethel's members is due to their experience of having women clergy in their midst. Since 1975 the associate pastor has been a woman, and more than half of the lay ministers of the church have been women.

The results of the survey on the church's involvement in political and social realms, civil rights militancy, and approval of women as pastors indicated how Bethel's "neo-Pentecostalism" differs from traditional Pentecostalism and from the charismatic movement in white churches. The latter movements tend to be more otherworldly, withdrawn, and focused upon the private sphere of religious experiences.

While Bethel maintains a strong focus on the inner spiritual life, that intense spirituality is balanced by its outreach programs and progressive political views.

Contemporary Lay Ministries

The uniqueness of Bethel's lay ministries lies both in the legitimation and in the organizational structure that the church provides. As mentioned above, the fifty or so lay ministries deal with the needs of women, pregnant teenagers, drug addicts, the homeless and the hungry, former convicts, prisoners, students, senior citizens, and the deaf. A newly formed public security ministry provides security for the church, its members, and their cars during worship services and other church meetings because Bethel is located in the heart of a poor black community. Each ministry is headed by a volunteer layperson who is formally called "minister" by others in the church; both the title and the ministry are thus legitimated by the church. Bethel's associate pastor, the Reverend Charlotte Clemmons, has the task of overseeing the lay ministries. Each lay minister is required to attend advanced Bible study and leadership classes provided by the church. Through its structure of lay ministries, Bethel Church has paved the way for about 100 of its lay members in a period of ten years to attend theological seminaries and become fully ordained clergy in the A.M.E. Church.

At one of the weekly meetings of the Freedom Now ministry for alcohol and drug abusers in August 1989, Sister Lillian Streeter introduced herself as Minister Streeter.[83] With the assistance of another Bethel lay minister, Vonda Guzman, the meeting began at 6 o'clock on a Thursday evening and lasted until 9:30. Beginning with a handful of members, people trickled into the small classroom throughout the evening until there were twenty present, fifteen men and five women. The Freedom Now ministry has adapted the twelve-step program of Alcoholics Anonymous to include drug or substance abuse and to be more biblically based. Small cards entitled "Jesus Is Your Victory," describing the twelve-step program at Bethel, were distributed during the meeting. The format of the meeting included prayer, reading from the Bible (Psalm 30), singing, and the sharing of testimonies. The Reverend Ron Wright from Pastor Reid's former church, Ward A.M.E. in Los Angeles, was the guest speaker. Wright spoke from his own experience and struggle with drugs and recommended the need for God's help in a

4.2   Sanctuary Mural in Bethel African Methodist Episcopal
Church, 1992. Courtesy of Bethel A.M.E. Church.

"serious transformation, a life changed" through faith and patience
with God.

Seated in a circle, members spoke freely about their drug and alcohol addiction, describing the numerous failures and small victories in
their personal struggles. Paul said that he had been "clean" for seven
months now but before that had taken all kinds of drugs and alcohol; it
was cocaine that had done him in, because he had lost all control. He
had spent a year in the Baltimore jail and had been paroled by the judge
to Bethel's Freedom Now ministry. After being separated from his wife

for four years, he was now reunited with his family. "They are hurting and in pain," he said of drug addicts. "I know that pain very well." Brother Harold, a former member of Bethel, spoke of earning lots of money as an engineer and then blowing it all on three-day drug binges. He was trying to do it all by himself; he had "an angel on one shoulder and a demon on the other." Faced with the prospect of losing everything, Harold had returned to Bethel and joined Freedom Now's beginners' group.

During the altar call of the worship service the week before, a father and his two sons had been in a line of twenty people who wanted to join the church as new members. Pastor Reid had announced to the congregation that the father wanted to help his eldest son in his struggle with drug addiction. They had agreed to come to Freedom Now's meeting on Thursday. The father had shown up at the meeting early and was waiting patiently for his son to come. As the meeting ended and people departed, tears of disappointment glistened in the father's eyes.

Minister Streeter announced to the group that at next Sunday's eleven o'clock worship service there would be a special recognition of the Freedom Now ministry, and all members were encouraged to attend. Group members would be seated in the front pews reserved for them, and Pastor Reid would preach a special sermon, "From Slavery to Freedom," detailing the new forms of slavery in substance abuse and addiction. At the worship service the congregation applauded and shouted their enthusiastic support for the members of the Freedom Now ministry. Each member was warmly greeted by the pastor. In an interview, Streeter said that certificates of abstinence are awarded to members at intervals of five months, seven months, and one year. People are placed in a beginners' group or an advanced group, each of which meets once a week at Bethel. Between the meetings Streeter and her assistant are available at all times of the day or night for personal counseling and support. Asked whether she would like to have a church of her own, she said that she had thought and prayed about it. She knew that if she did start a new church she would do so with Bethel's blessing. Her immediate goal, however, was to establish a home or halfway house for drug abusers with Pastor Reid's help.

Esther Bailey is another of Bethel's lay leaders, serving in the educational ministry and as president of the Daniel Payne Scholarship Committee. She also represents the third generation of her family's connection to the church. (Her grandfather was the Reverend Daniel Hill, a pastor of Bethel, and her mother, Violet Hill, became the first black police officer in Baltimore in 1937.)[84] The scholarship committee was organized by John Bryant in 1975 in order to give financial encouragement to high school graduates of Bethel Church who were entering college. The early awards were "book scholarships" amounting to $50 each. Since 1975 the amount and number of awards have expanded greatly. In 1989 twenty-eight awards were made, totaling $20,900. At the eleven o'clock worship service the recipients and their families were called to stand before the altar and receive their awards from the pastor. The congregation gave them a standing ovation. Young people at Bethel who have made outstanding contributions to the life of the church are given supplementary monetary awards for the first year of college. Bailey stressed that it was not enough for a student to have a good academic record; the fifty-five committee members felt that the student also needed to be active in church programs.

Since 1975, the Daniel Payne Scholarship Committee has given over $100,000 in book scholarships and monetary awards. In order to raise the money, the committee held fund raising events like a "Showcase of Stars" talent show, a luncheon and fashion show, and its annual December Penny Rally. On the first Sunday in December, all of Bethel's members are asked to bring the pennies they have been collecting at home. In 1989 the Penny Rally itself raised $3,361. The committee has also contracted with the *Baltimore Sun* to sell its Sunday edition to church members after both services. With stacks of newspapers in the foyer of the church, members are encouraged to buy their Sunday papers from the committee, which raised $2,800. The committee has also solicited and received donations for educational awards from different groups within the church.

Besides raising funds, the Payne Scholarship Committee hosts a reception for graduates and sponsors a financial aid workshop. Through the Bethel Educational Incentive Program, which the committee initiated in 1987, it also encouraged students from grades six through twelve to develop goals for securing an education and recognizes their academic progress.[85] The church's concerns for education have also resulted in Bethel's expansion of its own private elementary school, the Alphonso MacLaren Christian Academy; the school now serves 130 students from prekindergarten to the fifth grade. The founding of the school grew out of a desire that Christian principles and values be part of children's education and out of a concern about the decline of quality in Baltimore's public schools.

These examples of lay ministries in substance abuse and education represent only a small portion of a larger social and spiritual phenomenon at Bethel. Some lay ministries like the TeenPep Program for pregnant teenagers have achieved a national reputation. Used as a model by social welfare agencies, TeenPep is one of the few programs in the country to involve teen fathers in its efforts to combat the highest rate of teen pregnancy in black communities nationwide.[86] Other lay ministries have been flexibly designed to include people's interests, aptitudes, and needs. Examples include the drama ministry, a modern dance ministry (the Hands to Glory Dancers), and the television and radio ministries.

Pastor Reid has contributed to the lay ministries by emphasizing Bethel as a unique place for ministry to black men. With headlines blaring the high rates of unemployment, homicide, and incarceration among black men, Reid has mobilized and encouraged the men in the congregation to develop lay organizations for men. Bethel's Black Men's Chorus of sixty voices is one of the largest choirs for men in any black church in the nation. Plans have been made for a men's center, a men's Bible study, and a Manhood Rites of Initiation group for young males to learn more about responsibility. Since 1988 male membership at Bethel has increased from 25 percent to about 40 percent of all worshipers (the average black church nationwide has a male membership of less than one third).[87] Bethel's efforts to increase and sustain its male members are being eagerly watched by other black congregations. Bethel's ministry to men, it should be noted, adds to—and does not replace—the church's ministry to women, which already includes special women's groups, female clergy, and a women's center.

The lay ministries give congregation members increased opportunities to practice their Christian beliefs daily, and the ministries have also empowered the laity in an institution that is often centered on the authority of the pastor. Through its lay ministries Bethel Church has become a "seven-days-a-week church," with groups constantly meeting on its premises. The varied lay ministries support the congregation's attempt to be holistic, to be involved in every aspect of life and society.

Conclusion

In 1985, the congregation at the Bethel A.M.E. Church in Baltimore celebrated its 200th anniversary, dating its founding from the establishment of a separate and independent prayer group for African Americans when the Strawberry Alley and Lovely Lane meetinghouses of the Methodist Episcopal Church began to segregate their black members. Bethel's faction of black Methodists in Baltimore was always a little more radical and independent than some others; hence, they played a leading role in establishing the African Methodist Episcopal Church, the first historic black denomination. The major theme in the congregation's history has been its struggle toward freedom, embodied in its attempts to abolish slavery and to acquire political, economic, and social justice in the nineteenth and twentieth centuries. The theme is intertwined with the lay ministries of the contemporary Bethel congregation as its members struggle against new forms of slavery like drug and alcohol addiction, teenage pregnancy, extreme poverty, and more subtle types of racial and sexual discrimination.

Composed of many families of the black elite of nineteenth-century Baltimore, Bethel Church often dominated the spiritual and secular affairs of the black community. Its worship services and talented preaching frequently attracted large numbers. Several of Bethel's lay leaders were also the prime political leaders in the community, and five church members established the first black-owned drydock company in the United States. Bethel Church was also the catalyst and the womb for numerous social and intellectual groups that met at the church—the lodges, beneficial societies, literary groups, and debate societies. It also provided an alternative status system for a people whose history and achievements were largely invisible or unrecognized within American society.

The subthemes of accommodation and resistance to the dominant culture also run through the church's history, sometimes leading in one direction and sometimes in another. The Reverend Daniel Payne's attempts to suppress the folk religious rituals of blacks, like singing "cornfield ditties" and dancing at Bethel's worship services, and his emphasis upon an educated clergy and laity represented a major thrust toward the Americanization of a congregation made up of descendants of freed and enslaved Africans. What occurred at Bethel in the mid-nineteenth century also happened to the A.M.E. denomination as a whole and to other black churches; many of the African-influenced rituals and songs were dropped in favor of the "order and decorum" of mainstream white churches. Only a small segment of songs called "Negro spirituals" were preserved from the earlier era. Bethel was one of the first black churches to have organ music and the first to sponsor concerts of sacred music. On the other hand, the members of Bethel also resisted complete assimilation and explicitly identified with the African heritage of the first independent black denomination. Some of the church's pastors and leaders—Henry McNeil Turner in the late nineteenth century, William Sampson Brooks during World War I, and John Bryant and Frank Reid III in the contemporary period—were avowed advocates of Afrocentrism, black nationalism, and black pride.

As a church that often served as a stepping-stone toward the bishopric in the denomination, Bethel has been blessed with highly talented lay leaders and pastors. Always a very large church, Bethel has become in the contemporary period (1975 to the present) a megachurch of more than 7,000 members. A neo-Pentecostal influence has been felt at Bethel, and the power of the Holy Spirit has been emphasized in all its activities, from prayer, Bible study, sermons, and music to its diverse outreach ministries. The neo-Pentecostal movement has also revived to some degree a few older black folk religious rituals like enthusiastic shouting, falling out, and even the "holy dance." The reason for the church's rapid growth lies in its potent combination of an enthusiastic black evangelical tradition and socially progressive lay ministries. Older and more traditional black Christians are attracted to Bethel's emphasis on the spiritual life, including intensive Bible study and prayer conferences. Relevant and dynamic preaching has also made an important contribution. College-educated members and younger people are impressed by the political and social involvement of the church and the pastor in the larger community, its emphasis on the African American heritage, and the modern gospel music supported by an instrumental group in worship services. In addition, Bethel Church's unique structure of more than fifty lay ministries has involved its members both in the internal life of the church and in its social outreach. In the A.M.E. denomination, Bethel is at the fountainhead of a growing neo-Pentecostal movement that has already produced five of the largest and wealthiest A.M.E. congregations in the nation.[88]

The triumphs and tribulations of an oppressed people are reflected in the history of Bethel A.M.E. Church in Baltimore. Throughout the long and arduous journey toward freedom, Bethel Church has remained a tower of strength and resilience, an anchor of stability in Baltimore's black community. The church has continuously attempted to meet its people's physical, social, and spiritual needs. African American history and indeed the history of the nation as a whole would be much poorer without the contributions of congregations like Bethel.

APPENDIX

TABLE 1

Membership in Bethel Church, 1816–1860

YEAR	NUMBER OF MEMBERS
1816	633
1824	715
1842	980
1845	1,302
1850	1,460
1852	1,504
1860	1,400

Sources: James W. Wright, 1971, p. 227; Daniel Payne, 1891; James A. Handy, 1901; and the Bethel Quarterly Conference Records.

TABLE 2

Pastors of Bethel Church

*Daniel Coker	1808–1818**
Henry Harden	1818–1824
Moses Freeman	1825–1827
Samuel Todd	1828–1830
William Cornish	1831–1833
William Miller	1834–1835
Jacob Richardson	1836–1837
Edward Waters	1838–1839
Richard Robinson	1840–1841
***Edward Waters	1842
H. C. Turner	1843–1844
***Daniel A. Payne	1845–1849
William H. Jones	1850–1851
J. R. V. Morgan	1852
***James A. Shorter	1853–1854
Alexander Wayman	1855–1856
Levin Lee	1857
***John M. Brown	1858–1860
***Alexander Wayman	1861–1863

TABLE 2
(continued)

Savage L. Hemmond	1864–1865
***Benjamin T. Tanner	1866–1867
W. D. W. Schureman	1867
Daniel W. Moore	1868–1869
John A. Warren (died in office)	1870
Willis R. Revels, M.D.	1870–1871
George T. Watkins	1872–1873
William Lankford	1874
***James A. Handy	1875–1877
John W. Beckett	1878–1880
***Levi J. Coppin	1881–1883
***C. T. Shaffer	1884–1885
Daniel Draper	1886–1887
Theophilus G. Steward	1888–1889
Daniel P. Seaton	1890–1891
James H. A. Johnson	1892
John W. Beckett	1893–1898
***John Hurst	1898–1903
***Abraham Lincoln Gaines	1902–1908
Daniel G. Hill	1908–1913
Robert Fickland (died in office)	1913
Louis Flagg	1913–1915
William Saunders	1915–1917
***W. Sampson Brooks	1917–1920
Frederick Douglas	1920–1925
C. Harold Stepteau	1925–1930
A. Chester Clarke	1930–1933
Clarence C. Ferguson	1933–1940
James Reese	1940–1948
***Harrison J. Bryant	1948–1964
***Frank M. Reid, Jr.	1964–1968
Walter L. Hilderbrand	1968–1975
***John R. Bryant	1975–1988
Frank M. Reid III	1988–present

*Elected bishop but resigned.
**From 1808 to 1815 Coker led the prayer group that preceded the official
establishment of Bethel.
***Elected and consecrated as bishop.

TABLE 3

Maryland Churches That Grew Out of Bethel

CHURCH	YEAR FOUNDED	LOCATION
1. Ebenezer A.M.E. Church	1827	Baltimore
2. Waters A.M.E. Church	1843	Baltimore
3. Campfield A.M.E. Church	1844	Pikesville
4. St. John A.M.E. Church	1856	Baltimore
5. Mt. Gilboa A.M.E. Church	1859	Oella
6. Grace A.M.E. Church	1868	Catonsville
7. Evergreen A.M.E. Church	1868	Baltimore
8. Union Bethel A.M.E. Church	1871	Cecilton
9. Shiloh A.M.E. Church	1876	Baltimore
10. St. Stephen's A.M.E. Church	1878	Essex
11. Trinity A.M.E. Church	1882	Baltimore
12. St. Luke A.M.E. Church	1889	Ellicott City
13. Allen A.M.E. Church	1893	Baltimore
14. Payne Memorial A.M.E. Church	1894	Baltimore
15. Oak Street A.M.E. Church	1905	Baltimore
16. Douglas Memorial Community Church	1925	Baltimore
17. Davis Memorial A.M.E. Church	1939	Baltimore
18. Adams Chapel A.M.E. Church	1982	Baltimore
19. Handy A.M.E. Church	1982	Baltimore
20. Israel A.M.E. Church	1982	Baltimore

TABLE 4

Membership and Annual Budget Figures
for Bethel Church

YEAR	NO. OF NEW MEMBERS	BUDGET
1974–1975	12	$67,500.00
1975–1976	220	$130,961.97
1976–1977	597	$200,646.23
1977–1978	799	$300,713.24
1978–1979	1,197*	$409,348.93
1979–1980	1,070	$509,550.00
1980–1981	1,305	$517,600.00

TABLE 4

(continued)

YEAR	NO. OF NEW MEMBERS	BUDGET
1981–1982	1,313	$651,421.18
1982–1983	1,165	$665,130.85
1983–1984	1,109	$758,645.00
1984–1985	1,117	$900,975.32
1985–1986	1,110	$1,208,853.00
1986–1987	1,275	$1,295,939.46
1987–1988	1,150	$1,298,240.00
1988–1989	1,132	$1,643,666.00
1989–Aug. 1990	973**	$1,643,666.00

*Received 1,000 new members each year beginning 1978.
**Partial accession.
Bethel Church has had new members join every Sunday since 1975.

NOTES

The author thanks and acknowledges the contributions of the pastor, the Reverend Frank Reid III, the members of Bethel, and the church staff for making this study possible. The help of research assistants Ms. Daniste Hunte and Ms. Roxanne White, students at Vassar College, is also acknowledged. Ms. Hunte was supported by a grant from the Congregational History Project at the University of Chicago. Ms. White was supported by a Ford Scholars grant from Vassar College. Ms. Millie Lee, a work-study student at Vassar, entered the survey data into the computer.

1. The Reverend Dr. John R. Bryant, "We Are: Bethel African Methodist Episcopal Church," n.d.

2. James A. Handy, *Scraps of African-Methodist History* (Nashville: A.M.E. Publishing Co., 1901), p. 24.

3. Daniel A. Payne, *History of the African Methodist Episcopal Church* (Nashville: A.M.E. Church, 1891), 89.

4. The reasons for Daniel Coker's resignation from the bishopric were not included in the minutes of the first convention, but there have been two speculations: First, according to Daniel Payne, Coker resigned because as a mulatto he was considered too light-skinned to be the founder of a church for black people. Second, Richard Allen was not present on the day when the election took place, and Coker may have deferred to Allen's leadership upon his return.

A more plausible third reason would be a serious moral offense like adultery, which resulted in Coker's expulsion from the denomination and his resignation from Bethel Church in 1818, two years after the first convention.

5. Harry Richardson, *Dark Salvation: The Story of Methodism as It Developed Among Blacks in America* (Garden City: Doubleday, 1976), 81.

6. Each of the major classifications of ministerial positions can be modified by placing other qualifiers before it. For example, "local preacher" can be changed to "itinerant preacher," and the same can be done for "elder." Due to the circuit-riding tradition of its origins in the United States, most Methodists believed in the "itinerant ministry," constantly moving their clergy from one circuit to another after a set period of time, e.g., four or five years.

7. Melvin D. Williams, *Community in a Black Pentecostal Church: An Anthropological Approach* (Pittsburgh: University of Pittsburgh Press, 1974).

8. Robert J. Breckenridge and Andrew B. Cross, "The Condition of the Coloured Population of the City of Baltimore," *Baltimore Literary and Religious Magazine* (1838): 171.

9. Bettye Gardener, "Ante-Bellum Black Education in Baltimore," *Maryland Historical Magazine* 71, no. 3, (Fall 1976): 9; Anglo-African, September 3, 1859.

10. My own research of Bethel's records has turned up a membership figure of 1,155 for 1853, while Wright has reported the higher figure of 1,504. Official Church Records, Bethel A.M.E. Church, Baltimore, historical case #3. See James M. Wright, *The Free Negro in Maryland 1634–1860* (New York: Octagon Books, 1971). Bethel's growth to over 1,000 members is confirmed by the *Anglo-African*, which reported that the church had 1,300 members in 1848 (*Anglo-African*, October 7 , 1859, p. 3).

11. See "Dramatic Civil Rights Battle Waged Here," in the *Baltimore-Afro-American*, March 2, 1976, bicentennial edition, A-1.

12. Payne, *History*, pp. 3–4. Clarence E. Walker, *A Rock in a Weary Land: The African Methodist Episcopal Church During the Civil War and Reconstruction* (Baton Rouge: Louisiana State University Press, 1982), p. 22.

13. The major antagonists in the debate were E. Franklin Frazier and Melville Herskovitz. For a summary, see Albert Raboteau, *Slave Religion: The "Invisible Religion" in the Antebellum South* (New York: Oxford University Press, 1978). Herbert Gutman's work is an example of the revisionist consensus on the formation of a unique African American subculture. See Gutman, *The Black Family in Slavery and Freedom, 1750–1925* (New York: Pantheon, 1976). Also see C. Eric Lincoln, *Race, Religion and the Continuing American Dilemma* (New York: Hill and Wang, 1984).

14. Eileen Southern, *The Music of Black Americans: A History* (New York: W. W. Norton, 1971; rev. ed., 1983), p. 161.

15. Walker, *A Rock in a Weary Land*, pp. 22–26.

16. Southern, *The Music of Black Americans*, pp. 132–33.

17. Paul Svinin's narrative is found in *Reis naar Noord-Amerika*, which is translated in Avrahm Yarmolinsky, *Picturesque United States of America: 1811, 1812,*

CHAPTER FOUR

1813 (New York: 1930). Quoted by Southern, *The Music of Black Americans,* pp. 91–92.

18. Southern, *The Musical of Black Americans,* p. 92.

19. *Baltimore Clipper* June 17, 1840, p. 2; Leroy Graham, *Baltimore the Nineteenth Century Black Capital* (Washington, D.C.: University Press of America, 1981), p. 148.

20. Breckenridge and Cross, "The Condition of the Coloured Population of the City of Baltimore," pp. 173–74.

21. I am indebted in this whole section to Clarence Walker's insightful interpretation of Payne and the cornfield ditties incident. See Walker, *A Rock in a Weary Land,* pp. 23–24.

22. Payne was also a participant in the upheaval of attempts to introduce choirs and choral singing in the worship service of the Bethel A.M.E. Church in Philadelphia in 1841 and 1842 (Southern, *The Music of Black Americans,* p. 133). Bethel-Baltimore's records do not indicate any struggle over the introduction of choral music, but given the reactions of the congregation to Payne's other innovations in worship, it is highly probable that there was a similar struggle.

23. Payne, *History,* pp. 231–32. Wright, *The Free Negro in Maryland, 1634–1860,* p. 271.

24. Payne, *History,* Preface, vi.

25. For this section on George Hackett, see the following references in Graham, *Baltimore:* 149–51; 155–62.

26. *New National Era,* April 28, 1870, p. 2; Graham, *Baltimore,* p. 161.

27. See Bettye Collier-Thomas, "Nineteenth Century Black-Operated Shipyard, 1866–1884," *Journal of Negro History* (January 1974): 1–12. Graham, *Baltimore,* p. 162.

28. While some scholars may argue about whether this group fits the definition of congregation, it should be recognized that the phrase "congregation in the streets" usually consists of the actions of small groups of Christians who perform their ministry in the public arena. The term the "congregation at worship" may refer to all of those who attend a worship service. It is very seldom that a congregation as a whole acts in the public or political arena. Usually, political action is carried out by morally motivated individuals.

29. Graham, *Baltimore,* pp. 162–67.

30. Ibid., p. 198.

31. Carter G. Woodson, *The Education of the Negro Prior to 1861* (Washington, D.C.: Associated Publishers, 1921; New York: Arno Press and the New York Times, 1968 reprint), p. 130.

32. See Breckinridge and Cross, "The Condition of the Coloured Population of the City of Baltimore," pp. 169–71. Also see Bettye Gardener, "Ante-Bellum Black Education in Baltimore," *Maryland Historical Magazine* 71, no. 3 (Fall 1976).

33. For the section on Isaac Myers's activities and mutual aid groups at Bethel, see the following references in Graham, *Baltimore:* 178–79; 186; 198–200; 204–5; 210–11; 213–14; 259.

34. *American,* December 5, 1879, p. 1.

35. Enslaved persons in urban areas could legally join a black church like Bethel even in the South. They tended to have more freedom of movement than slaves on plantations. It is not clear from the church records which persons were slaves. However, the Bethel congregation was made up largely of freed persons and some slaves. Freed persons outnumbered slaves in Baltimore by a 4 to 1 ratio.

36. *Baltimore Afro-American,* July 2, 1985.

37. See the section on the black church as the womb of black culture in chapter 1 of Lincoln and Mamiya, *The Black Church in the African American Experience,* (Durham, N.C.: Duke University Press, 1990). p. 8.

38. *Baltimore Sun/Evening Sun,* February 10, 1987, p. 13.

39. Levi Coppin, *Unwritten History,* (1919; reprint, New York, Negro University Press, 1968), pp. 330–31. For the section on Coppin, see also pp. 245–46. Bishop Coppin's second wife was the famous educator of poor black youth, Frances ("Fannie") Jackson Coppin, after whom the city of Baltimore named the Coppin State College.

40. *Baltimore Afro-American,* July 2, 1985.

41. Official Board minutes, 1915 to 1918. Minutes of Bethel's Official Board are available from 1826 to the present.

42. Coppin, *Unwritten History,* pp. 245–48.

43. *Baltimore Afro-American,* May 30, 1953.

44. Coppin, *Unwritten History,* p. 247.

45. "Pastors of Bethel Who Became Bishops," Bethel Church publication, n.d., p. 6.

46. See Robert Hill, editor, and Carol A. Rudisell, assistant editor, *The Marcus Garvey and Universal Negro Improvement Association Papers* (Berkeley and Los Angeles: University of California Press, 1983), vol. 1 (1826–August 1919). There was a letter on the Bethel event from Major Wrisley Brown of Military Intelligence to Lt. Colonel H. A. Packenham which said, "It is reported to this office that Ida B. Wells-Barnett is considered a far more dangerous agitator than Marcus Garvey. Both of these people are being carefully watched."

47. For a summary of the criticisms of Garvey, see Lawrence H. Mamiya and C. Eric Lincoln, "Black Militant and Separatist Movements," *Encyclopedia of the American Religious Experience,* ed. Charles H. Lippy and Peter W. Williams (New York: Charles Scribners Sons, 1988), 2: 755–71.

48. Bethel A.M.E. Church, "Official Church Records," Permanent Data Book 1, 1918–32.

49. Robert Hill, *The Garvey and UNIA Papers* (Berkeley and Los Angeles: University of California Press, 1983), vol. 2 (August 27, 1919–August 31, 1920): 441–43.

50. The differences in spelling are shown in comparing Bethel's own list, "Pastors of Bethel, Baltimore," which uses the spelling "Douglas," with an article on the history of the church, "Bethel A.M.E. Church Proclaiming the

Gospel for Two Centuries," which uses "Douglass," *Baltimore Afro-American,* July 2, 1985.

51. "Tumult Marks Hearing At Trinity Church," *Baltimore Afro-American,* July 1, 1921. "Bishop Absolves Rev. Douglass From Charges," *Baltimore Afro-American,* July 8, 1921. The paper reported that while the trial went on downstairs, twenty-five church women from Bethel, including Mrs. Frederick Douglas, held prayer and class meeting upstairs. "Strains of 'I'll Live On,' and fervent prayers for the discomfiture of the pastor's enemies floated downstairs to the committee in session" (July 1, 1921, issue).

52. Baltimore District: Rev. J. W. Norris, P. E., Statistical Table (Financial), April 30, 1930, in *Official Church Record, Membership Record, Book 3 (1918–1932), Bethel A.M.E. Church.*

53. Gerald D. Jaynes and Robin M. Williams, eds., *A Common Destiny: Black Americans and American Society* (Washington, D.C.: National Academy Press, 1989), pp. 27–28.

54. *Baltimore Afro-American,* November 15 to 30, 1930.

55. Lillian Ashcraft Webb, *About My Father's Business: The Life of Elder Michaux* (Westport, Conn.: Greenwood Press, 1981), pp. 30–32.

56. See the elaboration of this tradition of "vicarious satisfaction" in C. Eric Lincoln and Lawrence H. Mamiya, "Daddy Jones and Father Divine: The Cult As Political Religion," *Religion in Life* 49, no. 1 (Spring 1980).

57. Juanita E. Jackson, "History of the City-Wide Young People's Forum," pamphlet, no date.

58. Ibid., 2.

59. See Gayraud Wilmore's thesis on the deradicalization of black churches in the interwar period, *Black Religion and Black Radicalism,* 2d ed. rev. (Maryknoll, N.Y.: Orbis, 1983), chap. 6.

60. For example, the entries of June 7, 1933 and October 7, 1933, referred to the need to borrow: "In order to meet emergency bills the Board borrowed $200.00 from the Mortgage Fund." Also see Bethel A.M.E. Church finance records and the Baltimore Annual Conference's Statistical Tables prepared by Rev. John W. Norris, 1925 to 1930.

61. Interview with Bishop Harrison J. Bryant at his home in Baltimore on July 1, 1989.

62. Alfred L. Henderson, "A Historical Resume of Bishop Harrison J. Bryant," in Bishop Harrison Bryant's anniversary book, *The Bryant Years, 1968 to 1978* (no publisher, date).

63. *Baltimore Afro-American,* February 25, 1961; *Baltimore Sun,* June 16, 1962.

64. "Minutes of the A.M.E. Preachers Meeting for Baltimore and Vicinity, 1958–1960"; Bethel A.M.E. Church Official Board Minutes (September 15, 1958).

65. See the advertisement for the march in the *Baltimore Afro-American,* March 28, 1964. Also see Ted Handy, "After Big March What Comes Next?" *Baltimore Afro-American,* April 4, 1964. For evidence of Reverend Harrison Bryant's participation in the civil rights struggle, see the summary during his

campaign for episcopal office: "Dr. Bryant Seeks Episcopal Honors," *Baltimore Afro-American*, April 18, 1964.

66. "AMEs to Mark 150th anniversary," *Baltimore Afro-American*, May 14, 1966.

67. This story was related to the author by Dr. Bettye Collier-Thomas. She spoke of using surgical masks and gloves to go through the records. The Maryland Historical Society helped to clean, microfilm, and preserve the documents.

68. In addition to the survey, interviews were conducted with the following key officials and members of Bethel A.M.E. Church during the summer of 1989: Reverend Frank M. Reid III, present pastor; Reverend Charlotte Clemmons, present assistant pastor, lay ministries and minister to married couples; Bishop Emeritus Harrison J. Bryant; Bishop John R. Bryant, former pastor; Reverend Marietta Ramsey, youth ministry; Reverend Joan Wharton, founder and director of TeenPep; Reverend Adella Holt, ministry to women; Mr. Daniel Diggs, chair of the steward board; minister Lillian Streeter, substance abuse ministry; Ms. Tessa Conwell, youth member; Ms. Geneve Bradshaw, church member; and Mrs. Esther Bailey, chair of the Daniel Payne Scholarship Committee.

69. Interview with Bishop John Bryant, July 8, 1989, in Baltimore, Maryland.

70. Ibid. Author's emendations in brackets. Subsequent quotations from Bryant are taken from the July 1989 interview.

71. Lincoln and Mamiya, *The Black Church*, chap. 11.

72. For articles on Freedom House, see the following: Pam Widgeon, "'Cong. Mitchell speaks at banquet honoring Dr. Lillie, Freedom House," *Baltimore Afro-American*, December 13, 1975. Elizabeth M. Oliver, "Freedom House program lauded," and "Freedom House awards of merit presented," *Baltimore Afro-American*, December 23, 1977.

73. For the section on the women's center and the Reverend Cecilia Williams-Bryant, see the following: Wanda L. Dobson, *Baltimore Sun*, March 24, 1976; DeWayne Wickham, *Baltimore Sun*, September 18, 1977.

74. For Bethel's Labor Day and homecoming services, see Frank P. L. Somerville, "Bethel launching unemployment fight," *Baltimore Sun*, September 1, 1979. Also see "Bethel AME serves the unemployed on Labor Day with jobs, school shoes," *Baltimore Sun*, September 4, 1979; Martin Evans, *News American*, 17 September 1984.

75. This issue of replacing John Bryant at Bethel was a concern to Bishop John Hurst Adams of the Second District in 1986. See Lawrence H. Mamiya, "The Second Episcopal District of the African Methodist Episcopal Church Under the Leadership of the Bishop John Hurst Adams: Evaluations of the Leadership Training Institutes and the Phenomenon of Church Growth in the District." Unpublished in-house study funded by the Lilly Endowment, Inc., January 1986.

76. About 1,300 attended the 8:00 A.M. service and 1,500 the 11:00 A.M. The full seating capacity of the church is about 1,700. Vassar College students Roxanne White, Daniste Hunte, Victor Mavi, and Philip Cooke assisted in the congregational survey. The high rate of return of surveys was due to the efforts of Pastor Reid, who constantly urged the congregation to complete and return

them. Because of financial limitations, a survey of church members who were absent on this particular Sunday was not done.

77. See Lincoln and Mamiya, *The Black Church*. Chapter 10 explains some of the problems that black churches have encountered in recruiting black men.

78. For data on church membership and rates of being churched, see *Emerging Trends*, published by the Princeton Religion Research Center, vol. 9, no. 5 (May 1987): 5.

79. See summaries of the Gallup surveys in Hart Nelsen and Anne K. Nelsen, *Black Church in the Sixties* (Lexington: University of Kentucky Press, 1975), especially chap. 5.

80. Ibid.

81. Mamiya, "The Second Episcopal District of the African Methodist Episcopal Church," p. 27.

82. Ibid. The results of clergy responses to the support of women pastors by denomination are found in Lincoln and Mamiya, *The Black Church*, chap. 10.

83. The participant observation of the Freedom Now ministry occurred on August 3, 1989.

84. Interview of Mrs. Esther Bailey by Roxanne White on July 31, 1989.

85. Sister Mary Elizabeth Robinson, *God's Rainbow of Women: Women's Day 1989* (Bethel A.M.E. Church publication, May 28, 1989). See the description of the Daniel Payne Scholarship Committee.

86. See Joyce Ladner, "Teen Pregnancy: The Implications for Black Americans," in *The State of Black America 1986* James D. Williams (New York: National Urban League, 1986.)

87. See Diane Winston, "A Powerhouse in the Pulpit: Bethel's Frank Madison Reid," *Baltimore Sun Sunday Magazine*, June 30, 1991, p. 25.

88. See Chapter 13, on future trends among black churches, in Lincoln and Mamiya, *The Black Church*.

Sugar House Ward
A Latter-day Saint Congregation

JAN SHIPPS, CHERYLL L. MAY, AND DEAN L. MAY

SOON AFTER THE MORMON prophet Joseph Smith was murdered, his followers were driven from Illinois. Brigham Young, who became Smith's successor, led many of the refugees to the intermountain west. When they arrived in the Great Salt Lake Valley, the political status of the virtually uninhabited desert region thereabouts was unclear. Before the outbreak of the Mexican War, it had been Mexican land; at war's end, the area would become United States territory. In the meantime, aside from scattered bands of Native Americans, practically the only people on the scene were the Mormons, members of the Church of Jesus Christ of Latter-day Saints. Since they were able to organize the area without opposition, they ordered it on "theo-democratic" principles that had been revealed to the Prophet Joseph as appropriate for Zion, God's earthly kingdom in the latter days.[1]

Nearly the first thing the Saints did was to mark the site for a temple, and because "Zion's tent" needs the support of "stakes," the Latter-day Saint (LDS) leadership designated the region surrounding the site as the "Salt Lake Stake of Zion." Led by Young, the leaders acted as ecclesiastical land distributors, laying out a city according to the plat Joseph Smith had drawn up for the "City of Zion" that the Saints once planned to build in Missouri. As many thousands of Saints made the trek across the plains and mountains to join the first 2,095 pioneers who had arrived in 1847, the Mormons built a city around the forty-acre square set aside for the temple.

The church leaders subdivided the stake into administrative districts called wards, and, coping with rapid population growth, repeatedly realigned ward boundaries and organized new wards. Between 1847 and 1849 alone, the number of wards increased from five to nineteen. Additional wards were created when large numbers of Mormon immigrants settled within the boundaries of existing wards and when Saints settled in new areas. One of these added wards, the Sugar House Ward, organized in 1854, is the focus of this study.

From its beginnings Mormonism had been much more than a church; it was a religio-cultural movement. Since this was the case, Mormon wards had civil as well as ecclesiastical status, especially between 1847 and 1857 when the Great Basin was not only the site of the institutional headquarters of the Mormon Church but also the seat of a latter-day "House of Israel" into which Saints were being gathered from out of the nations. The federal government tried to incorporate the area into the organized political life of the United States with the passage of the Compromise of 1850, but the appointment of Brigham Young as governor of Utah Territory and many other LDS leaders as territorial officers left the Mormons in charge. Even though they only held these federal positions until the outbreak of the Mormon War of 1857 (a conflict generated by the nation's realization that the Saints had established what amounted to a theocracy in the republic's recently acquired western lands), this initial decade of Mormon hegemony set a pattern. The ordering of things in this crucial period, a thorough blending of public and private, secular and religious, was enshrined in the creation of a Latter-day Saint system in which the practical and the spiritual were fused. Church and state were officially split apart in Utah Territory in 1858, but to a kingdom-building people inspired by the ancient model found in the Old Testament, the notion of making clear distinctions between religious and secular realms was so alien that, in Mormonism, the line between the two remained indistinct throughout the nineteenth and much of the twentieth century.

During the first decade of settlement, Salt Lake City grew rapidly, developing into a real metropolis. Most of the new wards in the immediate area were organized within the city limits. Sugar House was not one of these original city wards, however; instead it is one of the first organized outside the city itself. Located to the south along Canyon Creek, which emerges from the foothills of the Wasatch Mountains, it was a rural/suburban ward in its early years. Although it was later incorporated into the city and is now a metropolitan ward, it has a semi-rural pioneer history that distinguishes it from many of the other wards in the valley.

As did most wards, this one took a name that identified it by its locale. It became Sugar House Ward because it was located in the vicinity of a sugar refining factory that was part of an ill-fated Mormon effort to found a beet-sugar industry in the 1850s. Because the region where LDS settlement was taking place was some two or three months of difficult travel from the nearest American population centers, everything that could not be produced locally had to be hauled a thousand miles in wagons at great expense. In the early 1850s, yearly sugar imports cost over $240,000 of very scarce hard currency.[2] Brigham Young and his counselors decided that the best way to eliminate the cost of transporting sugar was to grow sugar beets and convert them into sugar, as had been done in France for several decades. Consequently, costly and heavy refining equipment was designed in France, fabricated in Liverpool, and, after its arrival in America, loaded onto forty huge Santa Fe prairie schooners, requiring four hundred head of draft animals to pull them during the arduous, four-month journey to Utah Territory.

After several false starts, the Saints decided to build their refining facility on Canyon Creek. Before construction began in 1854, about a dozen farm families had settled in the vicinity, diverting the creek waters to irrigate their crops. Brigham Young also had a plantation there that covered a full square mile south of the creek to help meet the food requirements of his own large family. To superintend the sugar project, Young selected Abraham O. Smoot, a convert from Tennessee whose impressive leadership skills and unflagging commitment to the faith had been demonstrated during the harrowing persecutions of the Mormon communities in the two previous decades.[3] The church president also asked Smoot to direct the work on his "Forest Farm" acreage, for he intended that this farm should set an example for others in growing sugar beets and other experimental crops.

With the prospect of the new refining center attracting a notably expanded population, church leaders established a ward in the area. This followed the usual Mormon practice of moving church organization forward in tandem with each new phase of settlement. The idea of establishing a community and not proceeding with religious organization until some later point would have been unthinkable to the LDS leaders, who, as the leading citizens of Zion, were organizing "a kingdom in the tops of the mountains" according to what they believed to be God's plan. To them, the blending of the community's secular and religious dimensions seemed perfectly appropriate; they were organizing administrative units, as necessary for conducting public business as for oversight of the spiritual welfare of the Saints. Although the way in which the business of the state was conducted shifted after 1858, the church's wards continued to be geographically based. Not unlike parishes in Roman Catholicism, their boundaries are established and their leadership determined by church authorities. Likewise, stakes resemble dioceses. The fact that wards and stakes both function as congregations and that all Latter-day Saints are members of both is a signal that Mormon congregational life differs considerably from that in other traditions in the Judeo-Christian family of traditions. In the Salt Lake Valley, the entire LDS community was initially one large congregation. Within its perimeter all Saints were sequestered, leaving outside only non-Mormons, persons the Saints called "Gentiles." As the LDS population in the area increased, Mormon congregational life took on what may be described as a multilevel character.

At first, the entire Mormon community often assembled to hear instruction and exhortation from their leaders. Figuratively, at least, the brethren addressed all Latter-day Saints when they spoke in such gatherings held in the "bowery" or, somewhat later, in the tabernacle constructed on a part of spacious Temple Square. In addition to coming together in these weekly general assemblies, the whole church was convened in semiannual general conferences in early April and early October every year, conclaves that continue and, to this day, treat the whole of Mormondom as a single congregation.

In the beginning, there were few formal gatherings for worship in the wards, but as more Saints settled in the valley, causing the distance to the center of the city to increase, the Saints also started holding ward congregational meetings for instruction and worship. When the numbers of Saints necessitated the organization of additional stakes as well as many more wards, regular quarterly stake conferences and other stake activities were added to bring the Saints in all the wards in each stake together at a second congregational level. At stake conferences, members of the highest level of the LDS hierarchy, usually members of the Council of the Twelve [Apostles], were assigned to preside. Whenever the church leaders concluded that the boundaries of the wards in a stake needed to be realigned, the reorganization of wards took place either in a ward conference or in stake conferences.

Aside from small "branches" that are formed when the number of Saints residing in an outlying area is sufficient to merit minimal ecclesiastical organization, the ward is the most intimate form of Mormon congregational life. Whether by design or as a consequence of the frontier experience, wards are congregations that function according to a village-life model. The ward bishop and his two counselors fill roles not unlike those of village elders, presiding over and ministering to the members of the ward, managing and overseeing ward activities. They, in turn, owe allegiance to those in higher authority, their own stake presidents and those above them in the church hierarchy. The ward leaders are also like village elders in that, as member of the LDS lay priesthood, they are not professional clergy. In addition to discharging their duties in the ward, they must earn their own livings. Perhaps it was this as much as the desire to keep congregations small enough for every member to have an assignment, a "calling," that led church leaders to begin limiting the size of LDS wards. For over a century the church has kept wards at village size by altering ward boundaries when the number of Saints in any ward gets much above 500 or falls below 250. This tinkering with boundaries is not unlike the periodic redrawing of boundaries of such political units as precincts and voting districts.

Church leaders called Abraham O. Smoot to serve as bishop of Sugar House Ward. As he had already been asked to superintend the sugar refining facility and Brigham Young's huge farm, his selection followed the normal Mormon pattern of choosing local secular leaders as religious leaders. President Young did not ask Smoot if it would be convenient for him to leave his new farm on Cottonwood Creek which, with great effort, he and his family had put into production only a few months before. Nor would Smoot have expected such a question. He had settled in Cottonwood and established a ward there at the behest of the church, and he resettled at Sugar House with the same conviction that Young—whose position in the church caused the Saints to regard him as a living prophet—knew the Lord's will. (That Smoot was a willing instrument of that will was again made obvious several years later when Brigham Young and the brethren called him to leave his spacious Salt Lake home to help settle the town of Provo and spearhead the establishment of the institution that became Brigham Young University.)

Smoot's appointment as bishop did not necessarily elevate him to a position in the priesthood higher than that of other Mormon men living in the Sugar House area. Without necessary reference to the positions they hold in the church, all worthy LDS males are ordained to the Aaronic (lower) priesthood. All have an opportunity to move up through the ranks of deacons, teachers, and priests within that order and to be ordained to the Melchizedek (higher) priesthood. Therefore, it would be incorrect to say that Smoot's appointment as bishop moved him from lay to clerical status; he simply received a call to preside over the ward. Nevertheless, as a bishop, Smoot had a clearly defined place in the LDS structure of authority that presided over Mormon life in the "Great Basin Kingdom."

At the pinnacle of this hierarchy stood the church president and his two counselors, the First Presidency. Then came the general officers: the "apostles" in the Council (or Quorum) of the Twelve, the presiding Quorum of Seventy, and the Presiding Bishopric. Together the men in these high church quorums were and are (the hierarchical structure of church governance remains essentially unchanged) the LDS General Authorities. The Saints know them more familiarly as "the brethren." Ranging downward in the LDS system of church organization are lesser authorities appointed to preside over Mormon stakes and wards. A presidency (a president and two counselors) presides over a stake; a bishopric (a bishop and two counselors) presides over a ward. The Mormons believe that ecclesiastical appointments at every level—known officially as church callings—are "effected through the gift of prophecy and by the imposition of hands by those who are in authority" and that they confer power on those who are called to administer in God's name.[4]

As ward bishop, Smoot presided over the Saints who lived in the Sugar House Ward area, serving as judge in the ward court, as well as overseer of the members' everyday existence and their spiritual lives. For all that, his independent authority—and the authority of all ward bishops—was more limited than that of many Protestant ministers. In addition to the control the General Authorities have always exercised over individual wards by virtue of the more or less continuous adjustment of ward boundaries, and equally important, the decisions they make about ward leadership, the church came increasingly to determine much about ward life through strict stipulations about the content of ward programs. The organization of classes, the plan of meetings in every age and gender category, the pattern of the Sacrament Meeting service, and practically every other ward activity is clearly specified in directions that issue from the headquarters of the church.

The effect of this level of attention to detail is the creation of wards all across the church that are essentially alike. When ward boundaries are redrawn, Saints are moved—horizontally, as it were—from one ward to another. But as one ward is so much like another, they do not feel lost; they are very much at home. Likewise, when Saints move vertically, going from the intimacy of the ward to a stake conference, they are not visitors. Members also experience stakes as their congregations. And when they attend the semiannual conferences of the church, either by traveling to Temple Square in Salt Lake City or by watching the proceedings on closed-circuit television in their local ward meetinghouses, everything is familiar; Saints are very much at home in a congregational setting that seems to encompass the whole people of God.

Because the Latter-day Saint congregational experience is so multi-layered, the history of any single ward becomes, in a sense, the whole story of Mormonism as seen from a particular geographic perspective. To a considerable degree, also, the history of any LDS ward is the history of every ward. Yet wards have their own histories and they do develop their own characters, personalities that allow them to transcend the regular alteration of leadership and "fruit basket turnover" of membership that reorganization generates, as well as the cookie-cutter effect of program standardization.

When current members of Sugar House Ward are asked about its distinctive character, they answer, nearly automatically, that it is "the sweetest ward in the church." This is a characterization easily tied to the ward's name, but it is more than that, for this is a ward that has always been friendly and unpretentious, humble and welcoming. Yet close examination of the ward's history reveals something more profound about its personality than a direct connection between its name and the nature of the interaction among members of the congregation.

This is a ward whose personality is rooted in its essential typicality. In an ironic turn, it is not some extraordinary or exceptional feature, some characteristic that sets Sugar House Ward apart from other LDS wards. Individuals, for example, do not dominate the ward's history or its life. With one notable exception, ward leaders have not moved up to positions of great prominence in the LDS hierarchy, causing members to think of this as the ward of President Grant, for example, and some other eminent church leader. Neither has the ward produced flagrant apostates nor members who turned out to be conspicuous criminals. Although the ward changed from a working-class to a middle-class congregation and, although the area in which it is located once had a stable population but now has one that is more transient, the ward has had no active members at the very top of the Mormon social ladder and not very many at the very bottom. It has never complained vociferously about a bishop who has been called to lead the ward; it has never whined unreasonably about any redrawing of ward boundaries, although it once came close; and it has never rebelled over Mormonism's uncompromising standardization. Instead, as a ward, Sugar House has always been reasonably unexceptional, almost archetypal.

As a result, this is a ward that has functioned effectively as a vehicle for "making Saints," for turning converts and immigrants into citizens of the LDS kingdom. As a Mormon melting pot in the nineteenth century, Sugar House became the ward home for a host of immigrants from all across Europe, providing an experiential learning situation for former Protestants, Roman Catholics, and "nothings" that allowed them to become Saints. The ward is still operating in this fashion in the late twentieth century, when the ward membership includes LDS converts from South America, Asia, and the Near East, as well as Americans of many different religious backgrounds. In short, this representative ward has always carried forward its appointed task of serving the Saints at the congregational level and building up the kingdom at the same time.

Recognition of its very typicality as its genius turns the history of Sugar House Ward into a lens for surveying the congregational life of Latter-day Saints everywhere, thereby providing a fine means of observing the role wards have always played in "making Saints." This close examination of Sugar House Ward inadvertently turned out to raise also the significant question of how effectively this, and by extension, other Mormon wards will continue to play this role in the late twentieth century and into the twenty-first.

I

Ward tradition maintains that it was Margaret, "Ma," Smoot, the bishop's first wife (he married four other women polygamously), who suggested the name Sugar House during the ward's initial organizational meeting on April 24, 1854. The name was approved by majority vote of the congregation, which initially met in the small one-room log schoolhouse built in 1852.[5] In 1855, the Saints erected a new combined schoolhouse and meetinghouse next to the sugar factory. Seats in the building were rough board benches. The citizens sprinkled sawdust on the floor on school days and swept up on weekends to prepare for Saturday night dances and Sunday church services.

The Sugar House area was still sparsely settled in 1854. For that reason, the ward boundaries enclosed a much larger territory than most other Mormon wards. The boundaries extended south from the southern borders of the city proper about five miles, to Mill Creek. East-west boundaries extended from the Wasatch Mountains looming on the east side of the valley to the Jordan River, which flows southward through the valley center to empty into the Great Salt Lake.

As the first of the Mormon suburban wards, Sugar House was unusual in nineteenth-century Mormonism, when the normal pattern was either a city congregation or a ward composed of village Saints who lived close together in town and traveled out to farm acreages located on the perimeter. But in the twentieth century, as residents fled city centers for more spacious suburbs, the suburban ward become the most common Latter-day Saint congregation. Thus, to a considerable degree, the Sugar House Ward presaged the pattern that by the 1950s would be most common. In Utah and other "Mormon country" communities, suburban wards (such as the current Sugar House Ward) often encompass only a few square blocks. But ward boundaries in areas where Mormons are scarcer often rival in extent those of the original Sugar House Ward.

Since the brethren take great care to keep the population of wards down to the size of a comfortable primary community, most everyone in the ward knows everyone else, and all active adults can have a "calling" (a commission from the bishop to teach, visit, preside, or perform some other service for the ward).[6] As the population increased in the area, ward boundaries had to be realigned so many times that historian Andrew Jenson claimed that of all the early wards established throughout the church, "no ward has had so many divisions and subdivisions as the Sugar House Ward."[7]

If the organization of Sugar House Ward went as expected, the high hopes of the brethren for refining sugar beets to solve the territory's need for sugar were soon dashed. Superintendent Smoot and his aides put the sugar factory into full operation in 1855, but after only six weeks it was clear that the sugar house, built at such great sacrifice by the Saints, would produce only unpalatable molasses.[8] The factory facility was not a complete loss, however. The valuable British-made machinery was used in subsequent years to help produce paper, textiles, buckets, and other products always in short supply in this remote frontier outpost, and paper mills and textile mills in the Sugar House area were to prove important to ward members.

Still, the anticipated rapid buildup of population in the area failed to materialize in the 1850s. Instead, growth took place at a gradual pace with the increase of farm settlement and the establishment of a few light manufacturing plants and mill works along the creek. Consequently, the boundaries of Sugar House Ward remained stable for a very long time. A "Farmer's Ward" was carved out of Sugar House to accommodate the cluster of farm families in the area west of Young's Forest Farm in 1877, but the great surge in population that caused the ward to be subdivided into scores of smaller geographical units did not take place until after the turn of the century.[9]

The history of Sugar House Ward in the early decades reveals that congregational life for those living in the ward in the early decades of settlement was all-encompassing. Sunday gatherings at the meeting-house were important worship activities; but, as the Saints were engaged in building the literal Kingdom of God, making sugar, stitching quilts, manufacturing woolen goods or paper, or digging irrigation ditches were also imbued with sacred meaning. The mundane daily acts that insured survival in the rugged new land were as important to the LDS enterprise as prayers, hymns, and sacraments.

Just as Brigham Young was governor and the leaders guiding the church were the same men who constituted the territorial legislature, so religious and civil authority were similarly entwined on the local ward level. The term "ward" derives from the municipal districts in Nauvoo, Illinois, where the Saints had lived between 1839 and 1847. There the major functions of ward bishops had been almost totally practical and public. Here the ward boundaries coincided closely with voting, judicial, postal, and school-district boundaries. Bishop Smoot, as administrator of each of these districts, exercised extensive civil authority over the citizens residing in his ward. He was in charge of allocating five-acre plots of land to new settlers as they moved in. He also had responsibility for the equitable distribution of precious irrigation water to each household. He was charged with maintaining an elementary school in the ward, and had the authority to levy and collect property taxes to support the school.[10]

Bishop Smoot also acted as "Judge in Israel." It was his duty to convene a "bishop's court" as needed to consider complaints against those who, because of doctrinal waywardness or moral lapses, were no longer considered worthy of church membership. Ward records indicate that cases of lying, stealing, or apostasy, where offending members were cut off from church membership, came up every two or three years. Those who were excommunicated were always urged to repent and make themselves worthy to rejoin the body of the Saints.

In the secular realm, bishops in early Utah were automatically elected as magistrates or justices of the peace by their ward members. During the early 1850s, many civil cases were turned over to county or federal courts, but bishops still served as probate judges, handling inheritances and divorce settlements.[11] Even after different civil judicial officers were appointed, church leaders urged members to take any disputes to their bishop first, resorting to civil action only when nonmembers were involved. Records of bishops' courts in the early settlement decades indicate that most of the Saints followed this advice, and a good many continued the practice into the twentieth century.[12]

Smoot and his fellow bishops also had major responsibilities for providing ward support for the many public works projects underway in the church/state of Deseret, the name the Saints had originally given to the Mormon kingdom. Each adult male in the ward was expected to contribute his labor every tenth day in "work tithing" to help to do his part in building that kingdom. Work-tithing crews erected major public buildings, bridges, dams, and other projects for the good of the general community. The church's presiding bishop would assign each ward bishop to a particular project on a certain day. The ward bishop was then expected to supply his quota of workers, and to furnish materials, teams, and food for his laborers.[13] Bishops also collected cash, or, more commonly, tithing in kind (defined as "ten percent of one's yearly increase") and other offerings from ward members. They distributed the donated grains, fruits, butter, and other foods to needy ward members. Surpluses not needed in the ward were turned over to the Deseret Store and Tithing Office in Salt Lake City, and used to meet the needs of the poor and to provide for the tide of immigrant converts, most of them destitute, which arrived in the valley each fall.[14]

Bishops in the early church visited each member family yearly to conduct a "tithing settlement." This yearly session between member and bishop still takes place every December, although a member now signs up for an interview time to see the bishop in his office at the meetinghouse. During such interviews members tell their bishops how much tithing they have paid during the year, indicating whether or not they are full tithe payers. Within the LDS church, tithing is considered to be not so much a free-will gift as a divinely mandated assessment put in place by the Lord to prepare his people for the "higher law" of total consecration of all their goods, an economic program which the Saints believe they will follow at the time of Christ's Second Coming. Because a Latter-day Saint must be a full tithe payer and be judged worthy in other respects to receive the "recommend" (written authorization) necessary to enter LDS temples and participate in the sacred ordinances there, an LDS bishop has a meaningful way of exercising sanctions over the members of his ward that can be very effective.

Sugar House Ward member Emily Hart records in her diary for January 5, 1862, and January 22, 1863, visits from Bishop Smoot to conduct a yearly tithing settlement with her husband James. The Harts' tithing payment for 1862 was 28 pounds of flour and a shoulder of mutton.[15] The bishop kept an account book with listings for each male member of the ward, with credit and debit columns showing a dollar value for all cash, in-kind contributions, and hours of "work tithing" completed. This book also recorded goods disbursed when members and their families were in need. In 1866, the most recent year for which tithing records have been opened to researchers, Sugar House Ward members paid the equivalent of $2988 in tithing.[16]

One of the most important reasons Mormonism prospered in the intermountain west was the success its missionaries had in making converts in northern Europe. No record has been located to indicate how immigrants were directed to the Sugar House area, but the general plan for settling those whose travel to the Salt Lake area was supported by the church's Perpetual Emigration Fund is clear. Brigham Young and Edward Hunter, the presiding bishop, acted as a sort of crude employment agency, questioning ward bishops about the work going on in their wards and determining needs and job openings. When immigrant trains arrived, immigrant skills and abilities were inventoried and the travelers were given direction as to where they should settle.[17] Since 73 percent of the adults in the Sugar House area in 1860 were of foreign birth, it stands to reason that Bishop Smoot helped to find work for many newcomers to Zion. Since he was the area's secular as well as religious authority, he was able to assign new arrivals to public works projects if their skills could not immediately be used for ward projects.

Bishops' responsibilities went beyond looking after indigent immigrants arriving in the valley. They were also responsible on a continuing basis for seeing to the needs of widows and others in strained circumstances in their wards. Within a few years, bishops adopted the practice of appointing "block teachers" (pairs of ward priesthood holders, called to visit all the families on their assigned block each month to ascertain their physical and spiritual welfare). These deputies were charged with helping in the administration of poor relief.[18] A Women's Relief Society had been organized in Nauvoo, but the trauma the Saints suffered in being driven from Illinois led to its discontinuance. When it was revived within the wards in the late 1860s, Relief Society presidents also assumed much of the burden for administering to the needs of the poor. Care of the poor was, therefore, as much a sacred duty as blessing and passing the bread and water of the Mormon communion or "sacrament."

The extraordinary commitment to missionary work that had characterized the church from its beginnings had a continuing impact on Sugar House Ward. Over the years, in keeping with the church's practice of calling young Saints to two years of missionary service, hundreds of missionaries have gone out from the ward to spread the gospel to the world. The first to be sent, however, was not a young person standing on the threshold of adulthood, but Bishop Smoot himself, who was engaged in a European mission throughout much of 1856. In these early years, it was not at all unusual for a leading brother to be called on a missionary assignment that could last anywhere from a few months to several years. At home, a bishop's counselors usually took over his duties. In Smoot's case, one of his counselors who filled in was his stepson, William C. A. Smoot.

Later, this same William C. A. Smoot was called on a mission to the southern states. The cost of these missionary journeys, both in terms of material sacrifice, and emotional pain, is revealed in one of "Ma" Smoot's letters to a friend:

> [William] has gone trusting in his Heavenly Father. He left his wife and nine children, three boys and six girls, the eldest a boy fifteen next February, and the youngest six weeks old. He committed them to the God who gave them to him. . . . My heart was sorely grieved at parting with my derling [sic] boy, and we wept bitter tears.[19]

Then, as now, missionaries often found that their faith and convictions were strengthened as they were shared. Despite her tears, Margaret Smoot could rejoice in this and in the fact that missionaries left with the expectation of returning within a "reasonable" time. The idea of a lifetime mission call to bring the blessings of Christianity to foreign lands has never been part of the LDS tradition. Then, also as now, the central church did not support missionaries financially. Neither, in most cases, did their wards. Family, friends, and individual ward members were (and are) expected to supply missionaries with whatever financial help they need to complete their missions. In the nineteenth century, moreover, ward members were often asked to assist with the care of the families missionaries left behind.

Wherever they were, the converts made by missionaries were expected to heed the revelation that all faithful Saints should leave their former homes and gather to the headquarters of the church. This was an arduous requirement for the poor English and Scandinavian converts who constituted the majority of new believers during the second half of the nineteenth century, but tens of thousands of them made the trek. Brigham Young believed that the rugged isolation of the American Great Basin provided the perfect environment for turning converts into Saints. In these Rocky Mountain valleys, free from Gentile influence, individuals from many cultures could learn in their ward communities the patterns of sharing and caring that would mold them into a true "Zion Community," a group that was "of one heart, and one mind." As a ward in which three of every four adults came from Europe, Sugar House was crucially involved in this Saint-making process.

Over the decades, the valleys of the Great Basin filled up, and by the turn of the century church leaders had decided that central Zion could hold no more. Declaring that Zion is where the people of God are, from that point onward they advised converts to stay at home to build up the kingdom in their own lands.[20] The long-range result of this policy is that Mormon stakes and wards have been organized throughout the United States and all across the world. The Saints continue, however, to make a distinction between stakes and wards in the mission field and those within Zion's historic confines.

In the early years, members were expected to aid in other ways as the human fruits of missionary labors made their journeys across the plains and mountains. The Sugar House Ward Manuscript History and the journals of several members tell of special calls every summer from 1862 to 1865 for ward members to make the trek to the advancing railhead in Nebraska or Wyoming, to take supplies to indigent immigrants and accompany them back to the valley. In each of those years, a contingent of men from the Sugar House Ward answered the call.

Once the new members arrived in the valley, they were frequently assigned to board with members of the Sugar House Ward and other wards in the vicinity of the city until early spring, when they could build their own accommodations, or head out to colonize one of the growing number of outlying settlements. For example, British convert James Kirkham records his arrival with his family in the fall of 1859 and their being provided with an adobe house for the winter by the Stringham family of Sugar House Ward. The next spring, the Kirkhams moved on to Lehi, a small farming settlement about twenty-five miles to the south. They must, however, have been impressed with their warm Sugar House Ward welcome, since they moved back into the ward in 1866.[21]

Some sense of the character of the ward population in the first decades after founding can be gained by examining the U.S. manuscript census, which in 1870 included a precinct called Sugar House Ward that covered roughly the same territory as the ecclesiastical ward. The occupational structure of this population is particularly revealing. By far the most pervasive employment in the ward was what the census takers called "keeping house,"i.e., taking care of the multitudinous tasks of maintaining a household and bearing, feeding, clothing, and training children. In a neighborhood consisting of 641 persons in 134 households there were 130 women and (small surprise) no men keeping house. Each woman was responsible, on average, for four or five persons other than herself, including children and husbands. Martha Crossgrove, for example, at thirty-nine, cared for her husband Byrum, their daughters, Wilhemina, eight; Mary, six; Martha, four; and a baby son, Byrum, Jr., nine months old. Since her husband was a farmer, Martha's work certainly included milking, making butter and cheese, gardening, cooking, cleaning, spinning, weaving, knitting, mending, and washing.

Yet Martha had her husband present to lend a hand as needed. Thirty-one of her ward sisters (23 percent of the households) did not. For instance, Sarah Burton, who was thirty-one, had six children, ranging in age from two to twelve, to care for, as well as an eighteen-year-old brother-in-law. Most of the weight of household management she bore alone, though she was fortunate in having a domestic to help out. She was likely not a widow or divorcée, but a plural wife—a woman whose husband, following the Mormon practice, had other wives and other families to provide for—and so she was alone except when his rotating residence with his other families brought him to Sugar House. (Generally, a polygamous husband lived with his first wife and visited the others; yet, even as a visitor, he maintained a head-of-household status in the minds of polygamous wives and children.) Though a precise measure is not possible, approximately 28 percent of all the households in Sugar House Ward were polygamous. And of the thirty-nine likely polygamous households, twenty-three were headed by women who, like Sarah Burton, carried the greatest share of responsibility for the family. The female-headed households averaged just over five persons—the same size, without husbands present, as the male-headed households.

Most of the plural wives, however, had a husband close by. Susannah Rockwood's husband, Albert P. Rockwood, the warden of the territorial prison, lived next door with another wife. The husbands of thirteen polygamous women were nearby, and thus present on a daily basis, but those of ten others apparently lived outside the ward boundaries and were less often in the home. The labor of these women was vital to the successful propagation of what Mormons proudly proclaimed to be their "best crop," their children. Though the census does not make it possible to know their completed family size, those women aged thirty-five to forty-five (and thus likely to have most of their surviving children at home), mothered households that averaged six or seven persons.[22] There were slightly more males than females in the district, 330 to 311, producing a sex ratio (males divided by females times 100) of 106, quite a low sex ratio for a frontier population but higher than that of many Utah localities at the time. The median age for women was eighteen, (mean, 22.7), and that for men nineteen (23.4), indicating a fairly young population.

Aside from women keeping house, the next largest occupational group, fifty-one mill workers, made up but 17 percent of those with occupations in Sugar House, most of them (forty-three) working in the textile mill as carders, spinners, dyers, weavers, fullers, or, in one case, as foreman of the woolen factory. Sixty-seven others (23 percent) worked at a variety of common trades—masons, carpenters, shoemakers, clerks, basketmakers, laborers, and one whip-maker. One man worked in the paper mill, and seven others were employed as unspecified mill hands or mill workers. There were, in addition, two brewery workers, and several territorial employees. A warden and three others guarded the eight prisoners at the territorial penitentiary, and a hospital steward and a nurse (his wife) cared for three mentally disturbed women in the territorial asylum.

Although Sugar House was not primarily a farming village, as so many Utah Mormon towns of the period were, the area retained a large rural component, some forty-four of the men (15 percent of those occupied) considering themselves farmers or farmhands. Still, the overall occupational structure supports our contention that this was a suburban neighborhood whose men were more likely to be factory operatives, civil servants, or craftsmen, than dirt farmers.

Seventy-three percent of Sugar House adults were from northern Europe, making the American-born a distinct minority. Of 337 persons eighteen and older, 245 were foreign born—153 from the British Isles, large numbers from Denmark, Norway, and Sweden, and several from German-speaking parts of Europe, especially Switzerland. As the Sugar House Saints gathered for ward meetings, one would have heard the people greeting one another in a rich variety of languages and English dialects. The large number of immigrants, many recently arrived in the United States, was no doubt a factor in keeping wealth rather low. Home and lands averaged $544 per household in value, other property $100, not including that of James Cummings, who listed himself as owner of the textile mill, valued at $40,000, with an additional $10,000 in personal property.

Until the 1890s the Mormon church did not support public schools, fearing that secular schools would not permit the religious training they believed was necessary for maintaining faith and group loyalty. Church leaders recommended instead that children attend schools maintained and taught under ward auspices. But the Mormon ward-based school system apparently was not serving its children well. Of all the 165 Sugar House children between the ages of six and sixteen less than half (45 percent) attended school and, of these, girls attended school in greater numbers than boys (53 percent as compared to 37 percent). Moreover, no one listed his or her occupation to the census taker as teacher, though teachers might have come from outside the ward boundaries; or more likely, teachers listed their primary occupations since they worked only part-time in the schools.

One can find in the census list a number of the wives and families of very prominent Latter-day Saints, including Youngs, Kimballs, Taylors, Snows, Van Cotts, and Cummingses. The presence of plural wives of high church leaders and their families, coupled with a large recent immigrant population, reveals wide diversity in the social status and wealth of those living in the district. Sugar House seems to have had two populations. At the upper end of the social scale were those who favored the area as a retreat from city life. Clustered near Young's Forest Farm, the social center of the district, some of the wealthier Saints may have been seasonal residents, who moved out to enjoy the shade and breezes along Parley's Creek (formerly called Canyon Creek) during the summer, but moved back into the city in the winter. In any event, many of these elites commuted to the city for church services and did not really take an active role in the local congregation, which means that ward membership in 1870 was not as strictly geographically based as it later became. At the lower end of the scale were the immigrants who sustained Sugar House Ward year-round. It is interesting to note, moreover, that although the larger society of which Sugar House was a part was probably 95 percent Mormon, Sugar House Ward was in the peculiar situation of having within its boundaries many who were not Latter-day Saints and, therefore, not members of the ward.

During its first forty years, what we might call the "pioneer" period in Sugar House Ward history, only the formation of the Farmer's Ward took place to change the ward's boundaries. But important changes took place within the ward during its early decades. In its first decade, and to some degree even into the 1870s, many church members within the ward boundaries had looked to meetings in the city center as their primary congregation. For them, the ward was a subsidiary administrative and worship center, which sponsored some devotional and social activities. By the mid-1870s, however, Sugar House Ward became their primary congregation.

One reason for this change is that while all aspects of life in the new Zion were considered part of a sacred calling, the early members of Sugar House Ward and its sister wards began to hold regular meetings explicitly devoted to worship and communion with the divine. Sunday meetings always included a communion or "sacrament" service in which bread and water were blessed in ritual prayers offered by priests as tokens of the body and blood of the Savior, and then partaken of by all assembled members who considered themselves worthy to do so. Sunday sermons by one of the brethren, or the bishop or other ward leader, could, when the spirit moved them, go on for several hours. Even in worship services, however, the fusing of public and private was manifest in the sermonizing. In typical Mormon fashion, Sunday speakers might preach one Sabbath on Christ's mediation and atonement and the next Sunday on the necessity of extending the Big Cottonwood Creek irrigation canal several miles north to give needed additional water to farms in Sugar House and adjoining wards.[23] Both themes were crucial to the building of the kingdom.

The first Thursday of each month was a day of fasting in early Utah for members of the Sugar House Ward, as well as for their brothers and sisters in the other wards throughout the church. Members were expected to fast and pray that day—donating the food thus saved to the bishop's storehouse for the poor—and to attend "Fast and Testimony meeting" in the afternoon. In this meeting members impelled by the spirit to do so stood in turn (rather in the manner of a Friends meeting) to "bear their testimonies."

As first Thursdays had no symbolic import and the rhythm of work in modern times makes the holding of general ward meetings on Thursday afternoon difficult, testimony meetings are now combined with sacrament meetings on the first Sunday of every month. These are unquestionably the most spiritually intense of the regular worship services held outside the temple. Members emerging from such meetings will speak of "feeling the spirit in great abundance" or of enjoying a "spiritual feast" during the meeting. Individual fasting and prayer prior to the meeting seem to attune those who attend to spiritual promptings, and the declarations of faith on the part of fellow members act to strengthen individual convictions. Fast and Testimony meetings also play a vital role in fusing a disparate group of believers, united only by the fact that they live in the same vicinity, into an actual communion of Saints.

As they shared their deepest spiritual feelings and most precious experiences, Sugar House Ward members forged strong spiritual bonds with one another. Under the rhetorical umbrella of bearing testimony to the LDS gospel, members shared their personal histories and affirmed their common history as a people. One good sister would tell of burying a child in the "wilderness" near Scotts Bluff; another would describe the hardship of the handcart journey; a third, a hardened pioneer, told of being with Brigham Young's pioneer company when the vanguard first spotted the Great Salt Lake shining mirrorlike from the floor of the Intermountain basin. Again and again, until it almost became a ritual, Sister Pyper, the Relief Society president, recalled a childhood memory of being among the weeping Saints who stood in the street and watched the funeral procession that brought the bodies of Joseph Smith and his brother Hyrum back to Nauvoo after they had been murdered.[24]

Less ritualized accounts of personal traumas—bare larders and hungry children miraculously dealt with through prayer and the assistance of other ward members—were staples of all the early testimony sessions. In May of 1886 Sister Cornelia Driggs thanked ward members for the milk and fruit they had sent when Bishop Driggs "fetched home" the legendary Mormon Apostle Parley Pratt at the end of his stay in the penitentiary for violating the antipolygamy statutes.[25] Such sharing brought the congregation together in a way that the sacrament meeting and Sunday school could not.

With other Mormons, Sugar House Ward members participated regularly in religious "ordinances," believed to be some of the most important religious duties of all Latter-day Saints. LDS ordinances are ritualized representations of divinely wrought changes. They can be generally divided into two main classes, ordinances of salvation and ordinances of comfort. Among the saving ordinances are baptism by immersion (the ordinance by which members are brought into the church), the laying on of hands for the gift of the Holy Ghost (a priesthood blessing usually conferred immediately after baptism), partaking of the sacrament, ordination into the higher priesthood, and temple ordinances such as eternal marriage (being "sealed for time and eternity") and receiving one's "Endowment" (temple rituals and covenants).

In the nineteenth century, baptisms were usually performed at a creek or pond, or as time went on at a central baptistery that served a number of wards. Confirmation, the laying on of hands for the gift of the Holy Ghost, was sometimes performed at the water's edge and sometimes the day after baptism at ward meetings. These patterns have changed little in the church over the last century and a half, although there have been changes in the wording in some of the liturgies. Priesthood ordinations usually take place at the ward level, but are sometimes performed at a stake center.

The only saving ordinance that virtually always takes place at the ward level is the administration of the sacrament. This ordinance, which recommits members to the covenants made at baptism, is considered the most sacred part of the weekly worship service called the "sacrament meeting." Sugar House Ward sacrament meetings, like those in most Mormon wards, usually have too many children in attendance to be very quiet, but older children are shushed most urgently during the sacrament service, and usually only the whimpers of an occasional unhappy infant are heard during this part of the meeting.

In Kirtland and Nauvoo, emphasis on the "restoration of all things" added a Hebraic dimension to the original Christian primitivist character of the Mormon movement. One manifestation of this Hebraic dimension is the importance of properly dedicated temples to the ritual lives of the Saints. Marriages "for time" can be performed by a bishop at a local meetinghouse. But Mormon doctrine says that these marriage bonds will last only for this life. For the husband-wife and parent-child relationship to last eternally, the ordinance of marriage, or sealing for time and eternity, must be performed in a properly dedicated temple.

Such edifices, or as the early Saints called them, Houses of the Lord, were constructed at great sacrifice, first in Kirtland, Ohio (1836), and Nauvoo, Illinois (1846), and after the Saints made the trek across the plains to the Great Basin, throughout the Mormon kingdom, in Logan, Manti, St. George, and Salt Lake City. Although the Salt Lake Temple was not completed until 1893, an Endowment House, where temple ordinances could be administered, was built and dedicated in 1855.

Central to the ordinances that the Saints often describe as "the fullness of the gospel" is the Endowment, which with sealing—the uniting of a man and a woman for eternity, with the Abrahamic promise of a numerous progeny to be a part of the eternal family unit—is essential to exaltation in the celestial world. The Endowment is a dramatic representation of humanity's eternal progression toward godhood. In the ceremony, actors portray critical biblical figures, important in the Mormon "plan of salvation"; as a part of this ritual, Latter-day Saints make covenants that are similar to final vows taken by those who enter a monastery or convent. After receiving their Endowment, faithful Mormon men and women wear next to their bodies, as a reminder and symbol of the temple covenants they have made, a "garment" that serves for them a function similar to that of a clerical habit.

The practice of wearing specially dedicated sacred clothing in the temple itself entered Mormonism in Nauvoo and it continues today. When participating in temple ceremonies, Saints wear white temple robes and ceremonial aprons. "Garments," however, are not temple clothes; they are articles of clothing that are worn under street clothes. Originally one-piece affairs that fit closely around the neck with sleeves to the wrist and legs to the ankle, with ritual markings sewn across the breast, at the navel, and on one knee, they are now two-piece undergarments with short sleeves and with legs that extend just below the knee. The wearing of garments has assumed a great deal of importance as a mark of LDS identity. Just as the "Word of Wisdom," which forbids smoking and the consumption of alcohol, coffee, and tea, is a reminder to the Saints that they are the "Chosen People," so wearing these white undergarments with special markings reminds Saints who they are.

Because these ordinances are reserved for the temple and because entrance to the temple is limited to worthy Latter-day Saints who possess "recommends" from their local bishops, they are not public events. So it is that one of the most sacred and most joyous of happenings within many congregational groups, the joining of one of its members to another in marriage, does not take place in the presence of the congregation. Generally only a few members of the immediate families of the bride and groom, and sometimes a few close friends, witness the actual marriage ceremony. The more public celebration of LDS marriages usually takes place at a wedding reception, a gala affair often held in the ward meetinghouse.

During the 1880s, however, a good many marriages of ward members in the Sugar House and hundreds of other Mormon wards were not only celebrated privately; they also were not publicly known or acknowledged. About one Sugar House Ward member in three was a member of a polygamous household. The leading men of the ward, Bishop Smoot, his successors Bishops Ira Eldredge and Apollus G. Driggs, who was bishop for twenty-two years, and many others had several wives, and families with each wife. As the U.S. government stepped up its anti-polygamy crusade in the 1880s, Driggs and at least three other ward members served time in the state penitentiary, which was located within the ward boundaries directly north of the meeting/schoolhouse. In 1870, this prison had been under the supervision of Mormons. Albert P. Rock-wood was warden and Charles Robson was first guard. Both were ward members and both were polygamists who lived at the prison with po-lygamous wives. Although the majority of ward households were not polygamous, the fact that the leading families in this and the other early Utah wards lived "the principle" gave the practice a great deal of legitimacy, and induced most ward members, even those not person-ally involved in a polygamous relationship, to support and defend the practice.

Another reflection of Mormonism's Hebraic character is the be-stowal of patriarchal blessings, one of the several ordinances of comfort that are generally administered in the ward. Patriarchal blessings are conferred by a patriarch, an older Latter-day Saint who holds a specially designated calling to this office which carries no line responsibility but allows him to bestow personal blessings that reveal their lineage in the House of Israel to individual Saints and disclose something of the direc-tion of their future lives if they remain faithful. Like several of the ordi-nances of comfort, patriarchal blessings institutionalize a spiritual gift, the gift of prophecy.

Another ordinance manifesting a spiritual gift is the practice of anointing (with olive oil that has been blessed for the purpose) and lay-ing on hands to heal the sick. Just as the patriarchal blessing is thought to be a manifestation of the gift of prophecy, priesthood administrations to the sick are thought to manifest the gift of healing.

Still another ordinance of comfort, one that has always taken place in a ward setting, is the blessing of babies. These blessings are adminis-tered during a special "ordinance work" time at the beginning of the Fast and Testimony meeting each month. From April 1854, when the ward was organized, through the end of 1855, eighteen Sugar House Ward babies were blessed.[26] In 1990 the total was thirty-four (which sig-nals the persistence of the "village" size of the ward across the years). Today the father is usually the one to give the blessing, while priesthood holders from both the paternal and maternal families, as well as a few members of the father's priesthood quorum, join him in the blessing circle. Fathers often feel inspired to bless their infants with healthy minds and bodies, with a continuing love for the gospel, and with the promise of worthy mates to whom they may be sealed for eternity in the temple. When the blessing is completed, the proud father usually lifts the infant up high enough so that the whole congregation can get a good look at the newest ward member, and the ward members respond with admiring "ohs" and "ahs." This ordinance reflects the Mormon belief that fathers holding the high priesthood have the right to receive revelation for their families, and to give family members priesthood blessings.

Funerals for ward members are usually held in the meetinghouse. Family members plan the service in consultation with the bishop, who typically presides at the funeral. Family members choose a high priesthood holder to deliver the prayer dedicating the grave, another ordinance of comfort. This dedicatory prayer often blesses the grave site as a place of comfort to loved ones, assuring them that the spirit of the departed is again with the Lord, and that spirit and body will be united at the time of the resurrection.

All Mormon ordinances must be administered by the proper priesthood authorities. In the first half-century of church history, women often experienced such spiritual gifts as the gift of tongues and the gift of healing, and regularly performed a "washing and anointing" ordinance of comfort for their sisters who were about to bear children. But as the nineteenth century progressed, women were discouraged from manifesting such gifts and bestowing such blessings. These activities were instead interpreted to be exclusive prerogatives of male priesthood holders.[27] In recent decades, a few Mormon women have become aware of what they consider to be a lost spiritual heritage, and some sisters have started joining their husbands in laying their hands on their children's heads as they are giving family blessings in the home. Although women may now lead the Saints in prayer in congregational worship services, any effort by women to impinge on priesthood prerogatives is being discouraged at the highest level of church authority.

Bishop Smoot, as the spiritual as well as the temporal leader of his ward, was frequently called upon to administer to the sick. An elder, J. V. Vernon, from the Sugar House Ward, related such an experience at a conference meeting at the Salt Lake Tabernacle in March 1856:

Whilst engaged in office business one evening, I experienced a mysterious attack which shortly took away all consciousness.

Bishop Smoot took me in his arms, and arrested the complaint by the power of the Priesthood, or mortality might have ensued before morning. But I was preserved alive, and I cannot help acknowledging the vigilant kindness of Bishop Smoot and Mrs. Smoot, and counselor Henry Wilde, who watched over me with the tenderest care during the night.[28]

Margaret Smoot's letters contain many references to healing blessings given by her husband. One account of such a blessing tells of Smoot's teenage son and a friend being struck by lightning while working in the fields one May afternoon in 1859. The family friend died immediately, but William Harris, the Smoot boy, survived. William was "hurt very badly," but Bishop Smoot administered to the boy, and he recovered. Margaret wrote to a friend that "we can own the preserving hand of the Lord in it, for he was killed to all appearances and was restored to life by the power of faith through the administration of the servants of God."[29] Journal entries of other ward members also mention healing blessings which is not surprising since authority to administer to the sick rests with all holders of the Melchizedek priesthood, not just bishops or other ecclesiastical leaders.

II

The imminent arrival of the transcontinental railroad at the end of the 1860s promised to breach the cocoon of isolation in which the Saints had been dwelling for twenty years. Though welcoming the railroad, Brigham Young was intent on shoring up the organizational defenses of his people against the coming influx of Gentiles with their tempting material goods and materialistic values. Young's first step in this organizational strengthening was to revive the Women's Relief Society on a church-wide level. Originally the society had been formed to give aid to the poor and sick, and to collect money to support the construction of the Nauvoo temple. It had been revived in a number of individual wards in the Great Basin, including the Sugar House Ward, but these small units received no central organizational support until 1867, when President Young called on one of his wives, Eliza R. Snow, to reestablish the organization on a church-wide basis.

Sugar House Ward's permanent Relief Society was established on May 12, 1868. Christiana Pyper was elected president; Martha A. Smoot and Catherine Staker were her counselors. For the first decade, Relief Society meetings were held in sisters' homes. The first order of business was setting up a "visiting teacher" system, in which pairs of society members made monthly visits to each sister in the ward.[30] The visiting teacher system, first established in the Nauvoo Relief Society, served several important functions. The visits gave women the benefit of regular social contact with sisters who cared about them, and who knew at firsthand the difficulties of bearing and raising children, and running a household in harsh frontier conditions. Visiting teachers also acted as door-to-door messengers, with the latest information and counsel from the bishop and the general authorities. For example, in December of 1872, visiting teachers were told to report to the sisters on their routes the latest news about efforts of the Grant administration in Washington to wipe out the practice of polygamy, and they were also told to "watch out for apostacy [*sic*]."[31]

President Pyper commissioned her teachers to report back to her if sisters on their routes were low on food or fuel, or needed nursing care, or winter coats for the children. The organization would then hold bazaars and organize other fund-raising projects to underwrite poor relief. They also made quilts, rugs, clothing, and other needed items to supply the needs of the less fortunate in the ward. The visiting teacher and "block teacher" programs helped to draw more tightly together the strands of the ward family. These ward programs—the priesthood visiting program is now called the "home teaching program"—play the same basic role today.

It was not unusual in the nineteenth century for church women to organize in order to aid the poor, but the efforts of the Relief Society in this and several other fields of endeavor went far beyond delivering hot casseroles and knitted sweaters to the needy. In addition to one-to-one acts of kindness, the society developed an extensive network of programs and institutions to meet the "welfare" needs of sisters and their families, programs that were obvious manifestations of the lack of division between the religious and secular dimensions of LDS women's lives.

The integration of public and private was particularly apparent in the field of community health. In 1873, President Young asked Relief Society presidents throughout the church to appoint three women from each Salt Lake City ward and one from each settlement to study physiology and nursing at classes held by women physicians in Salt Lake City.[32] In 1898, the society established the Relief Society Nurse School for more formal training in nursing, and these Relief Society programs continued until the 1920s, when college and university training programs were available to take their place. For decades afterward, ward Relief Societies maintained funds to support ward members receiving nurses' training. The Relief Society also contributed greatly to the improvement of hospital care. The society established the Deseret Hospital in 1882 and provided administration and financial support for the hospital until it was closed twelve years later. Sugar House Ward Relief Society minutes record a number of contributions to the Deseret Hospital during the 1880s. Many stake Relief Society organizations established maternity hospitals throughout the Great Basin. Other society activities in the field of public health included operating milk depots and sponsoring summer trips for malnourished children, conducting clinics for preschoolers, supplying layette kits for new mothers, providing payment, when necessary, for medical and dental care, and organizing an extensive program of health and child-care education.[33]

The Sugar House Ward Relief Society and its sister societies throughout the church were actively involved in many other welfare-related programs. Relief Society members were called by President Young in 1876 to carry out a systematic program of saving grain against a time of need. One of the official Relief Society histories recounts the many activities pursued by the sisters to fulfill this calling: "They raised wheat, gleaned in the fields, and bought wheat with funds raised through sale of such items as quilts, carpets, rugs, jam, and Sunday eggs. Sometimes they would follow the threshing machine with a team and wagon to gather in the wheat. They also solicited wheat from door to door."[34]

Society members in the Sugar House Ward pursued the wheat collection program with great vigor. By December 20, 1876, just two weeks after the campaign was initiated, $80 worth of grain, flour, and donations for the wheat drive had already been collected—nearly a thousand dollars ($977) in 1990 dollars.[35] Sarah Gibson, with six children still at home, was elected to lead the organization when Sister Pyper moved to another ward. She reminded sisters in February 1877 that the drive to store wheat was the result of a divine revelation to the prophet of the Lord, and that decisions by Sister Snow and her counselors about when and where to disburse the wheat would also be made by revelation.[36]

On both the central and the local ward levels, the Relief Society exercised more freedom of action than might have been expected in a church dominated by an all-male hierarchy. With its expenses raised from members' dues, the organization was financially independent of other church organizations. Decisions regarding disbursement of these funds and other Relief Society resources were made by the Relief Society sisters, not by the priesthood authorities. The organization published its own periodicals and lesson manuals. On the ward level, the independence of the women's organization was underscored by the separate Relief Society halls, built entirely with funds raised by the sisters.

In December, 1874, "Presidentess" Sarah Gibson proposed such a building for Sugar House. A motion to build a ward Relief Society hall was passed, and each sister was asked to contribute a dollar to the new building fund. By May 1876, $356.25 had been raised to support the construction effort and, in 1877, a 16′ × 27′ hall was completed.[37] Furnished with tables, quilting frames, a cook stove, a sewing machine, chests for storing sewing materials, and other items needed for Relief Society work, the hall served as headquarters for the Sugar House Ward Relief Society until 1924, when a new meetinghouse was completed that had a Relief Society room furnished by the sisters.

In the Mormon system, the Relief Society is known as a church auxiliary. On the church-wide level, Eliza R. Snow not only played a key role in reviving this organization, but she also helped launch several other auxiliary organizations. In 1874, she urged the young women of the church to form local "Young Ladies' Retrenchment Societies." As the name suggests, the purpose of these groups was to encourage a return to a simple lifestyle that stressed the virtues of home industry. The fancy silk dresses, factory-loomed carpets, and mahogany divans fancied by the young sisters cost the precious hard currency that the community needed for machinery and other eastern imports necessary for building the kingdom. These new organizations for young women soon expanded their scope to include recreational activities and weekly lessons. Snow told young sisters in the many wards she visited that their own activity would prove an effective spur to the young men. "As sure as the sisters arise and take hold of the work," she promised, "the brethren will wake up, because they must be at the head."[38] As she had predicted, soon Young Men's Retrenchment organizations were also established. When one of the sisters in the village of Farmington, Utah, suggested that similar efforts were needed to supplement children's religious instruction, Snow quickly procured the local bishop's permission for the sisters to found such a group. She then worked to see that the new organization, which was called "Primary," was organized in every ward throughout the church.[39]

Sister Sarah Gibson, Sugar House Ward Relief Society president from 1873 to 1904, played a similar role in encouraging the formation of auxiliary organizations for children and youth in her ward. At stake conferences, and at twice-yearly Relief Society presidents' conferences, Sister Gibson received instructions from central authorities about where and how these auxiliaries fit into the ward. The March 1876 Relief Society minutes note that President Gibson was urging the sisters to organize the young women. Sister Gibson returned to this theme several times during the next year, and finally announced with pride in March 1877 that the young ladies would meet the next week to organize themselves and select officers.[40] The corresponding young men's organization was established the same year.

Perhaps because the term "retrenchment" signified something negative to the adolescents who were potential members, the names of the new organizations were soon changed to the Young Men's and Young Ladies' Mutual Improvement Associations. By the 1880s the young men's and women's groups were frequently meeting together. A typical biweekly meeting included scripture readings, recitations, hymn singing, musical presentations, and, often, a sermon from a visiting leader from church headquarters, or from some other ward. But it took a while for these organizations to start flourishing. On December 9, 1892, the president of the general board of the Young Women's Mutual Improvement Association visited the ward and told the Sugar House girls not to be discouraged by recent low attendance at their meetings. She counseled the young women to "judge not lest they be judged," to make friendly visits to the shirkers, and to "take courage and press onward."[41]

Sister Gibson also mounted a campaign for the organization of a Primary for the younger children. Her first call for a Sugar House Ward Primary came in January of 1880. Few meetings went by during the next year where the Relief Society president failed to mention the need for this organization.[42] In June 1881, her urgings finally bore fruit and the ward Primary was organized. Sisters Eliza R. Snow and Zina D. H. Young, another prominent wife of Brigham Young, attended the organizing meeting along with Bishop Apollus G. Driggs. To emphasize their LDS heritage, Sister Snow showed the children a watch that had been owned by her first husband, the Prophet Joseph Smith. Sister Isabella McGhie was set apart as Primary president, and she and her counselors and teachers began holding Primary meetings for children from three to eleven years of age every Friday afternoon.

These organizations for children and youth were quite separate and distinct from the Sunday school, which held meetings on the Sabbath, either before or after the sacrament meeting. But the Sunday school was also defined as an auxiliary organization. Since auxiliaries had stake and general boards to which they reported, boards that reported, in turn, to the General Authorities, while the priesthood organizations reported more directly, the local ward administrative structure was somewhat complicated. This is a problem that was manageable as long as most of the Saints lived in the Great Basin, but one that became increasingly troublesome as the number of wards and stakes multiplied and the distance from the center to the periphery increased. Almost a century would pass before a program of priesthood correlation would streamline the ward administration by insisting that the leadership of ward auxiliary organizations must report to the ward bishop.

Before Brigham Young died in 1877, different administrative and organizational problems caused him to press an early effort to rationalize what was at the time a rather chaotic pattern of church organization. That year stakes were established throughout the church, and priesthood quorums were reorganized so that quorum jurisdictions coincided with ward boundaries. Because all priesthood holders (i.e., practically all the adult males in the church) had theretofore been members of priesthood quorums that were organized by priesthood rank and, thus, might include men from several different wards, this move strengthened individual wards. In effect, making priesthood quorum jurisdictions and ward boundaries coincide meant that there were several men's organizations in each ward.

At this time, the practice was inaugurated of ordaining boys as deacons in the lower (Aaronic) priesthood at age twelve, and their duties and lessons were framed as a preparation and training course for the higher priesthood. All Aaronic priesthood activities, and many Melchizedek priesthood activities as well, were placed firmly under the control of the local bishop.[43] These steps added greatly to the coherence of church organization. But the true order in church operations could not be achieved until an increasingly disruptive problem for the Sugar House Ward and its sister wards was dealt with. This was the problem of the antipolygamy persecutions.

For many Sugar House Ward members, the 1880s were years of pain and anguish. Federal prosecution under the Edmunds-Tucker antipolygamy act had reached a high pitch. "The Feds," as the Saints called federal marshals, were everywhere seeking men who were guilty of "cohabitation." They apprehended many Mormon leaders and brought them to trial. Large fines and jail sentences were imposed if a guilty verdict was returned—which it generally was. Between 1886 and 1889,

Bishop Driggs; his counselor, Martin Garn; George Crismon, a prominent wealthy rancher and miner; and several other ward members were arrested. All served four- to six-month jail sentences and paid $200–$300 fines.[44] Trying to escape prosecution, Mormon men went into hiding for long periods, or they fled with one or more of their families to Canada or Mexico. With so many of the fathers in the ward in hiding, in exile, or in jail, life became very difficult for Sugar House families. By the end of the 1880s, carrying on the organized activities of the ward was almost impossible.

Federal pressure on the general church leadership was equally intense. By early 1890 most church property had been confiscated and persons refusing to take an antipolygamy pledge had been disenfranchised. When LDS church president Wilfred Woodruff learned that no relief was available from the federal courts to redress what the Saints believed were the unconstitutional excesses of the Edmunds-Tucker Act, and when he saw the Mormon temples threatened, he issued a directive known as the "Manifesto," withdrawing church authorization for plural marriages, and urging all members to comply totally with federal law.[45] In the General Conference held in October 1890 the Saints accepted Woodruff's statement as divine revelation.

Church-wide compliance with the Manifesto did not take place overnight, but gradually the practice of plural marriage was eliminated among virtually all the Saints who continued to participate in authorized church activities. A few schismatic groups, long since excommunicated from the church, continue the practice even today. But the church abandoned plural marriage. At the same time, as the price of statehood for Utah, the federal government demanded that the church relinquish control of the major economic and political institutions in the Great Basin. With the forfeit of these distinctive elements of life in the kingdom, the church gained back its property and the opportunity for its members to resume their normal lives, again participating in their regular ward and stake activities.

III

After the 1890 Manifesto prohibiting plural marriage had been issued, Mormon leaders faced new opportunities and new problems. Federal prosecution and the disruptions it caused were over, but the two bastions—polygamy and the independent political and economic kingdom—that had effectively isolated the Saints from the Gentile world were now gone. The completion of the transcontinental railroad in 1867 had greatly diminished the physical isolation that the pioneers had come so far to achieve. Adherents of other faiths had for several years been moving into the Salt Lake Valley in notable numbers. In 1875, the Presbyterians had established Westminster College within the Sugar House Ward boundaries, and in 1892 they built an elaborate church just a few blocks from the still rustic Sugar House Ward chapel.[46] During the same period the discontinuance of plural marriage eliminated the biggest social obstacle between the Saints and the rest of the world.

Residing in Salt Lake City, or in one of the scores of Mormon settlements that now dotted the landscape from northern Mexico to Canada, no longer guaranteed—as it had in the early years of settlement—that one was safely encased in a Mormon community. Though the Mormon culture was still dominant, it was no longer exclusive. Secular entertainments proliferated, including dancing, theater, beer parlors, resorts, sporting events, and other activities that the church could not control or influence. The federal government had stipulated that political and economic institutions had to operate independently from the church. Yet church leaders were still convinced that it was absolutely necessary to keep the Saints an isolated and "peculiar people" if they were to fulfill their divinely mandated mission.

To maintain boundaries against the encroaching Gentile world, the brethren repeatedly emphasized the Word of Wisdom, which called on the Saints to forgo such hot drinks as coffee and tea, as well as the consumption of alcohol and the use of tobacco in any form, as a means of keeping separate "from the world." Indeed, this became an almost ubiquitous sermon topic. They also placed tremendous stress on tithing when the role of the church as ecclesiastical institution increased and institutional activity began to take on an importance it had lacked as long as the Saints had, despite the presence of federal officials, exercised dominion over the Great Basin. Church leaders developed a ward-and-stake-centered schedule of activities for members that kept them within a tight orbit of church influence. The activities of the auxiliary organizations were expanded on both the ward and stake levels to include organized sporting events, youth dances, scouting, speech contests, musical and dramatic presentations, and a centrally published set of lesson manuals. With such a welter of activity, hardly a night went by when the lights of the meetinghouse were not ablaze. In this period

5.1 Sugar House Ward meetinghouse, completed 1924. Courtesy of Sugar House Ward, Church of Jesus Christ of Latter-day Saints.

the ward community became the bastion against secularism that the entire Great Basin, behind its Rocky Mountain fortress, had been in earlier days.

The Sugar House neighborhood was undergoing its own transformation during the 1890s. With railroad lines adjacent to the business center, and the trolley line now extending inside the ward boundaries, the foundations were laid for rapid residential growth and commercial development. The old farms were gradually bought up and subdivided into house lots, and scores of new retail businesses and a few light manufacturing plants were established in the business district. The simple two-story meetinghouse that ward members had built on the old schoolhouse site in 1887 was soon perceived to be inadequate in size and facilities for the needs of the burgeoning neighborhood.[47] Projects to modernize and enlarge the building were constantly underway until the drive to build an entirely new chapel was initiated in the early 1920s.

As the Sugar House area population increased, the time arrived for the realignment of ward boundaries. In 1883, the Salt Lake stake authorities decided to extend the boundaries of Salt Lake City wards south about a mile in response to the southward creep of residential development. As ward subdivision always does, this move transferred a number of Sugar House Ward members to other wards, mainly the Salt Lake First Ward, but also to a sprinkling of several other city wards.[48] Further divisions of the ward took place more gradually. A familiar pattern was the establishment of satellite or branch Sunday schools, and sometimes other auxiliary organizations and priesthood quorums, in outlying areas not yet populous enough to sustain full ward organization. The Saints in the Forest Dale area south of Parley's Creek, formerly part of Young's Forest Farm, met in a branch Sunday school for several years until the group became populous enough for an independent ward in 1896.

In the northeast portions of the Sugar House Ward, located in the foothills of the Wasatch Mountains, the Pleasant View Branch retained its satellite status for a number of years before becoming a full-fledged ward. A separate Pleasant View Branch Sunday school was listed as early as 1895 in Sugar House Ward records, and in December of 1906 a meetinghouse was constructed.[49] The branch had its own Relief Society, priesthood meetings, and other auxiliary meetings for seven years after the construction of the branch meetinghouse before it was finally given independent ward status in 1912.[50]

The fact that Latter-day Saint congregations divided frequently did not mean that the divisions were accomplished without pain. The minutes of the Sugar House Ward, and of the new Emerson Ward, created from northwest sections of the ward in 1905, reflect the sadness (and perhaps even acrimony) that accompanied the partitioning of a group whose members had for years been enmeshed in a tight religious and social network. Apostle Hyrum N. Smith addressed the Sugar House Ward Conference at which the division was announced, acknowledging the ward members' "feelings of regret" at parting with old friends, but assuring them that "time can heal wounds." In what might have been a response to reports of grumbling about the new Emerson Ward leadership, the Apostle reminded the Sugar House flock that while it took a courageous man to oppose an appointee whom he knew to be guilty of a crime, it was a small man who would oppose someone due to personal feelings. Stake president Frank Y. Taylor added his own admonition that the members should give strong support to the new ward organizations.[51]

At the turn of the century, Sugar House Ward was placed under the jurisdiction of the newly formed Granite Stake, which in 1900 encompassed fourteen wards in the southeast suburbs of Salt Lake.[52] The organization of Granite Stake was a part of a larger effort by church authorities to energize and decentralize church organization. By this time total church membership was 268,331, and many of the old stakes had as many as ten or even twenty thousand members. Existing stakes were divided and new ones organized to create an average stake membership closer to five or six thousand. Following this change, which made it possible for stakes to be true congregations, both the number of stake officers and the importance of stake activities grew rapidly.

The twelve high priests constituting each stake high council had previously served almost exclusively as a priesthood court for imposing church discipline on errant Melchizedek priesthood members. Now their duties were expanded to include monthly speaking assignments in the wards. On their monthly visits, the Granite Stake high councilmen communicated to the members of Sugar House Ward the current concerns of the General Authorities and of the stake presidency. Stake boards were created to help each of the auxiliary organizations in planning stake-wide activities to supplement the already busy ward activity schedules, and to provide the systematic teacher training and support that were becoming an important part of the church's effort to upgrade the level of religious instruction.

The many changes that had taken place since 1870 are clearly reflected in the 1910 manuscript census for the Sugar House neighborhood.[53] In the intervening forty years, Sugar House had taken off its overalls and put on a white collar. Occupationally the neighborhood was much more diverse. As opposed to 1870 when only forty different occupations were reported, in 1910 well over a hundred different occupations were reported, including many wholly new white-collar positions, such as clerks, salespeople, stenographers, real estate agents, abstractors, and bookkeepers. Farmers had almost entirely disappeared; only 7 of 289 thought of themselves as farmers. The occupational array is, in fact, so diverse as to defy almost any reasonable classification scheme. About equal numbers were employed in white- and blue-collar jobs (72 and 79); and while fewer residents held factory positions, a good many of these worked in the candy industry ("dippers," they called themselves), an industry that would remain (appropriately enough) one of the Sugar House specialties until the 1980s. The textile and paper mills had long since closed, but a nearby brickyard employed a number of ward members. The furniture retailing business had become important to the district and would remain so into the 1990s. There were several professionals—physicians, teachers, and real estate brokers—and a number who worked in millinery shops, grocery stores, or other small retail establishments that hardly existed forty years before. The prison now employed ten persons, and there were various other civil servants, such as streetcar conductors and firemen, whose presence attested to the new urban character of Sugar House. No longer a country watering place for downtown elites, the neighborhood was developing its own shopping district and becoming a commercial center in its own right, while at the same time housing many who commuted daily to the city center on the streetcar.

Over the years the predominantly immigrant character of the neighborhood had changed. Now 51 percent of the 472 adults were Utah-born and 20 percent were from other parts of the United States, reversing the foreign-born proportion from what it had been in 1870. Eighteen percent were now from Britain, 9 percent from continental Europe, including Scandinavia, and the remaining 3 percent from places as remote as Samoa, New Zealand, Australia, and India. Most of the adults in 1910 were first-generation Americans. The fathers of 64 percent of the adults had been foreign-born, and the mothers of 65 percent had been.

Moreover, these children of immigrants seem not to have done too badly in America. Utah had recovered well from the 1907 recession and virtually all household heads had been employed during the previous year, 110 working for others (74 percent) and the rest working in a profession, trade, or running a business on their "own account." Only five had extended periods of unemployment the previous year, ranging from seven to twenty-six weeks. Sixty-five percent of the 152 reporting lived in their own homes, half of them paid for and the other half mortgaged. The rest (35 percent) lived in rented houses or apartments. Again it is clear that Sugar House, if not affluent, was solidly middle class.

Reflecting more a national than a local trend, the census takers had been instructed to consider housewives as having no occupation, and dutifully wrote "none" beside the name of each wife (the same for children and the unemployed men), suggesting that Americans had devalued the difficult and vital labor of maintaining a household and rearing children to a cipher. The "keeping house" designation of the 1870s at least had suggested that women worked at some worthy occupation, as opposed to the "none" reported in 1910. Indeed these women were well occupied. The average household was just over five persons, hardly changed at all since 1870. But the women no longer spun and wove, and if they gardened it was to raise flowers or fresh vegetables for the summer and not to assure survival until next harvest.

In the 1880s electricity had begun to lessen the troublesome and often hazardous use of kerosene lamps, and by 1910 many women had acquired labor-saving household appliances, which relieved to some extent the burden of home and child care. Of 147 married women 129 had borne children, averaging five each (5.2), and losing one to death before they were grown.[54] Women above forty-five, who thus had likely completed childbearing, had borne an average of 7.3 children each and suffered the loss of two. Susannah McGhie, the Primary president, lived at 1150 Downing Avenue with her husband James in 1910. She was forty-three; he was forty-six. She had borne ten children in twenty-three years of married life, eight of them surviving, and all eight, ranging in age from twenty-two to the twin girls, four, were still living at home. It would have taken many household appliances to make a noticeable dent in the burdens her "keeping house" entailed.

Before 1890, the Saints had been afraid that public schools would inculcate Protestant doctrines and values and so had refused to support them. With the end of polygamy and the demise of the political kingdom, this changed and the advent of the public school system in 1890 had positive effects. As Sugar House became more middle-class, parents began to send many more of their children to school than their parents and grandparents had done in 1870. There were 220 children between the ages of six and sixteen and 186 of them (85 percent) attended school, 81 percent of the 104 girls, and 90 percent of the boys. Such school attendance rates were high for 1910 and contrast sharply with the schooling pattern of the 1870 generation, both in the proportions attending and in the fact that more boys were now attending than girls, a reversal of the 1870 pattern.

Sugar House remained a youthful neighborhood; the average age of twenty-three (median nineteen) was almost exactly the same as in 1870. Obviously, while the 1870 generation aged, the new homes being built on their former fields and pastures were being purchased by young couples. Comparison of ward records and census lists indicates that about half of the families in the neighborhood were not Latter-day Saints, which was almost precisely the proportion of non-Mormons in the entire state at the time.[55] The old Sugar House neighborhood of 1870 had been similarly peopled by many who did not attend the local ward, but previously these had been what today would be known as "inactive" Latter-day Saints. Now the nonattenders were persons of other faiths or no faith, Gentiles. While their presence was evident on every street, instead of fostering Mormon-Gentile interaction and growing acceptance (on all sides) of those of other faiths, the mixed residence pattern probably helped occasion a retreat of Sugar House Mormons into their ward community.

The sex ratio had dipped somewhat, there now being 95 men for every 100 women, instead of the 106 in 1870. And both men and women took advantage of the relative balance between the sexes. There were only three households out of 177 headed by unmarried persons, men in all three cases. Only five homes had lodgers. Sugar House was definitely a family neighborhood. Divorce was a rarity, with only one person, a woman, reporting that she had been divorced. Fifteen women in the precinct had no husband at home, though all but three of these claimed they were widowed or (in the one case) divorced. Some may have been plural wives, who now, with polygamy officially abandoned, were unwilling to tell federal census-takers that they had a husband. Yet it is clear that polygamous households, comprising nearly a third of 1870 Sugar House, were now on the wane, and those remaining were keeping a low profile.

By 1910, the relentless federal campaign against plural marriage had very nearly accomplished its aims. The remaining polygamists would not be prosecuted, and any church members marrying henceforth into polygamy would be severely disciplined by the church itself. Once the subject of close scrutiny by the American public, amounting almost to voyeurism, the Mormon marriage pattern no longer was a distinguishing mark of the Saints. Yet, if Mormonism was no longer considered a danger to family life in the nation, Americans continued to regard the Saints as strange, odd, and somehow un-Christian.[56] For all that, outwardly at least, the Sugar House neighborhood looked no different from similar neighborhoods in Des Moines or Portland. In many respects, however, the similarity was more apparent than real because the public dimension of the lives of many LDS women, youth, and children was contracting while the private expanded. Except for the time spent on earning their livings, the same was also true for many Mormon men. Their church activity filled virtually all their free time, causing the lives of these Latter-day Saints to be centered around ward-sponsored activities to a degree that typical suburbanites elsewhere in the nation would have found quite exceptional.

IV

Despite an economic climate that went from poor to very bad in the intermountain west in the 1920s and 30s, the Sugar House area experienced considerable growth as a commercial and residential center during the Depression years. Wards continued to proliferate as people moved into the solid brick bungalows erected by suburban developers, and the number and variety of ward- and stake-sponsored activities reached their peak in the four decades from 1920 to 1960.

In 1911, the Boy Scout movement was adopted as an official part of the church program. The LDS-Boy Scouts tie has proved enduring, and scouting in the Sugar House Ward neighborhood is still generally a Mormon-led affair, though nonmember boys are invited to join the troops. In 1913 the church affiliated its young women's organization with the Camp Fire Girls, but probably because that organization seemed too secular this alliance proved less satisfactory and the affiliation was dropped after a year's trial. It was replaced by a church-sponsored "Beehive" program, which is similar to the Camp Fire Girls and Girl Scouts in promoting outdoor experiences, crafts, and homemaking skills, but also includes a large religious education component.[57]

By the early 1920s both programs were going strong in the Sugar House Ward. The neighborhood newspaper reported that the Sugar House Ward Boy Scout baseball team won almost every game against its Granite Stake rivals in the summer of 1921, and the troop's basketball team also ran up a creditable record in stake competition the following winter.[58] In May of 1921, the Granite Stake Boy Scout leaders established a new organization to supplement the broad array of scouting activities then in place. This new offshoot of scouting was called the "Sugar House Chums," with the name taken from the Edgar Guest couplet, "Be more than a Dad; Be a chum to your lad."[59] Though the Chums organization did not long survive, the enduring concern for maintaining warm parent-child ties has continued to manifest itself over the years in ward and stake father-son and mother-daughter activities, averaging three or four per year. About an equal number of special meetings and socials are planned for young people and both parents. In recent decades, great efforts have been made by ward leaders to see that the growing number of young people in single-parent families are provided with "adopted" parents for these occasions.

The Sugar House Ward Beehives in the early 1920s followed a program of instruction and activities that would seem familiar to the twelve- and thirteen-year-old young women who make up today's first- and second-year Beehives. In the winter months, they were given lessons, from *The Guide*, the standardized lesson manual from church headquarters, interspersed with special programs (to which the mothers were usually invited), "girls' parties" (taffy pulls and such), and parties with the scouts. The summer program stressed outdoor sports, outings, and recreation. For example, on Memorial Day, 1921, the summer season of girls' activities was kicked off by an outing attended by 400 Granite Stake young women between the ages of twelve and eighteen. Streetcars were chartered to take the girls (generally clad in their brothers' khakis, according to the local reporter) for a day's outing at Stephenson's Grove, a recreation area several miles to the south.[60]

In the early 1920s, ward- and stake-sponsored sporting activities went far beyond the Boy Scout League. A stake-wide Elder's Baseball League ("elders" were generally the younger Melchizedek priesthood members) was formed and there were also baseball games between the bishops, on one side, and the stake presidency and high council, on the other.[61] In May 1921, the Wandamere Golf Links, part of the old Forest Farm property, were opened under the administration of the Deseret Gymnasium, an extensive athletic complex which the church had built in downtown Salt Lake City in 1910.[62] By the 1920s, also, all plans for new ward houses included as part of the building a recreation hall suitable for indoor sporting events.

Teams of young men in the seventeen-to-twenty-four age group from Sugar House Ward began in the 1920s to participate in church-wide athletic competitions in baseball, basketball, and several other team sports, which culminated in championship matches at the auxiliary organization conferences in Salt Lake City each June. At the height of the program in the 1940s and 1950s, over a thousand teams throughout the church participated.[63]

These developments parallel the emergence of institutional churches in American Protestantism, but there is little evidence of direct borrowing of programs. Although the proliferation of ward and stake activities and the activities of institutional churches were both designed to provide an alternative to secular entertainment and to create a sense of Christian community, in Mormonism all these activities functioned as a barrier to social interaction between Mormons and Gentiles. Active Saints were left with little or no time for those who were not part of their stake and ward congregations.

In a typical week in the 1920s or 1930s, for example, the ward sponsored at least one dance at the ward house. Members could participate in the "Sugar House Ward Night" at the local movie theater, with a percentage of the proceeds going into ward coffers. In addition to the regular ward auxiliary meeting schedule, most members had a chance to attend at least one party sponsored by an auxiliary organization, often at a member's home. Two or three sports competitions were scheduled during the week, along with one or two pick-up basketball games arranged by ward teenagers. Other informal ward groups such as quilters, glee clubs, and dramatic societies also met weekly at the ward house or in members' homes. Several times a month, special stake programs, dances, and outings were also scheduled.

In a special week, such as an annual ward conference, the ward meeting schedule became even more intense since, in addition to a conference in which the business of the ward was conducted and instruction was given to the members of the priesthood, the various auxiliaries also held conferences attended by members of their stake boards and sometimes by members of their general boards as well. On these occasions, the auxiliaries took stock of their progress, conducted business, and presented elaborate programs. The Sugar House Ward Conference held in March 1922 began with an Aaronic Priesthood Conference on Sunday, March 5, at 10:30 A.M. Primary Conference was held at 4:00 Monday afternoon, and Home Night Conference was held that evening. The Relief Society Conference was held on the afternoon of Tuesday, March 7, and the Genealogy Conference was held later the same afternoon. The Young Ladies' and Young Men's "Mutual" Conference was held at 7:30 Tuesday evening, and the Religion Class Conference convened at 4:00 Wednesday afternoon. The ward choir rehearsed on Wednesday night for the big program to come on Sunday, and on Thursday evening all ward officers and teachers met in a special conference session with the stake presidency. Friday night a ward social was held to mark the conference. On Sunday morning, the twelfth, the Melchizedek Priesthood session was held at 9:00 A.M.; the Sunday School Conference at 10:30 A.M.; and the General Ward Conference at 6:30 P.M.

Each of these sessions had stake leaders, and in some cases General Authorities in attendance, and included sermons, readings, musical numbers, and other presentations. The Tuesday night mutual conference, for example, featured twelve young ladies dressed in "Alice-blue gown" costumes, complete with pantaloons, presenting a special musical number.[64] The "home night" and genealogy conferences reflect the addition to the array of ward activities of a family activity now called "Family Home Evening," and an individual activity that would assume increasing importance in the overall Mormon program in the years ahead. The former, a scheduled weekly gathering of family members for devotional and recreational activities, was a recommended weekly event that has now been institutionalized and made mandatory throughout the church. The genealogy classes, which instructed Saints in tracing their families back through the ages, were connected to the increasing emphasis on "temple work," a ritual activity in which Saints are baptized and participate in other ceremonies by proxy for persons who lived before the church's restoration in 1830 and, hence, did not have an opportunity for baptism under the auspices of what the Saints believe is the only legitimate priesthood authority.

Non-Mormons are often astonished to learn that this elaborate program of activities was—and continues to be—run entirely without paid staff of any kind. Although stake presidents, bishops, and auxiliary officers are all faced with enormous administrative responsibilities, even as they must also earn their own livings, the church has never made any effort to professionalize any of its leadership, with the exception of the instructors in the church educational system who teach seminary classes in local areas, as well as classes in LDS Institutes that are located near colleges and universities. Even this minimal professionalization of staff did not occur until after World War II.

That Sugar House Ward members have been supportive of all their bishops and appreciative of the sacrifices such volunteer service demands of both the bishop and his family is shown by the fact that the foyer of the Sugar House meetinghouse is lined with photographs of each ward bishop from Abraham Smoot to his present successor. One bishop, however, continues to evoke particular pride and love nearly seventy years after completion of his tenure. This is LeGrand Richards, who held the office from 1919 to 1925.

Richards, whose father and grandfather were both apostles, moved into the Sugar House area with his family in 1916. He was called to be ward bishop in 1919, when he was only thirty-three, and is remembered for his energy, infectious enthusiasm, and his unflagging commitment to what he saw as the work of the Lord. During his years as bishop, Richards successfully instituted programs to involve long inactive members, to increase attendance at meetings, and to improve the quality of ward life. The most memorable of Richards' many accomplishments was spearheading the construction of the new Sugar House Ward meetinghouse.

The previous chapel, constructed in 1887, was "an old rattletrap with dirty outside toilets attached to the back of the building," and the young bishop was determined to replace it. He said he knew this would be no easy task in a ward with many widows and families struggling hard just to get by, but when a high councilman living in the ward warned Richards that the members were too poor to build a meeting-house, Richards responded, "Then we'll die trying, because if we don't do it the ward will die, and we aren't going to let that happen."[65] Great sacrifices were required of ward members, and the building campaign faltered a few times when funds ran out, but Richards and his ward members successfully realized his vision of the kind of chapel they needed and deserved.

By the mid-twenties, the LDS Church was moving to develop standard architectural plans for use when new meetinghouses were constructed.[66] This not only created buildings that were distinctively Mormon, it was also economically beneficial since at a minimum cost the members of local wards could have access to architectural plans that needed only to be adjusted for particular sites. The Sugar House Ward meetinghouse, which was completed in 1924, was one of the first of the standard-plan buildings designed by church architect Joseph Don Carlos Young. Although standard in many respects, it had a number of distinguishing features. For example, there were the tall white columns and a carpeted entryway, a balcony at the back over the reception area, and a shallow vaulted ceiling. It also has circular arched windows through which the brilliant sunlight in the valley of the Great Salt Lake shines during daylight hours. This bathes the chapel in a warm glow that makes it unusually lovely.

A truly remarkable feature of the building is the polychromed plaster bas-relief mural at the back of what Mormons call the "stand," the raised area in the front of meetinghouses where the members of the bishopric sit and where the podium is located. In three panels, picturing the Hill Cumorah, the prophet Joseph Smith praying in the Sacred Grove, where he had his first vision, and a view of the Susquehanna River, where Smith was baptized, this elaborate work of art was executed by sculptor Torlief Knaphus, a member of the ward at the time of the building construction. Knaphus was a convert to the church from Norway whose sculptures and bas-reliefs are found in the Cardston, Arizona, Idaho Falls, and Salt Lake temples. His work is found in many buildings in Salt Lake City and elsewhere in Utah, and he sculpted the Handcart Monument, one of Mormonism's most easily recognized symbols, which now stands on Temple Square.[67]

The building cost $89,644. When it was fully paid for, it was dedicated by church president Heber J. Grant.[68] The bishopric's invitation to the dedication on Sunday, October 16, 1927, and the accompanying ward reunion the preceding Friday evening assured former and current ward members that the building represented "the last word in design and construction, for church and recreation purposes, with a beautiful chapel, seventeen classrooms, dance floor, well appointed stage, kitchen, lavatories, check rooms and closets." Today this meetinghouse, in which the ward continues to gather, is one of the best-preserved chapels in the church.

Many new ward house-models have come and gone in the more than sixty years since the Sugar House building was constructed, but this building contains all the elements considered essential to a modern Mormon meetinghouse: a chapel, a recreation hall (now called a "cultural hall") with a stage at one end, suitable for dancing, sports competitions, plays, etc., a Relief Society room, a kitchen, classrooms, and offices for the bishop. (When wards are divided, it is not unusual for both wards to meet in the same ward house, scheduling activities at different times. Therefore, it is also not unusual for newer ward houses to have offices for two bishops.) Although it is now one of the older chapels in the church, the Sugar House Ward meetinghouse wears her sixty-three years gracefully. Every surface shines. Signs on the bulletin boards remind members to "keep our historic chapel beautiful."

When the decade of the 1930s commenced, the poor economic climate that had afflicted Utah since the end of World War I became disastrously worse, as Utah was dragged into the depths of the Great Depression. It was not long before nearly half of the able-bodied Sugar House Ward members were either unemployed or underemployed. The traditionally large Latter-day Saint families made the burden of family survival particularly difficult. In the face of this crisis, the church drew upon its well-entrenched heritage of communal responsibility and cooperative enterprises, instituting a Church Welfare Program in 1936.

Featuring a massive program of farms, food-processing facilities, and basic manufacturing, all cooperatively purchased and managed, the program was designed to meet the needs of the destitute. The able-bodied in need of help were expected to do volunteer work on a church farm, or at the Welfare Square Cannery, about three miles to the west of the ward meetinghouse, or to work at the nearby multistake soap factory (which was still in production in the 1990s). Work at these facilities, especially during harvest, and other high-demand periods, was expected not just of the needy but of all able-bodied ward members. The goals of the program, according to church leaders, were to "help the people to help themselves," while at the same time abolishing "the evils of the dole."[69]

Bishops met weekly with priesthood quorum presidents and the Relief Society president to determine the needs of ward members in distress and to consider how these needs could best be met, but welfare dispositions of aid within the ward were always kept strictly confidential. Relief Society sisters sewed quilts and clothing for needy ward members, and contributed these items to central warehouses in readiness for responding to local needs. Though in recent years the church has cut back on its extensive agricultural holdings, and on some of its other welfare manufacturing and processing facilities, the program continues to operate to help ward members in economic difficulty under the same basic principles established in the mid-thirties.

Whenever Mormons and the Great Depression are mentioned together, non-Mormons almost invariably use an expression that seems first to have been applied to the Jews, "they take care of their own." Probably originally derived from articles outsiders read in the popular press, this phrase typically refers to more than the workings of the Church Welfare Program; it signals a generalized perception of the Latter-day Saint community as a sort of closed corporation that operates apart from the larger culture.[70] Initially resting on the church's rhetoric about self-reliance and the evils of the "dole," this changed understanding also developed in the years following World War II as a direct consequence of the incredible postwar mobility of the nation's population, which allowed non-Mormons to observe the Saints first-hand.

This was something new. Although a surprising number of non-Mormons had lived in the Sugar House section of Salt Lake City as well as elsewhere in Utah in the nineteenth and first-half of the twentieth century, during that time the Mormon population had been almost entirely concentrated in the intermountain west. Now, as the "gathering" scattered, non-Mormons had an opportunity to see for themselves the Saints who were settling alongside them in the many new housing subdivisions in Arizona, California, other parts of the American west, and elsewhere in the nation in the 1940s and 1950s.[71]

Physically isolated from the great majority of Americans for almost a century and culturally set apart by polygamy, the idea of which lingered on after the practice ceased, the Saints had long been perceived as weird, if not downright dangerous. In this changed situation they were still set apart. But at the very time when the "coffee klatch" was coming to characterize the lives of women in suburbia, and when smoking and drinking, if not the norm, were at least becoming socially acceptable for both American men and women, the Mormons were identified by their observation of the "Word of Wisdom" that called for the absolute avoidance of coffee and caffeine in any form, including tea and soda pop, tobacco, and all forms of alcohol. These restrictions made Saints appear definitively different, but different in a way that made them seem admirable rather than contemptible.

A new attitude toward "those amazing Mormons" replaced the negative picture of the Saints that had been a fixture in American minds for over a century.[72] This altered climate of public opinion was coupled with an LDS rate of growth that reflected a huge natural increase due to the baby boom as well as an accelerating rate of conversion to the church.[73] As a result, being a part of this movement in the 1950s and 60s became both exciting and satisfying in a way that was entirely new to Mormonism. This had a direct bearing on local ward activities everywhere since changing perceptions began to weaken the cultural barriers between Saints and outsiders, who were no longer set apart linguistically by being called Gentiles, but were simply described as non-Mormons. Ward activities opened up, as it were, and non-members were encouraged to participate.

Moreover, the situation in which the array of church activities that made wards function as Mormon enclaves was also transformed in the postwar years by an accelerating rate of church growth, a virtual explosion in Mormon family size, and the increased occupational and professional demands on the heads of households that the faster pace of an expanding economy generated. Everything combined to make church responsibilities seem more taxing and arduous than they had in earlier, less frenzied days. Being Mormon began to appear to some like being on a merry-go-round; the lives of adult Latter-day Saints began to be filled with meetings to attend, meetings to direct, and meetings to plan other meetings. As one Sugar House sister recalled, "during those years the definition of a Mormon was 'someone who is in a meeting, going to a meeting, or coming from a meeting.'"[74]

For many Saints, particularly those in "mission field" areas where Mormons were a small proportion of the population, the intense level of programming seemed worthwhile. Ward activities kept lines of communication among the Saints open and vital, allowing the ward to incorporate enormous numbers of converts without losing the sense of peoplehood that had always set the Saints apart. In other words, as long as there was almost daily interaction among ward members, wards remained efficient vehicles for "making Saints." But at what cost to Mormon families in which one or both parents had callings that sometimes took on the character of full-time assignments?

Even though some of the Sugar House Saints began to feel that they were being "run ragged," they carried out the church program with a great deal of energy throughout the 1950s.[75] The success of the efforts of the ward members and their leaders can be gleaned from the pages of the ward manuscript history, which records that in 1952 alone, in addition to all the regular programming at both the ward and stake levels (priesthood quorum meetings, women's Relief Society meetings, Sunday school, Primary meetings after school, the Young Men's and Young Women's Mutual Improvement Association (YMMIA and YWMIA) meetings, sacrament meeting, the church Welfare Program activities, visiting teaching), the Sugar House MIA mixed quartet won "superior" ratings in the church finals; the ward MIA won the yearly stake and church-wide road-show competition; and the ward prepared a float for the Pioneer Day parade depicting the coming of sugar-making machinery to Utah. In 1954, the ward celebrated its centennial with a birthday celebration that "consisted of a Primary party for the children, a roller skating party for the MIA, a dance, a banquet with a spectacular program afterward reliving the past of Sugar House Ward from its organization until today." The week of commemoration was climaxed by a sacrament meeting with Elder LeGrand Richards as speaker.[76] In 1955, for the first time, the ward presented its road show on television, and an exhibition basketball game was played between the bishopric and the M-Men teams for funds for the MIA. Basketball was a ward specialty, as is demonstrated by the fact that three years later Sugar House won the stake championship.

But trying to keep the church's full program of activity going was not always easy, and by 1960, it was becoming clear that the members of the Sugar House Ward were more likely to experience the thrill of LDS success at the general church level than in their local ward. The 1960 annual reports of the ward YMMIA and YWMIA reveal the average monthly figures for the year: there were twelve officers and leaders for the Young Women, but average attendance was only nine; there were forty-one young marrieds involved—husbands with YMMIA and wives with YWMIA—but their average attendance was only fifteen; teenagers belonging in the Gleaners, Laurels, and MIA Maids classes together only totaled thirteen, while only ten youngsters were in the Beehive group.

The number of Young Men was almost the same, with ten Explorers and thirteen Scouts, plus four M-Men. In spite of these small numbers, nine dances were held, a play was produced, five road shows and skits were performed, and twenty-one chorus presentations were given.[77] In comparison with the wards in the newer suburbs, for example, this was a disappointing record, as the reporting officer obviously understood: "General condition of our YWMIA [and YMMIA] is good considering small number of enrollment. . . . Our biggest problems include lack of teachers and lack of funds because of *our Ward being so transient and small*."[78]

While this was a report for the youth program only, it is possible to extrapolate from it the condition of the ward in the 1960s that, in turn, reflected the changing nature of the Sugar House area. No longer a neighborhood primarily made up of single-family dwellings, it was becoming an area in which many of the homes were being used as rental property. Also several apartment complexes were constructed within the boundaries of the ward. Residents at the upper and lower ends of the age spectrum—retired and single persons and young married couples with young children—were attracted to the neighborhood. Students at the nearby University of Utah were often among the latter. As had been the case since the early years of settlement, persons from other cultures still made up a prominent part of the Sugar House population mix. Rather than being permanent immigrants, however, many of the residents for whom English is a second language came as students with visas valid only so long as they are engaged in getting an education.

Because LDS ward memberships in predominantly Mormon areas are absolute reflections of the local population, the membership of the current Sugar House Ward includes above-average concentrations at the upper and lower ends of the age spectrum. But while more than one ward member described the current membership as a combination of the "newly wed and nearly dead," such a descriptive profile is more caricature than realistic portrait. Active Saints in the ward include many persons between the ages of thirty-five and sixty. A surprising number of persons from other cultures—South America, Asia, the Middle East— attend Sunday school and are present in the pews for the sacrament meeting.[79]

In the mid-1970s, the changing population patterns in the area led to a restructuring of wards within the stake; two wards were combined to form a single Sugar House Ward. Even so, the transient character of the younger population and the relatively small number of youngsters in the ward made it difficult to keep the church's full program of activities in a flourishing state. Consequently, although there is a certain nostalgia for the way things used to be, most ward members were pleased when, in 1980, the church made an extremely significant church-wide program modification that alleviated some of the meeting overload. From March 2, 1980, forward, a "consolidated meeting schedule" would, with the exception of certain youth activities, concentrate all major ward programs (priesthood quorum meetings, Relief Society, the young men's and young women's programs, Primary, Sunday school for all ages, sacrament meeting) in a three-hour block on Sunday.[80]

A principal purpose of this extraordinary change was to allow Saints, particularly adults, to spend more time with their own families.[81] Although not as clear at the time as it has since become, this pointed to a more than routine concern on the part of the brethren about the importance of the LDS family as the fundamental social unit within which Saint-making goes forward. At the same time, this program alteration signaled the General Authorities' recognition of the difficulty wards were experiencing in carrying out the full church program when necessity often required mothers as well as fathers to be employed outside the home. In recent years, moreover, under an elaborate restructuring of the church organization called Priesthood Correlation, the church-wide program has also been scaled back at the stake level, so that fewer meetings are needed and fewer specific assignments are placed on the Saints. This gives them more time to fulfill the callings they hold and to be more effective in fulfilling them.

V

While the consolidated meeting schedule and priesthood correlation program modifications were particularly welcomed by Saints in wards like Sugar House where program demands were such that active members had been fulfilling several callings simultaneously, a decade of following this reduced schedule of ward and stake activity is bringing tremendous change. In order to assess the impact of these changes as well as to develop a profile of the ward at the beginning of the twentieth century's last decade, the authors developed and administered a questionnaire to current adult ward members. Although their responses indicate that an intense level of love and caring among ward members unquestionably persists, it is also obvious these changes are having a striking impact on the congregational life of the ward. As Sugar House

5.2   Sugar House Ward meetinghouse, 1991. Courtesy of Cheryll May.

is a typical ward, following the church program without significant variation, its experience reflects the impact of the new meeting schedule and priesthood correlation on LDS wards everywhere. What that experience suggests is that where public and private, the secular and the religious, were once joined within Mormonism, they may be becoming as separate and distinct as they are in other religious traditions in America.

One signal of the dramatic difference in the life of the Sugar House Ward yesterday and today is that an analysis of census data can no longer depict the congregation. There are simply too many non-Mormons living in the area to make such an exercise useful. To provide a basis for comparison with the ward in former years, the authors developed a rough profile of Sugar House Ward at the beginning of this final decade of the twentieth century by analyzing the demographic data supplied in the responses to the questionnaire, which was administered to all the Saints attending the Gospel Doctrine (adult Sunday school) class on December 3, 1989. Although the respondents were selected randomly only insofar as the distribution of the instrument was not announced beforehand, the responses provide a fair representation of the age, marital status, number of children, and length of ward membership of adults in the ward.

With regard to age distribution, 11 of the 69 respondents (15.9 percent) were under thirty years of age.[82] Twenty-three percent were in their thirties; 14.5 percent were in their forties; 10 percent were in their fifties; and almost 35 percent were over sixty. Reported average length of membership in the ward is 10 years and 8 months, but this is misleading. The transient nature of the ward is revealed in the fact that although there were members who had been in the ward for many years—77 years (1), 54 years (1), 45 years (3), 38 years (1), 35 years (1), 32 years (2), 20 years (1)—the median number of years class members had been in the ward was only 3. Ten of the seventy persons attending the class had been in the ward three months or less; more than 37 percent had been ward members two years or less. The process of reorganizing wards by redrawing ward boundaries is easily seen in the data describing how long Saints have been members of this particular ward. A substantial block of current ward members (16 percent) were brought into the ward in the structuring that took place in the late 1970s. A later redrawing of boundaries brought in a smaller group (11.5 percent).

That Sugar House Ward is located in a Mormon area is obvious. Despite the fact that in every year since 1960 the LDS Church has grown overall more by conversion than natural increase, more than 75 percent of this adult group of Sugar House Saints was born in the church. Moreover, those who were converted to the church had been members for about twenty years. An overwhelming number (75 percent) grew up in a Mormon area, although four respondents had lived a part of their youth in the mission field. Over 80 percent of these adults were (or had been) married, another indicator of the traditional character of the ward, notwithstanding the transient nature of a considerable portion of the ward membership.

Even though several described Sugar House as "the sweetest ward in the church," the ward members' narrative responses to an open-ended question about the ward did not provide an unrealistic picture of sweetness and light. Problems addressed were mainly connected with the changing nature of the neighborhood, the transient nature of the ward population, and the difficulty of keeping a youth program going. With regard to the first, a ward member recalled that "as the Sugarhouse area was developed more and more apartment buildings were built. The congregation thus became very transient, a large percentage of the members stay for only a few months or years. The children tend to suffer from the lack of permanence." A ward member who had obviously served in a leadership role said that "the transient nature of the ward presents a challenge in seeing that everyone who comes within its boundaries receives the proper fellowship." And the current bishop added, "There is one faction that finds a difficulty feeling integrated and that is the youth who advance to elders quorum or young women into Relief Society. If they are not married, they find it hard to be part of those groups. This is probably a difficult area throughout the Church. Our youth when they reach this age have frequently gone to single or University wards were they feel the unity they need."

In response to the open-ended question, the metaphor most often used to characterize the ward is "family": "The Sugarhouse Ward is to me like my extended family. I cry with them, I laugh with them. We are all together for good things and bad things. . . . I am new and still getting to know the people, but when I got here the first time I felt welcomed, and I felt like I already knew the people from a long time, like they were relatives I was visiting after a long time spent far away," one said. Another wrote, "This ward is in essence, my family. [They] made me feel I belong, that I'm one of 'theirs.'" A third, referring to the elderly, added, "It's like having dozens of Grandpas & Grandmas. It's very comfortable and homey." Another, describing the 1977 recombination of two wards, added, "I was excited to become a member of the Sugar House Ward and felt blessed and impressed with the way we newcomers were welcomed in and merged as family members."

This characterization of the ward as family is marvelously evocative, bringing to mind the way the Saints have always called their fellow members Brother and Sister and the extent to which the symbol of patriarchy pervades LDS culture. But if what happened to middle-class families in America—the way they became private "havens," separate from the public world—is kept in mind, describing Sugar House Ward as a family is also extremely revealing. This extraordinary but very typical ward was once a precinct of a literal kingdom, drawing the whole world into itself. Then it became an enclave, creating an entire world for those inside its walls of ward activity. Now it seems to be separating the sacred from the secular, setting the ward apart from the world; Sundays become the occasion for reuniting the ward family and reminding its members that being Mormon means being "in the world but not of it."

All this suggests that in the future Sugar House Ward may function less effectively as a Mormon melting pot. Perhaps that is as it should be, since turning Swedes and Germans into Utah Mormons is not on the modern LDS agenda. Within the last decade, the LDS Church has re-defined its goals, expressing them in terms of a threefold mission. One goal is carrying the gospel to the whole world by means of a competent missionary movement. Another is "redeeming the dead" by means of the administering of ordinances by proxy in LDS temples. The remaining goal is "perfecting the Saints."

In this program for the future, every ward is to some degree the seat of a local "every member a missionary" movement. In ward meetings, members are encouraged, also, to fulfill their obligations to those who have gone before by doing temple work. But wards are only directly implicated in the church's program for the future in that they are one of the arenas in which Saints are being perfected, the other being LDS families, particularly those over which fathers who hold the priesthood preside. What these changes will mean for the members of the Sugar House Ward and, indeed, for the future of congregational life in the LDS Church is, as yet, not at all clear.

NOTES

The authors wish to acknowledge with gratitude the research assistance of student interns John Huber and Janet Ellingson.

1. The best modern histories of Mormonism are James B. Allen and Glen M. Leonard, *The Story of the Latter-day Saints* (Salt Lake City: Deseret Book Co., 1976); and Leonard J. Arrington and Davis Bitton, *The Mormon Experience: A History of the Latter-day Saints* (New York: Alfred A. Knopf, 1979). For an interpretation of Mormon history that focuses on the Mormon religious experience, see Jan Shipps, *Mormonism: The Story of a New Religious Tradition* (Urbana: University of Illinois Press, 1985).

2. Leonard Arrington, *Great Basin Kingdom: An Economic History of the Latter-day Saints* (Cambridge: Harvard University Press, 1958), pp. 116–20.

3. C. Elliot Berlin, "Abraham Owen Smoot, Pioneer Mormon Leader" (Master's thesis, Brigham Young University, 1955), pp. 10–67.

4. James E. Talmage, *The Articles of Faith of the Church of Jesus Christ of Latter-day Saints*, 11th ed. (Salt Lake City: Deseret News, 1919), pp. 187, 193.

5. Pauline Smith, et. al., *Sugar House Ward: 125 Years, 1854–1979* (Salt Lake City, n.p., 1977), p. 4. This is a folk history produced by ward members to commemorate the 125th anniversary of the establishment of the Sugar House Ward.

6. Douglas D. Alder, "The Mormon Ward: Congregation or Community?" *Journal of Mormon History* 5 (1978): 61–78.

7. Andrew Jenson, *Encyclopedic History of the Church of Jesus Christ of Latter-day Saints* (Salt Lake City, Deseret News Publishing Company, 1941), p. 843.

8. Charles L. Schmalz, "The Failure of Utah's First Sugar Factory," *Utah Historical Quarterly* (Winter 1988): 50–53.

9. Jenson, *Encyclopedic History*, p. 243.

10. Dale Beecher, "The Office of Bishop: An Example of Organizational Development in the Church," Task Paper in Mormon History, no. 21 (Salt Lake City, LDS Church Historical Department, 1978), pp. 16–19.

11. Ibid., 19.

12. Edwin B. Firmage and Richard Collin Mangrum, *Zion in the Courts: A Legal History of the Church of Jesus Christ of Latter-day Saints, 1830–1900* (Urbana and Chicago: University of Illinois Press, 1988), pp. 29–30.

13. Beecher, "Office of Bishop," p. 15.

14. Leonard J. Arrington, Feramorz Y. Fox, and Dean L. May, *Building the City of God: Community and Cooperation among the Mormons* (Salt Lake City: Deseret Book Co., 1976), pp. 59, 73.

15. Emily Ellingham Hart, "Emily Ellingham Hart Diary, 1856–1886," LDS Church Archives, Salt Lake City, Utah.

16. Sugar House Ward Membership Records, microfilm roll 6743, LDS Church Archives.

17. William Hepworth Dixon, *New America*, 2 vols. (London, 1867), 1:252–53.

18. Arrington and Bitton, *The Mormon Experience*, p. 209.

19. "A Short Sketch of the Life of M. T. Smoot," from a bound volume of the Paul Thatcher Family Papers, 1809–1972, University of Utah Marriott Library, Western Americana Collection, Salt Lake City.

20. Allen and Leonard, *The Latter-day Saints*, pp. 421, 497.

21. James Kirkham Journals, 1867–1929, LDS Church Archives.

22. Nonetheless their fertility was not exceptionally high for a frontier population, there being in the whole Sugar House area 1.65 children under ten for every woman aged sixteen to forty-four. In frontier areas elsewhere, including small towns in Utah, it was common for there to be two to three children per adult woman. This is not, however, the same as completed family size. Any snapshot portrait of a population, which a census is, captures unmarried women, infertile women, young women just beginning their families, and older women whose families have left the nest, all of them reducing the "child-woman ratio" to a number far below what the completed family size of fertile women would be. See John Mack Faragher, *Sugar Creek: Life on the Illinois Prairie* (New Haven: Yale University Press, 1986), pp. 88, 253n. Faragher has calculated child-woman ratios from data printed by James E. Davis in *Frontier America, 1800–1840: A Comparative Demographic Analysis of the Frontier Process* (Glendale: Arthur E. Clark Co., 1977), p. 169, showing ratios (normally reported standardized to a base of 1,000) for northern backcountry areas of 2,550 in 1830 and 2,091 in 1840. The 1860 ratio in the rural district of Sublimity, Oregon, was 2,385 (children under ten years per 1,000 women, ages sixteen to forty-five).

23. "Life of M. T. Smoot," p. 19.

24. Smith, *Sugar House Ward*.

25. Sugar House Ward Relief Society Scrapbook, LDS Church Archives. This incident is described on a page headed "May 5, 1886."

26. Sugar House Ward Membership Records, microfilm roll 6743, LDS Church Archives.

27. Linda Newell, "A Gift Given, a Gift Taken: Washing, Anointing, and Blessing the Sick among Mormon Women," *Sunstone* 6 (September–October 1981) 4:16–25.

28. Berlin, "Abraham Owen Smoot," p. 71.

29. "Life of M. T. Smoot," p. 25.

30. Minutes, Sugar House Ward Relief Society, 1868–1972, second meeting, May 20, 1868; tenth meeting, August 19, 1868, LDS Church Archives.

31. Ibid., 61st meeting, December 4, 1872.

32. Cheryll Lynn May, "Charitable Sisters," in Claudia Bushman, ed., *Mormon Sisters* (Cambridge, Mass.: Emmeline Press, 1976), p. 228.

33. Ibid., pp. 228–29.

34. *History of the Relief Society, 1842–1966* (Salt Lake City: Relief Society, 1966), p. 111.

35. Minutes, Sugar House Relief Society, 116th meeting, December 6, 1876, and 117th meeting, December 20, 1876.

36. Ibid., 118th meeting, February 7, 1877.

37. Ibid., 87th meeting, December 9, 1874.

38. Maureen Ursenbach Beecher, "Eliza R. Snow," in Bushman, *Mormon Sisters*, p. 29.

39. Ibid., pp. 29–30.

40. Minutes, Sugar House Ward Relief Society, 120th meeting, March 4, 1877.

41. Minutes, Sugar House YWMIA, December 9, 1892, LDS Church Archives.

42. Minutes, Sugar House Ward Relief Society, 165th–179th meetings.

43. William G. Hartley, "The Priesthood Reorganization of 1877: Brigham Young's Last Achievement," *BYU Studies* 20 (Fall 1979): 3–36.

44. Smith, *Sugar House Ward*; Martin Garn, Journal, LDS Church Archives.

45. Allen and Leonard, *The Latter-day Saints*, pp. 412–16.

46. *Tales of a Triumphant People* (Salt Lake City: Stevens & Wallis Press, 1947), pp. 177–78.

47. Smith, *Sugar House Ward*.

48. Jenson, *Encyclopedic History*, 843.

49. Sugar House Ward Historical Record, LDS Church Archives.

50. Granite Stake High Council Minutes, 1900–1920, LDS Church Archives, Salt Lake City.

51. Sugar House Ward Historical Record, series 11, roll no. 1, LDS Church Archives.

52. Jenson, *Encyclopedic History,* p. 843.

53. The census precinct called "Sugar House" or "Precinct 88" in 1910 obviously did not overlap perfectly with the ward boundaries, as we have determined from ward records. About half (89) of the families that were members of the ward lived in the Sugar House census precinct, and another 93 ward member families lived out in neighboring census precincts.

54. The child-woman ratio remained high for a twentieth-century urban population, at 1.42 children under ten for each woman fifteen to forty-four, only slightly less than it had been in 1870.

55. There were about 200 families in the ward altogether in 1910, and in the portions of the ward boundaries covered by the census precinct 51 percent were found in the ward records. The proportion of non-Mormons in Utah in 1910 had reached about fifty percent. It had reached its apogee and would decline steadily through the rest of the twentieth century, in 1990 reaching a level of 25 to 30 percent.

56. Jan Shipps, "From Satyr to Saint: American Attitudes toward the Mormons," paper presented to the annual meeting of the Organization of American Historians, Chicago, Ill., April 1973.

57. Allen and Leonard, *The Latter-day Saints,* p. 478.

58. *Neighborhood Booster,* March–December, 1921; *Sugar House Times,* January–March, 1922, University of Utah Library Microfilm Collection, Salt Lake City.

59. *Neighborhood Booster,* May 21, 1921.

60. Ibid., June 4, 1921.

61. Ibid., May 14 and 28, 1921; *Sugarhouse Times,* January–March, 1922.

62. *Neighborhood Booster,* May 28, 1921.

63. Dean L. May, "Social and Cultural History," *Encyclopedia of Mormonism,* 5 vols., ed. Daniel H. Ludlow (New York: Macmillan, 1992), 3:1378–85.

64. *Sugar House News,* March 3, 1922.

65. Ibid., 115–16.

66. Martha Bradley, "The Church and Colonel Sanders: Mormon Standard Plan Architecture" (Master's Thesis, Brigham Young University, 1981), chap. 1.

67. William G. Hartley, "Torlief S. Knaphus, Sculptor Saint," *Ensign* 10 (July 1980) 7:10–15.

68. The authors express thanks to art historian Paul Anderson, a former member of the staff of the LDS Church Museum of History and Art, who provided information about the meetinghouse.

69. *Semi-annual Conference Report,* Fall, 1936, p. 3, as quoted in Arrington, Fox, and May, *Building the City of God,* 343. Interesting and important to note is the fact that, despite their rhetorical distancing of the church from the "dole," church leaders encouraged Saints to take advantage of available government programs before applying for assistance from the Church Welfare Program.

70. Articles praising the Mormons were published in such mass circulation magazines as *Life, Coronet,* and especially *Reader's Digest,* which regularly in-

cluded items about the Saints on their "Life in these United States" page and among their filler items.

71. The changing LDS residence patterns are fully described in Jan Shipps, "The Scattering of the Gathering and the Gathering of the Scattered: The Mormon Diaspora in the Years after World War II," 1987 Juanita Brooks Lecture published in pamphlet form by Dixie College Printing Services, St. George, Utah.

72. "Those Amazing Mormons" was the title of a widely reprinted article first published in *Coronet Magazine*.

73. Current as well as historical membership figures are included in the *Deseret News Church Almanac*, which is published every other year by the church.

74. Discussion between Sugar House Ward members and the authors conducted in the ward during the Sunday school hour, December 3, 1989.

75. The expression "run ragged" was used by one of the ward members who was recalling what things were like before the introduction of the consolidated meeting schedule. See below.

76. Sugar House Ward Manuscript History.

77. YMMIA Records, microfilm roll no. 2, under Sugar House Ward, 1960 Annual Report Form, LDS Church Archives.

78. Ibid., under "Narrative Report." Emphasis ours.

79. Responding to a query in a questionnaire distributed by the authors, one ward member indicated that she was not surprised to hear at least four different languages being spoken when she came to church on Sunday mornings.

80. "News of the Church," *Ensign* 10 (March 1980) 3:75–78. The initial rationale for the new schedule was the fuel crisis; in wards outside Utah, Saints were using a great deal of gasoline traveling long distances to attend meetings practically every day of the week.

81. In the official announcement of the change, Saints were encouraged not to neglect Family Home Evening, the church's program in which all church members were directed to spend Monday evenings with their own immediate family members, socializing and holding a family worship service.

82. This age group was underrepresented because many of the young adults were engaged in leading youth activities that were taking place at the same time as this "Gospel Doctrine" class.

An Oak among Churches: St. Boniface Parish, Chicago, 1864–1990

STEPHEN J. SHAW

THE HISTORY OF American Catholicism is to a large extent the history of the myriad ethnic parishes that dotted the American landscape for more than 150 years. For Germans, Poles, and Hispanics, as well as for other groups, the ethnic parish provided a place where immigrants could express their Catholic faith precisely as Germans, Poles, or Hispanics, while slowly being nurtured as American citizens.[1] The history of St. Boniface Church in Chicago gives ample testimony to the important role of the ethnic parish in the United States, and the account of this congregation's growth and demise may be helpful to other faith communities which face change but seek to remain a harmonious whole.

The Establishment of Parish Life:
The German Era (1864–1917)

Chicago's history began when Jean Baptiste Pointe du Sable started a small trading center on the north side of the Chicago River in 1750. The city soon became a magnet for real estate speculators, as well as for Irish and German immigrants. The Germans, better prepared than their Irish contemporaries, possessed trade skills and some capital, and they soon set up small shops and businesses north of the Chicago River.[2] By 1846, the number of German Catholics in the city warranted the establishment of two German parishes: St. Peter's to the south, and St. Joseph's to the north. St. Joseph's became the "mother church" of more than twenty German parishes.[3] Germans continued to immigrate in record numbers after the Civil War. Between 1871 and 1890, nearly two and a half million Germans arrived to take their place as America's largest immigrant group. The German population of Chicago grew from 52,316 in 1870 to 170,738 in 1900. Poles increased dramatically from a mere 552 in 1870 to 16,008 by 1900. By the turn of the century Chicago was 77 percent foreign-born.[4]

Among the thousands of Germans who immigrated to Chicago in the early 1860s were some twenty-five Catholic families who lived west of the Chicago River on what is now Ashland Avenue. St. Joseph's Church was two miles away, reached by a difficult ferry trip across the river. Peter Suerth, a recent immigrant, soon formed a parish lay committee to inquire about the erection of a permanent parish west of the river.[5] Suerth and his wife, Anna, had moved into a small frame house on Cornell Street in the year 1860 and immediately had seen the need for a church of their own. With the encouragement of the Benedictines, Suerth, along with other prominent men of the area, went to Bishop Duggan to request a parish.[6] Father Ferdinand Kalvelage, Duggan's representative (and eventually a chronicler of St. Boniface's history), quickly responded, "You shall have it." A small frame structure roughly 125 feet square soon arose on the northeast corner of Cornell and Noble Streets. Peter Suerth was one of the first parishioners to greet the new pastor, the Reverend Phillip Albrecht.

Father Albrecht, who celebrated the first mass at St. Boniface on March 5, 1865, found himself in a small German community of about twenty-five families.[7] Life was simple, and men like Peter Suerth formed the first generation of Boniface's *Gemeinde,* or community. Suerth worked during the day at a furniture company and operated a barber shop on the second floor of his home. His house was often used as an annex for parish activities. Life for Peter Suerth centered around the parish and the local community. Chicago and Ashland Avenues, as well as the diagonal Milwaukee Avenue, evolved as central shopping districts. Germans soon opened up small retail shops, bakeries, butcher shops, fruit stands, and barber shops along these main arteries. The Lower Northwest Side, or West Town, as this area was called, grew steadily during the latter half of the nineteenth century.

The Growth of the Parish Societies

Parish voluntary associations, or vereins, were one of the most important characteristics of German Catholic life in America. They had their origins in Germany and were divided along religious and provincial lines; Catholics and Protestants were urged to join their own societies. The most important of these voluntary associations were mutual-aid societies, which not only offered insurance benefits but provided a focus for provincial loyalties—whether Bavarian or Hessian or Saxon. Many associations had their own flags and banners, went on picnics together, and took part in liturgical celebrations. While not directly linked to parish life, provincial societies did rely on local parishioners to join them.[8]

The St. Bonifacius Unterstützungs-Verein, or St. Boniface Mutual Aid Society, incorporated by an act of the Illinois legislature in 1865, played a significant role in the life of the parish. But tension soon arose between Father Albrecht and certain lay trustees of the society. Although the pastor welcomed the Polish members of the community—who were filling up the empty houses in the area but had no church of their own to attend—the trustees disdained anyone who even spoke to the Poles. To them, St. Boniface was a German community, and other nationalities would simply have to go it alone. This conflict over nationality soon forced Father Albrecht to resign his pastorate and move to Wisconsin, but the conflict over national loyalty plagued St. Boniface for decades to come.

Boniface's second pastor, James Marshall, arrived in 1867 and soon found himself at odds with the same elements of the Unterstützungs-Verein.[9] Fluent in German, English, and Polish, Marshall tried to incorporate the Poles into the parish, but the same troublesome trustees within the verein would not accept them. When Marshall refused to see a delegation from the verein, the trustees called the police to force him out. Marshall reluctantly resigned his pastorate to avoid a scandal. But he had accomplished many things during his brief pastorate: he had procured the Sisters of St. Francis (Joliet, Illinois) to teach in the parish school; he had begun the first mission, or weeklong retreat, under the Franciscan Fathers; and he had demonstrated the advantages of having a bilingual pastor.[10]

The Reverend Clement Venn, a native of Westphalia, was appointed as St. Boniface's third pastor in 1869.[11] But Father Venn soon found himself embroiled in the same power struggle that had plagued Father Marshall. Many social gatherings were held under the verein's auspices, but the picnics often ended up in "drunkenness and excess of every kind," and members were drunk and disorderly at church services. Venn expected his parishioners to follow his guidance in spiritual and moral matters, and he felt morally bound to deal with the drunkenness, "but they were determined upon their rights."[12]

The tension between pastor and laity came to a head on Easter Day, 1870, when Venn refused to allow the verein to receive Holy Communion as a body. The leading members then gathered forces—

banners and all—and forced their way down the center aisle. Venn, along with the prominent layman John Reisel, met them in the middle of the transept, fought with a few, and threw the verein members out onto the street. Father Venn, who suffered minor injuries, never again had trouble with the society, and he even established a *Liebesbund*, or federation of love, to counter its influence. Like most German pastors, Venn was practically appointed for life. A strong-willed but fair man, Venn's dealings with the lay trustees reflected his own vision of what a German Catholic pastor was supposed to be. He was willing to let the laity lead the societies and take an active role in the parish, but he insisted on being the spiritual head.

Although this episode could have been expected to sour his view of parish societies, Venn continued to encourage their establishment. The vereins nurtured leadership by men and women—at a time where there was little opportunity elsewhere for women to exert leadership roles. The earliest society at St. Boniface was the Mutter-Gottes Verein, or Married Ladies' Society, established in 1865.[13] No leader was as interesting as a certain Mrs. Splitthof. On one occasion, when a woman was about to be thrown out of church for lack of a paid pew, Splitthof brushed the usher aside and led the woman to her own pew. On another occasion, she convinced the associate pastors that she could be both portress and sponsor at a confirmation ceremony. When Father Venn objected, she said: "First, I will admit the Archbishop and then one of the fathers can announce in Church—make room for Mrs. Splitthof." Needless to say, she was both portress and sponsor at the confirmation. A generation of lay leaders was developed through the local vereins at parishes like St. Boniface.[14]

Pastors like Clement Venn could not function without the approval of Chicago's bishops. Fortunately Chicago was blessed with a succession of men who understood the immigrant mentality. Patrick A. Feehan, Chicago's first archbishop (1880–1902), guided Chicago Catholicism through the 1880s and 1890s.[15] His greatest accomplishment was to reconcile the various ethnic and national forces in his archdiocese, and he managed to placate the three most powerful immigrant groups within his city—the Irish, the Germans, and the Poles. Although Pope Leo XIII had declared the ethnic parishes could exist only for the first-generation immigrant, Feehan realized that each nationality needed time to become American, and thus he encouraged the establishment of ethnic parishes. For the Germans and the Poles, he established nineteen and fifteen national parishes respectively. But he insisted that these parishes remain Catholic, centered on the sacraments and devotional life of the church.

James Quigley, Chicago's second archbishop (1902–16), continued Feehan's policy of supporting ethnic parishes. He always took a deep interest in ethnic minorities and preached to them in German, Italian, Polish, or French. He said of America, "A young people, a people of composite stock, we have kinship with many different nations, but we are not identical with any of them, and are developing a separate national life."[16] Quigley consistently opposed immigration restriction as prejudicial to all foreigners. By the end of his episcopate, Chicago had thirty-six German, thirty-three Polish, ten Italian, nine Lithuanian, and eight Slovenian parishes.[17] Like his predecessor, Quigley saw the ethnic parish as an ideal way-station for immigrants on the path toward Americanization. Within these parishes children grew up as Germans or Poles but also as American Catholics. The genius of the ethnic parish was to provide a center for the ethnic, nationalistic, and religious feelings of its members.

On October 8, 1871, a small fire—which reportedly broke out at Mrs. O'Leary's barn—quickly spread north toward the Chicago River and soon engulfed most of the Near South Side. After the fire jumped the river, St. Joseph's Church was soon engulfed in flames, and thousands fled across the North Avenue Bridge to the western prairies. St. Boniface, the first German parish in the area, escaped the flames and quickly responded to the city's needs. An eyewitness tells of seeing Father Venn come into the school loaded with hams, bacon, and sausages, "strung together . . . over his shoulders, three in front and three behind . . . his face . . . black with cinders and smoke."[18] Venn was always aware that Boniface was part of the larger community, and he came to be viewed as a significant voice of the Near West Side.

But from the ashes of the Great Fire came new growth. The parish annals record that "it was from this eventful epoch that the rapid growth of the parish dates its beginnings. It received many new families, as this territory had not been touched by the flames of devastation and offered a place of refuge to those who had suffered loss in the fire."[19] The parish grew from 400 families in 1875 to 700 in 1895. St. Boniface's records clearly show an ever-increasing surplus of money during Venn's twenty-seven-year pastorate. By 1877, the debt was eliminated, and by 1889 the treasury held $21,652.

In 1895, when Father Venn's health began to fail, Archbishop Feehan appointed the Reverend Albert Evers to St. Boniface. A Westphalian like his predecessor, Evers had been an assistant in the parish since 1890, and he sought to maintain the German integrity of the parish.[20] For Evers, the parish was the community, and he often exhorted his parishioners not to leave: "It is important for our community that those who live within the parish stay there. Don't leave your mother church; don't leave the holy St. Boniface Parish." Father Francis L. Rempe, an assistant to Evers, echoed these sentiments in a sermon in 1903: "Be united as much in belief as in work for the good of this community. Remain true to your church, which has become your family; gather your friends and relatives who have left the old Homeland around you here in this community, so that it will be in the future as it was in earlier times a bulwark for your beliefs and a sign of the virtue and rectitude of your old homeland."[21] This remarkable sermon clearly points to the dual loyalty that attracted German Catholics to St. Boniface. For Boniface was a bulwark both of faith and of the fatherland.

St. Boniface was first and foremost a Catholic parish. And German Catholics, just as much as Irish or Polish Catholics, expressed their faith by participating in the sacramental life of the church. Yet the German language was essential to the expression of piety by these immigrants. Father Evers observed once that quick assimilation was "no blessing for the German people." He believed that church authorities were moving too quickly in pushing the German immigrants to learn English and that the whole process should be stopped, for "we have won nothing, and lost much."[22] Language was the link between faith and fatherland, and loss of language meant loss of faith.

Most Sunday services at St. Boniface were conducted in German through World War I, and week-long missions, or days of recollection, were periodically given in German into the early 1900s. But the holidays that came from Germany often stirred the most fervent devotion. The Feast of Corpus Christi, for example, introduced in Bavaria in the late eighteenth century, was brought to America in the early 1800s. It was, as one German observed, "a feast right for the German spirit, because it came from a German heart and a German soil . . . the Corpus Christi processions, which take place in spring under the clear-blue sky and in front of flower-bedecked homes, are such a rich experience to nature-loving Germans that whoever participates once . . . never wants to miss them again."[23] In time, however, these processions lost their German origins and simply became part of the American Catholic landscape.

Father Venn had left Evers a financially sound parish, with over 700

6.1   Laying the cornerstone, St. Boniface Church. The building was dedicated June 4, 1904. By permission of the Sisters of St. Francis of Mary Immaculate, Joliet, Illinois.

families, a strong group of voluntary associations, and more than $26,000 in the bank. Father Evers soon set his sights on the construction of a new church and rectory. Germans delighted in the theatrics of church liturgy, and a new church was a symbol of pride to the entire community. Engineers constructed the rectory and the north end of the church first, so that the basement could be used for church services after the old church was torn down. Designed by the noted ecclesiastical architect Henry B. Schlacks, the church was "a magnificent structure . . . large, stately, and imposing," comparing "in architectural beauty with the finest churches in the West." The main tower of the belfry was over 150 feet high; the church's interior was 160 feet deep, 40 feet wide, and 52 feet high. Furnishings were added gradually—stained-glass windows from Munich, oak pews, magnificent wood-carved statues from Bavaria. The Stations of the Cross were originals, painted on copper by the famous German craftsman Feuerstein.[24]

Accompanied by Archbishop Sebastian Messmer of Milwaukee, who gave the dedication sermon in German, Archbishop James Quigley dedicated the new edifice on June 4, 1904. More than 20,000 people—

members from over 200 Catholic societies as far away as Milwaukee—joined in the festivities. The church was decked with banners and flags on the outside, while the houses for several blocks displayed flags and evergreens. Other nationalities joined in as well—Poles, Italians, French, and Bohemians. The *Chicago American* described the event as "one of the most impressive religious spectacles in the history of Chicago." When some parishioners objected to the cost of the new church, Father Rempe reminded them that "it is not that we don't understand the glorious past, but that it is necessary to build a new and more worthy place of worship."[25] Indeed it was the crowning event in Father Evers's career as pastor.

The 215 societies that marched in the dedication parade certainly included St. Boniface's own vereins. Father Evers had built on his predecessor's work by expanding the number of vereins to seventeen. These organizations—for men, women, and children—promoted ethnic ties and solidified Catholic identity, while also serving as an Americanizing force to varying degrees according to the nature of the society. This trifold function of the vereins mirrored the function of the parish as a whole.[26] The earliest vereins were devotional societies. The Unterstützungs-Verein and the Married Ladies' Society each regularly attended Sunday Mass as a group. Most of the societies turned out for such important festivities as *Weihnachten* (Christmas), *Ostern* (Easter), *Pfingsten* (Pentecost), and above all, *Fronleichnamsfest* (Corpus Christi). Forty Hours, a popular Eucharistic devotion since the 1890s, was also popular at St. Boniface. After forty hours of exposition, a time of private prayer during which the Blessed Sacrament was exposed to the public, a public mass was celebrated, and a huge procession which included most of the vereins of the parish was held. The purpose of these devotions was "the praise of God in his wonderful sacrament, thanksgiving for all his deeds for life and soul . . . and for [forgiveness] of all the sins of our life."[27] Such services strengthened among these Germans a sense of being Catholic.

The Young Men's and Young Ladies' societies provided the young people a locus for keeping in touch with their German heritage. One of their principal activities during the early 1900s was the community plays, frequently performed in German and attracting a broad audience. These societies, by actively welcoming the young within the parish, insured future generations of faithful Catholics. But St. Boniface did not function as an entity unto itself. The Young Men's and Young Ladies' societies also encouraged Americanization by nurturing contact with other immigrant groups. Athletic societies became popular, and Bonifacians were pitted against other parish teams.[28]

In addition, societies like the Holy Name and St. Vincent de Paul connected the parish with the broader world. The St. Vincent de Paul Society was particularly active at this time. Founded by a small group of French Catholic laymen in 1833, this organization came to America in 1845. By 1883, there were 4,000 conferences with 45,000 members; by 1911, there were 7,500 conferences with 100,000 members. St. Boniface's branch bought food, clothing, and fuel for the poor of the neighborhood. By 1916, the parish's conference had an income of $488.96.[29]

As Germans became more conscious of being German in America, they joined other extraparochial organizations.[30] The Diocesan Union of German Young Men, established in 1889, "raised the standard of young manhood and laid a solid foundation for Catholic layman work." Archbishop Quigley lauded the organization as a model for other Catholic societies. This type of federation encouraged Americanization by gently nudging its members into American life, encouraging its members to be "ideal patriots" who would battle any force that threatened the freedom of the church or state. Women were not ignored either, as hundreds gathered in Chicago to form a national organization for German Catholic women. The Federation of German Catholic Societies in Illinois, established in 1893, included most of the vereins in Illinois by 1901. The avowed goal of the federation was "to demonstrate that German Catholic citizens are firmly united . . . in the study of the social question[s of the day] . . . with a view to advancing the interests of the laboring class."[31] The federation encouraged these Germans to look beyond their parish toward the greater good of the community, and Father Evers enthusiastically urged the parish societies to join.

To publicize all their activities, Father Evers established a parish journal, the *Pfarrbote der St. Bonifacius Gemeinde*. On the one hand, the *Pfarrbote* promoted German ways by enthusiastically publicizing all the activities of the vereins: their meetings, plays, and so on. On the other hand, it encouraged Americanization by including notices about elections and other community events. The election notices, it must be said, made no bones about commending the candidates' Catholic credentials. One article noted, concerning a candidate for circuit court judge, that he was "an upright Catholic Irishman, who attended St. Stephen's parochial school, St. Patrick's Academy, and belonged to the Ancient Order of Hibernians." The *Pfarrbote* also reflected on "the future of Catholicism in America." It congratulated Chicago's Catholics for "the congregations, the zeal, the activities, the business-like methods." [32] Another article pointed out the many contributions Catholics had made to America.

But the *Pfarrbote* also interpreted America for the German immigrant. Many articles deplored the growing threat to family life. Another decried the tendency to delay marriage, for "the trouble with people of today is that they are suffering from too much luxury." There was always a certain wariness about becoming too American, and this came out most clearly when Evers wrote about the mores of the day. Many articles decried the growing trend toward divorce; one society even put on a play entitled *The Divorce Question* ("Don't marry until you see this play . . . don't get divorced until you see it"). Another article noted the "shameless dress" of the day as well as the dangers of going to the theater. [33]

In the vereins many parishioners honed leadership skills that also served them in the broader community. The Venn family, which traced its origins to the very beginning of the parish, is one example. Joseph Dinet, a member of the original lay committee that visited Bishop Duggan in 1865, had one daughter, Louise, who married Father Clement Venn's brother, Charles Venn, a well-known Chicago physician. The Venns were descendants of a wealthy Catholic family who gained prominence in Westphalia shortly after the Reformation. Both brothers emigrated to America in the 1860s and soon found a home on the Near West Side of Chicago. They formed a literary club that attracted a number of intellectuals from Catholic parishes, including Father John Dunne, who was later appointed bishop of Peoria (Illinois). Dr. Venn had an abiding interest in the Reformation, and both men brought literary interests to the community. [34] In a certain sense both men were heirs of the Forty-eighters, German intellectuals who fled to America after the aborted revolutions of 1848. They were also examples of a German Catholic intellectual tradition that traced its roots to the seventeenth century.

Other parishioners' names also stood out at this time—the Suerths and the Fensterles, for example, who led through the local vereins. As one chronicler of the parish noted,

> A list of the German Catholics who have attained prominence in the social, political and commercial life of our city and the State of Illinois sounds like the roster of St. Boniface. Almost all the German Catholic families of Chicago have at one time or other

worshiped there. There their parents, grandparents and great-grandparents were baptized, made their first Holy Communion, and from there also the vast majority were carried to their last resting place. It is this fond association with the great past that has made St. Boniface so dear to all the German Catholics of Chicago.[35]

The Parochial School

The parochial school was a crucial link between the parish and the vereins, for the school cultivated the ethnic and religious feelings of the students upon whom the future of the parish depended. As the *Pfarrbote* noted, "For parents there is hardly any question more serious than that which regards the education of their children. To them God has entrusted the child they call their own. . . . Here then arises the question, 'Where can my child get a sufficient knowledge of that faith?' The answer is very clear . . . the Catholic School."[36]

Education was always important to German-Americans, and German educators had made significant contributions to public education. It was no wonder, then, that German Catholics were particularly interested in establishing parochial schools.[37] The first St. Boniface structure was actually built before the formal establishment of the parish; a combination church and school, popularly known as "the little white school house," was the only seat of learning west of the Chicago River when erected in 1862. Ludwig Fink, a Benedictine father, headed the first mission at St. Boniface. (A mission was often established before the formal inauguration of a parish; St. Boniface's Mission was staffed from St. Joseph's from 1862 to 1864.) Fink first called a meeting of laymen in the area to see if it was possible to build a school. With typical Germanic organization, the laity elected a school board and a finance and publicity committee, and under instructor Nicholas Dreyer the school grew from approximately 30 students in 1862 to 120 in 1863. Together with Father Fink, Dreyer was considered cofounder of the parish, "because of [his] prominence in the affairs of spreading the kingdom of God on earth."[38]

It became obvious that one teacher was not enough for St. Boniface's expanding population, so Father Marshall soon invited the Sisters of St. Francis of Joliet, Illinois, to staff the school.[39] On September 3, 1867, Mother Alfred Moes, with Sister M. Francis and Helen Droesler, a novice, arrived to organize the school. From the very beginning the sisters attracted young girls to their way of life. Statistics indicate that in 1880 there were no more than 2.5 million working women in the United

359

States and that slightly more than 86 percent of these were employed in only a few occupations—as domestic workers, laundresses, dressmakers, teachers, and restaurant and hotel workers.[40] Within a few years the first novice from St. Boniface entered the order. Johanna Fricker, a thirteen-year-old, was followed in 1868 by two companions, Christina Mueller and Christian Falkenberg. By 1917, forty-six young women from St. Boniface had joined the Sisters of St. Francis of Joliet.[41]

The school grew steadily during Father Venn's pastorate—from 440 students in 1874 to 587 students in 1894. With lower salaries than those of the laity, the sisters were able to operate the school on a substantially reduced budget, and even the poorest students could thus attend. (As the financial reports of the day noted, "One-third of the students are too poor to pay school money and a good many pay not regularly.") Without the Franciscan sisters, the school could not have existed. Financial records indicate that school expenditures remained at the same level from 1886 on, the year that the sisters took complete charge of the school.[42]

Parochial schools—like the vereins—were important vehicles for nurturing young Germans as German Catholic Americans. As expressed in the bulletin of another German Catholic parish, "children not only learn religion, but also reading, writing, arithmetic, history, and geography; in short, all those things which are necessary to succeed in this world. . . . In the German parish school, the children also learn their German mother tongue next to the language of the country—which is important not only for daily conversation but also for business and religious life."[43]

German parochial schools encouraged ethnicity through the use of German in the classroom. Mrs. Henry Hahn, a North Side German, recalled that all the subjects taught at St. Michael's School were in German (except English, of course). As she recalled, the nuns insisted that students speak German even during recess: "if someone started to speak English, they would tell them 'Du mußt Deutsch sprechen' [you must speak German]." Theresa Krutz, a member of St. Alphonsus Parish, recalled using German readers until she was in third grade. "I think everybody in school knew the Christmas chorales in German," she said. "We read and talked German, but not on a regular basis." As mentioned above, St. Boniface's young people regularly presented German plays. In 1915, at the close of the school year, they presented *Das Zauberglöckchen* (The Magic Clock); of eighteen graduates, at least thirteen were German.[44]

But German parochial schools were also way stations in the movement toward Americanization. English was introduced into the curriculum as early as 1869. In 1917 St. Boniface's parish bulletin printed an article written by James Clancy, school inspector for New York City, entitled "Efficiency of the Catholic Schools."[45] After examining all the classes, Clancy came to the conclusion that the large majority of parochial schools "were SUPERIOR to the public schools." The parochial schools excelled in the traditional disciplines of the day—penmanship, language, grammar, reading, arithmetic, history, and geography. Germans insisted that their schools were producing a "good product"—students who were prepared to enter the world of business and commerce.

In 1904 St. Boniface began a business school which prepared young women for jobs in Chicago's retail world. The business courses, which included shorthand, typing, and bookkeeping, were taught to the more advanced eighth-grade girls. Many eighth-graders then returned for a second year of courses, which were supplemented with advanced courses in arithmetic, grammar, and other subjects. One sister noted that these pupils, "while not being called high school students, really accomplished much more than an ordinary first-year high school student."[46] The courses served as a valuable resource at a time when there was little opportunity for immigrant children to attend high school.

The school, the parish, and the vereins were interrelated: each depended on the others for support. Venn and Evers supported the school as an integral part of the parish, and it became obvious during Evers's tenure that a new building was needed. By 1896 the old school had been removed and a new one built in its place, consisting of twelve classrooms, a large entertainment hall with a stage, a smaller social hall seating a hundred people, a large kitchen, a bowling alley, and several club rooms. The school was thus a natural location for parish and social activities. Many societies met in the club rooms (and even had a round of bowling after their regular meetings). The vereins assisted the school with their plays and provided music for their festivities. The sisters who taught at the school also contributed to the parish by assisting with liturgical activities, and one of the sisters played the organ at Sunday masses during Father Venn's tenure.[47] By 1902–3 the school's enrollment had reached a zenith of 991 students. But change was already on the horizon, as Chicago entered a new century of progress and rapid urbanization.

Ethnic Change and Conflict

St. Boniface could not escape the changes that were transforming Chicago into a major American metropolis. The city grew from 1,698,575 in 1900 to 3,396,808 in 1940. The percentage of immigrants in the population began to decrease as native-born outnumbered new arrivals. The number of German-born decreased dramatically, from 170,738 in 1900 to 83,424 in 1940. During the same period, Polish immigration increased from 59,714 to 119,264. The *Pfarrbote* noted that the Lower Northwest Side was becoming a place for business, while the people were moving to the suburbs, a movement made possible by the gradual extensions of the elevated train line and the Northwestern Railroad in the early part of the century. Census data show that West Town decreased in population as older German families moved north and northwest into Humboldt Park, Lakeview, and North Center. While the population within four miles of the downtown (an area that included St. Boniface) remained constant between 1910 and 1916, the population from four to ten miles beyond increased by 1,408,000.[48]

As older Germans moved north, they left behind a community that was already "old."[49] Much of the housing dated from the early 1880s, and three- and four-story apartment buildings offered "rooms where the sun never enters." Rear tenements were even worse: the rooms were dark and conditions filthy. Manufacturing continued to spread outward from Chicago's center, leaving West Town far from many available jobs.

Father Evers did what he could to maintain St. Boniface as a German parish. But "old St. Boniface" was inexorably changing, and Evers was unable to handle the change. As Poles, Slovaks, and Jews moved into the established community, they clashed with old-time Germans. Evers could not accept these newcomers and made his feelings known. He called Boniface "a wasted city" that had been "robbed of [its] best supports and [its] most beautiful jewels."[50] Enmity between Germans and Poles was common. Centuries of conquest by marauding Teutonic knights had left their mark on German-Polish relations. Father Marshall had quit his pastorate in the 1860s over just such enmity. But Father Evers, not ready to relinquish control, tried valiantly to keep St. Boniface's identity as a German parish.

In an illuminating letter addressed to Archbishop Quigley in 1914, Evers spoke plainly.[51] He noted that, when he had first come to the parish, the old buildings had been extremely unsafe. Things had improved for a time, but panic had set in when poor immigrants from Slavic countries moved into the neighborhood. Evers said that "experience proves that when this class of people settles in large numbers in a congregation, they bring financial ruin upon the parish." He complained to the archbishop that if he tried to get them to contribute, they would defect altogether. Evers saw the situation as particularly critical because there were "scarcely any old settlers of the parish [that is, the Germans] remaining." When the two largest German Lutheran churches sold their buildings to Poles, "this destroyed the last and best German Catholic section of our parish. The few Catholic Germans who still remain are scattered over such a large and densely populated territory that the pastor alone . . . is unable to control and remain in touch with them." Evers saw Boniface as a unique German community that had more in common with German Lutherans than with Polish Catholics.

The embattled pastor then recommended that the parish become a Polish missionary church and that he be allowed to stay on as pastor. But the Poles did not trust him. In their eyes St. Boniface had already been half-Americanized, for the language used in the services was no longer German but English, for the benefit of the young. The Poles, however, wanted a Polish priest who could speak to them in their own language. They would not support a German priest once the old Germans had left.

Enrollment figures for the parochial school between 1902 and 1919 tell of the parish's gradual decline.[52] In 1903 there were 991 students enrolled at St. Boniface School; by 1911, there were 669; by 1919 there were only 220. Several factors caused this dramatic drop in enrollment. First, Polish Jews began to move into the area at the beginning of the century, their numbers reaching a peak between 1913 and 1915. At that time 80 percent of the public-school children in the neighborhood were Jewish. By 1915 the Poles had become the largest group of immigrants in the neighborhood. Elizabeth A. Smyth, a catechist at St. Boniface, noted these changes in a letter to Father Evers: "A great change has come in the membership of our [public] school during the past year or so. Sometime ago our entire membership was German; then it changed to be largely Jewish, but now ninety per cent of the children attending our school are Polish Catholic children, hence the necessity of the catechism classes."[53] As the older and more established German families moved out, newer and poorer Polish families moved in and were simply unable to pay the tuition in the Catholic school. Those Poles who wanted to send their children to a Catholic school preferred St. Stanislaus Kostka directly north of St. Boniface. For the Poles of West Town, this was the Polish church, a place where their own ethnic and religious needs could be met.

Because Evers was unable to deal with his Polish parishioners, Archhbishop Quigley recommended that he resign his pastorate. But Evers felt that such a resignation would be a sign of weakness. He noted that "an indiscreet resignation would cause incalculable damage to the authority of ecclesiastical government." His health deteriorated badly, and according to all medical reports he needed an extended vacation. But the chancellor informed him that such a leave was unthinkable unless he resigned completely. Evers refused to resign from "the battlefield of so many conflicts and victories, hardship and sufferings." The pastor then suggested turning the parish over to a German Franciscan order. But a group of laity became so incensed at this idea that they forged a number of signatures on a letter to the new archbishop, George W. Mundelein, to keep the parish in the hands of the secular German clergy. Broken in health and spirit, Evers resigned his pastorate in 1916 and died in a Denver sanatorium in 1920.[54] The German parish he had struggled to maintain was no longer a German community but a parish in transition, a parish waiting to be home to another generation of immigrants.

While Chicago's West Town community was wrenched by ethnic change, the nation as a whole struggled with the prospect of World War I. Chicago's German community remained strong and vital through 1917. With its numerous societies to nourish ethnic life, Chicago's *kleines Deutschland* (Little Germany) seemed to face no threat of diminishment. During the early war years, the archdiocesan newspaper, the *New World*, consistently stated "Germany's case." In an article with that title, the newspaper asserted that "industrialism, not militarism, [was] Germany's aim" and that "German military expenditures do not come near those of the British Empire and France." According to a 1915 article, "Germany's greatest concern today is to preserve for itself the ideals and institutions that she has erected in the Fatherland during the long years of peace."[55] The German-American Alliance sponsored a Bismarck celebration to support Germany and to prepare to defend its aims to Americans. Within the German communities, especially the ethnic parishes, support for Germany was unequivocal.

But all changed in 1917, when, after repeated attacks by German submarines, the United States declared war on Germany. The *Chicago Tribune* declared: "Never was patriotism so feverish, so mindless, so nakedly jealous of the slightest qualification or mildest questioning." German societies began to curtail their activities or to go out of existence altogether. The *Illinois Staats-Zeitung* reported that "nearly every day we are informed that another German-American Society has given up its usual activities, that festivals . . . have been postponed, that meetings and conventions will not be held while the war lasts." There were even reports that leading German-Americans were interred for the duration of the war. At St. Aloysius Parish in North Center, Monsignor Aloysius Theile interceded for the German Sisters of Christian Charity, who had to register during the war years. And at St. Benedict's in Lakeview "nerves frayed and tempers flared" during the war. It would seem then, that at parishes like St. Aloysius and St. Benedict—parishes that had received former Bonifacians—German sympathies still prevailed. There was much anguish as "ties of blood and religion naturally inclined the German-Americans . . . to sympathize with their mother country and their relatives and friends abroad."[56] But there is little evidence that such anguish tormented the Bonifacians of 1917, for by that time the majority of parishioners were Polish.

The Consolidation of Parish Life:
The Polish Era (1918–1959)

The Transition of 1918–1932

Chicago was poised for prosperity after World War I. A new skyline rose, suburbs mushroomed, and the automobile changed the face of Chicago forever. Manufacturing spread outward from Chicago's center, while residential neighborhoods stretched north and south. The older residential areas within four miles of the city center lost 150,000 inhabitants between 1920 and 1930.[57] But neighborhood consciousness remained strong, as eastern and southern Europeans clung to their enclaves. By 1920, the Lower Northwest Side (West Town), St. Boniface's home community, numbered 218,130; of these some 90,299 were Catholic.

Poles had begun to arrive in the New World shortly after the Civil War. Most were peasants who had no intention of settling permanently in the United States; they had come to America to earn their fortune so they could return to Poland. By 1875, more than 200,000 Poles had settled in America, and they worshiped in 50 established Catholic parishes. By 1890, their numbers had increased to 800,000, with 132 churches, 126 priests, and 122 schools. By 1914, about 1.3 million had immigrated; Chicago alone boasted 32 Polish parishes.[58] A common language *and* religion made them more alike than German Catholics and Lutherans. Polonia, as this new society was called, grew rapidly in the late nineteenth century and the twentieth century, with heavy concentrations in the Great Lakes area from New York to Illinois.

Good transportation and employment opportunities attracted thousands of Poles to Chicago. Census data indicate that Chicago's Polish population grew from 1,205 foreign-born in 1870 to 59,713 in 1900. The Resurrectionist Fathers, one of the leading Polish religious orders, concentrated their efforts in Chicago, and the Polish Roman Catholic Union, a Catholic fraternal order, was organized in Chicago in 1873. The Polish National Alliance, established in Philadelphia in 1880, moved its publishing branch (*Zgoda*) to Chicago in the latter part of the decade. By 1910, Chicago had nearly a quarter-million Polish-Americans. By the end of the First World War, Chicago was the informal capital of this Polonia in America.[59]

The national parish was "the most important Polish-American institution in the United States, for it recreated the narrower village life from which most Poles had come." Providing a center for the community, the ethnic parish helped break down the anonymity of American life, and the societies and organizations grouped around the parish helped affirm the identity of its individual members.[60] At the heart of each parish was the pastor, who embodied the religion, language, and national culture so important to the Poles. Yet although the Polish parish nurtured the ethnic religion of its members, it was also a way station—like the German parishes before it—toward eventual Americanization. Father Vincent Barzynski, pastor of St. Stanislaus Kostka Parish directly to the north of St. Boniface, stressed this in the very first issue of *Dziennik Chicagoski* (Chicago Polish Daily): "[Among] the principles guiding us shall . . . be to regard highly the Constitution of the United States, as citizens of the country. We must participate actively in the public life of our country. . . . Specifically, we Poles must not consider ourselves as visitors but as an integral part of this country."[61]

Meanwhile, the American Catholic church at large was growing tremendously during the postwar decades. Chicago, which numbered 1,250,000 Catholics, was the second largest diocese in the country.[62] The trend within the American Catholic church was consolidation, symbolized by the formation of the National Catholic Welfare Conference in 1919. The influence of this conference was felt at the level of diocese and parish, and nowhere was this trend more evident than in Chicago.[63] Chicago's third archbishop, George Cardinal Mundelein (1916–39), was the quintessential bishop of the twenties and thirties. Although Feehan and Quigley had favored the establishment of ethnic parishes, Mundelein merely tolerated them. And while the first two archbishops ran a decentralized form of government, which allowed pastors like Venn and Evers essentially to run their own parishes, Mundelein favored a centralized form of government. Mundelein was an Americanizer par excellence, whose decisions had a profound impact on parish life. One of his first acts was to reform and organize the parochial school system. He required ethnic schools to teach the ordinary subjects in English, to use standardized texts, and to use native languages only to teach religion. After decades of relative independence, schools like St. Boniface now had to conform to archdiocesan norms.[64]

Mundelein encouraged Americanization by establishing archdiocesan organizations and societies. He elevated the Holy Name and St. Vincent de Paul societies as the principal organizations for men in the archdiocese. Acting through the parish, both of these societies brought Germans and Poles into the American mainstream. As Mundelein stated, "In the church today we have societies, sodalities, confraternities . . . but I have ever maintained that there is no body of laymen in the Church more Christian, more charitable, than the St. Vincent de Paul Conference." Through the inspiration of Bishop Bernard Sheil, an auxiliary to Mundelein, the Catholic Youth Organization (CYO) became one of the most significant youth organizations in the United States. The CYO Americanized thousands of immigrants in scores of American parishes. The *Chicago Herald-American* noted that it was "one of the most powerful influences for good citizenship in Chicago and one of the great forces for Americanism in America."[65]

Archbishop Mundelein appointed the Reverend Christian A. Rempe as St. Boniface's fifth pastor in 1916. The new pastor faced monumental difficulties: the average Sunday attendance had dropped to 400, and the parish debt stood at $128,392. The centennial history of the parish noted that "Fr. Rempe soon realized that it would be impossible for him to be pastor of a German parish in the old tradition." Because he spoke Polish, he tried to attract the unchurched people of this newer immigrant group. Father F. L. Kalvelage, one of the chroniclers of the parish, summarized the situation succinctly:

But while the census proved the insufficiency of the German element, it also showed that a large percentage of the Polish population was not affiliated with any parish. Some of them had made their First Communion, either in St. Boniface Church or some other non-Polish parish in the neighborhood . . . others had never been to confession or communion. There are literally thousands of these in our neighborhood. Most of them were born and raised in this country, scarcely understanding Polish. Others though born abroad have become lax in the performance of their religious duties; among these are generally the parents of the children who make their First Holy Communion in our Church. Here was indeed a large and legitimate field of labor and recruits for St. Boniface Parish. And it is from these that the parish has grown.[66]

Although many of St. Boniface's Poles had either lost sight of their Polishness or had strayed from Catholicism altogether, Rempe welcomed them to his community and began to attend to their needs.

But growth did not take place overnight. A year after he came, Father Rempe complained to Archbishop Mundelein that the obstacles he met at St. Boniface were insurmountable. "At the end of the year," he said, "I shall be in a position to say whether this parish is capable of existence." But Mundelein insisted that Rempe continue his work: "All that matter was gone over and thoroughly considered when St. Boniface was permitted to conserve its character as a German-speaking parish. As for yourself, I would be indeed disappointed to learn that you were not achieving the success I had been led to believe you were obtaining in the task that had been given to you at your own solicitation." Rempe interpreted this as a reprimand and quickly responded to the "unkind tone" of the archbishop's letter. He pointed out that he "did not know 'perfectly well' the conditions of this parish" and denied "that I ever solicited St. Boniface or any other parish."[67]

Father Rempe stayed, and St. Boniface revived; but the parish lost much of its German flavor. Rempe sought new parishioners among the Poles who lived directly north of St. Boniface, a move that angered both Germans and Poles. The Germans who remained in the parish were indignant about the new Polish members, while the Polish clergy accused the new pastor of stealing their parishioners. But the parish continued to attract new members from this unchurched group. Mass attendance rose from 400 in 1916 to 700 in 1921. The pastor was still concerned about enrollment and pleaded with his parishioners: "Have you ever asked your neighbors upstairs or downstairs to come to our church on Sunday? . . . If each of you brought only one it would make our attendance 1,500 a Sunday, a weekly income of $300; enough to pay

TABLE 1

St. Boniface Parish, Annual Reports

	NO. OF FAMILIES	YEARLY PEW RENT/ SUNDAY COLLECTION	SCHOOL ENROLLMENT
1917	200	$3,275.23	317
1919	250	$3,370.90	220
1921	300	$4,324.00	368
1923	300	$5,850.98	497
1925	400	$6,705.55	552
1927	450	$10,955.99	540
1929	500	$9,328.26	478
1931	800	$9,954.20	370

our running expenses. . . . Wake up a little! Put your shoulder to the wheel."[68]

St. Boniface's fiscal condition gradually improved to such an extent that Rempe was able to report that "the impossible has happened: Who, even including myself, thought that we really could raise $4,000? And now we are actually above it." Rempe was truly astounded that in a parish with "few wealthy members, 40 gave ten dollars and 330 gave five!"[69] In fact, the parish's growth could be traced to the large number of unchurched Poles who had sent their children to St. Boniface for First Holy Communion. The annual reports document the remarkable rebirth of St. Boniface during Father Rempe's sixteen-year pastorate (see table 1).[70]

Father Rempe reached out to all his parishioners, preaching to them in German, English, and Polish.[71] He set forth for them his vision of the church in a set of pastoral letters published between 1919 and 1926:

The whole world is divided into parishes. A Catholic, no matter where he lives, must belong to one of them. Only in his own parish can he receive the sacraments; only the priests of his own parish are bound to render him service . . . otherwise a Catholic cannot have his children baptized in any church; in case of sickness he cannot get a priest from anywhere; in case of death he cannot be buried from any Catholic cemetery; in case he wishes to be married no Catholic priest is allowed to perform the ceremony.[72]

To be a Catholic was to participate in the sacramental life of the church. Attendance at Sunday mass was part of being Catholic. Father

Rempe was insistent upon this point, and he chastised his parishioners in a pastoral letter for "the enormity of the sin of missing Mass on Sundays. . . . God gives you 168 hours every week, are you not ungrateful when you refuse to give him one on Sunday?"[73]

Connected with attending mass was contributing to the support of the parish. Rempe returned to this theme often: "For I am convinced that we must earn God's gifts, and that the best way to do this is to properly contribute to his Church. Some never give God a chance to reward them. Either they give nothing or the amount is small." This approach to giving was typical of the postwar years. The Catholic bishops had enumerated several precepts for Catholics, one of which was to contribute to the support of the Church. Rempe, like most pastors of his time, equated being Catholic with giving. He counseled the parents of the parish, "If you teach [your children] to be generous to the Church you have the assurance that they will never want. Above all things, however, you will know that they will never lose their faith or even become lukewarm in its practices."[74]

Like Father Venn of the 1880s, Rempe never questioned his own role as spiritual leader of the parish. And like Venn, he nurtured lay leadership through the verein structure. John Fensterle, the subject of a lengthy *Pfarrbote* article published after his death, was one such lay leader.[75] Fensterle's life was characterized by a "strong belief in Christ" and "a great love for his holy Catholic Church." There was hardly any undertaking of the community in which he did not take part. He belonged to all the vereins—and he was usually an officer in each of them! Men like John Fensterle exercised leadership through the vereins and became leaders of the broader community as well. Rempe did not see such men as a threat but as a source of leadership and support. And this was certainly one of the reasons he was able effectively to lead St. Boniface through these turbulent decades of ethnic change.

Rempe encouraged the continuation of the verein structure that had been so successful during the pastorates of Venn and Evers. These societies were important vehicles which continued to nourish ethnic traditions but at the same time encouraged Americanization. During this period the Young Men's and Young Ladies' societies showed the most vitality, growing enormously under the tutelage of Father F. L. Kalvelage. While chess and bowling were favorite pastimes at the beginning of the century, baseball became the most popular sport of the twenties. The Young Ladies' Society put on socials and various get-togethers for the young people of the parish, and sometimes both groups joined to put on plays, dances, and socials, including a midsummer carnival complete with dancing outdoors.[76]

The Holy Name and St. Vincent de Paul societies became the most important men's groups of the 1920s. Both groups grew substantially during this period, and it was probably not uncommon for many Holy Name members to be members of the St. Vincent de Paul Society as well. The latter took in hundreds of dollars to buy food and coal and to pay the rent for the indigent.[77] Although it is true that these societies were pushed onto the parish from above by the archbishop, they quickly became an integral part of Boniface's life. These national organization gently drew Rempe's parishioners into the American Catholic mainstream.

The societies were also important vehicles for social interaction. The Married Ladies' and Altar and Rosary societies put on innumerable socials, where one could breathe in the aromas of homemade cakes and sausages and drink *Schmierkaffee*, a German type of coffee. There one could "meet again an old friend whom [one] had not seen for a long time."[78] The highlight of this period was the annual *Herbstfest*, or fall festival, which brought parishioners and nonparishioners together for a week of fun and entertainment. The schoolchildren sold raffle tickets, and all the societies contributed their personnel and talents to the success of the venture. The *Pfarrbote* made specific appeals to the old Germans to participate in the *Herbstfest*. As Father Evers put it, "we may truly hope that all former members of old St. Boniface, who in course of time have moved to other parts of the city but who remain true and attached to her and her pastor, remember her with grateful hearts [and remember] that you are welcome in your old mother church."[79] The festival also provided a place where Poles and Germans could gather together and celebrate not only what they had in common—their attachment to St. Boniface—but what made them different.

Rempe tried deliberately to keep the ethnic roots of the parish alive. He instituted an annual St. Boniface Day celebration, which he called "a modest beginning towards the regaining of our self-respect." These programs continued through the 1920s, deliberately evoking the drama of days gone by. Strains of German lieder once again filled the streets near St. Boniface, and dramas like Goethe's *Faust* drew large crowds to St. Boniface's auditorium.[80] Festivities like the St. Boniface Day celebration kept the ethnic tradition of the parish alive and well.

During this period of ethnic change, the parochial school continued to be the principal means of assuring future generations of Bonifacians.

In 1915, the eighth-grade graduating class numbered thirteen German students and five Polish. By 1921, the Polish children outnumbered the Germans two to one. Rempe tried to attract the Polish children to his school, thinking that "if we get the children we will get the families eventually."[81] And so, paradoxically, the children led the adults back to parish life.

The school continued to cooperate with Archbishop Mundelein's Americanization program, and in that sense it became more like the schools around it. Although religion was taught in German, the other subjects were taught in English. St. Boniface was also part of the Twenty-eighth International Eucharistic Congress, held in Chicago in 1926.[82] This five-day event attracted Catholics from around the nation. For the Children's Day festivities, young Bonifacians joined more than 60,000 other children to sing the Mass of the Angels at Soldier Field. As part of a crowd of more than half a million, Boniface's youngsters certainly came to know a world much larger than Chicago and Noble Streets. They came to realize that they were not just Germans or Poles or Americans but Catholics who professed a truly international faith.

Father Rempe's pastorate was largely successful for a number of reasons. First and foremost, he kept the genius of the parish alive by nurturing the ethnic loyalties of both the Germans and the Poles. Events like the St. Boniface Day celebration strengthened the church's ties with many of its older parishioners. Second, Rempe continued the verein structure, which allowed all parishioners, male and female, to participate actively in the parish. Third, he continued to attract children to the parish through his continued support of the parochial school. He also reached out to the broader community; he was credited, for example, with helping to form a building and loan association for the West Town community.[83] And all these structures and activities were bound together by devotion to one Catholic faith, the faith of these parishioners that had endured through the decades.

Becoming an American Parish

On the very day of Rempe's funeral, Cardinal Mundelein appointed Father Alfred Milcheski, a German, as St. Boniface's sixth pastor.[84] Milcheski's task was to continue to deal with the German-Polish division within the parish. Mundelein felt that a German with a Polish name could continue the process begun by Father Rempe. Some fifty years later, his successor said of Milcheski that "he greatly loved the people and was greatly loved by the people and was very popular with them." Many of the parishioners were second-generation immigrants who did not fully accept their ethnic origins, but Milcheski helped "support the Poles in their Polishness." Liturgical services began to take on a Polish feel. Historian Kalvelage observed that the Poles seemed more devout during Lent: "the deep devotion of the congregation, their fervor, their emotion and sorrow in the sufferings of Christ" were quite different from the qualities called forth by the German service. While the Germans delighted in the pageantry of church worship, the Poles preferred to meditate on the sufferings of Christ. Milcheski also instituted Polish-American Constitution Day to further a sense of ethnic pride.

Father Milcheski came to St. Boniface at a time when the city and nation as a whole were reeling under the Depression. Chicago in the thirties was different from the Chicago of the twenties. The Urban League reported that "every available dry spot of ground and every bench on the west side of Washington Park [on Chicago's South Side] . . . is covered by sleepers. . . . Some were young, others were old, their clothes were shabby but not tattered."[85] Older neighborhoods like West Town continued their downward slide, as commercial and residential developments moved north and northwest. Between 1920 and 1940, more than one million people moved out of West Town.[86] St. Boniface's enrollment declined during the Depression and World War II but increased dramatically thereafter. Though parish income declined during the thirties and early forties, it rose sharply after the war.[87] Unemployment was modest, and personal incomes rose steadily. By the mid-fifties, parish income had nearly doubled from the prewar years.

In many respects Milcheski's pastorate was similar to those of other American pastors during this period. Archbishops like Cardinal Mundelein saw ethnicity as a remnant of the past, and though they tolerated the national parishes already extant, they established only a handful of new ones.[88] The verein structure that had been so strong during the 1920s began to lose its ethnic cast, and by the 1940s the societies at St. Boniface resembled those of most Chicago parishes. The efforts of Cardinal Mundelein to make the Holy Name and St. Vincent de Paul societies the principal societies of the archdiocese were largely successful, and by the 1930s most of the older societies at St. Boniface no longer existed.

Samuel Cardinal Stritch, who was appointed Mundelein's successor in 1940, also put his imprint on parish life.[89] Chicago's fourth archbishop (1940–1958), he actively supported the establishment of the

Cana Conference (premarriage instruction), the Christian Family Movement (CFM), and the Young Christian Students (YCS) in his archdiocese.[90] He also gave strong support to the Catholic Youth Organization (CYO), which continued during the thirties and forties to be one of the most powerful influences for Americanization.

Father Milcheski strove to make the CYO a significant force in parish life. During the 1930s, St. Boniface's school cooperated with the CYO in promoting citywide activities. A most impressive campaign was the CYO's demonstration for the Legion of Decency, called by one writer the "greatest demonstration of united Catholic Action . . . since the Eucharistic Congress."[91] The CYO also promoted scouting at the grammar school level, and records indicate that St. Boniface had an active scouting program promoted through the school.

But the most significant connection to the CYO was the Canteen, or youth center, which was dedicated in the school basement by Bishop Bernard Sheil in 1948. Father "Bob" Bobritzke, an assistant to Milcheski, was instrumental in having the center established at St. Boniface. Young people from throughout the community gathered every Friday night in the church basement for study and recreation. The Reverend Stanley Rokicinski, who came to assist Milcheski in 1950, noted that the Canteen was the greatest draw at the parish at this time. The Canteen was part of a CYO network of thirty-three such centers, which operated summer camps at neighboring parks. St. Boniface operated its own summer session at Eckhart Park, directly across from the church (a park that had been established by the city through the lobbying efforts of Father Evers). Like Venn and Rempe before him, "Father Rocky," as Rokicinski came to be known, was for and with the people. On summer nights he would sit outside on the steps of St. Boniface and talk with as many as 150 teens. On other nights, he took the teens out for ice cream after the study clubs. Both he and Father Milcheski were effective because they allowed the people to feel that St. Boniface was their parish. When asked why he felt that St. Boniface was unique, Father Rocky replied that "everyone was accepted there; it was a place where the priests truly loved their people."[92]

To understand St. Boniface Parish fully, it is important to understand the role of the Sisters of St. Francis who worked there for five generations. The sisters were a vital part of Boniface's life for more than a hundred years—through the Chicago Fire, outbreaks of typhoid, the decades after World War I. During Milcheski's pastorate, St. Boniface became a model for other Catholic schools and was often the first school in the archdiocese to offer new curricula. The school continued to foster Americanization during World War II through war drives, parades for the troops, and pageants and plays like *I'm an American . . . America for Me.* After the war, the sisters continued to invite outside organizations like the Chicago Fire Department, the Tuberculosis Institute, and the American Red Cross to the school.[93]

But the sisters never forgot that their mission was to impart knowledge within the context of the Catholic faith. The school was an integral part of parish life, and its goal was to graduate educated *Catholic* young men and women. All students thus participated in the liturgical life of the church. They attended mass and went to confession frequently and began every school day with prayers. Moral education was part of their daily training.

A main event of the school year was the annual May Day procession.[94] This event epitomized parish life at mid-century, for it joined the school and the parish in a grand celebration of Catholic belief and practice. The ceremony was conducted outdoors for all to see. The schoolchildren and parish societies gathered outside the church, with the First Communicants and eighth-grade graduates in formal attire. The large assembly then marched around the church, the schoolchildren said the rosary, and one girl placed a crown on the statue of Mary, honoring her as Queen of May. This ceremony gave witness to the highly individualistic and Marian emphasis of Catholic devotions before the Second Vatican Council. By fostering such liturgies as the May Day procession, Boniface's school nourished generations of immigrants within a framework of pre–Vatican II Catholicism.

Father Milcheski's pastorate was cut short by a serious car accident in 1949. Although he lived on until 1957 and was still able to administer the parish from his bed, Milcheski needed the sturdy hands of Father Rokicinski to run the parish. Cardinal Stritch appointed Rokicinski administrator in 1950, effectively giving him control of the daily life of the parish. Father Rocky was a builder, a traditional role for pastors of the time. One of his first acts as pastor was to complete the redecorating of the church begun by Father Milcheski. He built a new marble altar and erected statues of St. Boniface and Our Lady of Fatima on either side of the church. He brought the solid oak corpus of Christ from the original 1864 church building to a prominent place in the sanctuary, thus linking the old traditions with the new. The parishioners watched as the church was tuckpointed, the organ rebuilt, and the sanctuary renovated; they also saw numerous improvements to the school and the sisters' convent.[95]

Father Rocky wrote numerous articles on the parish and the role of the pastor in the parish bulletin. He saw the rectory as "the heart of the parish—the nerve center—from which Parish Life and Spirit spring. Visit your Parish Priest," he said. "He is Christ's Ambassador on earth." Father Rocky understood the pastoral role as many pastors before him had. But he was also influenced by the teachings of Pope Pius XII in his 1943 encyclical, *Mystici Corporis* (Mystical Body). According to these teachings, laymen and laywomen had an important role within the church, a vision of the church that had given birth to such movements as those mentioned above—the Cana Conference, the Christian Family Movement, the Young Christian Students, the Young Christian Workers. Like many other pastors of his day, Father Rocky was profoundly moved by this vision of the church and brought these movements to St. Boniface.[96] Father Rocky saw the parish as central to Catholic life. As he wrote of St. Boniface Parish in 1954,

> Three small words spelling out a first love, a *church* never to be supplanted, a *pastor* never to be forgotten, *Sisters* never to be equaled. Yet there are people who are ready to contribute heavily to other causes . . . while they refuse to turn a hand for their home parish. This involves a confusion of responsibilities. First things are no longer first. Values are distorted. . . . The way God wants it, the way he intends it, is that the Parish come first.[97]

The Reorganization of Parish Life after Vatican II: The Hispanic Era (1960–1990)

The vast dispersal of Chicago's population to the outer parts of the metropolis and beyond continued after World War II. As inner communities like West Town and Logan Square continued to lose population, outer communities like Lakeview, North Center, and Uptown peaked by mid-century. But most of this growth occurred outside the city limits, and suburban expansion drew away many taxpayers.[98]

Chicago's industrial strength continued to rest on its role as the midcontinent's transportation center. The extraordinary growth of its highway system (modeled in part on the German autobahn) in the postwar years made Chicago an important trucking and automobile center. The

6.2   View of St. Boniface Church. Reprinted from *St. Boniface Church on Its Centennial Anniversary, 1864–1964* (n.p., n.p.).

statistics are staggering: in 1945, there were 428,000 cars in Chicago; by 1953, the number had nearly doubled to 765,000. Only a massive construction program could handle the new traffic, and so block upon block of old housing was torn down to accommodate the Edens and Kennedy expressways to the north, the Eisenhower to the west, and the Dan Ryan and Stevenson to the south and southwest. By 1969, all but a few sections of this massive highway system were built. The Kennedy Expressway, which opened in 1960, split St. Boniface Parish in two and forced many parishioners to leave the area; many small businesses were destroyed.[99] But the Kennedy also signaled the arrival of thousands of

Puerto Ricans and Mexicans, who began to move into homes once inhabited by Germans and Poles.

The arrival of the Spanish-speaking at St. Boniface coincided with the decision by Pope John XXIII in 1959 to call the Second Vatican Council. Few realized how momentous this event would be, but in a few short years every Catholic parish was influenced by its decrees.[100] The council brought in a vision of a church that was not simply a hierarchy but the "people of God"—laymen and laywomen who were also called to take leadership roles within the parish. This vision—highly biblical, historical, and ecumenical—inspired Father Rocky throughout his lengthy pastorate. In many ways he was a man ahead of his time, enthusiastically accepting the decrees of Vatican II. For Father Rocky, "the voice of the laity must echo the authentic voice of Christ to the whole community."[101]

Father Rokicinski accepted the Hispanics just as he had accepted the Poles who were there when he arrived. He noted the friction between the Polish- and Spanish-speaking parishes; just as the Germans had resented the Poles after World War I, so the Poles resented the Spanish when they arrived in the 1960s. Father Rocky immediately started to learn Spanish, and he went from store to store putting up signs inviting the people to attend a Spanish mass. The Poles began to consider him "a Spanish pastor." Father Rocky relates a telling episode about going to St. John Cantius Parish (solidly Polish) one Sunday to go to confession in Polish. The priest curtly told him that it was Sunday and that he should come back at the appointed time. This lack of courtesy was a harbinger of the times, for as Father Rocky saw it, the Poles disliked his positive treatment of the Hispanics who had moved into "their neighborhood." "The Annals of the Parish" first note in 1959 "the great difficulties which confront our school with our non-English speaking people." By 1963, seventeen of the forty-six graduates were Hispanic.[102]

At St. Boniface during this period, the laity were allowed to take charge and make St. Boniface their own. Rokicinski developed this leadership in his own practical way: whenever he wanted anything done, he simply appealed to the people. He worked shoulder-to-shoulder with Poles and Puerto Ricans to sand the desks and floors in every classroom of the school. To keep the Canteen open, he fought the city fire department over alleged fire code violations. He welcomed one of the community's few black families, the Cunninghams, when St. John Cantius rudely turned them away as "non-Polish speaking." Mr. Cunningham soon became a Holy Name member and an usher in the church; Mrs. Cunningham joined the Ladies Auxiliary and became vice president; and the Cunningham children, who enrolled in the parochial school, presented flowers to Albert Cardinal Meyer, the fifth archbishop of Chicago (1958–1965), at the centennial celebration of the parish in 1964. From Rokicinski's point of view, St. Boniface was a community where "each group [was] able to maintain its individuality while appreciating the customs of the other."[103]

When Father Rokicinski was transferred to Our Lady of Grace Parish in 1968, Father George B. Roth was assigned to take his place. Fluent in both Spanish and Polish, Roth set forth his post–Vatican II vision of the church in the parish bulletin:

> St. Boniface is a "community" in that it is a fellowship of people who meet regularly at a given place and time for a given purpose. It is "church" in that its members are not merely a disconnected jumble of isolated groups, but, united through their individual service, form an all-embracing fellowship.[104]

The new pastor grasped the different ethnic and religious needs of his parishioners, and drawing on the experience of the past, he tried to maintain St. Boniface as a multi-ethnic parish. He called upon the church members to put on a series of ethnic masses and dinners, for the purpose of affording "all parishioners an opportunity to learn and appreciate the culture of their fellow parishioners and neighbors." The first cultural exchange was Polish—a mass followed by a typical Polish dinner. Polish arts and crafts, folk music, dancing, and a sing-along complemented the occasion. A feast in honor of Our Lady of Czestochowa was introduced in 1969.[105] The second series of festivals was for the Hispanics. The Mexican community began to celebrate the Feast of Our Lady of Guadalupe in 1969, and a Latin American supper and dance in conjunction with the Feast of the Three Kings (La Fiesta de los Tres Reyes) was begun in 1970.[106] Father Roth began the practice of publicizing all major events in three languages—English, Polish, and Spanish. He seems to have made a conscious effort to bring all three groups together.

Roth established a number of new societies and instituted new liturgical events for the changing parish. While older societies like the Holy Name and St. Vincent de Paul still existed, the newer societies brought fresh life into the parish. For the older members he began the Golden Pioneers. For the Hispanics, he continued the Damas del Perpetuo Socorro (Ladies of Perpetual Help), established by Father Rokicinski in

1965. He also established the Guadalupanas, an important social group for Hispanic women. For the youth of the parish he established a Latin Youth Club (La Juventud Latina) and began a guitar mass.[107] Through these societies St. Boniface's lay leadership evolved.

Father Roth was particularly concerned about the continuance of the parochial school. Despite new economic pressures, he firmly believed the parish school to be "not only the responsibility of the parents of the children in the school, but of all the parishioners, because the school helps the entire community of today and tomorrow." At a time when some were questioning the very existence of the parochial school system, Roth foresaw that it was an institution worth saving. Sending the results of a 1969–70 survey of parishioners to the Sisters of St. Francis, Father Roth noted that "we need [the parochial school] but I do not know whether we can pay the cost of it. The school keeps my people together; they are a lost people [without it]."[108] Roth was acutely sensitive to the needs of the Spanish-speaking, and together with the sisters, he formed a working alliance in their behalf.

Roth maintained a good relationship with the Sisters of St. Francis. The latter ran not only the school but an extensive Confraternity of Christian Doctrine (CCD) program. This program, revived by Pius X in 1904, offered religious education to Catholic public-school children. The superior general of the Franciscans, Sister M. Francine, agreed to find a Spanish-speaking sister for the CCD program and to consider for the school a model that had been tried at Lafayette School, another Chicago school with a "large number of Spanish-speaking children who have a problem with English." At Lafayette, according to Father Roth, "these children receive English classes all morning and in the afternoon they are taught the academic subjects in Spanish. In this way, these students are not falling behind in their academic courses—and with the crash program in English, they are entering their regular classes quicker." Roth requested the services of Sister Ana Marie, who had been "well received by the Spanish-speaking community," to start up just such a program at St. Boniface School.[109]

Sister Ana Marie did come, and together with the other sisters, she played an important role in educating the youth of the parish, both in and out of the parochial school. The sisters taught English classes for the children during the summer and helped form home-school councils as a link between parent, teacher, and child. According to Father Eugene Gratkowski, one of the parish associates during this period, St. Boniface "thrived because there was something special in those people all through the years. The combination of the leadership and the openness of the people made it thrive and blossom as it did."[110] Father Roth, like Venn, Rempe, and Rokicinski before him, was a good leader because he accepted the people who came into his parish and paid attention to their needs. All these priests accepted the Germans, Poles, and Hispanics as they were, and sought to meet their needs through a variety of societies and liturgical activities. They educated the young through the parochial school, and later through the CCD program. The parish seemed to have come full circle with the pastorate of Father Roth, as once again St. Boniface became a way station for ethnic groups in the process of being Americanized.

The forces released by Vatican II challenged not only the laity but the clergy as well. Father Roth, like hundreds of other clerics, began to question his decision to become a priest. He resigned his pastorate in 1972, and after a leave of absence he left the priesthood. St. Boniface was left with a "team ministry," or co-pastorate, headed by Fathers Eugene Gratkowski, John Hillenbrand, and Donald Stalzer. But before they could embark on this unique style of pastorate, they had to convince John Cardinal Cody, Chicago's sixth archbishop (1965–1982), that it was a practical endeavor. Cody wanted to control the archdiocese much like a business organization, where each subordinate was responsible to one person.[111] He disliked the idea of a co-pastorate, which diluted his ability to deal with one pastor. The situation came to a head when the people themselves confronted the personnel board of the archdiocese and demanded the team ministry. Cody approved the co-pastorate the next day.[112]

The team divided the responsibilities of the parish into three areas: Father Gratkowski headed the Spanish ministry and young people's groups; Father Hillenbrand took charge of the finances and the school; and Father Stalzer headed the English liturgy and publicity. Father Steven Chao, an assistant, headed the senior citizens' groups.[113] But the team realized that they could not succeed without the backing of the parishioners. And so they sought the advice of their own community. They began a series of home meetings, informal gatherings of five or six couples with one of the team priests present. They began a parish advisory board, with fifteen lay members. The latter group encouraged communication between priests, organizations, and parishioners; advised the priests on parish issues; and laid the groundwork for a parish council. These structures empowered the people to take charge of the parish alongside their co-pastors.

The pastoral team and parishioners created a statement of the "Vision of St. Boniface," which was prominently displayed in the church vestibule: "Our ideal is the development of a community in which each person is proud of his national, ethnic, and racial heritage, at the same time respecting the richness of other cultures . . . a community which will serve as a sign to others that life is good, that people are good, and that there is a reason for hope." Even parishioners outside of St. Boniface were attracted to this vision. One Sunday, the whole Hispanic section from Holy Trinity Parish marched en masse to St. Boniface and enrolled there as parishioners. According to Father Gratkowski, "they were wonderful people, and some of the best leadership came from that group."[114]

Many programs helped to make the church's vision a reality. Father Stalzer continued to publish the parish bulletin in English, Spanish, and Polish. The parish continued to celebrate Polish-American Constitution Day and hold Polish masses and dinners. They celebrated the Feast of Our Lady of Guadalupe for the Mexicans and the Feast of St. John the Baptist for the Puerto Ricans. They succeeded in getting the various groups to intermix and know one another, despite barriers of language and age. The Spanish began to emulate the Polish blessing of baskets, while the Polish enthusiastically attended the Live Stations of the Cross.[115] Father Gratkowski got all ages and nationalities together for a liturgical celebration of *Godspell*. They even resurrected the Feast of St. Boniface as a means of uniting the various ethnic groups. Father Gratkowski also instituted a popular "soup and bread" Wednesday during Lent. Once a week he showed a film (with little or no dialogue) that connected with the previous Sunday's gospel, and more than 150 Polish and Spanish members attended.[116]

The team ministry did not forget the young of the parish. Father Gratkowski reorganized the Canteen of the forties and fifties into a group called Re-Cycle. Its purpose was to recycle ideas about faith and community, and, like the Canteen, the group proved very popular among the teens of the neighborhood. In fact, most of the eighth-graders looked forward to joining Re-Cycle after their confirmation. It was through Re-Cycle that teens participated in such liturgical activities as the Live Stations of the Cross. The school contributed to the overall "vision" of the parish by holding a number of International Day celebrations. These celebrations featured the songs, dances, art, and folklore of many different groups—from French Creoles to African Americans, from Mexicans and Puerto Ricans to Polish. As the community grew, more and more parents wanted to send their children to the parochial school but simply could not afford it. As a result, the CCD program grew enormously during this period. Sister Therese Didier, the director, noted that "the growth of the CCD program caught us by surprise."[117]

By 1979 the team ministry had reached the end of its tenure. Father Hillenbrand had been reassigned two years earlier, and Father Stalzer took a leave of absence. Father Gratkowski was appointed permanent pastor that same year. Gratkowski saw that staffing the school was becoming ever more difficult and that a tuition increase would simply lower the enrollment to an unacceptable level. The inevitable solution was a merger with St. Stanislaus Kostka School. Both schools had fallen well below 300 students by 1983, so in order to avoid the closing of both, the two schools combined in the fall of 1983.[118]

The history of St. Boniface School mirrored the history of the parish itself, for the school, like the parish, had responded to the ethnic and religious impulses of all the immigrants who had come through its doors. It made them into American citizens but citizens who were still Catholic. The school was a mosaic of many nationalities and cultures, each proud of its own culture but richer for knowing others. There are ironies in the gradual decline of the school, for the school had been a primary source of vocations for the Sisters of St. Francis. But as Vatican II called women to holiness in other states of life, fewer and fewer joined religious life. And as vocations declined, there were fewer sisters to staff the school, and more laity had to be paid to take their place. As tuition went up to pay salaries, enrollments went down, for many simply could not afford to pay. And so a merger was the only way for the school to survive. After 1983, the Sisters of St. Francis discontinued their service on the school staff, and in 1985 their formal association with St. Boniface Parish ended.[119]

St. Boniface continued to be part of the broader community around it. Father Rokicinski was active in the Near Northwest Side Planning Commission, an early community organization. Meetings were often held in the Canteen to discuss various community problems. The group's first concern was to keep the community clean from litter; in addition, vandalism was rampant, and even the church had been broken into on several occasions. Father Rocky opened the parish halls to any block club that wanted to meet for community business. These clubs consisted of concerned parishioners who, together with Father Rokicinski, worked for the good of the community. Along with Father Hintenburg of St. Aloysius, Rokicinski was instrumental in organizing the twenty-three Catholic parishes of the Near North and East Humboldt Park communities into a cohesive whole.[120]

These early community efforts soon merged with the Northwest Community Organization (NCO), the most significant community group of the period. The NCO, established in 1962, included twenty-two Roman Catholic churches, fifteen Protestant churches, schools, settlement houses, local business leaders, and fifteen civic organizations representing more than 170,000 people. St. Boniface was a founding member of the organization and actively supported all its programs.[121] In fact, the parish was often used as a center for NCO activities. A health fair held at St. Boniface School in 1977 attracted more than seven thousand neighborhood schoolchildren. Senior citizens' groups often met for city tours at St. Boniface. A White House Conference on the Elderly was held at the Canteen. Parish halls often echoed with arguments about urban renewal, real estate practices, and community stability. St. Boniface took the lead in promoting low-cost housing for the neighborhood.

The pastoral team and the parishioners of St. Boniface vigorously supported the NCO's activities through the sixties, seventies, and eighties. The Sisters of St. Francis were in the forefront, involved in the Urban Apostolate and the Center for Urban Education. Sister M. Jovita, a seventh-grade teacher at St. Boniface, led a committee of sisters, parents, and concerned laity to force the Chicago Board of Health to correct serious health deficiencies in the twenty-two parochial schools of the community.[122] Many sisters spent long summer hours studying Spanish at the Archdiocesan Center for Latin America. They realized that faith was expressed through language and that it was just as important for the Mexicans as for the Germans and Poles before them to express that faith in their native tongue. Part of St. Boniface's strength through the years had been precisely its recognition of the important link between faith and language.

Father Eugene Gratkowski served St. Boniface for more than twelve years. When he was reassigned to St. Gregory Parish in 1985, Father Thaddeus Perzanowski was named to take his place.[123] Perzanowski established a consultation and ministry board representing all segments of the parish. He made the Feast of St. Boniface a bilingual parish celebration called *Opdust* (Polish and Spanish). He expanded the pastoral staff to include a Dominican sister (Harriet Agnew) and three Victory Noll sisters (Grace Marie Samblanet, Mary Ellen Descourouez, and Beatrice Haines). These women represented a new breed of sisters, women who wanted to assume leadership and responsibility within a team ministry. In an interview in 1990, Sisters Descourouez and Samblanet noted that they had come to St. Boniface to start a Hispanic outreach and evangelization program "for the marginals" of the community, those who had been largely forgotten by the society at large. Their idea was to form local *communidades*, or base communities, which would reflect on the meaning of Scripture and perhaps, they hoped, lead to social change.[124] This was the church of the future, they thought: small communities with their social and liturgical center in a parish like St. Boniface.

But the sisters arrived on the day that Father Perzanowski said his last mass at St. Boniface. Like Father Roth, Perzanowski decided to take a leave of absence, and he ultimately left the priesthood. Father Lawrence Collins, the new pastor, had a vision of the parish slightly different from that of the sisters. In their view, he wanted a pastoral team more than an outreach program. And so, although the sisters stayed and the *communidades* program was begun, it did not flourish as the sisters had hoped.[125] Father Collins was left with the unenviable task of carrying on the traditions of Boniface as the sole priest there.[126] But with the continued decline in priestly vocations and little likelihood of a married priesthood to take up the slack, the archdiocese had to act to consolidate its resources and manpower.

On January 21, 1990, Joseph Cardinal Bernardin, the seventh archbishop of Chicago (1982–), announced that St. Boniface Parish, along with thirty-six other parishes and schools, would either close or consolidate with other parishes. "Understandably, these closings will create a sense of loss," Bernardin said, "but great care has been taken so no Catholic will be without relatively convenient access to a parish church and a Catholic school." St. Boniface found itself targeted because it lay geographically between Holy Innocents and St. Stanislaus Kostka parishes. In addition, St. Stanislaus still had a functioning grammar school, the one that had merged with St. Boniface eight years earlier.

The closing brought an immediate uproar from the Catholic community, with some members vowing that they would not join another parish.[127] Many women were particularly concerned that the leadership roles they had enjoyed at St. Boniface would disappear at another parish. One ministerial leader said: "This is our church. Don't we have a say in it? You tell us we are the church, and yet you won't let us in on the decision-making process."[128]

But when Bishop Placido Rodriguez, an auxiliary to Cardinal Bernardin, came to discuss the issue, it was obvious that the decisions about the closings had already been made. St. Boniface, Chicago's fifth oldest Catholic parish, would close its doors. Its Hispanic members would be forced to merge with larger non-Hispanic parishes, and, without a parish to call their own, some parishioners would certainly be lost. Some might be drawn to Protestant fundamentalist groups that appealed to more personal religious experiences.[129] Others might simply drift away from Catholicism altogether.

St. Boniface had been strong because it had been proud of its heritage, and it had thrived in its belief that different groups could respect and appreciate the richness of other cultures. Its unique genius was its success in providing a focus for the ethnic and religious loyalties of its members, while encouraging their growing identity as Americans. And though its exact circumstances may not be duplicated elsewhere, the story of St. Boniface Parish can nonetheless help guide other Catholic communities in finding their own distinctive genius.

APPENDIX

Bishops of Chicago

1844–1848	Rt. Rev. William Quarter
1849–1854	Rt. Rev. J. Oliver Van de Velde
1855–1858	Rt. Rev. Anthony O'Regan
1859–1869	Rt. Rev. James Duggan
1870–1879	Rt. Rev. Thomas Foley

Archbishops of Chicago

1880–1902	Rt. Rev. Patrick A. Feehan
1902–1916	Rt. Rev. James Quigley
1916–1939	Rt. Rev. George Cardinal Mundelein
1940–1958	Rt. Rev. Samuel Cardinal Stritch
1958–1965	Rt. Rev. Albert Cardinal Meyer
1965–1982	Rt. Rev. John Cardinal Cody
1982–	Rt. Rev. Joseph Cardinal Bernardin

Pastors of St. Boniface

1864–1866	Rev. Philip Albrecht
1866–1869	Rev. James Marshall
1869–1895	Rev. Clement Venn

1895–1916	Rev. Albert Evers
1916–1932	Rev. Christian A. Rempe
1932–1958	Rev. Alfred J. Milcheski
1958–1968	Rev. Stanley J. Rokicinski
1968–1972	Rev. George Roth
1972–1979	Co-pastorate:
	Rev. Donald Stalzer
	Rev. John Hillenbrand
	Rev. Eugene Gratkowski
1979–1985	Rev. Eugene Gratkowski
1985–1986	Rev. Thaddeus Perzanowski
1986–1990	Rev. Lawrence Collins

NOTES

Martin E. Marty, my graduate school adviser, deserves my first thanks for imparting to me an enthusiasm for American Catholic church history. I am grateful for his continued support as this project evolved from its original form in my dissertation to this final essay. Special thanks are also due to Jay Dolan, Philip Devenish, and James Wind, whose comments on the original manuscript were invaluable to me as I completed this project.

This essay could not have been written without the cooperation and help of the staff of St. Boniface Parish. I am grateful to Father Lawrence Collins, who generously made the resources of the parish available. I am very grateful to Sister Marian Voelker, O.F.M., archivist of the Sisters of St. Francis of Joliet, who provided generous assistance and gracious hospitality while I worked in their excellent archives. I am also grateful to the archivists at the Archdiocese of Chicago who assisted with general archdiocesan materials. I would also like to thank my research assistant, Marilyn McCluskey, whose interviews provided useful insights on St. Boniface Parish.

1. See Stephen J. Shaw, *The Catholic Parish as a Way-Station of Ethnicity and Americanization: Chicago's Germans and Italians, 1903–1939* (Brooklyn: Carlson Publishing, 1991), vol. 19 of Chicago Studies in the History of American Religion, ed. Jerald C. Brauer and Martin E. Marty (hereafter cited as Shaw, *Catholic Parish*).

2. See Andrew J. Townsend, "The Germans of Chicago" (Ph.D. diss., University of Chicago, 1927); Rudolf Hofmeister, *The Germans of Chicago* (Champaign: University of Illinois Press, 1976); and Shaw, *Catholic Parish*, pp. 29–36; 39–46.

3. On the early history of Catholicism in Chicago, see Gilbert J. Garraghan, *The Catholic Church in Chicago, 1673–1837* (Chicago: Loyola University Press, 1921).

4. Theodore C. Pease, *The Story of Illinois* (Chicago: University of Chicago Press, 1925; rev. ed. by Marguerite J. Pease, 1965), pp. 186–87.

5. See "The Life of Peter and Anna Suerth" (manuscript), at the Archives of the Sisters of St. Francis (hereafter cited as ASSF), Joliet, Illinois. Primary source material on St. Boniface Parish is now found at the Archives of the Archdiocese of Chicago (hereafter AAChi). The early history of the parish is chronicled in F. L. Kalvelage, *The Annals of St. Boniface Parish, 1862–1926* (Chicago: privately printed, 1926) (hereafter cited as *Annals of St. Boniface*); *Centennial, St. Boniface Church, 1864–1964* (Chicago: privately printed, 1964) (hereafter cited as *Centennial Boniface*); and "A History of St. Boniface, 1864–1989" (mimeographed).

6. Kalvelage, *Annals of St. Boniface*, 7. Besides Suerth, the committee consisted of J. Klettenberg, B. Schuenemann, Anton Dettmer, J. Dinet, J. Hildebrandt, Peter Schommer, Peter Schmidt, and John Hellmuth.

7. On the life of Father Albrecht, see Kalvelage, *Annals of St. Boniface*, pp. 1–19.

8. Ibid., pp. 14–16.

9. Ibid., pp. 26–29.

10. The 1868 Parish Annual Report (AAChi) is the earliest extant record.

11. Kalvelage, *Annals of St. Boniface*, pp. 31–56.

12. Ibid., pp. 37–42.

13. Ibid., pp. 193–94.

14. Another lay leader was Mrs. Juliana Schueler, who tirelessly supported the many bazaars undertaken by Father Venn to raise money. She would single-handedly get a wagon and travel from store to store to bring loads of articles back to the parish hall (ibid., p. 53).

15. See Charles H. Shanabruch, "The Catholic Church's Role in the Americanization of Chicago's Immigrants: 1833–1928" (Ph.D. diss., University of Chicago, 1975), pp. 190–230.

16. *New World*, March 14, 1903, p. 14.

17. Joseph Parot, "The American Faith and the Persistence of Chicago Polonia, 1870–1920" (Ph.D. diss., Northern Illinois University, 1971), p. 301.

18. Kalvelage, *Annals of St. Boniface*, pp. 42–43.

19. "Annals of St. Boniface Mission" (handwritten journal, 1867–1920; mimeographed, 1921–1984), ASSF (hereafter cited as "Annals Boniface Mission"); Parish Annual Reports, AAChi, 1873–95.

20. Kalvelage, *Annals of St. Boniface*, pp. 57–86.

21. Ibid., pp. 65–68. This sermon, given on May 25, 1903, is printed in its entirety in German in the annals.

22. *Pfarrbote der St. Bonifacius Gemeinde* (Parish Bulletin of St. Boniface Community), January 1907, p. 11 (hereafter *Pfarrbote*). These weekly bulletins were published from 1898 to 1926 and provide a wealth of information on Chicago's German community.

23. *Pfarrbote*, June 1920, p. 3.

24. Kalvelage, *Annals of St. Boniface*, pp. 73–75; "The Dedication of St. Boniface Church," *New World*, June 4, 1904, p. 28.

25. Kalvelage, *Annals of St. Boniface*, pp. 69, 68.

26. *Pfarrbote*, May 1912, pp. 25–30.

27. Ibid., October 1905, pp. 11–15.

28. St. Boniface affiliated itself with the National Catholic Athletic Association (*New World*, August 26, 1910, p. 1).

29. *Pfarrbote*, February 1916, p. 6.

30. Philip Gleason, in *The Conservative Reformers* (South Bend: University of Notre Dame Press, 1968), persuasively argues this point. It was the appearance of the second generation that made the creation of these supraparochial organizations necessary (pp. 10–12).

31. *New World*, May 8, 1915, p. 1; July 7, 1914, p. 1; August 13, 1915, p. 1; June 9, 1916, p. 1.

32. *Pfarrbote*, June 1903, p. 10; July 1905, p. 9.

33. Ibid., January 1914; *New World*, April 21, 1915, p. 5.

34. Kalvelage, *Annals of St. Boniface*, p. 49.

35. Joseph Thompson, *The Archdiocese of Chicago, Antecedents and Development* (Des Plaines, Ill.: St. Mary's Training School Press, 1920), p. 361.

36. *Pfarrbote*, February 1915, pp. 36–37.

37. For an excellent survey, see James W. Sanders, *The Education of an Urban Minority: Catholics in Chicago, 1833–1965* (New York: Oxford University Press, 1977); Jay P. Dolan, ed., *The American Catholic Parish*, 2 vols. (New York: Paulist Press, 1987), 2:313–14.

38. Kalvelage, *Annals of St. Boniface*, pp. 1–6.

39. Valuable information on St. Boniface School was found at ASSF, including: Sister Cor Maria, O.S.F., *In the Service of Love: A Brief History of the Sisters of St. Francis of Mary Immaculate* (Joliet, Ill.), and Sister Helen Marie Beha, "Community History, 1865–1965" (Joliet, Ill., 1865).

40. Ruth Hernandez, "Women in the Labor Force: An Overview" (U.S. Department of Labor, 1986).

41. "Annals Boniface Mission," 1868; *Pfarrbote* 1917, p. 18.

42. Parish Annual Reports, 1888, AAChi. The parish annual reports indicate expenses of only $1,545 between the years 1886 and 1892.

43. German parochial schools grew from 2,700 students in 1870 to 14,311 in 1910. (Ironically, Polish enrollment began to rise dramatically after 1900—from 12,276 students in 1900 to 49,517 in 1930.) Sanders, *Education of an Urban Minority*, p. 45; *St. Augustine Pfarrbote*, September 1911, p. 9.

44. Interview, Mrs. Henry Hahn, Chicago, Ill., May 30, 1978; interview, Theresa Krutz, Chicago Historical Society, Chicago, Ill., August 20, 1978; *Pfarrbote*, June 1915, pp. 12–13.

45. *Pfarrbote*, September 1917, pp. 9–10.

46. From Sister M. Edith, O.S.F., to Sister Marie Ann, O.P., January 16, 1945, ASSF.

47. "Annals Boniface Mission," passim; Sister Marian Voelker, O.S.F., "It's

Hail and Farewell at St. Boniface," *Chicago Catholic* (in 1977 the *New World*, the archdiocesan newspaper, changed its name to the *Chicago Catholic;* in 1989 it became the *New World* again), November 15, 1985, p. 1. From Sister M. Alberta, O.S.F., to Father Clement Venn, January 9, 1891, ASSF.

48. *The People of Chicago: Who We Are and Who We Have Been* (Chicago: Department of Development and Planning, 1976), pp. 24, 37; *Pfarrbote*, June 1914, p. 5; Harold M. Mayer and Richard C. Wade, *Chicago: The Growth of a Metropolis* (Chicago: University of Chicago Press, 1969), pp. 212–18.

49. Mayer and Wade, *Chicago*, pp. 256–60.

50. *Pfarrbote*, January 1907, passim.

51. Letter from A. Evers to Archbishop Quigley, January 21, 1914, correspondence files, ACChi.

52. Kalvelage, *Annals of St. Boniface*, pp. 157–61.

53. Letter from Elizabeth A. Smyth to Father Evers, September 19, 1914, correspondence files, AAChi.

54. Letter from A. Evers to Archbishop Quigley, January 21, 1914; letter from A. Evers to Archbishop Mundelein, July 5, 1916, correspondence files, AAChi.

55. *New World*, October 30, 1914, p. 4; January 8, 1915, p. 3; February 12, 1915, p. 2; April 16, 1915, p. 3.

56. Townsend, "Germans of Chicago," pp. 113–15; 128–29; Shaw, *Catholic Parish*, pp. 62–65.

57. Mayer and Wade, *Chicago*, pp. 316–32.

58. Anthony J. Kuzniewski, S.J., "The Catholic Church in the Life of the Polish Americans," in *Poles in America, Bicentennial Essays*, ed. Frank Mocha (Stuart Point, Wis.: Wonzalla Publishing, 1978), pp. 400–401.

59. *People of Chicago*, 1870, 1900. On Poles in Chicago, see Edward R. Kantowicz, *Polish-American Politics in Chicago, 1880–1940* (Chicago: University of Chicago Press, 1975); and Joseph J. Parot, *Polish Catholicism in Chicago, 1850–1920* (DeKalb: Northern Illinois University Press, 1981).

60. William I. Thomas and Florian Znaniecki, *The Polish Peasant in Europe and America* (2d ed.; New York: Octagon Books, 1974), 2:203; 2:1521–24.

61. December 15, 1890, p. 2; as cited in Kantowicz, *Polish-American Politics*, 33.

62. Catholic church statistics by dioceses are found in the *Official Catholic Directory* (New York: P. J. Kenedy & Sons, 1886–). For Catholic statistics in Chicago, see Marvin Schafer, "The Catholic Church in Chicago, Its Growth and Administration" (Ph.D. diss., University of Chicago, 1929), map insert. Schafer estimates that 69 percent of West Town's Catholic population was Polish by 1920.

63. The NCWC inspired the foundation of forty-two national bishops' conferences and operates seven distinct departments. Most dioceses established diocesan councils for men and women, Catholic Charities, and other such organizations through the 1920s and 1930s. Dolan, *American Catholic Parish*, 2:239.

64. For the life of George Cardinal Mundelein, see Edward R. Kantowicz,

Corporation Sole: Cardinal Mundelein and Chicago Catholicism (Notre Dame: University of Notre Dame Press, 1982).

Mundelein saw the parochial school as "an anchor that steadies and holds the boat. A school will ensure the continuation of a parish more than anything else . . . more than that, it is the junior church." Cited in Mundelein's own memoirs, *Two Crowded Years* (Chicago: Extension Press, 1919), pp. 54–55.

65. *New World*, December 17, 1937, p. 5; *Chicago Herald-American*, July 12, 1940.

66. *Centennial Boniface*, n.p.; Kalvelage, *Annals of St. Boniface*, pp. 101–20, 103.

67. Letter from Archbishop Mundelein to Father C. A. Rempe, August 25, 1917; from C. A. Rempe to Archbishop Mundelein, August 27, 1917, correspondence files, AAChi.

68. *Centennial Boniface*, n.p.; *Pfarrbote*, September 1921.

69. Kalvelage, *Annals of St. Boniface*, p. 119.

70. Parish Annual Reports, 1917–31, AAChi.

71. Information on Father Rempe was scant: his pastoral letters have been lost, and only two parishioners could provide useful information on his life. In separate interviews conducted on October 30, 1990, in Chicago, Mr. Daniel Pasowicz and Mrs. Edward Eggler, both in their eighties, recalled that Father Rempe was a vigorous leader who tried to get people to join the church.

72. Pastoral letter, November 22, 1925. It is interesting that the sermons were in German and English for the nine years they were published; a Polish translation was provided after 1923.

73. Pastoral letter, December 1924.

74. Pastoral letters, December 21, 1919, April 6, 1924. In another letter, Rempe wrote: "The prosperity and happiness of a man is in proportion to his contribution to his church. More than that, God gives not only temporal but spiritual favors in the ratio of our generosity" (December 10, 1922).

75. *Pfarrbote*, April 16, 1925, passim.

76. Ibid., February 1924; July 1922. A history of these societies to 1926 is found in Kalvelage, *Annals of St. Boniface*, pp. 205–32. Daniel Pasowicz recalled that the boys' and girls' clubs were particularly vigorous at this time and attracted hundreds of young people to St. Boniface. (Interview, Daniel Pasowicz.)

77. *Pfarrbote*, February 1925; September 1921.

78. Ibid., January 1918; April 1923.

79. Ibid., November 1921; August 1915, p. 10.

80. Ibid., June 1917, June 1920. The 1922 celebration featured two German plays, an English play, and a potpourri of German music.

81. Ibid., June 1915; September 1921.

82. On the Eucharistic Congress and Chicago's ethnics, see my dissertation, "Chicago's Germans and Italians, 1903–1939: The Catholic Parish as a Way-Station of Ethnicity and Americanization" (Ph.D. diss., University of Chicago, 1981), pp. 184–96.

83. *Centennial Boniface; Pfarrbote,* December 1924, January 1925. In a letter to Rempe from the chancellor, Rempe was commended for his charitable work. As the chancellor noted: "I have personally been aware for some time of the very excellent work being done in your locality. I must admit however that I did not realize how extensive it was." From the chancellor to Father C. A. Rempe, June 3, 1930, correspondence files, AAChi.

84. The parish *Pfarrbote* abruptly stopped in 1926 but reemerged as a typical parish bulletin in 1968. Primary source material for Father Milcheski's era was reconstructed through personal interviews and archival material at the ASSF.

85. Mayer and Wade, *Chicago,* pp. 358–60; 344–52.

86. Census data for 1910–20 taken from Evelyn M. Kitagawa and Karl E. Tauber, eds., *Local Community Fact Book: Chicago Metropolitan Area, 1960* (Chicago: University of Chicago Press, 1963); data for 1930–40 taken from Louis Wirth and Eleanor H. Bernert, eds., *Local Community Fact Book of Chicago* (Chicago: Chicago Recreation Commission, 1938).

87. The parish annual reports (AAchi) from 1932 to 1956 indicate that the number of families at St. Boniface actually declined from 1932 to 1943 and then gradually began to increase, to 980, by 1956. The parochial school also increased to 485 students by 1956.

88. W. J. Madaj, "The First Cardinal of the Archdiocese of Chicago," *New World,* August 30, 1974, p. 8. Mundelein established only one German and one Italian parish during his tenure as archbishop.

89. Marie C. Buehrle, *The Cardinal Stritch Story* (Milwaukee: Bruce Publishing, 1959); W. J. Madaj, "The Second Cardinal of the Archdiocese of Chicago," *New World,* September 13, 1973, pp. 39–41.

90. The Cana Conference began in St. Louis, Missouri, in 1944. The Christian Family Movement was organized in Chicago in 1947 and soon spread throughout the country. By 1957, there were 25,000 CFM groups in the U.S.

91. "Annals Boniface Mission," 1934, 1940.

92. Interview, Father Stanley Rokicinski; see also *Centennial Boniface.*

93. Informal discussions with Sister Marian Voelker, O.F.M., June 1990, ASSF; "Annals Boniface Mission," 1923:35.

94. "Annals Boniface Mission," 1949.

95. *Centennial Boniface;* "St. Boniface Parish Views Past 100 Years of Service," *New World,* April 3, 1964, pp. 1–2.

96. *St. Boniface Parish Bulletin* (hereafter cited as *SBPB*), October 20, 1957.

97. Ibid., 19 February 1961.

98. Between 1950 and 1960, Chicago lost population to the suburbs, which grew from 3,550,404 inhabitants to 6,794,461. Mayer and Wade, *Chicago,* pp. 355, 376.

99. Ibid., pp. 432–42. Parishioner Daniel Pasowicz noted that his own coal business was destroyed when the Kennedy Expressway was opened. (Interview, Daniel Pasowicz.)

100. The Twenty-First Ecumenical Council opened on November 11, 1962.

The council set its seal on the chief movements of this century—the biblical movement, liturgical renewal, and the lay movement. The council was notable for its stress on ecumenism and its Christocentric foundation. Karl Rahner and Herbert Vorgrimler, *Concise Theological Dictionary* (London: Burns and Oates, 1965), pp. 478–79.

101. *SBPB*, June 3, 1968.

102. Interview, Father Stanley Rokicinski; "Annals Boniface Mission," November 11, 1959; 1963.

103. Interview, Father Stanley Rokicinski.

104. *SBPB*, June 1, 1968. Father John Hillenbrand came to St. Boniface as an assistant to Father Roth in 1970. He noted that Father Roth accepted a consultative style of leadership and shared his authority with Father Hillenbrand and Father Steven Chao. (Interview, Father John Hillenbrand, Chicago, October 30, 1990.)

105. *SPBP*, June 22, 1968. The dinner consisted of Polish sausage, sauerkraut, rye bread, and cheese-covered sweet breads.

106. An Italian Night was also held during Father Roth's pastorate, although there is little indication of a significant Italian presence at St. Boniface.

107. "History of St. Boniface," pp. 6–7. Father Roth was also instrumental in bringing the Cursillo movement into the parish. The Cursillo was a three-day weekend specifically designed to deepen parishioners' Catholic faith. See Dolan, *American Catholic Parish*, 2:250–53; 356.

108. *SBPB*, March 2, 1969; "Information from Pastors . . . to Srs. of St. Francis," 1969–70, ASSF. Roth realized that persons working at St. Boniface should be screened for their ability to work in an inner-city parish.

109. Letter from Father George Roth to Sister M. Francine, O.S.F., January 23, 1969 (ASSF).

110. Interview, Father Gratkowski.

111. On John Cardinal Cody, see Charles W. Dahm, *Power and Authority in the Catholic Church: Cardinal Cody in Chicago* (Notre Dame: University of Notre Dame Press, 1981).

112. Interview, Father Gratkowski.

113. According to an article in the *SBPB*, June 4, 1972, "they [the team ministry] will provide the type of leadership that the people of St. Boniface want and deserve—priests who respect their people, who listen to them, who are responsive to their needs." Father Hillenbrand noted that technically Father Stalzer was the administrator of the parish; but for all practical purposes it was a team ministry. The people felt that they got three pastors out of the deal. (Interview, Father Hillenbrand.)

114. "Community 21," May 1979 (mimeographed bulletin, ASSF). There is strong evidence that other parishes would not accept the Hispanics as Boniface did. When one young girl went to Holy Innocents to obtain a baptismal certificate, the priest noted that St. Boniface was the "junk parish" because they took anybody. The girl retorted, "That's right, it's the only Catholic parish around here." (Interview, Father Gratkowski.)

115. *SBPB,* April 21, 1974; December 1, 1974; April 27, 1975.

116. Interview, Father Gratkowski.

117. "Annals Boniface Mission," 1977. The pastoral team supported the school throughout this period, for the school was still seen as "the most substantial contribution our parish makes to the community" (*SBPB,* April 26, 1970).

118. "Merge St. Boniface School into St. Stanislaus Kostka's," *Chicago Catholic,* February 3, 1983; "Wrinkles Are There but Merger Works," *Chicago Catholic,* February 10, 1984, p. 14.

119. Sister Margaret Alice Martinek, who had served as teacher and principal at St. Boniface from 1973 to 1983, served as a pastoral associate until 1984. In 1985, the sisters announced at a parish staff meeting that they would leave St. Boniface after 118 years of service. Their parting letter read: "It is with greatest gratitude that we look back at all the years our sisters have served in your parish . . . yes, the list of Franciscans who taught at St. Boniface is long, and we are sad too that our ministry there has ended. But we promise that our prayers and love are not ended! You have shared so much life and goodness; you are a beautiful example of a true 'community of thanksgiving.'" (Mimeographed letter, ASSF.)

120. *SBPB,* June 15, 1958; March 1, 1959; April 26, 1959; May 3, 1959. Mrs. Eggler noted that Father Rocky "knew how to get along" with politicians and other community leaders. By placating them, he was able to get things done for the community. (Interview, Mrs. Eggler.)

121. "Annals Boniface Mission," 1964. Father Hillenbrand noted that the five Catholic parishes of the neighborhood formed their own subgroup within the NCO, Community 21. This community covered an area roughly equivalent to the area of the five parishes and acted as a neighboring planning committee. (Interview, Father Hillenbrand.)

122. Information on the sisters' contribution to the NCO found at ASSF.

123. On Father Perzanowski, see "History of St. Boniface," pp. 10–11. While Father Ted certainly adopted the spirit of Vatican II and enthusiastically served the parish, some parishioners felt that he unconsciously shifted the power of the parish back to himself. (Interview, Father Gratkowski.)

124. Interview, Sisters Mary Ellen Descourouez and Beatrice M. Samblanet, Chicago, June 15, 1990. T. P. Sweetser has written on this subject in "The Parish of the Future: Beyond the Programs," *America* 162 (March 10, 1990): 238–40. Sweetser maintains that the formation of such base communities is the hope for the revitalization of parish life in the U.S.

125. It should be noted that this was solely the point of view of Sisters Descourouez and Samblanet in their interview. Father Collins was unavailable for an interview.

126. Collins did continue to address ethnic religious needs through the celebration of the Mexican Posadas, the formation of charismatic prayer groups, and the development of the Rite of Christian Initiation for Adults (RCIA). See "History of St. Boniface," pp. 11–12.

127. Sister Cathy Campbell, "Cardinal Urges 'Sacrifice' for Sake of Future," *New World*, January 26, 1990, p. 1; Michael J. Behr, "Mixed Reaction Greets Back of the Yards Plan," *New World*, January 26, 1990, p. 2.

128. Interview, Srs. Descourouez and Samblanet.

129. Michael Hirsley and Jorge Casuso, "Hispanic Catholics Feel Pull of Protestant Fervor," *Chicago Tribune*, January 7, 1990, sec. 1, p. 1; "Troubled Hispanics Find Haven within Strict Pentecostal Rules," January 8, 1990, sec. 1, p. 1; and "Catholics Fighting Back to Hold on to Hispanics," January 9, 1990, sec. 1, p. 1.

SEVEN

¿Qué es esto? The Transformation of St. Peter's Parish, San Francisco, 1913–1990

Jeffrey M. Burns

ST. PETER'S CHURCH and St. Peter's parish are interwoven in the life of the vast majority of the Catholic men and women of the City of St. Francis."[1] So wrote one parish historian in 1920. A similar statement can be made in 1990, with one qualification. St. Peter's Church and St. Peter's parish are interwoven in the life of the vast majority of *Hispanic* men and women of la Ciudad de San Francisco. During the past eighty years, St. Peter's has changed dramatically—what was once the premier Irish parish in San Francisco is now the city's premier Hispanic parish. The transformation has not been without its difficulties and tensions, but throughout the period from 1913 to 1990, the genius of St. Peter's has been its ability to adapt and respond to the rapidly changing ethnic and social composition of the parish, and to make each new parishioner whether Irish, Italian, Latino, or Filipino feel at home at St. Peter's. It has inspired within each parishioner a sense of belonging, a sense that St. Peter's is his or her "own."

St. Peter's genius was put to the test not only by the parish's changing ethnic makeup, but also by the extraordinary changes that were occurring within American society during the 1960s, and within the Catholic Church as a result of the Second Vatican Council. As the 1960s progressed, as the parish sought to redefine itself in terms of its new ethnic groups, conflict arose over questions of what it meant to be American, and more importantly what it meant to be Catholic. Moreover, St. Peter's adjusted to these challenges within the well-defined structure of the Catholic Church.

A Catholic parish is not an isolated congregation; it is a subunit of the local archdiocesan church, guided by its archbishop, and of the international church, guided by the pope in Rome. Decisions made at levels beyond the parish will directly effect parish life. Change in the parish will not only be generated from within the community itself but will often have its source in these two bodies exterior to the local community. For instance, the Vatican's teaching on controversial issues such as birth control and divorce will affect the manner in which a parish deals with these problems. Basic doctrinal definitions emanate from Rome, not from the parish. The most significant impact an archdiocese makes on a parish is the appointment of a pastor. Clerical leadership originates outside the parish, not from within the community itself.

Equally as important, the parish has little control over who its members are. The territorial boundaries for St. Peter's are established by the archdiocese. Any Catholics living within these established boundaries are members of St. Peter's regardless of where they were baptized or confirmed. St. Peter's is not free to reject them. Nor do parishioners choose their own parish. They must go to the parish within whose boundaries they are living. The only exception to this rule is the "national parish." A national parish is a parish established to serve a particular ethnic group; it has no strict territorial boundaries. Thus, a German living within St. Peter's boundaries could choose to go to the German church rather than St. Peter's. In any case, membership at St. Peter's was dictated by forces beyond the parish.

St. Peter's genius has been its ability to incorporate a wide diversity of ethnic groups during a time of enormous turmoil. It has been able to respond effectively to local needs, while working within a larger church structure over which it has little control. Its genius has enabled it to hold all these diverse groups and interests together, and to invest in each parishioner a sense of belonging to and ownership of St. Peter's. St. Peter's has accomplished this task effectively through a combination of inspired clerical leadership and the hard work of countless men and women, lay and religious.

The Irish Enclave Parish, 1913–1960

St. Peter's was founded in 1867 in the heart of the Mission District of San Francisco. The Mission District is located in the southeastern part of the city, which surrounds the old Mission San Francisco de Asis. By 1900, the Mission District was a working-class, immigrant neighborhood peopled primarily by German and Irish families.[2] The Irish, working-class quality of the Mission increased with the Great Fire and Earthquake of 1906, which razed most of the downtown and South of Market areas of San Francisco, and sent refugees into the Mission, where many eventually resettled. St. Peter's served as a focal point in the post-earthquake period, serving as a general relief station, providing medical assistance, food, and clothing to the refugees, services which reinforced St. Peter's status in the community.

What characterized the inner Mission and St. Peter's parish after the earthquake and until the 1950s was its insulated quality. Urban geographer Brian Godfrey describes the area as having a "tightly knit, highly localized basis of community life."[3] Sister of Mercy M. Petronilla Gaul's memory of parish life in the 1910s and 1920s reinforces Godfrey's assessment; "The parish was the center of activity, and all our lives were tied up in the things that happened there. The families were very close. You knew everyone who went to church regularly."[4] All the social, religious, educational, and psychological needs were met right in the parish neighborhood, as were the material needs. Shops up and down 24th Street and Mission Street provided everything people in the Mission could want.[5] Longtime St. Peter's resident Warren Jenkins referred to St. Peter's and the Mission as an "encampment"; rarely was there need to venture beyond the parish boundaries.[6] Another resident called 24th Street a "Peterite village."[7] Local bars such as Pop's and the Green Lantern acted as neighborhood social clubs, where "everyone knew everyone else." The St. Francis Creamery, founded in 1918 (and still in operation) became a hangout for the nonalcoholically inclined.[8] Or one might drop in for a chat with "Sandy, the Barber," who rented his shop from St. Peter's, or for a counseling session with assistant pastor Nicholas Farana (at St. Peter's from 1945 to 1955), who could often be found in Sandy's chair. In short, St. Peter's and the surrounding Mission neighborhood provided a warm, nurturing place to live and raise a family, an environment insulated from an outside world which often seemed harsh and cruel. Another former resident of the Mission remembers the 1940s and 1950s, "We were dominated completely by family and church and we were absolutely secure. Everyone of our relatives from both sets of grandparents to each of our many cousins lived within walking distance of each other's houses. We were Irish Catholics, mostly civil service employees. . . . Our neighborhood was our world."[9]

Part of the security lay in the Irishness of St. Peter's and the Mission. By 1913, St. Peter's was operating as an unofficial Irish national parish. Three blocks south of St. Peter's, St. Anthony's had been established as a German national parish in 1893, and in 1912, just two blocks south of St. Anthony's, Immaculate Conception was established as an Italian national parish. St. Peter's became the Irish parish, a fact reinforced by its beloved Irish pastor Peter Casey (1879–1913). Moreover, the Mission

District had a distinctively Irish, working-class air. Historians Robert Cherny and William Issel write, "[From the 1910s] until World War II, many Mission residents were consciously Irish, often consciously working class, and very conscious of being residents of 'the Mish.'"[10] Not surprisingly, the Mission was the birthplace of over half the city's unions.[11]

With the death of Father Casey in 1913, a pastor perfectly suited to the Mission was named to St. Peter's, Irishman Peter C. Yorke. (Yorke had previously served as an assistant to Casey from 1901 to 1903.) Yorke, an extraordinary orator and writer, had achieved citywide fame in the 1890s by "vanquishing" the anti-Catholic American Protective Association (APA) as editor of the archdiocesan newspaper, *The Monitor.* His mythic status grew in 1901 as he championed the unions in the teamster strike of 1901, serving as spiritual adviser and major spokesman and publicist for the strikers. In 1902, he founded and would continue to edit until his death the Irish newspaper *The Leader,* which avidly supported the movement for a free and sovereign Irish republic. Yorke then, was ideally suited for St. Peter's and the Mission—the defender of Catholicism against hostile attackers, the champion of labor, and the pro-Irish advocate. One historian concludes, "Yorke was undeniably one of their [the Irish] own and they gloried in his attack on employers and religious bigots. They liked his style. He was a fighter and they could vicariously share in his victories over the respectables."[12]

From 1913 to 1960, St. Peter's reveled in its Irishness, celebrating Irish culture and nationalism and reflecting an unmistakably Irish ethos. The parish sponsored frequent Irish cultural events including classes in Irish dancing and music, in Gaelic, and in Irish history. In 1921, parents were encouraged to enroll their children in a Gaelic dancing class so "young Irish Americans may be brought up with the soul that is marching the men of Erin to victory today."[13] The familiar melodies of "old Irish airs" were common at parish dances and socials. This promotion of Irish culture was reinforced by several nonparochial Irish organizations, which offered similar courses and to which many parishioners belonged: the Knights of the Red Branch, the Irish Volunteers, the Ancient Order of Hibernians, and others. The Irish societies provided nonstop social outlets—dances, musical entertainments, and picnics.

The greatest parish and local celebration was St. Patrick's Day, honoring the patron saint of Ireland (and the copatron of the archdiocese of San Francisco). In the 1920s, because of Yorke's intimacy with the United Irish Societies, St. Peter's was the focal point of several city-wide celebrations. One typical St. Patrick's Day began with a high mass at St. Peter's, complete with Gaelic sermon and with the Irish "tricolor" hung proudly in the church beside the American flag.[14] Before the mass, the Irish societies paraded through the streets from Hibernian Hall to the church. The celebration culminated in the evening with a dinner dance and musical entertainment featuring Irish music. After Yorke's death, St. Peter's observed the day more modestly, but it remained a major parish event through the 1950s.[15]

What especially aroused the Irish fervor of St. Peter's parishioners was the cause of Irish freedom. In their battle against Great Britain, Irish republicans had no greater friends than Father Peter C. Yorke and the San Francisco Irish. In 1919, Irish leader Eamon de Valera made a triumphal tour of San Francisco, ushered around the city by Father Yorke. When the Irish Republic conducted a bond drive to raise funds to assist in its struggle for freedom, St. Peter's parishioners gave freely (Yorke himself gave $500), "without expectation of immediate return."[16] In 1920, the Friends of Irish Freedom, in which Yorke had been active, merged with the American Association for an Irish Republic to form the American Association for the Recognition of the Irish Republic (AARIR). Yorke was appointed California director of the association, and traveled the state stirring up enthusiasm for the cause of Irish freedom as defined by de Valera. In 1921, a branch of the AARIR was established at St. Peter's. Even St. Peter's High School did its part, sponsoring an essay contest on "Why the United States should recognize the Irish Republic."[17]

Irish nationalism, however, was intimately joined with being a good American. "The cause of Ireland is the cause of America,"[18] Yorke declared. At another Gaelic society meeting, he began, "I come tonight as an American citizen speaking to other Americans."[19] American ideals dictated support of a free Irish republic. Yorke's affirmation of his Americanism reflected a lingering suspicion in American society of Irish patriotism and loyalty to America.

The Irish quality at St. Peter's went beyond sponsoring Irish cultural and political events; St. Peter's was encompassed by an Irish ethos that combined varied elements of defensiveness, sacrificial piety, and civic involvement. Despite having "made it" in San Francisco by 1920, St. Peter's Irish maintained a defensive attitude toward an American society that regarded the combination of Irish and Catholic as doubly suspicious. The battle with the APA in the 1890s had become an integral part of the collective psyche of the San Francisco Irish. The rise of the Ku

Klux Klan in the 1920s, and the KKK-backed Oregon School Bill, did nothing to ease the Irish sense of defensiveness. The Irish regarded themselves as a besieged minority buffeted by such real villains as conniving anti-Catholics, scheming employers, and the false prophets of materialism and godlessness.[20] The struggle was simply a manifestation of the cosmic struggle between good and evil. Yorke reminded his people, "The Church of Christ was built as a beleaguered city against whose adamantine walls the gates of hell forever rage."[21] This was preaching the San Francisco Irish could understand.

To remain faithful in the struggle required sacrifice, and a deep strain of sacrificial piety runs through the Irish ethos. Sin and guilt were realities that had to be expiated through appropriate penances.[22] Prayer was essential, and every Irish child knew his or her prayers. Children were exhorted to "offer up" their sufferings in reparation for their sins. Frequent confession was encouraged. Respect for priests, sisters, and all things holy was demanded. At the name of Jesus every head would bow. Every action, no matter how small, brought one closer to or further away from God and Heaven. Yorke instructed, "Every deed we do, every word, every thought, has its eternal consequences."[23] The Catholic had to be forever on guard against temptation and the allures of a comfortable life. Yorke confided to his diary, "I think I must scrap the big chair" (his easy chair), as it was leading to a "lack of spirit of sacrifice, mortification and self control."[24] Long-time parishioner Warren Jenkins, related an incident from the 1920s that reflects how deeply the ethos permeated Irish culture. While his class was praying the rosary, two big Irish policemen burst into the room to pick up a youthful offender. When they realized the rosary was being prayed, they stopped, took off their caps, and joined in the concluding decades of the rosary, before hauling the offender off.[25] The rosary was the more important duty.

A corollary to the notion of prayer and sacrifice was the parishioners' devotion and love for the Sisters of Mercy and the Christian Brothers, whose lives personified prayer and sacrifice. Both orders won the hearts of countless students by their dedicated teaching. Vocations to both orders were common. The Sisters particularly endeared themselves to the parish by their selfless service during two great traumas—the fire and earthquake of 1906, and the influenza epidemic of 1918. The love and devotion of the Sisters and Brothers for the parish, and of the parishioners for the Sisters and Brothers, was a vital part of the St. Peter's ethos through the 1950s.

Prayer and sacrifice alone were not enough. The Catholic also had to know how to defend his or her faith from hostile attacks. To this end, Yorke wrote a textbook, *Apologetics* (though he died before finishing the text, it was completed several years later by an assistant at St. Peter's), that was used at St. Peter's High School. Yorke opined, "As our circumstances require not only the positive knowledge of our religion but also an acquaintance with answers to the common objections against it, there is need of emphasizing questions in dispute."[26] The *Apologetics* text would fill this need.

Despite the insulated quality of neighborhood life in St. Peter's and the Mission, the parish made its presence known in the city. One final element of the Irish ethos was a deep involvement in the civic life of San Francisco. Yorke, of course, was a major player in civic affairs, but he was not alone. Countless parishioners and alumni of St. Peter's were employed by City Hall. Many worked at civil service jobs; others became part of the police or fire departments. "Peterites," as they called themselves, could be found at every level of civic affairs. Service to the city provided a sure means of advancement for the Irish immigrant community. Though Yorke's successor, Ralph Hunt, was not as visible in civic affairs as Yorke had been, the number of Peterites "downtown" remained quite high.

Despite Yorke's penchant for the limelight, he took his pastoral responsibilities seriously, performing what he called "the humdrum duties of the Church's daily life"[27]—hearing confessions, visiting the sick, counseling the troubled, or visiting the school. Though a great deal has been written on Yorke, most writers have neglected Yorke the pastor. Yorke's eulogist in the *San Francisco Leader* did not, "[Yorke's] chief concern was always his parish. He was the good pastor. He knew his sheep and they knew him. He trained the children to know and love our Lord—to come close to him. He was an inspiration to the young men and women who came under his influence, a safe counselor to the old, and a messenger of mercy at the bed of death."[28] Yorke would greet his parishioners on his daily evening walk through the parish with his good friend and assistant, Father Ralph Hunt. Yorke was loved by his parishioners, though he was regarded with "awe" by many, especially the school children.[29]

Indeed, Yorke was held in such esteem by his Irish parishioners that it is difficult to determine where the man ends and the myth begins. Stories of his goodness are legion.[30] But Yorke was not without his faults. A man of strong ego, he was quick to take offense, and readily engaged in conflict. At various times he sparred with other local Irish leaders—Archbishop P. W. Riordan, Mayor and then Senator James D. Phelan, Garret McEnerney, attorney for the archdiocese, and Father D. O. Crowley, head of the Catholic Youth Directory, as well as others. Within his parish though, there is little evidence of conflict. Yorke's own attitude toward the laity indicates that he would brook little dissent. "By divine appointment the clergy rules. . . . There is a Church teaching and a Church taught. To the Church taught the laity belongs."[31] Despite this attitude, Yorke was loved by his Irish working-class parishioners. He lifted them beyond their isolated social position, and as one historian notes, "He made them proud to be Catholics."[32]

Like many pastors of his day, Yorke was a builder, obsessed with providing a complete parish plant.[33] Although Father Casey "bequeathed to his successor a parish, well equipped in everything necessary to carry on the work of religion,"[34] Yorke felt compelled to build additions to the school and rectory, and to build a new parish hall (St. Anne's, 1924). By the end of Yorke's pastorate the parish had a church that seated over 800, a girls' grade and high school, a boys' grade and high school, a convent, a rectory, and a hall. Nonetheless, Yorke's successor, Hunt, built additional classrooms for the school. The successful pastor had to build.

Along with building, came a parish debt. Operating two large schools added to the ordinary operating expenses of the parish. As in most parishes, fund-raising became an integral part of parish life. One regular fund-raiser hosted by the ladies of St. Peter's was the weekly "whist" card games. They became a standard feature of life at St. Peter's through the 1950s. Prior to the 1930s, the parish sponsored a major fund-raiser which took the form of a festival or bazaar. In 1917, St. Peter's rented the Civic Auditorium for two weeks to host their Golden Jubilee Bazaar. Thousands attended. In 1925, the parish held a week-long Harvest Festival. In the late 1930s, an annual festival was established. Though more modest than the major bazaars, the festivals provided the parish with additional yearly income. Significantly, a number of St. Peter's fund-raisers took place in major city arenas: the Civic Auditorium, the Mechanic's Pavilion, the St. Francis Hotel, and the Fairmont Hotel. The locations reflected St. Peter's position in the city.

Fund-raisers did more than merely retire the parish debt. By providing frequent parish socials, and a common cause for which to work, they also raised parish morale. Parishioners who worked and participated in the fund-raisers felt they were contributing to the well-being of the parish. The parish became more their own. Moreover, fund-raising was the

7.1 View of St. Peter's Church, c. 1946. Courtesy of the Archives of the Archdiocese of San Francisco.

major area of lay involvement. Though the pastor might "rule" his parish, it was the laity who paid the bills. Again, in seeing the tangible results (church, school, etc.) of their efforts, the congregation felt the parish to be more their own.

Besides building and fund-raising, the parish's main areas of concern during the 1913–60 period were education, liturgy, and devotions, with the latter reaching its greatest activity during the 1940s and 1950s. Participation in these three areas increased the parishioners' sense of belonging to St. Peter's. Integral to the parish even before 1913 were the parish schools. In 1913, the parish was operating a girls' elementary school with close to 500 students, begun in 1878 and staffed by the Sisters of Mercy. The Sisters also conducted a four-year girls' high school, with a separate two-year commercial department in which young women of the parish were taught bookkeeping, shorthand, typing, and other commercial skills. The parish also had a boys' elementary school, founded in 1886 and staffed by the Christian Brothers, with an enrollment of close to 400. By 1924, Yorke had added a four-year boys' high school, though enrollment was never very large. These schools were faithfully supported by the parish, which always considered the schools "the pride of St. Peter's,"[35] an attitude which has persisted to 1990.

The emphasis on the school bore abundant fruit for the parish, as St. Peter's alumni were faithful and loyal participants in and supporters of the parish and the school (even after they had left the parish). By the 1920s, St. Peter's girls' academy had an active alumnae club that met at least once a year for a mass and social.

St. Peter's dedication to Catholic schooling was reinforced by Yorke, who had a reputation as an innovative educator. He was one of the "founding fathers" of the National Catholic Educational Association, and served several years as its vice president.[36] He operated as the unofficial superintendent of Catholic schools in San Francisco, vigorously promoting teachers' institutes and workshops to upgrade the teaching quality in Catholic schools. His successor, Ralph Hunt, was the first superintendent of Catholic schools in San Francisco (1916–25), and like Yorke served as vice president of the NCEA.

Yorke's greatest contribution to Catholic education was a series of religion textbooks, which were adopted for use throughout the archdiocese. The textbooks were innovative in a number of ways. Yorke was unhappy with the *Baltimore Catechism*, the standard, approved catechism for the American Catholic Church, because it was ungraded. Yorke corrected this by arranging the material in the catechism according to grade level. A first grader could not be expected to digest the same material as an eighth grader. In addition, Yorke added scriptural passages and Bible stories, insisting that knowledge of scripture was integral to Catholic education. He also included illustrations, reproductions of classic paintings, claiming that art was an effective teaching tool.[37] Before publishing the textbooks, Yorke personally tested the lessons in his parish school. During his tenure at St. Peter's, Yorke was a frequent visitor to the classroom, where he would often teach a religion lesson. This practice was continued by Ralph Hunt. Both pastors got to know the students in their schools quite well, and the students got to know them.

Besides his grade-school texts, Yorke also wrote several high-school textbooks. While at St. Peter's, at the request of Archbishop Edward Hanna, Yorke developed a syllabus of religion for high-school students to be used in the high schools in the archdiocese. Again he tested his syllabus on St. Peter's students.

Education was always a top priority at St. Peter's. The devotion of the parish to the Catholic school resulted, in part, from its Irish-Catholic defensiveness. Catholic schools were necessary because of the inadequacy of the public schools. At best, public schools were inadequate because they neglected the central factor in the development of the child, namely, religion. Religion was replaced by "statism." At worst, the public school could be aggressively and unapologetically anti-Catholic. In 1923, Yorke wrote, "The intolerant character of the first public school teachers and demand that the children of immigrants should be decatholicized before they could be considered good Americans was the rule rather than the exception."[38] Catholic schools were a necessary correction to the aberrations of the public school. From a positive standpoint, the Catholic school was necessary to properly instruct the parish's children in the Catholic faith and to instill in them the discipline of religion, thereby enabling them to build a more Christian social order.

For Yorke, Hunt, and for St. Peter's, the primary duty of the Catholic pastor and the Catholic parish was to provide for the Catholic education of its children. The ideal was "every Catholic child in a Catholic school."[39] Yorke wrote, "The school is as necessary as the Church, nay more necessary. You can say Mass in a vacant lot, you can shrive penitents in a barn, but it is only in a well equipped parochial school that you can preach the word of God effectively to . . . children."[40] Further, Yorke asserted, "The parish school is the cornerstone of the Church. . . . [It teaches children] the only lesson of importance in the world—to know, love, and serve God is first and above all the reason for their existence."[41] The Catholic school was not only a duty, it produced splendid benefits for the parish, not the least of which were loyal, disciplined parishioners, who supported the parish and worked for its good.

Besides producing loyal parishioners, the Catholic schools provided much for the social life of the parish. Musical "pageants" put on by the schoolchildren were frequent occurrences, as were class plays. Each year the senior class presented a play. In the late 1930s, the high-school and parish alumni put on "minstrel shows." Beyond entertainment, the

schools' athletic teams provided a source of parish pride and entertainment. In a variety of ways, the schools were central to the life of
St. Peter's.

Yorke did not limit his efforts to the Catholic school. While close to
50 percent of the Catholic children in the neighborhood did attend the
parish school, a figure 10 percent higher than the archdiocesan average,[42] the other 50 percent did not. They too had to receive a Catholic
education. When Yorke arrived at St. Peter's he found a Sunday school
program for public-school children that met only once a week, a program he found woefully deficient. Yorke reorganized the Sunday school
program and hired two Holy Family Sisters to run it.[43] He drew up a
course of instruction divided into four levels: (1) communion class, (2) in-
termediate, (3) confirmation class, and (4) postconfirmation. Levels 1,
2, and 4 met once during the school week, and the confirmation class
met three times a week. All four levels met on Saturday morning from 9
to 10:50 A.M. All instruction during the week was conducted by the Holy
Family Sisters.[44] On Saturday, the Sisters were assisted by a "corps of
volunteers," who were themselves instructed at night classes during the
week.[45] Under Yorke, no child would lack the opportunity of receiving
proper instruction in the Catholic faith.

Integral to Yorke's educational outlook was his belief that the liturgy
had an important educative function. In 1901, while an assistant at St.
Peter's, Yorke inaugurated what came to be an essential part of St. Peter's
parish life, the Children's Mass. All the children in St. Peter's boys' and
girls' schools were required to attend the 8:30 A.M. mass on Sunday (in
later years, 9:00 A.M.), and "woe betide you if you were absent."[46] To
assist the children's understanding of the mass, Yorke printed a small
pamphlet entitled, *Hymns and Prayers for the Children's Mass*. The booklet
printed the various prayers of the mass in English, from the prayers at .
the foot of the altar to the final prayers. Then, while the priest offered
the prayers of the mass in Latin, a reader at the back of the church (usually a Christian Brother) recited the priest's lines in English; the boys
and girls, sitting on opposite sides of the church, then recited the responses in English, with the boys and girls alternating lines. The English
responses continued until the Sanctus; the children then remained silent
until after the Elevation. In addition to the English responses, the children sang appropriate hymns at various parts of the mass, concluding
with a hymn of thanksgiving. The communion hymn was always an
"anthem to the Blessed Virgin Mary,"[47] and one hymn was always sung
in Latin. Hymns such as "Regina Coeli," "Hail, Holy Queen," and

"Holy God, We Praise Thy Name," were popular. To assist with the singing, Yorke published another small booklet, *Hymns for the Children's Mass*. Yorke believed printed materials were essential to intelligent participation at mass. Each child was required to have his or her "little Mass book" with them at each Children's Mass. If they forgot it, they were given another and charged ten cents.[48]

To ensure that the Children's Mass went smoothly, Yorke instituted another weekly ritual, Friday afternoon liturgy practice. Every Friday the schoolchildren assembled in the church to be drilled in the proper responses to the mass. Yorke also used this time to instruct the children on the different liturgical seasons, or on the meaning of the hymns or of the priest's vestments. The St. Peter's child came to understand the meaning of Christian symbols and of the different sections of the church building. Before First Holy Communion and again before confirmation Yorke took the candidates on a tour of the sanctuary and sacristy to make them more familiar with these holy places. Yorke's insistence on understanding, participation, use of the vernacular, congregational singing, and the use of printed materials made him a pioneer in the liturgical movement in the United States.[49] The Friday practice for the Children's Mass became a standard feature of St. Peter's life through 1950.

Intelligent participation in the liturgy was not limited to children. By the time a child graduated from high school, Yorke believed, he or she should be able to follow and understand the mass in Latin with the assistance of a missal. Yorke wrote, "The faithful assisting at Mass are not mere passive spectators, for they too have a real part in offering the Holy Sacrifice. . . . The use of the missal at Mass is to be strongly recommended."[50] One way to involve the faithful in the liturgy was through congregational singing, which Yorke encouraged at St. Peter's masses. In typical Yorke fashion, he had a hymnbook printed to enable the congregation to assist with the singing at mass and devotions.[51]

Besides encouraging active participation in the mass, Yorke sought to provide his people with a rich devotional life. The sodality was the basic organization for encouraging parish piety.[52] Sodalities were organized at every age-level: the Infant Sodality for the lower grades, followed by the Holy Angels Sodality for the middle grades, the Children of Mary for the upper grades, the Young Ladies Sodality for high-school girls, the St. Anne's Confraternity for adult women, the Gentlemen's Sodality (later the Holy Name Society) for adult men. The goal of all the sodalities was to make "practical Catholics." Each sodality recited a set of prayers at their meetings; for the older children and adults the "little office of the Blessed Virgin Mary" was used. The St. Anne's Confraternity would meet at least one Sunday a month for group communion. As the *Leader* reflected, "What could be grander or more inspiring than five or six hundred women receiving Holy Communion in a body?"[53]

During the 1920s, the parish aggressively recruited members for the sodalities. Yorke confided to his diary, "If we could rebuild the [St. Anne's Confraternity], it would be worth much to the parish."[54] Aggressive drives resulted in doubling the membership of the St. Anne's Confraternity in the 1920s, and in greatly increasing enrollment in the Gentlemen's Sodality. By 1936, 470 women were enrolled in the St. Anne's Confraternity, 170 men in the Holy Name Society, 200 young men in the Junior Holy Name Society, 180 young women in the Young Ladies Sodality, and 500 members in the children's sodalities.[55] In a parish of approximately 7,000 people, 22 percent were officially enrolled in a sodality. Besides inspiring devotion, the sodalities also operated as social clubs and agents of charity. The St. Anne's Confraternity and the Young Ladies Sodality assisted the poor by providing clothing and other necessities. They also sponsored card parties, lectures, and socials. In sum, the sodalities attempted to organize the parish devotional and social life at every age-level. The effect was to improve the individual's personal prayer life while further incorporating the sodalist into the life of the parish.

The parish also hosted a whole series of devotions based on the liturgical seasons: devotions to Mary in May, to Mary through the rosary in October, to the Holy Souls in November, and special devotions in Advent and Lent. Lent inspired a whole series of devotions, most importantly, the Stations of the Cross, in which the participants meditated on the suffering of Jesus on his way to Calvary. The stations were offered at least twice a week during Lent. Special stations were conducted for public-school children at 1:30 P.M. on Sundays. In addition, a series of weekly sermons were preached during Lent. Lenten devotions culminated with the "Tre Ore," or Three Hours devotion, on Good Friday, commemorating the three hours Jesus spent on the Cross. Sermons were preached that were meditations on the Passion of Jesus. Good Friday concluded with the Stations of the Cross in the evening, and another major sermon.

Several devotions were not tied to any one season but were offered throughout the year. Each Sunday the parish would host afternoon and evening devotions consisting of prayers, sermon, and Benediction. An important devotion during this era was the adoration of Jesus in the

Blessed Sacrament. Once a year, Forty Hours Devotions were held, in which Jesus, present in the host, was displayed in an elaborate golden monstrance for forty hours over the course of the three days for adoration, prayer, and reflection. A series of congregational prayers and devotions would be held at various times during the Forty Hours. More regular was the weekly Holy Hour, usually held on Fridays, which consisted of prayers, a sermon, and concluded with exposition of the Blessed Sacrament. Other recurrent devotions included triduums (devotions held on three consecutive days), and novenas (devotions held on nine consecutive days). The triduum and the novena became essential parts of St. Peter's piety through 1960. By the 1920s, several triduums and novenas were established that became annual parish events: the triduum in honor of St. Anne (later it became a novena), the triduum in preparation for the Immaculate Conception (December 8), and the school novena to Our Lady of Lourdes. Triduums and novenas could also be used to ask special favors. For instance, when Yorke fell ill in 1925, the children were told that "we will storm heaven with our prayers."[56] Part of the storming was a novena to the Little Flower, St. Therese of Lisieux, a devotion then in vogue as a result of the Little Flower's recent beatification. In addition, triduums were offered for other needs, especially for vocations.

The most sacred space outside the church, and a center of a number of parish devotions at St. Peter's, was the grotto.[57] The grotto was a re-creation of the Blessed Mother's apparition to a young French girl, Bernadette, at Lourdes, France. No parish celebration or devotion was complete without a visit to the grotto. One tradition, the celebration of First Holy Communion on Thanksgiving Day, included a "pilgrimage" to the grotto in the morning before the mass. Each May and at various times during the year, the children would gather at the grotto in the morning for prayers.[58] The triduum in honor of the Immaculate Conception concluded with the crowning of Mary Immaculate at the grotto. In May, Mary would also be crowned Queen of Heaven.

One final aspect of parish devotional life was the parish mission, held at least every two years at St. Peter's. The mission was a form of parish revival.[59] A religious order, such as the Redemptorists, Dominicans, or Franciscans, would conduct a series of nightly sermons over the course of a two-week period. The first week was devoted to the women, the second to the men, with the children's mission conducted during the day. In the 1930s, the missions were often conducted by the Archdiocesan Mission Band, which was stationed at St. Peter's rectory.[60] The main thrust of the mission was to exhort the people "to live practical Catholic lives."[61] In the 1920s, the missions encouraged enrollment in the sodalities, but success at a mission was judged by the number of confessions and communions it inspired. The 1921 mission was judged a success as 6,000 received communion over the two-week period.[62] The missions were always well attended, considered by most parishioners as "a rousing good time."[63] The quality of the mission sermons was better than the typical Sunday sermon, and definitely more entertaining. The women's mission was always better attended, with "every pew filled," as a 1941 report noted. However, "The other sex is not so devout, but will undoubtedly be more so before the week is closed,"[64] if the mission achieved its desired effect. The mission then, was to rekindle the faith of the parishioners and to inspire them to greater involvement in the social and spiritual life of the parish.

The whole thrust of St. Peter's educational, liturgical, and devotional programs was to create "practical Catholics," and to reinforce the close-knit quality of St. Peter's life, by investing in each parishioner a sense of ownership of and responsibility for the parish. Yorke's description of the proper end of religious education can also be seen as the proper end of parish life: "good conduct must be established, the Sacraments must be frequented, Mass must be attended, prayers must be said regularly, and according to their age, all those habits or practices must be inculcated that in after years will be the mainstay of an upright life."[65] And it was the parish's duty to provide the structures within which these habits could be inculcated.

In 1925, Yorke died and was replaced by his close friend and long-time assistant, Father Ralph Hunt.[66] What most distinguished Hunt's pastorate was his promotion and perpetuation of the memory and spirit of Father Peter C. Yorke. Hunt evoked the memory of Yorke as a symbol to unite the parish, as well as to inspire the parishioners to maintain the ideals that Yorke held dear. Hunt's personal devotion to Yorke is best symbolized by the fact that, after Yorke's death, Hunt left the former pastor's rooms in the rectory untouched for twenty-four years, preserving them as a shrine to his fallen hero.[67] As Father Nick Farana, an assistant to Hunt, put it, Hunt "submerged himself in the shadow of his ideal, Peter Yorke."[68] On a practical level, Hunt sought to maintain the programs begun by his predecessor. As the parish historian in the *San Francisco Leader* observed in 1931, Hunt "has faithfully maintained the traditions in the parish that were begun by Father Yorke."⁶⁹ The memory of Yorke became an integral part of the identity of St. Peter's parishioners.

The two most significant developments during Hunt's pastorate both involved the perpetuation of Yorke's spirit and memory: the Yorke Memorial Campaign and the Yorke Memorial Mass. After the pastor's death, friends initiated the Yorke Memorial Campaign, whose purpose was to raise a million dollars to build a tuition-free Catholic high school for boys in the Mission District. Half of the money would be used to build the school; the other half would be used as an endowment to keep the school tuition-free. After an initial burst of enthusiasm in which close to $250,000 was pledged, including $30,000 plus from the parishioners of St. Peter's, and pledges from several San Francisco unions and Irish societies, the campaign fizzled out. The money that was raised was placed in trust with the Hibernia Bank as custodian. For many years, Hunt and Hibernia vice president John McArdle monitored the fund. While enough money was never raised to build a high school, the campaign did raise enough money to provide St. Peter's boys with a tuition-free high-school education. When the parish high school closed in 1952, the funds were used to assist St. Peter's parishioners in attending other archdiocesan high schools. This practice began eating into the capital, and in 1961 the remainder of the fund, $190,000, was used in the construction of a new St. Peter's elementary school, dedicated in 1963 to the memory of Father Yorke.⁷⁰

More important was the Yorke Memorial Mass. Begun in 1927, the mass became one of the major yearly celebrations of the parish and of the city's Irish. Each year on Palm Sunday, the day Yorke had died, various state and local dignitaries, union leaders, members of the United Irish Societies, schoolchildren, sodality members, and many others would assemble for high mass at St. Peter's at 11:00 A.M. After the mass, the whole contingent would make a pilgrimage to Holy Cross Cemetery in Colma (south of San Francisco) to the grave of Father Yorke. At the grave site, a series of commemorative speeches would extol the life and ideals of Father Yorke. Such dignitaries as Eamon de Valera, Mayor and then Governor James Rolph, and Mayor Angelo Rossi, appeared over the years to give speeches. Each year a St. Peter's student would receive the honor of reciting the poetic tribute to Yorke, "Rest, Warrior Priest": "the priest with the heart of the warrior bold, rest now for the battle is ended."⁷¹ In addition a mixture of "sacred and patriotic songs" would be sung. In 1938, "Come, Holy Ghost," was followed by the national anthem.[72] But whatever the festivities, the entire proceedings were to recall to mind, as one speaker in 1961 put it, "the lasting fruits of the work of Father Yorke."[73] The memorial had the desired effect on St. Peter's parishioners, as Jack Bourne remembered: "We learned to respect what he was."[74] Beyond merely celebrating Yorke, the memorial was an event which strengthened the ties of the groups Yorke represented—the Irish, Catholics, the working class, labor. For those who had moved beyond St. Peter's and the Mission, the memorial was a way of rekindling their ties with the parish and community.

The spirit of Yorke promoted by Hunt, reinforced St. Peter's sense of its own specialness. Parishioners referred to St. Peter's as "the Vatican of San Francisco." Even parishioners who had moved from the parish always considered themselves Peterites, regardless of their new parish.

During the 1930s and 1940s a large number of Italians became part of St. Peter's, providing the Irish parish with an Italian flavor. Italians had always been present in the parish, but had belonged to Immaculate Conception parish, which was an Italian national parish. However, Immaculate Conception did not have a grade school until 1957, and many Italians sent their children to St. Peter's schools, while they received their sacraments at Immaculate Conception. Nonetheless, involvement in the school drew Italians into a vital segment of St. Peter's parish life. The national restriction of immigration in 1924, which discriminated against Italians, slowed the growth of the foreign-born community in the Mission. By 1936, second-generation immigrants exceeded the number of first-generation immigrants at St. Peter's for the first time in its history.[75] Second- and third-generation Italians were less inclined to attend the Italian national parish, and so became involved with St. Peter's. The "Americanized" Italians blended well with St. Peter's stress on education, devotion, and community life. By 1950 the close-knit community of St. Peter's, of which the Italians had become a part, was on the verge of a turbulent era that would disrupt and transform the parish that people had known under Yorke and Hunt.

The Transition, 1950–1964

In 1950, old St. Peter's and the old Mission were changing. The upcoming transition, however, did not seem readily apparent to the Irish and Italian community. The appointment of Father Timothy Hennessy, whom one parishioner described as "100 percent Irish,"[76] to replace the revered Father Hunt, seemed to promise a preservation of the status quo. The parish priorities would remain the school, the traditional devotions, and the maintenance of the spirit of Father Yorke. Above all, the parish would retain its Irish tint, albeit with Italian shadings. Unfortunately, events in the Mission would soon eclipse these well-laid expectations.

An incident in 1953 proved to be a harbinger of the oncoming disruption of parish life. In that year, the traditional parish minstrel show, performed by the students and alumni, and directed by a Christian Brother, was picketed by a civil rights group, who felt the minstrel show demeaned black people. Such accusations seemed unfair to parishioners. The 1950 program asserted, "though our cast 'blackens up' in our *Minstrel Melodies*, we have never tried to offend colored people but wish to sing and laugh with them." [77] In reality, a deep if at times unconscious, undercurrent of racism ran through the Irish community that would be the source of continued problems as the complexion of the parish and neighborhood darkened. Typical of the early 1950s, the Christian Brother director felt vindicated when it was uncovered that the picketers had "communist connections." [78] However, a gentle letter from the assistant superintendent of Catholic schools, Monsignor John Foudy, suggested it was time for the parish to move on to other types of entertainments and fund-raisers, and the minstrel shows came to an end. [79] One final irony: the patroness of the minstrel shows, chosen in 1948, was Our Lady of Guadalupe! In her honor, a statue of the Latin American patroness was placed in the Brothers' gardens. Unbeknownst to the minstrel players, they had provided an excellent welcome mat for the incoming Mexican and Central American people.

The 1950s brought significant change to the Mission. Postwar prosperity prompted many of the Irish and Italians to move to the more affluent and newer Richmond and Sunset Districts of San Francisco. The move was hastened for many, as a freeway was constructed through the eastern portion of the parish, dislocating many old-time parishioners. [80] The vacancies created by people moving up and out of the mission were filled by new arrivals from Mexico, El Salvador, Nicaragua, Puerto Rico, Cuba, and other Central and South American countries. Hennessy observed in his annual report for 1958, "During the past 5 years there has been a very large increase in the number of Spanish type families, with a corresponding exodus of families of other national origins" (i.e. Irish, Italians, and Germans). [81] By 1960, 30 percent of the population within the boundaries of St. Peter's was first-generation Hispanic. As Hispanics were over 90 percent Catholic, they made up more than 30 percent of the total Catholic population in St. Peter's parish.[82]

The pull of Latinos to the Mission in the 1950s resulted from a number of factors. In the 1930s, a small Latino colony established itself in the Mission, having been relocated from Rincon Hill as a result of the construction of the Oakland-Bay Bridge. Unlike in Latino immigration to most parts of California, San Francisco's Latino community contained a significant number of Central Americans. While the majority of Hispanic immigrants and residents in San Francisco remained Mexican, large communities of Nicaraguans and Salvadorans existed by 1960.[83] By 1980, the Mexican and Central American communities were roughly equal in size; a new flood of immigrants in the 1980s would tip the balance toward the Central Americans.[84]

The attraction of the Latinos to the Mission District reflected the typical "push" and "pull" factors of immigration. As with many immigrants, a large number of Latinos came to San Francisco to find a better life. The rigors of Central American poverty drove many to the Golden Gate. In addition, recurrent political upheavals in El Salvador, Nicaragua, Cuba, Guatemala, and elsewhere, characterized by military dictatorships, repression, coups, and persecution, caused many to flee. The primary pull factor operating in the Mission was the presence of an already established Central American community. The success of the San Francisco coffee industry had resulted in a number of Central Americans settling in San Francisco for business purposes. By 1930, 3,200 Central Americans lived within the city.[85] When large-scale immigration from Central America to San Francisco began in the 1950s, the preexisting family ties made the city the preferred port of arrival. The Mission District also attracted Central Americans because its "good climate" most closely approximated Central American weather.[86] In addition, the newer immigrants were attracted by the working-class nature of the Mission, particularly its lower rents.

Unlike several areas that became black neighborhoods, the Mission did not experience "white flight;"[87] rather the exodus from the Mission was gradual, occurring over the course of the 1950s and 1960s. As the white exodus was in process, physical conditions in the Mission experienced a progressive decline. By 1965, the Mission was designated by the Economic Opportunity Council (EOC) as one of five poverty areas in San Francisco. The 1960 census revealed that 20 percent of Mission residents had a family income of less than $3,000, 12 percent were unemployed, and 7 percent were underemployed. Sixteen percent of the housing was overcrowded and close to 10 percent of the housing was substandard. In addition, the Mission was characterized by the youthfulness of its population and by great geographic mobility. In 1960 over 43 percent of the population was under eighteen years of age. In 1962 St. Peter's had more baptisms (344) than any other parish in the city. By 1960, over 60 percent of the residents of St. Peter's had moved into the parish in the previous six years.[88] By the mid-1960s the Mission faced classic inner-city problems.

The rapid increase of Hispanics presented St. Peter's and the church in San Francisco with enormous pastoral problems. In 1875, Archbishop Joseph Alemany had established Our Lady of Guadalupe Parish in North Beach as a national parish for the Spanish-speaking in San Francisco to serve the Hispanic remnant left from California's days as a Mexican province and the Latino immigrants who had been brought by the Gold Rush. Our Lady of Guadalupe remained the center of the archdiocese's apostolate to the Spanish-speaking until the 1950s. Modern ministry to Hispanics was instigated largely through the efforts of Father Charles "Pop" Phillips (ordained 1911, d. 1958), who almost singlehandedly began ministry to the migrant farmworkers and braceros in the archdiocese. (His first missionary work began in 1929 among immigrant Basque shepherds.) His example inspired the creation of a Spanish Mission Band, consisting of five young priests, who ministered to the needs of Spanish-speaking farmworkers.[89] Within the city in 1959, a group called the Catholic Council for the Spanish-Speaking was being formed to direct ministry to Hispanics in the archdiocese.

St. Peter's was fortunate in 1950 to receive the services of a Nicaraguan priest, Luis Almendares, who was appointed assistant pastor. Almendares had come to San Francisco in 1943. After serving at Stockton, and with Father Charles Phillips in Oakland, he came to St. Peter's. Noted as a brilliant speaker with a perceptive mind, Almendares hosted a Spanish Holy Hour on radio, reciting the rosary and giving a short sermon in Spanish, which was broadcast throughout the Bay area. The radio show also publicized "Mexican patriotic fiestas," and other news of interest to the Latin American community.[90] While at St. Peter's from 1950 to 1958, Almendares ministered to the Spanish-speaking community, hearing confessions and providing counsel in Spanish. He began holding weekly devotions in Spanish, and yearly, in December, would offer a triduum in Spanish in honor of Our Lady of Guadalupe. Almendares was reputed to be an exquisite dresser, severe in bearing. He maintained a traditional masculine outlook reflected in the fact that, "He did not allow ladies wearing pants inside the Church."[91] While Almendares' ministry to the Hispanics allowed them to feel part of St. Peter's, they remained on the periphery of the parish. Almendares left St. Peter's in 1958 to return to Nicaragua, where he met an untimely death, allegedly for being too outspoken politically.

Almendares was replaced by a Spanish-speaking priest of eastern European origin, Father Leopold Uglesic, who arrived at St. Peter's by a rather circuitous route. Before, during, and after World War II, Uglesic had survived death threats from the fascists, Nazis, and communists, before emigrating to Brazil, then Argentina, finally coming to San Francisco in 1954. In Argentina Uglesic learned Spanish, which enabled him to replace Almendares at St. Peter's. Uglesic carried on the devotions begun by Almendares, placing special emphasis on the feast of Our Lady of Guadalupe (December 12). He was troubled by the inter-Hispanic conflicts. Mexicans, Salvadorans, Nicaraguans, and other Central Americans in the parish identified with people from their own country but had difficulty mingling with other nationalities. Uglesic offered the Virgin of Guadalupe, whom he called "Reina de ambas Americas" (Queen of both Americas), as a unifying symbol; however, inter-Hispanic friction would remain a problem throughout the 1960s.[92]

Despite the Spanish services offered at St. Peter's, many Spanish-speaking gravitated to the neighboring parish, St. Anthony's. St. Anthony's had been a German national parish, but in 1948 it had reverted to territorial status. In the early 1960s Franciscan Father Ernesto Sanchez developed an active Hispanic ministry.[93] By 1962, St. Anthony's was the center of the Federation of Guadalupe Societies, a group specifically devoted to "promote the spiritual, social and temporal welfare of the Spanish speaking."[94] The Cursillo retreat, imported from Spain via Texas, was introduced at St. Anthony's and became immensely popular among Hispanics. At one mass each Sunday the readings and sermon were offered in Spanish; the parish was one of only three in the city to do so.[95]

In 1962, St. Peter's received an additional assistant who spoke Spanish, Father James Casey, a native of San Francisco. Casey and Uglesic visited St. Anthony's to learn from its success with the Spanish-speaking. At St. Peter's in the same year, Spanish-speaking parishioner Isaura Michel de Rodrigues began circulating a petition to request of the pastor, Father Hennessy, a Sunday mass with sermon in Spanish. Isaura had come to San Francisco in 1943 from Mexico, carrying vivid images of the persecution of Catholics in Mexico in the 1920s and 1930s. She worked in a variety of jobs, including teaching. She assisted Almendares and Uglesic in the various Hispanic services, but continued to attend Sunday mass at Our Lady of Guadalupe. Weary of the trip across town, in 1962 Isaura pushed for a mass in Spanish at St. Peter's. Hennessy was not an early enthusiast of the Spanish mass, preferring to leave most of his dealings with his Spanish-speaking parishioners to his assistant pastors. Hennessy had the typical Irish-American attitude—the good American Catholic would worship in English. He asked Isaura, "Why are your people so lazy? They should learn English."[96] In 1964, Isaura again petitioned Hennessy, sending a copy of the petition to Archbishop Joseph McGucken. She wrote, "I told you that most of the Spanish people, adults, they do not speak English at all, and they need to listen to the Word of God in the Spanish language."[97] She was particularly concerned about the inroads Protestant evangelicals were making in the Hispanic community. She counted at least nine Protestant churches that offered services in Spanish in the neighborhood. In addition, she pointed out that the monthly first-Saturday mass in Spanish at St. Peter's was well attended. With the additional prodding of Uglesic and Casey, Hennessy allowed St. Peter's to celebrate its first regular Sunday Spanish mass in September 1964. The inaugural mass was attended by a standing-room-only crowd of over one thousand.

In response to the Rodrigues petition, Hennessy sent Archbishop McGucken a report of the work being done at St. Peter's on behalf of the Spanish-speaking. His report provides a snapshot of St. Peter's services provided in Spanish: each Friday a Holy Hour with a sermon, hymns, and Benediction; every first Saturday of the month a dialogue mass with a sermon; during Lent, a weekly Way of the Cross with a sermon; on Holy Thursday and Good Friday, a sermon, prayers, and hymns were offered. Each year a triduum was held in honor of Our Lady of Guadalupe. Cursillos were being promoted. Confessions were available in Spanish. Preparation for First Holy Communion and confession were being offered in Spanish. English classes were offered for adults and children. And in September a Sunday mass would be offered with readings and sermons in Spanish at 11:00 A.M.[98] In sum, Hispanic ministry was well underway at St. Peter's by 1964.

The development of Hispanic ministry and the increased presence of Latinos in the neighborhood did not sit well with many old Peterites who resented the "infiltration" of "their" parish. After Uglesic preached a sermon in Spanish, he was accosted by an irate Irish woman who reminded him, "This is an Irish parish." Uglesic responded, "Not anymore, it isn't."[99] In a similar instance, when the aging pastor, Timothy

Hennessy, practiced and recited an announcement in Spanish at mass, an older parishioner asked, "Why did you give in to them?"[100] Nonetheless, Irish resentment was generally limited to words; overt conflicts were generally avoided between old-time Peterites and the newer Hispanics.[101] The peaceful coexistence was attributed in no small measure to Hennessy, who called on the affection he enjoyed with the older Irish to smooth out relations between the groups, reconciling the older parishioners to the need for Hispanic ministry.[102] The hostility of the Irish was not lost on the Spanish-speaking, who described the Irish attitude as "agria" (sour),[103] or their treatment as being put "a un lado" (to the side).[104]

Resentment of the Hispanics was more than mere racism, though racism was undeniably present. For decades, St. Peter's had prospered as an Irish parish. The spirit of Yorke and Hunt was imbedded deep in the hearts of every Peterite, even those who had left the parish. St. Peter's was *their* parish. Now all they had known was disappearing. One old-time parishioner observed that the parish was "alien" to him now.[105] And another reflected of the Mission in general, "The place where I grew up doesn't exist anymore."[106] Beyond the racial differences, Hispanic Catholics seemed a different species of Catholic. While Sunday mass attendance and parish support were highly valued qualities of the "good Catholic," Irish-American style, they were not values the Hispanic seemed to observe. Equally as galling to the Irish was the apparent refusal of many Hispanics to learn English. The change in St. Peter's struck at deep convictions and attachments held by the Irish-American community, which at times seemed to forget its own immigrant ancestry. The conflict was ultimately resolved by simple numbers. By the mid-1970s St. Peter's was over 70 percent Hispanic; most of the Irish and Italians had left the parish. The greatest bitterness had passed by the 1980s. By then, many of those who chose to live or remain in St. Peter's did so precisely because of its cultural diversity.[107]

From 1950 to 1964, despite the growing numbers of Hispanics (they accounted for about half of the parish), and despite the attempt to develop a Hispanic ministry, they remained on the periphery of parish life, as St. Peter's maintained its Irish/Italian aura. At the very time of transition, St. Peter's had reached the acme of Yorke's and Hunt's parochial aspirations for the school and devotions. Like his predecessors, Hennessy made the school a top priority. Unfortunately, during his pastorate, both the boys' high school and the girls' high school were closed, in 1952 and 1966 respectively, as a result of increasing costs, declining enrollment, and competition from archdiocesan-sponsored central high schools. Nonetheless, the parish's commitment to Catholic education remained high. Hennessy built a new elementary school and convent, buildings that he dedicated in 1963 to Father Peter C. Yorke. Two of the more active parish organizations remained: the Mothers' Club (founded in 1931), which hosted an annual Halloween bazaar in October for the schoolchildren to raise money for school supplies; and the Fathers' Club, which organized the annual spring festival. The Fathers' Club also ran the athletic program, which offered vigorous programs in basketball, baseball, and boxing. Bingo was introduced in 1953 to raise money for the school. Bingo flourished in the 1950s and 1960s, albeit illegally. However, bingo as a major fund-raiser collapsed in the early 1970s, when it was made legal. Legal competition ended the Catholic-school monopoly on bingo, and St. Peter's was unable to compete.[108] What all this activity suggests is that the school remained a major commitment and focal point for the parish, and, as in the past, lay men and women worked hard, if somewhat anonymously, for the success of the parish and school.

Traditional parish devotions such as novenas, triduums, and missions continued to flourish in the 1950s. In addition, the 1950s were marked by an increase in Marian piety, an increase sparked by the international Marian year in 1954. Devotions to Our Lady of Fatima enjoyed a brief vogue in the parish, but the biggest devotion centered around the rosary. Each October in the 1950s, a novena to the Holy Rosary was offered, and subsequently a rosary group developed, consisting of approximately thirty families who pledged to say the rosary daily. All this mirrored the national rosary crusade, inspired by the dynamic Father Patrick Peyton ("The family that prays together stays together"). At the parish, the May procession, which included the crowning of Mary at the grotto, continued through the 1950s, complete with procession, hymns to Our Lady, the Litany of Loretto, and the rosary.[109]

The greatest beneficiary of the Marian revival was the Young Ladies Sodality, now called Our Lady's Sodality. Besides the seasonal devotions to Mary, the highlight of the sodality year was the annual Sodality Ball. In February 1957, the ball was reestablished after a hiatus of seventy-nine years. The ball was a typical high-school dance except for the decorations, which consisted of blue and white trim and various Marian symbols. During the intermission Mary was crowned amidst Marian hymns. The ball epitomized the sodalist as "a grace-filled vessel of holiness and beauty mirroring the Divine Life."[110] Or as one orchestra leader assessed the ball, "This is the only place I know where religion, loveliness, and good social usage remain today and are blended into such a wonderful experience."[111]

Three final elements marked parish life in the 1950s. First, the parish experienced the general societal emphasis on the family through the family rosary and other events such as the Forty Hours Devotion to celebrate the feast of the Holy Family, and the Family Communion Sunday. The Children's Mass was phased out in the 1950s, as emphasis was placed on the family worshiping together. Second, the parish reflected the widespread missionary impulse in American Catholicism. Prosperity brought concerns about spreading the faith and material riches to less fortunate countries. Pagan babies could be "adopted" for an appropriate price through the school to assist the foreign missions. Several parish organizations raised funds to send materials such as books and medical supplies overseas. Finally, the 1950s saw the creation of several small study clubs and social action groups, including Father Nick Farana's study club in the early 1950s and the Young Christian Students and Young Christian Workers. These groups were forerunners of the small-group spirituality that would flourish in the 1960s and 1970s at St. Peter's.

Though the neighborhood had begun to change, the Irish and Italian community struggled to maintain the close-knit community they had grown up with. More debilitating to the community than the new immigrants was affluence. In the 1950s, the Irish and Italians were, in the words of Nick Farana, "the cock of the walk";[112] however, they chose to strut in other parts of the city. The Mission would now become the preserve of newly arriving Hispanics. For the unobservant, the switchover became painfully clear in the fate of the Yorke Memorial Mass. Though the mass continued through the 1950s and 1960s, the enthusiasm and crowds that had characterized the celebration in the 1930s and 1940s were gone. By the mid-1960s the numbers had dwindled to a faithful few, who insisted on keeping the celebration at 11:00 A.M. on Palm Sunday. Unfortunately, the 11:00 A.M. mass was now the Spanish mass, and no one had informed the Spanish-speaking community that the Spanish mass had been cancelled. As a result a throng of bemused Hispanics attended the Yorke Memorial Mass, honoring the parish hero of a bygone era. After the Hispanics sat quietly through the entire Yorke liturgy, in which the traditional hymns were sung quietly in English,

Father Jim Casey invited the congregation to conclude the celebration with a Spanish hymn. The congregation exploded into noisy singing "almost taking the roof off the church."[113]

The future of the parish seemed evident.

The Parish Turns Outward, 1964–1970

Given the influx of Latinos to the parish, and the Mission's declining economic condition, St. Peter's faced more than enough challenges as the 1960s began. On top of these practical realities, the parish was rocked by the dual revolution that shook Catholicism and America: the Second Vatican Council and the social turmoil of the 1960s. The result: deep divisions, as the cohesive parish of yesteryear shattered into contending factions. The old Irish/Italian parish was at odds with the new Hispanic parish. The old pre-Vatican II Catholics clashed with those imbued with the elusive "spirit of Vatican II." Within the Hispanic community divisions continued to exist between competing nationalities.

The central conflict was personified in the division between the pastor, Timothy Hennessy, and his two assistants, Jim Casey and John Petroni. Hennessy represented the old Irish parish and those reluctant to enact the changes brought on by Vatican II. In contrast, Casey and Petroni both spoke Spanish fluently, having received instruction in Spanish at the language institute in Cuernavaca, Mexico. Both were deeply sympathetic to the Hispanic community. Both were ready to move beyond the old Irish-Catholic ghetto to explore the new vistas opened by Vatican II. Serving as a buffer between Hennessy and his young assistants was Monsignor James Flynn, director of Catholic Charities for the archdiocese of San Francisco, who was in residence at St. Peter's beginning in 1964. Flynn was sympathetic to Casey and Petroni but was able to speak to Hennessy in a language he could understand. Hennessy respected Flynn's status as a monsignor. To Hennessy's credit, though often bewildered by his two younger associates, he rarely interfered with their programs, particularly their programs with the Spanish-speaking of the parish. In addition, Hennessy often soothed his more traditional parishioners, who were equally bewildered by Petroni and Casey.[114]

Casey and Petroni embodied the future direction of St. Peter's. Both repeatedly attempted to push St. Peter's and its parishioners beyond the confines of the traditional Catholic parish into the community in order to address the community's needs. In conferences with the Sisters of

Mercy, they urged the Sisters to be more attentive to "wider community relations."[115] They urged longtime resident (and future deacon) John Bourne "to move out from St. Peter's, and not just be involved in things that were strictly St. Peter's-oriented."[116] Bourne did move beyond, becoming an active participant in the Mission Coalition (see below).

Casey and Petroni complemented each other. Casey became more active in the civil sphere, serving as chaplain for the Archdiocesan Council for the Spanish-Speaking and later moving into community action. Petroni was more involved with the religious sphere, devoting much time to the liturgy. His greatest love was to develop small groups, where problems could be dealt with at some depth. Both were exploring new concepts of church and inviting St. Peter's parishioners to come with them. Lay Catholics were no longer simply to "pay, pray, and obey," they were now "co-responsible" for the church and were urged to actively engage the world as Catholics. Salvation no longer came solely through the reception of the sacraments; it also came through faithful witness to the gospel teachings of Jesus.

Essential to Petroni's vision was the development of "little parishes" within St. Peter's. In theory, the "little parish" broke the large, impersonal parish down to small "neighborhood cells," where people were able to deal more personally with the issues of religion and with each other. Organized as discussion groups, the little parishes consisted of eight to fourteen people and met in parishioners' homes. Scripture was discussed in practical terms and was directly applied to the people's lives. The same was done with the sacraments. The participants were encouraged to seek "personal answers," and then to see the "social dimensions" of Scripture and the sacraments. The hope was that the little parishes would multiply as people's "consciousness" was raised,[117] and that the multiplication of the little parishes would transform the community.

Petroni based the little parish program on a course developed by Father Leo Mahon, director of the Cardinal's Committee on the Spanish-Speaking in Chicago. Mahon developed his program to provide for a more effective evangelization of Latin American Catholics, whose main problems, he believed, included a distance from the institutional church, a lack of formal knowledge of the faith, and a lack of leadership. Mahon believed that it was not enough to teach Latin Americans to be "practical Catholics." A basic problem with ministry to the Latin American Catholic, Mahon contended, was that the means (i.e., the sacraments) were confused as ends in themselves, rather than means to the end (i.e., "to build the Kingdom of love and justice").[118] The Mahon approach seemed ideally suited to the St. Peter's community, with its increasing numbers of Hispanics and its older, more "practical" parishioners. The little parishes would help to unify the different areas and factions at St. Peter's, and push them outward to renew the larger community.

Petroni began the program at St. Peter's in 1965 with the assistance of eight seminarians from St. Patrick's Seminary.[119] Each seminarian hosted a bible study group, which met in the home of a parishioner. The ten-week sessions ended with a mass in each of the little parish centers. Six of the groups were conducted in English, two in Spanish. The following year, six groups were conducted in Spanish, six in English.[120] The little parish program was not an overwhelming success in terms of the parish, but it did have a positive effect on many of the participants who became more active in the parish and community. Whether successful or not, the little parishes were a creative attempt to respond to the problem facing St. Peter's in the mid-1960s.

Less enthused about the philosophical implications of the program was Archbishop Joseph McGucken, who had more practical concerns. When granting permission for mass in Spanish, or for home masses at St. Peter's, McGucken clearly delineated his criteria for successful Hispanic ministry. In 1964, he approved of mass in Spanish, writing, "It might be a way of bringing a number of people to Confession and counteracting the intense amount of proselytizing activity that is going on in the Mission District."[121] The following year, while he approved the home masses for the little parishes, he requested that Hennessy inform him as to "whether or not they [home masses] have the effect of bringing more negligent Catholics to the parish church."[122] The following year, in requesting the home masses, Hennessy assured McGucken that the little parishes had increased mass attendance and increased CCD enrollment.[123] Not so easily appeased, McGucken warned, "Our reports on dispensations requested in similarly situated parishes indicate that there are many more validations in the parishes where priests spend less time holding meetings, and more time maintaining apostolic contacts."[124] The thrust of the little parishes seemed lost on McGucken. The little-parish philosophy highlighted the conflict between the old notion of the church, in which success was judged by the number of sacraments received, and the post-Vatican II notion that success was to be judged by the quality of one's faith. The latter criterion was more nebulous and conducive to greater concern among those accustomed to quantifiable judgments.

McGucken was no more comfortable with the interest Casey and Petroni took in the burgeoning farmworkers' movement (though the archbishop would later endorse the United Farm Workers). St. Peter's parish, through the promptings of Casey and Petroni, and later Flynn and Jim Hagan, became ardent supporters of Cesar Chavez and the UFW, providing material support (food, clothing, and money), and marching in local demonstrations in support of the grape and lettuce boycotts. Though some opposition to the UFW existed within the parish, the majority of Peterites endorsed the union. Casey, with a group of parishioners, joined Chavez in his march from Delano to Sacramento in 1966. Casey's participation in these protests was not without some misgivings. Casey confided, "people thought that maybe this was not the role of a priest . . . that the priest should stay at the parish and send the people out into the community." [125] That was definitely McGucken's feeling, but Casey believed he could not send the people out alone; he had to accompany them. By participating personally, people became more involved. Without clerical participation, lay involvement in the community was not as great.

The proper role of the priest and parish was soon at issue in a controversy brought on by the development of the Mission Coalition (MCO), an Alinsky-inspired coalition of community groups in the Mission. The coalition grew out of the city's attempt to impose "urban renewal" on the Mission District through the San Francisco Redevelopment Agency (SFRA). In the early 1960s, the creation of a new light rail line called BART (Bay Area Rapid Transit) to run beneath Mission Street, provided the SFRA with an opportunity to redevelop the Mission. In 1966, fearful of "massive relocation and a bulldozer approach," [126] a number of groups united to form the Mission Coalition on Redevelopment (MCOR) to oppose the SFRA's plan for renewal. They insisted that any redevelopment be controlled at the neighborhood level. At a meeting of the San Francisco Board of Supervisors the coalition succeeded in stopping the redevelopment plan by one vote. The MCOR then dissolved.

Two years later, newly elected Mayor Joseph Alioto promoted redevelopment through the neighborhoods. He announced that he would apply for federal Model Cities monies for the Mission if a "broad-based community group" requested him to do so. In response to Alioto's request, remnants of the defunct MCOR reemerged as the Mission

Coalition. More than simply sponsoring a Model Cities proposal, the MCO strove to be the "representative voice of the Mission."[127] At its height the MCO consisted of over 115 community groups and held a yearly convention to address community concerns. The Mission would become part of the Model Cities Program in 1971.

St. Peter's became involved early on in the MCO's struggle, as the parish council, created in 1966, became a charter member of the MCO. St. Peter's was the most active of all the church groups in the MCO.[128] Father Jim Casey headed the Mission Housing Committee of the MCO and led the fight for tenants' rights, an activity that did not make him popular with many landlords. He succeeded in having a "tenant-landlord pact" signed that guaranteed tenant rights.[129]

Besides Casey, Jack Bourne, a wholesale hardware dealer and a parishioner since 1930, at the prompting of Petroni and Casey, became part of the MCO Planning Council, where his interest turned to the issue of housing. Bourne was deeply involved in parish activities. As a youth he served as an altar boy, and played on the parish athletic teams; as an adult he was a member of the St. Vincent de Paul Society, served as president of the Men's Club, taught CCD, and served on the first parish council (1966). The Mission Coalition was his first activity beyond the parish. Bourne would go on to be the executive director of the Mission Housing Development Corporation, "a community based development corporation," from 1971 to 1989.[130] But in 1969, Bourne's efforts became the focal point of conservative opposition to the MCO. On July 10, Bourne preached at all the masses at St. Peter's on the problem of housing in the Mission District, and promoted the MCO's program to produce more low-cost housing. The novelty of a layman preaching in a Catholic church was overshadowed by the presence of picketers in front of the church protesting Bourne's sermon. A group of merchants and realtors carried signs reading, "Churches are for Worship, Not for Politics."[131] They followed their protest by filing a challenge to St. Peter's tax-exempt status, claiming that St. Peter's had violated its status as a nonprofit religious organization by supporting the MCO. The city attorney assured McGucken the challenge was nonsense, and it was eventually dismissed. Nonetheless, McGucken cautioned Hennessy about his priests becoming too involved in the political realm. The Bourne incident and Casey's activism reflected St. Peter's increasing involvement in the public sphere, an involvement that made many uneasy.

Beyond involvement in community organizing, the parish also became home to several federally sponsored programs aimed at uplifting the Mission District. The parish and area benefited from a number of the War on Poverty programs and programs sponsored by the Economic Opportunity Council. The parish school received funds for field trips, books, reading assistance, and bilingual education. In 1966, Head Start, a program designed to assist the preschool children of low-income families develop fundamental learning skills, operated at St. Peter's.

Great use was made of the space in the old high-school building, which became a parish and community center. The downstairs was used as a community day-care center. Other rooms were used for the two most significant federal programs housed at St. Peter's: Arriba Juntos and Horizons Unlimited. Both programs addressed major problems in the Mission District: unemployment, an increasing high school drop-out rate, and a lack of recreational, counseling, and community services. Arriba Juntos was an offshoot of the OBECA (Organization for Business, Education and Community Advancement) founded in 1965 to develop and upgrade small businesses in the Mission. Arriba Juntos began in May 1967 with seed money from Catholic Charities of San Francisco. In September, both organizations moved their offices to St. Peter's. Arriba Juntos (literally "Up Together"), attempted "to prepare Hispano Americans to enter the job market, to ease their assimilation into the Anglo community, and at the same time to preserve the values and traditions of the Spanish culture."[132] To accomplish this, Arriba Juntos offered job-training programs, counseling services, referrals to community agencies, and courses in English. Horizons Unlimited geared its energies toward potential high school dropouts. Funded by the EOC of San Francisco, it developed a counseling and guidance program to encourage Mission youth to get their high school diplomas, and to pursue worthwhile careers. The program provided part-time work for high school students through the Neighborhood Youth Corps. Both programs attempted to "provide self determination for a better life in a better neighborhood in the Mission."[133]

St. Peter's also provided office space for the primary archdiocesan department in charge of ministry to the Spanish-speaking, the Catholic Council for the Spanish-Speaking. More important, the director of the council was Roger Hernandez, a St. Peter's parishioner and Nicaraguan immigrant, and the chaplain was Father Jim Casey. The council was begun in 1959, but Roger Hernandez did not become director until 1966. Hernandez tried to fashion an organization that would respond to the needs of the Spanish-speaking in the archdiocese. Parishes with Hispanic communities would each send two representatives to the council meetings, but Hernandez was the driving force. Under his direction the council saw itself as a voice for the Spanish-speaking within the church and within the community. Within the church, they agitated for more Spanish-speaking priests, and more Spanish services. On a practical level, they offered a course to assist in the validation of marriages and sponsored leadership-training institutes. The development of Hispanic leaders within the church was a primary concern of the council. Within the community they fought discrimination against Hispanics, challenging the Post Office, the city transit system, and Pacific Gas and Electric.[134] The council also supported many of the concerns of St. Peter's parish; it worked hard in support of the UFW. It was also active in the Mission Coalition, and it assisted Arriba Juntos by advertising job opportunities and training workshops in its newsletter. On occasion, the council would sponsor special workshops to assist the Spanish-speaking obtain jobs. For instance, it joined the archdiocesan Department of Education in offering a course to prepare people for the civil service exam (civil service as a means of advancement had a long tradition at St. Peter's). In all its activities the council sought to uplift the Hispanic community. Each year it would host a Latin American Unity Day to bring the various Latin American groups together. Often they would celebrate a specific ethnic tradition at the unity day such as Salvador del Mundo (El Salvador), El Senor de Esquipulas (Guatemala), the Immaculate Conception (Nicaragua), the Lord of the Miracles (Peru), and Our Lady of Guadalupe (Mexico). The council tried to respond wherever it perceived a need in the Hispanic Catholic community.

The "new" church at St. Peter's in the 1960s not only pushed outward, the internal operation of the parish also changed. In November 1966, a parish council was formed to increase lay input into the operation of the parish. The council would address a variety of issues in its brief three-year existence, including social action, the CCD program, programs for the Spanish-speaking, and so on. It even established a free dental clinic that was open on Saturday mornings for parishioners who could not afford to see a dentist.[135] Petroni and Casey were enthusiastic about the parish council; Hennessy was noncommittal until the council attempted to alter Sunday mass times. Hennessy felt such decisions were his prerogative and were not the business of the parish council. Relations between the pastor and council steadily deteriorated after this until the council was abandoned. Lay council members were discouraged by Hennessy's intransigence over mass times. Many believed that if they encountered so much opposition over such a minor issue, significant change would be impossible.

Another factor which militated against groups such as the little parish and the parish council was the rapid geographic mobility in and out of the parish. In 1960 over 60 percent of the people had resided in St. Peter's for less than six years; 37 percent less than two years.[136] These figures would increase slightly during the 1960s. With such mobility the priests provided the most stable leadership within the community.

Inaugurated at the same time as the parish council was a new method of parish fund-raising, the Stewardship Program. Emanating from the Archdiocesan Chancery Office, the Stewardship Program sought to rid the parish of the "crasser" forms of fund-raising—raffles, bazaars, card parties, bingo—which made the church appear too "money-grubbing." Stewardship would be a more dignified way of funding the parish, as the parish would rely solely on the commitment of its parishioners. Funds would be raised by having parishioners pledge to give so much money a week in their Sunday envelopes. The object was to provide a more secure and regular income for the parish. The annual festival sponsored by the Men's Club was discontinued in 1967. The festival would resume in 1977 with the parish facing a severe debt, as stewardship proved inadequate to meet the parish financial needs.

The new look of the post–Vatican II church consisted of more than changes in church leadership, or in changes in the role of the church vis-à-vis society. What struck the average Catholic most was the change in the liturgy. Mass was now said in English, or Spanish, as was the case at St. Peter's 11:00 A.M. mass, instead of in the traditional Latin. The priest celebrated mass facing the people, rather than with his back to the congregation. (At St. Peter's, Father Casey had to buy a portable altar in order to begin saying mass facing the people. Hennessy was not enthused).[137] After the "Our Father," Catholics would now greet one another with a sign of peace. A variety of changes in the mass and sacraments were designed to increase the participation of the parish community in the liturgy. One would think that such changes would be welcome at the parish of Peter C. Yorke, but change came hard for many old-school Peterites. Equally as important as community involvement in the liturgy was a newfound emphasis on Scripture, a phenomenon readily evident at St. Peter's where Bible study had flourished. The old paraliturgical devotions were deemphasized or altered. In 1965, the

Stations of the Cross were "Biblicized"; a short Scripture passage was read prior to each station. By 1969, the stations were eliminated and replaced by a mass in the stations' time slot.[138]

In tune with the new theology of the laity was a renewed emphasis on parents as the primary Christian educators of their children. No longer could parents leave their child's preparation for the sacraments "to Sister." Parents had to attend baptism classes before their children could be baptized. Parents were responsible as never before, in preparing their children for confession and First Holy Communion. Parents of candidates for confirmation had to attend adult education classes at night. Much of what had been done by the priests and sisters was now thrust back upon the parents.[139]

Equally as difficult to digest for some old-school Catholics, was the new openness toward Protestant churches. In the 1960s and 1970s, St. Peter's participated in a series of pulpit exchanges with Lutheran, Episcopal, Presbyterian, and Methodist churches. Such events seemed unthinkable to people raised in the tradition of Irish defensiveness.

The stress on the Bible, parental participation in the religious education of their children, and ecumenism all reflected the new stress of Vatican II: each Catholic was "coresponsible" for the church; the success or failure of the church was not the sole responsibility of priests and women religious. Religion had to be more "personally authentic." That these innovations met resistance at St. Peter's suggests the perpetuation of Yorke's theology of the church teaching and the church taught.

Ironically, the new liturgical emphasis and ecumenical thrust of St. Peter's occurred at a time when many of the newly arrived Hispanics retained a pre–Vatican II piety devoted to triduums, novenas, and sacramentals. The increased presence of Hispanics also undercut the ecumenical movement, as Catholics accused Protestant evangelicals of undue proselytizing among the Hispanic community. The attempt to usher Hispanics into the post–Vatican II church, without leaving them susceptible to Protestant evangelization, would remain a basic pastoral challenge for St. Peter's through 1990.

Crucial to the evangelization of the Hispanic was the liturgy. Casey and Petroni worked hard on the liturgy, "so it would speak more to the Spanish-speaking."[140] One means of speaking to the Hispanic community was to celebrate their traditional feasts. In the 1960s, St. Peter's celebrated the Nicaraguan feast of the Immaculate Conception, hosting a triduum from December 6 to December 8, concluding with the "misa Pan Americana." The custom of "La Griteria" was also observed. In the traditional Griteria, people would go from home to home shouting, "Quien causa tanta alegria?" (Who causes so much joy?), to which the response would be "La Concepcion de Maria." Little packets of sweets and fruits with Nicaraguan flags would be distributed to the visitors. The Griteria was celebrated in a modified form at St. Peter's.[141] Two days later the parish would celebrate the Mexican feast of Our Lady of Guadalupe with a triduum from December 10 to December 12. This celebration included a procession through the streets of St. Peter's with an image of Our Lady of Guadalupe. The celebration would include "mananitas," an early morning serenade of the Blessed Virgin Mary, or "nochecitas," an evening serenade.[142] St. Peter's also sponsored a "Las Posadas," a reenactment of Mary and Joseph's search for lodging before the birth of Jesus. A Christmas party, complete with traditional Hispanic treats, would conclude the Posadas.

In 1967, the parish council established a Spanish-speaking liturgy committee to assist in the preparation of Spanish liturgies. Petroni envisioned the weekly Sunday liturgy as a means of bringing the diverse elements of the Hispanic community together. The recurring contention between Hispanic groups mystified the Anglos, who saw little difference between such groups, generally referring to all Hispanics as "Mexican." Within St. Peter's, however, the people considered themselves Nicaraguans, or Salvadorans, or Mexicans, or whatever. These national identities often formed the basis of conflict or jealousy. (The closeness of the Immaculate Conception and Guadalupe celebrations was often a source of conflict.)[143] Petroni hoped the Sunday liturgy would be a means of uniting the Hispanic community. He fought attempts in 1967–68 to add another Spanish mass on Sundays, insisting that the single liturgy was essential in binding the Hispanic community together.[144]

The more basic division at St. Peter's was the split between the Anglo and Hispanic communities. In fact, what developed were parallel parishes, one for the Spanish-speaking and one for the English-speaking. During Holy Week there were two complete but separate schedules. On Holy Thursday, the Mass of the Last Supper was held in English, and then at a different time in Spanish. The process was repeated on Good Friday. On Christmas, both communities had Midnight Mass; the English mass was in the church, the Spanish mass in the auditorium.[145] As one Spanish-speaking parishioner observed, "They had their groups and we had ours."[146] The "separate" parishes reflected more than just pragmatic needs. Petroni recalled that the relationship between the Anglo and Hispanic communities was "not a good relationship at all . . .

and in some cases, downright hostile."[147] Another parishioner suggested the basis of conflict lay in the Irish desire to maintain control of the parish, while making little attempt to understand the Hispanic people and their customs.[148] The parish council frequently discussed what could be done to bring the two communities together.[149] In 1967, a special bilingual mass was held on the feast of the Epiphany[150] in an attempt to bring the groups together. A discussion followed the mass, but little was resolved. The influx of a large group of Filipinos in the late 1960s and early 1970s made intergroup relations even more interesting, and led to trilingual celebrations in English, Spanish, and Tagalog, the main language of the Philippines.

One program that did unify the two communities to some degree was the Cursillo. "A short course in Christianity," the Cursillo was a weekend retreat that invited the retreatant to make a deeply personal commitment to Christ and his church. Cursillos were very popular in the Hispanic community and were regarded as a prime means of bringing the Latino Catholic closer to the church. But the Cursillo also flourished in the Anglo community at St. Peter's. Both men who were ordained deacons at St. Peter's in 1979 claim the Cursillo deeply affected their lives. Roger Hernandez, the Spanish-speaking deacon, called the Cursillo "a source of total change,"[151] and the English-speaking deacon, Jack Bourne, reflected that, after his Cursillo, "I began to feel that religion was more than attending Mass on Sundays."[152] The Cursillo partially achieved what the little parish had set out to do—make the participant a better Christian. After the weekend retreat, the Cursillistas met once a month for a follow-up, and some groups met as often as once a week. The Cursillo produced a number of parish leaders, and according to Monsignor Flynn served as "a bridge between the Anglos and the Hispanics."[153] Despite the breakthrough occasioned by the Cursillos, the need to unify the English and Spanish communities would remain an ongoing problem for St. Peter's. As late as 1986 a parish report noted, "The Hispanics and English people of our parish must become more one in the things they do."[154]

The Open Parish, 1970–1978

In 1970, Father Timothy Hennessy retired. Replacing him was Monsignor James Flynn, director of Catholic Charities for the archdiocese. Flynn had been in residence in the parish since 1964. In 1972, he would become director of the Social Justice Commission for the archdiocese.

Flynn continued the parish in the direction begun by Petroni and Casey, though both previous assistants had gone elsewhere by the time Flynn was named pastor.[155] They had been replaced by two young priests, both fluent in Spanish, Jim Hagan and John J. McCarthy. Father Hagan's personality would come to dominate the spirit of the parish, but Flynn set the tone.

In a sermon on the "Qualities of a Priest," Flynn highlighted what would become major themes in his pastorate. Above all, Flynn asserted, the priest should be a man of prayer. Moreover, the priest should be "open," parishioners should regard him as a friend, as someone they could trust in time of trouble. He concluded, "Priesthood doesn't always mean being at the helm as much as being at the center."[156] The priest and pastor had to know how to use authority. Authority was not a club to beat parishioners and associates over the head with to get one's way. Real authority empowered people to be better. Flynn operated his pastorate on a "team ministry" basis, rather than in the "dictatorial style" of a traditional pastor. By 1976 he had brought into the team three full-time parish sisters. The team would meet to discuss parish priorities and to set parochial policy.

One of the tasks Flynn and his team tackled was the dual parish they encountered. To unify the Anglos and Hispanics, and Filipinos as well, bilingual events became much more common in Flynn's era. The separate celebration of Midnight Mass at Christmas ended, being replaced by one bilingual mass. The following year the mass was trilingual, as was the yearly Thanksgiving mass. These liturgies were a means of the community celebrating as a unified whole, instead of celebrating in separate groups. In 1975, the school sponsored a Heritage Night potluck dinner, celebrating the various cultures present in the parish. The Latin American countries, Ireland, Italy, the Mideast, and the Philippines were all represented. The following two years the celebrations continued. The celebrations and the liturgies attempted to point toward parish unity despite the diversity of cultures.

At the heart of Flynn's pastorate was the notion of St. Peter's as an open community—open and at the service of the Mission community. Flynn explained that he was constantly hearing how "rich" St. Peter's was despite the fact that it faced a huge debt and lacked the money to do anything other than survive. As he reflected, he realized St. Peter's was in the situation of having the "largest house on the block." Whether the people in the largest house are rich or not doesn't matter; people assume they are rich. Flynn realized that what St. Peter's was rich in was properties and facilities. In order to "share the wealth," Flynn decided to make the facilities of St. Peter's as open as possible to the local community.[157] Over the next eight years a motley assortment of organizations would hold meetings at St. Peter's. Flynn recalls, "You had every organization in town using the hall, some of them rather questionable."[158] "Questionable" seemed an understatement to many parishioners! The auditorium housed or had meetings for UFW organizers, members of the Third World Liberation Front (student strikers from San Francisco State College), Iranian students who opposed the Shah, Vietnam War resisters, communist labor unions, international solidarity groups, and others. The FBI became a frequent visitor to St. Peter's. This was the way a parish should be, reasoned associate pastor Jim Hagan, whom Flynn credits for making St. Peter's such a "welcoming place" during those years.[159] In Hagan's assessment, "St. Peter's at that time was part of the neighborhood, part of its culture, of its history, of all its involvement. The major things happening in the neighborhood were there at St. Peter's."[160] The logical conclusion of Casey's and Petroni's efforts had been reached. Flynn's open parish was the logical extension of the parish's policy of making the old high school available to community groups.

Two of the more controversial groups allowed to meet at St. Peter's were Dignity and Los Siete de la Raza. Dignity, a support group for gay and lesbian Catholics, had its first mass in San Francisco at St. Peter's in January 1973. Flynn had allowed the group to use the parish auditorium at 3:00 on Sunday afternoons. When news of the meetings became public, a storm of protest broke out, with most of the noise coming from beyond the parish. The incident prompted an editorial in the archdiocesan newspaper, *The Monitor*, reasserting the traditional Catholic teaching on homosexuality. Flynn defended his action in a letter to Archbishop McGucken, saying "Our involvement at St. Peter's is limited to making available to the group our meeting rooms," and warned that refusal to allow Dignity to hold a mass would cause greater publicity and disruption.[161] Dignity was allowed to continue meeting at St. Peter's. Equally as important was what did not happen. The Hispanic community has been stereotyped as rabidly anti-gay, but at St. Peter's no conflict ever surfaced between Hispanics and gays.

More controversial was allowing a group called Los Siete de la Raza to meet at St. Peter's and to run their breakfast program for children from the parish auditorium. Los Siete was an organization formed in 1969 to defend seven Hispanic youths who were accused of assaulting two police officers in the Mission District (one policeman died, the other was critically injured). The defendants were dubbed Los Siete de la Raza and the defense organization took the same name. Los Siete, the organization, became a radical political group modeling itself after the Black Panthers, with whom it had an ongoing dialogue.[162] Besides protecting "Brown rights," Los Siete established community programs including a medical clinic and a breakfast program for children, the latter of which operated at St. Peter's.[163] To the older Irish and Italian parishioners, supporting a group that seemed to glory in the killing of a police officer was almost too much to bear. Many Peterites had served in the San Francisco Police Department, which was often referred to as an "Irish club." Pastor emeritus Tim Hennessy urged several parishioners to go to the archbishop, but no formal protest ever got organized.[164] Flynn again reasserted his philosophy: he was not supporting Los Siete, but it was a community group providing a useful service; therefore, it was allowed to use the facilities.[165] Mercifully for the elder parishioners and former pastor, the program lasted slightly less than a year. Nonetheless, the open policy of St. Peter's had enabled the church to establish contact with groups that previously had little contact with the church. St. Peter's reputation spread. Hagan remembers, "[St. Peter's] was known at all different places as a church that was open to workers, and to the poor."[166] The St. Peter's community did not meet these new developments with total support. Many older parishioners began attending mass at several of the more subdued neighboring parishes.[167]

Despite some opposition to Flynn's open-door policy, the majority of the parish seemed to support it. In November 1971 the parish held a referendum as to whether it should serve as a "sanctuary" for deserters from the Vietnam War. To the question, "Should St. Peter's offer 'sanctuary' to servicemen who refused duty in Vietnam according to the dictates of their conscience?" the parish voted 620 "yes" to 180 "no." (Only four other Catholic parishes in the archdiocese served as sanctuaries.) The overwhelming support for the radical proposal suggests how widely accepted the open parish was at St. Peter's.[168]

At the heart of the open parish was associate pastor Jim Hagan. Hagan had begun working at St. Peter's in 1965 as a seminarian, guiding one of Petroni's little-parish Bible study groups. In 1968, he returned for his diaconate year and in 1969 he was ordained; he then remained stationed at St. Peter's through 1975.

During Hagan's stay at St. Peter's he was regarded by many as an "eccentric" or an "oddball."[169] His eccentricity stemmed from his desire to be with the poor and despised, to be the least, and in the Mission this meant being with the Spanish-speaking. Rarely would he dress in clericals, rather he would wear black jeans, T-shirt, and work boots. Hagan's other trademark was grease under his fingernails, obtained from working on people's cars, or fixing their stoves or washing machines. Though many of the English-speaking parishioners had their doubts about Hagan, he was deeply loved by the Spanish-speaking community. One Spanish-speaking mother, when asked about "Padre Jaime," as Hagan was known, sighed lovingly and exclaimed, "San Francisco de Asis."[170] Another woman observed, "He gives his heart to everyone."[171]

Guiding Hagan's apostolate was the Catholic Worker belief that the poor had to be served at a personal sacrifice. Hagan once wrote, "The lifestyle of the Catholic Worker is what I would wish for myself."[172] In the Catholic Worker philosophy, each person was responsible for the transformation of society; he or she could not transfer that responsibility to the state or to some other institution. Personal service and personal responsibility were, for Hagan, grounded in a personal and loving God. His description of a conversation he had with a dying friend reflects his image of God. "She began to talk to me about her life and about God. You could see the union between God and humankind . . . a God who cared about people, a God who brought people together, that stood for justice and for right."[173] And in another situation he would assert, "There is such a thing as grace, God's favor that lives within us."[174]

Hagan's notion of personal responsibility and a personal God convinced him that a major part of his priesthood was simply to be present and available to people. Juanita Alvarez remembers, "When he was here, you could call him at midnight and he would come; at whatever time you called him, he was always there."[175] And another parishioner, Maria Guerrero, mother of six daughters, remembers, "Padre Jaime was everywhere. . . . I remember one day he came here and I told him that my washing machine was out of order. He went, got a part and helped me. He left whatever he was doing to help others, and when he finished with you, he would go and help someone else."[176] The needs of the people were his primary ministry. His example of priesthood deeply affected all those with whom he came in contact, inspiring people to serve in the parish and in the community.

The ministry most closely identified with Hagan was his "mechanics ministry." Hagan enjoyed working with his hands. He was constantly helping people repair their cars, refrigerators, or washing machines. One parishioner remembers, "It was very rare when you didn't see [him with] his feet sticking out from beneath somebody's car or fixing a stove."[177] To assist in this ministry Jim was aided by "George the junkman," who would set aside parts especially for Hagan.[178] Hagan repaired a 1959 Chevrolet pickup truck which soon became the community truck. In keeping with the open parish, the truck was used by anyone in the community who needed it. In a poor, working-class neighborhood, Hagan's mechanical gifts were greatly appreciated.

Beyond personal service, Hagan sought to build small communities at St. Peter's that would empower the people to address their own needs and the needs of the Mission. He began with Bible study groups which soon evolved into "comunidades de base," literally base communities. The comunidade met once a week, to, as one member described it, "reflect on the gospel . . . and apply it to our work in the community. Through the gospel we saw the needs in our parish and we tried to find practical solutions to those needs, but always in light of the gospel."[179] The Bible-study/comunidade discussions were not lessons with the priest as instructor but creative and deeply personal discussions about the message of Jesus. At the height of this development, eight base communities, consisting of eight to twelve people in a comunidade, were operating (two in English and six in Spanish). The members of the comunidades worked hard in support of the parish, and were always available when work needed to be done.[180] Though only two exist as of 1990, they remain highly visible and active in the life of the parish.

The comunidades harkened back to the "little parishes" of the 1960s and the small groups of the 1950s. All three groups used similar formats, though they did not use the same terminology to describe what they were doing. In Jocist terminology, all three groups employed the observe-judge-act method of Catholic Action. ("Jocist" is the term given to the movement started by Canon Joseph Cardijn in Belgium in the 1920s. It came to America as "specialized Catholic Action," in the form of the Young Christian Workers [YCW] and the Young Christian Students [YCS].) The members of each group would "observe" their environment, "judge" whether what they observed was in accord with the gospel, and then "act" to lessen the gap between what they observed and what they had judged to be the Christian response. All three used a small-group dynamic which attempted to make practical applications of the gospel in their neighborhood. The comunidades were the most successful in showing tangible results.

The comunidades were made up of ordinary, working-class people—mechanics, longshoremen, day laborers, nurses, housewives.

Maria Guerrero was mother of six, Juanita Alvarez was mother of nine. Many of those involved knew little English. The comunidades not only allowed them to act on problems in their parish and neighborhood, they provided emotional and spiritual support to people considered marginal by American society. They assisted in incorporating these people into the parish, making them feel that they were not aliens being tolerated but that the parish was really theirs.

The Bible groups/comunidades and Father Hagan developed a variety of ministries designed to give people the opportunity to do things for themselves, to provide for their own needs and the needs of others. Leonor Solorzano, an original comunidade member, observed of the programs, "they were not something out of the blue, sponsored by some government agency, but they were there because the need was there."[181] One of the most successful programs was the food cooperative, created to provide food at cheaper prices than in the neighborhood markets. Comunidade members conducted a survey to determine the ten most-needed food items, and the co-op set about providing them. The co-op began in Hagan's garage, selling such staples as rice and beans. As the program expanded, the co-op moved into rooms in the old high school. At its height, the co-op had over 300 members with at least 50 attending its monthly meetings. People could join the co-op for $2 plus a pledge to work two hours a month, either staffing the store or picking up the food, which they purchased from another local co-op. The co-op continues to exist as of 1990, but at a much reduced level.[182]

Besides the co-op, the parish also ran an emergency food program and a supplemental food program out of the church and rectory. Feeding the poor and hungry was a high priority.

A less successful experiment, based on the same principle as the co-op, was the Fondo Comun, a community loan service, designed to assist people in need of emergency money. Since most people in the parish found it hard to obtain loans from local banks, the Fondo Comun was started. People would contribute to the common fund, then in times of emergency—unemployment, sickness, etc.—they could draw on the fund. They would pay the money back when they were able.[183] Again, the object of the Fondo Comun was for the community to provide for its own needs.

With the comunidades, Hagan also inspired the creation of several local "self-help industries" to provide jobs and income for the people (unemployment was a major problem in the Mission). A wedding industry was begun to provide young couples with an inexpensive wedding.

Women who could sew made wedding dresses, or altered dresses solicited from local department stores. Women who could cook prepared the wedding meal; others would decorate the hall.[184] The wedding industry never did flourish to any great extent. A candle-making industry was also initiated, which enjoyed little success at St. Peter's but which would blossom into a successful industry for the Catholic Worker farm at Sheep Ranch, California. Home gardens were also encouraged. People planted fruits and vegetables in their own yards, thereby supplementing their food budgets. All these programs encouraged people to provide for their own needs rather than relying on outside agencies.

A parish recycling program, operated by the youth of the parish, was also begun. The program was designed not only to help clean up the neighborhood but to provide the parish kids with something worthwhile to do. Successful youth activities had to have a point.[185] The year before, the young people painted the auditorium. Hagan picked up the ministry to the parish's street kids where Jim Casey had left off. (Casey had frequently taken children from the projects on trips to his parents' cabin on the Russian River.)[186] Hagan's and Casey's youth ministry was vital in a neighborhood where gangs were a major problem. They assisted in establishing the Real Alternatives Program (RAP) in the Mission by securing a storefront for the program. RAP attempted to provide counseling, jobs, education—whatever was necessary to enable youth to break out of the culture of poverty and self-destruction.[187]

Hagan was also instrumental in bringing Dorothy Day's Catholic Worker movement to St. Peter's. The Catholic Worker movement was established in New York City in 1933 by Dorothy Day and Peter Maurin.[188] Hagan and Rich Bonnano of the Catholic Peace Fellowship contacted Chris Montesano, who had recently returned to San Francisco after having worked for a year and a half at the New York Catholic Worker House. They convinced him to begin a Catholic Worker House of Hospitality in an old barroom and inn they had been able to lease. Montesano set about creating a house with definite countercultural aims, "where violence is met with love and the needs of our brothers take precedence over money."[189] At Hagan's urging, the house was named St. Martin de Porres House, to reflect the ethnic makeup of the neighborhood. The house began serving two free meals a day, breakfast and dinner, as well as holding "round-table discussions" once a week for "clarification of thought." St. Peter's was quite involved in the early days of the house, providing workers to cook a meal at least once a week. Other parishioners worked more often. Garage sales were held to raise money for the house. For their part, the Catholic Workers felt at ease in a parish like St. Peter's. The Worker's anarchist philosophy and radical political outlook often alienated it from ordinary parish life in many places, but at St. Peter's they felt "very welcome."[190]

Over time, the neighborhood became less welcoming, as the free meals brought a constant stream of unemployed, homeless transients into the neighborhood. Hispanics had difficulty accepting the sight of healthy young men accepting such charity.[191] In the mid-1980s, Martin de Porres House moved out of the parish to another location in the city, where it continues to operate its free-meal program. In 1976, Montesano and a group of the original San Francisco Workers established a Catholic Worker farm at Sheep Ranch, California. Part of the Worker vision was to "get back to the land." Sheep Ranch accomplished this. The Farm, among other things, actualized Hagan's candle-making industry, which as of 1990 provides a significant amount of the farm's support.[192]

An offshoot of the Worker at St. Peter's was "Padre Jaime's dormitorios." With the help of Francisco Alvarez, Hagan renovated an old garage to serve as a shelter for homeless men. Hagan himself slept there three nights a week. Hagan and the Catholic Workers established several other short-lived shelters. At one point, Hagan even considered converting the basement of the priests' rectory into a shelter, but this idea received little support from the parish team.[193]

All of the comunidades' and Hagan's programs were based on the principle that the parish should provide for the needs of the community, and for its own needs as much as possible. "We tried to do things not only to benefit our Church, but to enhance the entire community. The Church should reach out and respond to all that was happening in the community."[194] On a much more basic level, the parish sought to practice the corporal works of mercy.[195] In Hagan's words, "I was just interested in the basic things we ought always to take to heart—that the poor are fed, people are clothed, and the sick taken care of."[196] The message inspired many St. Peter's parishioners to act to lessen the ills they saw in their own neighborhood.

While Hagan's personal style endeared him to many, it annoyed many others. His outspoken opposition to the Vietnam War, and his support of the UFW, enraged some parishioners, particularly because of the radical nature of his protests.[197] His protests ranged from such traditional means as fasting, to the novel act of writing "GOD" in the blank for a social security number on a bank application,[198] to more drastic protests in which he was arrested. In 1970, he distributed to the parishioners of St. Peter's a two-page statement, preparing them for his arrest, and explaining his resistance to the Vietnam War. "The only power which will change the hearts of men is the power of love. . . . I do not believe in violence as an activity that will resolve human problems."[199] On one occasion he was arrested for blocking the entrance to the Oakland Army Induction Center. In 1973, he was arrested and spent two weeks in jail during a UFW protest. His most famous arrest involved an attempt to prevent the enormous aircraft carrier the USS *Enterprise* from leaving San Francisco Bay to go to Vietnam. Early one morning, Hagan and others set out in a ragtag flotilla of rowboats, and small motorboats, intending to "blockade" the *Enterprise*. The flotilla was easily brushed aside by FBI boats, and the participants were arrested.[200]

Hagan's arrests were hard for some parishioners to understand; they were unused to the idea of a priest going to jail. Harder to understand was Hagan's adherence to the Catholic Worker precept "Jail, no bail"; the jail sentence was to be served, no bail provided. On one occasion, despite Hagan's protest, a parishioner bailed him out of jail, unable to accept the thought of Padre Jaime in jail.[201]

While parishioners were divided over Vietnam, they were more unified in the support of Cesar Chavez and the grape and lettuce boycotts. As one parishioner remembers, "we walked and walked."[202] In 1972, Chavez spoke one Sunday at all the masses, stirring up support for his movement. The following year Dorothy Day made her second visit to the parish, during her protests in support of the UFW. The parish actively supported the UFW; according to Hagan, "St. Peter's was one of the main support parishes [for the UFW] in the whole country."[203] On one occasion, several hundred UFW workers lived in the St. Peter's auditorium for a week while they organized city-wide demonstrations. The parish joined other Catholic groups, most notably the Catholic Council for the Spanish-Speaking, and the Archdiocesan Social Justice Commission, in the demonstrations against Safeway and other supermarkets that continued to sell nonunion products.[204] St. Peter's tradition of strong union support was evoked on behalf of the UFW.

One of the novel elements of Hagan's protests was adapting traditional customs and devotions to protest. On one occasion, he sponsored the traditional Las Posadas at the San Francisco Federal Building. Accompanied by about 200 parishioners, "Mary and Joseph" knocked on the door of the Federal Building, to request lodging. No one answered. A Christmas party and games were then enjoyed in the Federal Plaza.[205]

In another instance, the traditional image of Our Lady of Guadalupe was transformed from the Mother of Solace to a beacon of liberation. According to one comunidade member, Our Lady of Guadalupe "fought to defend the Mexican natives from the oppression of the Spanish."[206] On Good Friday, Hagan led a group of people on a modern Way of the Cross through the city, stopping to pray at oppressive factories and war-related industries where Jesus was currently being crucified.

Hagan's sermons also caused controversy. He regularly commented on "current events": capital punishment, the Vietnam War, etc.[207] On one occasion, Hagan led the congregation out of the church, and around the neighborhood to show them the garbage and trash in the streets. He stressed the need for the parish to keep the neighborhood clean and urged the people to participate in the recycling program.[208]

Hagan's sermons "definitely galled a lot of people," and on occasion someone would walk out of the church in the middle of the sermon.[209] Neither was Hagan's personal style of ministry without its detractors. Many people were upset by his handling the Eucharist and distributing communion with grease under his finger-nails. Others were upset by the constant flow of "weirdos" through the parish hall.[210] Nonetheless, as radical as Hagan was, it is surprising that he did not encounter more opposition. He himself marveled at the tolerance of Flynn and Hennessy: "Anybody else would have kicked me out long before!"[211] Overriding any dissatisfaction with the priest, however, was the love and respect most of the community, particularly the Spanish-speaking, had for him. When he was transferred in 1975, several parishioners (Irish, Italian, and Hispanic) sent a petition to Archbishop McGucken requesting him to let Hagan remain at St. Peter's.[212] Several of the parish women threatened to go on "strike," but Hagan was transferred nonetheless.[213] He worked in several parishes before becoming a missionary in Tijuana, Mexico, in the early 1980s. Parishioners still run fund-raisers to support his work there.[214]

Many others contributed to St. Peter's during this period beside Hagan. While lacking Hagan's flair they worked hard in keeping people attached to St. Peter's. Sister Ruth Marie Bareda, a Peruvian, worked hard among the Spanish-speaking. Father John J. McCarthy, a more conservative man than Hagan, replaced Casey as chaplain to the Catholic Council for the Spanish-Speaking, and actively promoted the Christian Family Movement (Movimiento Familiar Cristiano) and the Marriage Encounter (Encuentro Conyugal) at St. Peter's. Sister Ana Maria Pineda, a Sister of Mercy, also worked with the Hispanic community, with MFC and EC, and with National Hispanic Encuentro. The parish school continued to struggle along though it no longer enjoyed as central a place in the parish as it once had.

By the 1970s, a small Filipino community had established itself at St. Peter's, making up a little more than 10 percent of the parish. Their presence was acknowledged, as already indicated, by trilingual masses on Thanksgiving and Christmas Eve. Their presence was also acknowledged by two Filipino deacons being stationed at St. Peter's. In 1973, a parish Filipino Club was established. The driving force behind establishing a Filipino identity at St. Peter's was the family of Carmen and Mariano de la Cruz. They worked hard to provide Filipino social events, and even planned and orchestrated the traditional Filipino devotion and celebration, Flores de Mayo. Through their efforts the Filipinos found a special niche at St. Peter's.[215]

In 1976, the parish received two new assistant pastors, Thomas McElligott and Tom Seagrave. In the same year, Flynn embarked on his last major endeavor as pastor, the Community in Action program (CIA). Jim Purcell of Catholic Social Services and Fred Ross, Jr., of the Community Services Organization were hired to organize the CIA. Using community-organizing techniques, they organized a series of parish home "clusters," in which parishioners gathered to express their impressions of the needs and condition of St. Peter's. After several months of these "listening" sessions, a town meeting was held. Over 200 parishioners attended. Reports were read summarizing what had been said in the cluster meetings. Committees were then formed in the areas of the greatest needs—youth, elderly, crime, neighborhood, and church—to fashion specific responses to the needs the CIA had brought to light.[216] As the parish began to answer the needs, Flynn was transferred. A new era was about to begin.

By 1978, the demographic transition was just about complete. Seventy-one percent of the parish was Hispanic; another 17 percent was Filipino. The old Irish and Italian community had moved up and out of the Mission. Nor did the influx of Hispanics slow during the 1980s as wars in Nicaragua and El Salvador ensured a fresh stream of new Peterites. The years 1964–78 had placed extraordinary burdens on St. Peter's—the ecclesiastical transformation mandated by Vatican II, the unending social turmoil and protests, and the constant stream of people entering and leaving St. Peter's. Few remained who remembered Father Peter Yorke. Nonetheless, the two new pastors would attempt to return the parish to its traditional concerns: education and devotions.

The Era of the "Two Toms": Back to the Mainstream, 1976–1985

St. Peter's "avant-garde" tradition seemed to be intact when, in 1978, assistant pastors McElligott and Seagrave were appointed co-pastors of St. Peter's, making them the youngest pastors in the archdiocese, and the first co-pastors ever. The concept was so new that there was no provision in canon law for it, so McElligott and Seagrave were officially appointed "canonical administrators."[217] Seagrave and McElligott had petitioned the archbishop to appoint them as co-pastors. Having experienced the collegiality of Flynn's pastorate, they felt well prepared to pioneer this new form of parish leadership. The co-pastorate was aided by the fact that Seagrave and McElligott complemented one another well. Seagrave was a "dynamo," outgoing and gregarious; McElligott was more introverted and reflective. Seagrave had a basic knowledge of Spanish, but worked primarily with the Filipino and English-speaking communities. McElligott was fluent in Spanish, and dealt mainly with the Spanish-speaking community. Other responsibilities were divided between the two men, but ultimate responsibility was shared by both. For seven years, the two, affectionately known as the "two Toms," directed the parish amiably together.

Despite their pioneering status, the two Toms brought to St. Peter's some very traditional notions of parish life. Seagrave believed that the parish, under Hagan and Flynn, had neglected the "more mundane aspects of parish life" and thereby put itself "out of the mainstream of things."[218] The traditional features of parish life were in decline: mass attendance was down, as was participation in the other sacraments, school enrollment was declining, and the parish was staggering under an enormous debt (over $200,000). In addition, neighborhood evangelical churches continued to raid the Hispanic community. Seagrave and McElligott set out to bring St. Peter's back to the mainstream by establishing three basic goals: (1) increase the sacramental participation of the parish, (2) revive the parish school, and (3) pay off the parish debt. In many ways, their plan echoed the pastoral advice given to St. Peter's by Archbishop McGucken some fourteen years earlier—make people more regular and practical Catholics.

For fourteen years the parish had thrust itself into the community and its affairs; under the two Toms, the parish would become a place of refuge from the violence of the neighborhood and from the struggles of daily living. The church was to be a welcoming, comforting place, personified by the welcoming, personal style of the new pastors. Seagrave remembers, "Our pastoral approach . . . was very personal. It was not real programmatic."[219] Both Toms would be out in front of the church before and after every mass to greet their parishioners. Both priests distributed communion at every mass so the people would have a personal experience of them as ministers. They attempted to trade in every shop and restaurant along 24th Street, but above all they tried to visit people in their homes.[220]

The chief means of getting into people's homes was the age-old technique of the parish census. Ostensibly designed to obtain basic information about the parish, the census was used by Seagrave as a means of making personal contact with the people. Motivating Seagrave was his belief that although "the people [at St. Peter's] had a strong, basic Catholic faith, *the message must be carried out to them*. The priests cannot sit back and wait for the people to come to them."[221] The Jehovah's Witnesses and others were out going door to door. Following their example, Seagrave visited around 4,000 homes during his pastorate. "My whole style," he once observed, "is to push doorbells."[222] As a result, Seagrave encountered a lot of people who were alienated from the church, mad at it, or simply indifferent to it, while gaining a personal awareness of the problems his parishioners faced. Contacts made through the census also increased sacramental participation, inspiring many people to have their marriages blessed or their children baptized. By 1982, St. Peter's was celebrating 500 baptisms a year, a large number by archdiocesan standards. Mass attendance was also up.[223]

What distinguished St. Peter's during these years was its continued sensitivity to its Spanish-speaking parishioners and their cultural traditions. The number of Sunday masses in Spanish was increased to three. Seagrave reflected, "People like to pray in their native language even if they are bilingual and speak perfect English. That's one time it shouldn't be an exercise in language. You should be able to concentrate on the spiritual experience."[224] The co-pastors showed an equal sensitivity to the Hispanic penchant for sacramentals and paraliturgical devotions— scapulars, medals, novenas, relics—that seemed to many like superstition and magic more than religion. Rather than demanding that people abandon their devotions and become modern American Catholics, St. Peter's accepted the people where they were. McElligott remembers, "Our first response to people was not to change their attitude, but to accept them, and to try and take these customs and develop them into a way more appealing to modernity but never disrespecting their culture."[225] Or as Seagrave put it, "If these things are important to these people then, first of all, let's find out what is of value in these things, and affirm them."[226] Practices that brought people closer to God and helped them to lead better lives were not to be discouraged.

The Hispanic love of ceremonials kept the co-pastors busy. Seagrave and McElligott found themselves performing ceremonies "all the time." They would say as many as five masses on Saturday. Hispanics were particularly fond of memorial masses. Following a funeral, many Hispanics observed the custom of a rosary novena that would conclude with a mass. Then they would try to have a mass for the thirty-day, one-, two-, and five-year anniversaries of the death. "Quinceaneras" celebrations also became frequent in the parish. The quinceaneras was a coming-out party for a young Hispanic woman when she reached the age of fifteen. The celebration was as elaborate and as formal as a wedding, complete with attendants, godparents, extended family, and formal dinner party. Some pastors discouraged this practice, but the two Toms did as many as possible.[227]

St. Peter's was fortunate to receive two Hispanic assistant pastors: Guadalupe Moreno (1979–81) from Mexico, and Mamerto Sigaran (1981–85) from El Salvador. Both were greatly loved by the Hispanic community.

Ethnic celebrations became a central feature of parish life in the 1980s. While the feast of Our Lady of Guadalupe and the Nicaraguan feast of the Immaculate Conception, as well as various others, had been established during the 1960s, during the period from 1978 to 1990 the number of celebrations increased and flourished. Though different saints and patrons were honored, the festivities usually followed a similar pattern. A procession would carry the sacred image through the parish streets to the church, where mass would be celebrated. Mass would be followed by "un gran Kermess," a party with traditional national foods, music, and dancing. National flags were often displayed. All the celebrations were regarded as ways of passing on the religious and cultural traditions to the children, an important function in an immigrant community. In addition, the procession provided a public witness of immigrant faith and pride to the larger San Francisco community.

St. Peter's celebrated a variety of feasts. The Nicaraguans celebrated the Immaculate Conception (December 8) with "La Griteria"; the feast of St. Dominic de Guzman, in late July; and the Procession of Men on January 1, in which the men of the parish would follow in procession the Blessed Sacrament carried by the priest.[228] In the late 1970s, the parish received an influx of Salvadorans as a result of the political turmoil in El Salvador; this heightened the Salvadoran feasts of Santa Ana in July and the major celebration, Salvador del Mundo, in August. In this feast, patriotic songs and sacred hymns are sung as a statue of El Salvador is carried through the streets. Those in the procession are grouped according to their native town in El Salvador. The national flag of El Salvador is carried. Between songs a leader shouts, "Viva el Salvador del Mundo," to which the crowd responds, "Que viva!" The parish also celebrated memorial masses in honor of the slain Archbishop Oscar Romero, and for the four American missionaries murdered in El Salvador in 1980. Additional feasts would be celebrated for the smaller immigrant communities, as well as masses in honor of town saints. For instance, the people from San Ysidro would have a special mass on the feast of St. Isidore.[229]

The greatest ethnic feast during this era, undoubtedly, was the feast in honor of Our Lady of San Juan de los Lagos. The devotion originated in the small town of San Juan de los Lagos in Jalisco, Mexico, and centered on the miraculous power of a small statue of Mary.[230] People would pray for various favors; if the favor was granted, the person would have to express his or her gratitude by making a pilgrimage to the statue of Our Lady residing in San Juan. This proved to be a hardship for people living at great distances from San Juan. The promise to Mary could be satisfied by visiting the "pilgrim Virgin," an exact replica of the original statue, which traveled to outlying areas of Mexico. Until 1980, the statue had never left Mexico.

The devotion to Our Lady of San Juan de los Lagos was carried into California as Mexicans from Jalisco migrated there. San Francisco experienced a revival of the devotion in the 1970s through the efforts of George Martinez, a lay office-worker at Mission Dolores who had grown up in San Juan and had a tremendous devotion to Our Lady of San Juan. He began passing a statue of Our Lady of San Juan from home to home, with a novena being prayed at each home. Soon the statue was circulating throughout the Bay Area. Martinez began an association to promote the devotion, sponsoring a monthly mass and a yearly celebration in honor of Our Lady of San Juan. With the assistance of Roger Hernandez, the devotion became a yearly feature of St. Peter's. The annual celebration was held on the feast of the Assumption (August 15), preceded by a novena (August 7–15).

In 1979, Martinez convinced the bishop of San Juan to allow the "pilgrim Virgin" to come to San Francisco, specifically to St. Peter's. He argued that the many Mexicans in California were unable to travel to

San Juan to repay their debt for a favor granted. In 1980, the pilgrim Virgin was allowed to come to San Francisco.[231]

For three days in August, 1980, wave after wave of worshipers from all over the Bay Area flooded St. Peter's. An estimated 30,000 people visited the Virgin. At one point some 2,000 candles were lit, making the church incredibly hot.[232] Since that year, the pilgrim Virgin has returned every year to St. Peter's, but the Virgin's U.S. itinerary has expanded, so St. Peter's is no longer the focal point for the celebration in northern California. Nonetheless, impressive crowds still attend the devotions.

The celebration surrounding Our Lady of San Juan de los Lagos at St. Peter's is similar to other ethnic celebrations held at the parish. A rosary and novena are prayed for nine days prior to the Assumption. Then on the feast of the Assumption, mananitas are sung in the morning. In the evening a procession carrying the statue of Our Lady proceeds through the streets of St. Peter's to the church, where a mass in honor of Our Lady is celebrated. A fiesta with mariachis, Indian dancing, and Mexican foods completes the celebration.

The association begun by Martinez continues to meet on the eighth of each month for mass, with about twenty people attending regularly. In the mid-1980s, a permanent statue of Our Lady was enthroned in St. Peter's Church. In addition, to raise money for the yearly celebration, the association, through the efforts of Frances Guillaumin, a Mexican immigrant, opened a religious-goods store at the back of the church, which is open on Sundays. The store is well stocked with rosaries made by Frances, scapulars, holy pictures, statues, novena prayers, and mementoes of Our Lady of San Juan de los Lagos.[233] As evidenced by the goods sold in the store, devotion to Our Lady of San Juan clearly reflects pre–Vatican II spirituality.

Besides the traditional ethnic devotions, the co-pastors emphasized Ash Wednesday and Good Friday, stressing the tangible and visual symbols associated with these devotions. While the Marian quality of Hispanic piety has often been stressed, equally as important in Hispanic piety is the suffering Jesus. St. Peter's initiated the practice of "all-day ashes." On Ash Wednesday, the first day of the Lenten penitential season, Catholics receive ashes on their foreheads accompanied by the words, "Remember, you are dust and into dust you shall return," to remind them of their mortality. St. Peter's began the practice of having a priest present in the church on Ash Wednesday from 6:00 in the morning until 12:00 at night, to distribute ashes. Up to ten thousand people would arrive each year to receive the ashes at some point during the day. On Good Friday, in a practice inspired by an article in *Modern Liturgy* magazine, a small piece of wood was hung around each person's neck during the veneration of the cross in the Good Friday liturgy.[234] The wood was something the people could take home, a tangible reminder of the reality of the cross in their lives.[235] Many parishioners placed the piece of wood in a prominent place in their homes. The visual was also stressed: "the altar of repose was lavishly decorated in the Hispanic tradition."[236] More impressive, the youth of the parish began dramatizing the Way of the Cross, the passion of Jesus. Good Friday liturgies had standing-room-only crowds. In a similar mode for Easter, one parishioner built a tomb-and-cave setting signifying the resurrection of Jesus. All these events stressed personal and physical contact as a means of inspiring devotion and attachment to the church, and reflected an interesting blend of traditional devotions and modern innovations.

The second goal of the two Toms was to remove the parish debt of over $200,000 and to repair the physical plant at St. Peter's. Many of the newly arrived Hispanics and Filipinos were unused to the Sunday envelope method of church support. St. Peter's struggle to retire its debt greatly benefited from an archdiocesan program that allowed poorer parishes to "twin" with wealthier parishes.

St. Peter's received little benefit the first couple of years of the program. Then in the last year of Flynn's pastorate, Seagrave and McElligott took over St. Peter's "twinning" program. Over the next few years they succeeded in twinning with several parishes, receiving $230,000 in twinning funds, in addition to $40,000 the parish had raised to meet its quota. Not only was the parish debt paid off, the parish was also able to paint the church, the school, and the convent. The whole program had a "wonderful" effect on the morale of the parish, and on the morale of the two new co-pastors. The archdiocesan program was a major boon to St. Peter's, relieving the parish of its financial burden and giving it a fresh financial start.[237]

Not content with merely twinning, the parish also worked at increasing the Sunday collection, which by 1981 had increased from $800 a week in 1978 to $2,000 a week.[238] The annual parish festival was also reinstated in 1977. In 1981, the festival cleared more than $40,000, double what any previous festival had cleared. By 1985, the parish was out of debt, but finance remained a major concern.

The third goal of Seagrave and McElligott was to revive the parish school. During the 1970s, although the parish subsidized the school by $30,000 a year plus bingo receipts, the school had not been the parish's central concern, as it had been in the days of Yorke and Hunt. The school was left to the direction of the Sisters of Mercy and the Parents Club. Seagrave and McElligott sought to reestablish the school at the center of the parish, where it would provide a refuge from the harsh world of the Mission and provide a loving, Catholic environment in which the children of the parish could grow. Sister Roseann Fraher, S.M., principal from 1980 to 1989, spoke of the school and its programs as "islands" designed to provide an environment "free from the violence of the neighborhood."[239] At the same time, the school served as a bridge between the Hispanic and American communities, enabling second-generation Hispanics to become part of the American community. McElligott recalls, "We felt that a solid, Catholic education was the only hope for those kids. It would provide the resources necessary to confront the world. It was the future we could give them."[240] The school would build up the community and the students. Seagrave asserted, "The whole emphasis of the school was to affirm the personal value of those children, so that they will have a sense of personal worth,"[241] defeating the negativism bred of the inner city. The school would enable the children of St. Peter's to succeed in America while remaining true to their Catholic faith. In the tradition of Yorke and Hunt, Seagrave and McElligott became frequent visitors to the school and the schoolyard.

The school did more in the 1980s than merely educate the children. It also provided services that reflected the changing nature of the neighborhood and parish. The school sponsored parent-support groups for single parents, one in English, one in Spanish. It offered English classes, and in 1987 it offered classes to assist undocumented residents in filing for amnesty. The school also reflected a sensitivity to the bilingual character of the parish. Though bilingual education was not offered, the first-grade class was grouped according to language ability, and all the parent meetings were conducted in English and Spanish. The school also adjusted to the high poverty level of the area, providing 30 percent of the students with scholarships.[242] As in the days of Yorke, "St. Peter's School does provide a source of encouragement, support and pride for all the people of St. Peter's parish."[243]

Despite the renewed emphasis on the school, it faced enormous financial problems, like other inner-city Catholic schools. Also indicative of Catholic schools everywhere, St. Peter's had fewer Sisters teaching in the school in the 1980s than it did in the 1950s. The need to hire lay teachers involved a major increase in the school's operating budget, and required a greater subsidy to the school from the parish. During the

1980s, the parish subsidy increased significantly, including the addition of a monthly second collection at all the Sunday masses for school support. In 1980, however, Seagrave informed the teachers that St. Peter's would not be able to give them the raise suggested by the Archdiocesan Department of Education. To Seagrave's surprise, when he informed the archdiocese of this, it agreed to subsidize St. Peter's School to cover the raise. From 1980 on, St. Peter's would receive a regular subsidy as part of the archdiocese's commitment to keep inner-city schools open.

As he had done with parish finances, Seagrave worked hard to increase other school revenue, and he found a great deal of support from former parishioners. In 1980, an alumni club was begun, different from the Girls' Academy alumnae. All past members of the St. Peter's schools were encouraged to support the current parish school—to repay their debt to St. Peter's. Thus began a yearly mass and fund-raiser for all the old Peterites. More innovative, Seagrave placed ads in the *San Francisco Monitor* and the *San Francisco Progress* requesting support for the school. One ad read, "Be an Angel this Easter—Please Help Save Our School— St. Peter's School in the Mission District cannot survive much longer without substantial help from people who believe in the value of good Catholic education and who live outside our parish."[244] The appeal to the alumni and the general public produced a steady flow of small donations—$5, $10, $25, many including notes such as, "Enclosed is a donation . . . in the memory of your late pastor, Peter C. Yorke."[245] While the present generation of St. Peter's might not know Yorke, his spirit still motivated many old-time Peterites. Finally, in 1982, a "Support-a-Student" program was begun, whereby a parishioner would contribute to the support of a student from a low-income family.

Under Seagrave and McElligott the strong bond between the school and the parish, a major tradition at St. Peter's for so long, was strengthened. Besides fulfilling their three major goals, the two Toms allowed many programs to continue. Several of Hagan's programs, the food co-op, and the Fondo Comun, struggled on, if at a much reduced level. At least one of the comunidades de base survived, and the outward thrust of the parish was not completely abandoned. In 1983, at the instigation of a committee from Old St. Mary's parish, St. Peter's established a Housing Committee, designed to assist tenants with indifferent landlords, similar to Casey's committee in the late 1960s. Even during the era of the two Toms, some complained the parish was too political. In 1984, a charismatic prayer group was established at St. Peter's. Reflecting the general right-wing inclination of the charismatic movement in America, the group complained that several groups at St. Peter's were using the "teachings of Christ" to promote "communism."[246] All the radical elements were not gone from St. Peter's.

Nonetheless, the era of the two Toms marked a definite turn away from the direction of the previous fourteen years at St. Peter's. The radical, open parish of Casey, Petroni, Flynn, and Hagan was redirected to what Seagrave and McElligott perceived to be the mainstream of parish life, even if they did not make it quite all the way. However, the parish could not be confused with the usual post–Vatican II parish. St. Peter's sensitivity to its newly arriving immigrants, and its accommodation to their cultural traditions and needs, made it more akin to an old-style national parish than a typical post–Vatican II parish. In addition, while parish leadership reflected post–Vatican II concerns, the devotional life clearly reflected pre–Vatican II theology.

In 1985, Father William Justice was named pastor, and under his direction the parish reflected the varied contributions of the past seven decades. The school remains a major priority. Two comunidades de base continue to contribute to the life of the parish. The Housing Committee continues to counsel troubled tenants. Emergency food programs continue to provide food for the hungry. The parish hall is opened every evening to shelter homeless young men. The St. Anne's Confraternity remains a link to the past, operating as a Senior Citizens' Club. The various ethnic celebrations—Salvador del Mundo, la Griteria, Guadalupe, Our Lady of San Juan de los Lagos, et al.—continue to be celebrated. All that has gone before has contributed to the St. Peter's of today, a parish that continues to be called upon for creative responses to poverty, high geographic mobility, typical inner-city problems, and a continuing wave of new immigrants. The developments under Father Justice indicate St. Peter's will continue to respond to the problems of its congregation and neighborhood, and continue to invest in each parishioner a sense that St. Peter's is his or her own.

Conclusion

During the years from 1913 to 1990, St. Peter's was transformed from an Irish parish to a multicultural Hispanic parish. The transformation did not come easily, and was made more difficult by the changes inspired by the Second Vatican Council, the social turmoil of the 1960s, and the decline of the Mission District. As the parish received increasing numbers of Hispanics, the civil rights movement and Vatican II insisted on a greater sensitivity to, and awareness of, people of color. As it welcomed the new Hispanics, St. Peter's thrust out from its insulated enclave to confront the world and participate in its transformation. The parish began confronting such unchurchly issues as housing, racism, war, poverty, urban renewal. The problem the church encountered was, as John Petroni put it, "There were too many needs."[247] The era of Jim Hagan also called the parish to assist in the transformation of the social order, but Hagan emphasized personal responsibility and personal service. The gospel injunction to feed the hungry, to clothe the naked, to shelter the homeless—more simply, to love one's neighbor—was made tangible by Hagan and his co-workers in the comunidades de base. Under Seagrave and McElligott, the parish no longer felt compelled to change the world, rather it opened its arms as a refuge from the world's difficulties. The attempt to insulate the parish, and to stress the importance of the school, brought St. Peter's full circle back to the Yorke era. Whatever its orientation, the genius of the parish has been to bestow on its parishioners a sense of belonging, of being at home in St. Peter's.

Several lessons may be learned from the history of St. Peter's. First, while the laity there have always been active, the pastors and priests have played a key role in determining the direction and spirit of the parish. With each new pastor and priest, St. Peter's took a different direction and style. The priests, however, were limited in what they could do by the needs of their people and of the community. In Yorke's time, the accepted ecclesiology made the pastor the unchallenged leader of the parish, but even Yorke worked hard to develop a close relationship with his people. Parishioner support for Yorke was due in no small measure to the fact that he articulated the deeply felt needs of his Irish working-class parishioners. In the post–Vatican II era the ecclesiology changed; no longer was the pastor the "unchallenged leader." The laity was to be "coresponsible." The styles of Casey, Petroni, Flynn, and Hagan reflected the new orientation. As priests, they played important leadership roles in the parish, but they also sought to empower the laity. As with Yorke, success depended on their ability to respond to the needs of the parish and of the community.

Second, St. Peter's became the premier Hispanic parish because of its commitment, at times grudging, to make a place for the newly arriving Hispanics within the parish. The parish made a real effort to provide for the needs of the Hispanic congregation. Several Spanish-speaking parishioners expressed their gratitude, "This parish has helped me grow a lot because I've been able to develop spiritually in my own language";[248] according to another parishioner, the best thing about St. Peter's is "that we've had priests that understand the Hispanic and they have made us grow."[249] At the heart of ministry to the Hispanic community at St. Peter's was not a fancy theory, or "strategy," but a basic acceptance of the people where they were, as they were. Hispanic ministry was successful ultimately because the newer Latino groups came to feel welcome at St. Peter's, to feel they were a vital and valued part of the parish.

Third, such acceptance was not always the way at St. Peter's. The clash between the Irish and the Hispanics was not only a clash of races and national cultures, it was also a clash of religious cultures. The practical Irish Catholics had difficulty understanding their "erratic" Hispanic compadres. Much of the clash could have been avoided had the Irish not been stricken with "immigrant forgetfulness," forgetting that they were descendants of immigrants themselves. Striking similarities exist between the two immigrant communities. Both faced a hostile environment that spawned anti-Irish, anti-Catholic, and anti-Hispanic attitudes. Both remained intensely interested in political developments in their own countries. Both tried to perpetuate certain of their cultural traditions and demonstrated their attachment publicly through parades and devotions. Both promoted the value of the family and maintained strong family ties. Both took immense pride in being St. Peter's parishioners. The most significant difference between the two groups is that the Irish had priests and pastors of their own, the Hispanics did not. Except for Almendares, until 1979 the priests who ministered to the Hispanic community were Anglo/Irish. In addition, most of the Irish spoke English, while a large number of the Hispanic immigrants did not. Nonetheless, the basic similarities between the communities have been overlooked by Irish Catholics who have forgotten their past.

Whether Irish, Italian, Filipino, or Hispanic, St. Peter's has been successful because it has made successive generations and groups of Catholics feel the parish was theirs. When asked what is the best thing about St. Peter's some parishioners said the people; others said the school. But again and again the people stressed the best thing about St. Peter's is that they felt "valued," "trusted," and welcomed there. In sum, St. Peter's parish has projected the loving face of God, and God's son, combining the two Gospel images, "Come to me all you who are weary and find life burdensome, and I will give you rest," and "When you do this for the least of my brethren you do it for me." St. Peter's has sustained the tension of making the parish a warm, loving refuge and at the same time thrusting outward to assist those in need. The struggle continues.

NOTES

Typed transcripts of the interviews with Jack Bourne, Rev. James Casey, Rev. Nicholas Farana, Msgr. James Flynn, Sister M. Petronilla Gaul, Sister M. Claude Gillis, Rev. James Hagan, Roger Hernandez, George Martinez, Chris Montesano, Rev. John Petroni, Rev. Thomas Seagrave, and Rev. Leopold Uglesic are in the Archives of the Archdiocese of San Francisco (AASF). The interviews with Indiana Blandon, Frances Guillaumin, Warren Jenkins, Merced Juarez, Frank Quinn, Don Ramiciotti, and Leonor Solorzano are on tape and are in the AASF. The interviews with Juanita Alvarez, Rafaela Canelo, Maria Guerrero, Lupe Martin, Isaura Michel de Rodrigues, and Esther Sandoval were conducted in Spanish, and typed transcripts, in Spanish and English, are in the AASF; the English translations were done by Mary Lou Zola. Notes of the interview with Sister Rosann Fraher are in St. Peter's file, AASF.

1. "St. Peter's Parish," *San Francisco Leader*, June 19, 1920, p. 11.

2. William Issel and Robert Cherny, *San Francisco, 1865–1932: Politics, Power and Urban Development* (Berkeley: University of California Press, 1986), pp. 63–66.

3. Brian Godfrey, "Inner City Neighborhoods in Transition: The Morphogenesis of San Francisco's Ethnic and Non-Conformist Communities" (Ph.D. diss., University of California, 1984), p. 186.

4. Sister M. Petronilla Gaul interview, June 19, 1989, at Mercy Convent, Burlingame, Calif.

5. Frank Quinn, *Growing Up in the Mission* (San Francisco: San Francisco Archives, 1985).

6. Warren Jenkins interview, July 18, 1989, at St. Peter's Rectory.

7. Rev. Nicholas Farana interview, July 7, 1989, at Archives of the Archdiocese of San Francisco (hereafter AASF).

8. Merced Juarez interview, August 5, 1989, at home in Stockton, Calif.

9. Geraldine Fregoso, "Growing Up in the Mission," *San Francisco Examiner and Chronicle*, California Living Section, April 21, 1974, p. 14.

10. Issel and Cherny, *San Francisco*, p. 66.

11. Lynn Ludlow and Mireya Navarro, "The Mission: Poor Streets, Proud Streets," *San Francisco Examiner*, October 20, 1981, p. 6.

12. James P. Walsh, *Ethnic Militancy: An Irish Catholic Prototype* (San Francisco: R & E Research Associates, 1972), p. 6.

13. "Miss Daley Opens Gaelic Dancing Class," *San Francisco Leader*, March 23, 1921, p. 8.

14. "Program for St. Patrick's Day," *San Francisco Leader*, March 11, 1922.

15. St. Peter's file, AASF.

16. "Women Hold Great Meeting for Bond Certificate Campaign," *San Francisco Leader*, February 28, 1920, p. 1.

17. "St. Peter's Branch AARIR," *San Francisco Leader*, March 12, 1921, p. 1.

18. "The Scotch Irish," *San Francisco Leader*, June 25, 1921, p. 4.

19. "Great Irish Meeting in Santa Clara," *San Francisco Leader*, April 11, 1921, p. 1.

20. See Walsh, *Ethnic Militancy*.

21. "Father Yorke's High Tribute," *San Francisco Leader*, November 11, 1922.

22. This sacrificial ethos was typical of many Catholic groups in the pre–Vatican II era.

23. "Sermon on Death," Yorke Papers, University of San Francisco Rare Book Room (hereafter Yorke Papers).

24. Yorke Diary, September 24, 1922, Yorke Papers.

25. Jenkins interview.

26. Yorke Diary.

27. Peter C. Yorke, "The Parish School and the Catholic Parish," in *Educational Lectures* (San Francisco: Textbook Publishing Co., 1933), p. 195.

28. "Father Yorke—Editorial," *San Francisco Leader*, April 11, 1925, p. 6.

29. Gaul interview; Jenkins interview; Sister Mary Claude Gillis interview, July 20, 1989, at Marian Convent, Burlingame.

30. See St. Peter's file, AASF.

31. Cited in Walsh, *Ethnic Militancy*, p. 33.

32. Ibid., p. 5.

33. See Jeffrey M. Burns, "Building the Best: A History of Catholic Parish Life in the Pacific States, 1850–1980," in Jay P. Dolan, ed., *The American Catholic Parish: A History from 1850 to the Present* (Mahwah, N.J.: Paulist Press, 1987).

34. Ralph Hunt, unpublished "History of St. Peter's" (1934). In the AASF.

35. "St. Peter's Harvest Festival," *San Francisco Leader*, October 17, 1925, p. 1.

36. Joseph Brusher, S.J., *Consecrated Thunderbolt: A Life of Father Peter C. Yorke of San Francisco* (Hawthorne, N.J.: Joseph Wagner, 1973), p. 92.

37. Yorke, "The Teaching of Religion," in *Educational Lectures*, p. 173.

38. Yorke, "The Parish School," p. 213.

39. "Catholic Educators Re-Elect Father Yorke," *San Francisco Leader*, July 16, 1921, p. 1. The goal of every Catholic child in a Catholic school was mandated by the Council of Baltimore in 1884.

40. Brusher, *Yorke*, p. 85.

41. Sister Mary Camilla Fitzmaurice, B.V.M., "Historical Development of the Educational Thought of the Reverend Peter C. Yorke, 1893–1925" (Master's thesis, University of San Francisco, 1963), p. 56.

42. Ralph Hunt, Annual School Reports, AASF.

43. The Holy Family Sisters were an order founded in San Francisco in the nineteenth century, whose primary apostolate was the Christian education of public-school children.

44. Hunt, "History of St. Peter's."

45. "Father Ralph Hunt of St. Peter's," *San Francisco Leader*, March 22, 1924, p. 1.

46. Frank Quinn interview, July 7, 1989, at AASF.

47. Peter C. Yorke, "Teaching Liturgy in the Elementary Schools," in *Educational Lectures*, p. 53.

48. Quinn interview.

49. See R. W. Franklin and Robert L. Spaeth, *Virgil Michel: American Catholic* (Collegeville, Minn.: The Liturgical Press, 1988).

50. Yorke Papers.

51. Hunt, "History of St. Peter's."

52. The term "sodality" is derived from the Latin "sodalitus," which means fellowship or brotherhood. The earliest sodality was founded in Italy in the sixteenth century. By the twentieth century they were common features of parochial life in America.

53. "St. Anne's Confraternity," *San Francisco Leader*, March 23, 1924, p. 6.

54. Yorke Diary, Yorke Papers.

55. St. Peter's file, AASF.

56. Quinn interview.

57. Grottoes were common in many Catholic parishes and institutions as a result of the popular devotion to Our Lady of Lourdes, which was begun in the nineteenth century.

58. Gaul interview.

59. See Jay Dolan, *Catholic Revivalism* (Notre Dame: University of Notre Dame Press, 1978).

60. The Archdiocesan Mission Band was a group of San Franciscan diocesan clergy created by Archbishop Mitty in the 1930s to preach parish missions, thereby reducing the number of religious order priests conducting missions.

61. "Capuchin Fathers Close Mission at St. Peter's," *San Francisco Leader*, November 19, 1921, p. 14.

62. Ibid., p. 14.

63. Quinn interview.

64. Sisters of Mercy, *Annals* (1941), Archives of the Sisters of Mercy, Burlingame, Calif. (hereafter *Annals*).

65. Yorke, "Teaching of Religion," p. 160.

66. Hunt was noted for his great personal holiness; he was reputed to have shoes that "always had holes in them." Jack Bourne interview, April 16, 1989, at home in San Francisco.

67. Farana interview.

68. Ibid.

69. "St. Peter's," *San Francisco Leader*, May 16, 1931, p. 1.

70. Timothy Hennessy, "Sermon at Dedication of School and Convent, May 25, 1963," St. Peter's file, AASF.

71. Bourne interview.

72. "Father Yorke Honored," *San Francisco Leader*, April 16, 1938, p. 1.

73. *Annals*, 1961.

74. Bourne interview.

75. Statistics, 1936 Census, AASF.

76. Don Ramaciotti interview, June 20, 1989, at home in San Francisco.

77. St. Peter's file, Christian Brothers Provincial Archives, St. Mary's College (hereafter SMC).

78. St. Peter's file, SMC.

79. Ibid.

80. St. Peter's File, AASF.

81. Ibid., 1958.

82. Eugene Schallert, *San Francisco Report II: The Catholic Parishes* (San Francisco: University of San Francisco, 1965), p. 542.

83. 1962 Report, Catholic Council for the Spanish-Speaking file, AASF.

84. Michael Fix and Steven Wallace, "Profile of the Central American and Mexican Immigrant Populations in the San Francisco Bay Area" (A Report to the San Francisco Foundation, by the Urban Institute, Washington, D.C., 1987). Copy in AASF.

85. Godfrey, "Inner City Neighborhoods," p. 173.

86. Roger Hernandez interview, June 21, 1989, at St. Peter's Rectory.

87. Godfrey, "Inner City Neighborhoods," pp. 173–86.

88. Statistics cited in Marjorie Heins, *Strictly Ghetto Property: The Story of Los Siete de la Raza* (Berkeley: Ramparts Press, 1972), pp. 25–26. Also Schallert, *San Francisco Report*, p. 541, and AASF records.

89. See Josephine D. Kellogg, "The San Francisco Mission Band, 1948–1961" (Master's thesis, Graduate Theological Union, Berkeley, 1974).

90. Isaura Michel de Rodrigues interview, July 17, 1989, at St. Peter's Rectory.

91. Ibid.

92. Father Leopold Uglesic interview, April 27, 1989, at St. Mary's, Oakland, Calif.

93. James Casey interview, March 20, 1989, at AASF.

94. 1962 Report, Catholic Council for the Spanish Speaking, AASF.

95. Ibid.

96. Rodrigues interview.

97. Rodrigues letter to Archbishop Joseph McGucken, July 12, 1964, St. Peter's File, AASF.

98. Hennessy to McGucken, August 14, 1964, St. Peter's file, AASF.

99. Uglesic interview.

100. Monsignor James Flynn interview, January 30, 1989, at St. Patrick's Seminary, Menlo Park, Calif.

101. Jenkins interview.

102. Casey interview.

103. Maria Guerrero interview, July 12, 1989, at home in San Francisco.

104. Juanita Alvarez interview, July 10, 1989, at home in San Francisco.

105. Quinn interview.

106. Fregoso, "Growing Up," p. 14.

107. Ramaciotti interview.

108. Ibid.

109. *Annals,* 1950s, passim.

110. *Annals,* 1960.

111. *Annals,* 1963.

112. Farana interview.

113. Casey interview.

114. Flynn interview; Casey interview; John Petroni interview, June 12, 1989, at office in San Francisco.

115. *Annals,* 1968.

116. Bourne interview.

117. Casey interview; Petroni interview.

118. Leo Mahon, "A Plan for Religious Instruction of the Spanish Speaking of Chicago" (1964). Offprint loaned to me by Father Ronald Burke, St. Bruno's Church, San Bruno, Calif.

119. Casey interview.

120. Hennessy to McGucken, February 2, 1966, St. Peter's file, AASF.

121. McGucken to Hennessy, July 15, 1964, St. Peter's file, AASF.

122. McGucken to Hennessy, July 14, 1965, St. Peter's file, AASF.

123. Hennessy to McGucken, February 8, 1966, St. Peter's file, AASF. The CCD is the Confraternity of Christian Doctrine, which conducts catechism classes for public-school children.

124. McGucken to Hennessy, February 9, 1966, St. Peter's file, AASF. Validations refers to the proper blessing of a marriage that had previously not been blessed by the church.

125. Casey interview.

126. Mission Coalition file, AASF.

127. Manuel Castells, *The City and the Grassroots: A Cross-Cultural Theory of Urban Social Movements* (Victoria, Canada: Edward Arnold, 1983), p. 110.

128. Robert Rosenbloom, "Pressure Policy Making From the Grassroots: The Evolution of an Alinsky Style Community Organization" (Ph.D. diss., Stanford University, 1976).

129. "Landlord-Tenant Pact in the Mission," *San Francisco Progress,* March 26–27, 1969, p. 1.

130. *Mission Housing Development Corporation: 15 Year Report, 1971–1986* (San Francisco: MHDC, 1986), p. 5.

131. "Pickets Outside St. Peter's," *San Francisco Examiner,* July 21, 1969, p. 21.

132. Arriba Juntos file, AASF.

133. Ibid.

134. Hernandez interview.

135. Parish Council Minutes, St. Peter's file, AASF.

136. Schallert, *San Francisco Report,* p. 545.

137. Casey interview.

138. *Annals,* 1965, 1969.

139. *Annals,* 1960s, passim.

140. Petroni interview.

141. Rafaela Canelo interview, June 15, 1989, at home in San Francisco.

142. *Boletino,* Catholic Council on Spanish-Speaking Bulletin (November 1967).

143. Petroni interview.

144. Parish Council Notes, St. Peter's file, AASF; Petroni interview.

145. *Annals,* 1965.

146. Esther Sandoval interview, July 19, 1989, at home in San Francisco.

147. Petroni interview.

148. Leonor Solorzano interview, March 30, 1989, at St. Peter's Rectory.

149. Parish Council Notes, AASF.

150. *Annals,* 1967.

151. Hernandez interview.

152. Bourne interview.

153. Flynn interview.

154. St. Peter's file, AASF.

155. Petroni left St. Peter's in 1968, Casey in 1969.

156. *Annals,* 1971.

157. Monsignor James Flynn, phone interview, August 23, 1989.

158. Flynn interview, January 30, 1989.

159. Ibid.

160. Father James Hagan interview, July 5, 1989, at Centro Juvenil in Tijuana, Mexico.

161. Letter of Flynn to McGucken, January 29, 1973, Dignity File, AASF.

162. See Marjorie Heins, *Strictly Ghetto Property.*

163. Ibid.

164. Ramaciotti interview.

165. Flynn phone interview.

166. Hagan interview.

167. Bourne interview.

168. Conscientious Objectors file, AASF.

169. Juarez interview.

170. Lupe Martin interview, July 13, 1989, at home in San Francisco.

171. Alvarez interview.

172. Vietnam Statement, January 13, 1970, St. Peter's file, AASF.

173. Hagan interview.

174. Ibid.

175. Alvarez interview.

176. Guerrero interview.

177. Solorzano interview.

178. Chris Montesano interview, July 14, 1989, at Catholic Worker farm in Sheep Ranch, Calif.

179. Canelo interview.

180. Hagan interview.

181. Solorzano interview.

182. Ibid.; Hagan interview.

183. Solorzano interview.

184. Canelo interview.

185. Hagan interview.

186. Ibid.

187. Castells, *City and Grassroots,* p. 114; Hagan interview. As of 1990, RAP still exists.

188. See Mel Piehl, *Breaking Bread: The Catholic Worker and the Origin of Catholic Radicalism in America* (Philadelphia: Temple University Press, 1982).

189. Quoted in Elizabeth Flynn, "Catholic Worker Spirituality: A Sect Within a Church" (Master's thesis, Graduate Theological Union, Berkeley, 1974), p. 92.

190. Montesano interview.

191. Solorzano interview.

192. Montesano interview.

193. Ibid.

194. Hagan interview.

195. The corporal works of mercy are to feed the hungry, give drink to the thirsty, clothe the naked, visit the imprisoned, shelter the homeless, visit the sick, bury the dead.

196. Hagan interview.

197. Juarez interview.

198. Montesano interview.

199. Hagan sermon in opposition to the Vietnam War, January 13, 1970.

200. Hagan interview.

201. Flynn interview.

202. Canelo interview.

203. Hagan interview.

204. NFWA file, AASF.

205. Hagan interview.

206. Canelo interview.

207. Ramaciotti interview.

208. Solorzano interview.

209. Montesano interview.

210. Juarez interview.

211. Hagan interview.

212. Letter to McGucken, June 23, 1975, St. Peter's file, AASF.

213. Guerrero interview.

214. Hagan interview.

215. Flynn interview.

216. *Annals,* 1976, 1977.

217. St. Peter's file, AASF.

218. Father Thomas Seagrave interview, February 6, 1989, at AASF.

219. Ibid.

220. Ibid.

221. Thomas Seagrave, "Proposal for Co-Pastorate at St. Peter's," 1978, St. Peter's file, AASF.

222. Ludlow and Navarro, "The Mission," *San Francisco Examiner,* October 19, 1981, p. 6.

223. Bourne interview.

224. Quoted in Don Lattin, "San Francisco: The Catholics," *San Francisco Examiner,* March 28, 1983, p. 4.

225. Father Thomas McElligott interview, July 21, 1989, at St. Elizabeth's Rectory, San Francisco.

226. Seagrave interview.

227. Ibid.

228. Indiana Blandon interview, July 18, 1989, St. Peter's Rectory.

229. St. Peter's file, AASF.

230. George Martinez interview, March 29, 1989, at Mission Dolores Rectory in San Francisco.

231. Ibid.

232. Seagrave interview.

233. Frances Guillaumin interview, July 20, 1989, in home in San Francisco.

234. McElligott interview.

235. Ibid.

236. *Annals,* 1985.

237. Seagrave interview.

238. 1981 evaluation, St. Peter's file, AASF.

239. Sister Rosann Fraher, S.M., interview, June 20, 1989, at St. Peter's School, San Francisco.

240. McElligott interview.

241. Seagrave interview.

242. Fraher interview.

243. Ibid.

244. Cited in *Annals,* 1983.

245. Letters on file at St. Peter's Rectory.

246. Charismatic Group to Archbishop Quinn, May 26, 1984, St. Peter's file, AASF.

247. Petroni interview.

248. Rafaela Canelo, quoted in Lattin, "San Francisco: The Catholics," p. 6.

249. Sandoval interview.

EIGHT

Making a Difference
Fourth Presbyterian Church of Chicago

MARILEE MUNGER SCROGGS

The Birth of Two Congregations

IT WAS 1848, AND Chicago needed a fourth Presbyterian church. The fifteen-year-old city was expanding north of the Chicago River, and those who lived on the "north side" found it inconvenient to cross the river to attend the First Presbyterian, Second Presbyterian, or Third Presbyterian churches. In addition, those congregations were affiliated with the "New School" branch of Presbyterianism, and some Chicagoans preferred the more conservative "Old School." (Ten years earlier, the Presbyterian Church in the U.S.A. had split over theological issues, church polity, and slavery. With both groups continuing to claim the original name, the only way to distinguish between them was by informal labels: Old School and New School.)[1] And so it was that the fourth Presbyterian church organized in Chicago was an Old School congregation located just north of the river. Known as North Presbyterian Church, it was officially organized with twenty-six members on August 6, 1848. Within two months they had built their first house of worship; two years later they had outgrown it and built another.[2]

The story of this congregation illustrates not only the Presbyterian Church's historic ability to attract and inspire city leaders but also the way in which those Presbyterian men and women understood the church itself to be an instrument for civilization, especially in the cities. As a result of their Calvinist "vocation" of public responsibility, Presbyterians sought to provide education, impose morality, dispense benevolence, and otherwise provide for the welfare not only of church members but of whole cities.

In fact, at least one of the founding members of North Presbyterian

Church expected this congregation to make a difference in the life of the *nation*. Inventor-industrialist Cyrus H. McCormick, who had arrived from Virginia in 1847, was deeply disturbed by the threat of a broken Union, brought on, he believed, by radical abolitionism. The key to saving the Union, he was convinced, was the growing frontier which was then the nation's Northwest, if it could be held to a conservative position on the issue of slavery in order not to push the South out of the Union. McCormick devoted his efforts to spreading conservatism, both theological and political, through his church and his political party, throughout the region.[3]

Recognizing the influence of the pulpit on public opinion, McCormick sought a preacher to champion his cause. When it became apparent that the first pastor of North Church was not such a champion, McCormick and other wealthy conservatives organized a second Old School congregation, known as South Presbyterian Church, in 1854. It was their intention to call Dr. Nathan L. Rice as its pastor. An opponent of abolitionism, Dr. Rice was a leader in the Old School and the editor of a Presbyterian journal; but he was unable to move to Chicago at that time. The preacher who was then called to South Church so disappointed McCormick that he considered organizing a third congregation. When the North Church pulpit fell vacant in 1857, however, McCormick held out such tempting financial inducements that Rice could no longer decline. Neither, apparently, could North Presbyterian Church. McCormick rejoined that congregation, bringing with him Nathan Rice and his journal, the *Presbyterian Expositor* (for which McCormick paid both debts and expenses).

Even before Rice arrived, the Chicago press was accusing McCormick of subsidizing the preaching of proslavery principles. Actually, McCormick opposed slavery in principle but felt that immediate emancipation by federal action invaded individual and states' rights and unnecessarily endangered the peace. Rice also denied being a proponent of slavery, but he preached that it was not a sin and that the church should not preach against it.

Although the city and the press were more and more abolitionist, the crowds who came to hear the controversial Dr. Rice quickly outgrew the building, which was enlarged and then replaced with a grand new edifice. When the large Romanesque brick building, complete with pipe organ, galleries, carpeted sanctuary, and central heat, was dedicated in 1861, the critical press had some justification for calling it "Mr.

McCormick's Church." But the $10,000 or more spent on the building was only part of his extensive support of the church and pastor.[4]

Meanwhile, in 1859, McCormick brought to Chicago an Old School seminary that had been forced by financial problems to close its doors in New Albany, Indiana. By endowing four professorships, McCormick revived the seminary with professors of his own choosing, and one of those professors was Nathan Rice himself. The seminary was meant to serve McCormick's "great cause." His purpose was "to keep that agitation [slavery] out of the church . . . for the preservation of the Union."[5] He envisioned each of the professors having a pastorate in the city, preaching regularly and contributing articles to the *Expositor*, spreading right doctrine and conservative influences throughout the area. And then he envisioned graduates of the seminary preaching conservative principles through all the Northwest.[6]

All his efforts and wealth, however, could not save the Union. In less than two years, the Civil War broke out. Most of the seminary students left to join the fighting, but three were induced to stay; and when North Church moved into its new building, the seminary took temporary quarters there. At the same time, however, Nathan Rice, tired of controversy and in ill health, left to accept a call to New York City's Fifth Avenue Presbyterian Church.

The congregation itself was sadly torn. Although "the conservatives had to be relied upon for most of the minister's salary," the majority of the members had become strongly antislavery.[7] McCormick was unable to influence the choice of the new pastor. While he and his wife were living in Europe during the war, his brother and family left the church because they could not endure the antislavery sermons and the applause of the congregation when the new minister, the Reverend J. B. Stewart, denounced the south. (When Cyrus McCormick and his wife returned from Europe, they lived in New York City until 1870, when they returned to Chicago, but not, at first, to North Church.)

National politics, however, was only one part of this congregation's life, as indicated by a description in an 1867 book by George S. Phillips, entitled *Chicago and Her Churches.*

> The society is composed of some of the best families in the city. . . . It is what is called a "rich church"; and most of the learned professions are represented. . . . No good cause in need of help pleads in vain at its doors. . . . They have been educated to the practice of

Christian benevolences, and sit under the preaching of the gospel of charity, with open purses in their hands. It is one of the most vital churches in the city. . . . Its Sunday schools are large and flourishing. . . . High and low, rich and poor, contribute their share of labor in the teaching and superintendence of them.[8]

One could indeed characterize this congregation as "a people with a cause"—but that cause was not so much political as philanthropic. It was education, Christian education, and relief of the poor. And the means for fulfilling this mission was simple individual generosity.

Meanwhile, North Church had ceased to be the only Presbyterian church north of the river. In 1853, a group of New School Presbyterians began meeting, first in a home and then at Rush Medical College—in exactly the same hall where North Presbyterian Church had held its first services. Taking the name Westminster Presbyterian Church, they were organized in July 1855. The economic depression of 1857 prevented them from building until 1860, when they at last completed "a little brown building of very humble and modest pretensions."[9] So it was that two very different Presbyterian congregations sprang up within three blocks of each other.

Both Westminster and North churches lost all their records in the Great Chicago Fire of 1871, and there is little available external evidence concerning the Westminster congregation, even in the 1867 book *Chicago and Her Churches*. Its author was so enthusiastic about the congregation's preacher, David Swing, that all he said about the congregation itself was that it would surely be "considerably enlarged" by having such a man in the pulpit.[10]

David Swing was an unconventional and compelling preacher. After studying the classics at Miami University (in Ohio), he had gone in 1852 to study theology in Cincinnati in the Old School seminary whose president was Nathan L. Rice. After one year, the seminary moved to Danville, Kentucky, and Swing returned to Miami University to accept the chair of Latin and Greek. Although deeply religious, he felt out of accord with current preaching and dogma. He did not like the hardness and pessimism of the doctrines preached by Dr. Rice and others—especially doctrines that pictured God as harsh and judging rather than as loving. He was also uncomfortable with the narrowness and intolerance that divided the different Christian denominations.[11]

Although uncertain whether to enter the ministry, he became a sought-after preacher throughout the Miami area. He preached at North Presbyterian Church in Chicago during the summer of 1862, after Dr. Rice had left the congregation torn over slavery and the war; but he turned down their invitation to become their pastor. Four years later, in 1866, he was persuaded to come as pastor to Westminster Church. Almost immediately, the little wooden church was too small to hold the audiences that came to hear him.

Merger and Tragedy

Just as time and the war were bringing the North and Westminster congregations closer together in their political views, so too the barriers were beginning to fall between the two northern branches of the Presbyterian Church in the U.S.A. As soon as the war was ended, the Old School and the New School (in the north) began to move toward reconciliation; and in 1869 the two groups voted to end the schism.

Seeing no need for two Presbyterian congregations so near to each other, the North and Westminster congregations immediately began working and worshiping together; and on February 12, 1871, they officially became one, taking the name "Fourth Presbyterian Church of Chicago." Although there were by now many more Presbyterian churches in Chicago, the name "Fourth" was not in use, and with the denominational schism ended, the congregation known as "North" could be acknowledged at last as the fourth Presbyterian congregation organized in Chicago. With an official membership of 351, and a worshiping congregation of some 800, the new congregation decided to use North Church's building and call Westminster's pastor, David Swing (the pastor of North Church having resigned to accept a call to Baltimore).

During the summer of 1871 the Fourth Church building was closed for expansion and renovation and the installation of a new organ. On October 8, the congregation worshiped for the first time in their refurbished building. Scarcely had the evening service concluded when fire broke out in the center of the city. The Great Chicago Fire left 18,000 buildings destroyed and 94,000 people homeless. Deaths numbered near 300. The Fourth Church building lay in ashes, as did the homes, stores, and offices of nearly all its members.

Most fortunes, however, were not completely lost, in part because what was in the banks was not lost. For instance, although McCormick's properties were destroyed and had to be completely rebuilt, his net loss (after insurance claims were settled) was about $600,000—compared to his assets of over $6 million.[12] And Henry King, also of Fourth Church and owner of a clothing company, lost stock worth more than half a million, but he managed to save some inventory by loading it onto a train the night of the fire and sending it to Indiana.[13]

Immediately after the fire, this same Mr. King accepted the responsibility of directing the Chicago Relief and Aid Society, which helped laborers find work (rebuilding the city) and distributed almost $5 million in aid. During those crucial months, he reserved but one hour a day for rebuilding his clothing business.[14] In addition to his leadership in business and in the city, Henry King was one of the congregation's most significant and respected leaders. First in Westminster Church and then in Fourth Church, he served as elder (an elected Presbyterian church officer). Another of Fourth Church's first elders was Roswell B. Mason, who was serving Chicago as mayor at the time of the fire. He had been elected as a "reform" mayor in a time of political corruption and rampant immoral business practices. Mayor Mason and director of relief Henry King were probably the two most important men leading the city's recovery from the fire.

Although nearly every member was homeless, the congregation of Fourth Presbyterian Church gathered only two weeks after the fire to take steps toward rebuilding. A resolution was adopted "to appeal to the church at large for aid" and to have Swing go East for that purpose. At the same meeting, "a committee of Ladies were chosen to relieve the suffering members of [the] congregation."[15]

Almost immediately they were able to secure, for their Sunday worship, a hall just south of the burned area. Although many members moved away, and although Sunday collections could hardly keep up with the expenses, church life continued. While Swing's preaching was filling Standard Hall with visitors, the congregation also met for midweek services, communion services, baptisms, prayer meetings, business meetings, and fellowship. At first they held these meetings in the vestry of St. James Episcopal Church. But as soon as possible they began meeting in the new home of Mr. and Mrs. Henry King. However popular Swing's preaching, these more intimate gatherings were what really kept the congregation together during the difficult days after the fire.

Far from destroying the congregation, the tragedy served to bring together the members from the two former congregations much more quickly than is usually the case in such mergers. Only four months after the devastation, on February 13, 1872, the trustees were instructed to purchase a lot at Rush and Superior streets at the cost of $20,000. On

April 18, the congregation authorized the trustees to borrow $25,000 in gold and to move toward building a new church home.

During that summer, Swing went on a preaching tour of the East, soliciting aid for rebuilding the church. The Presbyterian churches of the East were generous, and this experience of receiving aid from other churches was a formative one. Throughout the years, they were reminded, "Other Christians helped us to rebuild after the Chicago fire. It's our turn now."[16] Having received denominational support for its own beginnings, Fourth Church became one of the denomination's strongest financial supporters, a benefactor to many other churches in their own initial years.

When Swing returned from his preaching tour, McVicker's Theatre had been completed in the burned district, and the church began worshiping there. McVicker's was centrally located, convenient not only for the congregation but also for the businessmen who lived in the hotels in the rapidly rebuilding downtown. The popularity of Swing's preaching drew crowds every Sunday. Soon newspapers were printing his sermons every Monday morning. In addition, Swing became chief editorial writer of *The Alliance*, a new nondenominational paper known as "Professor Swing's paper," which quickly became a voice for liberal minds of all denominations.

Swing believed that the Christian faith needed a "restatement" if it were to be meaningful to the people of his day, particularly in Chicago. The spirit of Chicago was one of optimism and faith in progress through industriousness. The men of commerce were too rationalistic for rationally questionable dogmas and much too sure of their own power and free will to listen to dogmas of determinism, pessimism, or even damnation. Theirs was a down-to-earth spirit which called for, according to Swing, "a practical gospel . . . a mode of virtue, rather than a jumble of doctrines."[17] He was pleased to see people doubting the traditional dogmas, for he believed these doubts meant that faith was coming out of the abstract, "taking shape in a new sense of justice, . . . a new faith which affirmed that poverty, crime, disease . . . must not and need not be."[18]

Professor Swing (as he was popularly known) was able to reach those who were not otherwise being reached by the churches. Not only was his style compelling and learned, full of illustrations from poetry and science and history and the classics, but he sought to make faith reasonable and credible to those touched by the current skepticisms. Further, he deliberately and successfully set out to appeal to the rich and powerful in order that he might, through them, influence the shape of society. He appealed to their higher natures, challenging and inspiring them to humanitarian actions and spiritual virtues.

So great was the success of the services at McVicker's that the preacher and elders discussed whether there might be some method by which this downtown service could be continued; but the commitment of the congregation was to a church in and for their own community. The congregation worshiped in their new North Side building for the first time on the first Sunday of 1874.

The Heresy Trial

Now, however, the congregation faced another challenge. Less than a month after a joyous dedication of the new building, it was announced in a presbytery meeting that charges of heresy were to be brought against David Swing. (A presbytery consists of all the churches and ministers within a certain district. A synod consists of several presbyteries, and the General Assembly is the governing body of the entire Presbyterian denomination.) In the aftermath of the fire, the new congregation had been drawn closer together, but this new trial had consequences that were more complex. Although there were some differences of opinion, most of the members drew together around their leader. The real problem came with the eventual necessity of choosing between loyalty to that leader and to the Presbyterian church.

During the previous year Dr. Francis L. Patton, a recent graduate of Princeton Seminary, had been selected by Cyrus McCormick for the chair of theology at the seminary in Chicago. (McCormick exercised great control over the seminary by declaring that his endowment and support depended on the seminary's teaching only the Old School orthodox doctrines. In practice, therefore, faculty appointments depended on his approval.) In February 1873, McCormick also made Patton the editor of his newest publishing enterprise, the *Interior*. (One of the purposes of this journal was "advancement of the cause of reunion between the northern and southern branches of the Presbyterian Church," and it was perhaps the only Presbyterian journal that circulated in both the North and the South. This is particularly interesting in view of the vigorous crusade for reunion waged in the twentieth century by Fourth Church pastor H. R. Anderson.)[19]

Soon Patton was publishing reviews critical of the popular Swing. What disturbed him most was Professor Swing's evolutionary view of

the creeds: Swing believed that some doctrines could outlive their use-
fulness and be left behind. He also believed that morality had progressed past the morality of the Old Testament. For an orthodox
Presbyterian like Patton, it simply was not possible to question any Presbyterian doctrine nor any word of the Bible and still remain a Presbyterian minister.

In January 1874 a collection of fifteen of Swing's sermons was published, entitled *Truths for Today*. It became immediately popular across
the nation. In his New York journal, the popular Brooklyn preacher
Henry Ward Beecher hailed the book as a literary and religious event.[20]
Feeling pressed to take drastic measures, Patton announced his intention to bring heresy charges to the April meeting of the presbytery.
(There is no evidence that McCormick himself initiated the heresy
charges, but there is also no doubt that he supported Patton's actions.)

The trial's causes and implications went far beyond the bounds of
one congregation, one presbytery, or even one denomination. It represented the painful struggles that the nineteenth century witnessed in
almost every denomination. Christianity was being challenged by ratio-
nalism, science, especially evolution, contact with other religions, and
the scientific rational criticism of the Scriptures. Many responded to the
new ideas by doubting religion, and agnosticism became fashionable.
Within the churches two responses competed: a conservative defense of
orthodoxy and a liberal incorporation of the new ideas into broader religious understandings. In their own ways Patton and Swing were both
defenders of the faith: the one defending it against change, and the
other changing it to defend it against irrelevance and irrationality. The
tragedy was that they went so far in opposite directions that they could
not understand each other at all.

According to Joseph Fort Newton, Swing's biographer, David Swing
made the mistake of thinking that "no one" really still believed the dogmas that he had abandoned. Although he was a man "at home with the
age" and in tune with the progressive spirit of Chicago, he had greatly
underestimated the strength of Presbyterian confessionalism, the loyalty to the Westminster Confession of Faith of 1646 and other Presbyterian standards, particularly the writings of John Calvin.

This struggle was not new for the Presbyterian Church. Early in the
nineteenth century, some preachers had begun to break away from the
strict doctrines of total depravity and salvation by God's election (especially the implication that some are condemned by God's prior decision).
Instead they emphasized human worth and goodness, salvation avail-

able to everyone (through Christ), and human free will (the ability to choose salvation). Not only were these ideas more in accord with democracy and the confidence of the American spirit, but, more important, they transformed the conception of God as a capricious despot into that of a loving God who desired the salvation of all. This was the tradition in which David Swing stood.

Such convictions caused New School theologians and preachers to see that the formal, historical creeds of the Presbyterian church could no longer be accepted in their entirety.[21] They desired not to do away with the creeds but to accept them "in substance," rather than word-for-word, recognizing them to be historical documents. Old School theologians, on the other hand, rejected the idea of human free will, seeing it as a threat to the sovereignty of God; they remained steadfastly loyal to the creeds as essential for Presbyterian faith.

In 1835 Lyman Beecher, president of Lane Seminary in Cincinnati, was tried for heresy, as was another Presbyterian minister, Albert Barnes, in Philadelphia. These trials and the doctrinal divergences they represented had contributed to the 1837 split between the Old School and the New School. When the two "schools" reunited in 1870, the theological differences remained. A gentleman's agreement was made to tolerate divergent types of Calvinism, but the first years after reunion were a time for testing this policy of diversity. Those (especially of the New School) who feared for their theological freedom in a reunited church soon had their apprehensions justified. David Swing and Fourth Presbyterian Church were the first to fall victim after reunion to the conservative attempt to enforce orthodoxy throughout the denomination.

The trial attracted great attention in Chicago and throughout the nation. The Chicago press gave verbatim reports of it, and both secular and religious press freely discussed it. Afterward the presbytery printed a verbatim report of the entire trial. More significantly, an independent press published *The World's Edition of the Great Presbyterian Conflict: Patton vs. Swing.*[22]

The trial began on May 4; the jurors were all the ministers and one elder from each church of the Presbytery of Chicago (sixty-one voted). Patton charged that Swing had not been "faithful in maintaining the truths of the gospel . . . and [did] not sincerely receive the Confession of Faith."[23] Swing pled not guilty, claiming that he held "the general creed as rendered by the former New School Theologians." In his opening speech, Swing declared: "A creed is only the highest wisdom of a particular time and place. . . . Chief among the doctrines which our

473

Church has passed by . . . are all those formulas which . . . indicate the damnation of some infant, or that God, for His own glory, foreordained a vast majority of the race to everlasting death."[24] He was accused of preaching salvation by good works instead of by faith, because he emphasized morality and had criticized the doctrine of salvation by faith for seeming to promise salvation while condoning evildoing.[25] Also in question were his views on the developmental nature of the Old Testament. He held that the morality of the Israelites, especially their wars and treatment of enemies, was an underdeveloped, though developing, morality—not to be bound into a contemporary "rule of faith and practice."[26]

Witnesses called by the prosecution included four elders from Fourth Church who were asked whether their pastor preached Presbyterian doctrines. Their support for Mr. Swing was expressed in a paper signed by every member of the session (the congregation's governing body of elders) and distributed to religious journals, affirming their "undiminished confidence in the orthodoxy and ministerial fidelity of our pastor."[27]

One of the elders, Oliver H. Lee, expressed his feelings in the trial "that an outrage has been committed, not only upon the pastor of this church, but upon the whole membership of the church. Our church loves our pastor; and we rally around him with perfect unanimity." And he added ominously, "If he goes, I shall say to him as Ruth did: 'Where thou goest, I will go.'"[28]

After thirteen days of testimony and argument, on May 20, 1874, the Presbytery of Chicago acquitted David Swing by votes of 46 to 15 and 48 to 13. The outcome had hardly been in doubt: the jurors were Swing's friends, and Patton was regarded as a young Easterner with the audacity to tell Chicago preachers what to preach. Swing represented liberal Chicago Presbyterianism and Western freedom, and from the beginning the presbytery, city, and press were all against Patton. Yet it is historically significant that a preacher of decidedly liberal views was acquitted in Chicago at a time when such preaching was soundly condemned in the wider Presbyterian Church and in many other denominations.

The ordeal, however, was not over. Before the presbytery adjourned, Patton indicated that he would appeal to the Synod of Northern Illinois. Everyone knew that the largely rural synod would probably find in favor of Patton. Swing had no taste for controversy. Although the elders of his church had steadfastly supported him throughout, the trial had been hard on the congregation and had left Swing weary and discouraged. Faced with seemingly endless litigation, he decided to withdraw his membership from the Presbyterian denomination. His friends begged him not to give up. Around the country, liberal journalists and clergy like Washington Gladden wanted him to "make the fight" on behalf of "thousands who are chafing in the bonds of old-time creeds."[29] The presbytery did not want his resignation, and the congregation did not want to lose him. But Dr. Patton pressed his appeal to the synod and won. The Presbytery of Chicago had no choice but to suggest that the congregation seek a Presbyterian pastor in good standing. Although the elders urged him to return to membership in the Presbytery, Swing would not compromise "his truth" nor give up his "intellectual liberty." In the fall of 1875 he regretfully tendered his resignation.[30]

Immediately fifty "leading citizens" from among those who had heard him at McVicker's pledged $1,000 each toward organizing a center-city church. Only a month after Swing left Fourth Church, Central Church (nondenominational) was organized with 500 charter members. Clearly the most popular preacher in the city, Swing was soon preaching regularly to audiences of five to seven thousand.

Obviously, Swing's leaving and the organization of Central Church presented a dilemma for many. Where did their loyalty lay—to Swing or to the congregation? And how should they respond to the denomination's censure of Swing—by leaving the denomination or by continuing to claim their own Presbyterian witness and heritage? Although a "goodly number" of the members of Fourth Church left to join Central Church,[31] the officers and majority of others felt their first loyalty was to the congregation for which they had sacrificed and prayed after the fire, which served their families in their community, and for whose new building they were still in debt. This loss of members was probably less harmful to the spirit of the congregation than such splits usually are, because it did not represent a serious conflict between those who left and those who stayed. The evidence is that, for the most part, both groups had been united in their support for their pastor throughout the trial. Some had undoubtedly considered Swing too "liberal," but they had probably not welcomed the outside interference in the church's affairs, and it was not they who left the church.

In fact, the history of Fourth Church (excepting the years of North Church) has never been one of overt conflict. This may be due to the Presbyterian respect for "order" or to the tendency of businessmen to respect centralized authority and to use power behind the scenes rather than in open confrontation, or to a high value placed on propriety and gentility, or to the strong spiritual leadership of certain individuals like Henry King and, in the twentieth century, the pastors of the church. It may even be due to a strong sense of unity and pride in the congregation. Probably all of the above are true.

Much later, a memorial to Henry King recalled:

> After Professor Swing left the Church a meeting of the Congregation was called to consider the future of the organization. . . . Mr. King's unquestioning courage and faith . . . inspired all who were present and before the meeting adjourned most of the large financial deficit of the year was provided for, and no question remained that the church would survive the Calamity.[32]

A Generous People

The church not only survived; it thrived, directing its strength and energy both inward to its own congregation and outward in a generous, natural philanthropy. Because of its wealth, Fourth Presbyterian Church has, throughout its life, earned a reputation for high quality in all it does. In its worship life, outstanding preaching and fine music have been the norm. For most of its life, its physical facilities have been not only adequate but impressive—in architecture, furnishings, and utility. When a need has been felt, it has usually been met in "style." Significantly, however, this congregation has always felt the needs not only of its membership but also of less fortunate people in nearby communities and throughout the world.

The congregation's wealth may be an accident of history and membership, but its benevolence has been intentional. Its members have done much more than respond to human need; they have sought out needs to respond to. Further, although they have sent money for missions around the world, Fourth Church philanthropy has never been limited to giving money. Theirs has been an activist congregation, particularly distinguished by the amount of volunteer personal effort on behalf of, and in direct ministry with, people from all walks of life. Members have taught Bible classes, English classes, and sewing classes. They have sewed and made bandages for others. They have knocked on doors and entered the homes of immigrants, lonely young people, and the very poor. They have built church buildings in other communities, particularly for people speaking other languages—and they have invited immigrant congregations to share their own facilities. They have gone out into the neighborhoods to invite people to join their congregation, and they have built their facilities to serve the needs of the young and the poor as well as the rich.

The congregation's sense of responsibility for others had probably been influenced at least in part by its Presbyterian heritage and preaching. Calvin believed the church should be the shaper of civic life, and Calvinists retain a strain of optimism about the possibility of Christian influence in civic life. According to the Genevan Confession of 1536, "all Christians are bound . . . to promote welfare, peace and public good."[33] Further, wrote Calvin, "All the endowments which we possess are divine deposits entrusted to us for the very purpose of being distributed for the good of our neighbour."[34] This was the theology preached at Fourth Church.

The church's sympathies, it should be noted, were extended to individuals and not to the labor unions or movements that sought to change the social and economic system from which they benefited. An underlying assumption seems to have been that the world's problems could be solved by charity; and that charity, therefore, is the Christian's calling, responsibility, and privilege—from providing Christmas baskets to building hospitals and neighborhood houses, from personal tutoring to endowing educational institutions. Fourth Church has never, however, assumed that charity is the calling only of individuals. The church understands itself as called to be a *philanthropic* institution and a *service* institution (in addition to being a worshiping, witnessing fellowship). The church's life has been shaped by this understanding and, in fact, this church has been a leader and model for other churches throughout the nation.

Even before the merger that created Fourth Presbyterian Church, George S. Phillips had written in 1867 of North Church's reputation for charity and active involvement, both personal and financial, in mission Sunday schools.[35] The first description of Fourth Church, as found in the letter to "the Churches in the East" after the Great Fire, claimed: "This church was supporting a missionary in Africa and one among the Germans in the home field, and was each Sabbath teaching about six hundred children in mission schools."[36]

The Howe Street Mission had been started by North Church in a building donated by Mr. and Mrs. Wesley Munger. Its building escaped destruction by the fire. In 1875, the women of the church engaged Emily Betz as "authorized missionary" for the mission. Soon, under her leadership, there were, in addition to the Sunday school classes, sewing classes attracting 200 girls, and separate prayer meetings for boys and girls attracting 75 to 100 to each meeting. In 1884 Fourth Church hired a minister for the mission; and in 1885 (only seven years after paying off their own building debts) the church purchased lots and built Christ Chapel with a Sunday school large enough for 1,500, at a cost of $45,000. In 1900 the mission became Christ Church (Presbyterian), but for many more years, Fourth Church trustees still had a "Christ Church building committee" for repairs and maintenance, and members of Fourth Church often gave gifts, taught classes, and helped in other ways.

In 1873, two months before they moved into the building at Rush and Superior, the Ladies' Benevolent Society of Fourth Presbyterian Church had held its organizing meeting. At that meeting they sewed for the Half-Orphan Asylum and made plans to raise money for pulpit chairs for the new sanctuary. From that day they continued both mission work and support of the congregation. In 1876 they started Mothers' Meetings as an outreach to the women and children in the nearby neighborhood known as "Little Hell." They engaged the help of Vera Eberhart, a city missionary supported by Mrs. Henry Willing. Every week the mothers met and sewed materials provided by the benevolent society, and Vera Eberhart taught a Bible lesson. They soon changed their name to the Mothers' Mite Society and continued until well into the twentieth century. At the request of the mothers, in 1878, the churchwomen initiated "cottage meetings" in the immigrants' homes in order to involve husbands. When men of the church were not available to teach the Bible lessons, Vera Eberhart taught. She also organized children's meetings.

For fifty-four years, until her death in 1930, Vera Eberhart worked for the church as a bridge between the rich and the poor. She went daily into the streets and homes of the poor, averaging over a thousand calls each year. Through the generosity of the women and the church, she was able to provide milk, coal, and medical and living expenses for hundreds of needy families—in addition to her teaching witness to the gospel.

The women of the church also raised money to support missionaries in the United States and in the world. The Fourth Church Woman's Foreign Missionary Society was organized as early as 1876. In addition, several of its members were leaders of the regional Presbyterian Women's Board of the Northwest, among whose first six presidents were four from Fourth Church. The women raised substantial support for missions, including gifts from Mrs. Cyrus McCormick which often equaled or exceeded the total gifts from all the others. She and her husband had rejoined the church in 1877. After Mr. McCormick died in 1884, Nettie Fowler McCormick lived forty more years, giving generously of her fortune and of her talents for leadership, particularly for the mission societies.

The women supported several women missionaries, some of whom came from their own membership. They corresponded closely with these missionaries, educating themselves concerning the conditions of the peoples served. In 1886 a Home Missionary Society was organized to support women missionaries throughout the American West and South, among "Mountain Whites, Freedmen, Indians and Mexicans"— and in Alaska too.[37] The congregation as a whole also supported missionaries (usually men) and hosted missionary speakers.

The men of the church, too, raised money, volunteered time, and organized benevolent institutions in the city. In 1869 Henry King and others were among the founders of the Presbyterian League, which raised money for new church buildings throughout the Chicago presbytery. In 1883, Cyrus McCormick, Jr., and Henry King were among the organizers of the Presbyterian Hospital. Others supported and served on the boards of the Presbyterian Home and other institutions, including Presbyterian neighborhood houses, which were developed by the Presbytery of Chicago during the nineteenth century to combine Christian witness with the settlement house model.

In 1907 Andrew Stevenson, a Presbyterian elder, published a book entitled *Chicago Pre-eminently a Presbyterian City*, in which he made the claim that practically every nondenominational philanthropic work in Chicago was "largely dependent upon the generosity of members of the Presbyterian Church" and that such works were even more dependent upon Presbyterians for their volunteer workers. He declared, for example, that at a very conservative estimate, 50 percent of the income of the Chicago YMCA was derived from Presbyterians.[38] Though Stevenson may have been biased in his observations, his book testifies to the philanthropic activities of the men of Fourth Church and at the same time shows that Fourth Church was not unique among Presbyterian congregations. His list of philanthropic Presbyterians includes a good number from Fourth Church. In addition to Cyrus H. McCormick, Jr., noted for "his devotion to the seminary and the YMCA," the presidents of American Cereal and Mineral Point Zinc, two bank presidents, and other financiers were from Fourth and served as presidents of the

Chicago YMCA, the House of Destitute and Crippled Children, the Tuberculosis Institute, the Presbyterian Hospital, the Chicago Foundlings Home, the board of the University of Chicago, and even the Moody Bible Institute.

Much has been said here about the leadership and contributions of the laity, without any mention of pastoral leadership, because the lay leadership was extraordinary and because from the time of Swing's departure through the remainder of the nineteenth century, Fourth Presbyterian Church experienced unusually frequent changes of pastor (see the Appendix for a complete list of the pastors). In twenty-three years, two pastors had tenures of three years, one had seven and a half years, and one had four years. They were not inconsequential men, and all were striking preachers, but their brief tenures left much of the leadership to the laypeople.

The first pastor, John Abbott French, left because of "exhaustion." The strain of serving a congregation recovering from a heresy trial may have been augmented when, in 1877, the McCormick family returned to the congregation. But if some resented McCormick's behind-the-scenes role in the trial, he seemed not to notice; he immediately headed a drive to pay off the debt on the building. And although Cyrus McCormick's relationship to the congregation was primarily financial and political, the rest of his family became more involved, over the years, in the life and mission and spiritual leadership of the church.

The next pastor, Dr. Herrick Johnson, brought a measure of national recognition to the congregation when he served as moderator of the Presbyterian General Assembly in 1882. He apparently made an impression on the city as well, according to one who called him the "scourge of the Chicago theatre."[39] He accused the playhouses of "a murderous assault on all that the family circle holds most dear and sacred."[40] But after only three years, during which his time was split between his church responsibilities and teaching at the seminary, he yielded to the temptation to become full-time professor of homiletics at the seminary, in order to have "less arduous" duties and "greater influence."[41] The next pastor, Melancthon Woolsey Stryker, spent a most fruitful seven and a half years with the congregation before becoming president of Hamilton College. Then Thomas C. Hall's pastorate was cut short by a nearly fatal illness.

These brief pastorates contrasted strikingly with the long service of other staff and congregational leaders. The quartet's director-soloist served for thirty-three years, the organist for thirty-six. Other soloists in the quartet sang for twenty-nine, twenty-seven, fifteen, and ten years. Even the sexton served for twenty-nine years. Henry Willing and Charles Mulliken volunteered as teachers and superintendents in the mission school for more than forty years, while Emily Betz and Vera Eberhart served as church staff, performing the tasks of social worker, Bible teacher, program administrator, and visitor for half a century each, spanning six pastorates.

In the absence of strong, continuous pastoral leadership, the spiritual leadership of the congregation fell to some of the laity. For instance, Horace F. Waite, one of the original elders, testified on behalf of Swing and continued as an elder until his death at the end of the century. Of him it was said, "In the day of [Fourth's] weakness, he gave it strength and in the days of its prosperity he gave direction to its work and wisdom to its councils."[42] Mrs. J. R. Trowbridge served as president of three of the women's societies and earned such respect that during the illness of the pastor, Thomas C. Hall, she was appointed by the session to visit members when needed. Probably the most influential layperson was Henry King. The high regard in which he was held and the influence he wielded is evident in his having been chairman of every committee to secure a new pastor from the founding of the church until his death in 1898, while he was chairing a committee to replace Hall. Although King was a wealthy man, his leadership was the result of his spirit and his hard work within the congregation—teaching Bible classes, visiting, serving on committees. He was also active in the presbytery and in 1888 was elected a delegate to the General Assembly meeting. For twenty-five years he was a member of the presbytery's Home Mission Committee. His memorial testimonial declared: "So innumerable were the calls made upon his attention by persons interested in Christian work . . . that the Clerks in his office called his private office 'the Presbyterian Headquarters.'"[43]

By 1885, when Melancthon Stryker arrived as pastor, the neighborhood around the church was changing from homes to rooming houses, as Chicago's wealthy families moved northward. Stryker helped the congregation to reach out to the "strangers" in the neighborhood. For the sake of evangelism among those with lower incomes, he led the congregation to abolish the pew-rental system for the Sunday evening service. Within six years, the membership at evening services had doubled, with an "unusual preponderance of men"; and "scores" of those attending in the evening had joined the membership. Stryker also organized the young adults into a Christian Endeavor Society with an emphasis on bringing strangers in. The Fourth Church Sunday school also attracted children and adults. During Stryker's years the membership doubled from three hundred to six hundred; and many of the new members were not from the wealthy classes.[44] However, the continuation of the pew-rental system at the Sunday morning services (until 1964) perpetuated a social and economic class difference between the majority of those who attended morning services and those who attended at night.

By 1897 it was estimated that about ten thousand young working-men lived in hotels and boardinghouses within easy walking distance of the church, and a group of younger businessmen in the church decided to form a Men's Club to reach out to them.[45] This club took charge of the Sunday evening worship service and organized club meetings and a Bible class. Their invitation committee met with good success, and the class and evening services grew. In spite of great social and economic disparities, the Men's Club provided positive personal interaction between the rich and the poor. For instance, Cyrus McCormick, Jr., and others spent their Saturday evenings tutoring immigrant men.

About the same time, a Bible class was started for young women of the boardinghouses, out of which grew a "gymnasium class." By 1907 the group had grown to fifty, and Miss Bertha Wood was hired to work with the Young Women's Club, which offered classes in subjects ranging from domestic science to stenography, art, and French. By 1909 club membership reached ninety. In 1907 the men of the church also organized a Boys' Club.

In 1899 Dr. William Robson Notman became the pastor. Although he suffered from poor health, he stayed for nine years, longer than any pastor before him. (He died in 1908, a few months after resigning.) In addition to his support of the clubs, he was remembered for leading the congregation to support a mission among Chicago Assyrians. He also gave extensive service and leadership to the Presbytery of Chicago, particularly in organizing the new Church Extension Board to oversee the presbytery's mission projects and new churches. Like Henry King and like most of the church's pastors before and after him, Notman was a servant and a leader in the Presbyterian Church.

The life of this congregation has been inextricably bound to the life of its denomination: one thinks of its origins in denominational schism and its involvement in denominational struggles over truth and heresy, the nationwide Presbyterian generosity that helped it rebuild after the fire, its own support of Presbyterian missions, and the involvement of its pastors and members in the denomination's mission and leadership.

In 1908, Fourth Church's leadership in the denomination took on new dimensions.

A Grand Era of Expansion

In 1908 the search committee decided to call as pastor Dr. John Timothy Stone, a recognized author, pastor, and preacher who was well known for his interest in evangelism. A graduate of Amherst College and Auburn Theological Seminary, he was serving his third pastorate, at Brown Memorial Church in Baltimore. When the committee talked with him, he challenged them to "a larger work and a new and better equipped edifice,"[46] but when he received their call, he turned it down, saying he was still needed in Baltimore. The men of Fourth Church immediately called a congregational meeting—two days after Christmas—and raised $100,000 toward a new building. With this pledge as an answer to Stone's challenge, Cyrus McCormick, Jr., went to Baltimore to call upon Stone in person. This time, he agreed to come.

When Stone began his twenty-year pastorate in May 1909, evangelism and membership growth were the first concerns on his agenda. The cornerstone of his strategy was the invitation committee. Every week a group of thirty or forty young businessmen met to report their progress ringing doorbells and entering places of business in order to invite young men to church or Bible class or a men's meeting. As one religious journal reported, "Clerks, stenographers, mechanics, students and even discharged prisoners have been recipients of calls."[47] In one winter the committee made calls on over 1,100 men. Attendance rose immediately. Soon the elders were meeting to receive new members every Wednesday after the midweek service. In the first two years of Stone's pastorate, two hundred men joined the church. Within five years, the membership had doubled from 638 to 1,303.

The special emphasis on recruiting men probably was a result of the presence of so many young men living in the area, as well as of Stone's personal emphasis on a "virile" Christianity and his conscious effort to counter the nationwide trend of there being more women than men in the churches. Stone was a leader in the nationwide ecumenical Men and Religion Movement, which focused on that issue:

> The present condition of the church has resulted from a program which over-emphasized the feminine. Emotional revivals and all the other things of the past century that laid stress upon the emotional have helped to divorce the church from men.[48]

Fourth Church, then, was both intentional and successful in attracting men. Through efforts like Swing's appeal to business and city leaders, the outreach of Stryker and the Men's Club to workingmen, and Stone's challenge to manliness, the congregation appealed to men of both upper and lower classes.

Stone appealed to their virility and daring and generosity. Again and again he quoted William Cary, saying, "Expect great things of God. Attempt great things for God."[49] His sermons were a constant challenge to lead the way, to meet opportunities and responsibilities, "with all manly fervor" and with the power of God. He challenged them to the "costly expenditure of hard personal work" for winning people to Christ. And Stone was one who could command such commitment and actions: whether the need was money or action, he had only to ask, and the challenge was met.

And so Fourth Church took on not only the task of building a great new edifice but also a large-scale program to "make an impress" on the social conditions of the surrounding communities. Fourth Church was expected to serve as a model, a pioneer, a leader in "the attack . . . on local problems." *The Continent,* a Chicago religious journal, commented in 1913:

> The great mission of Fourth Church will be to grapple with the conditions by which it is surrounded. If Fourth Church can make an impress upon the life of this community, and if it can lead the way in demonstrating that a thoroughly evangelistic appeal may be coupled up with a distinct social message, it will perform one of the greatest services for the church at large that has yet been rendered. This, it has been determined, shall be done.[50]

The church undertook in 1912 an exhaustive survey of their community, of such scope that it attracted the attention and admiration of the *Chicago Tribune,* which published the survey results.[51] The survey pointed to the existence of several distinct neighborhoods. The church stood between two: the neighborhood known as the "Gold Coast," where Chicago's social elite were building their new brownstones, and the neighborhood that same elite had left behind, now a community of crumbling mansions that had been converted into furnished rooms. In the latter area, the survey found twenty thousand young people between the ages of eighteen and thirty-five. Two slum areas lay to the south and to the west—areas of extreme poverty, overcrowding, crime, and prostitution. Fourth Church had been helping poor families in these slums for forty years; and it was here that they used their political influence to try to control vice, including dance halls, particularly for the sake of the young workers nearby.

In December 1912, for instance, the Men's Club sent a resolution to the city protesting any reopening of the recently closed "resorts" in the "vice district."[52] Henry P. Crowell and D. R. Forgan from Fourth Church were members of the "Committee of Fifteen," along with Jane Addams and other civic leaders. The work of this committee was to investigate and proceed against the vice resorts, primarily through a "superintendent" hired to collect evidence against houses of prostitution and to present that evidence to the police.[53]

After studying the results of the 1912 survey, the church decided to focus on those in the boardinghouses. This was not a new ministry, but now the "roomers" became a congregational priority. By 1913 they had hired Superintendents of Men's Work and Young Women's Work, and plans were under way to provide an appropriate space for this ministry.

Fourth Church's approach to ministry in its community was changing from the traditional model of evangelism through Sunday schools to a new model influenced by the YMCA movement, with its attempt to reach unattached young people through the use of four emphases: physical, educational, social, and religious. (It was the YMCA that pioneered in defending the values of athletic recreation in the face of some "puritanic criticism.")[54] The church seems also to have been influenced by the concept of the "institutional church," an outgrowth of the Social Gospel movement that had developed in New York to serve the needs of the crowded working-class areas of that city through continuous weekday social-service programs and a large professional staff.[55]

This commitment to community ministry as well as the rapid growth in church membership required new, expanded facilities. Early in 1911 the congregation had elected a building committee. At the time, grave doubts were expressed about the location chosen. Although it was only a few blocks from the new mansions of Chicago's wealthiest citizens, Pine Street, on which the property fronted, was merely a sandy road along the lakefront, unconnected by bridge to the center of the city. On the property was an abandoned tile factory and a tavern, with rooming houses nearby. (In 1920, the Michigan Avenue bridge was built, connecting Chicago's grandest street with Pine Street itself. The church was soon to be surrounded by grand hotels and attractive shops—some built on landfill in the lake—and Pine Street was to become Michigan Avenue, with its "Magnificent Mile.")

485

The building committee had clear priorities. First, only the best would do. Their building would compare with the world's great cathedrals; it would be unlike anything west of New York City. It was built of solid limestone masonry with huge buttresses supporting the walls and gabled slate roof. Complete with Gothic arches and a spire, the sanctuary was cruciform in shape with three balconies and seating for 1,400 persons. Twelve massive stone columns held up six arches and were surmounted by carved figures of angels, under an elaborately painted ceiling. The stained-glass windows were in the thirteenth-century style known as *grisaille*. Ground was broken on June 1, 1912, and the building that was completed two years later, May 10, 1914, is still the congregation's home.

In addition to the church sanctuary, the edifice included a Sunday school building (also with a capacity for 1,400), a courtyard with a fountain, and an elegant three-story manse. Yet part of the plan was to build for the church's ministry to the community. Specifically, the church's vision was to provide a "home away from home" for the single young working people in the rooming houses—an alternative to lonely rooms and dance halls—so the new complex also included a clubhouse, complete with gymnasium, dining hall, classrooms, and club rooms for men, women, boys, and girls.

The quality of the clubhouse was that to which church members were accustomed. It provided an opportunity for any young man to "sit in a Morris chair before an open fire, beneath an imposing pair of antlers and read a book from the club library or listen to the player piano or to the Edison diamond point machine."[56] The Men's Club included a writing room, classrooms, a game room large enough for shuffleboard, and a music room for their orchestra, glee club, and quartet. There was also a gymnasium and quarters for a resident staff. It is easy to see why, soon after the clubhouse was opened, the YMCA was referring newcomers to Chicago to the Fourth Church Men's Club.

In the young women's clubhouse there was one parlor in which women could entertain their men friends under the eye of a chaperone and another for playing the piano or visiting by the fire. There were classrooms, a library, a kitchen, a sewing room, and a music room for their orchestra; and they shared the gymnasium. The basement area included club rooms for boys and girls. The youth clubs required attendance at Sunday school, with each teacher spending one evening a week with his or her class.

With the opening of the new building in March 1914, every program expanded overnight. On the first Sunday 387 came to Sunday school, almost a hundred more than ever before. Almost 200 women attended the first young women's club night, and during the first week 450 men showed up for programs, gym activities, and informal visiting. The new dining room with its dark oak tables and benches was soon serving 500 people each week. The community, the city, and the press admired the great building, which would enable the church to carry out its mission in unprecedented style and extent. A visitor wrote in the *Sunday School Times* of "the highest efficiency that modern equipment and modern methods of service can give." He was impressed with everything from the number of pianos and Bibles and drinking fountains to the individual linen towels in the lavatories—"just as you would find in [a fine hotel]." [57] By the end of the first year, Sunday school enrollment had increased to 603; the boys' clubs enrolled 120; the women had a membership of 255; and the average attendance at men's meetings was 145, while many more dropped in during the week.

A Broader Ministry

Even during the years of building construction, rapid membership growth, and community ministry development, Stone found time to serve on the boards of denominational and ecumenical organizations, including the Chicago Tract Society, the Presbyterian Hospital, the presbytery's Church Extension Board, and Amherst College. As a designated "college preacher," he often spoke at colleges and universities from Yale and Princeton to California. In 1912 the *Syracuse Post-Standard* observed that "Dr. Stone is one of the most prominent men in the Presbyterian Church. He has made the Fourth Church one of the largest institutions in religious circles west of New York." [58]

In May 1913, the General Assembly bestowed the denomination's highest honor on him by electing him its moderator. In that capacity he presided over the assembly and the monthly executive committee meetings in Philadelphia and traveled to state synods, Presbyterian institutions, and special events across the nation.

During his one-year term as moderator, the Presbyterian Church and its executive committee were involved in a significant organizational change. Until that time, each of the denomination's agencies (such as those concerned with home missions, foreign missions, and Sunday schools) did its own separate fund-raising. Now, along with several other denominations, the Presbyterian Church organized its benevolences into one system of "unified giving" and carried out the first "Every Member Canvass," in March 1914, to secure financial pledges of regular support for the local congregation and denominational programs.[59] Annual pledging, regular giving, and unified denominational budgets have become such accepted practices that it is hard to realize the great hopes with which they were introduced, expressed by Stone's expectation that, with such regular giving, "the church will enter upon a revival greater than any we have known in centuries that are past."[60]

Not only was Stone involved in the development of these innovations, but he claimed that the "wisdom and generous backing" of an anonymous member of Fourth Church had provided for the first tests of the plan before its adoption. This project is another illustration of the intimate involvement of Fourth Church in the leadership and activities of the denomination as well as the influence of the denomination in the life, work, and organization of the congregation.

In May 1914, exactly five years after Stone's arrival, the new sanctuary was completed at last, and a week of celebration followed. The building cost $740,576 (of which $300,000 had come from the McCormick family) and was completed without debt, with an additional $25,000 from the sale of the Rush Street building for the beginning of an endowment fund. At the dedication service, Thomas E. Jones, chair of the building committee, said that justification for the expenditure would be proven by the service and spirit that would "enter into the life of the community," and he expressed the "hope that these structures may have a silent ministration of their own" and that members and passersby might find "an awakened sense of reverence of the presence and power of the unseen."[61]

The building was completed just in time for the church to host the General Assembly meeting, May 21–29. Receptions, organ concerts, and worship services welcomed 865 delegates along with many visitors from across the nation, and some observed that the building was the finest in the denomination at that time.

The sanctuary, the music, the preaching, and the formal elegance of the worship services at Fourth Church have continued to attract and inspire members and visitors from around the world. The architecture evokes an atmosphere of reverence, carefully preserved by the orderliness and dignity of the liturgy and enhanced by the quality of the music. When the church moved into the new sanctuary, the quartet was replaced by a full choir, under the leadership of Eric DeLamarter, who served as organist-choirmaster from 1914 until 1935. Services were held every Sunday morning, afternoon, and evening, and special emphasis was given to music in the afternoon service, which continued for fifty years.

In those first five years of Stone's Chicago ministry, not only did the congregation double in membership, build its "cathedral," add staff, and expand programs, but while the new building was under construction, Stone led the trustees to erect two other church buildings in Chicago (using two generous bequests): one for the Persian mission that had been begun earlier, and one for a Bohemian mission, which was Stone's special interest.

As with the Howe Street Mission (which had become Christ Church in 1900), many members of Fourth Church were involved in these immigrant missions, teaching sewing and English classes and helping with Sunday schools, providing financial help for needy members, and assuming responsibility for building maintenance and repairs. In return, the members of Fourth Church were kept aware of, and given a chance to help, the suffering people of Europe, particularly the Armenian Persians, during the First World War.

In addition to these missions, which received the church's direct support, the congregation also generously supported the work of the Chicago presbytery, which included (during Stone's years) approximately 112 churches and missions in five counties. Each year about a third of these received financial aid to start new congregations, to build, or to serve their communities. Presbytery missions also included neighborhood houses, particularly among the foreign-born. Each year between 1910 and 1940, Fourth Presbyterian Church contributed at least a fifth, and sometimes almost a fourth, of the total congregational support for presbytery missions.[62] The tremendous significance of the financial contributions of this one congregation for the mission work and the building of churches in the Chicago presbytery is largely unrecognized because it was done indirectly, through the presbytery's budget.

In 1921 it was reported that in its first fifty years Fourth Church had received a total income of $7,222,867, less than half of which was used for their own buildings and congregational life. The rest was given in response to appeals concerning home missions, foreign missions, church erection, education and colleges, Sunday school work, relief, evangelism, freedmen and temperance, and after 1914, for the General Assembly (unified) mission budget, which included most of the preceding.[63]

Yet the contributions of this congregation were not only financial.

489

Many members gave their lives to Christian service as ministers and missionaries. There were often as many as ten to fourteen young men of the congregation studying for the ministry. An interest in foreign missions was actively promoted by the mission societies, visiting missionaries, a missionary library, and an annual mission study (four or six Wednesday evenings), which drew as many as three hundred to its classes. The monthly newsletter published long letters from missionaries. In 1915 the general secretary of the Student Volunteer Movement for Foreign Missions spoke to an audience of six hundred young people, and the next year three women and one man were listed as "among the young people soon to go to the foreign field from our church." There is no complete record of how many missionaries have gone out from Fourth Church, but one illustration is a 1926 list of eight missionaries who were at that time being supported by the church, ten more who were members, and twelve who had been associated with the church while studying or working in Chicago.[64] Over the years men and women from Fourth Church have worked in hospitals, YMCAs, schools, orphanages, and churches in Iraq, Thailand, China, Puerto Rico, Korea, Africa, and elsewhere around the world.

The power of John Timothy Stone's personality and preaching also had its effect. A young woman wrote from shipboard on her way to China: "I yielded fully to His will during the sermon you preached May 21st, 1916. The following Tuesday I decided for China."[65] His persuasiveness was particularly evident when it became clear that the United States would enter World War I. It was during Holy Week. Two young men wrote that the sermon they heard at the Good Friday evening service convinced them, and two other friends, that they should enlist in military service.[66] Another wrote that Stone's sermons "left no alternative; service was righteously demanded. I chose Navy."[67]

The entire congregation seems to have been energetic in the war effort. Gym classes were changed to "drill and military training"; an army recruiter spoke to the Men's Club. Within a month, Friends of Fourth Church had sent two ambulances to France, and five young men had gone to do "ambulance work." Thousands of bandages and medical supplies were made by the women's organizations and even by the young girls. If there were any who questioned involvement in the war, it was certainly not evident in *The Fourth Church* monthly magazine, which emphasized patriotic poems, addresses, symbols, sermons, and letters from "the Front." Special prayer services were held each week. By the end of the war the service roll totaled 298 men, and eleven had given their lives. But the end of the war did not mean the end of the effort: the newsletter was still filled with pleas to "Help Belgian Babies" and to help the starving Armenian, Greek, and other refugees.

Even during the war, the congregation maintained a wide range of activities that displayed an interesting combination of the evangelistic and the social. For instance, the church was involved in the Anti-Saloon League campaign to ratify the national Prohibition amendment. The session urged church members to vote for candidates favoring "dry legislation"[68] and provided $10,000 for the temperance movement between 1911 and 1920.

In a very different endeavor, Stone—even while serving as chaplain at Camp Grant in Rockford, Illinois—served as a vice chairman of the Chicago evangelistic campaign of Billy Sunday in the spring of 1918. Thirteen subcommittees coordinated the congregation's supporting role in that ten-week event. Although this controversial evangelist often attacked established churches, education, Christian efforts to address urban ills through social services, and even formal worship services, churches like Fourth Church helped him organize his campaigns in the hope that he could influence those beyond their own reach. *The Fourth Church* magazine explained: "We may or may not like his method of presentation, but we can all in our own way work for the Kingdom of God in the campaign."[69] The apparent contradiction between the church's orientation toward social service and its sponsorship of Sunday's evangelistic crusade is clarified by the church's view of Billy Sunday as a missionary to "others" who would probably not come to Fourth Church. It was another way of carrying out temperance work, and fighting vice and poverty.

In truth, it was easier for this church to support Billy Sunday's campaign for the souls of the "lost" working class than it would have been for it to support the labor union movement. Although John Timothy Stone challenged his members to bring the Kingdom into being in the world through their generosity, and although the church adopted an approach to ministry addressing the physical, social, and educational aspects of life, the church did not take the further step of addressing the economic problems of the working classes—except as individual cases. And although the church was capable of calling for government-enforced prohibition of alcohol, there was not within the church a corresponding movement calling for government protection of the worker. One could not expect to hear from this pulpit the social gospel's criticism of the evils of unrestricted competition, laissez-faire government, or even the exploitation of the laboring class. On one occasion Stone's remarks at a father-and-son banquet included criticism of labor unions, offending the working-class fathers.[70]

Yet Fourth Church is fairly typical of large urban churches that pioneered in social service ministries, as illustrated by the staff roster, which included directors of women's work, men's work, boys' work, the Mothers' Mite Society, and the Bible School Home Department (family social services), plus a parish visitor, a Bible school visitor, and a church deaconess. Forty years before "street ministers" were hailed as a new idea in the 1960s, David Primrose was seeking out boys on playgrounds and streets, inviting them to scouting, sports activities, and Sunday school. There was even a summer camp built at Lake Geneva in 1915 to serve primarily the clubs and Mothers' Mite Society.

Its social-work orientation led the church to recognize and hire deaconesses; it was one of the few Presbyterian churches to do so. As in several other denominations, Presbyterian deaconesses were set apart primarily for ministries like nursing and social work: "for the care of the poor and sick, . . . widows and orphans."[71] In fact the General Assembly that met at Fourth Church in 1914 had recognized the office of deaconess as one to which a "woman graduate of an approved training school" should be "inducted by a Presbytery."[72] Within six months a deaconess was added to the church staff. Between then and 1963, Fourth Church was served by five deaconesses (in succession); the last was succeeded by the church's first woman minister.

The city, however, was not standing still, and a neighborhood of rooming houses is almost as transient as its occupants. After 1920, when Pine Street was paved and became Michigan Avenue, the area immediately surrounding the church became more and more a place of businesses and expensive apartment buildings, pushing the rooming houses further and further west. By 1929 the Men's Club no longer existed, and the Young Women's Club had become the Business Women's Club with members who came from as far away as the city's suburbs. With a membership of 230 and an average weekly attendance of 121, it appears to have been an important ministry but very different from that "home away from home" of fifteen years before.

It would be unfair to say that the grand experiment of the clubs failed; there is much evidence of their helpfulness. But the clubs did not last—because of the changing neighborhood but also because of the difficulty of overcoming the gap between people of different economic levels. However generously Fourth Church people gave of themselves and their money, and however committed they were to including all people in the church, they could not escape the division between the rich and the poor, between those who gave and those who received. As late as 1929, sociologist Harvey Zorbaugh wrote of Fourth Church:

> The "community" feels keenly the barrier between itself and the world of fashion of which the church is a part; and the church is commonly referred to about the "community" as the "Millionaires Club." The Gold Coast attends the morning service; the "world of furnished rooms" the evening service. . . . How little a part of the church these people . . . feel themselves to be.[73]

This is not, of course, the whole story. Stone exhorted his congregation to invite the clerks and shopgirls they met to join them in their pews, and there certainly were personal relationships and friendships between people of different groups, and acts of helpfulness and caring. Many young people from the surrounding community appreciated being a part of "old Fourth." Particularly the ministries of the staff made a difference in countless young lives. Yet the barriers of social and economic distinctions have been a problem with which Fourth Church has struggled throughout its years.

Changes, Depression, and War

In April 1928, John Timothy Stone accepted a call to serve as president of McCormick Theological Seminary, on the understanding that he would continue his pastoral duties at Fourth Church part-time, with the aid of a co-pastor. Within two months the church had chosen Harrison Ray Anderson, a pastor in Wichita, Kansas. While a student at McCormick Seminary from 1914 to 1917, he had worked at Fourth Church and developed a friendship with Stone that had continued through Anderson's war chaplaincy and two pastorates.

Well aware of the church's character as a Gold Coast church run by a small group of powerful men, Anderson envisioned a congregation that truly included the broad range of society in its membership and leadership as well as in its programming. Before accepting their invitation, he made it clear to the officers that if he came, he would expect changes. They assured him they were ready for his leadership. He arrived in September 1928 and remained until his retirement thirty-three years later.

Anderson moved quickly to revise the bylaws to open up the church leadership. The church soon adopted a growing Presbyterian practice of three-year terms for the officers, with no possibility of reelection until after a year had passed. Further, each board was significantly expanded. (In the Presbyterian system, the session, composed of the elders, governs; the deacons provide services for the congregation and individuals who are ill or needy; and the trustees manage the money and property.)

A year after his arrival, Anderson set in motion a plan to broaden the outreach and membership of the church by focusing on Streeterville, the poor community just southeast of the church. The Streeterville invitation committee was ultimately successful in bringing more diversity to the membership.

One of Anderson's deepest commitments was to provide pastoral care and develop a sense of community, even in such a large congregation. To this end, in 1929, he instituted a parish plan by which the congregation was divided into groups along geographical lines. Each group had several leaders who kept in touch with them; and each group met with the church staff, once every two years. About half the time these meetings were hosted by the pastor and his wife, in the manse. Although one could question whether biannual meetings could actually "create an intimate fellowship," they did help to sustain relationships, particularly with the pastor; and as long as Anderson remained, the plan was greatly appreciated. Anderson also took pastoral calling very seriously, in spite of the size of the still-growing congregation, and many of his parishioners remembered him first of all as pastor and friend.

In May 1929, John Timothy Stone was honored for twenty years of service as pastor, during which time the church's membership had increased by 2,000 members (to a total of 2,624). This extraordinary growth was not only due to the attraction of the new building and its programs but was in large measure due to Stone's personality and preaching and his leadership in personal evangelism. One year later he resigned in order to give full time to the seminary, and Harrison Ray Anderson continued as pastor for thirty-one more years.

The nationwide Depression brought new challenges. The board of deacons, expanded to forty-eight men, found employment and odd jobs for church members and distributed clothing, food, and furniture. It was said of them, "doctors have given medical service, lawyers have given legal assistance and business men have given business advice."[74] With the help of deaconess Viola G. Baker, they provided milk, food, and medicines and paid bills for doctors, coal, electricity, gas, and even rent. During the year ending March 31, 1932, for instance, the deacons expended $4,899 for "extended relief" for thirty families of the church and parish and temporary relief to twenty-five families and 120 individuals. In the 1940s it was reported that "during the depression the deacons assisted 200 families directly connected with our church" and spent "$42,000 for the poor of this parish."[75]

The national economic situation had its impact on the income and budgets of the church. In the year ending March 31, 1929, expenses had been $111,907, while $107,969 had been given to benevolent causes. By 1932 expenses had been cut 5 percent, and benevolences had fallen to only $45,935, with further cuts made in following years. The inability to raise more for benevolences was of great concern to the church officers, as they demonstrated by sometimes transferring money from other funds to benevolent giving. They discussed the matter with the congregation, as in 1936, when the president of the trustees said in his annual report: "Fourth Church is one of the largest and strongest Presbyterian churches in the U.S. and I believe we have a sacred obligation to raise our share of the expenses of the important activities of the great Boards of the Presbyterian Church."[76] Even though unable to contribute the amounts it had given earlier, the church was still by far the strongest supporter of the work of the Chicago presbytery; one year Fourth Church's contribution amounted to one-third of the presbytery's mission receipts.[77] Finally in 1947, the expense budget had returned to the pre-Depression level, and the benevolent giving was even greater than the expenses.

The church was also active in the war effort. Long before the U.S. entered the Second World War, a Red Cross unit had been organized at the church; the congregation had already been giving generously to the Presbyterian World Emergency Fund; the educational programs of the church often focused on "the crisis"; and the staff were carrying on ministry among the naval midshipmen being trained at nearby Navy Pier.

Soon after the attack on Pearl Harbor, Anderson led the church to accept the responsibility of inviting a congregation of Japanese-American Christians to meet in the chapel on Sunday afternoons. As a member wrote later, "a long, long story could be written of the numerous times our church and her pastor were misunderstood because of protecting this little church."[78] Some still remember the pastor himself keeping guard outside the chapel on Sunday afternoons as the Japanese-American worshipers gathered. Although a number of church members were uncomfortable with the arrangement, any objections were far outweighed by Anderson's personal strength and stature, the loyalty of his officers, and the tremendous respect in which he was held by the congregation, the denomination, and the city. As a result of its relationship to Fourth Church, the nondenominational Japanese-American congregation became a Presbyterian church in 1947 (and continues to this day).

Prayers were said each morning for the 425 men and women members of Fourth Church in the military, fifteen of whom lost their lives. On the day of victory in Europe, the sanctuary filled spontaneously with grateful people from across the city. And a few months later the victory over Japan saw once again a steady stream of prayerful people pouring in through the doors on Michigan Avenue.

In 1945 church membership reached three thousand. Adult religious education flourished. About three hundred persons attended classes on Sunday mornings, and that many or more came to Sunday evening events. The School of Missions begun by Stone had been changed in 1932 to a School of Religion, with a broader range of topics; classes met five Wednesday evenings each winter. In 1947, for instance, 325 to 380 attended. Later a School of Lent was added and was just as popular. These schools were taught by professors from the universities and seminaries of Chicago, including some of the nation's best theologians. Other educational opportunities were sponsored by the women's organization and the young adults; some of their subjects were the Bible and communism, the atomic bomb, the Negro, Cuba, and the World Council of Churches, and courses on the Christian family, missions, and the Bible were also offered. Church members also heard some of the nation's best preachers, particularly during Holy Week. At Fourth Church the assumption was strong that education in theology, Bible, ethics, and current events was important for Christian faith and life.

The Sunday school for children flourished, too, although enrollment began dropping in the 1950s because there were fewer and fewer children in membership and in the neighborhood. The weekday programs still served primarily youth from the community, and in 1955 over two hundred boys and girls participated in gymnasium sports, scouting, and other activities.

Of special interest to Anderson were the students in the area. In the late forties and fifties some fifteen thousand students lived within a mile of the church, enrolled in universities, medical schools, and art schools. In 1947 the church hired a minister to students, and by the early fifties, between 350 and 400 were attending three Sunday evening groups (for high school students, for ages 18–24, and for ages 25–30), with the oldest group the largest. In addition, retreats, social outings, service projects, and "cell" (small-group) meetings filled the calendar. The ministry was so successful that Anderson began to dream of a Christian student center in the church, but the church's facilities were already overflowing.

In 1956 the trustees bought an old factory building on an adjacent lot; in 1958 it was demolished, and construction was begun on a new building. Like the clubhouse built forty years before, the new Westminster Student Center was to be a "home away from home" for students. For the congregation there would be Sunday school rooms above and large meeting rooms below.

On November 29, 1959, Westminster House was dedicated. It had cost a million dollars (raised for that purpose), but it was owned free and clear, and an endowment fund of $200,000 was provided for its maintenance. At first, the student center was open day and night, but the vision of Westminster House as a home away from home for students was never fully realized. Still, the church continued to have a city-wide reputation for its large and active young adult groups; and the new building has had wide and continued use as an integral part of the total ministry of the church.

Another of Anderson's enduring accomplishments was the growth of the endowment fund. Established in 1914 to support the cost of maintaining the building, the fund had reached a half-million dollars when he became pastor. Then came the Depression and war, but as a result of his leadership, between 1950 and 1960 (at the same time the million-dollar building project was going on), the endowment increased by two million dollars. By the spring of 1961 it totaled over three million. The importance of this fund can hardly be overstated, as it provides today for about one-third of the total expenses of the church.

During the Anderson years, the church continued its strong interest in missions. Members and staff continued to go to the mission field, and forty-five men entered the ordained ministry in thirty years.

Although women could serve the church as deaconesses and directors and could give their lives in service to the church overseas, women had never been elected as officers of the congregation. Some Presbyterian churches had been electing women as elders, deacons, and trustees since 1930, but the officers of Fourth Church were all men until 1958 when, without any fanfare, three women were elected as deacons. From that day, more and more women served on the board of deacons; but it was fourteen more years before women were elected as elders or trustees.

A National and International Churchman

As it had thirty years before, the church once again hosted a General Assembly meeting, in 1944, and shared its pastor with the denomination. Anderson had been moderator of the Chicago presbytery and president of Chicago's ecumenical Church Federation, as well as serving on the boards of the Presbyterian seminary, hospital, and retirement home. Nationally, he served on important denominational commissions, and in 1943 he was appointed to serve the General Assembly as vice-moderator. After the war he became well known throughout the national church by conducting seminars and preaching schools, but he was best known as a champion of the cause of reunion between the Presbyterian Church in the U.S.A. and the Presbyterian Church in the U.S. (the "Southern" church), which had split apart at the time of the War between the States.

In 1948 he attended the first meeting of the World Council of Churches in Amsterdam, and later he chaired an international committee to raise funds ($16,000 was given by Fourth Church) for the restoration of a chapel in Geneva that had been used by John Calvin and John Knox (the father of the Presbyterian Church). Although in some denominations ecumenical activity may be seen as an indication of disloyalty to the denomination, that is not the case in the Presbyterian Church, which is a leader in ecumenical movements. Particularly at the local level, the pastors of Fourth Church have accepted active leadership in ecumenical affairs.

In 1951 Anderson was elected moderator of the General Assembly, which gave him further opportunities to travel and speak on behalf of Presbyterian reunion. Anderson's dream of a reunited Presbyterian denomination was not fulfilled in his lifetime; yet when reunion did come in 1983, four years after his death, the significant role he had played was publicly recognized. Long after his retirement, Fourth Church continued to be known to many as Harrison Ray Anderson's church.

Anderson's pulpit ministry, like Stone's, added to the reputation of the church. Although he claimed no partisanship in the pulpit, he left little doubt about his political, social, and economic convictions. He preached about wealth, waste, inflation, and the national debt. He preached about the need to combat the Nazi menace and, later, about the need for an international court to administer justice and to enforce that justice with arms if necessary. He preached against "the gravy train" and "subsidies," against "the growing power of the American state," and against the "Fascist demagogue" (Joseph McCarthy).

Although Anderson addressed broad political, social, and economic issues in his sermons, the session did not take public positions on such issues. It did, however, continue to take public stands—and even to use political means—on issues of personal morality. As in earlier years the elders had fought for Prohibition, for Sunday observance, and against prostitution, in 1934 the session records refer to "the matter of signing the 'Declaration of Purpose' for better motion pictures" to be "stressed at all services Sunday."[79] In 1943 the session passed a resolution opposing the proposed national lottery, urging all members to protest to their representatives in Congress. Then in 1961 a session committee made recommendations concerning corruption and the Chicago police.

During Anderson's pastorate, it would have been relatively easy for church members to avoid public responsibility, in the light of sermons that proposed private faith and morality (repentance and church membership) as the answers to the world's greatest problems, including war and nuclear threat. Month after month, "The Pastor's Page" of the church newsletter defined Christian service as worshiping every Sunday, praying and reading the Bible daily, contributing a portion of one's income to the church, bringing others to church, and living a Christian life during the week.

Yet during the fifties especially, there would have been some truth in claiming that "the city" paid attention to what was said, and not said, from the pulpit of the big church on Michigan Avenue. Because of the church's location (downtown yet in the center of Chicago's "money" and near to the Catholic cathedral), because of the size and constituency of the membership, and because of its impressive building, Fourth Church had come to be regarded by many as a symbol and "flagship" (perhaps even the "cathedral") of Chicago establishment Protestantism. In fact, by the middle of the twentieth century, Fourth Presbyterian Church of Chicago enjoyed a national reputation. On Easter Sunday in 1943, Fourth Church was one of four churches in the nation featured in a national sunrise service broadcast by NBC. When the 1952 political conventions were held in Chicago, numerous senators, governors, and other visitors came to worship—including both presidential candidates, Dwight Eisenhower and Adlai Stevenson. (Anderson himself served as chaplain to the Republican convention that year; another year he was chaplain for the Democrats.)

When Harrison Ray Anderson retired in 1961, after serving for exactly one-third of a century, the church was strong, with a solid endowment, a much-expanded building, numerous educational programs, and a very active young adult ministry. After reaching a high of 3,177 in 1957 during the "churchgoing fifties," membership was falling slightly, to 2,956. Although Anderson had been relatively successful in broadening the membership and congregational leadership, the church was very much identified with his personal leadership and with Chicago's wealthy and powerful people.

The Turbulent Sixties

The sixties were a challenging time in Chicago. It was a decade that included civil rights demonstrations, urban unrest, rioting and burning, the war against poverty, and the war in Vietnam. In the midst of the turbulence, Fourth Presbyterian Church stood for many as a sign of permanence, tradition, and stability in a rapidly changing world. For others, at a time when established traditions and institutions were suspect, the congregation represented propriety and "the Establishment." Fourth Church, however, did not stand aloof from the challenges of the decade, particularly the needs of the poor in the city around it.

The new pastor, Dr. Elam Davies, was a native of Wales and had been educated at the University of Wales, Cambridge University, and the Theological College at Bala, Wales. After two pastorates in his native land, he had come to the U.S. in 1952 as pastor of the First Presbyterian Church in Bethlehem, Pennsylvania. The church, he preached, exists primarily for those who are outside of it. It is the church only when it is in mission—"to the least, the last, the lost and the lonely." These often-repeated words became his trademark.

Because of its resources and its location Fourth Church was uniquely situated for leadership in such a mission. It was surrounded by luxury apartments on the east and north (many of which had been built in the 1950s), exclusive shops to the south, and restaurants and clubs immediately to the west. But a few blocks further west were tenements occupied by Puerto Rican, African-American, and southern-white families; and only ten blocks away were the Cabrini-Green Homes, a 3,600-unit public housing complex with a reputation as one of the worst places to live in the city. Its residents, most of whom were African-American, were among Chicago's poorest, and the neighborhood among the most dangerous.

As the city's churches directed their attention to urban problems and race relations, Davies joined with others in seeking solutions. A member of the presbytery's Department of Urban Church and its planning committee, he also became vice president of the ecumenical Church Federation. Within the congregation he established a committee on evangelism which did survey-calling in nearby high-rises, and a city ministry committee which gave support to several community organizations and block clubs in the area and after several years of study and preparation initiated programs to benefit the church's urban neighbors. Within a few years, Westminster House (the 1959 addition) was as full and busy as any settlement house or institutional church could be.

The first program, begun in 1964, offered religious instruction on a "released-time" arrangement with the nearby public school and served twenty-five to sixty children annually for the next twenty years. A one-on-one tutoring program began with 60 grade-school children, was soon serving over a hundred, and later expanded to two evenings a week. The year 1966 saw the beginning of a summer day-school, which like the tutoring program continues to the present.

In 1965 two programs for youth were established. The Culture Center ministry served primarily the African-American youth from the housing projects with weekly instruction in music, drama, dance, sewing, typing, photography, and woodworking. Serving seventy youths in its first year, the center continued for sixteen years. "The Pres," a drop-in center in the church basement, attracted primarily Hispanic youth. About eighty-five to a hundred teenagers would drop by on Friday nights to talk, play, and dance. In spite of the occasional discovery of lead pipes and knives in pockets, and even Molotov cocktails outside in the bushes, the church served some fifteen hundred teens through "The Pres" in the three years before urban renewal demolished the community where the Hispanic teens lived, and "The Pres" was replaced by a smaller Spanish Teen Club for several more years. During the week, teens stopped by the office to chat or seek advice, and parents called for help. Staff and volunteers went with the kids to "ballparks, hospitals, police stations, court rooms and detention centers." They helped to find jobs, schools, social services, and even runaway teens.

Not all the new programs were for the young. In 1965 a senior center opened. At that time senior centers were a relatively new idea, but the deacons had discovered that the heaviest concentration of retired persons in the city was within a few blocks of the church. Open two days a week for lunch, classes, lectures, parties, and field trips, the center soon had over two hundred participants, about 75 percent of whom were not members of Fourth Church. In 1968 a preschool was organized for the young families who lived in the nearby high-rise apartments.

All these programs (particularly the tutoring) called for a great many volunteers. In addition, in 1969 the pastor announced from the pulpit the need for volunteers to serve weekly in Cook County Hospital. Within two weeks, sixty-eight volunteers had come forward; soon there were enough recruits to serve the hospital two nights a week. In 1970 a number of men began Fourth Church's involvement with the county jail tutoring program. And the women's organizations continued their traditional volunteer work, giving hundreds of hours each year for the Presbyterian hospital, retirement home, neighborhood houses, and other institutions.

Even though its members and programs served the community in so many ways, Fourth Church continued for many people to represent the Establishment and so became a target for some sit-ins and demonstrations. During the 1968 Democratic convention in Chicago, protestors of the Vietnam War disrupted worship services. In 1971 a group of Native Americans staged a sit-in in the church, demanding city action on an apartment building without heat or electricity and money from the presbytery to support a school and housing. After Davies himself called city and presbytery officials to initiate action, the sit-in was brought to an end, with everyone, including Davies, sitting in a circle and sharing a peace pipe.[80]

Four months later they were back. This time they told reporters: "A lot of power comes out of this church; the vice president of U.S. Steel is a member here."[81] And indeed it was he, Edward Logelin, who acted as intermediary, bringing to the church a director from the governor's office to listen to their concerns.

The extensive involvement of Fourth Church members in the needs of others was a Fourth Church tradition, but it was also a consequence of the leadership and outstanding preaching of Elam Davies. According to the *Chicago Tribune*, "Dr. Davies, whose resonant voice retains clear traces of Welsh lilt, has been an unabashed dramatist in the pulpit . . . commanding . . . attention with sweeping gestures, spiritual passion and vivid oratory."[82] He was a guest preacher on many distinguished occasions and in many places including Australia, Germany, and Wales. In 1979 *Time* magazine featured him as one of "seven star preachers";[83] and in 1981 the *Chicago Tribune Magazine* featured him on its cover as one of "ten spellbinding preachers."[84]

While his preaching style attracted many people and further enhanced the reputation of Fourth Church's pulpit, Davies's message furthered the church's understanding of its calling. "There is no church at all," he taught, "unless it has a 'sense of mission.' The Church . . . can only serve Him as it 'loses its life' for the sake of others."[85] Further, he explained, "Worship is much more than an aesthetic experience. It is a deliberate setting of oneself side by side with people who spiritually are poor, maimed, blind and halt."[86] He even called for "a change of heart over the distribution of wealth . . . so that . . . we shall fight the trend whereby those who have, have more and those who have not, have less."[87] In Davies's preaching Fourth Church began to hear some criticism of the injustices of the economic system.

Davies was concerned about Fourth Church's reputation as a "club for the rich." Although the very wealthy were definitely a minority, still the perception persisted that it was a church of "minks and millionaires." One of the first traditions that had to be changed was the pew-rental system, which was still in effect long after most churches had forgotten such a thing had ever existed. The reason given for its continuance was that it enabled regular members to be sure of a seat. Visitors sat at the back or waited until just before the service to move into the unfilled pews. However well it worked for the members, many visitors were offended; and Davies understood the need to change a system that communicated privilege and exclusivity instead of openness and welcome. He was further "encouraged" in this resolve by some students who threatened to "sit in" until the system was changed. In January 1964 the session announced that no more new pew sittings would be rented, though they would allow the continuance of rentals already in effect. Most of the congregation responded positively, voluntarily giving up their sittings. Today, not many even know that a small number of open hymnbooks lying in the pews before the service is the last remnant of the old tradition.

Another tradition at Fourth Church was ushers in "tails." Many a visitor remembered the warmth and friendliness of the ushers, yet some saw their formal dress and their regimented processions as old-fashioned, at the least. One small concession was made: the tails were replaced by the morning coats and striped pants still worn today.

Another change, however, put the church ahead of its time. Fourth Church was among the first Presbyterian churches in the nation to install a woman as a minister. Davies selected Lesslie J. Anbari for a staff position in 1963 and encouraged her ordination the next year. About the thirtieth woman to be ordained in the denomination, which had ordained women as ministers only since 1956, Anbari was the third to be ordained in the Presbytery of Chicago and may have been the first to serve on the staff of a large city church. In the tradition of the deaconesses, she worked with the deacons in their calling ministry and in the Parish Plan. Although she did not preach at the Sunday morning service, she participated in leading worship, thus introducing the congregation and hundreds of visitors to the reality of a woman minister. If any members disapproved of the idea of women clergy, it is not remembered. Anbari probably posed little threat in a church long accustomed to deaconesses and to young assistant ministers generally thought of as being "in training."

Another change was a lowering of the average age of the membership. New high-rise residences were being built in all directions from the church; and the "Near North"—the center of the city's night life, with easy access to downtown business centers and several universities—became the choice location for the city's young professionals. Although many young people were uninterested in or openly antagonistic to organized religion, and although the Fourth Church worship service made no concessions to the times, the congregation's average age dropped from fifty-seven to thirty-five in less than a decade. In 1969, over 50 percent of the membership was under forty, and about a third of the congregation were young professionals from the high-rise apartments of the Near North Side. Some were attracted by the church's aura of success, wealth, and power; others, by the church's ministries to those in need. Further, the young adult programs were a well-known place to meet other young adults.

About the same time, the congregation began to show small signs of racial inclusiveness. Quietly, almost without notice, a few African Americans began to attend and then to join. People of various national backgrounds, especially Asian, found themselves welcomed, although they were still a tiny minority.

At a time when many churches and denominations began a steady decline in membership that has continued to the present, Fourth Church membership remained steady, at around three thousand, receiving and losing over two hundred members annually. This steady state was partly due to the continuing work of an active invitation committee in a highly mobile community. Many churches in this period were also beginning to lose interest in foreign missions, but Fourth Church continued its strong participation in worldwide mission, sending missionaries and financial support around the world. In 1966, for instance, they raised $600,000 for a denominational campaign. Their gift helped build a nursing school in Taegu, Korea, where Fourth Church members were serving as missionaries, and other members visited and volunteered.

A New Decade and a New Century

In 1971 the congregation celebrated its centennial with the dedication of a new organ, a renovated chapel, special services, a drama, and a dinner attended by Mayor Richard J. Daley, Governor Richard Ogilvie, Senator Charles Percy, and former pastor H. R. Anderson. The moderator of the Presbyterian General Assembly, William R. Laws, Jr., was the keynote speaker.

Across the nation during the 1970s activism was being replaced by inwardness. Fourth Church's commitment to its service programs did not waver, but time and resources were also spent on enriching its worship and spiritual life. In the fall of 1970, some three hundred people enrolled for the first semester of study in the Bethel Bible Study Program, a two-year overview of the Bible. In 1973, nearly three hundred members participated in "Key 73," an ecumenical evangelistic movement which used small-group Bible studies as its method of inspiration and outreach. The School of Religion attracted several hundred each year, and an average of 120 adults attended Sunday morning classes, primarily Bible studies.

The 1970s also saw, at last, the election of women as elders and trustees. Presbyterian law had allowed women officers since 1930; but at Fourth Church no woman had ever been nominated as elder or trustee. In the light of the women's movement and the advancement of women in professional and business careers, the absence of women in the church's leadership had become, according to Davies, "a glaring exclusion" perpetuated by tradition and a few of the elders. Until 1969, officers had always been nominated by a committee of the session, but Presbyterian government had been changed, clearly prescribing a nominating committee elected by the congregation and representative of the congregation (that is, including women). Even under this new system, the congregation's nominating committee continued to nominate only men for three more years. In 1972 the slate included, at last, two women elders and two women trustees, and they were elected without controversy. Election as elders finally made it possible for women to be delegates to presbytery, synod, and General Assembly. In 1976, Nina L.

8.1 View of sanctuary and cloister of Fourth Presbyterian Church, Chicago. Courtesy of Fourth Presbyterian Church.

Hermann was the first Fourth Church woman member to study for the ministry and become ordained under the church's sponsorship.

After the war in Vietnam, the church sponsored eight Cambodian families, with the help of a part-time coordinator. A member of the church, Neal Ball, founded the American Refugee Committee, and when he turned to his church for help, individual donors made possible the sending of a ten-person team of medical personnel to a refugee camp in Thailand for two months in 1979.

When Elam Davies expressed his vision for a professional pastoral counseling center, member Luther Replogle donated funds to buy a house next door and to finance the first years of the center, which opened in 1976 with a staff of two. With an expanded staff, the Lorene Replogle Center serves church and community through individual counseling, seminars, and support groups.

The next project was to provide racially integrated affordable housing for low- and middle-income families in the area between the housing projects and the Gold Coast. A joint effort with four other churches, the project required over a decade of planning and negotiations to obtain state and federal funding, community involvement, and city approval. The Atrium Village, completed in 1979, cost $10.5 million and includes 307 units in eight three-story buildings and one nine-story building, as well as a day-care center, pool, playgrounds, parking, and small shops. The churches turned over administration of the village to a residents' board, and a quota system maintains economic and racial integration. Atrium Village testifies to what churches can accomplish even in such difficult areas as housing and human community.

In the early eighties, as a response to the continuing challenge of transients coming for help, an apartment in the church basement was remodeled as a social service center. A part-time director and several assistants provide food, clothing, counseling, and referrals for employment, public assistance, mental health, and shelter. The Elam Davies Social Service Center was dedicated on May 1, 1983, and continues to the present—a fitting tribute to a pastor who for twenty-three years urged his congregation to reach out with compassion to "the least, the last, the lost and the lonely."

When Davies retired in 1984, the church was serving nearly five thousand people weekly in the social service center, counseling center, senior center, preschool, programs for community children and for young adults, music programs, worship, and congregational life. There were 2,850 members (about the same number as when Davies arrived, though it had been higher in some years), and the staff had grown to include three associate ministers (one a woman) and three assistant ministers, a director of education, several program directors, and several seminary students.

A Church for the City

In the summer of 1985, Dr. John McCormick Buchanan became the church's new pastor. A graduate of Chicago Theological Seminary and the University of Chicago Divinity School, he had served two pastorates in Indiana and an eleven-year pastorate at Broad Street Presbyterian Church in Columbus, Ohio. Vigorous, intense, and in his middle forties, Buchanan had a reputation for outstanding preaching and congregational leadership and had served the denomination in many ways. His vision for Fourth Church included its being more consciously inclusive and Presbyterian, continuing the mission programs, and becoming a recognized presence and participant in the city, especially on Michigan Avenue.

Buchanan brought a new style of leadership. Rather than continuing a centralized, staff-led administration, he emphasized shared leadership and a much greater degree of lay involvement. To accomplish these ends, he reordered the administrative system. There are now twelve session committees, each with at least ten members, thus engaging dozens of church members (in addition to the elders) in planning and carrying out the activities of the church. This change has resulted in a new sense of vitality and involvement, as well as more leadership opportunities for women and minorities, young and old.

Another early task was to increase the visibility of women in the worship service. Although women "greeters" were sometimes at the doors, the ushers in the sanctuary were all men, and when fourteen men marched up to the front to collect the offering, the message sent was far from being inclusive. More important, although a few women elders served Communion, policy assigned them to serve in and under the balconies, and only those men who served the center aisle had seats around the table at the front when the elders received Communion. The congregation was ready for the new pastor to make changes. At Buchanan's first Communion service, he invited women elders to serve the elements in the center aisle, and it was not long before women were also serving as ushers. By the second year of his pastorate, three of the six associate ministers on the staff were women, so every Sunday one or two of the worship leaders are clergywomen.

Buchanan also made changes in the worship service. Since 1914 the liturgy had remained essentially unchanged, both because it expressed the congregation's tradition and because members felt satisfaction and pride in the service as it was. Some Presbyterian visitors and new members, however, noticed minor differences between Fourth Church services and more recent Presbyterian tradition, which seemed to set the church outside of, or "behind," the Presbyterian mainstream and modern movements in liturgical renewal. For example, there was no lay leadership in the services, and the liturgy did not include a unison congregational prayer of confession. Soon after Buchanan's arrival, the service followed the order used by most Presbyterians and similar churches. The congregation easily accepted the changes.

Lay liturgists now share the leadership of the evening service and, on a monthly basis, morning worship. Special "family" services have included folk songs and innovative liturgies. Even a liturgical dancer leading the Palm Sunday procession was accepted with equanimity.

Not only is Buchanan himself in close accord with contemporary Presbyterian styles of leadership, inclusiveness, and worship, but he has sought to strengthen the congregation's understanding of itself as Presbyterian. He believes a congregation is helped to find its own identity when it claims its denominational heritage and participates in its denominational "family." This is especially important at Fourth Church because many members have not been raised as Presbyterians. Connections to the Presbyterian denomination are becoming clearer: through educational courses and a fuller interpretation of denominational mission programs; through publishing a congregational history; through using the new Presbyterian hymnal, the new Statement of Faith, and other worship resources; and through the expanded participation of pastors and members in the life of the presbytery and the General Assembly. Associate minister Deborah Kapp served as moderator of the Chicago presbytery in 1989, and the entire clergy staff serves at various presbytery, General Assembly, and ecumenical levels.

The congregation is also beginning to grapple more openly with difficult and controversial social issues. The church leadership is learning to trust the congregation's strength and ability to deal openly with life's hard issues and to respect people with different points of view. The pastor has dealt frankly in his sermons with such matters as abortion and AIDS. He led a study of the language of worship, including "inclusive language." As a result of a church task force on AIDS, the session extended a statement of concern and now provides community memorial services for AIDS victims. The entire church staff participated in a workshop on understanding AIDS and its victims. A task force on racism has also been established.

In early 1990, after lengthy discussion, the session agreed to host a "Fast for El Salvador" sponsored by the Chicago presbytery and several other organizations. The decision was explained to the congregation in this way:

The Session is aware that people of faith and integrity differ . . . it does not presume to know the solution. . . . Its action specifically expresses concern for and solidarity with El Salvadoran Christians who are suffering [and] abhorrence of the murder of clergy, invasion of church buildings and harassment of church workers.

In making this decision, the Session was acting in the best

Presbyterian tradition. From the days when John Calvin commented on the laws of Geneva, . . . we have understood our calling to speak and act our sense of God's will in the world.[88]

In this decision, the session was carrying on the Fourth Church tradition of moral leadership in society, but it was breaking with the church's previous practice of speaking primarily on "private" issues. To address a public issue like foreign policy (however obliquely) was a relatively new step for this congregation, though to do so was quite in keeping with Presbyterian tradition.

In a variety of ways Buchanan has sought to make the church a presence on Michigan Avenue. On Palm Sunday the children process up and down the avenue waving palms and shouting "Hosanna!" During the summer, the courtyard that faces Michigan Avenue is the location of twice-weekly free concerts, and the fellowship hour after Sunday worship has been moved outside, both for the enjoyment of parishioners and as a way for the neighborhood to see the church as people, not stone.

A more direct outreach has been the Michigan Avenue Forum, discussions of important issues to which the public is invited. Five or six hundred people came to hear the U.S. surgeon general speak on the subject of AIDS. Other forums have focused on the fall of the Berlin Wall, the film *The Last Temptation of Christ*, euthanasia, and public education.

Similarly, the annual fine arts festival which began in the early eighties has been expanded. The public is invited for the art exhibits, drama, and music, including such major performers as Dave Brubeck. Each year an artist has provoked attention and some controversy with an outdoor artistic display or sculpture on Michigan Avenue.

The church also serves the public through its music program, which continues to provide frequent recitals and concerts, from Mozart's *Requiem* and Bach's *Magnificat* (with the city's finest instrumentalists) to organ recitals, chamber music, and instrumental soloists. Through this long-standing tradition of musical events many people, including members of other churches, have been given the opportunity to enjoy the best church music from the world's greatest composers.

The church's community ministry is no less important than in the past. In 1990 the Center for Older Adults celebrated its twenty-fifth anniversary by expanding its services to five days a week. The tutoring program celebrated the same anniversary by serving 350 children per

8.2   View of Fourth Presbyterian Church, Chicago, looking east toward Lake Michigan.

week and hiring its first full-time director, who also oversees the summer day-program, the scholarship program (to send children to summer
camp), and the church's involvement in the city's adopt-a-school program. The church's task force on homelessness brings volunteers together every Sunday evening during winter to cook meals for overnight
shelters, and the church helped a nearby Presbyterian mission agency
to set up a shelter.

Fourth Church continues to engage volunteers in many ways. Older
programs (like those serving the schoolchildren, the hospital, and the

jail) continue in strength. In recent years the church has become involved in Habitat for Humanity, providing the manual labor to build two
townhouses and the financing for one of them. They have also participated in a program with the Chicago Housing Authority: along with
several other churches, a team of church members repairs, cleans, and
paints apartments in the Cabrini-Green housing complex.

The congregation continues its fine programs of adult education,
from Bible study groups to series on environmental concerns. To accommodate busy schedules and to help business and professional people
apply their faith in the workplace, the pastor leads book studies at
weekly breakfasts; and a Loop breakfast series, led by church members,
meets downtown. A number of young adult groups meet throughout the
week, and a thriving women's program has managed to bridge the gap
between women who work outside the home and women who don't.

In Buchanan's first five years, membership grew by five hundred
members (membership stood at 3,340 at the end of 1989, with an average
of three hundred new members joining each year), but even more significant is the age of those who join: the trend toward a younger membership has continued. From 1986 through 1989, over 55 percent of the
new members were between twenty and forty years of age. At the end
of 1989, 34 percent of the total membership were under the age of thirty-
five, compared to 25 percent in most Presbyterian and other Protestant
"mainline" churches; and only a third of the congregation was over fifty,
while in most Presbyterian churches those over fifty make up one-
half.[89]

The number of children is also increasing; around fifty infants are
baptized each year. With an enrollment of 261, the Sunday school can
no longer be contained in Westminster House, so some children's classes
are once again being held in the original Sunday school building.

The leadership of the congregation is also much younger than it
once was. The officers are an interesting mix of older men and women
who remember "the way it has been" and younger people who appreciate Fourth Church as an institution with heritage and traditions yet
who bring new perspectives of inclusiveness, new styles of family life,
and an awareness of today's economic realities. The officers are conscious of the necessity to teach the new membership the traditions of
generous giving. With fewer really wealthy members and the traditionally strong "older" givers now in the minority, the work of the church
depends more and more on support from every member, with regular
"percentage of income" pledging. One of the greatest challenges before

the congregation will be to continue the spirit and level of generosity that has characterized the congregation in the past and made possible over the years a nursing school in Korea, a chapel in China, a hospital in Thailand, chapel furnishings in Geneva, Switzerland, church buildings in Chicago and Montana, and much more.

Conclusion

Among the reasons for Fourth Church's continued strength are many factors that could be considered accidental to the church's faith and ministry: its location and demographics, its wealth and endowment, its attractive and enduring building. Nevertheless, the church's stability has been the result of internal factors as well. In seventy-five years, the church was served by only three pastors, all of whom have been impressive preachers, with strong leadership qualities, and highly respected within the congregation and beyond. Further, the congregation has suffered remarkably little internal conflict. Although discomfort has been felt by those on both sides of many issues and changes, and some have chafed at the slowness of change, this has not been a congregation of factions or open conflict (except in its distant beginnings). The congregation apparently places a high value on *not* having conflict. Its self-image simply does not allow for fighting within the ranks, not only because of the importance of propriety and order but also because of the conviction that the mission and worship life of this church should not be endangered by disunity.

The church's image of itself as philanthropist has remained one of its distinctive characteristics. Because of its location and wealth, this congregation has not experienced the city around it as a threat (as have so many inner-city churches); rather, the church sees itself as benefactor toward the city. Of course, urban transition has been completely on its side: Fourth Church has not been the victim of urban blight, white flight, or the disappearance of a residential community. Therefore the church regards the city not so much as a shaping force as the arena within which the church is called to act out its faith—that is, to "glorify God," to "do those things which are good and useful," and "to promote welfare, peace and public good."

Of course some have criticized this assumed role of benefactor as being patronizing and of the "Band-Aid" and "Christmas basket" mentality. It has always been possible to assume that the people of the congregation could do more than they have done, and to question the source of the wealth that has made their generosity possible. Some have thought the church should look more seriously at questions of lifestyle and the root causes of economic injustice, poverty, and institutionalized racism. Others suspect that the aura of wealth and power automatically sets the church over against those less fortunate. Elam Davies wrote that the church's work with black families was criticized by the left as tokenism and by the right as "do-goodism."[90]

Yet men and women have testified, "I am where I am today" because of Fourth Church's tutoring program, and countless more could make similar statements about other ministries of the church. Hospitals, schools, and church buildings stand as evidence of the influence of this congregation around the world. Without the support of Fourth Church, the work of the presbytery and even the denomination would have been diminished. This congregation as an institution and its members as individuals have accomplished much through generous financial gifts and countless hours of personal involvement as volunteers. In addition, there is no way to measure what the church through its life and its worship has added to the spiritual lives of individuals and, through them, to the life of the city.

With more members than ever before, the Fourth Presbyterian Church of Chicago today continues to display the attributes that have been part of its distinctive character from its beginning: the high standards it sets for itself in all it does (music, worship, preaching, education, and service programs) and the spirit of philanthropy and volunteerism that expresses its concern for others and its belief that people can indeed make a difference.

APPENDIX

Ministers of Fourth Presbyterian Church, Past and Present

North Church

1848–56	Richard Higgins Richardson
1856–57	Robert Alexander Brown
1858–61	Nathan Lewis Rice
1862–64	John B. Stewart
1864–66	David Xavier Junkin
1866–70	David Calhoun Marquis

Ministers of Fourth Presbyterian Church, Past and Present (*continued*)

Westminster Church

1855–57	Ansel Doane Eddy
1858–61	William Henry Spencer
1861–65	Edward A. Pierce
1867–71	David Swing

Fourth Presbyterian Church

1871–75	David Swing
1877–80	John Abbott French
1880–83	Herrick Johnson
1885–92	Melancthon Woolsey Stryker
1893–97	Thomas Chalmers Hall
1899–1908	William Robson Notman
1901–3	James M. Duer
1905–9	John N. Freeman
1909–30	John Timothy Stone
1912–14	Claude Porter Terry
1913–30	Harold A. Dalzell
1918–19	Samuel Martin Gibson
1920–22	Ezra Allen Van Nuys
1920–23	Rudolph Samuel Schuster
1921–22	Calvin Pardee Erdman
1923–27	Alfred Samuel Nickless
1928–61	Harrison Ray Anderson
1930–35	William Samuel Meyer
1931–40	Clarence N. Wright
1935–37	Alexander B. Allison
1939–46	Allan A. Zaun
1942–48	Kenneth N. Hildebrand
1947–52	Ralph S. Hamilton
1947–57	Calvin DeVries
1949–52	William Faulds
1953–63	Robert Bent Hayward
1953–67	Donald K. Safstrom
1957–66	Paul S. Allen, Jr.
1961–84	Elam Davies

Ministers of Fourth Presbyterian Church,
Past and Present (*continued*)

1963–71	Gerald E. Hazelrigg
1963–66	Lesslie J. Anbari
1966–71	Andrew D. Tempelman
1968–72	John M. Miller
1971–76	David W. Robertson
1971–84	James M. Fleming
1973–81	David S. Handley
1974–78	Robert E. Wheat
1984–86	R. Milton Winter
1976–	John H. Boyle
1978–	David A. Donovan
1981–	Deborah J. Kapp
1985–	John M. Buchanan
1986–	Linda C. Loving
1986–	Christine A. Chakoian
1987–	Thomas E. S. Miller

Source: Marilee Munger Scroggs, *A Light in the City: The Fourth Presbyterian Church of Chicago* (Chicago: Fourth Presbyterian Church, 1990), p. 169.

Note: The names indented under the names of the ministers are those of assistants or associates.

NOTES

1. For information on the division of the Presbyterian Church in 1837, see Lefferts Loetscher, *A Brief History of the Presbyterians* (Philadelphia: Westminster, 1978). See also Maurice W. Armstrong, Lefferts Loetscher, and Charles A. Anderson, *The Presbyterian Enterprise* (Philadelphia: Westminster, 1956).

2. James G. K. McClure, "The History of Fourth Presbyterian Church of Chicago, an address delivered May 12, 1914." *The Fourth Church*, May 1914, p. 2. Much of the information about the church and its organizations is from *The Fourth Church* magazine which began publication in 1909. The source of such information will not ordinarily be noted. Information from before 1909, especially about the organizations, is found in the fiftieth anniversary edition.

3. William T. Hutchinson, *Cyrus Hall McCormick: Harvest, 1856–1884* (New York: D. Appleton-Century, 1935). All information about Cyrus H. McCormick is taken from this book.

4. Ibid., p. 15.

5. Ibid., p. 20.

6. Ibid., p. 29.

7. Ibid., p. 32.

8. George S. Phillips, *Chicago and Her Churches* (N.p.: E. R. Myers and Chandler, 1968), p. 329.

9. Ibid., p. 323.

10. Ibid., p. 333.

11. Joseph Fort Newton, *David Swing, Poet-Preacher* (Chicago: Unity, 1909), pp. 45–49.

12. Hutchinson, *McCormick*, p. 507.

13. Paul Thomas Gilbert and Charles Lee Bryson, *Chicago and Its Makers* (Chicago: F. Mendelsohn, 1928), pp. 104–6.

14. Memorial tribute, session records, May 1898.

15. Session records, Fourth Presbyterian Church, October 22, 1871.

16. H. R. Anderson, "The Pastor's Page," *Fourth Church*, November 1946, p. 2.

17. Newton, *Swing*, p. 59.

18. Ibid., p. 73.

19. Hutchinson, *McCormick*, pp. 253f.

20. Newton, *Swing*, p. 82.

21. For Presbyterians, the "creeds" included (and still include) primarily the Westminster Confession but also other confessions such as the Scottish and the Heidelberg as well as the writings of John Calvin.

22. *The World's Edition of the Great Presbyterian Conflict: Patton vs. Swing* (Chicago: George MacDonald, 1874).

23. A Committee of the Presbytery, ed., *The Trial of the Rev. David Swing Before the Presbytery of Chicago* (Chicago: Jansen, McClurg, 1874), pp. 8–14.

24. Ibid., p. 18.

25. David Swing, *Sermons* (Chicago: Jansen, McClurg, 1884), pp. 103, 107.

26. Newton, *Swing*, p. 79.

27. Session records, 1874.

28. *The Trial*, p. 266.

29. Quoted by Newton, *Swing*, p. 109.

30. "Prof. Swing's Reasons for Withdrawal," in Helen Swing Starring, comp., *David Swing: A Memorial Volume. Ten Sermons* (Chicago: F. Tennyson Neely, 1894), pp. 370ff.

31. McClure, "History," p. 5.

32. Memorial tribute, session records, May 1898.

33. "Genevan Confession of 1536," excerpted in Clyde L. Manschreck, *A History of Christianity* (Englewood Cliffs, N.J.: Prentice-Hall, 1964), p. 93.

34. John Calvin, *A Summary of the Christian Life: Of Self-denial, Institutio III*, quoted in J. S. Whale, *The Protestant Tradition* (Cambridge: Cambridge University Press, 1955), p. 165.

35. Phillips, p. 329.

36. Session records, October 22, 1871.

37. *The Fourth Church, Fiftieth Anniversary Number*, February 1921, p. 53.

38. Andrew Stevenson, *Chicago Pre-eminently a Presbyterian City* (Chicago: Winona, 1907), pp. 18–20.

39. James G. K. McClure, "Historical Address, the Fiftieth Anniversary of Fourth Presbyterian Church, 1921," *The Fourth Church*, February 1921.

40. Marilee Munger Scroggs, *A Light in the City* (Chicago: Fourth Presbyterian Church of Chicago, 1990), p. 50.

41. Session records, July 1883.

42. Memorial tribute (Waite), session records, May 1898.

43. Memorial tribute (King), session records, May 1898.

44. "Farewell Sermon," *The Fourth Church*, April 1931, p. 309. In the magazine this sermon is incorrectly attributed to Herrick Johnson. Stryker's farewell would have been in the fall of 1892.

45. *The Fourth Church*, February 1921, p. 77.

46. "A Summary of the Sixty-Fifth Anniversary Celebration," *The Fourth Church*, February 1937, p. 7.

47. Editorial, *Congregationalist*. Reprinted in *The Fourth Church*, June 1912, p. 7.

48. "Religious Movements in Chicago," *The Fourth Church*, November 1911, p. 12.

49. Quoted by Stone, "Preparation for Service," *The Fourth Church*, November 1916, p. 339.

50. Charles Stelzle, "A Modern Church to Meet a Modern Situation," *Continent*, February 27, 1913. Reprinted in *The Fourth Church*, March 1913, pp. 4–6.

51. Editorial, *Chicago Tribune*, March 12, 1913. Reprinted in *The Fourth Church*, March 1913.

52. *The Fourth Church*, December 1912, p. 7.

53. S. P. Thrasher, "Closing Vice Resorts," *The Fourth Church*, July 1913, p. 10.

54. Sydney E. Ahlstrom, *A Religious History of the American People*, vol. 2 (Garden City, N.Y.: Image Books, 1975), p. 200.

55. Charles Howard Hopkins, *The Rise of the Social Gospel in American Protestantism, 1865–1915* (New Haven: Yale University Press, 1940), pp. 154–55.

56. Frederick Hall, *Sunday-School Times*. Reprinted in *The Fourth Church*, October 1914, p. 5.

57. Ibid.

58. Editorial, *Syracuse Post-Standard*, December 23, 1912. Quoted in *The Fourth Church*, January 1913.

59. *The Fourth Church*, December 1913.

60. *The General Assembly Herald*, March 1914. Reprinted in *The Fourth Church*, March 1914, p. 9.

61. Thomas D. Jones, *The Fourth Church*, May 1914, p. 6.

62. Annual reports of the Church Extension Board, 1910–1940, Presbytery of Chicago.

63. McClure, "Historical Address."

64. *The Fourth Church*, January 1926, p. 269.

65. Minerva S. Weil, "Missionary Letters," *The Fourth Church*, August 1917, p. 636.

66. James M. Gillet, letter, *The Fourth Church*, February 1918, p. 859, and Clyde Winegart, letter, *The Fourth Church*, January 1918, p. 808.

67. Robert McCormick Adams, letter, *The Fourth Church*, March 1918, p. 889.

68. "National Prohibition," *The Fourth Church*, June 1918, p. 106.

69. "The Fourth Church William A. Sunday Campaign Committee," *The Fourth Church*, January 1918, p. 819.

70. From an interview with a church member.

71. Lois A. Boyd and R. Douglas Brackenridge, *Presbyterian Women in America* (Presbyterian Historical Society; Westport, Conn.: Greenwood Press, 1983), p. 111.

72. *Digest of the Acts and Deliverances of the General Assembly of the Presbyterian Church in the United States of America*, vol. 1, December 1930, p. 386.

73. Harvey W. Zorbaugh, *The Gold Coast and the Slum* (Chicago: University of Chicago Press, 1929; Midway reprint, 1983), p. 184n.

74. *The Fourth Church*, May 1937, p. 32.

75. *The Fourth Church*, December 1943, p. 3, and May 1944, p. 3.

76. "Report of the Board of Trustees," *The Fourth Church*, May 1936, p. 8.

77. Annual reports of the Church Extension Board, Presbytery of Chicago.

78. "The Church of Christ Japanese," *The Fourth Church*, March 1947, p. 2.

79. Session records, 1934.

80. "40 Indians Go to Presbytery," *Chicago Daily News*, March 11, 1971.

81. "Ousted Indians Find Temporary Shelter," *Chicago Sun-Times*, July 2, 1971.

82. Bruce Buursma, "Famed Preacher Davies to Retire," *Chicago Tribune*, March 23, 1984.

83. *Time*, December 31, 1979.

84. Bruce Buursma, "Pulpit Power," *Chicago Tribune*, August 16, 1981, sec. 9.

85. Elam Davies, Introduction to *One Hundred Years, The Fourth Presbyterian Church* (anniversary booklet) (Chicago: Fourth Presbyterian Church, 1971), p. 3.

86. Elam Davies, quoted in *Fourth Focus*, April 1984, p. 3.

87. Davies, "Some Reflections on the Nation's Need," sermon preached on June 9, 1968.

88. "From the Boards," *The Fourth Presbyterian Church of Chicago Newsletter*, April 1990.

89. "A Presbyterian Profile," *Presbyterian Survey*, September 1987, p. 26. See also Wade Clark Roof and William McKinney, *American Mainline Religion* (New Brunswick, N.J.: Rutgers University Press, 1987), p. 152.

90. Davies, "For Reflection," *The Fourth Church*, Spring 1968, p. 2.

NINE

The History of the Greek Orthodox Cathedral of the Annunciation

GEORGE PAPAIOANNOU

Introduction

THE AGELESS BELIEF OF THE Orthodox Church is that the purpose of the Church is salvation in Christ. In its doctrine and worship the Orthodox Church is today fundamentally unchanged from its beginnings. Indeed, the adherence to an immutable tradition and a sense of living continuity with the ancient Church are essential characteristics of Orthodoxy. "The thing that first strikes a stranger on encountering Orthodoxy," writes Timothy Ware, "is its air of antiquity, its apparent changelessness."[1]

However, tradition is also the source of Orthodoxy's ability to adapt to the present and the future. Holy Tradition is regarded by the Orthodox as nothing less than the direction and teaching of the Holy Spirit who has been abiding in the Church since Pentecost.[2] As such, it is not an external authority but rather an internal principle that illuminates the will of God for the Church on its earthly pilgrimage. As the "conscience" of the Church, it draws on the wisdom and experience of the past as it acts to reinterpret the changeless truths of the faith to address the needs of the present.[3] Furthermore, one of the strengths of the Orthodox Church has always been its ability to incorporate or, more accurately, to "baptize" into Orthodoxy the national customs and languages of the peoples it evangelizes without in any way altering the Christian beliefs it so carefully guards. These characteristics of changelessness and adaptability are evident in the Greek Orthodox congregation of Annunciation Cathedral of Baltimore, Maryland—the subject of this chapter.

The people of Annunciation do not comprise a community of believers in the Protestant sense. The Orthodox Church cannot be seen as a confederation of local churches, nor does the local church exist independently of other Orthodox churches. The Church is a eucharistic society.

Apart from the Eucharist, the people of Annunciation are not a church but only a group of individuals. But in coming together to celebrate the Eucharist in the name of the one, holy, catholic, and apostolic Church, the people of Annunciation become the Church. There is no distinction between "local" and "universal" church in the Eucharist; there is only one altar, one Eucharist, one Church, one Lord.[4] This one Church finds its expression in the communion of the many local churches.[5]

Furthermore, the unity and catholicity of each local church is guaranteed by the bishop. As the head of the eucharistic community and as the living image of Christ, the bishop is the unity and the source of all the ministries in the Church.[6] The pastor of the local congregation derives his spiritual and administrative authority from the bishop and acts on his behalf.

In the Old World, practically all Orthodox churches have their own system of administration based on the Holy Canons of United Orthodoxy, and the presiding bishop holds the title of patriarch or archbishop. These independent jurisdictions are united to each other by the bonds of doctrine, worship, and discipline. In America there is not yet a completely self-governing church. Practically all of its ethnic branches remain under the jurisdiction of the Old World mother churches. The Greek Orthodox Archdiocese of North and South America (of which Annunciation is a part), established in 1922, is under the jurisdiction of the Ecumenical Patriarchate of Constantinople.

Although Annunciation congregation is, in the celebration of the Eucharist, the one Church in its fullness, it is also a concrete, historical expression of the one Church, with its own particular history and way of doing things. As one of the pioneer Greek Orthodox congregations in the country, Annunciation Cathedral, founded in 1906, set an example for many of the immigrant Greek Orthodox communities which followed. A look at its history will both illuminate the life of Annunciation congregation and also aid in understanding the fundamental experience of the Greek Orthodox in the United States.

The historical development of the Annunciation congregation may be divided into three periods: from 1906 to 1937, from 1937 to the mid-1950s, and from the 1950s to the present.

The first period began on March 18, 1906, when the Divine Liturgy was officiated by Father Joachim Alexopoulos in a Union Hall in Baltimore, marking the beginning of Annunciation congregation. This period covers the years of the congregation in a little church at Homewood Avenue and Chase Street to 1937, when it moved to a new and more prestigious location at Maryland Avenue and Preston Street. The first twenty years were marked by a mixture of religious and patriotic enthusiasm, but also by a struggle for survival, by poverty, and by divisions rooted in Greek politics, in which the parties sought to destroy each other. The church was the center of the Greek immigrant's activity, but that activity was not always religious. Greek ethnicity and the preservation of the Greek language sometimes took precedence over religious matters.

The second era covers the period from 1937 through the mid-1950s. Following the years of the Great Depression, the Greek congregations throughout the land entered the mainstream of the American way of life. The Greek Americans began to reconcile their differences. For Annunciation, the years between the late thirties and the mid-fifties saw the development of strong spiritual leadership supported by wise laymen.

The dawn of the decade of the fifties found the Annunciation congregation preparing for the passing of the torch from the immigrant to an American-born generation. This passage demanded a new spiritual leadership coming from the ranks of the native Greek-American generation. Although this transition was at times difficult, it was ultimately achieved. Since the mid-1950s, Annunciation Cathedral has been playing an increasingly important role in Baltimore's religious, social, cultural, and educational community life. Although the church is located in the heart of the city of Baltimore, with most of its parishioners residing in the suburbs, it has never lost its vitality. It is, perhaps, one of the very few inner-city Greek Orthodox congregations that is thriving and has expanded its educational and cultural facilities.

The Beginnings: 1906 to 1937

Like some other European immigrant groups, the Greeks came to the United States not because of religious persecution but because of economic realities and arrived without any church structure or guidance to provide for their spiritual needs. When the new arrivals began to seek spiritual direction, they were forced to establish the congregations themselves, thereby breaking with the traditional reliance on episcopal initiative for the founding of parishes. The theologically unsophisticated lay organizers and administrators adopted a Protestant type of church polity in which the local congregation takes the lead, especially in administrative matters. By contrast, in traditional Orthodox ecclesiology, spiritual and administrative authority is centered in the bishop, who may then delegate it to the priest. The importance of the laity in the leadership of the Greek Orthodox congregations in America from their very beginnings was both a departure from the way things were done in Greece and the first step towards a distinctively American way of doing things.

After a failed attempt in 1894, a second attempt was made to organize a Greek Orthodox congregation in Baltimore, Maryland. Sunday, March 18, 1906, marks the beginning of a congregation that was to play an important role not only in the life of the local Greek community but also in the life of the Baltimore community at large and the entire Greek Orthodox Archdiocese of North and South America. On that historic day, a highly regarded and educated priest serving the Greek community of Washington, D.C., Father Joachim Alexopoulos, visited Baltimore and celebrated the Divine Liturgy. About 150 Greeks attended. Joy and tears, enthusiasm and excitement filled the air. The Divine Liturgy was followed by an organizational and fund-raising meeting. The collection tray and the membership contributions on the first day brought in $407.15, a very respectable amount for that time.[7]

The very act of fund-raising signaled a departure for the Greeks from the traditional way church finances were handled in the old country. In Greece, Orthodoxy was the official state religion, the government paid the salaries of the priests, the clergy were in control of the finances, and religious education was taught in the public schools. The only financial responsibility of the parishioners was the occasional repair of the church building. In contrast, if the Greek Orthodox congregations were to survive in the United States, they would have to supply and administer the money themselves for the church structures and operation. Raising funds on such a large scale came as a shock to the Greek immigrants and continued to be a sore spot as each new wave of immigrants was told, to their surprise, that what they had received for "free" in Greece now had to be funded from their own pockets. It was not a question of generosity—the Greek immigrant sacrificed much for his church. It was rather a question of reeducation and an awakening to the new responsibilities thrust upon the laity by the American system of separation of church and state. But with these responsibilities came empowerment: the laity could hire and fire the priest and determine how the parish funds were to be utilized.

Shortly after the first inspiring and encouraging Divine Liturgy celebrated by Father Alexopoulos in Baltimore, the ad hoc committee that had organized the event was replaced by the first elected governing body to run the affairs of the new congregation. The parish council in America was very different from its counterpart in Greece. In Greece, the parish council was appointed by the bishop, upon the recommendation of the priest, and had little to do but pass the offering tray and stand proudly in the narthex of the church. But in America, the council was elected by the laity and was the legal authority in charge of all the affairs of the congregation. Those elected were: George Sempeles, president; George Giovannis, secretary; and Constantine Diamantopoulos, treasurer.[8] The governing committee moved swiftly to consolidate the progress achieved and began to function, on a limited basis, as a Greek Orthodox congregation. The committee had arranged to share the services of a priest with the Greek Orthodox congregation of Washington, D.C., until they were able to support a permanent pastor. They offered to pay the Washington congregation the amount of $100 per month for six months so the priest, Father Alexopoulos, could visit Baltimore once a month to celebrate the Divine Liturgy and serve the other religious needs of the parish.

This time, the Greek Orthodox congregation in Baltimore was founded on solid foundations. Father Alexopoulos was a symbol of stability, and with his direction the lay committee worked diligently to solidify the progress and look to the future. Even the name of the new congregation, "Evangelismos," the Greek word for Annunciation, projected a bright period ahead. It refers to the good tidings brought to the Virgin Mary by Archangel Gabriel, and, to the Greeks of Baltimore, signified the bringing of the "good news" of the Orthodox faith to their new country. Religious services were held in the Union Hall at 500 East Fayette Street, with Father Alexopoulos continuing to serve the spiritual needs of the parish until the spring of 1907.

The congregation by then had grown to some sixty-eight families and felt strong enough to seek a permanent priest, using the same procedure that other congregations in the country used. Without a bishop to govern the churches and assign or transfer priests, individual parishes petitioned either the Church of Greece or the Ecumenical Patriarchate to send a priest from the jurisdiction of Athens or Constantinople. The congregation of Baltimore made its request to the Church of Greece, and in the spring of 1907 the Reverend Constantine Douropoulos arrived in Baltimore to become the first full-time priest of Annunciation.[9]

The new priest had limited theological training but was well respected. A contemporary historian wrote that Father Douropoulos was "known as a model priest, due to his humility and goodness."[10] Like his fellow priests serving in other Greek Orthodox congregations in the United States at the time, he found himself to be under the authority not of ecclesiastical superiors but of a board of directors. Although Father Douropoulos had been serving as the spiritual leader of the Annunciation several months before the certificate of incorporation was received from the state of Maryland on June 4, 1909, his name was not included. The certificate included only the names and signatures of laymen. These laymen resisted any attempt to return to the ancient Greek Orthodox tradition in which the administrative authority of the local congregation was vested in the clergy. When priests arrived, they faced a new reality. Their authority was limited to matters of spirituality.

After three years of holding services in the Union Hall, the parishioners decided to acquire a permanent place of worship, a church they could decorate in the Orthodox tradition. A Methodist church was for sale for $12,000, and they purchased it.

October 1909 is a historic date for the Annunciation congregation. The Greek immigrants, the vast majority of whom owned no home of their own, became the owners of a building and made it a house of God. One of the few parishioners who owned his own building mortgaged it for $4,500 to secure the $12,000 transaction.[11] In this humble location they were to worship God, to be sanctified by the sacraments of their faith, and, especially, to raise their children in the sacred traditions, customs, and language of Hellenism. Indeed, it can be argued that, in this early period, the perpetuation of their Hellenic identity and especially the Greek language was the foremost concern of the immigrants. The Greeks not only took pride in their language as that of the great ancient philosophers and of Holy Scripture, they also saw it as the key to their continuing identity as a cohesive group. Their language and Orthodox faith had held them together throughout four hundred years of Turkish occupation and had played a significant role in their successful fight for freedom from Turkish rule. The Greek language now had to be perpetuated among the Greeks in America if their unique and ancient Hellenic character and virtues were to be preserved amid the melting-pot pressures of American life. That the Greek Orthodox Church should serve as the guardian of Hellenism seemed natural, since it had taken on that role throughout the many centuries of Turkish domination, from 1453 until 1821.

Annunciation congregation in Baltimore, like so many other Greek Orthodox parishes in America, took up the torch of Hellenism and established the Greek school before developing any separate formal religious school, such as the Sunday school. The first Greek school at Annunciation opened its doors in the church hall in 1912. The first teacher hired was a Mr. Karas. As was the case with all the Greek schools in America, the curriculum was patterned after the public schools in Greece, where religion was compulsory and taught along with the other lessons. Thus the lessons about the faith were interwoven with the language lessons. The Greek school became the pride of the congregation. In addition to teaching Greek and religion, the school was charged with giving plays with ethnic themes to entertain the Greeks.

It is remarkable how well this young congregation was able to organize, function, and expand in only a few years. Three years after acquiring a church building of their own, the Greek Orthodox of the Annunciation moved to purchase their own burial grounds, which they named the Greek Circle, in Woodlawn cemetery. Again, leadership was provided by a layman, Antonios Konstantopoulos, who was serving as president of the congregation when the transaction took place.[12]

Although an Orthodox funeral is necessary for the faithful, burial in land owned by the church is not considered essential to the Orthodox since the grave site is blessed at interment. But the purchase of burial grounds by the congregation was important as an expression of the unity of the ethnic community and its sense of identity as an extended family unit. In Greece, burial practices differed substantially from what was now encountered in America. In the old country, the dead were never embalmed, and were buried quickly in church grounds. After a period of a few years, the bones were unearthed, washed by the family, placed in a small box, and stored with the bones of other family members. Several generations were thus gathered together in a relatively small space. But in America, where the beloved dead were buried permanently in vast cemeteries, there was a sense of isolation from the group that did not sit well with the Greeks. Furthermore, Orthodox theology stresses the unity of the worshiping community, living and dead, and this seemed better expressed by burial of the members of the congregation close to one another.

Decades later, in 1943, Annunciation purchased fourteen acres for its own cemetery and, in 1981, built a chapel dedicated to the Resurrection on these cemetery grounds.[13] In the chapel of the Resurrection, not only funerals but also eucharistic liturgies are celebrated, especially liturgies occurring on "Psychosabata," or Saturdays of the Souls, that include special prayers for the dead. At these times, and during other memorial services, the parishioners of Annunciation experience in a personal and deeply meaningful way the gathering together of all worshipers, living and dead, in the life and worship of the Church.

Throughout the early years of Annunciation congregation's existence the laymen continued to provide the leadership and set the goals and objectives for the parish. Some were highly regarded for their education, and others for their professional or business achievements. Aristo M. Soho, for example, was a professor of romance languages who had received his Ph.D. from Johns Hopkins University. Described as "bearded, muscular, and more temperamental than most scholars," he was the pride of the Greek Orthodox community of Baltimore and played a leading role in the founding of Annunciation, serving as the congregation's president in 1910.[14]

Another leader, Elias Mavromihalis, exuded an air of superiority, being a descendant of the famous Mavromihalis family of revolutionary leaders in the war of independence of Greece against Turkey. Well educated in Greek and eloquent, he was the poet laureate of the Baltimore Greek community. He was given permission to deliver the sermon on occasions of ethnic observances.

Theodore Agnew opened a restaurant that brought him economic success and gave him prominence in the Greek community. Agnew had special affection for Greece and Greek culture but, unlike most of his fellow Greeks, he advocated the Americanization of the Greeks in America. Although very active in the formative years of the Annunciation congregation, from the early 1920s he devoted his time and energy to AHEPA (American Hellenic Educational Progressive Association), an association which strongly promoted a new Greek-American identity that adopted the American way of life. Agnew married a non-Greek woman who was Episcopalian, and his son, Spiro (who became vice president of the United States in 1968), was baptized in the Episcopal Church.

The strong leadership of the laymen often led to conflicts with the priests. Indeed, any priest who tried to assert a leading role in the congregation's administration found himself in deep trouble. For years there was a humorous story circulating in Baltimore about a certain leader at Annunciation who was known as the "papadospastis" (priest-breaker). He was so adamantly opposed to the clergy's involvement in the congregation's administration that any priest who attempted to change the status quo was chased out of town by the papadospastis.

These occasional conflicts led to a rapid turnover of priests. Between

1910 and 1913 three priests came and went. They were Fathers Douropoulos, Parthenios Rodopoulos, and Chrysanthos Kaplanis. Of the
three, only Rodopoulos is supposed to have had a theology degree, for
he signed all documents as "Doctor of Theology." Between pastoral
transitions, the congregation remained unified. However, the assignment of Father Iakovos Leloudas in 1915 coincided with the beginning of
new problems and deep divisions. Following the conclusion of the Bal-
kan Wars (1912–13), most of the Greeks who had settled in America and
had then left to fight for their mother country returned with wives and
families.[15] Patriotic enthusiasm ran high, but so did political animosities
that eventually polarized Greek communities and divided Greek Orthodox congregations.

The Battle Between Royalists and Venizelists

The eye of the storm was located in Athens. At the beginning, it involved two principal actors, King Constantine and Prime Minister
Venizelos, men of great ability and charisma, but of diametrically opposed views. Aside from being an opponent of the monarchy, Prime
Minister Venizelos clashed with King Constantine in handling the Greek
struggle for the liberation of Greek territories still occupied by Turkey.
Another major issue was Greece's entry into World War I. Prime Minister Venizelos strongly advocated Greece's entry into the war on the
side of the Allies, whereas King Constantine, a German sympathizer,
advocated neutrality. It was a political controversy, and the Orthodox
Church, being a state church, was hopelessly involved. This had tragic
consequences not only for the faithful in Greece but also for the faithful
of the American diaspora. When Prime Minister Venizelos declared a
revolution against King Constantine, Archbishop Theokleitos of Athens
and of all Greece excommunicated him in a public ceremony. Unfortunately for Theokleitos and royalist sympathizers, the revolution was successful. King Constantine was forced to leave the country. Theokleitos
and his royalist bishops lost their positions. The synod of bishops then
moved to elect Meletios Metaxakis, a Venizelist sympathizer, as the new
head of the Greek Church.

The new Archbishop Meletios, in the midst of his problems in
Greece, showed great concern for the Greeks of America. He paid two
visits to the United States. During the first (1918), he studied the conditions and installed one of his assistants, Bishop Alexander of Rodos-
tolou, to administer the area. On his second visit (1921), he set the

foundation for the Greek Orthodox Archdiocese of North and South America. Although a controversial personality in Greece and in the Greek diaspora, Meletios was elected Ecumenical Patriarch of Constantinople, and from that position he officially declared the Church in America to be an archdiocese and placed it under his jurisdiction. His faithful friend, Bishop Alexander, was chosen by the Holy Synod of bishops as the first archbishop in America.

This promising start was immediately frustrated by pro-royalist clergy and laity in Greece and America. Both Patriarch Meletios and Archbishop Alexander were considered to be linked to Venizelos and thus unacceptable. Although the majority of the parishes followed the new archbishop, there were many who remained fanatically devoted to the royalist cause. There were also many divided congregations which fought each other legally and even at the sanctuary of the holy altar.[16]

In Baltimore, the political-ecclesiastical controversy resulted in the physical division of the Annunciation congregation. It started when the parish priest, Father Iakovos Leloudas, ignored the instructions given by Archbishop Alexander to cease the commemoration of the king's name during the Divine Liturgy and to commemorate, instead, the Greek nation and its army. The Venizelist faction was offended and demanded his removal from the Baltimore congregation. Ironically, they charged him with "injecting Greek politics in the church worship."[17] Archbishop Alexander charged Father Leloudas with insubordination and ordered him to leave in June 1920.

Although the majority of the congregation in Baltimore seemed to favor Venizelos, the royalists were more vocal and more fanatical and at times their dedication to the cause gave them a majority. This happened in the spring of 1921 when the board of directors, with a royalist majority, refused to receive any instructions from the archbishop. Instead, they expressed their allegiance to the representative of the Church of Greece, Metropolitan Germanos. The first order of business was the dismissal of the priest, Father Polycarpos Marinakis (who had arrived in early 1921), which opened the way for the second coming of Father Iakovos Leloudas. A desperate Father Marinakis sent a telegram to Archbishop Alexander asking for instructions:

Reverend Leloudas arrived here by invitation of Trustees, who, as I hear, are about to discharge me as I do not recognize the Synod of Athens. Many members of the community want me to establish a new church. Let me know what to do. Must I stay here or not?[18]

The archbishop did not allow Father Marinakis to physically divide the community and organize a separate congregation. Instead, he instructed him to go to Somerville, Massachusetts. The split was avoided, but what the Venizelists didn't do the royalists accomplished.

Following the departure of Father Marinakis, the royalist Father Leloudas regained his pastorship at the Annunciation, but his tenure was brief. The frustrated Venizelists were energized and in 1922 they regained the majority. When the Ecumenical Patriarch proclaimed the Church of America an archdiocese, the board of directors voted to submit to the authority of the new archbishop. Under the direction of the archbishop, the general assembly of the congregation convened on May 13, 1923, to accept the charter granted by the Ecumenical Patriarch, which proclaimed the Greek Orthodox Archdiocese of North and South America to be the superior ecclesiastical authority of every Greek Orthodox congregation in America. Father Leloudas, who continued to alienate the parishioners with his pro-royalist views, opposed this new arrangement. After consulting with Archbishop Alexander, the congregation informed Father Leloudas, through a registered letter, that he was dismissed.[19]

This time, Father Leloudas and his royalist friends were prepared to fight. They brought a civil suit against the church arguing that Father Leloudas's dismissal was illegal because the Holy Synod of Greece, not the Ecumenical Patriarch, was in charge of the transfer of priests in America.[20] A civil suit such as this against the church was unheard of in Greece and unusual even in America, where it was made possible only by the irregularity and confusion in the administrative authority of the church in America. However, the attempt of Father Leloudas to recapture the pastorate did not succeed, and he was forced to leave Baltimore and find employment elsewhere. Even so, the royalists of that city did not accept defeat.[21]

Under the leadership of John P. Prevas, the royalists determined that Annunciation was now too closely identified with the Venizelist views of Archbishop Alexander and that the only way to advance their cause was to form their own congregation and hire a priest who adhered to their political ideology. Prevas's suggestion was enthusiastically accepted and royalist supporters began searching for a priest. An advertisement in the pro-royalist daily *Atlantis* for a royalist priest was answered by Father John Magoulias, and he was hired. A building was rented and converted into a Greek Orthodox church named Holy Trinity. To further separate themselves from the progressive Venizelists, the royalists adopted the Julian calendar, whereas Annunciation followed the Gregorian calendar.[22]

The split became official on Sunday, July 1, 1923, when Father Magoulias arrived in Baltimore and celebrated the first Divine Liturgy. As occurred in so many other cities, the division of the congregation had a devastating effect on the people. It disrupted peace and unity in families and broke up friendships and business and personal relationships. Some of the people who had important roles in the development of Annunciation were now supporting Holy Trinity. Elias Mavromihalis became president of Holy Trinity in 1924.

The departure of the royalists from Annunciation did not bring peace and tranquility to the congregation, however. Conflicts arose between the clergy and laity as the priests finally began to demand recognition of their rights in church administration. From the time of the split to the end of the 1920s, there was a constant succession of priests in Baltimore. Such a frequent change of the parish priest is not the norm in the Orthodox Church, nor was it a common occurrence in Greece, where decisions about a priest's assignment were made by the bishop. But in these early years of the Church in America, the administrative authority of the archdiocese was still virtually powerless and could rarely back up the priest when a dispute arose. From the perspective of the hierarchy, the laymen sometimes abused their power. If a priest did not follow the will of the laity, the laymen found a new one. At Annunciation, between 1922 and 1935 eight priests came and went, the shortest stay being six months and the longest two and a half years.[23]

Was the situation better in other Greek-American congregations? In many of them it was even worse. The centralized authority in the archbishop and his synod of bishops that had been expected to bring order out of chaos failed to meet those expectations. Many blamed the system and others blamed the archbishop. In actuality, many factors had combined to create the deplorable situation of the Greek Orthodox Church in America. But one thing was certain: the complete identification of Archbishop Alexander with the party of Venizelos had tarnished his reputation as a spiritual leader, and as long as he remained the leader of the young American church the existing conditions could not improve.

The ecclesiastical war in the Archdiocese of North and South America was embarrassing and destructive not only to the Greek Orthodox Church in America but also to the Church in Greece and to the Ecumenical Patriarchate. In response to the cries of despair from all sides, church leaders joined forces with the political leaders of both parties in Greece to find a solution to the Greek-American problem. It was this effort that set the stage for the restoration of harmony in the Greek Orthodox community in America. A saving force arrived in the person of Metropolitan Damaskinos of Corinth who, in the spring of 1930, was dispatched to America as the exarch (a representative with full authority) of the Ecumenical Patriarchate to restore ecclesiastical order. After many months of consultations and negotiations with parties involved in the dispute, Metropolitan Damaskinos presented to Patriarch Photios II a plan that called for the repatriation of Archbishop Alexander and his auxiliary bishops to Greece. Damaskinos then recommended the election of Metropolitan Athenagoras of Corfu as the new archbishop of North and South America.

The plan of Damaskinos was accepted and Archbishop Athenagoras arrived in New York on February 24, 1931. He received a wildly enthusiastic greeting. His reputation as a remarkable man and a leader with great dedication, dynamic energy, farsighted statesmanship, and visionary enthusiasm had preceded his arrival in America. The greatest challenge of the new archbishop was in visiting the politically divided communities throughout the United States and Canada. His goal was to eliminate the labels of Venizelist or royalist, and to create strong, united congregations that would embrace all people.

The Greek Orthodox of Baltimore welcomed the change that the new archbishop symbolized. They had suffered enough from political divisions and animosities. They had even tried in 1927 to reunify their congregation on their own, but had failed because the royalists had demanded that Annunciation renounce Archbishop Alexander.[24] Even so, people were tired of the hostilities and were unwilling to support two churches and two schools. Two years later, a second attempt at reunification succeeded. The meeting was held on December 13, 1929, with the participation of the boards of directors of both churches. The agreement was simple, decisive, and final: Holy Trinity Church would be closed, Holy Trinity's priest would receive a three-month salary compensation and leave Baltimore, and, finally, all possessions and property of Holy Trinity would be moved to the Annunciation church.[25] The conclusion of the agreement brought tears of joy to the participants, who rose, embraced each other, and took an oath to work together in harmony for a united congregation.

The unity agreement was received with enthusiasm by the Greek Orthodox of Baltimore, who celebrated the event in a gathering on Sunday, December 22, 1929. An unprecedented fifteen hundred persons were present. The *Baltimore Sun* reported the reunion celebration: "Differences among Greeks of Baltimore, arising from political strife in their native land ten years ago, ended at Lehman Hall last night."[26]

The reunification of the Annunciation congregation was a landmark not only for the Greek Orthodox of Baltimore but for the entire Archdiocese of the Greek Orthodox Church of North and South America. Baltimore had set the tone for other divided congregations to follow. The authenticity of the unity was manifested in the eased tensions and positive attitude that prevailed in the new congregation and in the election of its new leadership. Prevas makes the following observation:

> An example of the relaxed feelings between the two factions is the fact that Leonidas P. Christakos, who had been an active Royalist member of Holy Trinity and served as president of its parish council in 1929, was elected to serve as president of the reunited Evangelismos (Annunciation) church in 1930, and, again, in 1932.[27]

A New Foundation

Having learned from its mistakes, the congregation offered its complete support to the new archbishop of North and South America in his efforts to set the foundation of the Greek-American church on sounder grounds and in accordance with the canonical tradition of Orthodoxy. When Athenagoras called a Clergy-Laity Congress in New York City on November 14, 1931, Annunciation sent its priest and two lay delegates.

The idea of the Clergy-Laity Congress, initiated by the founder of the archdiocese, Meletios Metaxakis, was a Greek-American innovation. It became a biennial event, with the archbishop presiding. Except for questions of doctrinal or canonical nature, the congress concerns itself with all matters affecting the life and growth of the Church, her institutions, her finances, and her administrative, educational, and philanthropic concerns.

The congress of 1931 was of great importance because it debated a new plan for the administration of the parishes and for the perennial, thorny issue of the authority of the priest. The new archbishop was convinced that the cause of the existing chaos in Greek-American congregations was not so much the political struggle in Greece as the poor administrative system, the domination of the laity, and the exclusion of the clergy and their humiliating status.

His proposed bylaws defined, among other things, three important areas—the local parish (congregation), its laity, and the authority of the clergy—that would affect the congregation of Annunciation and change, at least in theory, its administrative practice. According to the adopted Archdiocesan By-Laws of Holy Churches and Communities, the parish is the local congregation, which is canonically dependent on the Greek Orthodox Archdiocese of North and South America, whose ecclesiastical authority is the canonical archbishop.[28] Article IX states that the archbishop is the authentic interpreter not only of matters of faith but also of the bylaws. The same article also dictates that every parish shall be governed by a board of trustees composed of the priest and of as many laypersons as required by the needs of the parish.[29] Article VI reasserts the authority of the priest, whose prestige and power had been seriously eroded in America. It states that the priest is an inseparable part of the administration of the parish. The bylaws strongly suggest, however, that in the performance of his duties he must cooperate with the board of directors, peacefully and harmoniously.[30]

The bylaws were reluctantly adopted by the majority of delegates in New York but became a difficult issue in every congregation in the country. The decision of the Clergy-Laity Congress required the acceptance of the uniform bylaws by parishes which had previously developed their own. Each parish viewed the problem from its own standpoint and found it difficult to accept the changes brought about by the bylaws. Having worked independently for so long, they feared that submission to the archbishop and sharing authority with the priest would bring an end to perceived lay domination. Throughout the country there were signs of defiance of clerical authority.

But the archbishop would not be thwarted. He attacked the problem in a uniquely American way: he personally visited countless parishes—especially the pacesetting parishes such as Annunciation—to lobby on behalf of the new bylaws. In Baltimore the leadership was sympathetic to the archbishop and its relations with him were cordial, but they hesitated to force the issue and ask the parish assembly to accept the bylaws. On Sunday, July 14, 1935, Archbishop Athenagoras came to Baltimore to be present at the general assembly of the congregation and to answer any questions regarding the bylaws. It was an important meeting for the embattled archbishop; he had visited other parishes, and their assemblies had rejected his appeal. Baltimore received him with love, respect, and affection. The adoption of the bylaws was unanimous, marking for Annunciation a new era of real community life.[31] The cooperation with the archdiocese was rewarded when the archbishop assigned one of the most learned and highly respected priests in the country, Father Joachim Papachristou, a graduate of the famous theological school of Halki, Constantinople. During his tenure (1935–50), the congregation of Annunciation experienced progress, harmony, and growth in membership and programs.

The Second Era: 1937 to mid-1950

Perhaps the greatest achievement of Father Papachristou and his board of directors was the acquisition of a new church building. There had been an ongoing debate over building expansion in the community for a long time. Plans and ideas had been presented at different times to the general assembly, but were rejected by the membership as either too costly or unsatisfactory. In 1937, however, Annunciation was presented with an opportunity to acquire a church building that was spacious, centrally located, and architecturally attractive. It was a Congregational church built in 1889. The building had been sold in 1936 to the Continental Oil Company, which intended to demolish it and build in its place a gasoline station. The Greeks were determined to stop the demolition and make the building their house of worship. Under the leadership of Niketas A. Konstant, the general assembly accepted a five-year plan, authored by Harry G. Pappas, to bring a successful end to the deal for the acquisition of the new edifice.[32]

By 1937 the Greek population had grown, and the Greeks had become a political power both in Baltimore and in Maryland. Continental Oil Company could not build a gasoline station in the Congregational church's location without an ordinance from the city. Although the city council had passed the ordinance, the mayor had not yet signed it. The Greeks, with the help of Mayor Jackson, succeeded in rescinding the motion, and so opened the way for this church structure to become the center of Greek Orthodox religious, cultural, and educational activity. This action marked the beginning of a new era. It brought unity, enthusiasm, and a sense of pride to the congregation. The building and property were purchased for a total of $40,000, and on March 4, 1937, became the property of the Greek Orthodox congregation of the Annunciation. The members were so pleased that within five years they donated well over $25,000 for renovations and expansion, and paid the mortgage in full.[33]

What made the building so attractive to the Greek Orthodox faithful of the Annunciation congregation was its Byzantine architectural

9.1 Exterior View of the Greek Orthodox Cathedral of the Annunciation, 1992. Courtesy of Dennis F. Paxenos, Photography (Baltimore, Maryland).

structure. One observer noted that "The circular sanctuary has been described as the only example of pure byzantine architecture in the area, reminiscent of early Greek temples."[34] The transformation from a Protestant to Greek Orthodox church began immediately. The exterior stone was cleaned, the interior was cleaned and painted, and the altar and iconostasis (a full icon screen) were brought from the old Homewood Avenue church.[35] Then, on Friday, April 23, 1937, the faithful of Annunciation, holding candles, icons, and other sacred items of the faith, walked in solemn procession from the old church to the new. The Baltimore populace was informed of the event from the columns of the *Baltimore Evening Sun:*

> Carrying three icons, one of which came from Mount Athos, members of the Greek Orthodox church, Evangelismos (Annunciation), last night moved from their old house of worship at Chase and Homewood Streets into the edifice purchased recently at Maryland Avenue and Preston Street. . . . The congregation first held a farewell service in the old church.[36]

Approximately one month later, the congregation of Annunciation celebrated Easter in the new church. The press took notice of this event and, from that time on, the Greek Orthodox Easter became an important religious event for the city of Baltimore. Again, the *Baltimore Evening Sun* reported on the uniqueness of the Orthodox Resurrection service:

At twelve midnight, every light in the church was extinguished, save that of the Altar, from which the priest, the Rev. Joachim Papachristou, lighted a candle and gave the invitation, "Come and receive the light from the unwaning light, then glorify Christ who rose from the dead." Young boys and girls of the church then came forward, lighted the candles, and passed through the congregation, lighting the candles of the other worshipers. At last, each person in the edifice stood with a lighted taper. Then the priest, followed by the congregation, proceeded to the lawn of the church, where the services of the Resurrection continued. The priest chanted "Christos Anesti" (Christ is Risen), and the congregation repeated the chant. At the close, red dyed eggs, typifying new life and joy, were given to members of the congregation.[37]

The community worshiped in the new building for over a year before its formal dedication. On Sunday, May 8, 1938, Archbishop Athenagoras officiated at the consecration of the new church of the Annunciation congregation. The elaborate ceremonies, which all Greek Orthodox churches follow, included the ancient practice of sealing a relic of a saint in the altar, a link to the past when chapels were built over the tombs of saints. The archbishop also cleansed the altar and blessed the edifice with holy oil, and concluded the ceremonies by celebrating the Divine Liturgy. Even though these consecration services lasted some nine hours, the parishioners still found the energy for a celebration ball that evening.[38]

Worship at Annunciation

The purchase of the new church building forced the parishioners to examine some of the customs that accompanied worship in the old country but seemed awkward in this new structure and, in fact, in the American environment. In particular, the use of pews and a pipe organ provided means by which the parishioners were able to alter their customs to allow for a greater expression of their more Americanized way of life.

In the Old World, the Orthodox churches used no pews. People stood during services. There were some benches, but they were re-served for the elderly. In the Annunciation church at Chase and Home-wood Streets, the congregation had followed this tradition strictly. There were no pews. Would there be pews in the new church? The decision actually was not difficult. Other Greek Orthodox churches in the country had already begun using pews. Then, too, there were pews in place and the parishioners were happy to accept this innovation for their own comfort. Also, the pews helped to discipline worshipers, es-pecially children, who easily became restless by standing during the long hours of Orthodox worship.

The use of the pews forced the congregation to change another of the Old World customs, the separation of the men from the women and children. Traditionally, women stood on one side of the aisle and men on the other. Families came to church together, but in the church they were separated. In the new Annunciation there was no central aisle. Families were forced to sit together, and they liked it. When the idea was suggested a few years later to create a central aisle for bridal proces-sionals and recessionals, it was rejected out of fear that the central aisle would bring back the old custom of separating families during worship.

Another item that the congregation of the Annunciation inherited from the former owners of the church was the pipe organ. In Greece, the organ was considered to be a Western innovation and was not used, except in the cathedral on the island of Corfu, where it had been intro-duced, despite the objections of the synod of bishops in Greece, by Bishop Athenagoras (who was destined to become archbishop of the Greek Orthodox Church in America in 1930). When Athenagoras be-came archbishop of America, he had among his major objectives the improvement of Orthodox worship. The use of the organ in worship was encouraged. Annunciation became the beneficiary of this policy, and the congregation decided to leave the magnificent pipe organ in place.

Undoubtedly, the organ has played a very important role in the de-velopment of some fine Orthodox liturgical choirs. At Annunciation it has helped to create a unique musical tradition. Since there was no Greek Orthodox organ music at the time, the choir directors at Annun-ciation composed their own music by transposing the hymns of Byzan-tine chant into organ music—not an easy task, since Byzantine music uses an entirely different scale than that of Western music. Athanasios P. Theodorides, who was choir director at Annunciation from 1937 to 1948, was considered a pioneer in the composition of choir music for Orthodox churches in America.[39] Following in his footsteps at Annunciation were Georgia Topol Tangires (choir director from 1950 to 1956, and again from 1965 to the present), and Anna Gallos (1956 to 1965), both of whom are noted for having arranged and composed many liturgical works.

The changes in these customs surrounding worship should not be minimized. Worship at Annunciation took on a distinctively American veneer, looking and sounding different from that in Greece. The services in America were more organized and quiet, and the movement of the worshipers was regulated so that they stood and sat at specific times in the service, remaining in the pews at all times. Women and men sat and prayed together, and children joined both parents, which reflected the greater equality women experienced in general in the New World. The music, sung by a choir of mixed voices, sounded with the even, harmonious tones of the Western scale rather than the more plaintive tones of the Byzantine scale sung by two or three male chanters. Yet, these changes, and the others that have occurred over the years in the externals of Orthodox worship, never threatened the vital center of Orthodox belief and practice. Along with these new practices there was also continuity with the past through an unswerving adherence to the inner content of worship and the basic structure of the liturgy.

The essence of worship at Annunciation did not change with the move to the new building because the basic worship of the Church belongs to the ancient and timeless dimension of Orthodox tradition. For Annunciation, as for every Greek Orthodox congregation, the celebration of the sacrament of the Holy Eucharist in the Divine Liturgy is the very center of its life. It is in this worship experience that the people of Annunciation become the Church. It is in the celebration of the Eucharist that each worshiper claims membership in the Kingdom of God, and is called to "put away all worldly care, that we may receive the King of all."[40]

The Divine Liturgy is conducted today in Orthodox churches in the same way it was conducted in the early centuries of the Church. The worship experience begins even before the actual service, as soon as one enters the church and reverences the icons. The use of icons by the Orthodox testifies to the belief that the invisible and indescribable God can now be depicted because he has become visible in Christ, and to the belief that the material world is included in Christ's transfiguring and redeeming work. The Orthodox do not worship the icons, but only reverence them, reserving worship for the Divine reality depicted in the icon. However, the icons convey a sense of the living presence of God and an experience of the community of saints gathering for the eucharistic celebration.

At Annunciation, one strong link with tradition is the role of icons, which have always been important to the worship experience. Although the first icons of the church were painted in a Westernized style, commonly preferred by the early immigrant parishes, the current icons (completed in the 1970s and 1980s) are in the fourteenth-century Byzantine style; they not only reflect Annunciation's greater understanding and pride in its Byzantine heritage but also are more truly Orthodox in that they focus on the spiritual rather than the physical qualities of the person or event depicted. In fact, the entire church inspires a sense of awe and touches a spiritual chord in those who enter. The spacious and elaborately decorated interior of the church, with its full icon screen, several large icon frescoes, four magnificent Tiffany stained-glass windows, huge triple arches in front of the sanctuary, carved oak woodwork, and gold leaf decorations creates a dramatic, spellbinding effect. The ethereal setting lends much to the worship experience.

At Annunciation, the continuity with the past becomes especially palpable when one enters the church on Sunday morning to celebrate the Divine Liturgy. One detects the sweet aroma of incense, along with the warmth and glow of numerous candles lit by the worshipers upon entering, as a reminder that Christ is the light of the world. Soon the glorious voices of the choir will join with the chanter and priest in the celebration of the service, which is mostly chanted or sung. In a commanding voice the priest chants, "Blessed is the Kingdom of the Father, and of the Son, and of the Holy Spirit, now, and forever, and to the ages of ages." Thus begins the Divine Liturgy. At its center is the story of the Last Supper which Christ shared with his disciples before his betrayal and crucifixion. But it is also a recapitulation of the entire doctrine of salvation, and is, in the words of the great Orthodox theologian, Alexander Schmemann, "the joyous gathering of those who are to meet the risen Lord and to enter with him into the bridal chamber."[41] The elements that adorn the Liturgy—the elaborate and colorful vestments, the singing, the incense, the repetition and ritual—are expressions of this joy. The grandeur of the Liturgy also reflects its importance as the pinnacle of spiritual experience for the Orthodox faithful.

The Divine Liturgy is centered around the sacrament of the Eucharist, but it is not usual for every worshiper to come forward and receive

9.2   Interior View of the Greek Orthodox Cathedral of the Annunciation, 1992.
Courtesy of Dennis F. Paxenos, Photography (Baltimore, Maryland).

Holy Communion. Only those who are prepared may receive. A regi-
men of prayer and fasting is undertaken for some days, and a strict
fast—nothing at all to eat or drink—is required in the morning, before
the sacrament is received.[42] Holy Communion is received with great
solemnity, awe, and quiet joy. The faithful approach "with the fear of
God, faith and love."[43] In the Orthodox Church, the laity as well as the
clergy receive both the bread and the wine, the Body and Blood of
Christ, from a common cup. Each person receives in the Eucharist new
life: the forgiveness of sins and the promise of life eternal. Even those
who are not prepared to receive the sacrament are renewed by the eucharistic experience. Parishioners describe the Divine Liturgy as the one
time in the week when they put aside the cares and strife of ordinary
life, enter a haven of peace, and experience the presence of God in
their lives. For a short time, the heavenly Kingdom is glimpsed here on

earth. Whatever else may change at Annunciation, this celebration of the eucharistic Divine Liturgy, this encounter with the Eternal, remains essentially unchanged.

Annunciation and the Wider Community

By the end of the thirties, the Greek Orthodox community of Baltimore was in good condition, unique but also an integral part of the larger American community. Several clubs that had been founded by members of Annunciation were key to the congregation's participation in the wider Greek-American community and in the community's outreach to non-Greeks.

Among the greatest accomplishments of Annunciation congregation in the 1930s was the founding of the Ladies Philoptochos (Friends of the Poor) Society. It was begun by Archbishop Athenagoras as a national movement in 1932 in the midst of the Great Depression, and the Annunciation chapter was formed on February 4, 1936, with Kalliope H. Pappas as president. The work of the Philoptochos was initially limited to rendering aid to the poor and needy in the local Greek community. However, the end of World War II created new opportunities and also presented the congregation of Annunciation with new challenges. The scope of the Philoptochos became wider and covered every area of community life. The women sponsored various events to assist the growth of the church. They assisted in education by sponsoring scholarships for young people and rendering financial support to Holy Cross Theological School. One of their most important projects, unique in the entire archdiocese of some six hundred parishes, was that of a social service suite. It began in the 1970s when the Philoptochos purchased a home across the street from the church and donated the property to the congregation, which renovated the building and incorporated it into the magnificent Annunciation Orthodox Center. The Philoptochos provided funds for furnishing the section that was used by the church's department of social services. More recently, the Philoptochos provided funds to purchase a van for transporting senior citizens of the Golden Age Group to various functions.

The Ladies of the Philoptochos have also served as witnesses for Greek Orthodoxy to the community of Baltimore at large. Their present membership in Church Women United enables them to enter into dialogue with members of other religious groups in the community and advance the cause of Christian kinship and ecumenism.[44]

Another organization, founded in November 1936, that provided great services to the Annunciation congregation was the Hellenic University Club. Established by several Greek Orthodox students at Johns Hopkins University, its goals were to foster fellowship and promote educational and cultural growth.[45] A strong bond was formed between the Hellenic University Club and Annunciation, with the club creating a tradition for learning within the church which continues to this day. The first efforts to establish a Sunday school program in Baltimore came from the Hellenic University Club.

In addition to these closely connected church organizations, in the 1930s Annunciation witnessed the establishment of several other organizations, known as the "topika somatia," the local clubs. They represented a town, village, or a specific region of Greece. Their primary objective was to serve the social needs of their members, establish new friendships, help their hometowns in Greece, and maintain their local customs and traditions. These clubs were crucial to the immigrants in preserving continuity with the ethnic customs and values of the old country. Also, for many Greeks, these local clubs were central to both their social and their religious lives. It was through the social activities of these clubs that their members engaged in the life of the larger Greek community, and through the religious activities that they were involved in the church.

The topika somatia played an important role in the Annunciation community's life by making contributions, offering gifts, and by participating in a unique way in the congregation. Each club set a Sunday aside every year to attend the Divine Liturgy as a group on the feast day of the club's patron saint. At the conclusion of the Liturgy a special Litany of Artoklasia (Blessing of the Five Loaves) was given.[46] The litany was offered for the health and prosperity of the club members and for the welfare of their Greek hometown. A representative from the club addressed the congregation, reminding them of their local history and urging them to maintain their Greek customs and traditions.[47] However, the clubs were unable to make the old ways meaningful to the next generation and for the most part faded away after World War II.

Perhaps of greater significance than the local clubs were two national organizations, AHEPA and GAPA. AHEPA, the American Hellenic Educational Progressive Association, was founded in Atlanta, Georgia, in 1922. About a year later, on October 5, 1923, an AHEPA chapter—the Worthington Chapter, Number 30—was formed in Baltimore. GAPA, the Greek American Progressive Association, began in

1923 in Pittsburgh, Pennsylvania. Three years later, on November 29, 1926, the Koraes Chapter, Number 14, of GAPA was established in Baltimore. These two organizations were never formally affiliated with the church, yet they have been influential, sometimes constructively and sometimes destructively, both locally and nationally.

The members of AHEPA and GAPA were, first of all, members of the church. But in these organizations they were rivals. Each organization promoted a different vision and way of being Greek-American. GAPA chose to emphasize Greek ethnicity over anything American. GAPA's primary objective was the preservation and proliferation of everything that was Greek: language, religion, traditions, culture, and so on. In contrast, AHEPA had adopted an almost exclusive use of the English language and placed its emphasis on educating its Greek members to identify themselves with America. It accepted the reality that America was now the permanent home for the Greek immigrants and called for a new expression of Greek identity in the American context. In 1928, emphasizing the importance of the adoption of the American way of life and the role of AHEPA in achieving it, one of the founders of the AHEPA movement in Baltimore, Theodore Agnew, made the following prediction: "AHEPA is worthy of the fate which awaits her because she cherished, in her heart, the sweet longing of one day seeing in the White House a president of this mighty democracy, a son of hers, who will be proud of his origin."[48] The dream of the senior Agnew was almost realized by his son, Spiro, a member of the junior order of AHEPA in the 1930s. Spiro Agnew served as Baltimore county executive and governor of Maryland, and was elected vice president of the United States in 1968, but was forced to resign in October of 1973.

Through the 1930s there was a fierce but basically friendly competition between AHEPA and GAPA in every area, especially in organizing the youth. To advance their causes, both organizations formed auxiliaries and junior orders. There were juniors and juniorettes that gave stage plays. There was a GAPA patrol. There also were junior orders of AHEPA, known as the Sons of Pericles and the Maids of Athena, whose activities and programs prompted Americanization. Despite their philosophical differences, these groups rendered valuable service by gathering together the youth and offering them cultural and even religious programs.

The dawn of the decade of the forties brought new challenges to Annunciation. The resistance of Greece to the Axis powers on October 28, 1940, not only aroused sympathy, but also respect, admiration, and even appreciation from Americans and other freedom-loving people throughout the world. The Church and Greek local and national organizations united efforts to assist their Motherland.

In Baltimore, on November 3, 1940, the Greek Orthodox gathered in Annunciation to pray for Greece and the Allies. In an eloquent and moving sermon, Father Papachristou urged his parishioners to join the local chapter of the Greek War Relief Association (GWRA) and provide money, food, and clothes for the stricken nation.[49] The Greeks of Baltimore were generous and gave of their resources to the Greek cause, not only during the war and the occupation of Greece, but also after the war ended, helping in the reconstruction of Greece. Greece was not the only beneficiary of Annunciation. When the United States entered the war, the congregation of Annunciation collected $250,000 to help the war effort.

With all these war relief programs, Annunciation did not completely forget its service to the faithful, especially the youth. When a building near the church became available in 1942, the congregation purchased it, renovated it, and used it for church offices, rooms for the Greek School, social activities, and the Maryland branch of the GWRA.[50] The acquisition of the building opened a new horizon in the life of Annunciation congregation. The youth that for so many years had been neglected by the church became the focus of the community.

This awakening of the community to the needs of the youth was forced by the young people's change of attitude toward things thought to be unchangeable for the elders. The latter part of the 1930s and particularly the 1940s became years of questioning within the Greek Orthodox family and church life. Up to that time, it had been taken for granted that the young people would remain Greek and Orthodox. Dating and marriage to non-Greeks was anathema. Even the dating of Greek youths with Orthodox Christians of a different nationality was not acceptable.[51]

This was the prevailing attitude, but things started changing. Young people who had been away at college or in the armed forces returned home with different ideas and were prepared to challenge the ideals, traditions, customs, ethics, and practices of the church. Young and old began blaming the church for its inability to satisfy the social, cultural, and religious needs of the young. In response to this challenge and the urgent need of the Greek youth, EONA (Elliniki Orthodoxos Neolaia Amerikis, Greek Orthodox Youth of America) was formed in February 1946. Responsible for this historic accomplishment was Athanasios P. Theorides, who was serving the congregation in a multiple capacity as

Greek School principal, chanter, choir director, and executive secretary. This remarkable man helped the youth draft their bylaws and formulate an attractive youth program. The goals set by the founder were the same for all members: "To foster fellowship among the youth of Greek Orthodox descent; to further the cause of tolerance; and to achieve the principles of clean living and fair play."[52] Theodorides remained the chief adviser, but had the wisdom to allow the young people to run the affairs of the organization themselves.

Annunciation's attempt to serve its youth was not an unqualified success. To advance its youth program and strengthen its ties with the church, the board of directors of Annunciation decided to hire an assistant pastor from among the American-born clergy. He was a fresh young graduate of Holy Cross Seminary, Father Soterios Gouvellis, who, upon his arrival at the church in 1948, became an instant celebrity, especially among the EONA members. Young, married, energetic, and aggressive, he posed a sharp contrast to the older priest, who was described as "extremely dignified and very imposing."[53] The new assistant priest spoke English, was humorous, developed an atmosphere of comradeship, and above all, played ball with the youth. His popularity began to overshadow the prominence of the senior pastor, Father Papachristou. It was not the senior pastor but his young assistant who became the focus of the congregation. There wasn't anything that Father Sam, as he was called, asked for that he did not get. For example, at his insistence, the social hall of Annunciation was converted to a gymnasium. Soon after, athletic and social activities attracted such large numbers of young people that the church was able to create its own basketball and softball leagues. Although some of the older members of the congregation were alarmed by this new state of affairs, the vast majority of the communicants were pleased with the activities of the young pastor. Annunciation had entered a period of transition in its leadership, from the Greek-American pioneer to an American-born generation that was not prepared to allow the senior pastor and his "old-time cohorts" to turn the clock backward. Father Sam was their hero, a symbol of change.

But the personal and professional relationship between the senior pastor and his young assistant quickly deteriorated. There was practically no communication between them. Father Papachristou accused Father Sam of insubordination. Father Sam responded by accusing Father Papachristou of placing obstacles in his way of saving the youth. The atmosphere became so tense that the *Baltimore Sun* reported: "recent allegations of improper actions by the Rev. Mr. Papachristou included an assault by the clergyman on the assistant pastor while the two were at the altar of the church."[54] The assault was not verified. However, it was well known that Father Papachristou did not allow Father Sam to assist him in the celebration of the Divine Liturgy, although the latter was on the altar during the service.[55]

Following these events, Father Papachristou asked the archdiocese to transfer his young assistant. This request was made without the knowledge and consent of the board of directors. Father Sam Gouvellis left Baltimore on January 15, 1950, but the worst for Father Papachristou was still to come. Almost two weeks after he succeeded in having his assistant transferred, the general assembly of the congregation (with Savas Kambouris, a friend of Father Gouvellis and leader of the Papachristou opposition, presiding), decided by a vote of 153 to 7 to dismiss Father Papachristou. The majority were angry over Father Papachristou's unilateral dismissal of Father Sam, and had found their pastor of fifteen years to be "spiritually and temperamentally incompatible" with their needs.[56]

The decision of the laity to fire their priest, however, was not an easy matter. The laity no longer could with impunity hire and fire priests. The Uniform Parish By-Laws, which had been accepted by Annunciation in 1935, gave the right of transferring and firing priests exclusively to the archbishop. Archbishop Michael, to whom the decision of the assembly had been communicated, refused to accept it. Father Papachristou remained in his position. Further confusing the matter was the arrival of Father Chrysostom Bogdis, on March 1, 1950, hired by the parish to serve for a few months but not authorized by the archbishop. The parishioners, led by those opposed to Father Papachristou, felt they had no choice but to ask the parish council, the legal arm of the congregation, to take action against Father Papachristou. But the parish council could not come to a decision on the matter, and, in fact, later resigned over it.[57] The members of the opposition then argued that the mandate of the general assembly entitled them to file suit on behalf of the congregation. They succeeded in having the court issue an injunction on March 24, 1950, that prohibited Father Papachristou "from usurping the functions, duties, and powers as Rector and priest of the Annunciation."[58]

Even among the Greek Orthodox in America, who were accustomed to the laity taking an active and sometimes aggressive leadership role in parish matters, a suit of the congregation against its priest was extremely rare and was considered an outrage. The people of Annunciation were confused, angry, and deeply divided over the issue. Some felt that the church itself had been violated. However, the legal action did succeed in convincing the archdiocese to respond to the will of the laity. Realizing that things were not improving but rather worsening, and wishing to restore peace and tranquility to Annunciation, the archdiocese reassigned Father Papachristou to Norfolk, Virginia.

After fifteen productive years, Annunciation congregation and Father Papachristou parted. The separation was a traumatic experience for both. It took several years for the congregation to recover from the experience, but Father Papachristou never did. The separation from his beloved Annunciation congregation, the accusations, and the rumors had demolished him both physically and emotionally. He died of a heart attack in February 1955, in Norfolk, Virginia. His body was brought to Baltimore and lay in state at Annunciation, where his former parishioners, many of them former adversaries, came to pay their last respects.

Many of the members of Annunciation felt the lay leadership had abused its power and mishandled the pastoral problem that ended in the dismissal of both priests. The pastoral controversy was even more devastating to the youth, EONA in particular. During the same era, Annunciation lost the services of another key person, Professor Theodorides, the founder of EONA, who had served for many years in so many important positions at Annunciation. Deeply affected by the pastoral dismissal, he accepted a similar position at another Greek Orthodox Church.

Father Philotheos B. Ahladas, who was assigned to Annunciation in 1950 as the permanent pastor, was not a stranger to Baltimore. He had served as an assistant priest to Father Papachristou during 1946 and 1947. He was not the type of dynamic priest to whom Annunciation was accustomed. He was, however, credited for restoring peace and tranquility, and had a special interest in helping the youth of the parish. In 1951, with the aid of the Hellenic University Club, he established Annunciation's first formally organized Sunday school program. Until that time, religion had been taught to the children through the Greek school or in an ill-equipped and poorly organized Sunday school which functioned in many ways like a Greek school. Although the archdiocese in 1931 had formed a separate Department of Religious Education and had made it mandatory for parishes to establish catechetical schools, many congregations, including Annunciation, resisted forming a separate school for religion. They believed that, if their children were truly Greek and learned the Greek language, they would also remain Orthodox.

In actuality, the separate catechetical school advocated in the thirties and the forties by the archdiocese was really but another form of the Greek school. The bylaws that mandated that every church have a catechetical school also made clear that its purpose was dual: religious and cultural. The Sunday school was not only to initiate the children into the Christian Orthodox teachings, but also to make good Hellenes of them by teaching the culture and customs of Greece and by using the Greek language.[59]

The first attempt to implement the archdiocesan directive was made by Father Papachristou in 1936. He began by teaching religion one day a week for each of the Greek school classes. Eventually, he separated the religious classes from the Greek school and moved them to Sunday, with the children attending half of the Divine Liturgy and spending the remaining time in classes.[60] Teaching materials were obtained from the newly established seminary of the Holy Cross in Pomfret, Connecticut, which had become the center of religious education activity. However, these materials were hastily produced and simplistic, inadequate in addressing the interests and capacities of the children. A second problem was the poor preparation of the instructors. But the greatest difficulty for the catechetical school of Annunciation and the other parishes was that the lessons were all in Greek. The idea that the promotion of Hellenism in the Sunday schools would save both Orthodoxy and the Greek national consciousness seemed to have the opposite effect, with the children learning neither their religion nor the Greek language.

Drastic changes were made with the introduction of the English language into Sunday school classrooms. In 1949, when Archbishop Michael came to America, Christian education became one of his main concerns. A man of extensive and varied education with strong Christian convictions, he immediately formed a committee to evaluate the situation of the Sunday school. This was a time of transition from the Greek immigrant to the Greek-American church. At the tenth Clergy-Laity Congress in St. Louis, Missouri (November 26–December 1, 1950), the education committee recommended the use of the English language in religious education. Archbishop Michael, a Greek scholar himself, painfully but eloquently emphasized this need. It passed by a great majority.

In Baltimore, the news of the adoption of English in the teaching of religion encouraged a number of well-educated people to volunteer their services. This time, both the pastor and the laity accepted the offers enthusiastically. A committee from the Hellenic University Club, under the leadership of Peter J. Prevas and the spiritual guidance of Father Ahladas, organized the first faculty of the Annunciation Sunday school. All of them were members of the University Club.[61]

In addition to the founding of the Sunday school, during the early 1950s EONA, which had remained dormant since the pastoral controversy, became an organization with national recognition. It developed a new, more American identity, its name was changed to GOYA (Greek Orthodox Youth of America) in 1952, and English became its official language. The formation of GOYA was followed by the formation of Jr. GOYA.[62] At the same time, Richard Contos helped Father Ahladas to establish the first Boy Scout troop at Annunciation.

To strengthen ties between members and the leadership of the congregation, a monthly periodical, *The Annunciation Herald*, began to be published in 1951. The driving force behind the periodical was Mary Bahadouris Kiladis, who served as editor-in-chief for some thirty-nine years. *The Annunciation Herald* to this day continues to be an excellent vehicle of communication.

In 1954 a dynamic layman, C. G. Paris was elected president of Annunciation. The greatest contribution of Paris and his 1954 administration was the selection of a new pastor who opened up a new relationship for the laity and clergy. The notion of divided authority, the spiritual belonging to the clergy and the temporal belonging to the laity, gave way to mutual respect and cooperation. The pastor was now not merely an employee of the church who had been endowed with the special gift of leading the worship. He was the head of the parish, involved in both the administrative and spiritual aspects of the parish.

Coming of Age: 1954 to the Present

Father George Gallos began his tenure as pastor at Annunciation in the spring of 1954. American-born and a graduate of Holy Cross Theological Seminary, he had served congregations at New Britain, Connecticut, and Rochester, New York. He was a gentle and courteous man whose emphasis was on spirituality, culture, and music. Married to the daughter of a priest and only thirty-nine years of age, he and his pastorship looked very promising. One Annunciation historian described the importance of his arrival:

> Other American-born members of the clergy had served the Baltimore church in the role of the deacon or assistant pastor, but he

(Father Gallos), was the first to assume chief responsibility for the parish. His appearance on the scene represented the realization of the dream held by the founding fathers that the guardianship of their religion might some day be entrusted to the hands of their children born in their newly adopted land.[63]

Father George Gallos, in negotiating his position with the board of Annunciation, suggested that both he and his wife, Anna, be hired as a team. Mrs. Gallos was to be responsible for the music program of the congregation and was to be the choir director, a paid position. Although it was fairly common in a small parish for the priest's wife to take on some duties such as choir director or Sunday school director (and some priests' wives took on several duties), it was less common in a large parish, and it was especially unusual for the wife to be paid for her work. But Anna Gallos had exceptional abilities; for example, she not only arranged and composed important liturgical works for the choir but also extended music education to the Sunday school.[64] A little more than a year after the couple's arrival at Baltimore, a third family member was hired. Father John N. Gerotheou, the father-in-law of Father Gallos, was hired as the assistant pastor. The congregation was pleased with the work of the trio, and in 1957 the parish assembly approved a decision of the board of directors to purchase a rectory for use as a residence for both Father Gallos and Father Gerotheou. Prior to 1957, Annunciation had only been able to provide rental housing for its priests.

With the advent of Father Gallos there was a drastic change in the administrative organization of Annunciation congregation. The church office was reorganized and professionalized by C. G. Paris, who hired an office manager. Also, unlike the previous clergy, who were not included in the decision-making process, Father Gallos was involved from the beginning of his tenure in all aspects of the congregation's life, including its administration and finances. There were two reasons for the change of the congregation's attitude towards the leadership of the priest. The first was the good will of the board of directors, and especially of C. G. Paris, who served as president for three consecutive terms, 1954–56. Paris felt that the pastor should be an inseparable part of the congregation's administration. Paris was succeeded in the presidency by Evan Alevizatos Chriss, one of Baltimore's most respected citizens. Paris and Chriss helped to create a tradition of mutual respect and cooperation between clergy and laity at Annunciation. A second factor in the positive attitude of the laity towards the priest's involvement was the pastor himself. He had a good way of dealing with his people. He was pleasant, knowledgeable, and used gentle persuasion. He earned the respect and the affection of his people and made them comfortable with him.

Almost immediately after coming to Baltimore, Father Gallos sought to change the giving (stewardship) habits of his congregation. This change was significant in moving the church forward towards a more reliable financial budget and a more modern and American approach to church finances. The Greek Americans had come to realize that stewardship of the Orthodox Church as a whole was lacking when compared to that of other Christian denominations. They found it distressing to constantly be forced to devote so much energy to fund-raising. Father Gallos instituted an organized and systematic fund-raising program, known as the envelope system, for the collection of Sunday offerings. Each parishioner received a package containing a numbered envelope for every Sunday of the year; records were kept and acknowledgments were made.[65] The success of the envelope system came to surpass the expectations of even its most enthusiastic advocates. The additional revenue enabled the congregation to meet its current responsibilities and think optimistically of the expansion of its building facilities and renovation of the sanctuary.[66] Later, in 1962, Annunciation initiated the pledge system for financial support of the church, and in 1974 the stewardship pledge became the sole required financial support for being considered a member in good standing.[67] With the pledge system, Annunciation reached a new maturity in financial stewardship, with each person pledging an amount of his or her own choosing.

The success of the envelope system especially helped to raise the prestige and the authority of Father Gallos. To his credit, Father Gallos did not abuse the trust the congregation afforded him, nor did he monopolize the authority which he had been given. Unlike the priests of the old school, he ruled by consensus and persuasion where possible, worked closely with the laymen, and was open to ideas and suggestions. This new style of pastoring was very appealing to the increasingly Americanized laity at Annunciation, who valued the democratic process and their own involvement in the development of church policy.

During his tenure, Father Gallos's focus was on the people of his congregation, and he sought to bridge the gap between the Greek-born and the American-born generations and to bring the youth into the church. Although the service itself continued to be conducted in the original Greek, the sermon was in English. Teachings, rituals, rules and regulations were explained in English. The people clearly thirsted for the teachings of their faith. They were taught the meaning of the Liturgy, to sing the hymns and responses, and to appreciate the beauty of the Greek Orthodox worship. They even recorded the Divine Liturgy of St. John Chrysostom, and the record was purchased by practically every family in the congregation and then distributed throughout the country.

The Sunday school that had been organized by the Hellenic University Club was given special care by the new pastor. Not only were the lessons given in English, but the children listened to the priest preaching in English and, at times, praying in English. Music played a special, perhaps unique, role in religious education at Annunciation. Anna Gallos organized a junior choir from among the Sunday school children.

The Greek school, which had been declining, was revitalized by C. G. Paris. He appointed a committee of Greek-American educators, under the chairmanship of Theodore George, a high-school principal, to evaluate the Greek school curriculum. The committee recommended some drastic changes. Greek was to be taught to the children as a second, not a first, language. Emphasis was to be placed on conversation and not on individual subjects.[68]

Despite the advances of the American-born generation, it was as late as 1956 when English replaced Greek at the board of directors' meetings as well as at general parish assemblies. But many of the pioneer Greeks, who were concerned that the innovations would lead to de-hellenization, accepted the changes out of necessity and respect for the pastor, who treated the senior members with love and respect.

The Annunciation of the late fifties was now increasingly American-born. It still valued its Greek identity and generally directed its attention and services to the Greek community. But it also began to emerge from its absorption with its own ethnic group and slowly extended its activities to the wider American community. A major step forward occurred in 1955 when the general assembly changed the bylaws defining membership requirements. No longer would a person have to be "of Greek descent" to qualify for membership; rather, one now was required simply to be "of Eastern Orthodox faith."[69] Annunciation had finally come to define itself as a religious rather than an ethnic community. This change was especially important in the reception of converts into full participation in all aspects of church life.

A change in attitude towards the other Christian faiths could also be seen. The beginning of Annunciation's ecumenical activity occurred in

1959 when the parish became a member of the Council of Churches and Christian Education of Maryland-Delaware, Inc. Shortly after, Annunciation also joined the Maryland Council of Churches. Annunciation expanded its role in the community by entering into dialogue with a Jewish congregation and helping it to establish a chapter of the National Conference of Christians and Jews in the Baltimore area. Also, during the late 1950s, there were exchanges of visitations between Annunciation and other Christian congregations. These helped to develop interdenominational understanding and appreciation of the Orthodox religion.

The Greek Orthodox Church in America not only sought to understand and dialogue with the other Christian denominations but also worked for recognition of itself as one of the major faiths in America. Of course, the Orthodox knew their faith to be the original Christian faith, but realized they were little known in America and were generally considered an ethnic oddity. The problem was highlighted during World War II, when the Selective Service did not consider the Eastern Orthodox Church to be a "regular church" and refused military exemption to a certain Orthodox priest.[70] In the 1950s a campaign was initiated by Archbishop Michael to have Orthodoxy recognized by every state of the union as the fourth major faith (the Catholic, Protestant, and Jewish faiths were already recognized). By 1959, twenty states had adopted such resolutions. Archbishop Michael's goal was realized in Maryland on March 11, 1957, when, in the presence of a Greek Orthodox delegation, Governor Theodore McKeldin signed a joint resolution passed by the General Assembly. As Theodore Saloutos points out, this campaign was helpful in teaching the American Greeks "the fine art of legislative pressure" and encouraged the Orthodox church "to identify itself with the greater American community as a means of warding off criticisms that it was an alien faith with a foreign orientation."[71]

The Question of Relocation

By 1956 Annunciation had grown to approximately 850 families. In the midst of its growth in numbers and programs the congregation began facing the problem of the rapid relocation of many of its parishioners from the city to the suburbs of Baltimore in the late 1950s. As the leadership of Annunciation was discussing the need for building expansion, it also had to face the question of whether to move the church to the suburbs, where most of the people now lived, or to remain in the city and face urban problems and possible decline. A special general assembly, held on March 10, 1958, was called to discuss all aspects of the question. After much discussion, the assembly decided that the present location still conveniently served the majority of Annunciation's parishioners, and that relocation would be too costly and unwise since Annunciation's neighborhood was included in the Downtown Renewal Program and would be a quite attractive area when the program was finished.[72]

Following the decision to remain in downtown Baltimore, the board of directors called another meeting of the parishioners, at which plans of the Expansion and Improvement Committee (under the chairmanship of James Mandris) for a new social and educational center were approved. Construction of the new center began on May 24, 1959, and was completed on June 17, 1960. The new building adjoining the church added a special dimension to the congregation. It helped to improve and expand religious and Greek educational programs. It attracted the youth to social and athletic activities and it became the place where social gatherings of the congregation took place.

Soon after the center was completed, the board of directors and the pastor decided to hire a youth director. In 1963 Steve Vlahos, a graduate of Holy Cross Theological Seminary, assumed duties as Annunciation's first youth director, starting a new tradition at the parish. A year later, Father Anastasios Voultos was hired as an assistant to Father Gallos.

The continued growth of the parish led to a reemergence of the relocation issue in a different guise some twelve years later. The first time that Annunciation had faced the question of relocating to the suburbs was in the relatively peaceful late fifties. But by the late 1960s and early 1970s new problems beset the community. In particular, racial tension in the city of Baltimore began to run high. In the spring of 1968, following the assassination of Martin Luther King, Jr., riots broke out in several major cities. Baltimore was literally in flames, with some of the rioting coming within blocks of Annunciation Church. The area surrounding the Annunciation building complex looked more like a combat zone than a church facility. Many families of the congregation moved from the city to the suburbs. The number of participants in the evening activities of the congregation, especially of the youth, was declining. In 1969 a young family man, Charles G. Pefinis, was elected as president of the board of directors. One of the first decisions of the new board was to hire armed guards, who were positioned in front of the church building during the Greek school classes in the afternoons and when the youth or choir groups met in the evenings. This practice of guarding the church continued until 1975, when Father Constantine Monios, upon his arrival at Annunciation, stopped it on the basis that it was not working and was actually generating fear.[73]

The deterioration of Annunciation's neighborhood helped Pefinis advance his idea for a community center in the suburbs. He envisioned a beautiful suburban site with a magnificent community center that would include modern social and educational facilities, a gymnasium, tennis courts, a swimming pool, and a chapel. His idea attracted a few enthusiasts, but the majority of the congregation remained reluctant. They feared that a community center in the suburbs would eventually dissolve the downtown church. In the early 1970s, a site committee, headed by Pefinis, recommended a lovely site known as the Emerson Farm, located in the suburbs north of Baltimore. At the general assembly of April 15, 1973, the report of the site committee was presented to the congregation. To his dismay, Pefinis, who had put much effort and time into finding a suitable site, was confronted with an almost united assembly in opposition to his recommendation. Evan Alevizatos Chriss had no problem convincing the participants that a suburban community center would result in the deterioration and ultimate closing of the downtown facility, a possible consequence which no one (including Pefinis) wanted. Chriss suggested that Annunciation begin to seriously consider the acquisition of properties around the present building to house a new community center.

Annunciation was not blind to the tensions in the surrounding community, however, and took steps to improve conditions in its immediate environment. It joined together with leaders from the community and from the various institutions of the area to form the Mount Royal/ Belvedere Association (named for a neighborhood street and landmark hotel). Father Constantine Monios recalled that when he came to Annunciation in 1975 there were massage parlors and porno shops a few blocks away. But through the combined efforts of the community, all that was changed. Each group decided to do something, and the surrounding property was bought and redeveloped in the 1980s. Since there was very little residential housing immediately around Annunciation (much of the property around the church houses institutions such as the University of Baltimore, the Lyric Opera House, and the new Symphony Hall), tensions in the immediate area were alleviated.[74]

Moreover, the congregation itself, in its racial attitudes, is progressive for a Greek parish. The church had a black sexton, John S. Green (who died in 1989), who was confirmed into Orthodoxy by Father Monios in 1976; a few interracial marriages have been performed by Father Monios; and the church has a few black parishioners.[75] Although the black presence at Annunciation is tiny, that it exists at all is astounding. The vast majority of Greek Orthodox parishes have no black members at all. This is due to several reasons, among them the ethnocentrism of the Greeks and the lack of any proselytizing by the Orthodox.

Evaluating the congregation's condition in 1981, almost eight years after the decision to remain downtown, one of its advocates and supporters, Dr. Thomas Gleason, made this appraisal:

> In the midst of secularism, suburban sprawl, and a tendency to withdraw into small family groups, this religious family with its home downtown in the city is growing and prospering. . . . The central location of the Cathedral is an important factor in making this possible. We can now clearly see that the decisions made over the years to remain in the city were correct![76]

New Directions

In 1965, the man who had served at Annunciation for eleven years, Father George Gallos, announced to his people that he was leaving Baltimore for a position at a young suburban community in Weston, Massachusetts. This marked the first time that a priest left Annunciation while still loved and on good terms with the lay leadership. Commenting on the peaceful transition of the pastorship from Father Gallos to Father Emmanuel E. Bouyoucas, Nicholas Prevas suggests that the congregation "had reached a new level of maturity and understanding which was accomplished, in part, through the strengthening of its relationship with the Archdiocese."[77]

Prevas's observation is correct. Except for the incident involving Father Gouvellis and Father Papachristou, the relations between Annunciation and the archdiocese have been unusually good. The congregation has always supported the Archbishop and the programs and institutions of the archdiocese. In fact, Annunciation became one of the exemplary congregations of the archdiocese, and one of only ten parishes in America that officially has over a thousand families.[78] In return, it was given special consideration in the assignment of pastors and associate clergy, and one of its leaders, Evan Alevizatos Chriss, was appointed to the archdiocesan council, the supreme advisory body to the archbishop in the administration of the national church.

The man who succeeded Father Gallos as pastor of Annunciation, Father Bouyoucas, was American-born and a graduate of Holy Cross Theological Seminary. He was one of the pioneer American-born clergy and was the valedictorian from the first class at Holy Cross. He was known as a brilliant man, who advanced the programs of his predecessor and witnessed for Orthodoxy, both as a lecturer at Loyola University in Baltimore and by participating in the ecumenical activities of that city.

The tenure of Father Bouyoucas could be labeled as the period of consolidation of the progress achieved during the preceding decade. There were, however, some monumental events that brought major changes to the congregation. The first occurred in October 1966, when the parish assembly voted to allow women the right to vote in parish assemblies and elections. Up to then, women's rights had been limited to membership in the Ladies' Auxiliary. But women had played an increasingly important role in fund-raising and philanthropy (through the Philoptochos and other organizations), had served on several committees, including the church PTA, the Library Committee, and the Education Committee, had taught in the Greek school and the Sunday school, and had been central to the development and activities of the choir.[79] They had proved themselves valuable and capable participants, vital to the life of the congregation, and there was no opposition to the decision to give them the vote. Since 1966, women have attended parish assemblies and have been elected to important positions of leadership. In 1986, Loretta Prevas became the first woman to be elected president of the parish council.

A second major event during Father Bouyoucas's tenure was the elevation of Annunciation Church to the status of Greek Orthodox Cathedral. The proclamation making it a cathedral was issued by Archbishop Iakovos and read by Metropolitan Silas in Annunciation Church on Sunday, March 23, 1975. The elevation of Annunciation and several other churches in America actually broke with the ancient Orthodox tradition of designating cathedrals only in cities to which a bishop is attached. Since there are very few bishops in the United States (about a dozen), and several major cities and states without a resident bishop, the archbishop decided to bend the canonical tradition and to choose the oldest and largest churches in the states to be named as cathedrals. There are currently some thirty-one churches in the United States that are designated as cathedrals, and Annunciation is one of the most active and influential.

The Baltimore city council congratulated the Greek Orthodox faithful of Annunciation on their new status with an official resolution:

By this step, the Church of Annunciation has become a mother church of the other Greek Orthodox churches in the state of Maryland and represents the primary spiritual center of Greek Orthodoxy in this area. This indicates the recognition by the Greek Orthodox Archdiocese of the significance and importance of the Greek Orthodox Community which has made many significant contributions to the religious and cultural life of Baltimore.[80]

Perhaps few other churches in America deserved the honor and recognition of cathedral status as much as Annunciation in Baltimore. Not only was it the most numerous congregation in Maryland (1,700 families), but it had a beautiful sanctuary and marvelous building facilities. It not only acted like a loving and obedient daughter to the archdiocese and provided leadership, it also helped in the organization of other Greek Orthodox churches.[81]

Also during Father Bouyoucas's tenure a popular and important event, the Athenian Agora, began at Annunciation. This festival, held annually in November, began in 1971 as a two-day bazaar. Today it is a four-day event that not only celebrates the Greek heritage of the parish but also provides the Baltimore community with a unique opportunity to learn about the culture and faith of the Greek Orthodox. From the beginning, Greek food and Grecian artifacts were sold. But Annunciation was not content to be known only for its Greek pastries. Annunciation currently devotes the first day of the Athenian Agora to the enrichment of area schoolchildren. Children are brought in from area schools and spend several hours learning about the Greek culture and Orthodox faith via lectures, tours, videos, a puppet show, and, of course, a luncheon of Greek foods. On the remaining three days of the festival, a variety of cultural activities are offered in addition to the bounty of Greek food, artifacts, and dancing. Lectures are presented on the diverse topics of Byzantine history, iconography, Greek antiquities, and travels in Greece. In addition, lecture-tours are conducted inside the church, and it is here that the Orthodox faith is discussed. This event is always a success, well attended and enjoyed by all of Baltimore, Greek and non-Greek alike.

In the midst of progress, Annunciation in the 1960s faced challenges that disturbed its peace and tranquility. Early in the decade of the sixties the congregation felt the need for some linguistic reforms at its Divine Liturgies. The use of English at meetings, in the teaching of the Sunday school, and in the delivery of the sermon had attracted the American-born to Annunciation. These changes, however, only partly met their needs. As time went by, there were demands for additional linguistic reforms. The Greek Orthodox Archdiocese of North and South America refused to change its policy and continued to regard the Greek language not only as an important part of the Greek identity of the faithful but, moreover, as an inseparable part of their Orthodox faith. To even suggest the use of English in the services was anathema to the Greek-born hierarchy and to the pioneer immigrants. To the cries of those who spoke only English, asking for the use of some English in the Liturgy and other sacraments, only a small concession was made: at the Clergy-Laity Congress in Denver, Colorado, June 28–July 3, 1964, upon the recommendation of Archbishop Iakovos, English was allowed to be used in conjunction with Greek for the Epistle and Gospel readings, the Creed, and the Lord's Prayer. This rule, which prevailed officially through the end of the 1960s, failed to satisfy and pacify the majority of Greek Orthodox parishioners.

The congregation of Annunciation tried to abide by the directive of the archdiocese, but, at times, Father Gallos responded to the appeals of his young people by expanding the use of English to other parts of the service. He made rather liberal use of English at weddings, baptisms, and funerals. This policy pleased the advocates of English but disappointed the conservative side of the congregation. Father Gallos, however, did succeed in preventing the language issue from becoming a matter of public debate in the congregation. His successor, Father Bouyoucas, being a man of conservative views and knowing that a significant segment of the congregation opposed the expansion of English, decided to abide strictly by the decision of the 1964 Clergy-Laity Congress.

During the second half of the 1960s there was open debate on the question of the use of English. The language issue was not in the pastor's hands any longer. The laity dealt directly with the issue. At a special parish assembly, held in February 1968, the proponents of English submitted a resolution requesting that the archdiocese allow English to be used in a substantial portion of church worship.[82] The assembly's decision prompted Bishop Silas, head of the First Archdiocesan District (to which Annunciation belonged), to visit Annunciation. The bishop's meeting with the board of directors was inconclusive. Silas expressed his willingness to permit some increase in the use of English, but he counseled caution in pursuing the matter, to prevent a division in the congregation.[83] The language issue was brought up for discussion at the regular general assembly on March 31, 1968. At this assembly one of its participants, Anestes Kampos, reported that he had taken the matter directly to Archbishop Iakovos, who advised him that the archdiocese remained firm on the language policy. The decisions of the Clergy-Laity Congress of 1964 remained in effect. Kampos made an appeal to his fellow members to abide by the archdiocesan decision and to avoid a split in the congregation.[84] This was the last public debate on linguistic reforms at Annunciation during the 1960s.

By 1970, however, the archbishop had reached a new conclusion. The church had to make drastic linguistic reforms if it was to be considered a serious factor in the creation of a new religious life in America. The opportunity for such reform was given when the Clergy-Laity Congress convened in New York in July 1970. In addressing the record-breaking Congress (1,000 delegates attended), Archbishop Iakovos suggested that, to be true to her mission, the church had to make sacrifices, and one of them was the replacement of Greek by English.[85] Having in mind this wish of the archbishop, the Committee on Linguistic Reforms made a recommendation, which was adopted by an overwhelming majority of the delegates: "Be it resolved that this Congress recommends that the Archdiocese permit the use of the vernacular language as needed in Church services in accordance with the judgment of the parish in consultation with the bishop."[86]

The editor of *Logos* periodical described the reaction that immediately followed:

A veritable furor has been sweeping the Archdiocese, from coast to coast, over what was termed as the "abolition of the Greek" from the Liturgy. Headlines in the Greek daily and weekly newspapers speak of an impending division in the Archdiocese, and cries for the replacement of Archbishop Iakovos have reached the church and government officials in Athens and Constantinople.[87]

For a time, it appeared that schism was inevitable.

During those crucial days for the national church, the leadership of Annunciation, both clergy and laity, handled the language controversy carefully. Although sympathetic to the reforms, they did not put them into effect until the controversy had subsided. The pastor, Father Bouyoucas, took part in the national debate and made a valuable contribution by helping to preserve peace on both the national and local levels.

Seeking to pacify the advocates of the Greek language at Annunciation, Father Bouyoucas wrote upon his return from New York, "Nowhere, at no time, was the abolishment of the Greek language considered. . . . We, here in our parish of the Annunciation, shall use a combination of Greek and English as we have been doing for the past few years."[88] Father Bouyoucas kept his promise during the remaining five years of his tenure in Baltimore. Seeking to safeguard the unity of his congregation, he did not expand the use of English. Although he was criticized by advocates of English for ignoring their needs, he felt that Annunciation could wait for the complete arrival of the English language. Annunciation was called to serve two linguistically (and somewhat culturally) different groups in the same congregation. The parish succeeded in that it introduced a system of flexible bilingualism, in which English is used more heavily at services and during times when listeners are mostly English, and Greek is utilized more heavily when the majority of listeners are Greek. In a loving, Christian way, the faithful of Annunciation have learned, over time, to share each other's burdens and even enjoy their sacred services in both English and Greek.

In 1975 there was a complete change in the spiritual leadership of Annunciation. Father Bouyoucas and his assistant left in a peaceful transition. In November 1975, a seasoned priest, Father Constantine Monios, highly respected for his service in parishes in Manchester, New Hampshire, and Pittsburgh, for his theological knowledge, and especially for his kind personality and humility, was assigned as dean of Annunciation Cathedral. Only two months before the arrival of Father Monios in Baltimore, a young assistant priest, Father Elias Velonis, had preceded him to Annunciation. The two clerics became a fine team. Father Velonis took over the youth programs and the Sunday school. Father Monios contributed his expert counseling and skills in dealing with people and oversaw the administration of the church.

During this time the issue of the community center, which had been dormant since the early part of the decade, again became the dominant issue. The suburban site proposal was not a matter of consideration. The leadership was concerned only with finding the proper location in the neighborhood for a new building. In fact, downtown Baltimore had changed quickly for the better. From the mid-1970s, the political scene in Baltimore had been dominated by its mayor, William D. Schaefer, who had set as the major objective of his tenure the revitalization of the inner city through an ambitious urban renewal program. Annunciation chose to become a partner in the mayor's undertaking, seeing this as an opportunity to preserve and expand its own facilities, while also extending itself to improving the wider community. Annunciation purchased four townhouses across the street from the cathedral with the purpose of renovating them and converting them into a cathedral center. The buildings were considered of historic architectural significance to the city, as they had been designed by John Appleton Wilson, one of the most prominent architects of Baltimore. Under Father Monios's inspiring leadership, the Baltimore congregation began in 1980 an ambitious expedition to solicit funds for the cathedral center. The pastor himself secured more than one-third of the amount. John Paterakis and Harry Tsakalos, brothers-in-law and business partners whose families had long been connected with Annunciation, donated half a million dollars. Boosted by this sizable donation, the committee went on to secure the rest of the funds from the membership.

The delicate reconstruction and conversion of the townhouses began in the spring of 1983 and was completed in April of 1984. The Annunciation Orthodox Center today consists of a library, ballroom, auditorium, banquet hall, kitchen, formal reception room, and several meeting rooms, all within the facade of the townhouses. The library has a prominent spot in the center of the complex, and rightly so. It is the pride of the congregation, and is considered to be the largest and most professionally organized parish library in the Greek archdiocese. The library specializes in literature related to Greek Orthodox history and theology, Greek culture, civilization, and art. One man, Theodore J. George, was chiefly responsible for the founding and organization of the library, and it is named after him. George began his efforts in 1959, and by November of 1962 the library was in operation. When it opened its doors in a small room, it had only about five hundred volumes. Today, its new facility houses over nine thousand volumes.

The new center gave the leaders of the congregation an opportunity to expand its human services. The Social Services Committee was established in 1978 to serve the Greek community of Baltimore. Its original goals were modest: to provide transportation for the elderly, to serve as interpreters for the non-English-speaking members of the congregation, to visit the community's shut-ins and bring them to church, to host luncheons for them and in general to make their lives more comfortable. A year later, in April 1979, the Social Services Committee created the Pan-Orthodox Blood Assurance Program to make blood available, at no cost, to its participants and their families.[89]

The enthusiasm with which the congregation received the efforts of the Social Services Committee encouraged the pastor and the board of directors to reorganize the program more professionally. In 1987 the Greek Orthodox Counseling and Social Services, Inc. (GOCSS) was established. Although housed at Annunciation Cathedral Center and funded by the congregation, it is governed by a board of directors composed of representatives from the three Greek Orthodox congregations in Baltimore.

The assistance offered by GOCSS is bilingual and covers such areas as translation, individual counseling, family counseling, case management, consultation, and education. It also covers liaisons between individuals and outside human services and institutions, such as hospitals, clinics, doctors, mental health organizations, welfare and social services, employment, disability entitlements, juvenile services, and so on.

Other programs developed at Annunciation in the late seventies and early eighties demonstrate the desire of the congregation to go beyond the ethnic group in aiding the needy. Opened in 1978, the Second Chance Shop sells used items at a low price. In the early 1980s, other projects were initiated. Project Philoxenia helps to support a soup kitchen at the Franciscan Center, and Project Zestasia collects and distributes clothing and blankets to the needy. In November 1990, Annunciation's Philoptochos society began Project Agape, which donated many items to members of the 85th Medical Battalion stationed in Saudi Arabia during the Gulf War.

In youth programs, Annunciation continues its tradition of devoting major resources to attract young people to the church. Since the mid-1970's three young assistant priests have been hired exclusively to serve the needs of the youth. Father Elias Velonis (1975–79) and Father Mark Benjamin Arey (1979–82) helped to organize retreats and educational, social, and athletic programs. From 1982 to the present, Father Louis J. Noplos has directed the youth programs. Father Noplos is credited with the founding of the Chesapeake Youth Council Annual Summer Camp, a very popular program which offers the children a variety of experiences—swimming, canoeing, horseback riding, soccer, basketball, arts and crafts, and Greek dancing. Above all, the camp offers children an atmosphere of Orthodox living and fellowship.[90]

In the midst of all these programs—the building program, the social services, and the youth programs—the spiritual life of the congregation was not forgotten. To his credit, Father Monios has never let his people wander from their center in Orthodox spirituality and worship. He reminded them that "No Christian can grow without the gifts of the Spirit. For this reason, creating a spiritual environment is the great priority of the Church."[91] Under his direction, the first formal adult bible-study class was begun in 1978–79. Lay people direct it on Sunday mornings, and the classes are taped so that Father Monios may keep informed and add his input.

The thorny question of the use of English in the worship services has continued as an issue. Even before the arrival of Father Monios, the congregation's membership had changed dramatically. This was no longer an immigrant church, and even though it still valued its Greek heritage it was now composed of members who were, in the vast majority, American-born, and whose language and thinking were more American than Greek. Orthodoxy was precious to them, but it did not have to be exclusively Greek. Furthermore, there were the converts who had adopted Orthodoxy but had great difficulty adjusting to worshiping in a language they neither spoke nor understood. A few months after Father Monios's assignment to Annunciation, a layman of Polish ethnicity and Roman Catholic background, Edward F. Jackovitz, was elected president of the congregation. His election was a manifestation of the change in the composition of the congregation as well as the maturity of the congregation in the treatment of its non-Greek members. In 1979, a young man who was born and raised as an Episcopalian, Mark B. Arey, was ordained an Orthodox priest and assigned to Annunciation as its assistant pastor.

The trend toward Americanization of the congregation continued in the 1980s when another convert, Dr. Thomas Gleason, formerly an Episcopalian, was elected president in 1981. In an article published in *The Annunciation Herald* in March 1985, Father Monios shared his thoughts about the change in the congregation's composition.[92] His analysis was based on the weddings performed in Annunciation between 1911 and 1984. Before 1940 it was extremely rare for a Greek Orthodox to marry a non-Greek Orthodox. Between 1940 and 1959, such marriages began to occur with greater frequency, but the number of marriages between two Orthodox was still greater than the marriages between an Orthodox and a non-Orthodox Christian. Since 1960, however, the trend changed. Of the thirty weddings solemnized in Annunciation's church that year, fifteen were between two Orthodox and eighteen were between an Orthodox and a non-Orthodox Christian. Since then, the number of mixed marriages has continued to climb. Of the sixty marriages performed in 1984, only nine involved two Orthodox partners, and fifty-one were mixed. Father Monios said many of the non-Orthodox spouses eventually become Orthodox, and the majority of their children are baptized in the Greek Orthodox faith. He cautioned, however, that the congregation must help the converts and their children feel comfortable in the Orthodox faith by making some adjustments, especially when dealing with the language question.[93]

Sensitive to the needs of the American-born Orthodox and to the difficulties that the converts face, Father Monios introduced a bold linguistic reform in the Divine Liturgy in 1979. The choir could sing hymns in the Liturgy and respond to the priest's petitions in English. Other congregations in the eastern United States had tried this before but had abandoned the practice because of membership opposition. But the surprising Annunciation congregation accepted this reform without serious opposition. Through a remarkable cooperation between the laity and the clergy, Annunciation has successfully avoided the bitter controversies over language that assailed some other progressive Greek Orthodox parishes in the United States in the late seventies and eighties.

Conclusion

It appears that the Annunciation congregation has dealt with the Americanization process without sacrificing the basic ethnic character of Greek Orthodoxy so important to its immigrant pioneers and their descendants. The genius of the Annunciation congregation is that throughout its history it has remained faithful to both its religious and cultural identity even as it adapts to the American environment and becomes a congregation that is truly both American and Greek. This recognition and preservation of the past has helped Annunciation maintain its vigor and vitality. It has allowed Annunciation to make the teachings and rituals of Byzantine antiquity relevant to contemporary men and women.

As Annunciation's identity shifted from ethnic Greek to an increasingly Americanized community, it also began to assert its religious identity, so that by 1955, when the requirements for membership were changed, group identity at Annunciation had finally shifted from an ethnic to a religious basis. This shift has enabled the congregation to succeed in making its converts feel welcome and in giving them the opportunity to assume roles of leadership in administrative and spiritual positions.

As it grew from a fledgling community to one of the largest and most successful congregations of the Greek Orthodox Archdiocese, Annunciation experienced important changes in its patterns of leadership. The strong, independent, and unilateral leadership of the laymen, prevalent in the early immigrant communities in America but antithetical to the clericalism in the Old Country, gradually evolved into a mutual and cooperative leadership shared by priest and laymen.

Annunciation has witnessed to the community mainly through its clergy, but also through religious, cultural, and philanthropic projects that involved many of its members. Annunciation, to a remarkable extent, has assisted the admirable efforts of the mayor of Baltimore in encouraging his fellow citizens not to flee to the suburbs but to participate in the physical and cultural renewal of their beloved city. The restoration of an entire section in the Mount Vernon area, for the Annunciation Orthodox Center, drew praise and applause from the Baltimore community.

Considering Annunciation's success and prestige, and the numerous and varied programs that it operates, it is amazing that the congregation did not lose sight of Orthodoxy's most fundamental teaching, that the main objective of the Church is humanity's sanctification and deification, and that this is accomplished by one's participation in the sacramental life of the Church. This progressive Greek-American congregation has much to offer Baltimore and the wider American community. But, of all it has to share, nothing is more valuable than its mystical treasure—its Orthodox faith.

NOTES

1. Timothy Ware, *The Orthodox Church* (London: Penguin Books, 1983), p. 203.

2. Ibid., pp. 206–7.

3. Cf. Gerasimos Papadopoulos, "The Revelatory Character of the New Testament and Holy Tradition in the Orthodox Church," in *The Orthodox Ethos: Essays in Honor of the Centenary of the Greek Orthodox Archdiocese of North and South America*, ed. A. J. Philippou (Oxford: Holywell Press, 1964), pp. 100–101.

4. Cf. John Zizioulas, *Being as Communion: Studies in Personhood and the Church* (Crestwood, N.Y.: St. Vladimir's Seminary Press, 1985), p. 133.

5. Ibid., p. 135.

6. Ibid., pp. 152–54, and the footnotes on p. 149.

7. Nicholas M. Prevas, *History of the Greek Orthodox Cathedral of the Annunciation* (Baltimore: John D. Lucas Printing Co., 1982), p. 20.

8. "Seventy-Fifth Anniversary Album of the Greek Orthodox Cathedral of

the Annunciation, 1906–1981," Archives of the Annunciation Cathedral, Baltimore, p. 18.

9. Prevas, *Cathedral of the Annunciation*, p. 21.

10. Spyridon A. Kotakis, *The Greeks in America* (Chicago, 1908), p. 159.

11. Prevas, *Cathedral of the Annunciation*, p. 26.

12. Ibid., pp. 32–33.

13. "Seventy-fifth Anniversary Album of the Greek Orthodox Cathedral of the Annunciation, 1906–1981," p. 62.

14. Prevas, *Cathedral of the Annunciation*, p. 13.

15. Theodore Saloutos, *The Greeks in the United States* (Cambridge: Harvard University Press, 1964), pp. 138–39.

16. Peter Kourides, *The Evolution of the Greek Orthodox Archdiocese of North and South America* (New York: Cosmos Greek-American Printing Co., 1959), p. 8.

17. Prevas, *Cathedral of the Annunciation*, p. 52.

18. Polycarpos Marinakis, Telegram to Archbishop Alexander, April 6, 1921, Greek Orthodox Archdiocese Archives, New York, N.Y.

19. Prevas, *Cathedral of the Annunciation*, p. 54.

20. Ibid. See also Appendix H, "The Very Rev. Iakovos Leloudas vs. The Evangelismos Church, 1922," ibid., pp. 243–52.

21. Prevas, in his *Cathedral of the Annunciation*, mentions "instances in which avid monarchist families of Baltimore chose not to have their religious sacraments performed at the Annunciation Church by the Reverend Christos Angelopoulos because he was considered to be a Venizelist" (p. 58). Prevas cites the example of Themistocles P. Prevas and Mary Petkovitis whose marriage on January 28, 1923, was held in a Polish hall with Father Leloudas officiating.

22. Ibid., p. 60.

23. Ibid., p. 263 (Appendix M).

24. Minutes of the Annunciation Board of Directors Meeting, April 26, 1927, p. 145.

25. Minutes of the Joint Meeting of Annunciation and Holy Trinity Boards of Directors, in Prevas, *Cathedral of the Annunciation*, p. 80.

26. *Baltimore Sun*, December 23, 1929.

27. Prevas, *Cathedral of the Annunciation*, p. 82.

28. "By-Laws of Holy Churches and Committees of the Greek Orthodox Archdiocese of North and South America Adopted by the Fourth Clergy-Laity Congress," New York, November 14–22, 1931, Article II.

29. Ibid., Article IX.

30. Ibid., Article VI.

31. Prevas, *Cathedral of the Annunciation*, p. 93.

32. Niketas A. Konstant, *A Synopsis of the History of the Greek Orthodox Community of Baltimore*, Dedication Memorial Book of the Greek Orthodox Community "Evangelismos," (Baltimore: 1938), p. 19.

33. Prevas, *Cathedral of the Annunciation*, p. 104. See also Konstant, *A Synopsis*, p. 5.

34. Rolan Fromes, "Five Congregations in Orthodox Group," *New American*, November 9, 1976.

35. Angeline Polites, "Another Milestone: Cathedral Building Turns 100," *The Annunciation Herald*, October 1989, p. 5.

36. *Baltimore Evening Sun*, May 1, 1937.

37. Ibid., May 2, 1937.

38. Ibid., May 9, 1938.

39. Prevas, *Cathedral of the Annunciation*, p. 112.

40. From "The Cherubic Hymn," in *The Divine Liturgy of Saint John Chrysostom*, trans. by a Member of the Faculty of Hellenic College/Holy Cross Greek Orthodox School of Theology (Brookline, Mass., 1985), p. 8.

41. Alexander Schmemann, *For the Life of the World* (Crestwood, N.Y.: St. Vladimir's Seminary Press, 1973), p. 29.

42. Some exceptions to the fast are allowed for the sick, those on medications, pregnant women, and others. The decisions about fasting should be made under the spiritual direction of the priest.

43. *The Divine Liturgy of Saint John Chrysostom*, p. 35.

44. "Through the Years," 50th Anniversary of Philoptochos Album, 1986.

45. Bylaws of the Hellenic University Club, Annunciation Archives, Baltimore.

46. The Service of the Five Loaves is based on the miracle of the five loaves of bread and the two fish by which Jesus fed the five thousand people in the desert (Luke 9:10–17).

47. Prevas provides a wealth of information on the Greek clubs of Baltimore in his *Cathedral of the Annunciation*, pp. 68–70 and 92–93.

48. Theodore Agnew, "Address to the Delegates of the District Convention," Baltimore, Maryland, 1928. See George Papaioannou, *The Odyssey of Hellenism in America* (Patriarchal Institute of Patristic Studies: Thessaloniki, Greece, 1985), p. 114.

49. Prevas, *Cathedral of the Annunciation*, p. 116.

50. Ibid., p. 126.

51. Theodore George, personal interview, July 23, 1990, Baltimore.

52. Prevas, *Cathedral of the Annunciation*, pp. 130–31.

53. Ibid., p. 135.

54. *Baltimore Sun*, March 25, 1950.

55. Prevas, *Cathedral of the Annunciation*, p. 139.

56. A Newsletter Addressed to the Parishioners of Annunciation, January, 1950, Annunciation Cathedral File, Greek Orthodox Archdiocese.

57. Prevas, *Cathedral of the Annunciation*, p. 141.

58. The State of Maryland, An Injunction served to Rev. Joachim Papachristou, March 24, 1950.

59. The Rev. Dr. George Papaioannou, *From Mars Hill to Manhattan* (Minneapolis: Light and Life Publishers, 1976), p. 143.

60. Ann Papadopoulos, "A Parish History" (The History of the Greek Orthodox Cathedral of the Annunciation, May, 1979, unpublished paper, Archives of the Annunciation Cathedral, Baltimore), p. 7.

61. Prevas, *Cathedral of the Annunciation*, p. 149.

62. GOYA was a young adults' organization. Jr. GOYA was the teens' organization. Jr. GOYA's motto was, "Learn your Orthodox faith." GOYA's motto was, "Live your Orthodox faith." The groups have changed over the years so that, as of 1991, there are now four national youth groups: HOPE is for children under the age of seven; JOY (Junior Orthodox Youth) is for children seven to twelve years of age; GOYA is now for teenagers thirteen to eighteen years; and GOYAL (Greek Orthodox Young Adult League) is now for those eighteen and above. (JOY Guidelines, Office of Youth Ministry, Greek Orthodox Archdiocese of North and South America, New York, N.Y., 1990, p. 7.)

63. Niketas Konstant, "Our History," Annunciation 50th Anniversary Album.

64. Georgia Tangires, "Choir History" (Baltimore, 1981), p. 1.

65. Rev. George Gallos, "Introducing the Envelope System," *The Annunciation Herald*, December 1954, p. 5.

66. Annunciation 75th Anniversary Album, p. 33.

67. Prevas, *Cathedral of the Annunciation*, pp. 169 and 194.

68. Theodore George, personal interview, July 23, 1990, Baltimore.

69. Minutes of the General Assembly Meeting, November 6, 1955 (Greek Orthodox Cathedral of the Annunciation: Baltimore), pp. 4–5.

70. Saloutos, *Greeks in the United States*, p. 374.

71. Ibid., p. 375.

72. Paul G. Stamas, "Report on the Special General Assembly, March 30, 1958," *Community Herald*, March-April 1958, p. 10.

73. Father Constantine Monios, personal interview, July 22, 1990, Baltimore.

74. Father Constantine Monios, telephone interview, February 28, 1991.

75. Ibid.

76. Dr. Thomas Gleason, "The President's Message," *The Annunciation Herald*, Spring 1981, p. 12.

77. Prevas, *Cathedral of the Annunciation*, p. 174.

78. When Annunciation celebrated its seventieth anniversary in March 1976, membership was about 1,100 families. The parish had probably reached the thousand mark in late 1975.

79. Prevas, *Cathedral of the Annunciation*, p. 167–68.

80. Baltimore City Council, "Resolutions on the Elevation of the Annunciation to the status of Greek Orthodox Cathedral of Maryland," *The Annunciation Herald*, April 1975, p. 1.

81. Annunciation extended its resources to help develop two other Greek Orthodox churches: Saint Nicholas (1952) in Baltimore and Saint Demetrios (1971) in Baltimore's suburbs.

82. Annunciation Special General Assembly, February 4, 1968, "Decisions and Resolutions," *The Annunciation Herald*, vol. 16, no. 2.

83. Minutes of the Board of Directors Meeting, March 12, 1968, pp. 219–20.

84. Annunciation Minutes of the General Assembly, March 31, 1968, p. 37.

85. Archbishop Iakovos, Keynote Address to the Delegates of the 20th Clergy-Laity Congress, June 29, 1970, New York, N.Y.

86. "Decisions of the 20th Clergy-Laity Congress," July 4, 1970, New York, N.Y.

87. *Logos* 3, no. 7 (August-September 1970): 14.

88. Father Emmanuel Bouyoucas, "Language in Our Worship," *The Annunciation Herald*.

89. Stephanie Panos, "The Social Services Committee of the Annunciation Cathedral," *The Annunciation Herald*, Summer 1980, p. 13.

90. Ibid.

91. Father Louis J. Noplos, personal interview, September 5, 1990.

92. Rev. Constantine M. Monios, "Spiritual Life, Administration, and Finances," *The Annunciation Herald*, September 1988, p. 31.

93. Constantine M. Monios, "Cathedral Weddings: An Analysis," *The Annunciation Herald*, March 1985, pp. 3–5.

TEN

Reducing the Distance: A Muslim Congregation in the Canadian North

Earle H. Waugh

No soul knows what it shall earn tomorrow
nor in what land it shall die.
Qur'an 31:33

THE LAC LA BICHE MUSLIM COMMUNITY in northern Alberta provides a remarkable example of Islam's transportability and flexibility in a North American context. Before its achievement can be fully recognized, however, it is necessary to examine the distinctive characteristics of Islamic institutions from a comparative congregational perspective.

Traditionally, Muslims have placed less stress on the local religious institution as a mechanism of identity than have their Christian counterparts. In Muslim countries, the local mosque might well be no more than a convenient place to pray with one's neighbors; one certainly never becomes a *member* of that mosque. One of the most crucial reasons for this is doctrinal: Islam accepts no mediating or authoritative role for a religious institution between Allah and the believer. Thus there is no role for an official priesthood in Islam, no need for an institutional body within which those officials may act on behalf of the believers, and no need for membership.

The term Muslims use to express the universal group to which they belong is *ummah*, and everyone who has any sense of being a Muslim is considered a member of that body. The local expression of the ummah self-consciously considers itself to be part of the whole and usually claims to be affirming the core of Muslim tradition, but it cannot claim to speak for the entire ummah. Like Christianity, Islamic tradition has created distinctive expressions of Muslim belief and fostered institutions that promote worship and education. Sectarian belief systems (for example, Sunnism and Shi'ism) and easily recognized architectural features like mosques are two such expressions, but they are not linked with a sense of belonging in the way that Christians *belong to* a congregation. Participation in the ummah thus has ramifications quite different from those associated with Christian congregational membership.

Likewise, rituals do not function in Islam as they do in the Christian context. To be sure, special patterns of behavior—prayer, almsgiving, fulfilling *ramadan* (the month of fasting), making the pilgrimage to Mecca, and affirming the oneness of God's existence—presuppose an integrated community life within which these activities are carried out, but no collectivity or powerful individual can claim universal authority to decide whether these patterns have been observed properly. Indeed, one may live out one's Muslim convictions apart from any "official" religious organization: a Muslim could conceivably have lived an entire lifetime and never have prayed in a mosque with the brethren. All organizational structures are construed to be incidental to the essential religious sentiment.

If the chief operative word for Christians is *salvation*, for Muslims it is *guidance*. It is the lifework of a believer to determine where God is guiding the community, because the individual is an integral part of the community. Sectarian differences have also affected the meaning of guidance. The larger of Islam's two main factions, the Sunnis (from the Arabic word meaning "custom"), see God's guidance residing in the collective insight of the ummah. For Sunni Muslims like the Lac La Biche Arabs, an individual is guided in and through the consensus views of the ummah. The Shi'is (from the word meaning "party" or "supporters of"), however, maintain that guidance comes only through the special directions God gives the ummah through an inspired leader called the *imam*. A person who claims an independent guidance is a prophet, but for Muslims there will never be another prophet like Muhammad. The guidance provided by any individual—a great leader, for example—can be given only for the immediate direction of the community; it can never replace the guidance of the Qur'an and the prophetic traditions.

For centuries, Islamic law functioned in Muslim societies somewhat like medieval Christian canon law, defining the proper relationship between the individual and the truths enshrined in the tradition. In general, guidance was expressed through the codified Islamic law, the *shari'a,* which encompassed all patterns of behavior in a Muslim's life. In

Muslim countries, the scholars interpreted the basic legal principles for the community, and it was the ordinary Muslim's task to apply them rightly to his own existence.

Applying these principles to one's life would seem to be fairly straightforward. But such a view ignores the complexity of everyday life; it also assumes that there can be no conflict in the application of varying principles of law to the minutiae of living. Muslims found this somewhat problematic. Was it possible for one part of the ummah to go wrong? The consensus was that although one individual or one group might, the ummah as a whole would never lose its purpose and wander from the path of God. Because the community's general direction was guided by God, the life of the group provided the best perspective on determining one's own spiritual state, whether in Lac La Biche or Delhi. It thus behooved the individual to heed carefully the lived values of the community.

Although the official status of the law has changed in Muslim countries, the basic relationship of the ordinary believer to the norms of the shari'a has not. Sometimes these norms are not clearly defined. In that case there is a dynamic between the individual and the community: one has a sense of what one thinks is the proper mode of behavior and acts accordingly. If one's views are acceptable, one will maintain good relations with one's neighbors and be accorded a proper place within the community. If they are not, one will be held accountable by the community. The believer knows that espousing behavior or ideology rejected by the group could lead to abandonment by God. Every Muslim therefore probes community values judiciously during daily life in order to be in tune with current norms: these constitute God's guidance.

At times, then, the official interpretation of the law has little direct influence on how the believer comes to understand true guidance. Being a good Muslim often involves debates on very insignificant matters, if not with the community as a whole, then within one's own soul about one's personal faithfulness. But it also involves "reading" one's position within family relationships, community ties, and group awarenesses that, from the Western view, would be regarded as secular, or at least neutral. This process becomes more difficult when one lives, as the Lac La Biche believers do, in a non-Muslim area. There the cultural environment either is ambivalent or does not aid one in detecting Islamic guidance.

The primacy of the sense of belonging to a worldwide brotherhood, the rejection of any ritually endorsed group for the carrying out of essential religious requirements, the theological prominence of guidance in the Muslim system, the centrality of law and proper religious behavior as the measure of true religion—all these reflect a religious ethos quite different from that fostered in the familiar congregational structures of the Christian church. At the same time, because traditional Islam assumed that culture would not be neutral but would contribute positively to the development of the ummah, the basic configuration of Islam's relationship to culture has had to undergo a change in North America, where public life has a secular character.

Given Islam's unprecedented growth in North America, both in numbers and in depth, we can now see a recently established and quite distinctive pattern. The successful founding of the ummah in Lac La Biche is an excellent example of this pattern. For by becoming firmly rooted in the Canadian north, the Lac La Biche Muslims have remolded the Muslim sense of belonging and in the process have recast both the public nature of the tradition and the private perceptions of their faith. Their experience helps to elucidate the ingredients of the faith that are essential to its existence in an entirely foreign environment.

But their experience also reveals ways in which North American influences have shaped the Muslim community in Lac La Biche. For North American congregational culture, this study suggests, has had a significant impact on the Lac La Biche Muslim community. To note but one example, the ummah has increasingly accepted an institutional, educational definition of mosque life and placed that mosque life at the center of its cultural development. The role of women has been very important in fostering this shift; indeed, we may credit women with pushing for institutional forms of Islam as the means for retaining traditional family values. The expanded roles of North American women (as compared with those of their counterparts in traditional Muslim societies) and the general influence of women's liberation have had at least some significance in this connection. As perceptions about Islam change among the larger population, the mosque structure may well move into greater conformity with the congregational structures of other North American religions. Such a process can already be observed in the various programs attached to the mosque such as Arabic language courses and converts' classes. In time the changes may also affect women's official leadership roles, just as they have in fund-raising and educational policy.

To understand the Lac La Biche Muslim community, we must examine its history, its internal dynamics, and its effort to define the domains of private faith and public expression so critical to the ummah. In doing so, we will begin to grasp the distinctive ways in which the congregation has held onto its religious roots and reduced the cultural distance between Islam and North America.

Being "at Home": Cultural Dimensions

The Lac La Biche region, approximately five hundred miles north of Great Falls, Montana, has a long and interesting history. The name, which can be translated roughly as Deer Lake, was given by French-Canadian explorers and trappers who marveled at the great number of deer around the lake. The lake itself lay on the main cross-country river system utilized by Natives, explorers, and early traders. The Catholic Church, through an order of lay missionary brothers known as Oblates, founded a mission there among the Natives (the Cree), and the area became important for the developing fur trade.[1] The town itself was initially Cree, with a small admixture of French-Canadians who had intermarried with the Cree (their descendants are known as Metis); a significant number of both these groups remain in the community and in the surrounding municipalities. The 1986 census shows 2,550 living in the town, of which the Cree are the largest group (490).[2] Also in the region are large minorities of British, French-Canadians, and Ukrainians. Anthropologist Harold Barclay estimated that the Muslims constituted 10 percent of the population in 1969.[3] Their number is now, in my estimation, closer to 8 percent, but the proportion of Muslims in the town's population is still larger than in any city in North America.

Lac La Biche is situated in picturesque countryside, poised on the edge of a delightful lake, in a region of marsh and wet grassland, tiny lakes, rolling hills, and scrubby trees. It continues to prosper, largely because of oil and gas exploration in the region; in earlier days it was almost exclusively a farming community, with smaller enterprises like mink farming, fishing, and logging.[4] Now it is the last major town on the road to the world's largest oil-sands development in Fort McMurray. Lying 140 miles northeast of Edmonton, it plays a significant role in transportation and in the service sector of the economy across northern Alberta.

The motivations of the first settlers from the Middle East have never been formally recorded. Archival records of the Hudson's Bay Company indicate problems with "the polygamous Syrians" who were undercutting the company's trading monopoly with their Native fur supplies.[5] The only information comes from sociologist D. M. Hamdani, who notes that the census of 1871 recorded thirteen Muslims in Canada, all in Ontario (where they were called "Mohametans"). Peter Baker (Ahmad Bakr) sketches his early life in the North in *Memoirs of an Arctic Arab;* he, too, traded heavily in the Lac La Biche region and records this conflict with the Hudson's Bay Company.[6]

The earliest Muslims from the Biqa'a region in Lebanon favored farming and so settled on farms in Manitoba, Saskatchewan, and Alberta. Hamdani notes that the Muslim population declined between 1911 and 1921 because 40 percent of the men died in the First World War fighting for Canada.[7] The result was that Arab women outnumbered men by 4 to 1. By 1931, much of the Muslim population (up to 76 percent) lived in Saskatchewan: the only "non-Anglo Saxons permitted permanent residence [in Canada] were farmers with means," and the earliest Muslims had established themselves on Saskatchewan farms.[8] Most of the immigrants had been farmers of small plots in their homeland. Because of the importance of land as a means of perpetuating the family, and because attitudes to land have quasi-religious meanings for both Canadians and the Lebanese, it is necessary to explore this dimension in greater detail.

The overwhelming majority of the Lebanese come from two villages, Lala and Kharbih Ruha in the Biqa'a valley in Lebanon. A beautiful area, with mountains rising impressively on both sides, the valley is the subject of myths and old tales still alive to the people. At the center of these tales is the main city, Baalbeck, which sits just a few miles to the north of Lala. Constructed on an imposing location overlooking the whole valley, the city, according to local custom, was built by the demon Ashmoun, and Adam lived on its outskirts. It was here that Cain killed Abel and fashioned the inner court or citadel to protect himself from God's wrath. Other tales tell of mastodons ten times the size of elephants being used to carry the stones required for the initial fortress. Later the valley itself was the backdrop for a number of biblical events: Elijah (in whose honor a small mosque was built) destroyed the priests of Baal; Jesus climbed Mount Hermon or Jabal Shaikh and was transfigured while flanked by Moses and Elijah; and John the Baptist used the waters arising in the Biqa'a valley to baptize Jesus. The area is thus steeped in religious lore.[9] Historian Abu-Izzedin writes that the people of the region were age-old tillers of the soil, and therefore they saw all aspects of their lives linked to the land.[10] The Lebanese may have been farmers, but the land was really more the result of their labors than a gift from God. In 1860 the historian David Urquhart had written:

Elsewhere man has cultivated the land: in the Lebanon he has made it. Elsewhere the harvest is the produce: here it is the soil. Man collects and carries to the hollow of the rock the vegetable mould; then hedges round with stones his wells of cunning fertility. . . . This is their arable land in the central range.[11]

Despite the arduous, painstaking work of farming, the meaning of having a little plot of land comes through clearly: when one has labored to build up a tiny farm, each inch of it represents family struggle. The value of land transcends both its size and its productivity; it represents family connections, long years of struggle, and fixed business relationships.

Sometime in the thirties, the Lebanese began to see that the traditional connection between a particular piece of territory and farming was very limiting, especially in the light of their growing population. Land was valued, and even held to be sacred, but it could not be the only means to a livelihood. A. I. Tannous, a sociologist, noted in 1941:

One gets the vivid impression that the farmer of Bishmizzeen has lost heart and has lost faith in farming. He is looking somewhere else for a possible solution of his problem, which is now the problem of his growing children—employment outside the village, engaging in business, or emigration.[12]

The Lac La Biche Arabs were part of this change; they retained their loyalty to the land of their ancestors, but they chose migration as a way toward finding a new livelihood.

Land has other meanings relevant for understanding these Arab Muslims. Islam itself has special attitudes toward geography. Orientation to Mecca, the birthplace of Muhammad and the holiest city of Islam, is absolutely essential for both prayer and the pilgrimage.[13] Land also has a direct impact on inheritance and marriage, for in many southern Lebanese villages, land is given as a marriage settlement. Anthropologist Emrys Peters notes that, in the village he studied, the land is registered in the bride's name and is, in effect, part of the husband's future inheritance from his parents. Such a practice allows for the gradual independence of the bride and groom.[14] Consequently, entitlement to land is a sign of the founding of a new family line and the recognition of community status. Commitment to ancestral land links one to the generations that have gone before and even to a tribal identity. With all these meanings, land cannot be conceived simply as a commodity to be bought and sold.

Thus immigrants to Canada may have been disenchanted with farming in Lebanon as a livelihood, but they certainly had lost none of their loyalty to the Lebanese homeland. Measures of this affection are the remittances sent home and the trips back; Lac La Biche people do both regularly. Many houses in the Lebanese villages have been rebuilt with money from Canada, and just about everyone in Lac La Biche from the two villages has made at least one trip back to the homeland.

But the special honoring of territory has begun to be associated with Lac La Biche, which is regarded not so much as a plot of land but as a remarkable "place" in one's emotional life and personal identity. This transference of loyalty is expressed by Mahmud (Bill) Tarrabain, a twenty-year resident of Lac La Biche who moved to Edmonton:

> We left Lac La Biche because my family has grown up and they wanted to go to university. My wife said there was no way the children were going to stay alone in Edmonton. We had to move there. We sold our business and moved with them. . . . But believe me, my heart is still there. I have a plan to live on that lakeshore again. You find peace there and I think that's what we all are looking for when we get old.

This affection does not end with the first-generation émigré; Mysoon, a second-generation daughter born and raised in Lac La Biche, visited the villages in Lebanon. She commented:

> It was a wonderful experience. I loved the mountains and the picturesque little villages. It helped me to understand who we are and where we came from.But I was glad to come back. This is my home. Lac La Biche is where I belong.

A distinctive affection and respect for the land (described as *geopiety* by David Carpenter)[15] has marked Canadians' attitude toward their country and has long played a role in Canada's literary and artistic traditions. The land is intellectually encountered and interpreted; it is given a cultural meaning that makes of it an artifact of identity. Thus the Lebanese immigrants found sympathetic attitudes toward land in their new home, which may well have reduced the foreignness of Canada and aided them in transferring their loyalties.

Building a New Home: The Pioneer Days

The pattern of disengagement from farming the ancestral land is seen in the life of one hero among the pioneer immigrants—Ali Ahmed Abouchadi, who was attracted first by the glitter of gold. The twelve-year-old Abouchadi was tending sheep in the Lebanese village of Lala in 1905 when he saw an uncle on his way to Canada to take part in the Klondike gold rush. He left his flock with a friend while he walked with his uncle to the port thirty miles away. During the walk, he decided that he wanted to go too, and with very little money and only the clothes on his back, he boarded the ship in Beirut. By the time he arrived in Winnipeg, the Klondike rush had petered out, and he began peddling dry goods. At thirteen, he had made enough to buy a horse and buckboard buggy, and he began to peddle extensively in the north. He and his uncle traveled the cow trails north to Lac La Biche, selling to the natives and the odd settler. At sixteen, he began operating a store in Lac La Biche for the natives, becoming quite proficient in Cree—he even created Cree words for several items he sold. (This facility in Cree is still a matter of pride for local Muslims.) At that time he changed his named to Alex Hamilton, apparently to make it easier to do business. Over the years, he engaged in "providing ties for the Northern Alberta Railway, in selling cattle, running an agency for the Ford Motor Company, a gas station, a saw mill and a floating store on the Mackenzie River." He moved to Saskatchewan, where he homesteaded, but the entrepreneurial lifestyle bewitched him again; he sold his farm for $1,000 and returned to Lac La Biche. Eventually he built a department store there which he sold to the Hudson's Bay Company in 1946. His second wife was a Ukrainian who converted to Islam. Finally he moved to Edmonton, where he engaged in the real estate business until his retirement. Asked whether he was happy with his move to Canada, he stated simply: "I'm proud of being a Canadian." [16]

The opportunity for wealth and a sense of adventure were Abouchadi's principal motivators, and his success paved the way for many more from the same region in Lebanon to try their luck in Canada. More and more, entrepreneurial values guided the Lebanese who followed him. Once loyalty to farming had dissipated, many reasons could be found to leave. Some immigrants testified that they came to Canada because they had difficulty obtaining water in their home villages. Others spoke of insufficient opportunities and the desire to be free of complex Lebanese family situations, in which decisions were based on family honor rather than on the merit of an enterprise. But the chance to develop entrepreneurial skills also surfaced as a reason. Bill Tarrabain was one who came for that reason.

Tarrabain recalls that when he arrived in Lac La Biche in 1957, the town had a population of 700, with no water or sewer lines and only dirt streets and wooden sidewalks. He was invited to immigrate by Amin Abu Ghouche, who, along with Bill's cousin Jimmy Tarrabain, sponsored him. About six Lebanese families lived in Lac La Biche at that time, including the family of Omar Fayad. Fayad owned a large home, and he encouraged the Muslim followers to use his home for prayers, especially the Friday noon prayer (the only prayer of the week which Sunnis are enjoined to perform together). The community had no imam, so Muhammad Mughrabi, another old-timer, acted as prayer leader.

Very few had come to Alberta from Lebanon before 1950. But, by the late 1940s, the social and cultural pressures in Lebanon were growing more intense. In addition, the founding of the state of Israel had a dramatic impact. With that event, the trickle of Palestinians into Lebanon became a flood, and social and political unrest followed. As a result, the largest group came to Lac La Biche after 1946, when thirty-five of these thirty-six heads of families immigrated. Of these, twenty-one came between 1951 and 1960.[17] With this influx, the Arab Muslims became a significant component of the town, and they set to work with ambition and vigor.

The Tale of Two Villages

Social anthropologist John Gulick has found that the strongest sense of values in Middle Eastern communities is attached to kinship, residence, nationality, religion, and language.[18] In the case of Lac La Biche, the strength of the common residence factor and its relatedness to the others is very evident. Village consciousness is not simply "locale awareness"; it integrates with strong kinship ties and the stability of village social order. All three have intertwining religious components.

The earliest village immigrants to be represented in Lac La Biche were from Lala. Since the 1950s, however, far more from Kharbih Ruha have made the town their home; more than 65 percent of the Lebanese heads of families come from that village.

Ancient loyalties to the separate villages of the Biqa'a are still reflected. Those inhabitants I interviewed insisted on a distinctive difference in status between the Lalaians and their compatriots from Kharbih Ruha, just as in the homeland. The former were inevitably better off and had higher social status in Lac La Biche. According to one source, the Lala group has been far more concerned than the people from Kharbih Ruha about the homeland. He pointed out that the Lala houses were in good repair and new ones had even been built because Canadian relatives continually sent money to kin and associates. Evidence also suggests that the Lala people are more likely to return home after they have made their retirement money in Canada.

Loyalties to the Lebanese villages are evident, too, in Lac La Biche business enterprises. No one from Lala has entered into business with someone from Kharbih Ruha in Lac La Biche. Some of this separation has to do with the sense of competitiveness among the Lebanese; they take pride in building something from scratch themselves, as Alex Hamilton had done. But it also relates to a preference for developing *family* resources and talents. When one commits family wealth to a partnership, the checks and balances within the family are thought to furnish the most reliable safeguards, and families are definitely village based.

It is difficult to stress too strongly the importance for the community of kinship and family ties. Lebanese sociologist Samir Khalaf insists on kinship's centrality to an understanding of the Lebanese people:

> If there ever has been a culture with an exclusive kinship orientation, Lebanon comes close to being such. Kinship has been and is likely to remain Lebanon's most solid and enduring [cultural] tie.[19]

Gulick formulates the way the average Arab would verbalize fundamental family values:

> The strongest tie which binds one person to another is the tie of blood, reckoned on the male line. The only people in this hard world in whom I can trust are my relatives. Therefore, the best people in the world are my relatives—my brother, my father, my father's brothers and their sons, and beyond them, everyone in my father's lineage. When one marries, one chooses the best person one can find, and the best person is to be found among one's kinsmen—the closer the better.[20]

Arabs invest a great deal of pride in family, traditionally tracing their ancestral lines back to Adam. Thus anyone who breaks a pledge or a vow, or who takes a political stand different from that accepted by the lineage, is held to be an individual of no origin, literally, of no family.[21] And anyone without family has no status and therefore no rights or personal meaning in the community.

The Lac La Biche Muslims still retain a strong *Arab* family identity. This manifests itself in loyalties to the Arabic language and in dedication to learn the Arabic of the Qur'an, the crowning achievement of the language. Indeed, for the other residents of the town, it is difficult to differentiate the Lebanese Arab characteristics from the Muslim characteristics. Because Muslim law expressly forbids women to marry outside the Muslim community, only Muslim men may seek spouses among the larger population. Those women who marry into the community have a difficult time without Arabic: it not only is used in prayers but often becomes the medium for true community interaction. The townspeople's general perception was that kinship values were so tightly bound to Islam that the two merged.

Family life is fundamental in the Qur'an and the traditions of the Prophet, and the Lac La Biche Arab family therefore has an essential religious component. Islamicist Arthur Jeffrey notes that several religious factors influence families among Muslims: Muhammad's *sunna* (normative practice) provides a direct model for behavior; Muslims genuinely strive to apply his standards of life in practical matters like marriage; Muslim law applies to one's life regardless of where one happens to reside; family life is *the* accepted ideal in Islam.[22] Thus among the Lac La Biche Muslims, marriage carries a special sacred meaning even if it is not sacramental in the Christian sense; it is a fundamental way of being Muslim.

Taken together, the values of village, kinship, Arabness, and religion shape life for the people in Lac La Biche, even where they diverge somewhat from the Lebanese norm in their lives. Indeed, some of these divergences reflect the modification of the community in Canada. A number of the young people interviewed commented on the sense of community that the village provided, and on the training they received in their families to think of their Canadian home as part of the Lebanese village from which they had come. Another second-generation informant, however, remarked on the "different attitudes even among first-generation people about maintaining village distinctions—some think it necessary, others not. Some kids don't know what village they belong to. It depends on the parents." Some scholars take such lack of uniformity concerning the home village to indicate the continuous erosion of village identity. For example, a study in Winnipeg by sociologists Jay Goldstein and Alexander Segall showed that as more intermarriage occurred among groups, the original identity became weaker; at the same time, the Canadian "ethnic" identity increased.[23] In Lac La Biche, where no marriages had occurred between the two villages back home in Lebanon or among the first-generation immigrants, three had taken place among second-generation community members.

Village consciousness among second-generation youth does seem to have declined, although not universally. One second-generation informant insisted that "the distinctions separating the two villages are irrelevant in Canada, and the young people respond accordingly." Members of the second generation tended to see Lebanese village identity as less significant for their identities; they were just Canadians living in Lac La Biche. But they realize that Lebanese village identity is important for their parents and for their own sense of having roots. Seemingly, then, the Lebanese village identity is the first to be modified by a new Canadian awareness of local identity in Canada. At the same time Lebanese village life is extended through life in the town of Lac La Biche.

Some Muslims from outside the town would argue on religious grounds against maintaining any alternate identity, village or otherwise. Canadian-born Muslims tend to view the adoption of a Canadian identity as necessary for Islam's survival. Saleem Ganam, a teacher in the Edmonton mosque and an important Canadian-born Arab leader, phrased it this way:

> Immigrant Muslims bring with them so much of their home ideas. They think that Islam has to operate like it does back there or it isn't Islam. It is tiring trying to get them to see that this is Canada, and Islam should be developed in Canada for Canadians. We really need a Canadian Islam for everybody but the first-generation immigrants.

Yet Islam is so intertwined with other senses of identity that the severing of village consciousness would be a difficult task. This is especially so if immigration continues to bring fresh believers from "back home" to continue the pressure for a Lebanese Islam.

Forming a Mosque-Based Congregation

Contributing to the construction of a new mosque for relatives in Lala expresses a sense of belonging to the extended village. But building a mosque in Lac La Biche expresses rootedness in another way; it is the ummah appropriating the territory for its own conscious purposes. Symbolically, a type of Muslim sacrality is established. Moreover, when the center of the community becomes the mosque, a shift of identity has occurred, a way of perceiving identity more in keeping with Canadian congregational patterns. Such a shift is necessary both for religious practice and for rootedness in the Canadian setting.

It is essential to note the critical change that mosque building in Canada brings. Establishing and maintaining the mosque is a means of institutionalizing the homeland in a new setting; the mosque becomes a way of reducing the distance from the community's true religious and cultural values. At the same time, constructing a mosque that rivals the other religious buildings in town is a visible statement of permanence, an affirmation that the Islamic identity can flourish in Canada even though not of this culture or place. It is also a statement to the believers themselves: their Islamic faith can be at least partially expressed in a building, as are other North American faiths. An acceptable mosque structure is thus an abiding symbol of the re-creation of the Lebanese Muslim environment on Canadian soil; its presence is a means of exteriorizing Islamic values in a region not necessarily associated with or committed to Muslim existence.

Some of the community's most crucial reorientations involve the mosque. The mosque becomes more than a building to gather the community together for prayer. Nor is it just the adding of a teaching component—mosque schools have existed since the first Muslim empire. What is new is that the mosque is called upon to provide a substitute culture to replace the Lebanese matrix that does not exist in Lac La Biche. This had two direct impacts upon believers: being Muslim could not just be left to ancestral traditions of kin, village, Arabness, or cultural religion in North America; and even as the ancestral tradition recedes, the mosque increasingly defines what is Islamic. With that process begun, we could expect some alteration of the meaning of mosque rituals to accord with North American lifestyle, including, perhaps, a shift to Sunday prayers. The mosque may well be on its way to being a concrete expression of a new vision of Muslim religious and cultural life in Canada and North America.

Nor is the host culture left untouched. The mosque is a statement to the larger community that the believers have appropriated that form as a means of integrating into Canadian culture. At the same time, the building insists that Islam is no longer foreign, and its adherents neither exotic nor inferior. If a synagogue can somehow be a daily reminder to the public of the Jewish foundations of the Christian faith, and therefore be part of the Christian family, the mosque states boldly that that religious solidarity is broken. A new sacred is present. In a small community, this fact must be dealt with. Society must now face the problem of alternate visions of faith and what that portends for the town's homogeneity.

In the Muslim community of Lac La Biche, prayers—especially the Friday prayers—were held in Omar Fayad's house until 1958. Most prayed the five enjoined daily prayers at home. With the coming of the Tarrabains and the Goodneys, and the loosening of Canadian government regulations on bringing in next of kin, seven families constituted a large enough group to establish a permanent place of prayer. In 1957 the Arabian Muslim Association had been formed with twelve male members. Elections were to be held once a year, with provision for a president, a vice president, a secretary, and a treasurer; the first officers were Sam Assef, Amin Abu Ghouche, Amin Fayith, and Bill Tarrabain, respectively. Because the community was growing very quickly, it soon became evident that they could no longer worship in Fayad's house. In addition, instruction for the youth required separate space. Members also wanted to replicate the amenities of village life in Lebanon, where they had been able to pray together; beyond that, they reminded each other of traditions of mosque construction that went back to Muhammad.

The earliest mosque was built by the Prophet as an enclosed courtyard attached to his house. As the ummah grew, the building of mosques was regarded as a public responsibility, and governments took over the financial burden. This was especially true for a city's official mosque, where the males gathered for Friday prayer. During and after Friday prayer, matters of public concern were expressed and acted upon. For example, after Friday prayers, any public chastisement of criminals took place. Traditionally, Muslim heads of states built mosques to signal their power and prestige or to fill their need for an official place to pray. Eventually, other motivations came into play: pious individuals bequeathed mosques for religious reasons, organizations built mosques as centers for their group, or regional governments built mosques as the population expanded. In Lac La Biche, none of these motivations obtained. The community built the mosque to express religious and social cohesion in the face of a culture that was fundamentally indifferent; the group needed to affirm its own religious roots.

Traditionally, the construction of Sunni mosques has been fostered by diverse motivations. Pious individuals or groups could establish *waqfs*, or religious endowments, and have them administered by a mosque council. This council arranged for and paid the mosque officials: a *muezzin*, who called the faithful to prayer, a *khattib*, who preached the sermon during the Friday prayer, and various cleaners and attendants. The only other significant individual was the *imam*, an individual distin-

586

guished enough to lead the congregation in its prayers. This was not likely to be a paid position, although some wealthier mosques had such a person on staff. Generally, though, Sunni Islam had very few rules for the imam: he was to be a man of character and knowledge who had the respect of the community. Technically, any mature male of sufficient religious stature within the community could function as prayer leader.

In Lac La Biche, North American demands for leadership skills have had a direct effect on mosque organization and religious authority. The many functions the imam is called upon to fulfill derive partly from the requirements imposed upon the community by governments, other religious groups, and public institutions. For example, an imam may have to appear before an immigration board to argue that the community can support new immigrants; he may have to insist that the community take steps to protect its children from some perceived problem in the larger population; he may have to function as an activist to urge the community to take some stand on an issue. From being a leader of prayers, the imam has become a professional religious functionary, with roles in counseling, representing Islam locally, nationally, and internationally, and interacting with other faiths as an equal partner. He now appears in court, interacts with public officials, presents his community's concerns to neighbors, and argues for an acceptable niche within the Canadian spectrum of religions. The North American penchant for specialists has profoundly influenced Muslim perceptions of mosque personnel; the imam himself is now evaluated by the congregation for his abilities in areas inconceivable thirty years ago—no traditional imam would have to worry whether young people were attracted to or repelled from mosque attendance because of his programs or personality.

We might expect the Islamic ideology of leadership to have expanded to include these new dimensions, but this does not appear to have taken place. No officially sanctioned definition of these roles in the mosque exists. The imam is not accorded a special liturgical role or given a sacramental meaning as an "evangelist" for Islam. Unlike Middle Eastern Muslims who have directed ideological and financial resources toward furthering the influence of Islam, the Lac La Biche Muslims have not adopted "salvific" aims to reach the larger Canadian community. Nor does the imam perceive himself to have such a purpose.

Where we do see structural change is in the modification of the imam's educational role. In Lac La Biche, teaching the youth was an important means of settling the community. The imam's teaching responsibilities, especially in teaching the liturgical language of Arabic, make his role somewhat different from that of the Protestant minister, even though other tasks of his may be quite similar. This teaching role may well make the imam distinctive among religious functionaries in North American religious circles.

Although it would be easy to point to models in the larger society as the locus for these leadership requirements (as, for example, the social service officer), Muslims do not necessarily perceive these new roles to be derived from that source. Indeed, if they were so perceived, they might be regarded as an unwarranted "secular" innovation. The models for the role of the imam may derive from Sunni sympathy for Shi'a conceptions of an inspired leadership directed from above. If that were the case the continuing metamorphoses of administration and authority could then still be considered Muslim and hence justified by the tradition, even if Sunnis reject Shi'i ideology about a divinely inspired Imamate, as expressed by one of its better-known proponents, Ayatollah Khomeini.

Nor has mosque organization been free of modification. This structure traditionally derives from the functions it carries out. Some mosque councils could be little more than those people designated to carry out the endower's will, while others could control everything down to the contents of the khattib's sermons. Generally speaking, the councils were to exercise discipline with the mosque and assure that proper decorum was preserved; they were also charged with maintaining the property. The people who attended the Friday prayer were under no obligation, however, to pay anything for the upkeep of the mosque or its officials, and the mosque council's discipline did not extend into matters of doctrine or behavior outside the mosque. Still, activities such as funerals took place at the local mosque, so even in traditional times people associated aspects of their identity with a particular mosque. Over time each mosque acquired a history and identity.

It is important to note that the Lac La Biche mosque could not impose discipline on its members in return for the benefits of ritual (an exchange some might associate with Christian churches). It could not, for example, demand endorsement of traditional beliefs about alcohol, adherence to a particular line, or material support from those who attended. It did not have within its tradition the notion of voluntary affiliation in order to construct an institution that would provide "salvation" for believers, as have many churches within Christendom since the Reformation. There was no "theological functionality" involved. Nevertheless, the Lac La Biche congregation did accept the affiliation aspect of the model and determined to develop a center for the community's religious life. The Arab Muslim Association, headed by its officers, was registered with the province, and planning began.

What was to be built? The mosque had to be large enough to accommodate the whole group when it prayed together on Fridays. This need dictated style. Because a Muslim must prepare for prayers by performing washing rituals, washing facilities were required. Minarets, although stylistically significant, were a later addition to mosque design, as the means by which the muezzin could call all the surrounding faithful to prayers. In Canada, such public calling to prayer would be frowned upon, and besides, muezzins no longer climb to the top of minarets but broadcast through public address systems from the floor of the mosque. On Fridays in traditional mosques, the khattib preached, so a raised platform or pulpit was needed. The only other common architectural feature was the *mihrab,* the niche in the end of the mosque indicating *qibla,* the direction of prayer. Very few mosques traditionally had office space, although mosques connected with the mystical orders could have attached quarters where the faithful met and performed their rituals. No other features were required or necessary. Thus the building in Canada had to represent only the barest of elements to be functional, and to that task the Lac La Biche community turned its attention.

The association bought a small piece of land on the north side of town for $250, and with the members acting as labor, a contractor built the mosque for $2,000. A rectangular building with a washroom, the mosque was exceedingly spartan. It had a mihrab, a small raised dais, and a curtain at the rear, behind which women could pray. The first prayer service was held there in the fall of 1958.

In later years, these pioneering days took on a mythic character. Linked by ties of religion, language, and Lebanese village culture, and allied against a Canadian environment that had not yet been conquered, the little community struggled valiantly. They relied instinctively on each other, and that knit the community together in a way that would not have been possible even in Lebanon. As Bill Tarrabain recalled that time,

> In the early days, we had a great spirit. Everyone was really friendly; we had many dinners together, we knew everybody, and everyone smiled at you when you met. You never had to ask anyone for help; they just automatically knew you needed something,

and they gave it to you. To my mind, the memory of those first years are like it must be in heaven.[24]

Two primary concerns pressed upon the fledgling Muslim community: youngsters were growing up without any official training in Arabic or Islam, and some members had married non-Muslims who had converted but who knew little or nothing about Islam. Mothers became particularly concerned that a generation would grow up without any depth of religious understanding. After all, they could not count on the influence of a surrounding Islamic environment as in Lebanon. The answer seemed to be to hire a religious functionary who could serve all these special needs. Hiring someone to be imam and educational leader and mentor was the ultimate solution. While it was an innovation, and innovations in religious matters were frowned upon, the community saw it as crucial to their proper development and even their survival. After several fruitless years, they were able to attract such an individual. A twenty-eight-year-old teacher, Muhammad Shibley from Los Angeles, was hired to be imam, with a levy agreed upon by each family. They paid him $200 per week and purchased a trailer for his residence. He arrived in 1962 and served for seven years.

Shibley made a strong impression on the congregation. A quiet man, he pursued the educating of the community with great fervor. What followed was surely an innovation in Canada: regular Saturday and Sunday classes in the Arabic language and Islamic training for children. In addition, weekly evening classes were instituted for converts. Shibley was the chief architect of these programs, and it is said that one can still recognize those in Lac La Biche who learned to pray from Shibley because they perform prayers so precisely.

Encountering the Publics of Canada

Building a mosque and hiring an imam were steps taken for the congregation and its religious life. What steps were taken to become part of the larger culture of Lac La Biche and Canada? One integrator was a women's council, formed in 1960. Modeled on Canadian church ladies' societies, the organization was developed by the women themselves. Partly a response to the loneliness that women faced in a society that lacked the cohesion of Lebanon, and in which their husbands spent long hours at work, the forming of the council was also a recognition that most converts were women and needed the support of a religious network.

For the Lebanese, the council was a natural outgrowth of the women's role in organizing the community for Ramadan celebrations or weddings. Traditionally, they also were responsible for the education of their children, and they were sensitive to religious requirements.

Very few women in the community worked outside the home in those early days. A few wore kerchiefs over their hair when outside their homes, or wore long dresses with sleeves that covered their arms, but they were not conspicuous by their dress; they did not fit the stereotype of Middle Eastern women now familiar from television. They were energetic and dynamic. Led by the wives of the association's officers, the women were a key force in raising funds for educational programs and other mosque endeavors. The vehicle they chose was the community supper.

From the beginning the community supper was popular with the townspeople. The Muslim women had the opportunity to exhibit some of their considerable culinary talent, for which many of them were privately hailed within the town. But it also brought the Muslim community into touch with the town's populace in a new way. The suppers were usually held as fund-raisers and the whole town was invited to attend. They were a huge success. For the Muslims, the suppers were a significant outreach to their new environment; for the other ethnic groups, their first engagement with a group that had kept very much to itself. And the community suppers paved the way for more integration into Canadian society.

The presidency of the women's council passed from one woman to another as the association offices passed among the males—rotating among the "principal families." The council was active or not depending upon the perceived need. Because of its loose organization, the council did not encounter problems of individuals exercising too much control. On the other hand, it brought into play traditional Muslim cohesion when the community was in need. The women's council was a mechanism for marshaling resources for good causes—raising funds for the local mosque, helping the Edmonton Muslim community raise money to move a historic mosque to a heritage park, assisting one of the home villages in Lebanon that needed a new mosque. Such voluntarism was common among Canadian ethnic groups, and the Muslims followed the pattern. The women, through their talents, provided the community with its first real entrée into Canadian culture.

But another public world—one far more formidable—was that of international politics. The expansion of Israel had wide ramifications for the Lac La Biche Arab Muslims, as for other parts of the Arab world. In Lebanon, after the founding of Israel, both home villages had suffered a great deal from the social dislocation brought by the flood of refugees from Palestine. Inhabitants of both villages were deeply moved by the plight of their fellow Arabs. Yet they resented the demands their presence made on the economy, on their lifestyle, and on political life in Lebanon. In Canada, they also had to deal with conflicts between the policies espoused by the federal government (which had welcomed them to Canada) and the policies they believed to be right from their religious or Arab nationalist viewpoint.

During Shibley's time a critical principle of far-reaching significance was enunciated: Middle Eastern politics should not dominate the congregation's relationship to Canada. The rationale: the community here had to develop on its own and adapt to its new environment, and it could not do so if the affairs of the international ummah caused friction within the Canadian congregation. Debate raged within the community—after Friday prayers, when they gathered for celebrations, during family birthday parties, at the cafés, in their shops. The problem was not just how to cope with the tragedy of learning that a relative or friend had been killed or wounded. It was how they could influence the policy of their new homeland without alienating its people. Finally the association had a community meeting, and the policy of separating politics of the homeland from the community's relationship to Canada was adopted. No minutes were kept of the meeting, but, following traditional practices, the consensus won the day. During his tenure, Shibley tried to balance commitments to rights with commitments to Canada. By and large, he followed this principle carefully.

Not all agreed with the policy. A vocal minority, related to Alex Hamilton's family and supported by others from the village of Kharbih Ruha and their relatives, argued for a more vigorous defense of Arab rights. In June 1967, the Six-Day War broke out between Israel and the Arab states. Badly mauled by Israeli troops, the Arabs were thrown back, losing the Sinai, the West Bank, and the Golan Heights. From a Muslim standpoint, the greatest loss was Jerusalem's Old City, where the Dome of the Rock, Islam's third most important shrine after Mecca and Medina, was located. By 1969, the Arab world's most powerful army, the Egyptian, had been pushed back to the Suez, and Israel had built the Bar Lev line (particularly odious to Arabs as a symbol of their impotence) to mark its victorious territorial expansion. Arabs in Lac La Biche, as well as around the world, were in shock and mourning. Frustrated and greatly fearful because they knew that Canadians had little sympathy with the Arab cause, and hurting because they felt so powerless, the congregation turned inward.

Several families in town were affected by the outcome: they had kin in the embattled regions, and the war left them defeated in spirit. They had no encouragement from the Canadian press or from the federal governments of the United States and Canada. Israel received universal accolades.

For the Lac La Biche Muslims, these events in the Middle East were a direct challenge to the Qur'an. God's word spoke of justice; a true Muslim state was the expression of what was right. Verse after verse reminded believers that God's hand of judgment would be upon those who trampled on the poor and defenseless. The Lebanese associated such unfortunates with their kinfolk in Palestine who were now refugees because of Israel's power. Shibley reminded them that Allah controlled the affairs of the world and that justice would prevail, but few members, even those who were opposed to speaking out, could see God's justice in such a debacle. Several members wanted a dramatic public statement about the wrongs being perpetrated in Israel. The association officers resisted this approach, and the imam—naturally quiet and studious anyway, and mindful of who controlled the pocketbook—continued to observe the policy. His sermons stressed Qur'anic themes and concentrated on the great principles of guidance found in the traditions. He mentioned political events in his sermons, but his comments never went beyond the norms established by the gentlemen's agreement among the members. Feeling powerless, and finding no outlet through the mosque, the dissidents simmered. The issue festered.

The association officers justified the policy on the basis of practicality: if powerful Muslims in North America could not dent the pro-Israeli stance, and if Arab countries could not contain Israeli aggression, there was little hope that a few Arabs in the Canadian north would change world opinion. Indeed, there was good reason to think that the group could become the focal point for Canadian hostility, just as the Jews had become the target earlier when the Canadian government refused to take them as refugees from Hitler.

The policy also had an economic rationale. Because none of the community could speak English very well, they all were dependent upon their entrepreneurial connections. In some way they were all very vulnerable; their movement into business had made them so. For example, in 1966, twenty-four of thirty-six Lebanese-born males were engaged in mink farming; nine were small shopkeepers.[25] But by 1978 just about all were heavily involved in businesses with direct public contact, an occupational profile confirmed by my own survey of the community in 1989. These were the community's occupations in 1978:

Store owners	
supermarket, grocery, meat market, confectionary	6
specialty, furniture, menswear	4
department store	1
Restaurant owners	2
Teachers	2
Leaseholder (car dealership)	1
Theater owner	1
Banker	1
Imam	1

In a small town, in a rather conservative part of Canada, Lebanese businessmen may well have been justified in having some concerns about their businesses if the group became voluble about the Middle East. Continuing growth in business depended upon access to finances, and they knew how easy it was for the banker to turn down their requests for funds. None had Middle East contacts for such funding. For good or ill, the policy remained in effect throughout Shibley's term.

Meanwhile Shibley was active on other fronts. As with every immigrant group, the Muslims had forever to deal with government bureaucracy. Few felt comfortable in English; none were confident in anything beyond a simple conversation. As the government relaxed its immigration policies, kinfolk could be sponsored. Shibley pioneered in what became almost a requirement of his position: dealing effectively with bureaucrats. Business issues demanded comprehending the nuances of English, so Shibley became the community translator. Municipal and provincial institutions needed a spokesperson from the Muslim community: Shibley stepped in. The imam's roles as confidante, counselor, assistant, and mediator between the larger Canadian public and the Muslim community became the norm. It was the beginning of a professional religious role for their imam.

Wherever one looked in Alberta, one found prosperity. Oil, one of the chief exports of the province, was pouring millions into provincial and local coffers. Oil-rich Lac La Biche was poised to receive great wealth from the oil-sands plants in Fort McMurray. The oil sands, potentially with more oil than Saudi Arabia, were touted as the next megaproject in a country already wealthy from petroleum products. Several Lebanese invested in land and became relatively wealthy. The association bought a house for the imam, and they recognized that the little square "shack" they had for a mosque did not express to townspeople the importance they accorded to their religion. Moreover, it had none of the facilities that had become necessary: it was too small for the various classes the imam had to give; it had no room for offices for the imam; it had no facilities for the women's suppers or for nonprayer activities. Drawing upon the wealth of the members, the association bought land on the south side of town, in a decidedly residential area somewhat away from the center of the business section. Because most drove to the mosque, they purchased two lots, one of them for parking. The community began the process of building.

Late in 1969, Shibley, troubled by poor health and weary of the pressures of a major building campaign, left to take up the imam's role at the urban mosque in Calgary. The community, facing several months without an imam and seeing the advances in education already beginning to be reversed, contacted al-Azhar University in Cairo through the Egyptian embassy. The Egyptian government sponsored imams for minorities throughout the world, paying their salaries and travel costs. Muhammad Amin Abdul Samad, a graduate of al-Azhar and a student at McGill University in Montreal, agreed to come. Unfortunately, he was unable to take up the task for more than eight months (for reasons that remain unclear). It became evident to the association that the community could not both complete their building program and pay the salary necessary to attract a good imam.

At about the same time, various Muslim governments became increasingly troubled by the growth within their own countries of conservative Muslim groups. Reformers with many different programs, these conservatives were united in criticizing their governments for using state funds for megaprojects while turning a deaf ear to Islamic causes. Western writers have generally labeled these reformers "fundamentalists," but this term is not strictly accurate: the reformers' understanding of their "return to fundamentals" differed markedly from that of Christian fundamentalists. Nevertheless, as a response to this conservative criticism and an increasingly "Islamic" agitation within their populations, these governments formed international Muslim outreach organizations. One function of these organizations was to send imams to fledgling Muslim groups around the world.

Interestingly, although these countries wanted to appear to their constituencies to be spending their money on Islamic development, they also took pains to assure that they did not export fundamentalist imams. The Muslim community abroad was fragile enough without having to deal with the activism of these reformers.

Saudi Arabia opened an office in 1970 in New York known as the Rabi'at al-'Alim al-Islamiyya (Muslim World League), an instrument to further the growth of Islam in North America. Libya fostered the Islamic Call Society as an equivalent organization. There was a price to be paid, however; the initiatives and concerns of the imams could no longer be controlled by the local mosque committees. Imams began seeing their role not only as prayer leader but as missionary and ambassador for Islam. The concept of "evangelists for Islam" had not been part of Sunni Islamic tradition. Shi'is, on the other hand, especially the Isma'ili branch, had promoted their cause with advocate-preachers (da'is) almost from their inception in the tenth century, and the Shi'a belief in a hierarchical structure by which the truth passed down to the uneducated and unaware promoted the notion of religious superiors. The current Sunni imam in Edmonton, Youssef Chebli, comments upon the relationship between imams, mosque councils, and government sponsorship:

> If they [a mosque council] hire you, they can fire you. You are compromised by their money. An imam must be the leader in religious affairs, and nobody has the right to interfere in these affairs. He is above the administrators. We [imams] consider ourselves as the representative of Islam; we are not representing the local, small community. We represent Islam; we represent the Prophet; we represent Allah. If I make a mistake, you have the right to correct me, but I represent Islam. Wherever I [as imam] go, I spread Islam. Under the [Libyan] Islamic Call Society, I have the freedom to speak out, I am free to go and carry the message. But they don't control me. When I was under the [Saudi Arabian] World League, they said, "Why did you go to such and such a place?" I sent them my resignation. Only my conscience and my God can tell me where to go to spread Islam. Even so, it is much better to be under a government-organized society than a local community. When you are controlled by a local group, it is much more difficult to do and say what you think is right.[26]

As every Protestant clergyman knows, the freedom to speak one's mind is sometimes curtailed by those who pay the bills. The association now recognized that its leadership options were very few indeed; most of their power to choose a leader for their community was now draining away to the international Muslim government programs. More and more they were to be subject to the men who went through training programs in powerful Muslim countries, and who came to them through the largesse of those countries. The new circumstances were not universally recognized as beneficial.

Policy Formation and Community Cohesion

Meanwhile, problems were multiplying for the tiny congregation. The cost of construction was high, especially because the region was economically so strong. Daunted by the prospect of building a new mosque, the association cast around for the means to pay for it. As businessmen, they naturally turned to the bank. Islamic law has traditionally forbidden usury, even if there were differences of opinion on what constitutes usury. The association acknowledged that borrowing money and paying interest for individual enterprise was one thing, but for building a mosque it was quite another matter. Despite their best efforts, they saw no other way of financing the building. Consequently, the mosque construction committee approached the Canadian Imperial Bank of Commerce, with whom several of the businessmen had accounts, requesting a loan. They were turned down, ostensibly on the grounds that the bank did not fund religious organizations; to the Muslims of Lac La Biche, the reason was blatant religious and ethnic prejudice. To them, there was no doubt: events in the Middle East were having a direct effect on their survival. The community banded together and borrowed or raised the money among themselves through pledges and personal loans.

Those who had expressed fears about the impact of speaking out now argued that the principle of restraint had been correct: Canadian society was indeed prejudiced against the community, and they had been wise to keep a low profile on the Middle East. Others rejected the contention. If restraint still brought prejudice, why not speak out? They had not been public in their criticisms, but they were still being denied funding. The community feared that Canadians were biased toward them because of the situation in the Middle East. What other rejections would be visited upon them if they spoke out?

Finally, in 1971, al-Azhar was able to provide the congregation an imam: Ahmed al-Sharkawi, a recent M.A. from that university. Sharkawi was a scholar in the old Islamic mold. He spent long hours in

Qur'an and shari'a studies, and eventually began studying education at the University of Alberta. He continued the extensive teaching program in the community and taught at the elementary and high schools when heritage and religious days were held. The new mosque, completed in 1970, afforded much greater educational possibilities. In the full basement, classes for several levels could be held simultaneously, and there was ample room for the women's suppers. The mosque could also provide a venue for the young people's social activities, limited as they were. Having a place available meant a big step forward for the youth. Old-timers shook their heads: there had been no facilities like that back home. Educational policy was on the front burner.

In the late 1960s, the Alberta and Lac La Biche governments had begun much greater investment in multicultural programs in schools. Funding was made available from the province to develop specialized education for minorities. The local school board, mindful of the large number of Arabic-speaking children, saw an opportunity to be in step with the times. The Arab children, of whom there were now ninety-six, were a sizable minority within the local school district. They were an ideal group for the multicultural program.

The superintendent of schools was not sure how the initiative would go. He expressed his concern plainly to Soraya Deeb, an Egyptian teacher in the local school who was being interviewed for the program: This is a very closed group; they are scared they might have to learn something they don't want; they keep almost totally to themselves. Deeb's mandate was to organize and teach Arabic classes at the elementary level and to include in the curriculum cultural components from Lebanese society. The women in the congregation were especially supportive of the initiative. The program went well, but the difference between the classical Arabic of the Qur'an and the vernacular Lebanese dialect meant that the children did not immediately take to the language training. As with every other language from antiquity, the modern dialects constitute almost another language. Although the language classes were not an unqualified success, the program did instill pride and confidence in the congregation. Tentative gestures toward rapprochement with the larger community began to bear fruit, and the Arab Muslims began to feel more at home.

One result was that the women's council began participating in the heritage-day festivities in town, an annual celebration of the region's ethnic diversity. The council provided special dishes and worked in the booths during this cultural fair. Another was that Bill Tarrabain, encouraged by town businessmen, ran for and won a seat on the local school board. Such a move was unprecedented, and despite the strains within the Muslim community brought on by status differences between the Lala and Kharbih Ruha factions, the congregation almost unanimously supported his candidacy. Tarrabain led the way in other areas: he joined the chamber of commerce and the country club. He learned to play golf because he saw its importance within the business structure of Lac La Biche. Eventually, he became president of the Curling Club. He was the only Muslim to participate, but his election was nevertheless an important first: his success indicated that a Muslim could be accepted.

Some within the community were critical. They pointed out that Tarrabain seldom had time to attend regular prayers and had less and less to do with the internal politics of the Muslim community. He did not spark religious leadership, and internal community matters were left to drift. Al-Sharkawi could do nothing about the Lebanese tensions within the community. First, he was Egyptian and an outsider in terms of the group's Lebanese village mentality. Second, Islam—whose representative he felt himself to be—apparently did not provide an in-group feeling in the community, even though it was the principal ideology of the congregation. Family and village identities were still the most powerful vehicles for community meaning. In 1975, al-Sharkawi left to complete his Ph.D. studies at the University of Alberta.

The internal cohesion of the congregation was further strained by Egyptian president Anwar Sadat's mission to Israel in November 1977 and the subsequent Camp David negotiations involving Egypt, Israel, and the United States. Those in the community who had opposed the principle of silence on Middle East issues had a new ally: the new imam, Muhammad al-Qasibi. Al-Qasibi had his M.A. from al-Azhar University, and he had been sponsored by the Egyptian government through that university, but he was an outspoken critic of Sadat's policies. Almost immediately the situation in Lac La Biche changed. A vocal and well-spoken man, al-Qasibi came out of an Egypt that had reeled under Israeli bombing and the resurgence of a fundamentalist Islam. His sermons on Friday applied Qur'anic principles of justice to the Middle East situation, and he urged a far more sophisticated and critical stance on the part of the members. His stand split the community. Some thought it high time that a spokesperson address the issues, and even do so publicly. A group of Arabs who were not in charge of the association supported al-Qasibi's initiative, and families attached to him gave him, as evidence of their support, extra funds beyond those allocated from

Egypt. The old power brokers managed to win the association's elections or trade leadership among the "old" families, and they never lost control of the mosque to the other faction, but the cracks within the congregation became open fissures. Members who did not agree with al-Qasibi had one very good option: they could stay home. They did.

Programs sputtered; the association's leadership was unable to marshal sufficient resources to overcome the malaise within the community. The imam could not do it, because he had become part of the problem. When Israel invaded southern Lebanon in Operation Litani on June 6, 1978, it was too much for the imam. Al-Qasibi left. He had served two years. During his tenure the congregation had learned that the association could not control what was done by the imam if they did not pay him; their only recourse was to complain to his program director. Moreover, the community was fractured enough that pledges for the mosque dropped off or were not paid. Costs were escalating, and the congregation could not afford to pay a full-time imam at a level that would attract the skilled people they wanted. From that time on, imams were financed from abroad.

But other changes were occurring. First, the population at large began to see the Muslims in a different light: they had the opinion that, as a group, the Muslims were well-heeled. The trend among the Muslims had been toward business ownership or entrepreneurial activity. Some had been more successful at it than others; only two members were now in laboring occupations. Moreover there was a further division between "uptown" and "downtown" Arab merchants.[27]

Second, the family structure among Lac La Biche Muslims was changing. Family ties had determined many elements: one's status within the community, one's claim to leadership within the association, whom one's children should marry, how successful the husband and father was. Traditional family structure played an essential role in the mosque's politics. Now both the numbers of Muslim families and their makeup were changing. Whereas in 1968 Barclay's research had identified thirty-six "Arabic-speaking male heads of families," by 1978 there were only nineteen. This number included units which the Arabs considered families but which differed significantly from the original definition. For example, there now was one Druse (a minority sect deriving from Islam and found only in the Middle East) who participated in the social life of the community but who was not Muslim; there were also two retired heads of families and one widow whose views were important. Significantly, there were two male heads of Muslim families who were not Lebanese—one Egyptian and one Canadian convert. A number of families had moved to Edmonton or elsewhere in Canada. None had permanently returned to Lebanon, although at least one was contemplating the move in order to marry the children to "proper" mates. The youths were growing up and taking a more active role; young people were reaching marriageable age. The Muslim community was in transition to its second generation.

Internal Tensions and Proper Islamic Values

The initial purpose of my study of Lac La Biche Muslims in 1978 was to develop background for a film on Islam in Alberta.[28] The Lac La Biche Muslims were asked to participate in the project and to select a representative family who could help to illustrate the story of Muslim life in Canada. The association, headed by Amin Abu Ghouche, chose Bill Tarrabain and his family. The film crew began shooting.

It soon became evident to everyone connected with the film that all was not well. Whenever probes were made to ascertain the trouble, a host of quibbles surfaced, all focusing upon the Tarrabain family: questions whether the Tarrabain family strictly adhered to what the Qur'an said, differences of opinion on whether young women should pursue higher education, contentions about whether the young people talked about religion outside of the mosque, pointed statements that the Tarrabain family did not truly represent the Muslim family in Lac La Biche.

It was evident to the film crew and me that issues not specifically religious also had a role in the conflict. Because the film was to play to a national audience, the community wanted a family that would project a good image. The Tarrabain family, and Bill in particular, had made significant strides in relating to the townspeople. He had been financially successful, and his family was known, even beyond the town, as one of the elite of the Lac La Biche Arabs. Village rivalry entered in, because Bill's connections were in Lala, and some who belonged to the other village felt resentment. There was also some religious resistance to the family's upward mobility at the perceived expense of their piety.

The Tarrabains had several daughters of marriageable age. During the course of the filming, the family moved to Edmonton to be near the university, where the children, including the daughters, were to attend. In effect, they were no longer "in the village." The move exacerbated the alienation.

Criticisms surfaced about Bill's Muslim behavior; some spoke darkly of the father's alleged deviation from the Islamic standard of abstaining from alcohol; others argued about the girls' attitude toward "marrying out," a sure sign of secularity. The congregation appealed to the association president to form a special mosque committee to monitor what the film said. One of Imam al-Qasibi's last acts was to serve on the committee. The group asked to receive a copy of the script so they could edit it, and conflict ensued. Omar Mughrabi, who later served as president and whose family had had reservations about the selection of the Tarrabain family from the beginning, stated it bluntly:

> Nothing in our history has split us like that film. Before you sent the text, we had a meeting in the mosque. Some members complained loudly about it, and people started pushing and shoving. Finally fisticuffs erupted. This should never happen in the mosque. We all knew how serious it was because two years later one of the men involved died of cancer; another had a son die. You just don't do things like that in a mosque. There are still bad feelings about it.

The mosque was holy ground whose sanctity was disrupted by the squabble, bringing God's judgment down upon the principals. The problems over the film had rent the fabric of unity in the mosque, the central focus of Muslim identity. A look at the modifications requested in the filmscript reveals some of the issues at stake.

The majority of the proposed changes to the text concerned what the family had said, not what the narration had added. Thus the meaning of family and Muslim protocols of family behavior were the central points of contention. Significantly, a primary dispute arose over the difficulties of finding the daughters suitable mates in Canada. One of the daughters remarked in the filmscript,

> My parents think your language, your culture, everything should be the same as the person you marry. The older kids and I don't agree with that. . . . I don't agree because there aren't any guys around. If I marry out of my religion I'd like him to convert; I'm not going to say, "If you don't convert, I'm not going to marry you"—but I'm not going to change my religion.

A note on the returned script, however, read: "A Muslim woman *can not* marry outside her religion." This rule is established by Muslim law and has been adhered to with great diligence by the ummah throughout history.[29] This issue is obviously one with strong potential to create conflict in the Canadian situation. A 1983 Gallup poll revealed that tolerance levels in Canada toward interracial and interfaith marriage increased substantially between 1968 and 1983: between Catholics and Protestants, from 61 to 84 percent; between Jews and non-Jews, from 52 to 77 percent; and between blacks and whites, from 36 to 70 percent. Maintaining ethnically and religiously based marriages in the Canadian environment appears to be even more problematic than in the American: Canadians are far more tolerant of interracial marriage (70 percent versus 43 percent) and are slightly more tolerant of Catholic-Protestant marriages (84 percent versus 79 percent). The younger the age group, the greater the tolerance level.[30]

The Lac La Biche community also feared losing the sense of uniqueness arising out of the Middle Eastern marriage heritage. Their concerns would appear to be well founded. Canadian notions of multiculturalism encourage retention of religious and ethnic differences on the one hand, but Canadian cultural attitudes appear to be placing less value on the importance of marrying within one's own religious and ethnic group, a prime factor in retaining differentiation. The first-generation members of the committee recognized the challenge and reacted with alarm.

But differences of opinion also surfaced concerning the role and importance of religion in the community, especially for the youth. Ali, a Tarrabain cousin then in his twenties, said:

All my friends know that I am a Muslim. The people I associated with respect me for it, and I respect their religion. In my age group, I don't think religion is talked about as much. I feel that you talk about religion when you're in a mosque, or when you're at home.

The script committee took exception to this, writing in: "Islam should be talked about or discussed anywhere." The youth were reflecting the Canadian view that religion is not a normal conversation topic. Religion is respected, but it is a matter of private concern. The filmscript crystallized this conflict about the place of religion in one's conscious relationships with others. At another place in the script, a daughter, Salwa, said:

We grew up as kids in Lac La Biche. There's a lot of Lebanese families here and that's where I really grew up with my Lebanese culture. I learned a lot [about it] and the cultural aspects of everything, the unity between all cultures. It was easy to be a Muslim there because you had so many people around you all the time. I have a lot of good memories about Lac La Biche. But now that I'm living in Edmonton, the unity isn't there anymore; it's sort of just a family unity.

The committee inserted the comment that "a Muslim is a Muslim and can practice his or her religion any place. It does not matter where the person is." Evidently the notion that cultural homogeneity in Lac La Biche would make the practice of Islam easier challenged the committee. For were that true, they would have to agree that Islam was more difficult to practice in Canada than in Lebanon, bringing to mind also the question of the legitimacy of migrating to Canada. It is interesting that the committee here was maintaining that Islam was a religious belief solely—that is, one did not need an Islamic ethos. This notion jibes quite well with the North American conception of the position of religion but is in sharp contrast to the Middle Eastern norm. Religion was seen by the daughters as having a cultural component and by the committee as being an ideal system applicable everywhere.

Other differences arose about the practice of Islam. Concerning prayer, Tarrabain had said:

I practice prayer, but I don't practice it during the working hours or in the office. I do practice it at home and on Sunday in the mosque. Well, I feel it's okay, because God didn't make things hard on human beings. As long as you know you have to worship Him, it doesn't matter in my belief what hour.

The special script committee wrote in the margins: "The Qur'an states, 'set up regular prayers. For such prayers are enjoined on believers at stated times' (Surat el-Nissa, Chapter 103)." This conflict went to the heart of Islamic values—did one have to obey the letter of the Qur'an, or did God understand your situation and approve your prayers whenever you could get to them? The committee favored an ideological interpretation of Islam, the one they saw as congruent with tradition and normative practice in the Middle East; Tarrabain obviously had responded to Canadian realities.

But it should be pointed out that the values of the script committee were not consistently Middle Eastern, nor were the family's values consistently Canadian. While it is evident that the family had not expressed the ummah's ideological beliefs about the society and the family as other Muslims would have liked, they had only differed with interpretations of their meaning, not the fundamental application of Islam to the Canadian experience. At bottom, both the Tarrabain family and the script committee had evidenced a Canadian accommodation: The Tarrabains that their religious views were their own, the script committee that religion could be separated from culture. These views are decidedly not Lebanese, and not Muslim in the traditional sense, but certainly Muslim. The Lac La Biche Muslims were not being *assimilated* into Canadian culture: they were formulating a new mix of Canadian and Lebanese Muslim traits in Canada, balancing several different values in the Canadian environment.

Transition to the Second Generation

The tenure of the next imam, who arrived in the spring of 1979, was a reprieve from the contentiousness that had characterized al-Qasibi's term. Dr. Muhammad Ansari was an Indonesian graduate of al-Azhar. A quiet, calm man, he kept out of the interfamily squabbles and stressed the application of Islamic principles to life. He took encouragement of the community as a whole to be his responsibility, and he tried to focus on the Islamic nature of the congregation rather than on its Lebanese nature. He felt that the ummah should develop in its own locale and that ties to another place would undermine the growth of Islam in Canada. Although he continued the strong teaching program of the mosque and promoted classical Arabic language training, he felt more at home in English than in Arabic. This isolated him from the first-generation believers, while it appealed to the second, who were better in English. Ansari remained in Lac La Biche for four years and oversaw the continuing interaction of the mosque with other religious organizations in town. With Ansari, the interfaith connections entailed in North American life became another factor in the imam's evolving role. He spoke at World Day of Prayer gatherings and participated in cross-cultural funerals and community celebrations. At the same time, the women increased their participation in bazaars and other town activities. Their involvement became an accepted and expected part of Lac La Biche life.

When Ansari left in early 1982, the congregation went through another difficult time trying to locate an acceptable imam. Local people filled in as best they could until Muhammad Aziz, an Egyptian scholar from al-Azhar, arrived in late 1982. His ability in Arabic was appreciated by most in the congregation, but now those in the second generation were beginning to move into positions of responsibility in the town and in the mosque. Arabic was valued by them primarily as a link with the past generation and the Lebanese homeland. Their own skills in the

Arabic of the Qur'an were minimal. It became a matter of ideology: language was first and foremost the basis of Muslim consciousness. But the loyalty to Arabic was given greater emphasis as a cultural and social dimension of the Lebanese Arab community including non-Muslim Arabic speakers, rather than exclusively as a religious language. An identity marker, it fit more into the multicultural model accepted within Canadian society. Unfortunately, the Arab identity was not always viewed in a complimentary light. One second-generation Arab leader from another city who was familiar with Lac La Biche and the Lebanese scene, and who requested anonymity, summarized his views of the problems in a 1981 interview:

> Canadian Arabs are embarrassed by the extremes of the Middle Eastern Arab immigrants. Most of them don't want any part of the whole Middle Eastern scene. Most of them are business-oriented and want to succeed. Consequently, they don't want to be identified with such a controversial area. Moreover, I find most non-Canadian-born Arabs are not sensitive to the nuances of feeling in the Canadian context: they mistakenly argue with Canadians over issues that the Canadians are not predisposed to listen to, or they pick issues that have little legitimate appeal for Canadians. For Canadian-born Arabs generally, religion is not all that important. Being Muslim or Christian can be worked out in a different and better way than being identified as an Arab. If they are Muslim, they want a genuine Canadian Islam, not an import.
>
> Leadership is also hampered by lack of commitment. Most of the time it is haphazard and disorganized. It pays little attention to details, and tends to stress the "public" image and the limelight rather than the substance. Organizations of a pan-Arabic kind have problems with various political or tribal factions trying to take control. If they do take over, they use the organization for their own purposes, splitting into pro-this or that country or political faction. The reaction of most people like me is "A plague on all your houses!"

Clearly, opinions differ about the split between Lebanese-Arab and Canadian identities. But in the Lac La Biche case, the congregation's context remained Lebanese and thus Arab in character; members did not regard belonging to an Arab community as contradictory to being a Canadian. What Lac La Biche provided for the Muslims was the opportunity to move out of their distinctive village identity slowly enough that they did not feel the disjunction between their former Arab identity and the new Canadian Islamic identity they were constructing. But they still clung to village connections in ways that Canadian-born Muslims found unnecessary and hampering.

During the eighties, people from Lala continued to send sizable financial assistance back to Lebanon—to build new homes, to shore up old family houses, to aid relatives or friends who needed assistance. The homeland still had solid meaning. One young woman from the community, after a failed marriage to a Lebanese Muslim in Canada, decided to visit Kharbih Ruha. She stayed, remarried there, and is now a permanent resident in Lebanon. This is a good example of the way in which the extended village notion became concrete. In effect, Lac La Biche and its sister villages of Kharbih Ruha and Lala became part of a larger kin structure, with intermarriage sealing the international links. Certainly the "village size" of the Muslim community in Lac La Biche must have been important for this across-the-seas connection; at the same time, the inner cohesion of the community must have contributed to the ease with which the mosque congregation was crafted. The village ties add a dimension to the community not possible in most other North American congregations.

By the time Aziz left in 1984, the Muslims had seen the death of Amin Abu Ghouche, one of the pillars of the first-generation families, as well as the relocation of several others and a modified relationship with the Lebanese homeland. As if compelled to enshrine the new situation in a permanent manner, the congregation began plans to replace the old mosque.

As early as 1978, it was evident that the building no longer served the community well: it did not have adequate space for differentiated classrooms for Arabic, and it lacked offices for the association and the women's council. Also, when it was built, the community was unaware that the shortest distance to Mecca was north, over the pole, so the building faced the wrong direction. By the beginning of the eighties the community generally felt it should have a building more representative of the status that Islam had in the world, a building that stressed a perceived modern aesthetic quality. Funds were collected to purchase land across the street from the old mosque.

A building committee was formed and various building types were examined. On the south side of Edmonton, a new mosque had been built whose design seemed adequate for their purposes, and the plans

10.1 Muslim Community at Lac La Biche, Alberta, Canada, 1992. Photograph by Agape Photographics.

were obtained. A fund-raising campaign, sparked by the women's council, swung into action. The community launched its third building program in its short history.

Construction began in 1988. Projected costs were $400,000. Rather than go to Middle Eastern countries as other Muslim groups had, the Lac La Biche congregation adhered to its tradition of independence: it appealed only to nearby Muslims. The Muslims of Edmonton gave $100,000 (some from members who had moved to Edmonton, and some from relatives from Lala who lived in Edmonton, indicating the close connection still obtaining between village and religious identity), and the local community raised the remainder by receiving pledges from each family or individual member. Pledges ranged from $1,000 to $10,000, and some non-Muslims from Lac La Biche also contributed.

The new mosque is far more elaborate and impressive than the building it replaced. A driveway allows worshipers to get out of their cars near the entrance, a convenience for an aging population, given

Alberta's cold winters. A fully developed basement provides multiuse facilities. The two-level congregational prayer area has a balcony level reserved for women (an architectural feature, incidentally, much favored by the women in several Muslim congregations). In addition, the building has ample office and classroom space, along with elaborate kitchen facilities. Functionally, then, it is similar to the buildings of other religious groups in the town. The mosque is not ostentatious, and its simplicity and dignity indicate a sense of peaceful existence. Lac La Biche Muslims speak with considerable pride of their new place of worship.

When Aziz left to take up duties at Edmonton, Ahmed al-Sharkawi returned. With a doctorate, he has more education than any of the other town clergy. Among his accomplishments are many that his Muslim members wish to stress; he brings to his position excellent Arabic, competent English, a sophisticated knowledge of the Muslim tradition, and an awareness of the position of religion within Canadian society. A respected father-figure, al-Sharkawi is seen to be sufficiently connected with the older generation to represent their views. And although younger members would like a more dynamic imam, they appreciate the stability afforded under the man honorifically called "the good shaikh." With the troubles of the past behind it, the congregation was contented with his return. The community had become a congregation with the next generation firmly in place. In a special sense, they had reduced the distances around them; they were at home.

NOTES

I wish to thank the Lac La Biche Arab Muslim Association, the members of the community, Bill and Bahija Tarrabain and their family, and many other members and former members for their assistance with this project. The interview with Imam Chebli was led by Professor David Goa, whose efforts I appreciate. All other interviews took place in 1978 or 1989 in Lac La Biche and Edmonton.

1. *Alberta Community Profiles* (Department of Economic Development and Trade, Government of Alberta, Edmonton, 1983); Michael Maccago, *Rendezvous: Notre Dame des Victoires*, (Lac La Biche Mission Historical Preservation Society: Lac La Biche, 1988).

2. *Census Canada: Alberta Profiles*, Part 2 (Ottawa: Ministry of Supply and Services, 1988), p. 312.

3. Harold Barclay, "An Arab Community in the Canadian Northwest: A Preliminary Discussion of the Lebanese Community in Lac La Biche, Alberta," *Anthropologica*, n.s., 10, no. 2 (1968): 144.

4. Barclay, "Arab Community," 143–144.

5. Personal communication from Dr. Frank Tough, Native Studies, University of Saskatchewan, March 1989.

6. Peter Baker, *Memoirs of an Arctic Arab: The Story of a Free-Trader in Northern Canada* (Yellowknife: Yellowknife Publishing Company, 1976).

7. D. H. Hamdani, *Muslims in Canada: A Century of Settlement 1871–1976* (Ottawa: Council of Muslim Communities of Canada, 1978), p. 29.

8. Lila Fahlman, "A Study of the Lebanese Muslim Community in Edmonton" (paper, Department of Religious Studies, University of Alberta, June, 1979), p. 9.

9. Fahlman, *A Study*, p. 8.

10. H. S. Abu-Izzedin, *Lebanon and Its Provinces* (Beirut: Khayats & Company, 1963), p. 13.

11. David Urquhart, *The Lebanon: A History and a Diary* (London: Oxford University Press, 1860), vol. 1, p. 1.

12. A. I. Tannous, "Social Change in an Arab Village," *American Sociological Review* 6, no. 5 (1941): 662.

13. See Xavier De Phanol, *The World of Islam* (Ithaca: Cornell University Press, 1959), and comments by Oleg Grabar, *The Formation of Islamic Art* (New Haven: Yale University Press, 1973), especially chapter 1. Juan Campo, *The Other Sides of Paradise* (Columbia: University of South Carolina Press, 1991), argues that Islam's sensitivity to spatial symbolism has influenced the construction of believers' homes.

14. Emrys L. Peters, "The Status of Women in Four Middle East Communities," in Lois Beck and Nikki Keddie, eds., *Women in the Muslim World* (Cambridge: Harvard University Press, 1976), p. 341.

15. Recorded in discussion summary in *Crossing Frontiers*, ed. Dick Harrison (Edmonton: University of Alberta Press, 1979), p. 7.

16. "Old-timer remembers young days as a pedlar [sic]," *Edmonton Journal*, Monday, August 25, 1980, section B3.

17. Barclay, "An Arab Community," p. 143.

18. John Gulick, *Social Structure and Culture Change in a Lebanese Village* (New York: Fund Publications in Anthropology, no. 21, 1955), p. 127.

19. Samir Khalaf, "Family Associations in Lebanon," *Journal of Comparative Family Studies* 2 (1971): 236.

20. Gulick, *Social Structure*, p. 145.

21. See Fuad I. Khuri, *From Village to Suburb: Order and Change in Greater Beirut* (Chicago: University of Chicago Press, 1975), p. 24.

22. See Arthur Jeffrey, "The Family in Islam," in *The Family: Its Future and Destiny*, R. Anshen, ed. (New York: Harper, 1959), emphasis added. For a fuller discussion of Muslim family life in North America, see Earle H. Waugh, Sharon M. Abu-Laban, and Regular B. Qureshi, eds. *Muslim Families in North America* (Edmonton: University of Alberta Press, 1991).

23. Jay Goldstein and Alexander Segall, *Intermarriage and Ethnic Identity: A*

Comparison of Adult Offspring of Mixed and Non-Mixed Marriages (Winnipeg: Winnipeg Area Study Report no. 2, 1983), p. 20.

24. Interview, July 1989.

25. Barclay, "An Arab Community," p. 152.

26. Interview, July 1989.

27. Ibid., 152.

28. The program was one of eleven half-hour films on religious diversity in Alberta which I developed in conjunction with Donald Spence of the Department of Radio and Television, University of Alberta, Edmonton. The films were built upon the notion that a distinctive religious group would choose a family, and the religious life of the group would be explored through that family and community.

29. See Salem Qureshi, "The Muslim Family: The Scriptural Framework," in Waugh et al., *Muslim Families*, pp. 12–60.

30. "Canadians today are more tolerant to intermarriage," *The Gallup Report* (Ottawa: Canadian Institute of Public Opinion, June 2, 1983).

Swaminarayan Hindu Temple of Glen Ellyn, Illinois

RAYMOND BRADY WILLIAMS

O N MEMORIAL DAY WEEKEND in 1971 ten Swaminarayan Hindus from Chicago joined about forty newly arrived immigrants from the Indian subcontinent on the banks of the Mississippi River at Davenport, Iowa. There they immersed some of the ashes from the cremation of their spiritual leader, Jnanjivandas Swami (1891–1971), who had died earlier that year in their native state of Gujarat in India. Leaders in India had decided that portions of the ashes would be sent to sanctify major rivers where Swaminarayan Hindus lived: the Ganges in India, Murchison Falls in East Africa, the Thames in London, and finally the Mississippi somewhere near Chicago. The small group gathered at a park in Davenport, where, in the presence of astonished fishermen and onlookers, a brahmin follower performed the appropriate final rites and lowered the ashes into the river. Now some two hundred people from the Bochasanwasi Swaminarayan Hindu Temple in Glen Ellyn visit that sacred spot each July for a worship service and picnic in an annual celebration of the founding event.

A few months before his death, Jnanjivandas Swami, who was affectionately called Yogiji Maharaj, had traveled to install Swaminarayan images in the group's first temple in England. Pilgrims from several countries came to see Yogiji Maharaj and to celebrate the occasion. One of the pilgrims was K. C. Patel, a chemistry instructor at Brooklyn College in New York who had been an active participant in Swaminarayan youth affairs before he emigrated to the U.S. Yogiji Maharaj commissioned Patel to organize the Swaminarayan followers in the United States and appointed him founding president.

At that time Swaminarayan Hindus were very few and widely scattered in America. Yogiji Maharaj had the names of twenty-eight followers, mostly students, and he wrote to each one, asking that they contact K. C. Patel. He also sent to the U.S. four *sadhus* who were traveling with him—young men who had taken vows to "renounce the world" and serve as Swaminarayan religious specialists—along with a leader having long experience among Swaminarayan Hindu immigrants in Kenya, to assist in the task. The group arrived in August 1970 and toured for forty-five days—in New York City, Buffalo, and Webster, New York; Newark and Hoboken, New Jersey; Cleveland, Youngstown, and Cincinnati, Ohio; Boston and Chicago— attempting to contact the twenty-eight and any other devotees or potential followers they could locate.

In India sadhus travel from village to village on tours called *padhramani*, and in each village they bless any homes that are opened to them. During their brief stay in Chicago in 1970, the sadhus visited six Gujarati homes, made the Swaminarayan followers known to one another, and encouraged them to begin regular meetings and to observe Swaminarayan discipline. Three started to meet regularly every Sunday in their homes, and similar small gatherings were started in other cities at the same time.

These pioneers were the first of the "new ethnics" from India to take advantage of the dramatic structural changes incorporated in the U.S. Immigration Act of 1965, a law proposed by President John F. Kennedy and signed by President Lyndon Johnson in the shadow of the Statue of Liberty. Before 1965, only a hundred people from India were admitted per year as permanent residents, even though many Indians had studied in American graduate schools. These restrictions had been established by the Immigration Act of 1924 and the Nationality Act of 1952 (McCarran-Walter Act), which assigned to each country an annual quota based on the national origins of the U.S. population in 1890. Approximately 90 percent of the places were reserved for persons from northern and western Europe, thus perpetuating the pattern of the "old immigrants" that figures prominently in the other congregations of this study. From 1820 to 1960, only 13,607 persons emigrated from India to the U.S.[1] The Immigration Act of 1965 changed all that by admitting immigrants equally from every country, with each country permitted a quota of at least 20,000 persons a year. The quota from India is always filled, with a long waiting list, and immigrants from India, along with other new ethnics from Asia, are rapidly changing the religious landscape of America, as did the old ethnics of previous generations.

Swaminarayan Hindus entered America after 1965 as part of a well-educated, technologically and scientifically trained, and upwardly mobile immigrant group. Two of the preference categories established in the new act shaped the character of the new community. One dictated that preference be given to top graduates of universities and professional schools and to those with scientific and technical skills needed in the American economy of the late 1960s and 1970s. Thus, the first new ethnics from India were not "your tired, your poor, your huddled masses, yearning to be free" but scientists, engineers, computer programmers, doctors, lawyers, and other professionals looking to expand their skills and opportunities in a First World country. They were competent, energetic, and soon affluent, and they were able to establish themselves quickly and successfully, along with institutions to serve their growing community. By 1979, as reported in the 1980 census, the median household income of the 387,223 persons designated for the first time as "Asian Indians" ranked second highest among ethnic groups in the country at $25,644; the median income for the country was $16,841. Many of these young professionals went back to India or England for arranged marriages and brought brides to the U.S. Since 1980, however, most new immigrants have come under the preference category for family reunification, which admits "brothers and sisters of U.S. citizens (at least 21 years of age) and their spouses and children," a provision that is changing the educational, professional, and economic profile of the Asian-Indian community. Some who come under the family-reunification provision do not have the elite educational or professional standing of the earlier immigrants. Relegated to low-paying jobs or remaining unemployed for long periods, they must rely on their extended families for long-term support. This has created a two-tiered social and economic structure among Asian Indians. Some of the participants in the Glen Ellyn temple are very successful engineers, scientists, and researchers; others, who have come more recently to join family members, work for minimum hourly wages in shops and restaurants. A revision of the immigration law in 1990 increased the total number to be admitted and strengthened the preference for highly educated and skilled immigrants, which will again change the character of immigrants. Official statistics are not available for the number of Gujaratis who have entered the U.S., but my informal estimate is that 40 percent of Asian Indians are Gujaratis (many of them with the surname of Patel), although they may have entered the country after long residence in Bombay, East Africa, or England.

The close relation between Swaminarayan religious commitment and Gujarati cultural identity at the Glen Ellyn Swaminarayan Temple is clear in a profile of those in attendance in September 1990. All were Asian Indians, and most were born in Gujarat state. More than 90 percent used Gujarati as the primary language at home. Almost half had lived in the U.S. for less than five years, and over half had participated in the temple for fewer than five years. Hence, the Swaminarayan group is growing rapidly because of the continued immigration of Gujarati Hindus from India.

The placing of ashes of Yogiji Maharaj in the Mississippi by some of these new immigrants was a symbolic way of connecting their new home with the sacred traditions, places, and people of India, and of marking the introduction of a novel, energetic, and successful religious community into the U.S. The Swaminarayan temple eventually built in Glen Ellyn and the people who worship there represent one of the "new religions"—new from the perspective of most of their neighbors—of the new ethnics. It was probably the case in 1970 that not one person in Chicago outside the universities, and very few within them, knew anything about Swaminarayan Hinduism. If a little girl says to her playmate, "I am Southern Baptist. What are you?" and the reply is, "I am Swaminarayan," what kind of answer is that?

Swaminarayan Hinduism

Hinduism as an immigrant religion is so new to the U.S. and so varied in its manifestations that it is necessary for both the immigrants and those who study them to distinguish one Hindu group from others. Swaminarayan Hinduism results from a religious reform movement begun in the nineteenth century by Sahajanand Swami (1781–1830), who was worshiped by his followers as a divine manifestation (*avatara*) for the modern age and the human form of the highest divine reality (*purushottam*).[2] Sahajanand Swami was born in the Hindi-speaking area of what is now the state of Uttar Pradesh in India. After a pilgrimage to visit the sacred temples and holy men throughout India and after taking initiation as a sadhu, he settled in Gujarat in 1802 to reform religious practices and establish a new religious community.

British control was extending into Gujarat at that time, and Gujarati society was moving from medieval to modern structures. Sahajanand Swami traveled through most of what is now the state of Gujarat to reform elements of religious devotion (*bhakti*) and discipline (*dharma*). He inspired in followers an intense devotion to manifestations of the Hindu god Vishnu. Several forms of images of Vishnu were placed in the temples he built and dedicated, along with the popular images of Radha and Krishna that are in all the temples. This divine couple is prominent in the Hindu pantheon and literature, Krishna being a manifestation (*avatara*) of Vishnu and Radha being the primary devotee. Krishna is the wise teacher of the *Bhagavad Gita* and the hero of one of the most widely known collections of sacred stories, the *Bhagavata Purana*. Images of Krishna and Radha are found in all Swaminarayan temples. It seems that in the early days some followers thought of Sahajanand as a manifestation of Krishna, but now Sahajanand is given preeminence in both ritual and doctrine. He also reinstated acts of public and private devotion: singing devotional songs, serving the images in the temples, prostrating before the images of gods, listening to religious discourses, and mentally worshiping god. The line separating the human from the divine is very narrow in India, and even during his lifetime followers accepted Sahajanand as a modern manifestation of Krishna, a manifestation of Vishnu, or the perfect manifestation of the highest reality. He was given the title Swaminarayan (Narayan is one of the names of Vishnu), and images of him were installed in temples throughout Gujarat. His reform, which was somewhat puritanical but not fundamentalist, was one mode of Hindu adaptation to modernization in India, sometimes called neohinduism, and it has proven very adaptable to the American religious scene.

Sahajanand Swami's message of religious devotion and fervor, linked with a strict discipline, attracted a large following. The ritual of initiation includes the pouring of a little water over the right hand, a vow ("I give over to Swaminarayan my mind, body, wealth, and the sins of previous birth"), an introduction to the Swaminarayan mantra, and a gift of a double strand of tulsi beads, to be worn around the neck as the sign that one is a devotee (*satsangi*), which most followers in Chicago import from India and wear. Aspects of the discipline for lay followers, known as *householders*, are summarized in five primary vows instituted by Sahajanand Swami; these form the basic structures of discipline and moral teaching in the Glen Ellyn temple. The first vow, not to eat meat, has corollaries in injunctions to follow a nonviolent manner of life (*ahimsa*). Swaminarayan teaching about nonviolence in word and deed parallels teachings of Mahatma Gandhi, the later, most famous son of Gujarat. As an extension of the doctrine of nonviolence, leaders in the temple in Glen Ellyn avoid, whenever possible, any conflict, controversy, or court action. The second vow is to avoid all intoxicating drinks and drugs. Sahajanand Swami opposed the opium trade of the British and decried its malevolent effects in Gujarat. It is common now for the temple to sponsor "anti-addiction campaigns." The third vow is to avoid adultery, and many accompanying restrictions are intended to reduce the occasions for and temptations to promiscuity. Men and women are separated in Swaminarayan meetings, and modesty in dress and behavior is encouraged. The fourth vow is to respect the property rights of others and not to steal. Honesty in business and truth-telling are virtues implied by this vow. People are enjoined in the temple to conduct their personal and business affairs in strict honesty, and speakers report with pride their sense that Swaminarayan businessmen are highly respected for their honesty. The final vow was, originally, not to eat or drink anything served by a person from a defiling caste, but now that prohibition has been broadened and softened, both in India and in the U.S., to say that followers will never defile themselves or others. Caste distinctions are not attacked in the temple, but such distinctions are muted by many aspects of practice in this sect: for example, common meals are prepared by non-brahmins but eaten by all present, and men are initiated as sadhus from castes previously thought to be polluting.[3] Much study remains to be done in the Asian-Indian community regarding the role of caste in community affairs. With the exception of the final vow, the discipline encouraged by these vows undergirds both economic and social success by Swaminarayan immigrants and provides a core of ideals for transmission to children of the second generation in the Glen Ellyn temple.

Sahajanand Swami's major reform was to institute a strict code of behavior for some two thousand men who "renounced the world" and became sadhus in an attempt both to gain salvation and to become religious leaders. Sadhus constitute an elite corps who enhance values by their acts of renouncing family ties, prosperity, appetizing food, and social involvement, thereby providing a mirror image of what many Gujaratis, including Swaminarayan householders, value highly. Swaminarayan followers say they are "successful" in family, business, and society "through the blessings of god." This paradox is at the heart of the relationship between the householders and the "world renouncers" and is a very important aspect of the relation between the lay-administered temple in Glen Ellyn and the religious leaders and institution in India. According to one traditional pattern in the ancient Vedic scriptures, men of the three "twice-born" groups—brahmins (priests), kshatriyas (warriors and rulers), and vaishyas (merchants and craftsmen)—go through four stages of life: student, householder, religious seeker, and world-renouncer. In sects of modern Hinduism it is more common for a young man to choose to become either a householder or world-renouncer (sadhu) and to follow his chosen path for the rest of his life. Some older men and women among the Swaminarayan satsangis have now begun to live celibate lives and devote themselves entirely to religious activities, in a kind of modified world-renunciation. A few in the U.S. have done that, including some in Chicago.

The sadhus, who are called "saints" by the householders, take a strict vow of celibacy that also involves many prohibitions of contact with women or with any object of sexual desire. They cannot even look at or stand close to a woman. Sadhus renounce all family ties and never return to their homes or engage in conversation with their parents. Their new status is signified by a new name given at the time of initiation. The name includes the suffix *das*, which means "servant," to indicate that they have taken a vow to avoid the pride of ego. The ideal is a humility expressed by nonaggressiveness and by service to god through service to the satsangis. A visible expression of self-denial is the renunciation of attachment to objects of the senses, demonstrated in regulations regarding fasting and controlling the intake of food. Sadhus regularly mix their food with water in their bowls to mask the taste of fine Gujarati food, even though the very best of Gujarati cuisine is offered to the deities in the temple. Especially in the nineteenth century, the sadhus entered a very hard life because they traveled through the villages of Gujarat, begged for their food, preached in the face of strong opposition, and engaged in physical labor to build temples and temple water reservoirs.

By the time of his death, Sahajanand Swami left a substantial legacy in a reformed Swaminarayan Hinduism. A large corps of sadhus provided religious leadership to scores of thousands of followers throughout Gujarat. Eight major temples contained images of Vishnu, Krishna, and Swaminarayan. Four sacred scriptures were added to the large Hindu canon: *Shikshapatri, Vachanamritam, Satsangijivan,* and *Lekh*. The first three are read in meetings in the Glen Ellyn temple and are sectarian literature, but the important and more universal Sanskrit Hindu scriptures, like the Vedas and the *Bhagavad Gita,* are also quoted as sacred scripture. Thus the major institutions of Swaminarayan Hinduism were established in Gujarat during the nineteenth century.

Yogiji Maharaj and the immigrants who honored him with final rites at Davenport in 1971 and later established the temple in Glen Ellyn were, however, members of a reform group that broke away from the leadership of the Vadtal temple in India because of differences in doctrine and practice. In 1906 a sadhu named Yagnapurushdas (1865–1951), popularly known as Shastri Maharaj, left the Vadtal temple and was

TABLE 1

Line of Succession and Pictures in the Temple Shrine

Gunatitanand Swami	1785–1867 (brahmin, priest caste)
Pragji Bhakta	1829–1897 (shudra, tailor caste)
Yagnapurushdas (Shastri Maharaj)	1865–1951 (vaishya, merchant caste)
Jnanjivandas (Yogiji Maharaj)	1891–1971 (vaishya, merchant caste)
Narayanswarupdas (Pramukh Swami)	1921– (vaishya, merchant caste)

expelled from the fellowship along with a few sadhus and householders because his efforts to reestablish strict discipline for the sadhus in matters of poverty, chastity, and ritual observance were disruptive. Shastri Maharaj also taught a doctrine considered heretical by leaders in Vadtal, that Swaminarayan had appointed one of his close followers, Gunatitanand Swami (1785–1867), to be his spiritual successor. He taught that Swaminarayan promised he would always be manifest in the world among his devotees in the person of his chief, perfect devotee, who thereby becomes the "abode of god." The doctrine involves interpretation of two terms in Hindu philosophy: *purushottam*, the highest supreme person or reality, of which Swaminarayan is the manifestation, and *akshar*, the abode of god.[4] Shastri Maharaj taught that akshar has two forms: the impersonal form as a heavenly abode—so that followers speak of the deceased as "going to *akshardham"*—and a personal form always manifest in the perfect devotee, who is the legitimate spiritual leader of Swaminarayan Hinduism. The collected talks of Gunatitanand Swami in the *Swamini Vato* are an additional sacred scripture for this branch of Swaminarayan Hinduism and are read and commented on in the Glen Ellyn temple. Affirming this doctrinal position, the legal name in India of the sect founded by Shastri Maharaj is the Bochasanwasi Akshar Purushottam Sanstha. A significant temple associated with this group is in the town of Bochasan (and *sanstha* is the word for "organization"). The legal name in the United States is the Bochasanwasi Swaminarayan Sanstha.

Yogiji Maharaj is revered as the fourth in the spiritual hierarchy following Gunatitanand Swami; Pragji Bhakta (1829–97), who was not a sadhu; and Shastri Maharaj (see table 1). An image of Gunatitanand Swami is placed in the central shrine of each Akshar Purushottam temple, at the side of the image of Swaminarayan. Pictorial images of his successors are placed in the temples for worship, and the current representative of the hierarchy, Narayanswarupdas (1921–)—known by followers as "Pramukh Swami"—is given honors as the divine abode of god. Some followers call him god. Shastri Maharaj and his successors have been both spiritual leaders (*gurus*) and administrators of this organization.

Although not as large in membership or number of temples, nor as wealthy as the two dioceses of Amdavad and Vadtal (which are represented in the U.S. by the International Swaminarayan Satsang Organization and the International Swaminarayan Satsang Mandal), the Bochasanwasi Akshar Purushottam Sanstha grew rapidly in India during the tenure of Yogiji Maharaj. He was particularly effective in gaining the allegiance of young students, some of whom traveled with him on tours through the villages during their school vacations. Indeed, a few of the men who became leaders in the U.S., including leaders in the Glen Ellyn temple, had been initiated by Yogiji Maharaj or had spent vacations with him and other sadhus. The dedication of the new temple in London in 1970 provided the occasion for the gathering of people from India, East Africa, England, and the U.S. who had been influenced by him, and out of that meeting came the new initiative to establish Swaminarayan Hinduism in the U.S.

Yogiji Maharaj's death in early 1971, only a few months after he returned to India, was a severe blow to the entire organization, but especially to the nascent group in the U.S. Nevertheless, allegiance was quickly transferred to Narayanswarupdas, who, it was said, had been designated by Yogiji Maharaj and confirmed by leaders in India. Narayanswarupdas was born in the village of Chansad in the Baroda district of Gujarat, and, after four years in the village elementary school, he joined a group of Swaminarayan ascetics. He was initiated by Shastri Maharaj in 1940 and spent some time in Sanskrit studies. Following assignments as an administrator of the large temple in Sarangpur and three years as private secretary to Yogiji Maharaj, he was appointed president of the Bochasanwasi Akshar Purushottam Sanstha in 1950, when he was only twenty-eight years old (hence his title Pramukh Swami, which is translated as President Swami). He was intimately involved in plans and strategies for growth from that time. As one leader in Chicago said: "Yogiji Maharaj was the heart, and Pramukh Swami was the head. They worked in perfect harmony." Since 1971, Pramukh Swami has been accepted as the abode of god and has been both spiritual guide and the chief executive officer of the sanstha. Growth has been dramatic worldwide under his guidance, as exemplified in the U.S. and Chicago, where the beginnings had been so small.

Gathering the Sanstha: Group Formation (1970–1974)

As with some earlier immigrant groups, Swaminarayan Hindus did not bring their religious leaders with them when they came as immigrants— indeed, their sadhus have not been permitted to establish residence abroad, even though the satsangis request them to stay for extended periods. The leadership of the movement and the temple in Glen Ellyn has thus been in the hands of students and householders who have administered the institution, performed the rituals, taught the sacred scriptures, performed menial service, and propagated the religion at the same time they were establishing themselves in professions and fami- lies. The Swaminarayan movement, both in Chicago and nationally, has been developed and led by laymen (householders) appointed by Yogiji Maharaj or Pramukh Swami, and that is a distinctive characteristic of the group. No seminary or similar institution for theological education could exist in the U.S. for this group, and none is contemplated. The training of religious specialists must be done in India, and any young man who wishes to become a sadhu must reside there permanently.

In February 1971 the Bochasanwasi Swaminarayan Sanstha was in- corporated as a nonprofit religious organization in the state of New York and licensed to operate in several states, including Illinois; in June of that year, K. C. Patel purchased a house in Flushing, New York, which became both the national headquarters and a place of meeting for fol- lowers on the East Coast.[5] The decision to have one national headquar- ters and a board of trustees that has control of all activities of satellite temples and centers throughout the country determined the adaptive organizational strategy of this ethnic-religious group. A similar structure would have been imposed on American Roman Catholicism if an 1890 petition made to Pope Leo XIII had been approved. In the petition some American Catholics asked for the establishment of ethnic dioceses so that each nationality could worship in a separate church where the mother tongue would be used and taught in the parochial schools.[6] Bo- chasanwasi Swaminarayan Hindus do have a national ethnic-religious diocese, and decisions about all activities are taken by a single national board of trustees. Hence, the Glen Ellyn temple in Chicago is not an independent institution but a satellite of the national organization. It seems unlikely that such a strategy could survive for a large and growing organization apart from centralized authority vested in the guru and validated by the history and theology of the group.

About the same time as the incorporation, three families began to have weekly meetings every Sunday evening in Chicago, moving weekly from home to home, a practice that continued until growth in numbers made it impractical. Invitations to other Gujarati immigrants were extended by word of mouth and in makeshift advertisements placed on community bulletin boards of grocery stores and shops that began to cater to the immigrants from India and Pakistan. These provided the first ethnic media centers.

Homes were the first meeting places and continued to be used for weekly meetings until the temple was built in Glen Ellyn. Most families associated with this branch of Swaminarayan Hinduism have home shrines containing images of Swaminarayan along with Gunatitanand Swami and other religious leaders. The shrine is the focus of daily morning and evening worship and of regular offerings of food prepared in the home. These shrines became the worship centers on Sunday evenings: the images were placed on a couch or table, and people sat on the floor before them. The simple services, led by one of the men, included devotional songs, chanting of the name of Swaminarayan, readings from the sacred texts, and, if anyone was prepared, a talk about the text or some aspect of Swaminarayan doctrine. After the concluding formal ritual of waving a flame in front of the images, the families enjoyed a Gujarati meal provided by the host family.

The structure and content of these meetings were adapted to the new situation of the families. Holding regular meetings on Sundays and observing festivals on the weekends were adaptations both to American work schedules and to the long distances followers had to travel to get to the temple. Some who led in these early meetings had been trained in the youth groups in India and had observed the sadhus, but they were not of the age, training, or standing that would have led them to take on major responsibilities in India or East Africa. In the States, however, they were thrust into leadership roles and had to learn by doing.

Religious commitments and gatherings helped to shape and preserve personal and group identity for these recent immigrants. As a group, they were "Made in the USA." No group with the same educational, professional, economic, and religious profile could be found anywhere in India or even in East Africa or England.[7] The challenge—indeed, the necessity—was to construct a new identity that would have as a component some reformulation of their memory of a past. The reformulation could conceivably entail a complete rejection of the past, but for most immigrants the process involves both constructing a new identity and reformulating the memory. Swaminarayan Hindus have intentionally preserved elements of Gujarati identity in this process of reconstruction. Weekly meetings, even in small groups, were very important early in the process. Such meetings provided the only occasion outside their family circle where they could without self-consciousness speak Gujarati, wear Gujarati apparel, sing familiar songs, and meet people from similar backgrounds who were facing many of the same problems of establishing themselves in a foreign land. These were not simply feasts or social gatherings; here the immigrants reinforced a strong memory, anchored their identity in a transcendent realm, and provided a secure base from which they could negotiate their entry into the larger society.

Newly arrived immigrant groups are highly mobile in American society, and the membership was in constant flux in Chicago during the early days. New members were attracted from the growing Gujarati community, and if a sadhu in India or a leader in another city learned that a follower was moving to Chicago, a Chicago contact helped the newcomer get settled. Few newcomers had families to join in Chicago in the 1970s, so satsangis helped them get settled in a job and apartment and provided a small, familiar, ready-made social group, fulfilling many of the functions of an Indian extended family. The most appreciated service of the group during this period was to help Gujarati immigrants with housing, jobs, and friendship, providing an important network. Newcomers often stayed in homes of satsangis, after having been introduced by a letter from a relative or an acquaintance in Gujarat, but that was part of the general Gujarati hospitality rather than a specific Swaminarayan duty. Several were transferred by their companies into or away from Chicago, and those who tell the story of those early days can remember when each person arrived to contribute to the growth in numbers and programs. Some moved to other cities and established Swaminarayan meetings in their new homes in Boston, Toronto, Cleveland, Florida, and Connecticut. This migration provided a network for expansion, leadership, and administrative development. Personal knowledge of leaders and groups in other cities also helped to overcome the sense of isolation felt by many immigrant groups.

A goal that inspired enthusiasm across the country in the early 1970s was to establish a Swaminarayan temple. Leaders in the U.S. relied heavily on the earlier experience of Gujarati immigrants in establishing and sustaining a strong organization in East Africa. In September 1973, Mahendrabhai Patel, a prominent lawyer and Swaminarayan leader from Nairobi, Kenya, came to advise leaders and to review prospects for building a temple in New York. He visited Chicago and raised $3,500 for the temple project. This and other support from across the country made possible the purchase of additional property in Flushing as the site for the first temple and national headquarters in February 1974. During that summer Pramukh Swami came with a few sadhus to dedicate the site and to install images of Swaminarayan and Gunatitanand Swami in a temporary shrine in the basement of one of the houses on the property. Several satsangis rented a car, left Chicago on Friday evening, drove to New York, attended the ceremony, and drove back to Chicago in time for work on Monday morning. During the meeting, Pramukh Swami appointed Navrit Bharot and Ghanshyam Patel as officers in Chicago and the latter as one of five national trustees. Ghanshyam, a relatively young engineer, had been prominent in Swaminarayan affairs: he had traveled to Davenport in 1971, had been the first appointed secretary of the Chicago satsang and the first priest in the Glen Ellyn temple, had been the first to resign his job to give full-time service to the satsang, had served on the board of trustees of the national organization from the beginning, and hence was a prime example of the lay leadership of the movement. He persuaded Pramukh Swami to visit Chicago for several days during his first visit, a five-week stay in the U.S.

The same intellectual and administrative skills of the young men that enabled them to advance in their secular professions were successfully applied to organizing and leading their newly formed religious group. But the success was always attributed to the guidance of their leader: "It is because of the grace of Pramukh Swami." Pramukh Swami has a major role in both spiritual guidance and administrative decisions. Every major decision about organization and strategy is forwarded to him for final action—when and where to build a temple, its design, the appointment of officers, the allocation of resources. Before his followers take a matter to him, they analyze the elements of the situation, propose alternatives, and perhaps recommend a course of action. However, the final decision is his. He is worshiped because he is thought to be the perfect devotee of god and thereby the chief guide and exemplar for those who would do god's will and gain salvation.

Even though he is not engaged in worldly affairs, he responds to requests for advice about all institutional matters. His vow of poverty does not permit him to possess anything except clothing, worship and study articles, and simple eating utensils; nevertheless, he makes decisions for the sanstha involving millions of dollars. He has renounced householder status, but he advises individuals on a wide range of personal, professional, and financial decisions. Satsangis ask his advice about marriage contracts, decisions about having children, family disputes, and educational decisions. His life of renunciation contrasts in many ways with the "good life" the immigrants came to the U.S. to find, and his life and that of other sadhus provide a check on the worldliness of the immigrants' experience.

The role of Pramukh Swami, and of other sadhus to a lesser extent, is that of an "intimate stranger": he follows a discipline that removes him from all normal intercourse in human affairs, but that distance is precisely what allows him access to the most intimate details of personal, professional, economic, and religious life. Nothing is outside the scope of his influence and guidance, and his teaching and advice are received by satsangis as the word of god.[8] The juxtaposition of remoteness and intimacy is important in validating religious leadership in Hinduism and some other religions. That is intensified for immigrants because visits of Pramukh Swami and sadhus have been relatively rare, especially in the 1970s; when these leaders do visit, however, satsangis have more direct access to them than they would have amidst the huge crowds in India. One follower in Chicago said, "Pramukh Swami has nothing to gain from me because he has renounced the world, so I can share all my secrets and concerns with him, and he will deal with them without attachment." Followers trust his objectivity, and many believe he has divine powers. His private advice has many public effects, as followers carry out his advice in professional, social, and political affairs. He is the guru, and hence his visits are, as one leader said, "like a battery charge that energizes us."

Pramukh Swami came to Chicago for the first time in 1974 and visited ninety homes. The men who drove Pramukh Swami around remember the hectic schedule of driving him from place to place all day and staying up all night to plan the next day's visits. They remember his patience and good humor when they got lost, when families were not prepared to receive him, or when he faced rebuff by people who did not welcome his visit. He blessed the homes he visited by talking to the men of the family, performing a ritual of worship at the home shrine or before the image of Swaminarayan that always accompanies him, and occasionally by performing the simple ceremony of initiation for new followers. Such tours are important for cultivating the "market" for the satsang and, just as important, for bonding and training those who are already members and evaluating them for leadership. In 1974 followers went out from their homes for the first time to a public gathering in Chicago's

River Park District Hall. About 150 people attended, some 50 Swaminarayan satsangis joined by about 100 members of the Gujarat Cultural Association, a social group formed in 1973. Satsangis considered the first visit a great success because it increased their visibility in the Gujarati community.

Longing for a Home (1974–1984)

In 1974 the group asked for Pramukh Swami's blessing to obtain a place for a temple in Chicago, but he told them to wait until they were strong enough to obtain a suitable temple. For the next ten years about twenty-five staunch satsangi families could be counted on for financial support and attendance at the weekly meetings. The group met on Sundays in homes throughout the city and suburbs, taking the meeting to new areas and reaching new potential participants. They began also to have four or five general meetings (*samaiyo*) in rented halls—apartment-complex activity halls, YMCAs, and park district halls. These meetings were generally held on the weekend nearest a major festival in the general Hindu or specific Swaminarayan calendar. Most Swaminarayan satsangis and many other Gujaratis joined in these public meetings. Only after they obtained their own temple did they start eight or nine such large meetings a year.

Pramukh Swami returned to the U.S. in 1977 to install the images and dedicate the new temple in Flushing, New York. It was a $200,000 structure, for which many in Chicago had given contributions. Earlier in that year the Gujarat Cultural Association proposed to the Chicago satsangis that they jointly purchase a property that could be used for a temple and cultural center, because the Swaminarayan group was the strongest Gujarati religious group in the area. The satsangis took the proposal to Pramukh Swami in New York, but he told them not to join in that project. The policy everywhere is for Swaminarayan Hindus to have their own temple. He did, however, give them permission to start looking for property.

After the dedication in New York, Pramukh Swami visited Chicago for five days and visited over a hundred Gujarati homes. He reorganized and expanded the leadership base by appointing a committee of five men to lead in Chicago and the Midwest. During Pramukh Swami's visit they held a public meeting every evening in River Park District Hall, and between 600 and 700 people attended the weekend meetings. About fifty-five people had been attending the weekly Sunday meetings in the homes before 1977, but each visit by the sadhus increased the group's visibility. The number of people attending meetings and becoming sat-sangis continued to grow. Pramukh Swami returned in 1980 to gain sup-port for the bicentenary celebration of Swaminarayan's birth and for a new temple in Los Angeles. He was in Chicago for five days, during which his morning worship was held in the Helen Keller High School before 200 people each day and his evening meetings in River Park Dis-trict Hall were attended by more than 900.

The growth of an ethnic immigrant religious group occurs in four ways: (1) *through immigration,* as new immigrants who have previously been satsangis arrive and become active, (2) *through conversion of immi-grants* from the same ethnic group who had no previous contact with the satsang, (3) *through the birth and the maturing of children* in families of satsangis, and (4) *through conversion of persons from the host society.* Growth occurs in these ways in successive stages, but growth continues among representatives of each stage and even increases as the next stage is reached. Swaminarayan Hinduism in Chicago has developed through the first three stages, primarily through immigration, some through con-version of Gujarati immigrants, and now increasingly among the second generation that is reaching the age of religious participation. Only one person from the host society became active in the Chicago temple, and that happened after her marriage to an immigrant.

Tours of sadhus gradually increased in frequency, and the tour groups became larger, the tours longer, so that almost every summer during the 1980s Pramukh Swami or another senior sadhu traveled in the U.S. for several weeks, touching most Swaminarayan centers. Hundreds of Gujarati homes were visited. One of a handful of "senior saints" of the satsang in India was assigned by Pramukh Swami to lead each tour, and each tour had a carefully defined focus and purpose—institutional development, raising support for building temples or hold-ing large festivals, holding youth conferences, or encouraging those in the remote centers. In 1979 Mahant Swami, a leading sadhu, toured to publicize and gain support for the large festival held in India in April 1981. By 1979 the mailing list of satsangis in Illinois included fifty-nine residences, and most of those received a visit. Mahant Swami returned to Chicago in 1986 to gather financial support for building the temple in Houston, and again in 1990 to inform people about plans for a Cultural Festival of India to be held in New Jersey in 1991 and to inspire them to volunteer time, money, and services to make it a success.

Each tour group was carefully composed to provide the service and guidance the satsang required at that time, and a householder always traveled with the sadhus to take care of financial matters and public relations. Some of the sadhus are specialists—in public speaking, religious education, cooking, public relations, vocal and instrumental music, and youth activities. The great need felt by immigrants whose children were approaching the teen years in the early 1980s was for development of youth activities. Thus a group of sadhus led by Doctor Swami (many sadhus have nicknames, this one coming from his training in medical school before he renounced that to become a sadhu) conducted a youth camp in 1982 for eighty-three young men in Chicago and organized a youth group, the Yuvak Mandal, under the leadership of a newly arrived immigrant who had been a leader of youth activities in the temple in London. (In Gujarat, such youth camps attract up to twenty thousand young people.) This camp brought youths from the area to Chicago for several days' training in the doctrines and discipline of the group and in the Gujarati music and dance that accompany some celebrations.

Several senior sadhus who assist Pramukh Swami with administration have visited Chicago. Atmaswarupdas Swami toured America in 1987 to celebrate the tenth anniversary of the dedication of the first temple in Flushing, New York, and visited museums in several cities, including Chicago, to obtain advice about displays in a cultural center being built in India. In 1989 Doctor Swami returned to Chicago, visited over two hundred homes, presided at a general meeting for 900 people, and conducted a four-day conference for Chicago satsangis at the Vivekananda Ashram near Fennville, Michigan. More than two hundred sadhus came in 1991 for a Cultural Festival of India. Much of the formal and informal instruction of leaders is given by sadhus in public meetings and in personal conversations during these tours. Many of the prominent sadhus are well known to the people in Chicago; indeed, some sadhus and leaders in Chicago are from the same Indian village, attended the same schools, and even participated in Swaminarayan youth activities or Yogiji Maharaj's tours together. Twenty-six people in Chicago reported that they have a "close relative" who is a sadhu. The sadhus are, indeed, "intimate strangers."

About the time of Mahant Swami's visit in 1979, the women in Chicago began separate meetings in order to conform to the practice in India. Before this time the women in Chicago had taken an active part in leading the singing of sacred songs and other elements of the programs, in part because the meetings were very much like family services of worship in which the women normally take a leading role. The regulations for public Swaminarayan meetings everywhere are that, although women attend general meetings, they do not take leadership roles when men are present. Rather, they conduct separate women's meetings, which they organize and lead. Two reasons are given for this separation: it assists the sadhus in maintaining their vows not to have contact with women; and it provides for the advancement of women by giving them their own organizations and opportunities for leadership. The result is that now women are not a part of the local or national administrative structure as coordinators of activities or as board members. Women only "overhear" what the sadhus say to men in lectures, in the U.S. as in India, because sadhus are forbidden to speak directly to women, and women do not give lectures when men are present. The educational program for children and young people is arranged so that men teach boys and women teach girls in separate meetings.

The strict separation of women and their exclusion from leadership roles in mixed gatherings is not common among Hindus, so this regulation creates some negative responses and requires defense. And although the practice receives little overt criticism from either male or female satsangis, it is a practice that attracts some criticism from outsiders. Members generally respond that women are among the most devoted followers of Swaminarayan and that women's activities, over which the men have no control, provide the best training in religious leadership and freedom. Swaminarayan Hindus have not weakened these restrictions because of opposition in the U.S., nor have they moved to conform to American mores regarding participation of women in general meetings.

The men and women householders lacked detailed knowledge of the scriptures and traditions of the sanstha required for teaching and propagating the religion. A leadership training program in the form of a series of study books and graded examinations for youths and adults was therefore introduced to centers throughout the world from Amdavad, Gujarat, in 1973. The four-year program covers the following topics: in the first year, basic worship rituals, the life of Yogiji Maharaj, and the childhood of Sahajanand Swami; in the second year, important chants, basic rules, stories of Sahajanand Swami as a young ascetic; in the third year, continuation of the basic rules, the adult ministry of Sahajanand Swami, the life of Pragji Bhakta, and the sacred scriptures; and in the fourth year, biographies of saints, the life of Gunatitanand Swami, continuation of the adult ministry of Sahajanand Swami, the sacred scriptures, and elements of the akshar-purushottam doctrine. Examinations covering these topics are administered on the first Sunday of July each year at ten centers in the U.S.; approximately 25,000 people appear for the examinations each year at 400 centers worldwide. The papers are sent to Amdavad and are graded by "honorary teachers," most of whom are retired principals or teachers. From 1973 to 1989 people in Chicago have taken 121 of these examinations, and 91 received certificates for passing. This educational program was begun and is still administered by a school principal in Gujarat, who has given life-service to the project. Although the study books were of uneven quality during the early period and the standard of English problematic, the program has been very important in providing both the information and the confidence the householders in Chicago needed to lead the various programs of the satsang.

Search for a temple site in the Chicago area intensified in the early 1980s, and the members investigated many properties—abandoned church buildings, motels, business properties, and schools. K. C. Patel came to Chicago for a meeting in 1982 at which $50,000 was pledged for a temple, greatly boosting the confidence of local satsangis. They soon found a property near Des Plaines and prepared a plan of purchase and renovation that would have required $300,000, but when five leaders went to New York expecting to get approval, the site was rejected as unsatisfactory. They were given permission to raise an additional $150,000 for a temple project. (The typical financial arrangement has been that each center must be self-sufficient for regular expenses, but for purchase of properties for temples the national headquarters provides approximately one-half the cost as a loan.) The Chicago group started the long drive back from New York somewhat discouraged.

What then transpired had a Keystone Kop quality. In conversation in the car on the return trip, one person mentioned that he had seen a property for sale in Glen Ellyn, a suburb about twenty miles west of Chicago, so they decided to drive directly there. The building belonged to the Veterans of Foreign Wars, and the night's activities were well under way, but they gained entrance by asking, "Is Dr. Patel here?" (Patel is a very common name among Gujaratis.) Without revealing their purpose, they then inspected the entire building. Satisfied by the inspection, they contacted the agent the next day and began negotiations. They raised more money by obtaining mortgages on their homes, borrowing on their credit cards, and taking out personal loans. They asked

11.1 Bochasanwasi Swaminarayan Hindu Temple, 1992. Photograph by Raymond B. Williams.

a relative of the local president to contract Pramukh Swami in India to "get his blessing." They received his permission, and in April 1983 they purchased a property of six acres with a large building in Glen Ellyn for $250,000. They now had a home.

Members did much of the work of remodeling, removing the bar and dance floor (appurtenances contrary to their discipline), installing pictures of the deities in a temporary small shrine, and transforming the building into a Swaminarayan Hindu temple, all of which cost approximately $100,000. They now had ample space for more than the 80–100 people who had been attending on Sundays, and the numbers began to increase. The first formal meeting in the new temple was held on May 29, 1983, attended by 1,500 people, exactly twelve years after the ceremony at Davenport.

When the temple was opened, Ghanshyam Patel (mentioned above as one of the early members in Chicago), the first secretary, and a member of the national board of trustees, along with his wife, offered their life-service to the satsang without remuneration. It is not unusual for satsangis in India to offer volunteer service (*seva*) for periods of time or for people to move to the temple at the time of retirement to donate life-service, but Ghanshyam and his wife were relatively young to become the first to donate their life-service in the U.S. Pramukh Swami instructed them to move into a small apartment in the temple building to act as caretakers and appointed Ghanshyam to care for the images and perform the rituals of the temple as priest, or *pujari*. The couple donated all their possessions, including the wife's dowry of gold jewelry, which were put toward the construction of a memorial to Shastri Maharaj at Sarangpur in Gujarat. They served full-time in the temple in Glen Ellyn for several years, performing the daily rituals and supervising the weekly meetings. Most of the Swaminarayan temples in India have resident sadhus who perform the daily rituals and brahmin householders who perform some special rituals. Appointment of a person who is neither a sadhu nor a brahmin represented an adaptation to the situation in America. The couple also visited other cities in the Midwest—Racine, Milwaukee, Detroit, Indianapolis, and St. Louis—in attempts to establish centers where Gujarati immigrants lived.

The gala festival of dedication for the temple provided a strong statement to their neighbors about the presence of a large Asian-Indian community, the vitality of immigrant religion, and the new face of Hinduism in their midst. Pramukh Swami stayed in the U.S. for four months in the summer of 1984, during which he installed new images in the temple in New York and performed the formal rituals of installing the images in the new temples in Chicago and Los Angeles. The rituals were performed in the Glen Ellyn temple before a huge crowd. On the day before the installation, a large procession, with floats carrying both Pramukh Swami and the statues of the deities, intrigued bystanders as it moved down Chicago's Michigan Avenue, men dancing in front and women marching at the rear in beautiful saris with water pots and coconuts on their heads (a traditional Gujarati action of celebration), some performing joyful Gujarati stick dances. Few in Chicago had ever seen a display of this type, although such processions are common in India. A meeting of approximately 3,000 people at McCormick Place, the major convention center in Chicago, introduced Swaminarayan Hinduism to community leaders, to representatives of the media, and to members of the Asian-Indian community. Finally, four training seminars were held in a school building in Glen Ellyn for approximately 650 people from across the country. At the time of the dedication, all the loans and expenses for renovations of the temple had been repaid in full, and the satsangis were ready to consolidate their gains in their new home in Chicago.

Consolidation and Growth (1984–1988)

A striking growth in Asian-Indian religious organizations and the establishment of temples generally occurs when the immigrant population reaches a critical mass and when the children of the second generation begin to move from the home into contexts where they are influenced by peers and not just by their parents. New immigrant groups made up of relatively young professionals are confronted with a series of challenges, according to their age and family status. When they first arrive and become settled in jobs, they face the problem of arranging a marriage—most go back to India to choose a bride—and bringing the young wife to America. Then they need a way to care for their children without the support of grandparents or the extended family, especially if both parents work. When their children are from seven to twelve years old, the parents face the problem of helping them to become successful by American standards and still protect their ethnic identity. When the community reached that stage in the mid-1980s, a flurry of activity created Sunday schools, study groups, and temples. The most significant correlation at the time of temple building is the coming of age of the children of the ethnic or religious group. The temple in Glen Ellyn opened at about that stage of development of the Asian-Indian community in Chicago, and it was the first to do so because the Swaminarayan group was well organized and had a single leader who could make decisions for the satsang.

The Temple as Sacred Space

Even though it is quite different from Swaminarayan temples in India, satsangis are proud to show the Glen Ellyn temple to visitors and to introduce them to their deities housed there and to the concepts embodied there. Three types of Swaminarayan temples require different ritual attendance, and each occupies a different status. Temples or shrines that contain pictorial images of the deities are called Hari Mandirs and do not require the constant presence of a priest to perform the daily rituals; they are very much like home shrines in their ritual importance. The images first installed in the temple in New York were of this type, but these were subsequently replaced by a third type. A more elaborate temple has freestanding images of the deities. These images require the constant presence of sadhus, who act as priests and clothe the images in beautiful garments each day. The images are served food and drink and cared for in a royal manner. Because sadhus do not reside permanently abroad, none of the temples or centers in the U.S. has free-standing images. The temple in Glen Ellyn is of a third type: its images are statues, prepared in India and shipped to Chicago for installation, but these are not freestanding. They are painted as clothed and hence do not require the daily clothing and service by sadhus. This third type is a recent development both in the U.S. and in India; the images do require, however, the constant presence of a person, not necessarily a brahmin, to perform the daily rituals.

The images are at the front of the meeting hall on the ground floor of the Glen Ellyn temple, and they form the focal point of worship, framed by a beautifully carved wooden canopy. The central images are of Swaminarayan and Gunatitanand Swami, signifying the presence in the temple of the two eternal principles, purushottam, the supreme reality, and akshar, the abode of god. At the time of worship, attention is given to all the images by offering food and drink or by waving a flame in front of the images, but the image of Swaminarayan is given priority. To the viewer's right are framed pictures of the four successors of Gunatitanand Swami as the abode of god—Pragji Bhakta, Shastri Maharaj, Yogiji Maharaj, and Pramukh Swami—in a square, two above and two below.[9] These figures are portrayed in pictures in all the temples in the U.S., and the pictorial form indicates the status of the four as servants and perfect, humble devotees of Swaminarayan. Worship is ritually located in the devotional tradition of Hinduism, and the primary purpose of acts of worship is to gain personal salvation—release from the bonds of the world and entrance to the abode of god. It is thought that Pramukh Swami is the primary avenue to god and mediator of salvation. Hence, a large photograph of Pramukh Swami is displayed in front of this portion of the shrine, which reflects Pramukh Swami's status as the guru of the worshipers and the current manifestation of the akshar as the abode of god. Such pictures are prominently displayed in homes, offices, and businesses, thus uniting the worship, family, and work of satsangis.

Facing the viewer, left of the central images, are representations of Krishna and Radha. These images attract to the temple many Hindus who are not satsangis, including some who are not Gujaratis; they come to worship, to fulfill vows, and to participate in festivals. The presence of the Krishna image locates the Glen Ellyn temple squarely within the "great tradition" of Hinduism; it is not an isolated "little tradition." It is a new form and, satsangis would say, a reformed Hinduism, but not a new religion. Before the Swaminarayan temple was dedicated, the only Krishna images in an area temple were in the International Society for Krishna Consciousness temple, located first in Evanston and then on Chicago's North Shore. Now a Krishna shrine has been dedicated in the Hindu Temple of Greater Chicago at Lemont. Still, many devotees of Krishna, especially among the Gujaratis, find it convenient to visit the temple in Glen Ellyn. All these major images are adorned with garlands of flowers and donated jewelry, and gifts of flowers are placed before the images by the priest and by some worshipers when they enter the temple.

Against the side walls at the front, beside the canopy sheltering the main images, are two shrines, one for Hanuman and the other for Ganesh. Ganesh, the elephant-headed son of Shiva (one of the two major deities of the Hindu pantheon), is the most widely worshiped deity in India, with small shrines in temples, on sidewalks, and in village lanes. He is the god of prosperity and helps those who worship him to be successful. Hanuman is the monkey god, one of the figures of the epic *Ramayana*. In the epic, Hanuman aided the god Rama in defeating the demon-king and rescuing Rama's wife, Sita. Hence, Hanuman is thought to aid worshipers in overcoming evil powers, sickness, and other difficulties. In larger temple compounds, these shrines are at the entrance, where devotees stop to leave an offering and look at the images before going to the main shrines. The explanation for the presence of these two shrines slightly to the front and at the side of the main shrine is that worship at these shrines prepares worshipers to approach Swaminarayan freed from concern with worldly affairs so that they can focus fully on spiritual growth and salvation. Little attention seems to be paid to these shrines by worshipers who come to Sunday evening meetings, but on special days in the Hindu calendar reserved for festivals of Hanuman and Ganesh, they receive special worship and attention.

Rituals and Worship

The images require daily service by a resident priest, an office filled by Ghanshyam Patel from the temple's opening until 1989. Ghanshyam was an engineer from the merchant caste and an early immigrant under the professional preference category of the immigration law who had no training or qualifications to be priest except his long association with the Swaminarayan movement and his devotion. In 1989 Pramukh Swami assigned him and his wife to go to New York to give full-time service preparing for the Cultural Festival of India, and a new priest, Kiran Brahmbhatt, was appointed. Kiran is representative of the newer immigrants who entered under the provisions for family reunification. Sponsored by his sister in Racine, Wisconsin, he lived for a while with her family, took care of the children while she worked, and also worked at night at a doughnut shop. He had been an active participant in Swaminarayan activities in Baroda since 1972, and, after moving to Racine, he traveled to Chicago each weekend to participate in Swaminarayan meetings. One day in October 1989, Prakmuh Swami spoke to him by telephone from India and told him to move to the temple to donate full-time service as the priest and caretaker. He has been living in the temple since that time.

An important part of the Hindu tradition is the performance of certain Sanskrit rituals that accompany life-cycle ceremonies (*samskaras*) of Hindu families, such as the ceremonies for pregnancy, birth, marriage, and death, and also for some occasional events like house-warmings, the opening of a business, or the completion of a vow. It is customary that these Sanskrit rituals be performed by brahmins, and priests of neighboring Hindu temples in Lemont and Aurora, Illinois, and several independent brahmins advertised their availability to perform these rituals. In the spring of 1990 it was announced that Hemant Patel, a recent immigrant, was permanently available for the rituals. He came to the U.S. in 1985 after working for four and a half years in the Swaminarayan temple in the Dadar section of Bombay. His responsibilities were primarily in reception and cooking, but he traveled a great deal with Mahant Swami and learned from the sadhus how to perform some of the Sanskrit rituals. His services mean that satsangis at the Glen Ellyn temple do not have to attach themselves to religious specialists outside the group in order to observe these important Hindu rituals. The program of the temple is thus more comprehensive.

It would be customary in Hindu temples generally and in Swaminarayan temples in India that either sadhus or persons from the brahmin caste would act as temple priests. Caste distinctions were ignored, however, in the selection of Kiran and Hemant; devotion to Pramukh Swami and knowledge of Swaminarayan ritual derived from long participation took precedence over heredity. Each received some minimal direct instruction from sadhus about conducting the rituals, and Ghanshyam gave the new priest instructions for a week before he left for New

York. The rituals are somewhat attenuated from the full Sanskrit forms performed in large temples in India.

The priest's daily schedule is fixed by the rituals to be performed before the deities, in which he serves the deities as a servant would minister to a reigning monarch. The priest arises in time to wake the deities at 6:30 and perform the first morning worship (*puja*). He offers the deities food and drink, after which the curtain covering them is removed and they are prepared for visits by any devotees who come to the temple. Then the priest performs his morning worship and sings hymns before the deities. He then prepares food and at 11:30 makes an offering of the food to the deities. At noon they are prepared for the afternoon rest, which gives the priest freedom to leave the temple briefly to get supplies or run errands. At 3:30 the priest must return to the temple to prepare fruits to be offered to the deities at 4:00, when they awake from rest. He generally sings for a period between 4:30 and 5:00. After 5:30 he prepares food for the evening. At 6:00 he performs the evening worship (*arti*) and offers food again at 7:00. He cleans up from cooking by 8:00, when he performs the last act of worship and covers the images for the night. After that, he is free to read, study, or perform other duties around the temple until bedtime. It is a rigorous, exacting schedule, and during the week a lonely one. The rituals are performed even when no one else is present, and the same ritual schedule is observed even while the Sunday meetings are in session. The physical acts of service by the priest represent the mental worship that devotees are supposed to perform regularly as servants of god. Except for brief trips out in the afternoon, the priest stays in the temple all day, seven days a week. Occasionally people will come to the temple during the day to look at the images, "to have darshan," as they say. Or a person may come for a special ritual; it is the custom, for example, when a satsangi buys a new car, to bring it to the temple for blessing and then to take the priest for a ritual drive around the temple property. A few people who live nearby come after work for the evening worship. (Because only a few satsangis live near the temple, only ten or fifteen come to the temple daily.)[10]

The morning worship is incumbent upon sadhus as well as householders, but daily temple worship by householders is not required because each person is supposed to have a home shrine and ritual paraphernalia to perform morning worship. The prescribed ritual includes chanting, prayer, offering of food to the deities before having breakfast oneself, and reading of sacred texts. Some of the more devoted satsangis spend a longer period in puja than others, studying the texts, singing hymns, and meditating. A few spend an hour or more reading the *Vachanamritam* or some other sacred text. A surprising 90 percent of the Chicago satsangis reported that they perform the puja each day. A prescribed part of the puja for men is placing the sect mark (*tilak*) on the forehead, a U-shaped mark of yellow sandal paste with a red dot of kumkum powder in the center. The mark is similar to other marks associated with the god Vishnu, but the exact form is unique to the Swaminarayan movement. It is difficult for satsangis in Chicago to wear the sect mark to places of their secular employment or education, so only the most devout wear the mark during the week. A few of the young men have started to wear it at schools and universities. More, but not a majority, wear it on the weekends when they are with family and friends in the Glen Ellyn temple.

Recently Pramukh Swami instructed followers to conduct evening family worship in their homes. Families gather after supper in front of the picture of Pramukh Swami and other images for the singing of hymns, a reading of a chapter from one of the sacred texts, and silent meditation. The purpose of these periods of worship is to strengthen the family, to preserve the children in the Hindu tradition, and to increase the knowledge of satsang doctrines. Although the services are held by satsangis in India and other countries, they are particularly important for immigrants who are widely scattered, who face significant tensions in adjusting to a new cultural setting, and who are deeply concerned that their children will be led astray by American peers. The family in India is the primary locus of a person's identity and social welfare because relatively few resources to assure security—for example, care for the elderly or support during unemployment—are available outside the extended family. Asian-Indians generally see a major threat to family security in the individualism of American society, which many view as the source of its ills. Thus they have an overwhelming concern and strong desire to provide moral and religious training for the children that will preserve the unity of the family, traditional roles between parents and their children, and traditional attitudes toward sexual behavior and intoxicating drinks and drugs. Parents fear that they will have gained a whole world of material benefits and status in the U.S. but will lose their children. Thus the parents desire assistance from temples and religious groups in resisting complete assimilation.

The weekend meetings in the temple attract larger crowds than do the daily rituals. To the right and left of the images in the temple are platforms from which laymen conduct the weekly Sunday evening meetings from 4:30 until around 6:30. The meeting begins with chanting and an opening verse (*sloka*). Then an extensive account of Pramukh Swami's travels, activities, and pronouncements during the past fortnight is read. (Sadhu secretaries traveling with him prepare detailed minutes of all his activities and conversations, and these are distilled by sadhus in the headquarters temple in Amdavad into a report that is sent to all the temples and centers throughout the world to be read during the Sunday meetings.) Those present are very attentive and seem to identify with Pramukh Swami's actions and words, which bond the satsangis to him and also to leaders, groups, and temples in India and other parts of the world mentioned in the reports. On some occasions a videotaped message is presented. A reading from the *Vachanamritam* follows, designated for all the temples by a notice from Amdavad, and a lecture on that text by one of the men is given. A period of singing of hymns (bhajans) follows; some of these hymns were written by companions of Swaminarayan and others written more recently by sadhus. Men and boys study vocal and instrumental music in the temple and lead the singing. The singing is interspersed with lectures on topics of current interest; a program in 1990 included a talk on the life of Yogiji Maharaj and another about plans for the Cultural Festival of India. A second prescribed reading from sacred scripture is included, this one from the *Swamini Vato*, the collection of teachings of Gunatitanand Swami. In the earlier days in the U.S., the entire program, including lectures, was in Gujarati, but now some of the lectures are in English "so the young people can understand them more easily." An active attempt is made to involve the younger boys, and occasionally a boy, even as young as twelve years old, is invited to prepare a lecture for the group. After the concluding hymn, a closing chant is followed by the ceremony of waving a flame before the images of the deities.

A locked metal box for offerings rests immediately in front of the images, and people place offerings in the box as they enter or leave the temple. The treasurer or his representative sits near the entrance to receive contributions from any person who wishes to give and provides receipts. Annual income for the temple is estimated at $75,000 for regular expenses, but that does not include special contributions for such things as travel for sadhus when they visit, purchases of temples in other cities, special festivals and conventions held in other cities and countries, schools and hostels, or relief work in India. Some of these offerings go directly to the national office or to India, and there is no local accounting. Currently, the satsang seems to be very prosperous, and lack of funds does not seem to restrict its ambitious expansion programs.[11]

The Gujarati meal that is served in the basement fellowship hall following the meeting is a great attraction. Leaders joke that many people may not be present for the beginning of the meeting, but they are all present in time for the meal. The food is ritually presented to the deities upstairs and is therefore holy food (*prasad*). It is still customary for the meal to be provided by a family who pays for the food, but the crowds are too large for a single family to prepare the meal. Women come to the temple earlier in the day to cook. The type of food served helps to maintain ethnic identity and ties, but it has religious significance as well. Only vegetarian food is served in the temple and homes—lentils, rice, potatoes, cauliflower and other vegetables, breads, lentil soup, chutneys, fruits, and sweets—and part of the food is typically offered to the deity before being eaten as prasad. Some of the satsangis will eat only food that has been prepared in a satsangi home or in the temple and dedicated to the deity; they will not "eat outside."

Followers prepare the best of Gujarati foods for the special Annukunt ceremony, in which foods are displayed before the temple deities. The food is carefully prepared in the homes, beautifully displayed on risers before the temple images as a decoration, and then eaten by the satsangis, either in the temple or in their homes. Just as there is a complex relation between householders and sadhus, a corresponding complexity exists in the relation between the abundance, beauty, and tastiness of cuisine in the temples and homes and the denial of these qualities by the sadhus regularly and by the householders during fasts. The best is both affirmed in daily life and denied in special ritual circumstances, and both the affirmation and the denial enhance the ritual value of food.

The meal provides a reasonably accurate count of attendance because people in the kitchen count the number of plates used. Leaders send a detailed report of each meeting to the national office in New York, giving the attendance, names of participants, and information about any special visitors or guests. Attendance at the meetings has grown steadily since the temple was dedicated; discounting the highest and the lowest attendance in 1989, the numbers ranged from a low of 175 to a high of 450 for the Sunday meetings. The average attendance for July 1990 was 350, whereas the average attendance in 1986 was around 150.

People at the Glen Ellyn temple are very young, and visitors regularly remark on how few elderly people are present at meetings. Of those responding to the author's survey taken in September 1990, only 22 were over fifty years old, and only 4 of these were over sixty. Many children present were discouraged from completing the questionnaire, so only 14 persons under the age of eighteen responded, and an additional 17 people were under twenty-five.

Major sacred times in the general Hindu calendar or the special Swaminarayan calendar are observed with general meetings on the Saturday closest to the date in the lunar calendar. These events enable the devotees to recover the sacred dimension of existence by participating in the primordial past of Hindu mythology and the historical events from the career of Swaminarayan and the leading sadhus. Approximately ten of these are held each year, smaller ones in the temple and larger ones occasionally in rented halls. Diwali (the New Year festival of lights in October/November) and the birthday of Krishna (July/August) are the Hindu festivals that occasion the largest attendance (approximately 2,000), with the largest number of nonsatsangis. Holi (a festival of general merrymaking in February/March) is celebrated in a restrained manner in the Swaminarayan temple because Sahajanand Swami objected to the erotic songs and bawdy behavior during the Holi festival and instituted purified rituals that are now performed in Chicago by approximately 1,200 persons. These ecumenical Hindu festivals are significant for the temple because they provide the opportunity to inform and impress many people in the Asian-Indian community who may not yet be satsangis but who are favorably inclined to the Swaminarayan movement. If the festivals are conducted well, Swaminarayan Hinduism gains a good reputation within the larger community and reaches many potential members.

The celebration of Swaminarayan's birth coincides with the celebration of Rama's birth at Ramanavami (March/April), so the event is both ecumenical and sectarian, and attracts some 1,500 people. Other festivals are specific to Swaminarayan Hindus and generally attract a smaller attendance of 600–1,100 people. These events include Gurupurnima (June/July), when all Hindus show respect to their gurus and these Swaminarayan followers revere Pramukh Swami; Pramukh Swami's birthday (November/December); Gunatitanand Swami's birthday (September/October); and Yogiji Maharaj's birthday (April/May). These occasions punctuate the year with special emphases that break the monotony of weekly meetings. They are similar to the Christian observance of Christmas and Easter in that most people who are going to be active anytime during the year will be present for these events.

The programs of these general meetings are similar to the Sunday meeting, with chants, songs, and lectures. They conclude with the ritual of waving a flame before the images and partaking of sacred food in a Gujarati meal. Some of these festivals include the ritual offering of food on specially constructed platforms in front of the image. All types of Gujarati food, especially fruits and sweets, are brought from the homes and arranged in a beautiful display that extends across the front of the temple. The dynamic optimism of the Swaminarayan group is fueled by the steady rise in attendance at both the weekly and monthly meetings. Participants say that they always see new faces and new families, and many of these become active members after they first attend one of the festivals.

Respondents to a questionnaire in the Glen Ellyn temple report a very high level of religious devotion. Three-quarters report that their family has a home shrine (although a large number—about 10 percent—failed to respond to this question), and a surprising number (about 88 percent) report that they perform daily puja, which does not require a fixed shrine. A large number (69 percent) visit the temple at least once a week, and another group (22 percent) visit at least once a month. Over half (54 percent) live within twenty miles of the temple, and three-fourths within thirty miles. Regular fasts are a part of Swaminarayan religious discipline, and many (38 percent) fast at least once a week, and a few more (41 percent) fast at least once a month. Only a few (8 percent) indicate that they never fast. Travel to attend religious festivals is common, and a large number of respondents (35 percent) attended the bicentenary celebration of the birth of Swaminarayan in Amdavad in 1981. It is common for people to travel to other temples for festivals and major celebrations.

Almost all the respondents (96 percent) indicated that they are Swaminarayan satsangis. A significant number (32 percent) indicated, however, that they were not Swaminarayan satsangis prior to arrival in the U.S.—a vast majority were Hindus of a general tradition associated with Vishnu—which indicates the success of the Bochasanwasi Swaminarayan Sanstha in reaching Gujarati immigrants who were not associated with them in India. Some Swaminarayan members follow a religious tradition not shared by members of their family in India (19 percent) or in the U.S. (17 percent). A majority (57 percent) indicate that they are more active in religious affairs now than before they came to the U.S., and 21 percent say their level of activity is about the same. Having a relative who is a sadhu is thought to be especially auspicious, and about 17 percent of the worshipers in Chicago report that a close relative is a sadhu.

Programs and Organization

Religious education programs are held every week at the temple. The meetings for boys and girls began when the group was still meeting in homes. Now there are two groups for boys and two for girls. The Bal Mandal is for boys up to the age of thirteen, and twenty-five or thirty boys meet in the temple every Sunday from 2:00 to 4:00 P.M. Study includes Gujarati language, fundamentals of Swaminarayan rituals, chants, prayers, and songs, and basic moral instruction. Classes emphasize the importance of working hard in school, and the older boys help the younger ones with difficult schoolwork. The Balika Mandal for girls meets at the same time and has the same curriculum for about twenty-five girls.

The Kishore Mandal is for young men between the ages of fourteen and twenty-three and meets in the temple on Saturday evenings from 7:00 to 10:00. They have an hour-long class in Gujarati language; an activities period; study of the *Vachanamritam, Swamini Vato,* and other sacred scriptures; and a period for asking questions, discussing various subjects, and observing rituals. They are assigned homework or lectures to prepare, and a few practice Indian musical instruments. The group serves the satsang by serving meals, cleaning the temple and grounds, and directing parking for the large meetings. Six of the twenty-five youths who participate in Kishore Mandal contemplated taking the step to become Swaminarayan sadhus at the time of the Cultural Festival of India in 1991.

Youths who wish to become sadhus must have the written permission of their parents before Pramukh Swami will allow them to be initiated. They must spend a probationary period of at least six months living with the sadhus in India, gradually following their discipline, and engaging in their activities. If they still wish to become sadhus, they assume *parshad* status, when they wear white clothing and receive instruction in a temple in India. When the leaders of the training program think they are ready, Pramukh Swami decides to initiate them into the status of sadhu. It would be a dramatic change for young men raised in the U.S. and educated in American universities to "renounce the world" and take up the very demanding life of a sadhu in India. Many of the sadhus of this group are university-trained in India, East Africa, and England, but only a handful from the U.S.—and none yet from Chicago—have sought initiation.

The young women ages fourteen to twenty-three meet in the Kishorike Mandal on Sundays from 2:00 to 4:00 P.M. and have a program of instruction and activities similar to that of the young men. All of the programs are segregated: men teach boys, and women teach girls. A meeting of the young women with their mothers at the temple in 1990 included a very intense discussion about restrictions placed upon the young people regarding dating and friendships with people of the opposite sex. Such meetings facilitate discussion between the generations on these and similar issues of concern.

The young people of the second generation are just arriving at the age for marriage negotiations, which appear to be delayed in the U.S. both because of the extended period of higher education and because the procedures and prospects for marriage negotiations have not yet been worked out. It is expected that most of the young people will follow the wishes of their parents and enter arranged marriages. It is not essential that the young people marry Swaminarayan Hindus; indeed, caste, profession, educational, and economic standing, and even the concerns of traditional village marriage associations seem more important to the parents than sect affiliation. Nevertheless, anxiety about "proper marriage prospects" is high among parents and young people alike. National and international Swaminarayan gatherings provide the context for preliminary contacts regarding marriage, and marriage partners are available in India, East Africa, and England as well as the U.S. Occasionally Pramukh Swami gives advice about marriage partners, a function served by traditional marriage brokers in the past. In semiarranged marriages, the young people become acquainted, and the parents then follow their wishes in arranging the marriage. Too few of the young people in Chicago have married to make possible a prediction about what pattern will develop.

The meeting for adult women is from 2:00 to 4:00 P.M. on Sundays. Many of the women are at the temple earlier to cook the meals, and such preparations continue through the day. The women's meeting is organized and led by local women who occupy positions of honor among the women. The meetings include songs and hymns, study of the major sacred scriptures, lectures on the texts or other topics, and discussion of issues of concern to the women. No man is present for these meetings. In India, some Swaminarayan temples have separate shrines for the women, where no men are allowed, and the large festivals have periods when the program is conducted by women for women only. The young women develop deep respect for the older women who lead the meetings, and a strong attachment is formed.

The educational program is supplemented by a book stall at the temple entrance that is open for business during the meetings. Some of the books and pamphlets, published in Amdavad in both Gujarati and English, are directly related to the annual examinations given in the temple, and all the major aspects of doctrine, discipline, and ritual are dealt with in the published material. Audiocassettes of devotional music performed by some of the sadhus who have attained professional quality in their work and of lectures by Pramukh Swami and other learned sadhus are sold at cost. Recently, videocassettes of lectures, sacred concerts, and major festivals have also become available in the temple book stall. A publications coordinator directs the book stall as well as the annual examination program and any local printing and publication. All these media materials extend the educational program of the temple into the cars and homes of the people.

Leaders appointed by Pramukh Swami from among the male householders conduct the local program through a hierarchical administrative structure that reaches from the local temples and centers to the national office in New York. A new administrative system of coordinators was established in "Policy and Procedures" approved by Pramukh Swami and issued from the national office in June 1989, and the structures have become more complex as membership and the number of centers have increased. At first two officers headed the Glen Ellyn temple, a president and a secretary, and then a committee of five. Now in all temples a center coordinator directs the volunteer work of ten activities coordinators. They meet together in the temple once a month to give reports and discuss the program of the temple. As they sit in a circle for discussion, the coordinator of meetings reports on arrangements of programs for meetings and on the selection of men to lead and give lectures. The Bal Mandal coordinator reports on programs for the children, which give special emphasis to teaching the Gujarati language and involving parents in the religious education of their children. The coordinator of the Yuvak Mandal reports on plans for young people, with emphasis on Gujarati language, cultural programs, service activities (*seva*), and vocal and instrumental music—the larger centers are encouraged to develop a marching band. Training for children and young people is valued greatly by satsangis.

Other coordinators report on details of public relations and the upkeep of the temple. The public relations coordinator discusses relations with other Asian-Indian groups, with representatives of the news media, and with local dignitaries. The coordinator for general administration functions as a secretary, keeping records and mailing lists and communicating reports to the national office. The primary responsibility of the kitchen coordinator is to ensure that all functions of the kitchen—plans, procurement, and execution—run smoothly and flawlessly. He has a difficult charge because several hundred people eat at the temple each week. A committee of four or five women plans the menus and oversees the cooking. The maintenance coordinator acts as caretaker of the property, and the finance coordinator handles all the money, making the disbursements in accordance with guidelines from the national office.

The women's program does not have appointed coordinators, but respected women in the Chicago satsang direct local activities under the authority of the center coordinator. A gender difference is apparent in that a few women in the Glen Ellyn temple still exercise charismatic leadership, recognized because of their devotion, wisdom, and saintliness, whereas the recent administrative change has routinized the leadership positions of the men. On one occasion, women in the temple were engaged in communal work without an obvious "boss," but when one of the respected women got up to start a new activity, the younger women hastened to complete the work she had undertaken. She obviously had the respect and deference of the other women, and she organized the entire enterprise without giving any verbal instructions. That the role of women in the satsang is a sensitive issue is demonstrated by the fact that an administrative structure for conducting the Mahila (women's), Yuvati (young women's), and Balika (girls') activities in the U.S. is still being formalized. The forthcoming statement of policy could result in a similar routinizing of female leadership.

The administrative structure reaches from the Glen Ellyn temple to Pramukh Swami. The center coordinator for the Glen Ellyn temple and coordinators for other centers report to the regional coordinator, currently a Cleveland physician. Two national coordinators implement the decisions of the national board of trustees, which is the highest policy-making and governing body below Pramukh Swami. K. C. Patel continues to serve as president of the Swaminarayan Hindus in the U.S. Pramukh Swami is at the apex of the administrative structure and has final authority for all decisions. The authority of all these volunteers to perform their tasks—none is a salaried officer—is derived from Pramukh Swami's absolute authority in the sanstha. The centralization of administrative authority is one of the reasons that Swaminarayan Hinduism has developed so rapidly in Chicago and in other cities.

The local group in Glen Ellyn is firmly situated in a larger national and international network. Leaders and active members in Chicago are well acquainted with officers in New York and with their counterparts at other centers and temples. Conferences and workshops, for both young people and adults, bring members together from across the region and nation. Annual lengthy visits by sadhus provide occasions for people to gather, and some even travel with the sadhus to other parts of the country, both to visit friends and relatives and to participate in the programs conducted by the sadhus. In addition to personal contact, regular reports about Pramukh Swami's travels in India, East Africa, Europe, and North America provide information about leaders and programs everywhere and make the individual in Chicago feel part of a dynamic international movement.

In Indian culture it is difficult to separate secular tourism from religious pilgrimage because people customarily visit sacred shrines and holy men as they travel around India. In a similar manner, the trips of those returning to Gujarat to visit relatives and friends become also pilgrimages to visit Pramukh Swami, several major temples, and respected sadhus. A stopover in Bombay may include rest and worship at the Dadar temple, and a transfer of trains in Amdavad may permit a visit to the temple that serves as headquarters for the movement. Families from Chicago regularly return to India during school vacations—the flights are fully booked over the December vacation, which is the best time to visit Gujarat—and a group of young boys toured the major temples during the summer of 1990 before they visited individually with their relatives in Gujarat. A few men travel with Pramukh Swami for several days when they visit India. All these visits are occasions for strengthening Gujarati identity, forming close ties with Pramukh Swami and other sadhus, learning more about doctrine, rituals, and organization from experts in India, and, if the schedule permits, obtaining advice from Pramukh Swami about personal or family matters. Gujarat is the sacred land, the setting of events recorded in the sacred scriptures and stories told in the Glen Ellyn temple. Temples and shrines, with marble "footprints" of Swaminarayan and other saints, mark places where significant events of the sacred history took place. Tours link these sites in Gujarat with the sacred story told in the temples, and the link is more immediate for these immigrants who came directly from that land than are pilgrimages to Jerusalem for earlier immigrants from other lands and their descendants, who are Jews or Christians.

Swaminarayan Hindus make explicit in pilgrimages to holy sites a component of religious devotion still present in the tourism of many Americans, but ignored because it is thought of as a secular activity. Vacations to India are properly understood as sacred pilgrimages, not only for Swaminarayan Hindus but for other Asian Indians as well. Moreover, they are establishing new sites of pilgrimage in the U.S., as, for example, when they visit Davenport, Iowa, each Fourth of July— an unlikely pilgrimage site, except that it sits on a "sacred river"—and when they take vacation time to visit various temples in the U.S., usually when the sacred site is newly empowered by the presence of sadhus, most of all by Pramukh Swami. Other Hindus visit the major Venkateswara Temple in Penn Hills, Pennsylvania, the Ganesh Temple in New York, the two South Indian temples in Lemont and Aurora, Illinois, and the Meenakshi Temple near Houston. A study of the function of pilgrimages to Hindu temples in the adaptation and self-identification of the new Asian-Indian community would be an important contribution to understanding recent religious history in the U.S.

Strong ties of identity between the individual member in Chicago and Swaminarayan Hindus elsewhere is enhanced by large international festivals, which draw hundreds of thousands of participants. The first major festival held by the Bochasanwasi Akshar Purushottam Sanstha was at Amdavad for a month in 1981 on the bicentenary of the birth of Sahajanand Swami. It was a major statement of the recent growth and prosperity of the sanstha worldwide. A Cultural Festival of India was held at Alexandra Palace in London in 1985, during which Pramukh Swami was weighed in gold that had been contributed by followers to support the sanstha. Later that year another festival was held in Amdavad to mark the bicentenary of the birth of Gunatitanand Swami. These festivals are like religious state fairs, with imposing temporary monuments, cultural performances, food stalls, large meetings, and thousands of people. They provide a forward thrust, which seems to characterize the attitudes of active members, because they are usually focusing attention on an upcoming major event. Devotees from several countries donate time and money to support the festivals, and many travel to participate. Much of the consultation and interaction between Chicago satsangis and those from other centers and countries, along with many of the administrative decisions, takes place in the contexts of dedications of temples and these large festivals. The satsangis feel part of something grand, and some members describe one or another of the festivals as "a once-in-a-lifetime experience." Thirty-four satsangis from Chicago attended the festival in Amdavad in 1981, thirty-eight the festival of the birth of Gunatitanand in Gujarat in 1985, and sixteen the Cultural Feast of India in London in 1985. Leaders encouraged support and participation in a Cultural Festival of India in New Jersey in August 1991.

Public Relations

These tours and pilgrimages to Gujarat demonstrate the strong attachment to Gujarati culture that undergirds the ethnic strategy of adaptation followed by Swaminarayan Hindus at the Glen Ellyn temple. Immigrant religious groups from India are likely to adopt one of several strategies of adaptation: (1) National strategies focus on all-India festivals, deities, sacred texts, and religious leaders. They support a civic religion that synthesizes aspects of the religions of "Bharat," (the name for India as the sacred land), and celebrate major national holidays. Some temples include shrines of Jains and Sikhs as evidence of this national unity. (2) Ecumenical groups emphasize the "great tradition" of Hinduism and mute local or sectarian elements. Temples built according to this strategy include all the major Hindu deities and have programs in English to attract the widest possible ethnic diversity of people from India. English is the preferred language for worship and social gatherings. (3) Sectarian groups stress loyalty to a particular religious leader, who may unite people from many ethnic or national groups. (4) Ethnic strategies identify religion with elements of regional, language-based culture and deities that are at home in that culture. Gujarati or Tamil Christian groups demonstrate elements of this strategy.[12] These strategies are not mutually exclusive, and immigrant groups may move through more than one of these as numbers grow and time passes, moving unevenly through national, ecumenical, sectarian, and ethnic periods, and then perhaps back to ecumenical. Ethnic and sectarian groups attract the highest emotional response and attachment from members of the first generation. The beliefs of sectarian and national movements are more powerfully transmitted to members of the second

649

generation, in part, in the case of the latter, because they embody a new ethnic identity as Asian-Indian.

Swaminarayan Hindus in Chicago are following an ethnic adaptive strategy that attempts to maintain close ties between religious devotion and Gujarati culture. The key element in this strategy is the attempt to preserve Gujarati language through classes in the temple and by conducting all the meetings in Gujarati. The temple advertises in the Gujarati media and in newspapers and television programs that reach large numbers of Gujaratis. The songs, hymns, musical instruments, dress, and cuisine in the temple are Gujarati. A little bit of Gujarat exists in Glen Ellyn. The strategy has been remarkably effective in preserving the emotional attachment and loyalty of members of the first generation, who need not work to be at home with Gujarati culture, in part because the strategy combines ethnicity with sectarian loyalty to a personal guru, Pramukh Swami. The combination seems to be successful also among many of the older young people of the second generation. The younger children, however, have a difficult time appreciating Gujarati culture and understanding Gujarati, especially in its written form when it is used to deal with complex theological and philosophical concepts. An important test will come when few of the young people are familiar with Gujarati and when, as a result, too much of the time and resources of the satsang are required to remedy that deficiency.

But for now, the group negotiates its relations with other religious and cultural groups from a clearly defined ethnic and sectarian position: its ties to Gujarat and its loyalty to Pramukh Swami. Two other Swaminarayan groups, the International Swaminarayan Satsang Organization (ISSO) and the International Swaminarayan Satsang Mandal (ISSM), meet regularly in Chicago. They are affiliated with the dioceses of Amdavad and Vadtal in India and do not accept the leadership of Pramukh Swami or the doctrines supporting his position. The head of the Amdavad diocese, Acharya Tejendraprasad Pande, has visited Chicago several times. During the 1970s all Swaminarayan satsangis met together, but as the number of Gujaratis grew, greater social differentiation took place, and the two groups began to meet separately about 1980. The ISSM dedicated a temple in April 1992. The ISSO is a much smaller group and still meets in rented halls. They are about a decade behind the group in Glen Ellyn in size and organization.

Swaminarayan followers participate in some all-India associations, but serious divisions afflict these organizations in Chicago, and they

are largely ineffective. Groups sponsor competing parades on India Independence Day each August. Satsangis have little contact with the
programs of the Hindu Temple of Greater Chicago in Lemont or the
Venkateswara Temple in Aurora. In the early days, some leaders of
the International Society for Krishna Consciousness came to Swaminarayan meetings to invite the immigrants to visit the Hari Krishna
Temple, but they were not successful. No contact now exists between
the two organizations, even though the Hari Krishna devotees did act
as religious specialists for a while for some Asian-Indian immigrants.
The Swaminarayan group is noted among Asian Indians for their skill in
organizing large gatherings, for the wealth of the satsang, and for their
well-organized volunteer corps, which others envy. Other organizations
request the assistance of Swaminarayan leaders in planning and conducting large gatherings. In 1989 the Glen Ellyn temple received the
annual community award for public service given by the *India Tribune*, a
major weekly newspaper for Asian Indians in Chicago.

As an institution, the Swaminarayan temple in Glen Ellyn has not
had much contact with those outside the Asian-Indian community.
Members did invite Glen Ellyn residents to visit the temple soon after its
opening to see the improvements and to enjoy a Gujarati feast, but only
a few accepted the invitation. With the exception of a very few random
acts of vandalism in the early days, there has been little interaction.
Aside from a few specially invited guests, no non-Asian Indians attend
meetings in the temple. A strategy for gaining understanding and support of the power structure of the community is to invite public figures
to be "chief guests" at large gatherings, especially when Pramukh
Swami is present. Politicians know the value of good relations with their
ethnic constituencies, and several local politicians and bureaucrats have
made contact with the Asian-Indian community through the Swaminarayan temple. Congressman Henry Hyde was an early and occasional
special guest at the temple. Nevertheless, neither the Swaminarayan
Hindus nor the Asian Indians at large have gained much general public
notice. Satsangis are knowledgeable about governmental actions, especially regarding immigration regulations and requirements for certifica-
tion of foreign physicians, but the institution does not take positions on
political issues. Relatively few Chicagoans know about the presence of
the Swaminarayan Hindus, who go out of their way not to "make
waves" or disturb people. The group has grown quietly and steadily,
away from the glare of publicity.

Membership and Discipline

Formal membership boundaries of Swaminarayan Hinduism in Chicago are relatively flexible. Most members go through the simple ritual of initiation—96 percent of the people responding to the 1990 temple survey considered themselves Swaminarayan satsangis—but no formal record of names and addresses of those initiated is kept. Nor do all who go through the ceremony continue active participation in the temple. No "transfer of membership" exists, and people come and go into and out of more active participation, depending on family situation, stage of life, job demands, and life experiences. (In this regard Swaminarayan Hindus are similar to those who attend Calvary Chapel in California, another relatively new religious organization that does not keep exact records of membership.) A religious group, even one growing rapidly, seems relatively stable in structure from the outside, but inside people are moving all the time, toward or away from active participation, in and out of leadership positions. Such movement is not recorded precisely when the formal boundaries are ill-defined and what serves as a membership roll is essentially a mailing list for notices.

Prior to 1987, an annual membership, with a fee of $11, or a life membership, with a fee of $151, gave persons the right to vote at the annual meeting of the Bochasanwasi Swaminarayan Sanstha, a New York corporation. Membership provides legal rights in the corporation. As the programs of the sanstha expanded and the financial value of corporation holdings increased, it seemed wise to limit the ability of an outside group or splinter group to influence policy through very cheap annual membership. The annual membership was therefore abolished in 1987, and the fee for life membership was raised to $1,001 (these odd numbers are considered to be auspicious in Gujarati culture). Of the 400 life members in the country, 60 to 70 are from the Chicago area.

Even though the formal boundaries are relatively loose, informal boundaries are strong. Cultural boundaries are related to Gujarati ethnicity. The ability to communicate in the Gujarati language and to appreciate Gujarati culture makes one an insider at the Glen Ellyn temple, and lack of such ability makes one an "outsider guest" regardless of one's religious inclinations. The primary religious test is allegiance to Pramukh Swami as guru and current embodiment of the spiritual hierarchy, but various levels of commitment and obedience to his guidance and teachings are present in the temple. Ultimately, the board of trustees and Pramukh Swami have the authority to withdraw fellowship from an individual or group, but this has never been exercised in the Glen Ellyn temple or anywhere in the U.S., though it has been carried out with a schismatic individual and his followers in India. No such exclusion is contemplated or mentioned in the temple for less disruptive infractions of religious rules or administrative procedures.

An important but more private aspect of discipline concerns regulations about what is taken into the body as food or drink. Swaminarayan Hindus are vegetarians, and, although visitors to the temple are rarely asked what they believe, they are often asked if they are vegetarians. Vegetarianism is a corollary of the doctrine of nonviolence that rules out killing, even to provide food. Talks given in the temple suggest that vegetarianism is supported by recent medical reports about the dangers of eating meat. The eating of meat would disqualify any person from positions of leadership or honor in the temple. Some of the men speak about times when, as young graduate students and professionals, they were tempted to assimilate to the mores of the host society, and meat-eating and alcohol-drinking are most often mentioned as lapses. Now members commonly inspect labels in supermarkets to make sure that no animal ingredients are in products they purchase, and they strain water from faucets, even in the U.S., to observe the prohibition against ingesting small insects.

A regular pattern of fasts is observed in the temple and homes. Some members observe two days of each lunar month as Ekadeshi days when no food or drink is taken. Others observe as fast days the new moon day, the full moon day, and the ninth day of the bright half of the month, which is the birth date of Swaminarayan. Four of ten people in the temple fast at least once a week, and eight of ten fast at least once a month. On certain fast days it is permitted to eat different, lighter food as snacks. More extensive fasts for penance or to fulfill vows are occasionally undertaken, but they are not public. This discipline of fast days is a constant reminder of the group's religious identity. By fasting, lay people in Chicago imitate and participate in the more exacting form of discipline undertaken by sadhus in India.

Anti-addiction campaigns and messages against drinking intoxicating beverages are prominent parts of the program in the Glen Ellyn temple. They are part of the outreach into the Asian-Indian community and receive very positive responses from parents. When people are asked to explain why they participate in the temple, they say that it "brings peace" and provides "good moral training for the young people." The young people who are active in the temple express some satisfaction and pride in these aspects of discipline that distinguish them from their peers in school and college.

Festivals and Future as Sacred Time (1988–1991)

Sacred time is not so much "time outside of time" or a liminal state as it is the energy or engine that motivates a religious person through time toward a defined future. Preparations for the next events in the temple calendar—weekly and monthly fasts and meetings, annual festivals like Ramanavami (birthday of Rama) or Krishnajayanti (birthday of Krishna), or occasional pilgrimages—force the individual and the entire group toward a future. Moreover, throughout the twenty-year history of a Swaminarayan presence in Chicago, a series of special events has focused the attendance, support, and service of devotees, beginning with the placing of Yogiji Maharaj's ashes in the Mississippi River and including the dedication of various U.S. temples, several pilgrimages to India and England, and then the large-scale Cultural Festival of India to signal their significant presence in the United States.

During his visit in 1988, Pramukh Swami announced that the Bochasanwasi Swaminarayan Sanstha would sponsor a Cultural Festival of India in the summer of 1991 that would involve volunteers from the Glen Ellyn temple and others around the country. Such festivals motivate people toward a future by relating that future to both a specific event in the past and an attachment to their religious leaders. The Cultural Festival of India was planned to celebrate the centennial of the birth of Yogiji Maharaj, just as the beginning of the story of Swaminarayan Hinduism in America was marked by his death. He had initiated most of the people who are now leaders in Chicago, so the festival associated with his birth attracted an outpouring of emotion and support. That devotion was also transferred to his successor, Pramukh Swami, the sponsor and "inspirer" of the festival. People in the Glen Ellyn temple committed themselves to it with high expectations and optimism because the presence of over two hundred sadhus, the cultural and religious displays, artistic works and performances, and religious discourses for the large crowd of people who visited the site celebrated their Indian heritage, marked their success as recent immigrants, recognized their place in the American ethnic landscape, and contributed to the prominence and visibility of their religion. The volunteer service that supported the birth and growth of the temple in Chicago was for several years focused on the Cultural Festival of India.[13] Except for the regular services in the temple, all other plans and activities were in abeyance or subsumed under preparations for the festival.

The budget for the festival is not public information, but many in Chicago made monetary pledges and donations to the project. Recent tours of sadhus were intended to generate support in time and money. In addition, several money-making projects were undertaken in the temple. The basement of the Glen Ellyn temple was rented out for meetings and ceremonies. Women prepared elaborate flower garlands in the temple and sold them to families for weddings and other festive occasions. They also organized an outside catering service to provide Gujarati vegetarian meals for families and organizations. All the work was done by volunteer labor in the temple, and all the income was allocated for the Cultural Festival of India.

The temple undertook an extensive public relations campaign in Chicago to encourage members of the Asian-Indian community to attend the festival. A promotional videotape detailing plans and illustrating them with scenes from previous festivals in England, East Africa, and India was taken to many meetings of Asian-Indian organizations in Chicago. The emphasis was upon celebrating and preserving the cultural and religious heritage of India. Fifteen organizations responded that they were willing to be involved in the festival. Swaminarayan leaders expected that such cooperation would enhance unity among Hindus and the larger Asian-Indian community in Chicago as well as involve a new generation in religious and cultural affairs. A second promotional initiative was to train volunteers to go out two-by-two to visit every Asian-Indian home in the Chicago area, beginning with Gujaratis, to encourage each family to attend and perhaps to give some volunteer service. Women were trained to visit homes where they were not known, which was something of an innovation. It would be difficult to reach even a majority of the 25,000 Gujaratis through home visits, much less the other Asian-Indians, so the attempt was a major public relations initiative.

The festival as sacred time beckoning toward the future provided an impetus for leadership development in the Glen Ellyn temple through training courses and other activities. Young people learned to play Indian musical instruments, practiced as a marching band, performed Gujarati folk dances, and sang hymns to present in various programs at the festival. One young man left college for a year to spend six months in India learning to perform Gujarati folk dances; another completed his premedical studies a semester early so that he could give nine months of volunteer service. Six young men from the Glen Ellyn temple indicated that they were prepared to present themselves to Pramukh Swami for training and eventual initiation as sadhus. It seems that each individual in the temple was challenged to reconsider the level of his or her devotion and service to Swaminarayan and to Pramukh Swami in the context of preparations for the festival, with a concomitant increase in levels of activity and commitment.

The immediate result of this activity was an increase in attendance and participation in the weekly and monthly services in the temple. Focused activity generated a sense of success and optimism for the future that seems rare among longer-established religious groups. It also generated wider contacts within the Asian-Indian community of Chicago, so that the Swaminarayan temple is becoming more widely known as prosperous, well-organized, growing, and successful.

Ties between the temple in Glen Ellyn and the national and international networks of Swaminarayan Hinduism were enhanced by participation in this and other festivals. No single temple in the U.S. could have undertaken such a large project, and having the advice, encouragement, and support of temples and devotees from abroad was critical. Thus, at every step toward the festival, people in Chicago were reminded of their important place in Asian-Indian Hinduism in America, their significant ethnic identity as Gujaratis, and the importance of their place in an international community of followers of Pramukh Swami.

In preparing for the festival, a new generation of leaders of the temple in Chicago were trained who will be able to take over from the founding members. Their transferable skills will be used to sustain both the program of the Glen Ellyn temple and the Swaminarayan agenda throughout the U.S. Sometime soon, followers expect Pramukh Swami to announce a new project for the temple in Glen Ellyn, either local or national, that will propel them into another period of intense activity and open new avenues for expansion.

Conclusion

Swaminarayan Hinduism has been in Chicago for only twenty years, beginning with three young graduate students and growing into a worshiping community with its own temple, a very active program, and hundreds of participants. They have been at the front of the wave of Asian-Indian religious and social organizations because they were called together just five years after the new immigration law invited them for permanent resident status. They are very self-aware and proud of their status as members of the "new ethnics" who are establishing Hinduism in Chicago, even while other new ethnics from India and other parts of Asia are emigrating and bringing along their own cultural and religious commitments. The Swaminarayan local history is short.

Growth has accelerated in the very recent past, primarily through the arrival of new immigrants. It is easy to think of an ethnic congregation going through the stages of first generation, second generation, and third generation in a fairly predictable manner as the community ages, but, in reality, rejuvenation is brought about by a constant stream of immigrants who bring fresh contacts with Swaminarayan practices and Gujarati culture in India and thus refresh the ethnic identity of the satsang. Rapid growth and mobility are potentially destabilizing, but the Glen Ellyn temple has thus far avoided the conflicts and divisions that have plagued some other Asian-Indian religious groups in Chicago.

One aspect of their organization has helped them avoid schismatic tendencies, even though they do not have a hierarchy of resident religious specialists: the centralized national structure that has both legal and spiritual authority over affairs of the temple in Glen Ellyn. The national structure has not been remote, however, because Ghanshyam Patel, once their resident priest and still a full-time volunteer, has been from the beginning one of five members of the national board of trustees. The national organization has provided a network of leadership, one with the ability to call upon a larger international network, to assist with any part of the local program. Satsangis in Chicago have never felt isolated or alone. Their vacation travel is often to attend Swaminarayan affairs at other centers, and they have hosted satsangis from all over the country and abroad. Moreover, financial support comes from all over to support local projects, including the purchase of the temple. This national and international religious network has been even more important than contacts with the large local Gujarati community and its institutions.

Nevertheless, one of the strengths of the religious group is that it reinforces Gujarati ethnic identity of members of the first generation and facilitates its transmission to the second generation. The boundaries established by language use and cultural forms clearly restrict active membership to those who have grown up in that culture or who have immersed themselves in it in both home and temple. Much of the educational activity of the satsang is directed toward that end. The importance of the visits of sadhus in this regard cannot be overestimated, because they coherently combine Gujarati culture—even their avoidance of some accoutrements of that culture makes them special—and Gujarati religion. The visits of sadhus represent "quality time," as they reinforce ethnic identity and religious devotion for both parents and youth. Pilgrimages to India reinforce ethnic identity and tie home, temple, and holy land together as part of one commitment. A projection for the future is that the strategy of adaptation based on ethnic identity may increasingly be replaced by the strategy based on sectarian identity, which is already present but more readily accessible to members of the second generation. That projection will be largely determined by patterns of future immigration from India and Gujarat.

The genius of the temple in Glen Ellyn is its blend of a particular religious tradition (a reformed Hinduism) with a clearly defined ethnicity (Gujarati) in a strategy of adaptation in the U.S. The temple is also unique in its reliance upon lay leadership in both the administration of the program and in the transmission of the ethnic and religious tradition. These leaders and their programs present a number of continuities and discontinuities with the other new ethnics and with the wider American immigrant religious experience: (1) The presence of the temple is a public announcement of a new religious tradition on the American scene, one of many that are growing and gaining more visibility. (2) The temple and its worshiping community demonstrate the way in which ethnic identity is both reinforced and transformed by a regionally and linguistically based religious tradition—in this case, the combination of Gujarati identity and Swaminarayan devotion. (3) Both sadhus and householders follow discipline regarding personal conduct, modes of worship, relations between the sexes, and family obligations that they perceive to be in conflict with mores of American society. (4) Swaminarayan Hinduism in America has been a lay movement, founded and led by lay people, and thus it has been part of an intricate relationship with the religious specialists and leaders in India. (5) Swaminarayan Hinduism in America is an example of an ethnically based organization under centralized national control, a system that was avoided by earlier Roman Catholic immigrants when they rejected ethnic exclusiveness in parishes and dioceses. (6) The group illustrates strategies and patterns of growth among a highly educated, prosperous, mobile elite. Their experience is similar to that of earlier immigrants—Irish Catholics or East European Jews, for example—but both the character of the immigrants and the social context into which they moved are quite different. They make a significant contribution to the religious and ethnic diversity of greater Chicago.

GLOSSARY

ACHARYA: a spiritual preceptor or teacher; the hereditary leader of the Amdavad dioceses of Swaminarayan Hinduism and leader of the ISSO.

AKSHAR: the abode of the supreme person; an eternal state; thought to have an impersonal form as a state of being and a personal form as an abode of god.

AKSHARDHAM: the heavenly abode or state of the supreme person; equivalent to akshar in the impersonal form.

ARTI: a waving of a lighted lamp before the deity; the ceremonies of daily worship in the temple or before the home shrines in which the lamps are waved before the images.

AVATARA: a descent or manifestation of a deity; specifically a form assumed by Vishnu.

BHAKTI: religious devotion as a way to salvation.

DARSHAN: the act of looking at the image of a deity in a shrine; sometimes the act of seeing a holy person.

EKADESHI: the eleventh day of the bright and dark halves of the lunar months; a fast day.

JATI: the name for castes, as distinguished from the four main classes (varnas) of the Hindu social system.

PADHRAMANI: a visit to the home or business of a devotee by a religious leader.

PARSHAD: the first stage of initiation into the ascetic life.

PATEL: a name for members of a prominent caste in Gujarat.

PRASAD: a gift; food distributed after having been offered to the deity in the temple or home shrine.

PUJA: an act of worship; daily worship in household, temple, or shrine.

PUJARI: one who performs the act of worship; the priest who cares for the deities in the temple and performs the daily rituals.

PURANA: a class of Hindu sacred writings containing ancient myths and legends about gods and holy people.

PURUSHOTTAM: Supreme [para], Reality [sat], Self [atma]; the supreme person, the highest divine reality.

SADHU: a Hindu ascetic; one who has renounced the world.

SAMAIYO: the general meetings of Swaminarayan followers, generally on one Saturday evening of a month.

SATSANGI: a companion of the truth; follower of the religious path; member of a religious fellowship or satsang.

SAMSKARA: one of the life-cycle rituals of Hinduism; sixteen rituals prescribed in the sacred texts, including birth, sacred thread, marriage, and cremation.

SEVA: service; volunteer work out of devotion to the deity or guru.

SLOKA: a stanza or verse of a sacred text.

TILAK: a sectarian mark on the forehead, generally affixed as a part of morning worship.

VAISHNAVA: associated with the god Vishnu.

NOTES

1. United States Immigration and Naturalization Service, *Statistical Yearbook of the Immigration and Naturalization Service* (1982), pp. 2–4.

2. For additional information about Swaminarayan Hinduism in India and its development in East Africa and England, see Raymond B. Williams, *A New Face of Hinduism: The Swaminarayan Religion* (Cambridge: Cambridge University Press, 1984).

3. Swaminarayan Hinduism attracts people from several castes. While most are from the vaishya *varna*, many brahmins and sudras are also followers. Traditional rules for higher castes restrict associations with people of lower castes, especially regarding commensality and marriage. For example, brahmins should not eat with untouchables. Although Sahajanand Swami did not attack caste rules, his emphasis on devotion reduced the importance of caste. See Williams, *A New Face of Hinduism*, pp. 146–50.

4. For additional information about the akshar-purushottam doctrine, see Raymond B. Williams, "The Holy Man as the Abode of God in the Swaminarayan Religion," in *Gods of Flesh, Gods of Stone: The Embodiment of Divinity in India*,

ed. Joanne Punzo Waghorne and Norman Cutler (Chambersburg, Pa.: Anima Press, 1985), pp. 142–57.

5. For additional information about Swaminarayan Hinduism and other religions of immigrants from the Indian subcontinent in the United States, see Raymond B. Williams, *Religions of Immigrants from India and Pakistan: New Threads in the American Tapestry* (Cambridge: Cambridge University Press, 1988).

6. Sydney E. Ahlstrom, *A Religious History of the American People* (New Haven: Yale University Press, 1972), pp. 830–32.

7. The survey taken in September 1990 showed that most respondents (79 percent) are married, and only one person is divorced. Only 5 of the 151 people between the ages of 25 and 60 are single, never married. A very large number (38 percent) have at least one graduate degree—45 percent of those between the ages of 25 and 60—and an additional number (23 percent) have a college degree. Of the 38 percent with graduate degress, nearly three-quarters are male, and about one-quarter are female, and of the 28 percent with only a high school education, the number of males and females is exactly the same. The respondents have primary occupations that reflect their educational background: practical/applied sciences (22 percent), business (17 percent), health and sciences (9 percent), legal services (5 percent), and education (3 percent). Others are students (13 percent), homemakers (12 percent), unemployed (4 percent), or retired (2 percent), but several (4 percent) are giving full-time service to the Swaminarayan satsang.

8. For additional information on the role of Pramukh Swami as counselor, see Raymond B. Williams, "The Guru as Pastoral Counselor," *Journal of Pastoral Care* 40 (1986): 322–30. (Also published in *Swaminarayan Magazine* 10 (1987): 6–7.

9. Statues of Shastri Maharaj and Yogiji Maharaj have been placed in separate shrines in some temples in India, but this is a recent development confined to India.

10. Seventy-five percent of the satsangis live within thirty miles of the temple in the western and northwestern suburbs of Chicago. Only a few live nearby in Glen Ellyn.

11. Of those responding to the survey taken in September 1990, a few (17 percent) neglected to answer the question about "current total family income." Some (27 percent) report a family income of less than $20,000, but most have larger incomes: $20,000–30,000 (20 percent), $30,000–50,000 (20 percent), $50,000–75,000 (9 percent), $75,000–100,000 (3 percent) and over $100,000 (4 percent). The income levels are roughly the same as those recorded in a survey at Swaminarayan gatherings in 1985, so recent immigrants have not caused a socioeconomic shift.

12. For additional information about strategies of adaptation, see Raymond B. Williams, "Sacred Threads of Several Textures: Strategies of Adaptation in the United States," in *A Sacred Thread: Modern Transmission of Hindu Tradition in India and Abroad,* ed. Raymond B. Williams (Chambersburg, Pa.: Anima Press, 1992), pp. 228–57.

13. Many respondents to the survey in 1990 reported support for festivals. A large number (39 percent) attended the bicentenary celebration of the birth of

Gunatitanand Swami in Amdavad in 1985. A few (17 percent) attended the Cultural Festival of India in London in 1985, but a great majority (80 percent) planned to attend the Cultural Festival of India in New Jersey in 1991 (15 percent were undecided, and only 5 percent responded that they did not plan to attend). Almost half (47 percent) made a vow to donate a month of volunteer service for the Cultural Festival of India—serving, for example, as groundskeepers, security workers, cooks, drivers, and public relations workers—and another group (11 percent) planned to donate two weeks. A surprising number had vowed to donate more: six months (5 percent), a year (4 percent), or more than a year (2 percent). Only a few (about 9 percent) had not pledged to donate some volunteer service. A few, such as a physician who could not leave his practice for an extended period, promised to donate a month's income to the project in lieu of service.

TWELVE

Calvary Chapel
Costa Mesa, California

RANDALL BALMER AND JESSE T. TODD, JR.

T HE FUTURE ALWAYS LOOKS GOOD in the golden land," Joan Didion once wrote in one of her haunting essays about California, "because no one remembers the past."[1] Didion could very well have had Calvary Chapel in mind when she wrote those words. A letter to one of the congregation's ministers inquiring about access to church records, archives, and membership lists elicited the following response: "I really don't know how much I can be of help in this matter. The archives or records that you asked about seem to be just in Pastor Chuck's memory."[2]

Calvary Chapel has no membership list, it turns out, because it has no members. No one—save, presumably, the paid staff—is formally affiliated with the church. Like residents in the contemporary California of popular imagination, people come and go as they please.

Such informality, however, is one of the defining characteristics of Calvary Chapel. The absence of membership status allows congregants to remain anonymous, if they so choose, and the sense of belonging to the congregation is entirely self-referential. There is, moreover, little discernible historical consciousness at Calvary Chapel. That coincides with what seems to be a genuine sentiment on the part of the senior pastor, Chuck Smith, and others that the congregation has flourished not by dint of human effort but by the providence of God. History also becomes unimportant because of Smith's strong apocalypticism, his belief that Jesus will return at any moment and thus render all of human history irrelevant.

Calvary Chapel's informality poses obvious problems for anyone trying to write a history of the congregation; the traditional tools of the historian are simply not useful. Because of its unique social location in the early 1970s, a number of sociologists have written about Calvary Chapel, but few have paid careful attention to its history. After a flurry of national attention, interest on the part of the media dropped off, and, despite large and elaborate local public libraries built on the ever-expanding tax base in Orange County, no library in the vicinity maintains a clipping file on Calvary Chapel.

This history of Calvary Chapel is based, then, on the small canon of published information—newspaper and magazine articles, sociological studies, and Chuck Smith's own published recollections about the early days of the congregation. It is also based on interviews with various individuals associated with the congregation.[3] Reliance on firsthand information, particularly from people still associated with the congregation, carries with it certain perils: selective, enhanced memory and, more frequently, a rhetoric that is so cloaked in spiritual language as to constitute providential history. Even this information is notoriously inexact. When Smith, the putative repository of the congregation's history, was asked by his office staff for the date of Maranatha Christian Academy's founding, he responded: "Oh, it must have been 1973 or so." When asked about KWVE, the church's radio station, he replied: "I think we bought that about three years ago."

The brief history of Calvary Chapel is actually part of a much larger story that includes the Jesus movement of the early 1970s, the recent resurgence of Pentecostalism in America, and the spectacular growth of suburban evangelical churches in the last two decades. Calvary Chapel has ridden the tide of the evangelical resurgence in recent decades.

The ability of Calvary Chapel to formulate an attractive, credible alternative to the counterculture, all the while purveying a conservative theology, ensured its success early in the 1970s, and that success, in turn, illustrates the adaptability so characteristic of American evangelicalism. The genius of Calvary Chapel lies in its ability to translate a very traditional, conservative theology into a form that appealed, first, to a younger, "hip" generation disillusioned with the counterculture and, more recently, to those who felt overwhelmed by the atomism of suburban life in Orange County. In that respect Calvary Chapel is very much typical of evangelicalism in general. Throughout American history evangelicals have proven themselves remarkably adaptable to cultural circumstances, from the open-air preaching of the eighteenth century to the circuit riders on the frontier to the urban revivalists at the turn of the twentieth century to the heavy-metal sounds of contemporary Christian music (much of which received its impetus from Calvary Chapel). Unconstrained by confessions, liturgical rubrics, or denominational hierarchies, evangelicalism has demonstrated its malleability throughout American history, its responsiveness to popular tastes and prevailing cultural norms.

Smith has, in fact, produced a kind of amalgam at Calvary Chapel, one that combines the tradition of American revivalism, the strict behavioral constraints of fundamentalism, the conservatism of Orange County, and the casual, emotive worship of Pentecostalism. Such an amalgamation defies easy characterization, but we shall refer to it as "soft Pentecostalism." Smith's own background is Pentecostal, and he shares with Pentecostals a conservative evangelical theology and a belief in spiritual gifts. At the same time, however, he does not insist upon speaking in tongues as a sign of regeneration or sanctification; in fact, he discourages such displays in public.

The theology at Calvary Chapel, despite its nuances, is quite traditional. The congregation's distinctive place in American evangelicalism, then, lies not so much in its theology as in its historical location. It remains the most significant and enduring institution of the Jesus movement and the cornerstone of a loose federation of churches that may very well be a new denomination in the making.

Religion and Culture in Orange County

Calvary Chapel, situated now in Santa Ana, had its origins in Costa Mesa (which accounts for the persistence of the moniker "Calvary Chapel of Costa Mesa"). Santa Ana is located southeast of Los Angeles in Orange County, one of the most affluent regions in the United States and even the world. Stretching along the Pacific Ocean from La Habra and Brea in the north, south to San Clemente, and as far east as the Cleveland National Forest, Orange County is the fifteenth largest metropolitan area in the United States, and its economy would rank thirtieth in the world if it were a separate nation. It ranks tenth in gross national product of all metropolitan markets in the United States, exceeding twenty-three of the fifty states and such cities as Atlanta, Newark, St. Louis, Dallas, and San Francisco.

Once lined with orange groves and bean fields, Orange County is now a tragic misnomer, a huge mishmash of housing tracts and shopping malls veined with highways that become virtually impassible in daylight hours. The character of the county itself has been evolving in recent years, from bedroom suburbs to a self-sufficient economy and culture, the most tangible example of which is the Orange County Performing Arts Center which opened in 1986 in Costa Mesa, just a short distance from Calvary Chapel.

Orange County also has its own distinctive religious culture. Evangelicalism in various forms thrives in this suburban, overwhelmingly conservative county, where Republicans hold a 55 percent to 35 percent advantage over Democrats in voter registration.[4] On March 27, 1955, a young seminary graduate named Robert Schuller held his first Sunday service at the Orange Drive-in Theater. Today Schuller presides over a vast religious empire, built upon his own Dale Carnegie theology, from his "Crystal Cathedral" in Garden Grove. Chuck Swindoll, pastor of the First Evangelical Free Church of Fullerton, another suburban megachurch, is also an author and radio preacher well known in evangelical circles. In Anaheim, Melodyland School of Theology is located about a block from the entrance to Disneyland. Also in Anaheim, John Wimber, once an associate of Smith's at Calvary Chapel, has begun a new church, Vineyard Christian Fellowship, which has grown greatly in recent years and, like Calvary Chapel has spawned satellite congregations around the country.

Such a salubrious religious culture in southern California belies the stereotype of Californians carousing in the secular shadows of Hollywood or engaged in an endless sequence of sybaritic dissolutions. Although such images may not be entirely unfounded, evangelicalism has managed to hold its own in the region, at least in Orange County. But it has held its own in a singular manner, quite unlike anywhere else in America.

For anyone unfamiliar with the beach culture of southern California, an initial encounter with Calvary Chapel's congregation can be startling. Sunday morning might be just another sunny day at the beach. Hundreds of automobiles have trolled a huge parking lot in search of a berth. Singles, couples, and families have clambered out, some pausing to retrieve lawn chairs from the trunk. But this is not just another foray to the beach (the beach can wait until the afternoon). These pilgrims have come not to bury their toes in the sand but to sing religious songs in cadences reminiscent of the 1960s and to hear the ruminations of a preacher whose folksy demeanor and sunny disposition match the character of both his congregation and the regional culture.

The preacher is Chuck Smith, a bald, avuncular man in his early sixties, who is known affectionately to his congregation at Calvary Chapel as "Pastor Chuck." Calvary Chapel sits on an eleven-acre campus at the corner of Fairview and Sunflower in Santa Ana. Built in the ersatz mission style evoking a romantic California past that disappeared long ago, the buildings of Calvary Chapel are virtually indistinguishable from the ubiquitous strip malls of Orange County. The church's architecture bespeaks a desire to blend into the surrounding cultural pastiche. Its slightly makeshift quality also reflects the disposition of "Pastor Chuck." The patchwork complex of Calvary Chapel is as unassuming as the Crystal Cathedral, its neighbor to the north, is ostentatious.

Much of the congregation arrives late, wearing anything from Ocean Pacific togs to Hickey-Freeman suits and everything in-between: knit polo shirts, Levi's, madras shirts, miniskirts, T-shirts. Hairstyles range from the meticulous and coiffed to the insouciant and sun-bleached. Compared with their audience, the pastors on the platform, dressed in business suits, look hopelessly formal, even on a Sunday morning. The congregation is generally young and, on a Sunday morning at least, overwhelmingly white. Outside the auditorium, some worshipers lounge on the grass in lawn chairs, listening to the service on speakers located at various points around the grounds. Some listen from their automobiles as security guards on bicycles patrol the parking lot. Virtually everyone carries a large Bible with some sort of casing—suede, hand-tooled leather, homemade quilting, vinyl with pictures of a cross and a dove—conveying at least the impression that these Bibles are consulted regularly during the week, not just on Sunday morning.

Historical and Cultural Context

In 1971, a series of startling photographs accompanied a lengthy *Time* magazine article about a new religious phenomenon known as the Jesus movement. The photos depicted the faces of a new generation of Christians at worship. These were the "Jesus Freaks," fugitives from a decade of social upheaval that began with the righteous energy of civil rights marches and ended with disillusionment, anger, and a great number of "bad vibes." In one of these photos, a smiling Chuck Smith was shown carrying a young paralytic into the sea for baptism at Corona del Mar as hundreds of other kids watch from the shore. This image suggests the safe arrival of these prodigal sons and daughters after a harrowing ride on the magic carpet of radical politics, Eastern esoterica, and psychedelic drugs. Wounded by their experiences but still searching, they were now safe—and forgiven—in the arms of the church.[5]

Calvary Chapel, along with hundreds of other churches, served as a port of reentry for thousands of young refugees from the tumultuous years of the 1960s. These youthful visionaries had once belonged to a movement intent upon revolutionizing the world, according to sociologist Steven Tipton, but their dreams ended "in squalor, bitterness and economic failure augmented by violent opposition from without."[6]

In his analysis of the 1960s, Tipton sees a revolt against two distinct yet interrelated American moral cultures: biblical religion, a system based on the notion of an authoritative God who issues divine commands, and utilitarian individualism, a system centering on the individual moral agent "seeking to satisfy his own wants and interests."[7] The counterculture challenged both, although its primary energy was directed at the latter, since biblical religion was regarded as largely irrelevant. The inequities and injustice that were the original targets of the protest stemmed from a mentality that many believed encouraged not cooperation but competition, not community but a willful antagonism toward others. In addition, the bureaucratization of life required to sustain an advanced economy also added to a sense of alienation and powerlessness. Tipton himself lends some warrant to the counterculture's protest. Utilitarian individualism was the fuel that fired America's industrial and commercial might, creating a great deal of wealth for a large number of its citizens. But such a moral system tends toward normlessness, Tipton writes, in its "incapacity to generate substantive values."[8]

In fact, many of the rebels of the 1960s began to question those very principles upon which American public life was supposedly ordered: the Enlightenment values of logic, rationality, and self-discipline. The so-called Protestant ethic also came under attack. It encouraged, many protesters thought, the senseless accumulation of capital toward no reasonable or meaningful end. Believing the system beyond repair, they set about radically to transform the American political and economic landscape.

In the beginning an alliance between middle-class youth and people of color provided a formidable vanguard for change. But the increasing radicalization of both groups drove a wedge between them as each began to pursue independent goals. By 1966–67, there was, at least among some student leaders, a noticeable shift away from political involvement to a rather passive "flower power." Former activists were becoming hippies.

In May 1967, the Council for a Summer of Love in the City of San

Francisco issued a letter inviting the youth of the world to join "a holy pilgrimage to our city, to affirm and celebrate a new spiritual dawn." Their plans included a Tolkien Festival of Elves and Hobbits, a Midsummer's Day observance, and events marking the summer solstice. The council, recognizing the powerful symbolism of the city's unofficial spiritual patron, also announced plans to import from Marin County a twenty-foot statue of St. Francis, carved from a California redwood tree. At some point during the summer, it was to be carried in procession across the Golden Gate Bridge and placed in the park at the foot of San Francisco's Haight Street, "facing East toward the place of Dawn."[9] The *Poverello*, the poor little beggar of Assisi who had once stripped naked to declare his dependence on God and his rejection of the material world, had become a central symbol of hip religiosity.

Although the Summer of Love failed to attract the expected throngs, its youthful promoters nevertheless captured a great deal of attention. Their laid-back idealism shifted the focus of their movement from active to passive protest. And their eclectic spirituality sparked the interest of theologians and religious scholars, some of whom began to reevaluate their judgment of America as an irredeemably secular nation. In *Feast of Fools*, Harvey Cox saw the Western world poised on the brink of some monumental spiritual awakening. He wrote admiringly, "Inspired by their gurus and holy men, the young people of today are fashioning their own celebrations and rituals. Rock music, guerrilla theatre, Dionysian dance, projected light and color—all play a part in the evolving rites."[10]

In an essay written in the same year as the Summer of Love, Huston Smith explored the emerging spirituality of the hippie movement in the context of American secular culture. Smith challenged the results of a 1967 Gallup survey revealing that 57 percent of Americans believed "religion is losing its influence." The poll's respondents, he claimed, had missed the point. The influence of institutional religion had indeed declined, but in multivalent forms at the margins of culture religion flourished. He wrote:

> For the first time since the Renaissance and the Reformation, western society is hearing . . . the suggestion that perhaps the contemplative life is the equal of the active one. With tribalism and Strawberry Fields Forever [hippies] seek the recovery of community. Turning on, they seek by their own lights the inner light. Tun-

ing in, they approach the natural order sacramentally. Dropping out, they assert . . . that their kingdom is not of this world.[11]

Hippie "be-ins," the rising interest in science fiction, along with tarot readings and *I Ching* divination at such unlikely places as the Massachusetts Institute of Technology, convinced Smith that America actually stood at the threshold of a spiritual renaissance. "Man remains *homo religiosus,*" Smith concluded, "not in the eighteenth century reading of the phrase to be sure, but in the sense of being by nature vulnerable to transcendence and the sacred."[12]

Few in the counterculture movement found themselves attracted to traditional Western religious systems, and even fewer churches made an effort to understand and interpret the new spirituality. With his long hair, beard, and sandals, Jesus was at times presented as the prototypical hippie, as he was at a memorable alternative liturgy at San Francisco's Glide Memorial Church in February 1967. During the service, an image of Jesus was projected over a dancing crowd while a naked hippie chanted. But the celebration ended rather abruptly when some worshipers were discovered making love by the altar.[13] For the most part, however, hippies simply stayed away from churches. According to Tipton, they believed Western religion offered nothing but authoritarian moralism, verbalism, intellectualism, and a lack of ecstatic experience.[14]

Although the countercultural rhetoric of change and transformation, of peace and love, was still quite strong as late as the Woodstock Festival in August 1969, the energy of the counterculture had begun to dissipate at some point in the late 1960s. The movement had lost its innocence, and many in the movement had lost their hope. It is difficult to chart with much precision the course of the movement's decline, but many interpreters point to challenges from the outside coupled with moral decay and exhaustion from within. The obstacles to change, recognized by many of the radicals who moved from political protest to the transcendentalism of the mid-1960s, had, if anything, grown more intransigent. The violence at the 1968 Democratic Convention in Chicago was just one indication of how far public authorities were willing to go to maintain order. Kent State would provide another, even more graphic illustration.

But the movement also began to crumble from within, perhaps because of its loss of direction and inability to institutionalize its goals and values. Joan Didion had seen the seeds of the movement's destruction as early as the spring of 1967, before the San Francisco Summer of Love.

In her remarkably perceptive essay "Slouching Towards Bethlehem," she described the chaos and aimlessness of the "Hashbury" culture that, she believes, had characterized it from the beginning. The acid trips she witnessed began with the "Wow!" of insight, but ended with trippers staring at their feet, wondering how many flowers they could find in a single grain of sand. Far too often, drug use had led to violence instead of love, self-gratification instead of self-transcendence, and irresponsibility instead of trust. "In the cold spring of 1967," she wrote, "adolescents drifted from city to torn city, sloughing off both the past and the future as snakes shed their skins, children who were never taught and would never learn the games that had held the society together." [15]

Although the youth movement's vision had become somewhat apolitical by the late 1960s, its rhetoric remained unabashedly millennial. In a number of ways the young were unlike their millennialist predecessors in American history, drawing their imagery not from the Christian tradition but from an ersatz Eastern spirituality; the millennium's hopefuls expected the dawn of the Age of Aquarius, not the coming of Jesus. But in other ways their vision was similar. They found America's injustice and inequities intolerable, its institutions morally bankrupt, its social and economic games meaningless and inhumane. They struggled for peace and longed for deliverance into a world transformed. But their great hopes led to disappointment and failure, and like other discouraged millennialists before them, these rebels began the slow process of coming to terms with a world from which they had found no release.

As the youth culture faded, the Jesus movement served to reintegrate burned-out hippies into the so-called "mainstream" of American culture. Indeed, Calvary Chapel itself, despite its apparent iconoclasm within evangelicalism, in that it welcomed erstwhile hippies into its worship services, nevertheless purveyed the theology of mainstream evangelicalism, with its emphasis on biblical literalism, premillennialism, and personal religious experience. Calvary Chapel, then, was a large—and largely successful—evangelical rescue mission to the troubled youth of the 1960s.

At the same time, however, the Calvary Chapel and the Jesus movement can be seen as an extension of the contentious spirit of the 1960s, especially in its adherents' appropriation of the counterculture dress and jargon. Many in the Jesus movement seemed unwilling to shed the trappings of the vast youth culture they had helped to build. Instead, they transformed their institutions along with their lives. By 1971 Christian surfer clubs had been organized, bands played Jesus rock, and

Berkeley coffeehouses dispensed Bibles instead of hashish. The Love Inn, a Christian commune in Freeville, New York, opened its doors, providing a "crash pad" for new converts. Some older Christians were disquieted by the movement's retention of the hip style, but others, such as Norman Vincent Peale, were so moved by the evidence of changed lives that they were willing to tolerate the movement's "rather boisterous message." [16]

The Jesus movement, then, was a complex phenomenon that included a bewildering range of groups, from radical millenarians like the Children of God to colorful individuals like Arthur Blessitt, who chained himself to a cross on Sunset Strip. Even at its peak, around 1970, the movement had no well-defined boundaries, just as it had no unified leadership. Calvary Chapel itself, arguably the primary cultural relic of the Jesus movement, retains at least a measure of that ephemerality. The church has institutionalized considerably since the early 1970s—indeed, the leadership is quite authoritarian—but it has done so in such a way that it does not appear institutional, at least to the casual observer.

Neither the Jesus movement nor Calvary Chapel, however, was one-dimensional. The gospel of a Jesus in long hair and blue jeans appealed not only to former hippies but also to very young teenagers, those not old enough to have adopted the "alternative lifestyles" of the sixties. And it made an indelible mark on people who had never met a hippie, including those in suburban congregations who were often the targets of the Jesus movement's protests. In those very churches, the youth-group meeting became a "rap session" and folk masses often displaced more solemn rites. These were "funky" times even for traditionally conservative groups. At the 1970 Inter-Varsity triennial at the University of Illinois, Champaign-Urbana, conventioneers sported bell-bottoms and beards and heard a black activist castigate Wall Street for its sins. [17]

In some sense the Jesus movement perpetuated the protests of the counterculture that spawned it: the Jesus movement insisted that it was both antibureaucratic and anti-institutional. And it successfully appropriated many of the images of the counterculture—the casual dress that many more traditional Christians found offensive, the unstructured worship and hip jargon, the bias against institutionalization. But it also served to resocialize and reintegrate some ex-hippies into the status quo. Billy Graham underscored this point in his 1971 book, *The Jesus Generation*. Graham tells of a teenager rebelling "against everything his parents stood for," who left his family's home in Florida for California and the allure of the youth culture. One day, lonely, despondent, and stoned, he was offered a ride by three "hippie types" who led him to Christ. "That boy's life was completely transformed," Graham wrote. "He went back to his parents, married a Christian girl, and is now attending a university. 'A new creature in Christ Jesus,' he is no longer a loser."[18] The prodigal son had returned, not only to the faith of his parents but also to an honorable world of responsible social roles.

Calvary Chapel and the Jesus Movement

When Chuck Smith took over a dying church in Orange County, he melded two unique strands of American religious culture: the Jesus movement and Pentecostalism. The strand of Pentecostalism provided access to the lexicon of traditional, conservative theology, while the accoutrements of the Jesus movement cloaked this traditionalism in a contemporary vernacular.

The mix was all the more congenial because of the populism and the iconoclasm inherent in both Pentecostalism and the Jesus movement. Historically, the Pentecostal movement in the United States can be seen as an explosion of popular religious sentiment and a kind of protest against mainstream denominations at the turn of the twentieth century. Especially in its early years, its anti-establishment views and its populist character manifested itself in criticism—implicit or explicit—of other churches, its emphasis on immediate experience with the divine, and its concerns with the workings of the Holy Spirit in the lives of individual Christians.

Although the history of American Pentecostalism begins with the 1901 eruption of miraculous tongues-speaking at Charles Parham's Bethel Bible College in Topeka, Kansas, California played an early and crucial role in the movement. The Azusa Street revivals of 1906 earned for Los Angeles a reputation among American Pentecostals as the New Jerusalem.[19] In the 1920s the city became home to Aimee Semple Mc-Pherson, the flamboyant leader of early Pentecostalism who built her Angelus Temple in Echo Park and eventually established the International Church of the Foursquare Gospel. McPherson's church, in fact, provided the link between early Pentecostalism and Calvary Chapel.

Chuck Smith, minister of Calvary Chapel since 1965, was ordained in the Foursquare church after graduating from the denomination's LIFE Bible College in 1948 with a G.Th. (Graduate of Theology) degree. His move to Calvary Chapel, as we shall see, resulted at least in part from dissatisfaction with the denomination and what he perceived as its ineffectiveness and trivial game-playing. Smith's ministry at Calvary Chapel marks a small "reformation" of sorts within Pentecostalism, an informal, even subtle, defection from an established Pentecostal denomination. At the time he left the Foursquare church, Smith was already something of a rebel, prepared to "follow God's call" and do something new. Even before his first encounter with a so-called Jesus freak, Smith was, in a sense, one of them—a rebel fleeing bureaucratic institutions. He sought what generations of Christian reformers have always sought: a more immediate experience of the divine unfettered by institutional constraints.

In the early 1960s Smith had begun to tire of church-growth schemes propagated by the denominational hierarchy. Typically, these notions (quite common in evangelical circles) involve dividing the congregation into two or more teams for a contest designed to fill their assigned pews by inviting the "unsaved" to church. Individual congregations within a denomination then compete against one another for the largest growth during the contest period. When promotional materials for yet another contest began arriving at his Foursquare church, Smith discarded them. "I couldn't face another Blues against the Reds," he said, resolving instead simply to teach the Bible.[20] In compliance with the requirements of the contest, however, the church secretary filed periodic reports about attendance, and at the conclusion of the contest Smith received a letter congratulating him as the winner—the church with the greatest increase—and inviting him to a rally to collect his trophy, even though his congregation had known nothing about the contest.

Disillusioned with denominational officiousness, Smith soon accepted a call to a nondenominational congregation in Corona, California, where he enjoyed similar success by continuing his emphasis on Bible teaching. In 1965 he received an invitation from Calvary Chapel in Costa Mesa, at that time a congregation of twenty-five, deeply divided and on the verge of disbanding. Smith accepted, even though he was forced to supplement his income by cleaning carpets several days a week. Under his ministry this tiny church, growing at a rate of 5 percent a week, soon had to look for new quarters.

The largest increase came from an unlikely source. At the time of the counterculture movement, with the beaches of southern California fairly swarming with hippies, Smith first discerned his call, although he later confessed that "these long-haired, bearded, dirty kids going around the streets repulsed me." Still, he felt drawn to them: "My wife and I used to go over to Huntington Beach and park downtown to watch the kids and pray for them. We wanted somehow to reach them, but we didn't know how." Smith remains oblique about his motivations for initiating an evangelical outreach to people who repulsed him, but there seems to be an almost voyeuristic quality to his fascination. He claims simply that his compassion for their plight overcame his revulsion at their appearance. A parental concern for his daughter may also have contributed to his resolve. At some point shortly before May 1968, one of Smith's daughters began dating a former acid-head who had once lived in the Haight-Ashbury district of San Francisco. John was now not only "straight" but a Christian as well, a believer who spent a great deal of his time witnessing at Huntington Beach. Smith told him, "John, we've got to meet a hippie!"[21]

John obliged, arriving at Smith's house one evening with Lonnie Frisbee, a "long-haired, bearded kid with bells on his feet and flowers in his hair." Smith was surprised to learn that Frisbee, too, was a Christian, having been converted while "tripping" in a California desert. Impressed with his piety and enthusiasm, if not his appearance—"I wasn't prepared for the love that came forth from this kid," he wrote—Smith invited Frisbee to move in with him and his family and soon hired him as Calvary Chapel's youth minister. Frisbee went on to lead the church's hugely successful outreach to the very kids Smith was once at a loss to understand. In addition, Smith's house became a "hippie pad," where Jesus freaks found both physical shelter and, in Smith's teaching of the Bible, spiritual sustenance.[22]

Oden Fong, now a staff member at Calvary Chapel, was another early convert. "I came out of mysticism. I used to study religions, and at the time I learned about Calvary Chapel I was living down in Laguna Beach where there was a different representative of every faith on just about every corner," Fong recalled. "You could walk down the street and talk to a Zen Buddhist, walk a bit farther and see a Krishna, a little farther and see a Satanist. It was a real hodge-podge of different faiths. I spent years in metaphysics, trying to attain perfection—fasting and that type of stuff, eating nothing but pure foods, meditating for hours and days, sitting in the same position for days. When I was doing yoga and things like that, I was just trying to get perfect. And there was just no way. I studied under the hierarchy of Tibetan Buddhism, Krishna Consciousness." Fong then heard about Chuck Smith and Calvary Chapel. "A lot of my friends had gone up to Calvary Chapel, and they invited me one day. I went, reluctantly, and it was just so real. It was so much more real than anything I had seen. I found compassion and love. There was a fullness in the hearts of the people I met—the Jesus people—and I wanted that, too." Fong claims to have found the answer to his searching in the grace of God. "There's no perfect man. By Jesus' simple act, we have the power to change and not to fall."[23]

Smith's message, his acceptance and compassion, caught on. L. E. Romaine, a retired military man and a longtime associate of Smith's, remembers that in the early 1970s "not more than five or ten percent of the crowd was over twenty-five. Everybody wore granny dresses and jeans and bib-overalls and tie-died shirts and long hair and beards," he said. "They were so wild it was scary. The news media couldn't understand it. Other churches couldn't understand it; some of them spoke against it."[24] Indeed, many churches struggled over how far they should go in tolerating the outward conformity of these hippies-turned-Christians. At Bethel Tabernacle in North Redondo Beach, for instance, older members continually voiced their displeasure with both the deportment and the attire of their new members. Many threatened to leave, but Bethel's minister, Lyle Steenis deterred them by promising "to whip anyone who tried to kick out a single kid."[25]

Although the opposition was never so fierce as it was at Bethel Tabernacle, even at Calvary Chapel there were those who did not share Smith's enthusiasm and openness. One long-time member was reported to have denounced the hippies because their bare feet soiled the carpet and the rivets on their jeans scored the pews. Some "straights" even left the church, but most members, doubtless influenced by Smith's acceptance and easygoing style, supported the congregation's youth outreach quite enthusiastically.[26]

Fong remembers that when he first came to Calvary Chapel, it met in a small building down the street from its present location. "I think the most they could pack in there if they filled up all the seats and filled up all the aisles—which they did, it was standing room only in those days—was about three hundred people. We ripped down the walls, tore down the side walls, and had people sitting outside. Even in the rain people would be sitting out there. It was just a great, massive revival; there was a great movement of people into Christianity at the time. Every month or so, the church would double."[27]

To accommodate the crowds, the congregation bought a parcel of land at the intersection of Fairview and Sunflower (their present site), put in a parking lot, and purchased a big, secondhand circus tent as temporary quarters while they constructed an auditorium. Here, once again, Calvary Chapel demonstrates its continuities with American evangelicalism. The tent, reminiscent of camp-meeting revivals in the nineteenth century, was a temporary structure, and just as the camp meetings were essentially conservative events in that they tamed the rowdiness of the frontier, so too Calvary Chapel aspired to tame the counterculture.

The night before their first service in the tent, Smith and others set up sixteen hundred chairs and planned double services. "I looked out at that sea of folding chairs," Smith recalled. "I had never seen so many folding chairs in all my life!" He asked an associate: "How long do you suppose it will take the Lord to fill this place?" The associate looked at his watch and answered, "I'd say just about eleven hours." [28] He was right. The next morning every seat was filled and people stood around the perimeter of the tent—for both services.

Oden Fong attributes Calvary Chapel's growth, in part, to the deflation of youthful ideals. The end of the sixties, he said, found people "totally disillusioned with the counterculture revolution, the 'peace,' 'love,' 'flower power' movement, LSD, and so forth. All the heroes of that time—the musical heroes of the youth and political leaders of the youth—were all dying off, either by heroin overdoses or suicide or assassination. People were turning on one another, turning each other in. It caused a lot of people to be extremely disillusioned with the counterculture revolution. But it was still a time of searching. The decade of the sixties was a time of looking inward and outward. We were trying to figure out who we were, what we were, where we were going as a human race." In the face of this disillusionment, Christianity became attractive to many, a haven of surety and security, even though the counterculture had consigned it to the scrapheap of irrelevance just a few years earlier.

Fong believes that this development was nothing short of an awakening. "The walls of the traditional churches that had not allowed certain elements of the society to enter—I'm thinking of the so-called hippies—began to crumble." One of the characteristics of this awakening, as Fong remembers it, was an emphasis on religious experience rather than doctrine, an emphasis that has been retained at Calvary Chapel. Experience was, of course, central to the counterculture, but it is also one of the central characteristics of American evangelicalism, especially in the Pentecostal tradition, where it has always enjoyed precedence over dogma.

Indeed, at Calvary Chapel religious experience, not simple orthodoxy, became the touchstone of faith. "Christians began to concern themselves with living for Jesus Christ on a day-to-day basis, rather than simply adhering to the dogmas of the church," Fong recalled."There were also incredible manifestations of spiritual power. I have seen people's legs grow out. I've seen blind and deaf people healed. These miracles added a lot of excitement to the movement, too. Calvary Chapel and Chuck Smith were just part of that broader movement. A lot of them, thousands of them, were hippies, people coming out of the drug culture. It was kind of like one hobo telling another where he can get a good meal. We got the name Jesus people or Jesus freaks from the media, primarily because of our baptisms."

Indeed, just as mass baptisms concluded camp meetings on the frontier, so too Calvary Chapel's baptisms in the Pacific at Corona del Mar signaled for many erstwhile hippies a final immersion into Christianity and symbolized their transition from the counterculture to the evangelical subculture. The baptisms, the focus of considerable media attention, also provided the church its early notoriety. "Dope addicts, panhandlers, and just regular kids who were confused have come through here and accepted Christ," Smith explained to a reporter at the time. "Baptizing is the symbol of this acceptance."[29] Fong remembers the chaos. "You pushed and shoved to get either into the parking lot or somewhere above the beach area. You'd walk all the way down over the rocks. You'd see this mass of humanity, thousands of people sitting on the rocks and down on the beach and all around the outsides of the cove. And then down by the water itself would be the pastors and hundreds of people lined up to be baptized—usually three hundred or more."[30]

Romaine, Smith's associate, also remembers the huge crowds. "The first big baptism down at Corona del Mar took place in 1970. We got down to Pirate's Cove on a Saturday around nine-thirty, ten o'clock, and there were thousands and thousands of people waiting there. These so-called Jesus freaks are climbing all over the rocks and into the adjacent residential area. They're knocking on doors and telling people about Jesus and hugging them. People were out there drinking iced tea in their swings, and these kids would just sit down and talk to them about the Lord. They had no pretenses whatsoever. They just loved the Lord, and if you'd sit still they'd tell you about the Lord," Romaine said.

"When we started the baptisms, the kids sitting on the rocks surrounding the cove started singing," he continued. "I'll tell you, I've never run into anything like that in my life. Four of us were baptizing people, and it took us two-and-a-half hours to baptize everyone who

12.1   Calvary Chapel, 1992. Photograph by Randall Balmer.

wanted to be baptized. I was so stupefied, I couldn't see straight. It was more than I could understand, more than I could handle."[31] At the height of the Jesus movement, baptisms in the Pacific took place about once a month. The baptisms occur less frequently now, but they are still well attended.

Calvary Chapel, then, was one of the primary beneficiaries of the movement of Jesus people into evangelicalism, in large measure because of Smith's encouragement. Convinced that the hippies had embarked on a spiritual quest that had been frustrated, Smith became persuaded that his church could satisfy their spiritual longings. At Calvary Chapel, Smith preached the gospel to hippies in an idiom that was both ancient and modern: Jesus is the Way. Alienated from families and even friends, searching for salvation from their disillusionment, these burned-out youths found rest in the arms of evangelical Christianity.

Worship and Theology

There is little about Calvary Chapel's appearance that would identify it as a church. The auditorium sits beneath a low-pitched roof with two large wings on either side to accommodate the crowds. The carpeted floors slope gently down to a platform with an unadorned wooden podium at center stage. There is no cross anywhere in sight, only a stylized rendition of a dove on the brick wall behind the platform.[32]

Liturgy at Calvary Chapel, like the building itself, is also simple, even spartan. When it is time for the Sunday morning service to begin, half a dozen men in business suits file onstage. Smith steps immediately to the pulpit to greet the congregation and offer an extemporaneous prayer. He then calls out a hymn number and everyone sings in unison.

While there is certainly no formal liturgy at Calvary Chapel—no prescribed prayers or choreographed kneeling—there is a kind of ritual. As with most evangelical congregations in America, each service at Calvary Chapel, no matter how spontaneous it appears, has its own rhythm and fairly standardized elements, although the chronology may be juggled from time to time. Sunday morning services at Calvary Chapel are generally organized as follows, with infrequent deviations:

Greeting and prayer by Smith
Congregational hymn
Prayer by one of the associate pastors
Announcement of activities for the coming week
Offering
Congregational hymn(s)
Reading of Scripture (Smith reads the first and all odd-numbered
    verses; the congregation reads the even verses in unison)
Sermon by Smith (an exposition of the Scripture text)
Benediction ("The Lord bless you and keep you . . ." sung respon-
    sively by Smith and the congregation)

During the benediction Smith walks down the middle aisle and to the rear of the church to greet members of the congregation as they file out of the building. The service thus ends as informally as it begins.

In keeping with evangelicalism's aversion to high liturgical forms, which dates back to the iconoclasm of some of the more radical elements of the Protestant Reformation, Calvary Chapel celebrates no sacraments in the Sunday morning services. The Lord's Supper (called simply "communion") is observed once a month, and then on a Thursday night. Baptisms, reserved for adults who have attested to some experience to spiritual conversion, are held irregularly in the Pacific Ocean at Corona del Mar. Child "dedications," where the pastor holds a child in his arms and "offers him to Jesus" by means of a public prayer, replace the baptism of infants, which the people at Calvary Chapel, borrowing from the long Baptist tradition, believe has no scriptural warrant.

Virtually without exception, the congregants we spoke with insisted that "teaching" is the focus of worship at Calvary Chapel, and Smith himself insists that biblical exposition has been the key to the church's success. The church's statement of faith, reproduced in the bulletin each Sunday begins:

> We believe worship of God should be Intelligent. Therefore: Our services are designed with great emphasis upon teaching the Word of God that He might instruct us how He would be worshipped.

Accordingly, Smith does not preach in the conventional sense of the term. His homiletical style involves a verse-by-verse exegesis delivered without the aid of notes. His knowledge of the Bible is impressive, and he digresses easily, almost acrobatically, from one chapter to another, one book to another, one testament to the other, frequently quoting from memory. He weaves disparate, often recondite, texts and manages to extract some practical application—all in a single discourse. Part of the genius of this approach is its simplicity, its accessibility even to un-lettered minds. Smith does not burden his auditors with historical-critical issues, nor does he provide reference to other theologians. There is a kind of guileless simplicity in his approach to the Bible, one that recalls the interpretive scheme of Scottish common-sense realism so popular among nineteenth-century Protestants and twentieth-century evangelicals. Scottish realism sought to confront the biblical text in a rationalistic way, without the filters of culture and theology; it insisted that the plainest, most obvious reading of the Bible was the correct one.

Many of Calvary's congregants go so far as to insist that the teaching of the Bible at the church involves no interpretation whatsoever. The Bible is simply God's Word; its meaning is clear and unambiguous. There is little mystery here. The whole enterprise of biblical study centers around an attempt to unlock the meaning of the text and thereby to discover the Word of God. In many respects, Smith's approach to the Bible recalls that of Martin Luther, who insisted that the Bible be available in the vernacular and be read by all believers. Luther's notion of the priesthood of believers made each individual accountable directly before God and not through the mediation of the church. Each Christian, then, must read the Bible for himself.

In this sense, of course, Calvary Chapel is thoroughly Protestant, but it is fundamentalist as well in its insistence that biblical literalism is one of the foundations of the Christian faith. Although Smith does not belabor the issue publicly, he believes in biblical inerrancy, that the Bible is wholly without error in the original autographs. It is the repository of objective truth and authority; it is God's Word (capital "W"). The doctrine of inerrancy does not appear explicitly in Calvary's brief statement of faith, but Rick Dedrick, one of Smith's associates, acknowledged that if one of the staff members denied biblical inerrancy, he would be called to account for his views.[33]

The teaching of the Bible, then, forms the core of Calvary's services, but the relative weightiness of this exegetical approach is leavened by music. Again, the statement of faith reflects this emphasis:

We believe worship of God should be Inspirational. Therefore: We give a great place to music in our worship.

Every service begins with hearty and sustained congregational singing. In the early days of the Jesus movement at Calvary Chapel, the church created its own distinctive musical style. It has spawned several "Jesus music" groups, including Gentle Faith, Love Song, and many others. This style, drawing on the folk music of the 1960s, has influenced American evangelicalism generally, but it remains a critical element of worship at Calvary Chapel, and visitors regard it as one of the more attractive features of worship at the church. "I was a stone-cold dead Catholic," Jim Barrow, a congregant who migrated from Chicago in 1968, said. When he first attended Calvary Chapel, Barrow recounted, "the thing I noticed first was the music. It was as though the people here knew who they were singing to."[34]

Both in the Sunday services and in small-group meetings throughout the week, music functions as a kind of invitation to worship and an invocation of the Holy Spirit. In a sense, no gathering is complete without a guitarist, who initiates singing simply by strumming a few chords. The congregation joins in unbidden. These songs, more than likely unfamiliar to an outsider, nevertheless constitute the oral tradition at Calvary Chapel. Although songbooks are not used at any time other than Sunday morning, everyone associated with the church for any length of time seems to know the words. When one song is finished, the guitarist provides a segue into the next with a few simple chords, thereby linking a dozen or more songs into a sustained musical offering.

As the singing progresses, the congregation settles into what appears at times to be a trancelike state—eyes closed, hands raised in the traditional Pentecostal posture of surrender to the Spirit. In many of these songs the name *Jesus* functions as a mantra of sorts; it is repeated over and over again, often in plaintive tones. Even though most eyes are closed, there is an element of autosuggestion at work. For these people the music serves as a catharsis, a unique mode of emotional expression. It marks the boundaries of sacred space. On a number of occasions we heard references to the harried pace of life in southern California, particularly the frustrations of freeway traffic. Then the music began, serving as a transition from secular life to a spiritual plane, from the profane to the sacred.

The music also reflects the community's highly traditional gender roles. The guitarist is invariably male. The men sing the melody, and the women often provide a counterpoint, a kind of musical embroidery that adds an unmistakable sweetness to the rendition. Many of the songs are responsive; the men sing one line and the women then echo precisely the same line.

Although the singing, therefore, is highly patterned in many respects, the music at Calvary Chapel conveys the impression of spontaneity. The worshipers insist that their music is inspired and directed by the Spirit. Another tenet of the statement of faith supports this claim:

> We believe worship of God should be Spiritual. Therefore: We remain flexible and yielded to the leading of the Holy Spirit to direct our worship.

Smith's own background is Pentecostal, a tradition that tolerates—indeed encourages—emotive outpourings inspired by the Holy Spirit during its worship services. Although Smith and many members of his congregation have attested to speaking in tongues and divine healings in the past, Smith's own position might be characterized as "soft Pentecostalism," which makes it more palatable to many. Luis Santos, a former Roman Catholic who recently began to attend Calvary Chapel, said that he had not known that Calvary Chapel was Pentecostal. "Had I known that," he said, "I probably would have been turned off." Now that he is a regular, however, he feels entirely comfortable with Smith's unique style of charismatic spirituality. Santos indicated that he had never spoken in tongues and had no particular interest in doing so. More important, however, he does not feel that others in the congregation regard him as spiritually inferior because he does not have that gift.

Smith elaborates his view in *Charisma vs. Charismania:* "There must be a middle position between the Pentecostals, with their overemphasis on experience, and the fundamentalists, who, in their quest to be right, in too many cases have become *dead* right."[35] While fundamentalists and most evangelicals acknowledge the spiritual gifts described in the New Testament, they, unlike Pentecostals, insist that these ecstatic phenomena were confined to the first-century Christians and no longer apply to the modern church. This controversy, based on divergent interpretations of the Bible, has occasioned acrimonious battles among conservative Protestants in recent years, with many a congregation torn asunder over the validity of spiritual gifts.

Smith's position represents a departure from traditional Pentecostal attitudes, which tend to equate the spiritual life with the demonstration of such gifts. The "soft Pentecostalism" at Calvary is an accommodation to mainstream, middle-class sensibilities. Smith insists that all of the New Testament spiritual gifts, from *glossolalia* to interpretation to prophecy to healing, remain valid in the present day; however, they are practiced at Calvary Chapel only in small groups apart from the Sunday services—the Upper Room Fellowship on Wednesday, various prayer meetings throughout the week, and on Saturday evenings when the elders gather to lay hands on the sick and pray for the gift of healing. Any other public demonstration of these gifts is discouraged. When we asked Dez Bowman, a former Nazarene and now a member of the board of elders at Calvary, what happens when someone begins speaking in tongues during one of the services, he replied quickly and emphatically. "We stop it," he said. "It's not to be done" because it is disruptive to the assembly. An usher would ask the individual to sit down, and, failing that, "we've removed them."[36]

Smith himself claims the gift of tongues, but he exercises it only, he says, in his private devotions. This view implies a kind of bifurcation between private and public spirituality, but it is necessary, several people alluded, in order not to offend newcomers. Rick Bender, ordained by Calvary Chapel of Costa Mesa and now pastor of a fledgling congregation in Yucaipa, California, acknowledged that he has "a private prayer language with the Lord," but he said that speaking in tongues has no place in the assembly. "We don't do that on Sunday morning because it would scare people away."[37] While Smith and others offer scriptural justification for this practice of downplaying Pentecostal gifts in their larger services—they point to Paul's admonitions to the Corinthians—it is clear that they are cautious lest they be perceived by the broader culture as a fringe group.

Another element of Calvary Chapel's theology does not appear explicitly in the statement of faith, although it arises implicitly from the congregation's literal reading of the Bible. Smith frequently refers to the coming "end times," the apocalyptic judgments predicted in the Scriptures. Like many other evangelicals in America, Smith believes in premillennialism, the eschatological doctrine that Christ will return for his church, the true believers (however variously defined in evangelical circles), at *any* moment. Smith frequently counsels his auditors to prepare for Christ's Second Coming, and this eschatology is arguably the most strongly held and consistently taught doctrine at Calvary Chapel, reflecting a fascination among many congregants with apocalyptic thought.

A large and colorful mural on the back of Calvary's bookstore faces the busy intersection of Fairview and Sunflower. It depicts a rainbow arching over the clouds, a dove, and the inscription: "GOD KEEPS HIS PROMISES. JESUS IS COMING SOON." An entire section of the bookstore is entitled "End Times," featuring the works of Hal Lindsey, a favorite among premillennialists, and several apocalyptic books by Smith, including *Dateline Earth: Countdown to Eternity.* "Now is the time to discover what Revelation has to say—because the end times have arrived!" Smith warns, "God is just about to pour out His judgment upon this world of ours."[38] *Dateline Earth* is fairly standard premillennialist fare; Smith predicts various calamities, and he sees many of the current political, economic, and ecological issues—the European Community, the AIDS epidemic, genetic engineering, global warming—as harbingers of the end times.

The final article in Calvary Chapel's statement of faith concerns what many evangelicals call "discipleship":

We believe worship of God is Fruitful.
Therefore: We look for His love in our lives as the supreme manifestation that we have been truly worshipping Him.

For many of the people associated with Calvary Chapel, their faith is not some distant, abstract commitment. The level of involvement is extraordinary, and it is manifest in the range of programs and activities that are sponsored by the church.

Programs

Over the past decade or so, evangelicals have invested a great deal of energy in the study of how congregations grow.[39] The mavens of church growth insist that one of the keys to success is establishing small support groups so that congregants feel a sense of identity within the larger congregation. Calvary Chapel has done this with a vengeance. In addition to Sunday school classes, three Sunday morning services, and the evening service at seven, the following is a sampling of the various programs and group activities available during the week: [40]

SUNDAY:
Junior High Fellowship (3)
High School Fellowship (3)
Spanish Service
Deaf Fellowship
Children's Special
    Education
Arabic Service
Children's Deaf Ministry
Korean Service (2)
College and Career Prayer
    Meeting

MONDAY:
Women's Intercessory
    Prayer Group
Working Women's Joyful
    Life Bible Study
Proverbs Class for Men
Bible Study (Chuck Smith)

TUESDAY:
Prayer Breakfast
Musicians' Fellowship
High School Mothers'
    Prayer Meeting
Music Ministry Bible
    Study
Bible Study
Men's Fellowship
50-plus [age group] Bible
    study

WEDNESDAY:
Men's Prayer Breakfast
Noon Bible Study

Korean Fellowship
Junior High
College and Career
High School
Becoming Disciples (for
    new believers)
Adult Study in Psalms
Arabic Study
New Spirit/Alcohol and
    Drug Recovery
Single Parents' Fellowship
Believers' Fellowship

THURSDAY:
Spanish Women's Bible
    Study
Bible Study
Adult Fellowship
Singles' Prayer Meeting
Bible Study and
    Communion (Chuck
    Smith)
Children's Special
    Education

FRIDAY:
Women's Joyful Life Bible
    Study
Singles' Group
Missions Fellowship
Spanish Study
Messianic Jewish
    Fellowship
Prison Fellowship

SATURDAY:
Men's Prayer Breakfast
Korean Prayer Meeting
Women's Prayer Meeting
High School Girls Bible
    Study

Physically Disabled
    Fellowship
Elders Pray for the Sick
    and Other Needs
The Outreach [musical
    program geared for
    young people]

Calvary Chapel's staff estimates that approximately 25,000 people pass through its campus during any given week.

In addition to these programs, the area from which Calvary Chapel draws its congregation has been divided geographically, and each unit has a "Home Fellowship" to provide more intimate prayer and study groups, which the people at Calvary regard self-consciously as churches within the church. Home Fellowships also cater to various "interest groups," including "new believers," "women's studies," "singles fellowship," "newly married," studies of various books of the Bible, and groups "following Chuck's Sunday night study." The Tuesday School of the Bible provides training for the laity in biblical languages, church history, theology, and practical ministry. The church also conducts summer camp programs, vacation Bible school, and various recreational outings for all age groups. Finally, the bulletin lists a phone number for "Prayer Watch," where prayer requests are taken daily from ten o'clock in the evening until eight the next morning.

Calvary Chapel also sponsors varied programs for the broader community, including a radio station (KWVE, "K-Wave") in San Clemente; a daily radio broadcast, "The Word for Today"; a television program; and a tape distribution network that sends out more than 20,000 cassette tapes every month.[41] Maranatha! Music, a publishing house and music distributor, was affiliated with Calvary Chapel for many years, although it is now an independent entity. The church also owns a farm north of Santa Barbara and two conference centers, one in Twin Peaks, near Lake Arrowhead, and another near San Diego.

Polity

Ministers, elders, and churchgoers insist that the only criterion for "membership" in Calvary Chapel is "a commitment to Jesus Christ as personal savior," which in evangelical parlance is the singular mark of a "Christian." Active participation in the host of programs at the church, however, appears to be the real requirement for affiliation, and even that is an entirely subjective determination, consistent, once again, with the congregation's attempt to remain as noninstitutional as possible. This appears rather confusing to those more accustomed to traditional patterns of church affiliation, but at Calvary Chapel it conforms to a kind of internal logic based on the conviction that the born-again experience confers membership in the church universal. In the minds of congregants, Calvary Chapel is merely a chapter of the universal body of Christ; therefore, the local church need not burden itself with the formalities of "membership."

Despite the casual attitude, such mundane issues do at times intrude on the life of the congregation. While the people at Calvary Chapel resolutely insist that there is no such category as "member," those who regard themselves as connected with Calvary Chapel gather each December for the election of elders, who oversee the operation and administration of the church. There is no attempt to regulate who attends this meeting and therefore who casts a vote. According to Dez Bowman, an elder, "if you feel yourself part of Calvary Chapel, you can show up and vote at the meeting."[42] Nine men sit on the board of elders, each serving a three-year term. Three elders rotate off the board each year. The elders, however, are a self-perpetuating group in that they nominate their own successors and place those names, usually no more than three, before the congregation. Those in attendance at the meeting, then, are asked simply to ratify the board's nominees.

Bowman indicated that the board was quite cautious in the choice of nominees. As in most other churches, the elders at Calvary Chapel tend to be drawn from the professional ranks of the congregation. Their responsibilities as elders are primarily financial; they rule on salaries, missionary allotments, and major purchases. Because they are considered spiritual leaders, however, matters of probity also figure into the criteria for selection. "We check into their spiritual lives and their personal conduct," Bowman said. "What kinds of places do they go to?"[43]

This suggests a measure of discipline that belies Calvary Chapel's easygoing mien. The church exercises little or no control over its congregants aside from its persuasive powers—its size alone would render that impossible—but the leadership, both lay and clerical, is held to strict doctrinal and behavioral standards. Although no one was willing to enumerate those standards, the same issues surfaced in several conversations. Leaders were expected to adhere to standard fundamentalist proscriptions against alcohol, tobacco, and extramarital sexual relations.[44] In addition, their views must conform to a conservative social agenda, one that is consistent with the conservatism of Orange County. One of Smith's associates, Bob Haag, indicated in the strongest terms that Calvary Chapel was, in his words, "pro-life"—during the summer of 1990 twenty-six congregants were serving jail sentences for having disrupted abortion clinics—and any leader who advocated a position to the contrary would be disciplined. The same applied, he said, to any toleration of homosexuality, which he called "an abomination to God."[45] In matters of theology, the doctrine of biblical inerrancy clearly is a central issue, and any deviation on that point would invite scrutiny.

This scrutiny intensifies with the clergy. Ordination at Calvary Chapel which is conferred by the board of elders, functions as a mechanism of control. Officially, there are no formal educational requirements for ordination because Smith believes that ordination is simply a recognition of a call from God. Typically, someone who has demonstrated leadership abilities through involvement in the church submits a request for ordination to the elders. The elders, with Smith's guidance, review the request, and, if they are satisfied that the candidate has indeed been called to the ministry, they ordain him. According to Rick Dedrick, one of Smith's associates, "the church puts a stamp on what God has already done."[46]

The church can also withdraw its approbation. Several pastors indicated that if someone ordained by Calvary Chapel should espouse ideas—theological, political, or social—that deviate from the positions staked out by Smith, he would doubtless be called to account for his views. Bob Haag, one of the pastors at Calvary Chapel, said that Smith would very likely talk to the person in an attempt to point out his errors. Although there seems to be no formal mechanism for ouster, Calvary Chapel has exercised a kind of "disfellowship" that resembles expulsion.

Lonnie Frisbee, a pivotal figure in the early history of Calvary Chapel, provides an example of this process. Frisbee left Calvary Chapel in October 1971, and it is fairly clear that he did not leave on good terms. Frisbee had always been more interested in the manifestation of charismatic gifts than had Smith, and during Frisbee's Sunday evening sermons he often emphasized the baptism of the Holy Spirit. Frisbee, therefore, violated Smith's "soft Pentecostalism." One contemporary observer reported that, before his departure, Frisbee seemed to be "kept in line" by the senior staff of Calvary Chapel.[47] When asked today about Frisbee, Smith's staff becomes noticeably evasive, and Oden

Fong emphasized that Frisbee—who became involved in the "shepherding movement" and now divides his time between Hawaii, San Diego, and Rio de Janeiro—has "absolutely no connection whatsoever" with Calvary Chapel.[48]

Discipline at Calvary Chapel, then, albeit informal, guarantees a measure of conformity, despite the veneer of toleration. Smith and his colleagues insist that theirs are not arbitrary standards; they are dictated by the Word of God. This leads to a certain intransigence, even absolutism that underscores the inherently conservative character of the church. Ordination, for example, remains a strictly male preserve at Calvary Chapel, reflecting a literal reading of Paul's writings. "Women have their own ministry to the women," Haag said. "The older women teach the younger women." Asked if that position might be revised, he said, "Not unless Scripture changes." How would he answer feminist critics who find those views offensive? "They have to talk with God about that," Haag responded, shrugging his shoulders dismissively. "He wrote it."[49]

In terms of leadership, the Bible even provides a kind of blueprint for succession. As he approaches retirement age, Smith acknowledges that a number of people have expressed interest in what will happen to Calvary Chapel, Costa Mesa, in his absence. He generally deflects such questions with a standard premillennialist response: "I still feel that the Lord is going to come before that happens."[50] Congregants also resort to spiritual language when asked about Calvary Chapel's future. "It's the work of God, not the work of Chuck" is a fairly typical response. "God will raise up a new leader." Beyond that, no one would elaborate or speculate either on likely candidates for succession or on the process itself.

Calvary Chapel as Denomination

The reach of Smith's ministry ensures that there will be no dearth of candidates. Success, especially in America, breeds imitation. Calvary Chapel has expanded greatly from the small band of contentious congregants in Costa Mesa in the mid-1960s to a huge church in Santa Ana, but it has expanded even further to include nearly four hundred satellite congregations across the United States and even around the world. Smith recalls that, in the early years of Calvary Chapel, people would drive considerable distances to attend the church. Eventually, with Smith's encouragement, clusters of people from faraway venues would begin Bible studies that evolved into churches. Other "members" would move out of the region entirely, according to Smith, and would pine for Calvary Chapel:

> As they would look for a fellowship similar to Calvary Chapel in these other areas, they were oftentimes discouraged in their endeavor to find a church. It seemed that their experiences at Calvary Chapel—receiving the warm, loving fellowship and the study of the Word—had spoiled them for any other kind of church. They would start sending for tapes and many times begin to invite their friends to come over and listen to the tapes. Soon a group would be meeting together listening to tapes. Their fellowship would grow, and they would write and ask if we could send someone to pastor. So, gradually, the Calvary Chapels have been extended throughout the entire United States.[51]

According to Richard Cimino, a longtime associate of Smith's in Costa Mesa, Smith functions as a kind of bishop—unofficially, of course—for these affiliated congregations. When a request for a minister comes in, Smith very often will pull one of his assistants aside and suggest that he take the post.

Given Smith's stated opposition to denominations, however, he and his associates insist that these churches do not comprise a denomination. Indeed, although Smith has designated one staff member, Oden Fong, to coordinate communications with these affiliates under the general rubric of "Calvary Chapel Outreach Fellowship," there is little evidence of any institutional or bureaucratic superstructure holding the churches together. It is clear, nevertheless, that these satellite congregations look to Smith and the original Calvary Chapel as their models. When asked about his relationship to these satellite congregations, Smith smiled and said, "I am the father."[52] He has a special telephone line for consultation; its number is available solely to the pastors of other "Calvary Chapels." Smith convenes occasional minister's conferences for these pastors, many of whom were ordained by the elders at Costa Mesa.

Smith retains nearly the same measure of control over these ministers that he wields over his pastoral staff at Costa Mesa. Bender, pastor of the Calvary Chapel in Yucaipa, explained the process. "If I was teaching something false and somebody had a tape of it or something and it got back to Pastor Chuck or Oden, then they'd call me up and say 'What are you doing? You're teaching contrary to the Word.' And if I didn't listen to them and I kept on doing my thing, then if someone called up Calvary Chapel in Costa Mesa and asked if there was a Calvary Chapel in Yucaipa, they'd say 'no.' I could still call myself Calvary Chapel, but to them it wouldn't be Calvary Chapel."[53]

The School of Ministry in Costa Mesa functions, in effect, as a seminary, whose purpose, according to the catalog, is "to train men to be church planters." Its teaching centers on the "discipling" process, where students undertake a kind of apprenticeship under Smith's tutelage. Although instruction includes biblical languages, theology, and church history, the school eschews traditional academic rigor in favor of practical training in ministry. This takes place in what the school calls "traveling discipling bands," which undertake field trips to other Calvary Chapels and forays to locales where Calvary Chapel missionaries are working.

Each Calvary Chapel sponsors missionaries. In Costa Mesa, a fellowship meets every Friday evening to sustain the missionaries with their prayers. Missionaries on furlough report informally to this group. Many work for established Calvary Chapel ministries throughout the world, in such places as Lagos, Nigeria; Sydney, Australia; and Alamos, Mexico. Others work under the auspices of established evangelical groups like Wycliffe Bible Translators, Campus Crusade for Christ, and the Navigators. A June 1990 directory listed forty-seven individuals or couples supported wholly or in part by the Costa Mesa congregation. Others in the congregation, especially high school students, participate in short-term mission teams. One member of the men's Saturday morning prayer breakfast has smuggled Bibles into the People's Republic of China.

Mission work is but one element of what people in Costa Mesa call the Calvary Chapel "movement." Smith professes a suspicion of institutions and bureaucracies—his refusal to keep mailing lists, his insistence that he is not part of any denomination—but the claim is something of a ruse. Calvary Chapel, succumbing to a kind of sociological inevitability, has indeed become an institution and, in fact, has become the fulcrum of a "denomination" that stretches across the country and even the world.

Conclusion

Lonnie Frisbee and Oden Fong were two of countless former acidheads and young dropouts who found a new life through the Jesus movement of the late sixties and early seventies. Like the student uprisings that preceeded it, the Jesus movement appeared somewhat unexpectedly but forcefully, drawing a great deal of media attention for a number of years.[54] Both the religious and secular press, from *Christianity Today* to *Seventeen*, picked up stories about Jesus rock festivals, Calvary Chapel's baptisms in the Pacific, hotlines for kids on bad trips, go-go clubs become Jesus coffeehouses, and churches offering a thirty-second cure for heroin addiction.[55] In one of the earliest stories on the movement, appearing in the February 9, 1971, edition of *Look* magazine, Brian Vachon explored the role of evangelical Christianity in transforming young lives. He concluded, somewhat sensationally: "A crusade—a massive, fundamentalist, Christ-as-personal-Savior revival—has caught hold in California, and it shows every sign of sweeping East and becoming a national preoccupation."[56] Surely the theatrical antics of some in the movement served to grab headlines, yet the media's mindfulness also reflected middle America's concern for the future of its youth after the turbulent, often violent years of the 1960s.

Some twenty years later, Calvary Chapel's urgent sense of mission to young people has not abated. Teenagers at a home fellowship spoke poignantly about the aimlessness of the youth culture in Orange County. "They seem like they're happy on the outside," one said of her peers, "but they're so empty." Several talked of acquaintances who had committed suicide, so vacuous were their lives. Like high school students throughout the country, those in Orange County grope for an identity in activities and interests dictated by their peer groups, which in turn are defined by fashion, musical tastes, or other elements from a vast sea of popular images.

Drawing from that very same reservoir, Calvary Chapel offers an alternative. Summer Harvest, an evangelistic campaign inaugurated in the summer of 1990, adroitly juggled contemporary culture and old-time religion. Held in the Pacific Ampitheatre on the Orange County Fairgrounds in Costa Mesa, Summer Harvest was a tent meeting packaged as a rock concert. Drawn to the event by slick handbills printed with Day-Glo ink, 19,000 came on a Sunday evening, with more than 45,000 in attendance over six nights. After a decidedly "hip" and contemporary warmup, featuring a galaxy of stars from the world of Christian rock, Greg Laurie delivered a fire-and-brimstone sermon replete with warnings about eternal damnation and the imminent return of Christ. Then Laurie, one of Smith's early and most successful disciples, now pastor of Harvest Christian Fellowship in Riverside, invited his auditors to come forward for Jesus.[57]

As thousands responded to Laurie's entreaty, Chuck Smith looked on. "These are the children of the Jesus people," he said. "It's happening to them just like it happened to their parents."[58] Indeed, Smith and Calvary Chapel have turned their attention to a new generation, and, in so doing, they are rekindling the fire of the church's early years. Without acknowledging it explicitly, Smith seems to be yielding to a younger group of preachers that he himself brought into the movement. "The young people have been coming out again," Smith said of Summer Harvest. "It's obvious God's anointing is upon Greg."[59]

Many young converts, however dimly aware of Calvary Chapel's unique history, nonetheless see themselves as spiritual descendants of Jesus People. Just as Oden Fong before his conversion had encountered a bewildering bazaar of religious options at Laguna Beach, which remains in many ways emblematic of southern California life, so too new converts see there a spiritual rootlessness typical of their own generation. "It's so dark down there," one teenager said at Calvary Chapel's high school fellowship. "It's Athens, straight out of Acts 17."

As the curtain fell on the 1960s, there had been a palpable sense of defeat and loss, especially among the young. Spurred by their alienation from the larger culture, many had felt compelled to transform it. No doubt to some degree they succeeded. However, their radical program, ill-defined as it often was, proved unworkable in a society largely hostile to it. The perceived failure of the counterculture demanded redress. For some of the sixties' refugees, evangelical Christianity provided just that. A formidable tradition in the very society the young had defied, evangelicalism proved to be for many rebels both a balm for their souls and a means of continuing their protest, however muted. Its strong current of apocalypticism, in many ways a doctrine both of despair and protest, coupled with its equally powerful message of hope and salvation, made evangelicalism an attractive alternative to the anomie of the late 1960s.

In the process, it allowed for the emergence of a new congregation—new, and yet quite old. Chuck Smith's genius lay in tying together various theological and cultural strands: premillennial apocalypticism, biblical inerrancy and literalism, fundamentalist behavioral codes, American revivalism, the social and political conservatism of surrounding Orange County, and, finally, a modulated Pentecostal worship with its strong emphasis upon experience and the accoutrements of the counterculture. The entire package defies easy description, but it clearly demonstrates the protean character of American evangelicalism, its ability to appropriate the language of the surrounding culture.

The Jesus movement began to lose momentum in the mid-1970s, but Calvary Chapel continues to thrive. The spirit of protest that Smith shared with those refugees from the counterculture has not really abated. This is due in no small measure to the singular vision of Chuck Smith, which he has passed along to hundreds of protégés now working around the world. Calvary Chapel's remarkable growth arose from Smith's reinterpretation of his Pentecostal upbringing and the successful link he has forged between that tradition and the otherwise chimerical eruption of spirituality known as the Jesus movement.

Traditional Pentecostalism shared with the Jesus movement a distrust of institutions and an emphasis on an immediate, affective encounter with the divine. It is not surprising, then, that some Pentecostals evinced an early interest in the Jesus movement, and vice versa. Indeed, Kathryn Kuhlman gave the Jesus People her blessing in 1971. On one of her telecasts she stood with Duane Pederson, Lonnie Frisbee, and Chuck Smith (whom she called "Daddy Smith"), and declared, "I'm one of you, too; I'm part of the Jesus Movement, too."[60] Kuhlman's endorsement, however, like that of most Pentecostal leaders, proved to be superficial and, ultimately, short-lived. Pentecostals were attracted by the movement's interest in charismatic gifts, but they were also frightened by its countercultural trappings. No matter how vigorously they might deny it, Pentecostals like Kuhlman had worked hard to gain a measure of respectability in a culture that had often delighted in ridiculing them. They did not want to compromise their personal achievements by supporting a religious movement that had not yet clearly defined itself or its relationship with the broader culture. For the most part, then, Pentecostals remained wary of the Jesus People.

Chuck Smith, however, was an exception. Despite his revulsion at the appearance of the hippies in Huntington Beach, he was in a sense one of them, at least in his impatience with institutions and his posture toward his own denomination's "establishment." Smith had left the Foursquare Church in disgust at its bureaucratic entanglements and ecclesiastical game-playing. Yet despite his rhetoric, his aversion to institutional life was by no means absolute. To be sure, Calvary Chapel thrives remarkably well without many of the bureaucratic trappings found in other large churches, and it remains a quirky operation—one without membership rolls, mailing lists, or even, at least to the casual worshiper, obvious theological dogmas. To a large degree, no doubt, this easygoing demeanor explains its appeal. At the same time, however, while Smith continues to denounce institutional church life, he has created a formidable institution, and, in so doing, he effectively harnessed the religious energy and spiritual ardor of the Jesus movement. Like a number of other churches that opened their doors to the countercultural refugees of the 1960s, Calvary Chapel channeled the disillusionment of the Jesus people toward rather more conventional ends. Chuck Smith took the Jesus people off the streets and the beaches, offered them a haven where they might continue their spiritual pilgrimages while retaining at least the trappings of their rebellion, and he thereby returned them safely into the arms of American evangelicalism.

NOTES

1. Joan Didion, *Slouching Toward Bethlehem* (New York: Pocket Books, 1968), p. 20.

2. Oden Fong to Randall Balmer, May 10, 1989.

3. Several requests to interview Chuck Smith were consistently denied by his protective office staff. On two occasions, however, we were able to question Smith briefly as he greeted worshipers following Sunday service.

4. Two of Congress's most persistently conservative members, William E. Dannemeyer and Robert Dornan, represent this area.

5. "The New Rebel Cry: Jesus is Coming," *Time*, June 21, 1971, pp. 55–63.

6. Steven M. Tipton, *Getting Saved from the Sixties* (Berkeley and Los Angeles: University of California Press, 1982), p. 88.

7. Ibid., pp. 6–7.

8. Ibid., p. 20.

9. The letter, dated May 13, 1967, and originally published in the *San Francisco Oracle*, is quoted in part in Robert S. Ellwood, Jr., *One Way: The Jesus Movement and Its Meaning* (Englewood Cliffs: Prentice-Hall, 1973), pp. 5–6.

10. Harvey Cox, *Feast of Fools* (Cambridge: Harvard University Press, 1969), p. 112.

11. Huston Smith, "Secularization and the Sacred: The Contemporary Scene," in Donald R. Cutler, ed., *The Religious Situation: 1968* (Boston: Beacon Press, 1968), p. 597.

12. Ibid., p. 599.

13. J. H. Plumb, "The Secular Heretics," *Horizon*, Spring 1968, p. 9.

14. Tipton, *Getting Saved from the Sixties*, p. 19.

15. Didion, *Slouching Towards Bethlehem*, p. 94.

16. See the condensed version of Peale's *Guideposts* article that appeared in *Reader's Digest*, December 1971, pp. 138–41.

17. Erling Jorstad, *That New-Time Religion: The Jesus Revival in America* (Minneapolis: Augsburg Publishing House, 1972), pp. 85–86.

18. Billy Graham, *The Jesus Generation* (Grand Rapids: Zondervan, 1971), pp. 98–99.

19. Martin E. Marty, *Modern American Religion*, vol. 1, *The Irony of It All, 1893–1919* (Chicago: University of Chicago Press, 1986), p. 245.

20. Chuck Smith, *History of Calvary Chapel* (Costa Mesa, Calif.: The Word for Today, 1981), p. 3.

21. Ibid., p. 6.

22. Ibid.

23. Interview with Oden Fong, May 11, 1987.

24. Interview with L. E. Romaine, May 11, 1987.

25. Brian Vachon, "The Jesus Movement Is Upon Us," *Look*, February 9, 1971, p. 20.

26. Ronald M. Enroth, Edward Ericson, Jr., and C. Breckinridge Peters, *The Jesus People: Old Time Religion in the Age of Aquarius* (Grand Rapids: Eerdmans, 1972), p. 88.

27. Interview with Fong, May 11, 1987.

28. Smith, *History of Calvary Chapel*, pp. 9–10.

29. Quoted in Richard Dalrymple, "Beach Baptism Helps Save the Young," *Los Angeles Herald-Examiner*, October 24, 1970, p. A7.

30. Interview with Fong, May 11, 1987.

31. Interview with Romaine, May 11, 1987.

32. During one of our visits to Calvary Chapel, there was a menorah on the communion table behind the pulpit.

33. Conversation with Rick Dedrick, August 10, 1990.

34. Conversation with Jim Barrow, August 11, 1990.

35. Chuck Smith, *Charisma vs. Charismania* (Eugene, Ore.: Harvest House Publishers, 1983), p. 9.

36. Conversation with Dez Bowman, August 12, 1990.

37. Conversation with Rick Bender, August 11, 1990.

38. Chuck Smith with David Wimbish, *Dateline Earth: Countdown to Eternity* (Old Tappan, N.J.: Fleming H. Revell, 1989), p. 13.

39. See, among others, Donald A. MacGavran and Winfred Arn, *How to Grow a Church* (Glendale, Calif.: Regal Books, 1973); and C. Peter Wagner, *Your Own Church Can Grow* (Glendale, Calif.: Regal Books, 1976).

40. This list was compiled from three Sunday bulletins: May 10, 1987, May 17, 1987, and July 30, 1989. The calendar of activities varies little from week to week. The number in parentheses indicates the number of such groups meeting on that day.

41. This is the figure Smith gives for 1981; *History of Calvary Chapel*, p. 11.

42. Conversation with Bowman, August 12, 1990.

43. Ibid.

44. Calvary Chapel, however, like many other congregations in America, has

found it increasingly difficult to enforce the traditional evangelical proscription of divorce. As an accommodation to the culture, stern judgment has given way to a tone of forgiveness.

45. Conversation with Bob Haag, August 12, 1990.

46. Conversation with Dedrick, August 10, 1990.

47. See Enroth et al., *Jesus People*, p. 93.

48. Conversation with Fong, August 9, 1990.

49. Conversation with Haag, August 12, 1990.

50. Smith's sermon, August 12, 1990.

51. Smith, *History of Calvary Chapel*, pp. 10–11.

52. Interview with Chuck Smith, August 12, 1990.

53. Conversation with Bender, August 11, 1990.

54. James Richardson writes, "[A]pparently no social scientist predicted the onset of the Jesus Movement and related phenomena. At the time when the Jesus Movement began, most social scientists were still reeling from the shock of the also unpredicted 'student revolution.'" Richardson, "Causes and Consequences of the Jesus Movement in the United States," in *Acts of the Twelfth International Conference on the Sociology of Religion* (Lille, France: Edition du Secretariat, CISR, 1973), p. 396.

55. See Anne Eggebroten, "Jesus Festivals," *Christianity Today*, August 6, 1971, pp. 38–40; Arnold Hano, "Who Are the Jesus People?" *Seventeen*, March 1972, pp. 136–37, 166–70.

56. Vachon, "Jesus Movement Is Upon Us," p. 15.

57. Harvest Christian Fellowship belongs to the Calvary Chapel "denomination."

58. Quoted in Tracy Weber, "Revival Concert Offers Christianity as an Encore," *Orange County Register*, August 16, 1990, p. 1.

59. Ibid., p. 18.

60. Enroth et al., *Jesus People*, p. 152.

CONTRIBUTORS

RANDALL BALMER is Associate Professor in the Department of Religion at Barnard College in New York City. His recent publications include *A Perfect Babel of Confusion: Dutch Religion and English Culture in the Middle Colonies* and *Mine Eyes Have Seen the Glory: A Journey into the Evangelical Subculture in America*. He was writer and director of *Mine Eyes Have Seen the Glory*, a three-part documentary for PBS.

CATHERINE BREKUS is Assistant Professor of the History of Christianity at the University of Chicago Divinity School. A 1993 recipient of the Ph.D. in American Studies at Yale University, her dissertation is entitled, "Let Your Women Keep Silence in the Churches: Female Preaching and Evangelical Religion in America, 1740–1845."

JEFFREY M. BURNS has been the Archivist for the Chancery Archives of the Archdiocese of San Francisco since 1983. He is the author of *American Catholics and the Family Crisis, 1930–1962: The Ideological and Organizational Response* (1988).

J. WAYNE FLYNT is currently Distinguished University Professor at Auburn University, Auburn, Alabama. The most recent of his seven books, *Poor But Proud: Alabama's Poor Whites*, was published in 1989.

KARLA ANN GOLDMAN, a 1993 recipient of the Ph.D. in American History at Harvard University, is currently Assistant Professor in American Jewish History at Hebrew Union College-Jewish Institute of Religion in Cincinnati, Ohio. Her dissertation is entitled "Beyond the Gallery: The Place of Women in the Development of American Judaism."

JAMES W. LEWIS is Executive Director of the Louisville Institute for the Study of Protestantism and American Culture. He is the author of *The Protestant Experience in Gary, Indiana, 1906–1975: At Home in the City* (1992).

LAWRENCE H. MAMIYA is Professor of Religion and Africana Studies in the Mattie M. and Norman H. Paschall Davis Chair of Religion at Vassar College. He co-authored with C. Eric Lincoln *The Black Church in the African-American Experience* (1990). He is currently engaged in a study of Islam in the African-American experience.

CHERYLL L. MAY is Director of Policy Planning and Public Information for the Administrative Office of the Courts in Salt Lake City. She is also Adjunct Associate Professor in the Department of Political Science at the University of Utah.

DEAN L. MAY is Professor of History at the University of Utah. He is the author of numerous articles on the history of the American west and Mormon history, the co-author of *Building the City of God: Community and Cooperation Among the Mormons,* and the author of *Three Frontiers: Family, Land, and Society in the American West, 1850–1900* (forthcoming).

GEORGE PAPAIOANNOU is a priest of the Greek Orthodox Church, currently serving St. George Church in Bethesda, Maryland. He is the author of *From Mars Hill to Manhattan* (1976) and *The Odyssey of Hellenism in America* (1985) as well as numerous articles related to Hellenism and Greek Orthodoxy in the United States.

JONATHAN D. SARNA is the Josph H. and Belle R. Braun Professor in American Jewish History at Brandeis University in the Department of Near Eastern and Judaic Studies. He has written and edited numerous books and articles and is currently working on a documentary history of religion and state issues affecting American Jews, an interpretive history of American Judaism, and an illustrated history of the Jews of Boston.

MARILEE MUNGER SCROGGS is a minister of the Presbyterian Church (U.S.A.), serving most recently as interim minister of a New York City congregation. In 1990 she published *A Light in the City,* a history of the Fourth Presbyterian Church in Chicago.

STEPHEN J. SHAW writes about the history of the Catholic parish in the midwestern United States and recently published *The Catholic Parish as a Way-Station of Ethnicity and Americanization: Chicago's Germans and Italians, 1903–1939.* He has been teaching religious studies and foreign languages at the secondary and community college levels since 1975.

JAN SHIPPS is Professor of Religious Studies and History at Indiana University–Purdue University at Indianapolis. The first non-Mormon to serve as President of the Mormon Historical Association, she is author of *Mormonism: The Story of a New Religious Tradition.* She is currently at Work on *Being Mormon: The Latter-day Saints since World War II.*

HARRY S. STOUT is the Jonathan Edwards Professor of American Christianity at Yale University, where he has taught American Religious History since 1986. He has written numerous articles and books, including *The New England Soul: Preaching and Religious Culture in Colonial New England* (1986) and *The Divine Dramatist: George Whitefield and the Rise of Modern Evangelicalism* (1991).

JESSE T. TODD, JR. is a candidate for the Ph.D. in the History of Religion in North America at Columbia University. His research interests include urban Protestantism, religious ecstasy, and the history of American Pentecostalism.

EARLE H. WAUGH is Professor in the Department of Religious Studies and Chair of the Canadian Studies Programme at the University of Alberta in Edmonton, Alberta. His book *The Munshidin of Egypt: Their World and Their Song* was published in 1989.

RAYMOND B. WILLIAMS is the LaFollette Distinguished Professor in the Humanities, and Chair of the Department of Philosophy and Religion at Wabash College, Crawfordsville, Indiana. His several books and numerous articles focus on the religions of Asian and Indian immigrants in the United States, including *Religions of Immigrants from India and Pakistan: New Threads in the American Tapestry* (1988).

JAMES P. WIND is a Program Director in the Religion Division of the Lilly Endowment in Indianapolis, Indiana. In addition to numerous articles and reviews, he has published *The Bible and the University: The Messianic Vision of William Rainey Harper* (1987) and *Places of Worship: Exploring Their History* (1990). With Carl S. Dudley and Jackson W. Carroll, he edited *Carriers of Faith: Lessons from Congregational Studies* (1991).